John Rawls, watercolor by Mardy Rawls

The essays in this volume offer an approach to the history of moral and political philosophy that takes its inspiration from John Rawls. All the contributors are philosophers who have studied with Rawls and they offer this collection in his honor.

The distinctive feature of this approach is to address substantive normative questions in moral and political philosophy through an analysis of the texts and theories of major figures in the history of the subject: Aristotle, Hobbes, Hume, Rousseau, Kant, and Marx. By reconstructing the core of these theories in a way that is informed by contemporary theoretical and practical concerns, the contributors show how the history of the subject is a resource for understanding present and perennial problems in moral and political philosophy.

This outstanding collection will be of particular interest to moral and political philosophers, political theorists, historians of philosophy, and historians of ideas.

RECLAIMING THE HISTORY OF ETHICS:
ESSAYS FOR JOHN RAWLS

Reclaiming the History of Ethics

Essays for John Rawls

Edited by

ANDREWS REATH
University of California, Riverside

BARBARA HERMAN
University of California, Los Angeles

CHRISTINE M. KORSGAARD
Harvard University

CAMBRIDGE
UNIVERSITY PRESS

PUBLISHED BY THE PRESS SYNDICATE OF THE UNIVERSITY OF CAMBRIDGE
The Pitt Building, Trumpington Street, Cambridge CB2 1RP, United Kingdom

CAMBRIDGE UNIVERSITY PRESS
The Edinburgh Building, Cambridge CB2 2RU, UK   http: //www.cup.cam.ac.uk
40 West 20th Street, New York, NY 10011-4211, USA   http: //www.cup.org
10 Stamford Road, Oakleigh, Melbourne 3166, Australia

© Cambridge University Press 1997

First published 1997
Reprinted 1998

Printed in the United States of America

Typeset in Times

A catalogue record for this book is available from the British Library

Library of Congress Cataloguing-in-Publication Data is available

ISBN 0-521-47240-7 hardback

Contents

Contributors

DANIEL BRUDNEY, *Associate Professor of Philosophy, University of Chicago*

JOSHUA COHEN, *Professor of Philosophy and Political Science, Massachusetts Institute of Technology*

HANNAH GINSBORG, *Associate Professor of Philosophy, University of California at Berkeley*

JEAN HAMPTON, *Professor of Philosophy, University of Arizona*[†]

BARBARA HERMAN, *Professor of Philosophy, University of California at Los Angeles*

MARCIA L. HOMIAK, *Professor of Philosophy, Occidental College*

CHRISTINE M. KORSGAARD, *Professor of Philosophy, Harvard University*

S. A. LLOYD, *Associate Professor of Philosophy, University of Southern California*

SUSAN NEIMAN, *Associate Professor of Philosophy, Tel Aviv University*

ONORA O'NEILL, *Principal and Professor of Philosophy, Newnham College, University of Cambridge*

ADRIAN M. S. PIPER, *Professor of Philosophy, Wellesley College*

THOMAS W. POGGE, *Associate Professor of Philosophy, Columbia University*

ANDREWS REATH, *Associate Professor of Philosophy, University of California at Riverside*

NANCY SHERMAN, *Professor of Philosophy, Georgetown University*

[†] Deceased

Introduction

John Rawls is known all over the world for the revolutionary achievements in political philosophy embodied in *A Theory of Justice* and *Political Liberalism*.[1] Almost immediately upon publication, Rawls's account of the aims and values of liberalism became the starting point for subsequent work in political philosophy. Many philosophers following Rawls have disagreed with him, taking issue with his methodological devices (e.g., the veil of ignorance as a device of representation), or the two principles of justice, or the account of primary goods as the proper basis of distribution. Others have denied that liberalism as he describes it draws on a sufficiently substantive conception of the self, or would lead to a sufficiently rich and supportive community life; or they have been skeptical of his attempts to show that those who disagree deeply on religious and metaphysical issues and favor different conceptions of the good life may still agree on principles of justice and political institutions. And many other philosophers have been convinced by Rawls's views, and have taken up their defense. There is little dispute on either side that these are the central issues and the appropriate terms of discussion. In this way, Rawls's work has provided the focal point for much of the political philosophy of the last twenty-five years.

It is also now fairly commonplace to credit Rawls's work with the revitalization of moral philosophy that began in the early 1970s. By the late 1960s, moral philosophy was in danger of becoming sterile and trivial. The prevailing emphasis on the analysis of ethical concepts and "metaethical" issues had turned the attention of philosophers away from practical questions. Indeed, the constraints that linguistic analysis imposed on philosophical method, combined with the bias against normative and systematic thought that grew out of ordinary language philosophy, discouraged philosophers from addressing substantive questions about what is right or good and related traditional questions about the nature of persons, the content and function of the moral sentiments, and the structure of human relationships, in any sustained and systematic way. Against the background of the social and political turmoil of the

1960s and the pressing moral questions raised by the war in Vietnam, the metaethical concerns of analytic philosophers seemed increasingly scholastic and unsatisfying. As Bernard Williams complained in 1972, "Contemporary moral philosophy has found an original way of being boring, which is by not discussing moral issues at all."[2] Even where philosophers began to reflect on substantive issues, it was a widely held belief that no useful advances in moral theory were possible.

In these conditions the publication of *A Theory of Justice* came to many as a kind of revelation. As a systematic theoretical work with significant political and economic implications, *A Theory of Justice* showed how the distinctive methods of philosophy might be brought to bear on important political and economic questions. Moreover, it showed how such issues could be addressed by twentieth-century philosophers who value clarity and rigor, and conclusions that can be expressed in accessible language. *A Theory of Justice* was eagerly read and discussed not only by philosophers, but also by political scientists and economists, taught in law schools, and eventually translated into every major European language and many others. In creating an audience outside of philosophy for its achievements, Rawls's work gave many philosophers themselves a kind of new confidence, a restored belief in the significance and value of the subject.

But for many of us who worked and studied with Rawls, what was so influential about Rawls's work was not only the confidence it inspired in the fruitfulness of the methods of philosophy and the potential practical value of its results. It was also a renewed confidence in the subject's tradition, in its classics. One place to see this, of course, is in the basic framework that Rawls adopts for approaching the question of social justice. For faced with a situation in which utilitarianism seemed the only "workable and systematic" substantive theory on offer, what Rawls had done is turn back to "the traditional theory of the social contract, as represented by Locke, Rousseau, and Kant"[3] and to develop his theory out of the concepts, tools, and theoretical structures that this tradition provided. Rawls had seen in the history of the subject a rich resource for dealing with substantive and contemporary problems.

No one who is aware of the wealth of historical reference in *A Theory of Justice* should be surprised by the fact that from the 1960s on Rawls's courses at Harvard were regularly devoted to the study of historical figures. They covered at different times virtually the entire range of writers in the history of moral and political philosophy, from Aristotle on. His lectures not only provided comprehensive readings of central texts that were remarkably clear, original, and deep. They offered reconstructions of classical arguments that reclaimed their power and their capacity to inform contemporary concerns. And it was this fact, this possibility of grappling with substantive normative problems through engagement with historical figures and texts, that captured the imagination, and shaped the careers, of many of John Rawls's graduate students, and of those who in turn have been influenced by their work. The purpose of this volume is to celebrate this, John Rawls's perhaps less well-known achievement: his extraordinary teaching, and the return to the history of moral and political philosophy that it has prompted. In the essays that follow, all written by people who have worked with Rawls, we hope to exemplify the attitude to the tradition of moral and political philosophy that for us has been so central a part of Rawls's achievement.

It is difficult to give a precise characterization of this attitude to the tradition. Perhaps the clearest way to convey it is through a contrast with another and quite opposite attitude toward classics of philosophy. It was common in the early and middle parts of the twentieth century, and in some circles still is, for philosophers to suppose that doing philosophy and doing the history of philosophy are two quite different activities, which lead to two quite different approaches to the classics of the subject. According to this conception, the historian of philosophy is primarily a scholar, whose aim is to reconstruct the philosopher's position as exactly as possible, or, if it developed and changed over time, to chart these changes as accurately as he can. A philosopher's views are treated as a theory, a certain body of doctrine organized in a logical way, with some of the doctrines derived from or dependent upon others, and inconsistencies noted only as blemishes in the final product. On the other hand the "real" philosopher, as opposed to the historian of philosophy, is interested in assessing the correctness of the view, its probable truth, and is committed to the principle that should a view depend upon absurdities or lead to inconsistencies, it should be committed to the flames.

By contrast, in his courses in the history of moral philosophy, Rawls always started by saying: "We are not going to criticize these thinkers, but rather to interpret their positions in ways that make the best of them, and to see what we can learn from them." And what he wanted us to see is the connection between the two sides of that formula: that it is by making the best of a philosopher's position that you can learn the most from it. This is less a methodology, in any formal sense, than a set of assumptions about what the texts and theories of the tradition have to offer, and a commitment to reading them in a way that brings out the deep insights and vision that were moving their authors. The aim might best be summarized as reconstruction of the philosophical core of the theories in question that is informed by contemporary theoretical concerns and addresses issues of enduring importance in moral and political philosophy – a kind of conversation with the historical tradition that uses it as a resource to understand present and perennial problems in the subject. It is based on the suppositions that the historical theories provide viable frameworks for addressing substantive questions in a systematic way, that working through these theories in the right way yields insights about important problems, and that historical work often provides a way of discovering facts about the structures of ethical theories that we still need to know even when, for other reasons, we no longer accept these views in all of their details. It is interpretation that proceeds under the unapologetic assumption that these theories contain at least some approximation to the truth about the matters that they address.

The attitude shows in Rawls's own work, although it is more explicit in his earlier papers, which contain lengthy footnotes remarking on the ways in which Hume, Kant, Mill, and Sidgwick treated the issues with which he is concerned. Looking at these footnotes makes it perfectly clear that Rawls learned a lot of what he knows about these questions by thinking hard about what his predecessors knew; looking at them, in fact, is one way for the reader who was never in Rawls's classroom to get some sense of what it was like to be there. In the *Protagoras*, Plato has Socrates complain of books that "they cannot either answer or ask a question on their own account."[4] In Rawls's lectures, this view, when applied to the works of Aristotle, Hobbes, Locke, Leibniz, Hume, Rousseau, Kant, Hegel, Mill, Marx, Sidgwick, and the other major figures in the tradition of moral and political philosophy, was challenged, for Rawls presented these works not as the repositories of theories closed and dead, but as the embodiments of voices that can be reawakened by a sympathetic but questioning reader. The essays in this collection aspire to follow Rawls in this, that is, in engaging the thinkers of the past to converse with us on the questions of the present.

A.R.
B.H.
C.M.K.

NOTES

1. John Rawls, *A Theory of Justice* (Cambridge: Harvard University Press, 1971). *Political Liberalism* (New York: Columbia University Press, 1993; paperback edition with new material, 1996).
2. Bernard Williams, *Morality: An Introduction to Ethics* (New York: Harper Torchbooks, 1972), p. x.
3. Rawls, *A Theory of Justice*, p. viii.
4. Plato, *Protagoras* 329a. Quoted from the translation by W. K. C. Guthrie in *The Collected Dialogues of Plato*, ed. Edith Hamilton and Huntington Cairns (Princeton: Princeton University Press, 1963), p. 324.

Aristotle on the Soul's Conflicts: Toward an Understanding of Virtue Ethics

MARCIA L. HOMIAK

Greek ethical theories are usually taken to be paradigmatic examples of virtue ethics.[1] But it is not clear what a virtue ethics is. A reason for the unclarity is that virtue ethics are usually described negatively rather than positively, by means of contrasts with "modern" ethical theories.[2] For modern theories, the primary question is, What ought I to do? and the answer is that I ought to do what is right. An action is right if and only if it is in accordance with the principles that specify right actions. Thus a modern teleological theory might say that a right action is that which promotes the best consequences, however that is defined, and a modern deontological theory might say that a right action is in accordance with whatever duties are specified by the theory. In both cases, the principles that specify right action – either those that specify which actions accord with duty or that specify which actions promote the best consequences – are discoveries of practical reason.[3] They are the principles that rational persons would accept. A morally good person, then, accepts these principles as the objects of rational choice and acts in accordance with them.

In these "principle-based" modern theories, what is the role of the virtues? Let us consider virtues as the ancients did, as states of character that involve both rational and nonrational desires, attachments, and tendencies – for the moment, let us just say they are dispositions to feel and behave, as well as to think. So understood, the virtues, viewed from the perspective of a principle-based theory, are secondary or derivative. First, they are secondary in definition. Virtues are identified as the dispositions that support right action; vices interfere with or hinder right action. Second, they are subordinate in their practical role. A person need not be virtuous in order to act in accordance with the substantive principles specified by her theory. It doesn't hurt if she is virtuous, for then she will have dispositions to feel and behave that support her recognition of what is right.[4] She can act properly, however, even if she has bad traits of character that impede her from doing the right thing. For example, she can rise above her cold and uncaring temperament and still help the homeless.

In contrast to principle-based theories, a virtue ethics is meant to focus on the agent in that it gives some kind of priority to being a virtuous person (that is, to having a virtuous character) over acting in accordance with the right principle. It is agent-centered in this sense, even though we can begin in the same way as with principle-based theories. That is, we can ask, What ought I to do? and answer that I ought to perform the right action. But then we move in a different direction. Right actions are not specified in terms of principles of action. Rather, right actions are those that virtuous persons would do, where virtuous persons are those with virtuous states of character that are complex combinations of the rational and the nonrational, of thought and feeling. In Aristotle, in particular, some kind of priority of character over principle is suggested by various passages: for example, that the virtuous person is the standard of what is fine and pleasant (*Nicomachean Ethics* 1113a29–33[5]), that virtue makes the virtuous person's end correct (1144a7–9; cf. 1144a31–36, 1145a4–6), that virtuous actions are those the virtuous person would do (1105b5–7), that ethics is inexact (1104a3–5).[6]

One problem that has arisen for virtue ethics is how to specify the states of virtuous character without invoking principles of action in the way principle-based theories do.[7] In Aristotle, the problem is clear once we attend to the complex nature of character. Any stable character is an intellectual-cum-affective state, which is formed by educating (well or badly) both the rational and nonrational parts of the soul. Can the two aspects of character (rational and nonrational) operate independently? They certainly seem to. We need only consider the incontinent agent, who, on the usual description, knows what is best to do but doesn't do it because of wayward emotion or appetite. The virtuous person doesn't have this experience, however, because her emotions and appetites have been educated properly to support the dictates of her reason. But if this is how we understand the virtuous person, it looks as though the virtuous person is specified primarily in terms of what she knows: She acts from an understanding of particular principles, which, in turn, identify the appropriate supporting nonrational tendencies.[8] By splitting character into independently operating parts, the alleged priority of character over principle is lost, for the individual virtues of courage, temperance, and so on, when considered as affective states, are now secondary in the ways we have described.[9] They are secondary in definition because they are specified by the governing principles of action, which are determined by practical reason. And they are secondary in practical role because they are, at best, necessary only to *motivate* virtuous action, since practical reason alone might not or cannot do so.[10]

If, especially in what is thought to be a paradigmatic example of a virtue ethics, virtuous character turns out to be secondary in these two ways, then it seems to me that there is no interesting theoretical difference between a virtue ethics and a principle-based ethics. I believe, however, that Aristotle's mature ethical writings do offer us a legitimate alternative to principle- or action-based ethical theories, since they suggest an ethics of virtue in which character is not secondary to practical reason. These writings contain a notion of character that can be articulated clearly enough to indicate, first, how character is not ultimately or primarily a matter of being guided by particular principles and, second, how character can function in a way that goes beyond providing motivation for the principles governing action. In this essay, I limit myself to the practical role of virtuous traits and do not attend to the question of whether they are or are not secondary in definition. I try to show that their practical role is not secondary, and that even if the virtuous person is guided by particular principles, a virtuous state of character can do more than provide motivation for those principles. Character can go beyond providing motivation if the nonrational emotions, attachments, and attitudes that partly constitute character guide and constrain the deliberations of agents so as to affect what they determine to be best to do. I argue that if this is the practical role of character, then we have some reason to think practical reason is guided by character rather than the other way around.

This essay is the fourth in a series whose overall aim is to show how the *Nicomachean Ethics* makes available to us an ethics of virtue.[11] Here, as I've said, I set aside questions about the extent to which virtuous traits are specified in terms of principles. I operate with a notion of character that I have defended in other papers in this series: On my view, virtuous character is understood in terms of what Aristotle calls true self-love, and this self-love consists of two fundamental nonrational attitudes, a stable enjoyment of practical rational activity and stable feelings of friendship with other self-lovers. I argue that character so understood (or its absence) accounts, in both virtuous and nonvirtuous persons, for the content of some practical deliberation and practical decision making.

My strategy is to consider in Section I Aristotle's discussion of *akrasia* (incontinence or weakness of will). I focus on incontinence for two reasons: First, incontinence highlights the complex nature of character by forcing us to consider what the nonrational and rational aspects of character are and how they are related. Here, if anywhere, we should be able to see whether and how one aspect of character has an influence on the other. Second, as I have already mentioned, the traditional description of incontinence seems to argue against a main claim of virtue ethics,

namely, that virtuous character is prior in some way to acting on principles. In Aristotle's discussion, the problem arises a bit differently, for
Aristotle seems to add to the traditional description that the incontinent
fails to know the "last premise" of a practical syllogism (1147b9);
alternatively, the incontinent fails to have "perceptual knowledge"
(1147b18). These characterizations of incontinence are Socratic in the
sense that they suggest that the incontinent's failure is a failure in practical knowledge or practical reasoning and also that the situation is put
right by better deliberation. But if the failure is repaired by better deliberation, then the primacy of practical reason is not threatened and the
nonrational aspect of character remains secondary to practical reason.
Better deliberation may preclude wayward emotions from arising, and
we can make a better effort to educate our passions to be more reliable
supporters of what reason dictates.

I argue in Section II, however, that we have no good reason to think
the incontinent's failure is Socratic in either sense. On the view I present
in Sections III and IV, the basic problem with the incontinent is that he
lacks self-love and has defective nonrational desires. In Section III I use
some familiar portraits from Homer to provide an intuitively plausible
description of the relevant defective nonrational desires. In Sections IV
and V, I show how this psychological defect matches the problems
Aristotle sees in persons who hate themselves. I argue that in a variety of
nonvirtuous states (including continence and vice, as well as incontinence), these defective nonrational desires cause agents to misperceive
the situation they face and to deliberate improperly. They also explain
why nonvirtuous agents are susceptible to wayward emotion. There is an
error in practical deliberation, then, but it is not fundamental, since it is
produced by a failure in nonrational desire and hence in character. In the
virtuous person, on the other hand, there is no failure in nonrational
desire, and her correct practical deliberation, I argue, is the outcome of
properly developed nonrational desires. In Section VI, I show how this
approach can explain why courage is a virtuous state, even though it
seems to be a conflicted state.

If I am right that some practical deliberation and decision making is
the result of properly developed nonrational desire, then we have reason
to think that character is not secondary to practical reason and that
Aristotle's ethics is a genuine alternative to principle- or action-based
ethical theories. Of course, for this reading of Aristotle's ethics to be
persuasive, the line of interpretation that I develop here would have to
be carried through other critical elements of Aristotle's view and that is
beyond the scope of this essay. Nevertheless, we can make progress on
resolving the question of what sort of ethics Aristotle's texts yield by

clarifying the ways in which character can account for the content of deliberation.

I. Incontinence and Ignorance

I begin with the parts of the soul, because Aristotle views incontinence as a conflict in the soul. An unconflicted soul is rare[12] – only in the virtuous person do the rational and nonrational parts of the soul agree (1102b27–28). The relevant nonrational part of the soul (viz., the part that shares in reason, 1102a32–33) includes the "appetites and in general desires" (1102b30), that is, what we might call the appetites and emotions (1095a4–11, 1111a27–28). The desires of appetite (*epithumia*) are for objects conceived of as pleasant, whereas the other nonrational desires (those of *thumos*, 1105b21–23) seem to be influenced by some conception of what is good but not by a conception of one's overall good.[13] The relevant rational part of the soul (viz., the rationally calculating part, *to logistikon*, 1139a12) also has its own desires. These desires (*boulēseis*) are for objects believed to contribute to the agent's overall good as she perceives it (1113a12[14] and 1113b3–5).

Because most human beings' souls are not unified, we would expect them to experience various forms of internal conflict. Incontinence, for example, seems a common phenomenon and easy to describe. Incontinence is thought to occur when the agent, believing it is best to refrain from X-ing, nevertheless intentionally and voluntarily X's. In Aristotle's terminology, the incontinent agent acts against his *prohairesis* (1150b30, 1151a6), his decision about what to do.[15] He acts against his *prohairesis* because appetite leads him on (1147a34), that is, because he has an appetitive desire that is contrary to correct reason (*orthos logos*, 1147b2).[16] (Cf. 1102b14–25 and 1111b13–16.)

Thus, according to Aristotle, the incontinent agent, though having judged correctly what to do, acts against that judgment and follows a contrary appetitive desire. His soul is in conflict: He is moved one way by *boulēsis* and in an opposing way by *epithumia*. So far there is no indication that the incontinent is ignorant or that he experiences any deliberative failure. Yet, at the end of his discussion of *akrasia*, at 1147b9–17, Aristotle claims that the incontinent does not know "the last premise" (1147b9) and that "the result Socrates was looking for would seem to come about. For the knowledge that is present when someone is affected by incontinence, and that is dragged about because he is affected, is not the sort that seems to be knowledge to the full extent, but only perceptual knowledge" (1147b14–19). In the end, then, the incontinent does fail to know something.

What exactly does the incontinent fail to know, and how, if at all, is his ignorance related to the presence of the relevant contrary nonrational desire? As a first step toward answering these questions, I now consider some of the details of Aristotle's discussion, and I remind the reader both of some familiar textual difficulties and of some recently proposed solutions. These discussions clarify the general nature of Aristotle's Socratic conclusion by showing that and how the incontinent's practical reasoning is defective.[17] But they do not explain how the defective reasoning is related to the contrary appetitive desire. As I shall explain, however, this issue is crucial for determining whether incontinence is fundamentally a deliberative failure.

Aristotle's specific description of incontinence, at 1147a31–34, outlines a disruption in the normal process of practical reasoning. Here is a literal translation: "Whenever, then, [(a)] the universal opinion is in us hindering us from tasting, and the other, [(b)] that everything sweet is pleasant, and [(c)] this is sweet, and this is active, and appetite is in fact in us, the one says to avoid this, but appetite leads us on." Unfortunately, it is unclear both what the incontinent thinks and when he thinks it. We do not know, for example, whether the incontinent has constructed two "practical syllogisms"[18] (of reason and appetite) or one (of reason only). Nor do we know the content of the universal premise(s). Nor do we know to which syllogism(s) "this is sweet" functions as the minor premise.[19]

If (a) above is the major premise of the syllogism of reason, it might take various forms, for example, "Avoid sweet things" or "Avoid an excessive number of sweet things." The major premise of the syllogism of appetite could then be (b), with (c) a minor premise common to both syllogisms. Alternatively, there might only be one syllogism (of reason). In that case, the major premise could take either of the forms above, and (b) and (c) could function together as the syllogism's minor premise.

In any case, Aristotle is clear that the incontinent person has the belief "to avoid this" (*pheugein touto*, 1147a34), that is, to avoid this sweet thing. The incontinent has, then, at least at some moment, drawn the conclusion to avoid this sweet thing, and so, at some moment at least, he has the knowledge that what he is doing is against his judgment of what is best. There is some sense, then, in which the incontinent person acts knowingly.

Yet a few lines later Aristotle refers to the incontinent person's ignorance: When the incontinent person is being affected, Aristotle says that he does not have "the last premise" (*hē teleutaia protasis*, 1147b9), which is a belief about the perceptible and controls action (1147b9–11). Alternatively, Aristotle says, the way in which he has it is not as someone who has knowledge has it; instead, he is like someone who is just saying the words, as the drunk says the words of Empedocles (1147b11–12). The problem is this: How can the incontinent be ignorant of the last premise (or how can he be like someone who is just saying the words) if, as we have seen, he has drawn the correct practical conclusion to avoid this sweet thing? (Indeed, Aristotle did not mention ignorance in his discussion of how incontinence occurs at 1147a31–34.)

We might be able to understand how the incontinent has or does not have knowledge if we can determine what Aristotle means by "the last premise" (*hē teleutaia protasis*) at 1147b9. There seem to be at least three possibilities:

(i) Because the practical syllogism consists of two premises and conclusion and because *protasis* is Aristotle's usual word for "premise",[20] "the last premise" ought to refer to the minor premise of the incontinent's (single) syllogism or to that of his syllogism of reason. If our representative syllogisms are accepted, the incontinent would not know either (a) that everything sweet is pleasant and this is sweet or (b) that this thing is sweet.

But Aristotle seems unwilling to admit that the incontinent can fail to know the minor premise. Aristotle tells us, for example, that the incontinent's recognition that this is sweet (*touti de gluku*, 1146b33) is active (*energei*, 1146b33). Hence it must contribute to his being able to draw the conclusion to avoid this (sweet thing). Certainly, then, at least at some time prior to action, the incontinent knew the minor premise.

(ii) *hē teleutaia protasis* may be better translated "the last proposition." If so, Aristotle may think that the incontinent does not know the conclusion of his practical reasoning, that is, to avoid this sweet thing, which is itself either the conclusion of his (single) practical syllogism or the conclusion of the syllogism of reason.[21]

This second interpretation faces a similar problem to the first, even if we set translation questions aside. Aristotle has claimed, at 1147a34, that the incontinent knows to avoid this particular sweet thing, for he has drawn the conclusion "to avoid this" (*pheugein touto*). At least at some point prior to action, then, the incontinent knows what conduces to his best interests.

So we seem to be back where we started. In what sense can the incontinent be ignorant of either "the last premise" or "the last proposition" if he has, at least at some point prior to action, drawn the correct practical conclusion to avoid this sweet thing? Perhaps the answer is this:

(iii) Although he has decided to avoid the sweet thing, now, at the time of action, his appetitive desire leads him on and his reasoning process is disrupted, with the result that he does not see that this particular sweet thing is one to which his general principle of avoiding sweets applies.[22] In effect, the incontinent does not entirely give up the general principle (he is still committed to the general principle of avoiding sweet things), but he also does not see the particular situation in a way that makes that general principle relevant to governing his action now. Because he does not entirely give up the principle, Aristotle can say, at 1147b15–17, that it is not knowledge to the full extent (*kuriōs*, 1147b15) that is dragged about by passion, but perceptual (*aisthētikēs*, 1147b17) knowledge. Appetitive desire interferes, so that we do not bring what would, in other circumstances, be relevant principles to bear on the practical situation we face.

If we accept (iii), the general direction of Aristotle's discussion remains Socratic, even though the mechanics of incontinence include a Platonic element.[23] During incontinence, a contrary appetitive desire leads the agent on, his reasoning is interrupted, and his perceptual knowledge is dragged about, with the result that he does not fully and completely know what he is doing. The difficulty is that we have isolated a new element in the situation, namely, the agent's failure to see that the situation he faces is one to which his generally held principles apply. (I shall now refer to this failure as the "recognition failure.") What produced this failure? Was it the agent's defective practical reasoning, some other nondeliberative defect in the agent, or some combination of them? If defective reasoning produces the failure, then presumably the defect is repaired and incontinence eliminated through a more complete or more determinate working out of what it is best to do. If the defect is repaired through better deliberation, then incontinence is primarily a failure in practical deliberation. But if the recognition failure is accounted for in some other way, it is not clear that incontinence is primarily, or even partially, a deliberative failure.

II. Is *Akrasia* a Deliberative Failure?

In this section I examine the view that incontinence is primarily a failure in practical deliberation. Call this the deliberative view.[24] On the deliberative view, the incontinent's recognition failure is produced by some defect or error in practical reasoning. Although there seems to be a problem with motivation (because the agent does follow a contrary desire), a proponent of this view can claim that better reasoning will preclude the desire from interfering. The problem of motivation is then subsidiary to the defect in deliberation.

If the recognition failure is produced by a defect in deliberation, we should be able to determine what this defect is. Since the virtuous person presumably has reasoned correctly, we should be able to determine what the virtuous person knows that the incontinent person does not know. We might think the incontinent agent could err about, and hence be ignorant of, any of the following: (1) a general expression of the appropriate conception of the best life; (2) an injunction against performing, or a recommendation to perform, specific types of actions; or (3) the expression of a general principle of rationality, such as a principle of prudence or a principle of continence, that could be common to various conceptions of the best life.

Although it might at first seem reasonable to think that the incontinent agent errs about (1), this cannot be the case. To be ignorant of (1) would be equivalent to accepting a different general conception of the best life, to accepting, for example, any of the lives Aristotle rejects in I.5. If the incontinent thought it best to pursue a life devoted to honor or pleasure, he would presumably be more like the morally vicious person than Aristotle describes him as being (1151a11–26). So we are better off thinking it is (2) or (3) that the incontinent person does not know.

If an agent is ignorant of (2), then he does not know that he should avoid or pursue specific types of action.[25] One might think the difficulty here is that the virtuous person's general conception of happiness is too vague or indeterminate to yield specific injunctions or recommendations. An agent may agree with the outline of happiness that Aristotle presents in I: He may agree that the best life consists of the complete realization of the human powers as achieved through virtuous action and as actualized in a community of fellow realizers, where each agent also enjoys various goods of fortune and external goods, including close friends, family, health, and material well-being.[26] The agent may be able to grant a general priority to some of these goods over others and to have determined that some are the consequence or expression of others. Aside from these general parameters, however, and some remarks on the organization of the best political arrangement for ensuring these goods, Aristotle does not give us guidelines for determining what individual good lives will look like.[27] The agent's general conception of happiness is thus eminently susceptible to delineation and refinement as determined by specific circumstances. This fact makes it hard to see how the knowledge the incontinent lacks would take the form of specific injunctions or recommendations. Specific actions to be taken or avoided seem more easily determined in Homeric ethics, where there is no accommodation to the idea of "hitting the mean."[28]

But one might grant that the virtuous person's conception of happiness is vague, in that her sense of what to do is determined by specific circumstances, and still think the virtuous person is guided by a recognition of types of action to avoid or pursue. Aristotle's virtuous person will, we assume, not only know what the important goods are but will also know why they are good, since to have a proper conception of human good isn't simply to have a belief that happens to be true. The virtuous person can explain, for example, why defending one's city is a good thing to do, whereas hiring oneself out as a mercenary is not, because the virtuous person can tell (roughly) when one should risk one's life in battle. To take a different example, the virtuous person can explain why his participation in political decision making is a good and why he should continue to participate, even if participation leaves him less time for other worthwhile activities, such as supervising his land. But if we grant that the virtuous person can be guided by principles like these, then these general principles cannot be what the incontinent person fails to know. This is because they are derived from the virtuous person's conception of happiness, which the incontinent person shares. There is no reason to think the incontinent person can't also come up with them.

This leaves us with (3). Here the error is an ignorance in how to apply relatively content-neutral principles of rationality.[29] Because many of the most common cases of incontinence seem to involve an abandonment of a prudential good in favor of the pursuit of immediate pleasure, perhaps it is some application of a principle of prudence that the incontinent person does not know: He does not know that he ought not abandon his considered judgments about what actions promote his future good in the presence of strong contrary desires. Or perhaps it is how to apply an even wider principle, say, a principle of continence, that the incontinent person fails to know. He does not know that he ought not abandon his considered judgments (period) in the presence of strong contrary desires.

This suggestion seems less helpful than (2), for it isn't at all obvious that Aristotle's virtuous person will want to apply a principle of prudence or continence, at least so rendered. For it is not clear that the virtuous person would experience a strong contrary desire, since her deliberations, as I shall argue in Sections IV and VI, will be prompted by a view of the situation according to which the tempting inclination will appear practically unimportant or uninteresting. Moreover, if, contrary to our expectations, she did experience a strong contrary desire, that would presumably be reason for her to reconsider the action she has judged best rather than to act in accordance with her judgment. Though not perfect, Aristotle's virtuous agent is a good deliberator, in part because she will recognize the need to revise her practical deliberations and will do so for the right reason (1151a29–b4).

We have not been able to find a specific policy or principle (or application thereof) that the incontinent fails to know. That is a good reason for thinking that incontinence is not fundamentally a failure in practical deliberation. But the proponent of the deliberative view might reply that our investigation is incomplete or unimaginative. There must, he could say, be an error in practical deliberation that accounts for the recognition error. Otherwise, the failure in recognition is implausible. To see why a deliberative error is needed to explain the recognition failure, consider the structure of the practical syllogism.

Although there is disagreement about the function(s) performed by the practical syllogism and the extent to which it represents the nature of practical thinking, commentators seem agreed about how roughly to distinguish its major and minor premises. The major premise is thought to specify a type of action to be done, whereas the minor premise indicates that persons or objects of the type specified in the major premise are present.[30] The performance of the action, or at least an intention to perform the action,[31] follows immediately as the syllogism's conclusion.

Aristotle has said that the incontinent fails to have the "last premise" and that his "perceptual knowledge is dragged about." We have interpreted these remarks to mean that, at the time of action,[32] the incontinent does not recognize his situation as one to which his generally held principles apply. Suppose that a deliberative error does not explain the failure of recognition. Does the incontinent then simply misperceive the persons or objects he confronts? This seems unlikely, because the content of the minor premise, which is acknowledged to be a matter of perception, is thought to be obvious.[33] So how can someone make this (perceptual) mistake? Indeed, the examples Aristotle offers of practical syllogisms suggest that any rational being could recognize that the relevant persons or objects specified in the major premise are present: "whenever one thinks that every man ought to walk, and that one is a man oneself, straightaway one walks" (*De Motu An.*, 701a14–15);[34] "if one ought to taste everything sweet, and this is sweet . . . necessarily the man who is able and not prevented does this at that same time" (1147a29–31). A straightforward error in perception, unmediated by an error in practical deliberation, thus seems implausible.

But one could reply that errors in perception are not implausible if, as David Wiggins has put it, "few situations come already inscribed with the names of all the concerns which they touch or impinge upon."[35] If agents must inscribe situations with the relevant concerns and then decide that these situations call for specific responses, they can misinscribe them, too. Then incontinence could occur when the agent misperceives the nature of his situation and constructs a new minor premise appropriate to a different practical syllogism, which then calls for a different practical response. Misconstrual of his situation is not, then, a simple perceptual error, as the proponent of the deliberative view claims. In the Aristotelian example, misconstrual does not imply that the agent fails to realize the thing in front of him is sweet. About that, he is undoubtedly all too clear. Rather, some other features of the sweet thing grab his attention, and he constructs a different practical syllogism to suit those features.[36] Because he mislabels his situation, he can be said not to have the last premise (1147b9). Finally, because nothing occurs to suggest that he has given up his general principle or that at some earlier point he failed to draw the correct practical conclusion, Aristotle can say, at 1147b15–17, that it is not knowledge to the full extent (*kuriōs*, 1147b15) that is dragged about by passion, but perceptual (*aisthētikēs*, 1147b17) knowledge. Thus we do not need to find an error in practical deliberation to make sense of Aristotle's description of incontinence.

III. Character and Perception

I have argued that the incontinent's recognition failure should not be seen as the result of a deliberative breakdown. How then to explain it? There seems to me to be only one plausible alternative: The recognition failure is caused by the incontinent's interfering nonrational desires, and proper perception is restored by altering one's desires, that is, by becoming virtuous. But for this explanation to be helpful, we will need some way to distinguish between the interfering desires of the incontinent person and the noninterfering desires of the virtuous person. Otherwise, all we have done is remind ourselves that incontinent persons are not virtuous.

In this section I shall focus on the interfering nonrational desires of the incontinent person. I shall use some familiar portraits of Homeric heroes to provide intuitively plausible examples of these defective desires and to show how they can account for distorted practical perception.[37] In Section IV I argue that these psychological defects match those of Aristotle's self-haters, whereas true self-lovers have the contrasting desires of the virtuous person.

Let's begin with a reconstruction of Paris's encounter with Helen.[38] If we assume that Paris believes that he, like other aristocratic Greeks, is bound by the traditional constraints governing the relationship between host and guest,[39] then the question is why Paris violates these constraints by sleeping with his host's wife and abducting her to Troy. If Paris is incontinent,[40] then his "perceptual knowledge" is dragged about by desire. What then does he fail to know? Certainly not that Helen is his host's wife. Rather, he must somehow fail to see that his present actions are violations of aristocratic norms. Paris could believe this if he viewed his attraction to Helen as a harmless and innocent flirtation.[41] But this also seems implausible, for if Paris is fully aware that Helen is Menelaus's wife, how can he think his attraction to her is harmless? It seems to me that we must construe Paris's thoughts differently. Paris might view his circumstances as exceptional if he thinks his sexual attraction to Helen is licensed by Aphrodite: Paris might think that, by rewarding him with Helen, Aphrodite has, so to speak, given him leave to ignore the usual constraints of the guest–host relationship. Divine intervention and divine sanction might make this situation, in Paris's mind, an exception to the traditional rules of aristocratic hospitality. Here his practical perception seems to be distorted by his sexual desire: Because he wants Helen, he can find a way to view his actions as exceptional.[42]

Paris's situation can be usefully contrasted to Odysseus's encounter with Nausicaa in *Odyssey* VI. Both Odysseus and Paris are offered hospitality by the rulers of foreign cities, and both find themselves in the company of beautiful female relatives of those rulers. Yet the thought of sleeping with Nausicaa does not occur to Odysseus. Odysseus doesn't view his circumstances as exceptional: He thinks they fall within the traditional parameters of the guest–host relationship. How are we to explain this difference in practical perception? Odysseus, like most Greek heroes, is not in the habit of restraining his sexual desires, or at least not to the extent that Aristotle's discussions of temperance suggest are appropriate for a temperate person. So we can't say that the difference in practical perception is due to Odysseus's temperance.

But I think this explanation is on the right track, for Odysseus and Paris are importantly different in the extent to which they fit the standard Homeric criteria of the admired man, or *agathos*.[43] Odysseus's strength, intelligence, cunning, and resourcefulness make him a great warrior. It is no surprise that the Greeks vote him the arms of Achilles at the end of the Trojan War. Paris, on the other hand, is weak, foolish, and cowardly. Although he is a prince, he is ridiculed by other heroes (as in *Iliad* III. 39–57). Odysseus has nothing to gain by sleeping with Nausicaa and much to lose if he offends her father. He wants most to get back to Ithaca, and he recognizes that a courteous and supplicatory relationship with Nausicaa can help him. He acts with his characteristically sound understanding of how best to achieve his ends and with his equally characteristic confidence in his ability to achieve those ends. But Paris does not (and cannot) have the same self-confidence, because the standard sources for the acquisition of confidence (namely, the deeds of an heroic warrior) are unavailable to him. This difference, I suggest, makes

it likely that Paris will abduct Helen (and without thinking that the
established rules of hospitality apply to his actions), because he will be
more inclined than the standard Homeric hero to think that his honor
and reputation lies in the possessions he has rather than in the deeds
coming from his own prowess.[44] Paris's sense of his own worth must be,
at best, unstable and precarious, and hence he will be more susceptible to
methods of strengthening it that depend on the fortune and circumstance
of divine intervention than on the use of his limited abilities as warrior
and protector. (In *Iliad* III, Aphrodite rescues Paris from death at the
hands of Menelaus. Paris *needs* rescuing; other heroes do not.)

Odysseus's and Paris's differing senses of what they are capable of and
of how they are viewed by others affect how they will perceive similar
situations, and because of that, these differences also affect their choices
and decisions. Features of a situation that seem practically salient to
Paris do not appear so to Odysseus: Paris sees an opportunity for
appetitive satisfaction, whereas Odysseus does not. This is the case, even
though both men presumably subscribe to the hospitality conventions
governing aristocrats. Paris and Odysseus are both *agathoi*; yet they
inscribe practical situations differently, in accordance with the degree to
which they actually fit the attitudes and values of the admired Homeric
man, that is, in accordance with the degree to which they fit the admired
Homeric character. If Paris is an example of the akratic in regard to
sexual desire, then his failure, though immediately one of perception
distorted by an occurrent sexual desire, is less directly, and more fundamentally, one of nonrational attitudes and attachments fundamental to
his character.

IV. *Akrasia* as a Failure in Self-Love

I have offered one example to indicate how an agent's character affects
his inscription of practical situations. Yet, because it is Homeric, it may
seem to draw upon a system of values and beliefs that Aristotle rejects.
(See, for example, 1095b22–1096a2.) But the example is not as foreign to
Aristotle's views as one might think. In fact, Aristotle's comments on the
attraction of appetitive desires reveal a connection between self-regard
and appetitive satisfaction not unlike the Homeric one.

Aristotle tends to associate the improper satisfaction of appetitive
desires with slaves and animals. At 1177a8, for example, he writes that
"anyone at all, even a slave . . . might enjoy bodily pleasures"; at
1095b19–20, he condemns those who choose a life of appetitive pleasure
as slavish, because they have chosen a life fit "for grazing animals."
Intemperate persons are described as enjoying appetitive pleasures im-

properly in that they enjoy them as animals do: They take most pleasure in the physical sensations of these pleasures and little or no pleasure in the rational activity (the discriminating and choosing) that surrounds tasting and touching (1118a30–b4). And in the *Politics* women are likened to slaves in so far as they are naturally defective. Their capacity for deliberation is not "authoritative" (*Politics* 1260a13). Aristotle seems to mean by this that women give too much weight to what is pleasant (rather than to what is good) and turn over their soul to its nonrational part. A woman's life will, as a result, always be slavish, since her life is not controlled by the deliberations of the rational part of her soul. These passages suggest that appetitive pleasures are especially appropriate for slaves, grazing animals, and women because they are, relative to other pleasures, lacking in rational activity. Even natural slaves, who lack the powers of deliberation and decision (*Politics* 1260a12), can enjoy appetitive pleasures.

But the capacities for deliberation and decision are characteristic of us as human beings (1166a17ff., 1170b12, b18–19; cf. 1095b26). When we realize these powers and engage in judging, choosing, deciding, and discriminating, we come to enjoy who we are, because "we are in so far as we are actualized" (1168a6) and the realization of our powers is enjoyable (1168a5–26). When we love the exercise of our characteristic human abilities most of all, we are true lovers of self (1168b35–1169a3). Moreover, we are morally virtuous: "the decent person likes this [what each person is] most of all. Hence he most of all is a self-lover (*philautos*)" (1169a3–4). The virtuous person, as a true self-lover, has a kind of positive self-regard and self-confidence: He enjoys himself and his life and does not wish to be different (1166a19–24). Finally, because the self-lover enjoys himself and his life in the way we've described, there is no reason to think he won't also take pleasure from the exercise of others' characteristic human powers.[45] He has no reason to grudge others their achievements; rather, he is more likely to develop friendly feelings with them. Because of the attitude he has toward himself, we can expect him to enjoy the pleasures of social fellowship and civic life[46] (1097b6–11, 1170b16ff). The absence of true self-love (not the bad self-love Aristotle condemns at 1168b15–28) is, on the other hand, appropriately associated with nonvirtuous conditions, whether those be conditions of continence, incontinence, or moral vice (1166b2–26). Vicious people are self-haters (1166b17–18), are full of regret (1166b24–25), and cannot form stable friendships (1159b7–10).

It is not possible here to argue fully for the connections between virtue and true self-love, on the one hand, and vice and self-hatred, on the other. But a few examples from Aristotle's discussions of particular virtues and vices may serve to indicate the direction the argument can take: A self-lover, because of her self-love, will be inclined to take the actions Aristotle thinks are morally virtuous and will be disinclined to take the actions or have the attitudes typical of vicious types, whereas self-haters, because of their self-hatred, will be attracted to the kinds of actions Aristotle thinks are morally vicious and will not enjoy the actions favored by the virtuous.[47] For example, some of Aristotle's vicious types care too much about what others think, which shows that they don't sufficiently enjoy what they do themselves: Flatterers want the favor of the more privileged (1127a7–9); vain people seek honor, though they are not worthy of it (1125a27–31); boastful and mock modest people want others' good opinion (1127a20–23); inirascible people accept insults to themselves, their families, and friends (1126a7–8). They are all contrasted to the magnanimous person, who has the right attitude toward herself and others (1125a1–3): If anyone determines her life, it is a friend, since friends identify with each other's decisions and actions (1166a32). Other vicious types do not care enough about what others think. They include cantankerous (1126b16), irascible (1126a14), and insensible (1119a10) people, who may be haughty or disdainful of others. These latter types cannot experience the pleasures of social life that come from the virtuous person's tendency to appreciate and identify with others' actualizations of their human powers.

For our general purpose of determining what the practical role of character might be, it is important to remember that the virtuous person's self-love is a love or enjoyment. Although both the source and object of self-love are the exercise of one's rational powers, the enjoyment of that exercise is itself nonrational, just as any other type of enjoyment is. The true self-lover is thus definitively characterized by a nonrational desire for rational activity. Because her desire is nonrational, it is not the product of deliberation about one's overall good. Such deliberation would produce rational desires, not nonrational desires. Nor can the nonrational desire be eliminated by deliberation about one's overall good, as rational desires can be. Indeed, the persistence of desire in the face of competing rational deliberation is an indication (as it is in akrasia) that the desire is nonrational.

Now we can understand why Paris and Odysseus act as they do. We have seen that Paris does not have the skills and cunning needed for Homeric success. In effect, the standard Homeric sources of honor and reputation are unavailable to him, and instead of being honored for victory in war, he is ridiculed by other heroes for being weak and foolish. For someone whose sense of his own worth is so low, the pleasures of the appetites will seem unusually attractive, because they are easy and immediate in contrast to riskier pleasures whose satisfaction requires the rational activity involved in skill and experience. In Paris's case, in particular, appetitive satisfaction is assured (even the usual rational activity of seduction is unnecessary), because Aphrodite is responsible for Paris's winning Helen. Unlike the clever and devious Odysseus, who clearly does enjoy the exercise of his human rational powers, Paris is more attracted to what Aristotle calls slavish pleasures. He sees an opportunity for appetitive satisfaction where Odysseus does not and ignores the hospitality conventions governing aristocrats whereas Odysseus does not, because he takes so little pleasure in the exercise of his human powers. But neither is Odysseus virtuous. Although Odysseus enjoys rational activity and thus seems to be a true self-lover, he enjoys even more the honor and reputation that other *agathoi* can bestow on him. Because he is an honor-lover, Odysseus exhibits the self-love Aristotle condemns: "Those who make self-lover a matter for reproach ascribe it to those who award the biggest share in money, honours and bodily pleasures to themselves. For these are the goods desired and eagerly pursued by the many on the assumption that they are best; and hence they are also contested" (1168b15–19).

Aristotle's lover of sweets is in the same general predicament as Paris. He does not enjoy the exercise of more difficult and complicated abilities and hence is attracted to easier, more immediate pleasures. Like the intemperate person, the incontinent enjoys sensations: "That is why a glutton actually prayed for his throat to become longer than a crane's, showing that he took pleasure in the touching" (1118a32–b1). His vulnerability to appetitive desire influences his perception of the sweet thing in front of him so that he does not attend to the harmfulness of eating it. He may think instead that the thing in front of him promises an unusually delightful culinary experience. What ought to be practically salient from the point of view of the agent's accepted and acknowledged principles of action becomes practically obscure.

I have argued that the incontinent's weak self-love accounts for his occurrent appetitive desire and causes him to misperceive (some) situations, so that he does not recognize them as falling under the general practical principles to which he subscribes. Were his enjoyment in the exercise of his rational abilities more stable and continuous, he would view situations of easy appetitive satisfaction with less interest and would be less likely to perform incontinent actions. Because his failure of recognition is caused by his weak self-love, we have good reason to think *akrasia* is ultimately a failure of character, not of deliberation.

V. Continence

Yet the association of virtue with true self-love, on the one hand, and of various nonvirtuous conditions with its absence, on the other, raises problems of its own. How can the various non-virtuous conditions be distinguished from each other if they are all examples of the absence of self-love? By accounting for everything, the absence of self-love seems to account for nothing in particular. And how are some virtuous conditions to be distinguished from the nonvirtuous condition of continence? If courage, for example, requires mastering one's fear in the presence of danger, then how is the courageous person different from the continent person, who acts on her recognition of what is best to do, though wanting to do otherwise (1102b14–28)?

I first take up the question of the various nonvirtuous conditions. On the view I have presented, the incontinent action is a departure from the agent's generally accepted and acknowledged practical principles. In the cases we have discussed, Paris acts against his generally held view that the guest–host relationship is not to be violated, and the akratic sweet-lover acts against her generally held judgment that eating too many sweets is harmful to her health. These departures from what agents normally take to be best result, I have argued, from defective self-love that causes agents to perceive other features as practically relevant and hence as action guiding. The incontinent agent acts in one sense knowingly and in another not – she retains her usual practical principles (she knows what it is best to do), but she does not recognize that this is a situation to which her principles apply (she lacks perceptual knowledge).

In contrast, the continent person's action doesn't violate her practical principles: She acts in accordance with her best judgment, though she wants to do otherwise. Though both she and the incontinent have contrary desires, she controls her contrary desire and does not act on it (1102b14–28). The contrary desire must be strong enough to issue in incontinent action. Otherwise, we cannot distinguish continent action from ordinary actions for which we have competing reasons, and we cannot see what is admirable about mastering the contrary desire. What then explains the failure to issue in action?

On the interpretation of incontinence that I have outlined, the incontinent person's defective self-love accounts for her occurrent appetitive desire and distorts her practical perception so that she does not recognize the kind of situation she is in and cannot apply her generally held principles to that situation. If this is correct, we should expect the continent person's self-love to be sufficient to enable her to perceive practical situations correctly, that is, in accordance with the principles to which she normally subscribes. Thus, for example, we can think of the continent sweet-lover as someone who has learned to take some pleasure in the exercise of the human powers, so that she is not always attracted by easy and immediate pleasures. Given that, the potential harm to her health will appear practically salient. Unlike the akratic sweet-lover, then, she will not fail to attend to her knowledge that eating an excessive number of sweets is harmful.

The continent's self-love must be sufficient to enable her to perceive practical situations in accordance with her judgments of what is best. But if it were sufficient always to have this effect, the agent would be virtuous. We should think, then, of the continent person's self-love as in the process of development: She has learned to take some pleasure in what she can do herself. But because she is only learning how to enjoy the expression of her human powers, her confidence in what she can do will be vulnerable to obstacles and setbacks and hence will be unreliable. Because her confidence is shaky, her perceptions of what is practically salient will not be consistent. Hence she will sometimes act as an akratic person does: Sometimes she will act against her generally held principles, namely, in those instances where her fledgling self-love fails her and her insecurities are pressing.

On this view, then, both continent and incontinent persons turn out to believe at the time of action that they are acting as their present circumstances warrant. This may seem a disappointing result. Neither experiences the conflict of desire that we pretheoretically associate with these states. This does not mean, however, that psychological turmoil will not arise later in the process of reflection on what one has done or that it will not arise indirectly. Someone who thinks that the specific circumstances she confronts warrant the action she takes, or that her actions are not a departure from her generally accepted principles, may express this conviction in ways that, to third parties, suggest misgivings and uncertainty. So one may, for example, project onto others one's own worries and self-criticisms (even a sense that what one has done is wrong) and invest considerable energy in defeating them. But these efforts are not equivalent to a conscious recognition at the time of action that what one is about to do is contrary to one's best interest. Thus psychological turmoil need not disappear from Aristotle's picture of continent and incontinent persons, but it will surface less directly.

On this picture, we can imagine a spectrum of moral transformation, with vice at one extreme and virtue at the other. Incontinence and continence lie in the middle, with continence further along the spectrum toward virtue. But everyone who falls outside of virtue is deficient in regard to the nonrational part of the soul: None takes the nonrational enjoyment in the expression of the human powers that enables a person consistently to act on practically wise principles. Although the non-virtuous types are alike in this way, continent and incontinent types share the virtuous person's rational desire for what is best, which means, at least, that they experience, indirectly or upon reflection, their own conflicting tendencies. Although the morally vicious person shares essentially the same nonrational psychology as the other nonvirtuous types, he does not share their considered view about what is best, and thus he is less likely to experience turmoil and to reflect on his own faults and failures. Reflection is less likely, but it is not unlikely. It is not unlikely, because it is hard to hide from oneself that one does not like who one is, and this condition may provoke reflection about what is better. Then morally vicious people begin to look more like the incontinent. Aristotle suggests as much at 1166b2ff. Morally vicious people, he says, "seek others to pass their days with, and shun themselves. For when they are by themselves they remember many disagreeable actions, and expect to do others in the future; but they manage to forget these in other people's company. These people have nothing lovable about them, and so have no friendly feelings for themselves" (1166b13–18).

VI. Courage

I now turn to the virtue of courage. Courage may seem to be a particularly troublesome virtue for an account like mine, since, as a conflicted state, it is hard to distinguish from continence in regard to fear. Here I argue that the conception of virtue I have developed so far can be extended to explicate courage and its related states. In so doing I provide further support for the view that the self-lover's nonrational desires and attachments crucially affect his practical perception and practical deliberation.

Aristotelian courage involves hitting the mean in regard to the emotions of fear and confidence (1115a7). That is, the courageous person is fearful or confident to the right degree, at the right times, toward the right things, and so on (1115b17–18). Although the courageous person stands firm against the most frightening conditions (death) in the finest circumstances (war) (1115a26, a30–31), he is not fearless. Rather, he is as unperturbed as it is possible for a human being to be (1115b11–14). The courageous person's courage thus seems to consist in mastering his fear and not running away. But if this is how his psychological state is to be described, how can he be distinguished from someone who is said to do the right thing, recognizing it is right, while wanting to do otherwise?

How, that is, can he be distinguished from the continent person as traditionally described?

Although Aristotle does not describe a continently brave person, we can extend the basic points of the canonical situation to accommodate continence in regard to fear and confidence. But when we do so, brave and continent persons continue to look alike. Both courageous and continent persons will have the same view of what it is best to do and for what reason. We can suppose, for instance, that when their city is threatened from outside, they both recognize that it is best to stay and defend their city, even at a risk to their own lives. We can imagine that they realize that the city offers the material and psychological conditions needed to live the kind of life that is genuinely complete and pleasant, that the city enables them, in other words, to actualize their human powers in a full and unimpeded way. The destruction of the city's political life thus amounts to the destruction of a virtuous and happy life for them as individual citizens. Moreover, both courageous and continent persons recognize the danger involved in defending their city against hostile forces, and both find the thought of death painful and fearful (1117b7–8) – neither wants to die (1117b10–15). But each stands his ground against the impending danger.

If we focus on their views of what is best or on their ability to master fear, continently brave persons and truly brave persons look alike. But if we look at confidence, the other nonrational desire relevant to courage, we can distinguish them. The courageous person's confidence is different from that of other would-be courageous types. Unlike the confidence of professional soldiers, it is not derived from a knowledge of particular facts (1116b3–6). Nor does it come from experience (1117a11). Nor does it derive from an insufficient appreciation of one's own life (1117b18–20). The brave person's confidence is continuous. It is not upset by failure of some planned action, by the recognition of the enemy's superior numbers, and so on. Now the brave person's confidence can be continuous if it is derived from an enjoyment taken in the expression of his human powers, for the expression of these powers is not a contingent feature of the agent who expresses them. That it is so derived is our best way of understanding why Aristotle emphasizes the brave person's love of life at 1117b10–15. And it is this love of life, that is, a love of what is essential to a human life, that carries him forward to defend his city against attack.

The continently brave person does not have this stable and continuous confidence. We can imagine, as we did for the simply continent, that the continently brave person is in the process of developing the confidence typical of the truly brave person. And because he is developing it within a city that makes it possible for him to be as fully human as possible (by giving him opportunities to express his powers in various ways, both small and great), he is able to begin to find the self-expression of others' powers pleasant, too, and to develop feelings of friendship for his fellow citizens (1097b6–11, 1170a4–10, 1170b16ff.). Hence he has growing and widening attachments to his city and its citizens. His affection for his city and fellow citizens informs his perceptions, so that what appears practically salient in situations of danger is not the risk to his body, but the risk to his city. Hence he does not flee. But because his confidence, and the attachments that are products of that confidence, are tenuous, his perceptions of what is practically salient will be inconsistent. Thus we can expect him, as we did with the simply continent person, sometimes to act as an incontinent person (in regard to fear and confidence) would: Sometimes he will act against his generally held principles, namely, in those circumstances where his self-love fails him and his insecurities are pressing.

For Aristotle, the courageous person is not fearless, but he is as unperturbed as it is possible for someone to be. Although he is like everyone else in finding wounds and death painful and in suffering them unwillingly (1117b–8), he differs from others in standing firm against frightening things for the right reasons. Still, he is said to be a type of fearless person (1115a17). We can understand the cause of his fearlessness in the same way we understood the cause of the incontinent person's ignorance. The brave person's concern and affection for his fellow citizens and his city influences his perception of what is practically salient. His attachments cause him to focus on the future of his city, not on his personal safety apart from the city. And this explains why he is not fearless in the way that Aristotle condemns. The condemnable sort of fearless person either is incapable of feeling distress (1115b26–27) or has no love of life (1117b17–20).

Concluding Remarks

I have given some reasons to think that we should understand virtuous character in terms of true self-love, a nonrational love of one's own rational activity. A true self-lover loves most the exercise of his own rational powers. As a result, he also loves the exercise of these powers in other persons, forms affectionate attachments to them as citizen friends do, and is not vulnerable to the kinds of desires Aristotle associates with akratic action. Incontinence, on the other hand, I have read as a failure of recognition that is caused by a failure of character. The underlying cause of that failure is the incontinent's defective self-love, which is incompletely developed and thus unreliable. The defective self-love explains why the agent has the nonrational desire on which he actually acts (the desire to sleep with Helen or to eat the sweet) and why he fails to apply his usual principles to the situation he faces. If he does not love the exercise of rational activity most, he will find other aspects of the situation more compelling and will construct new practical premises to match his distorted perception.

In addition, I have argued that the other nonvirtuous conditions (continence and moral vice) share in the nonrational psychology of the incontinent person. Continence and incontinence mark stages of developing self-love, with the morally vicious person characterized by the most extreme self-hatred. In my discussion of courage and cowardice, I argued that the courageous person acts from a self-love that is based in a love of the exercise of his own and others' characteristic human powers. The courageous person has developed attachments to his fellow citizens and to his city that cause him to be more concerned about the safety of his community than about his personal physical safety. I used the notion of defective self-love to explain the deliberations and actions of noncourageous types.

I have argued that *akrasia* is to be understood as a failure in character as opposed to a failure in practical deliberation. If *akrasia* were a failure in practical deliberation, the development of good character could be viewed simply as additional motivation, necessary to put into effect the directives of practical reason. In that case, character would be secondary in its practical role, and the place of virtue in Aristotle's ethics would not be substantially different from its place in principle- and action-based ethical theories. I have argued, however, that an agent's practical perception, and hence his practical deliberations, are constrained by the fundamental nonrational desires and attachments that constitute his character.

REFERENCES

Annas, Julia, "Plato and Aristotle on Friendship and Altruism," *Mind*, 86 (1977): 532–54.

    The Morality of Happiness. Oxford: Oxford University Press, 1993.

Anscombe, G. E. M., "Modern Moral Philosophy," *Philosophy*, 33 (1958): 1–19.

Barnes, Jonathan, ed., *The Complete Works of Aristotle*. Princeton: Princeton University Press, 1984.

Broadie, Sarah, *Ethics with Aristotle*. Oxford: Oxford University Press, 1991.

Burnet, John, *The Ethics of Aristotle*. London: Methuen & Co., 1904.

Charles, David, *Aristotle's Philosophy of Action*. Ithaca: Cornell University Press, 1984.

Charlton, William, *Weakness of Will: A Philosophical Introduction*. Oxford: Basil Blackwell, 1988.

Cooper, John M., *Reason and Human Good in Aristotle*. Cambridge: Harvard University Press, 1975.

"Aristotle on Friendship," in Rorty, Amélie, ed., *Essays on Aristotle's Ethics*. Berkeley: University of California Press, 1980, pp. 301–40.

Dahl, Norman O., *Practical Reason, Aristotle, and Weakness of Will*. Minneapolis: University of Minnesota Press, 1984.

Davidson, Donald, "How Is Weakness of the Will Possible?" in Feinberg, Joel, ed., *Moral Concepts*. London: Oxford University Press, 1969, pp. 93–113.

Farquharson, A. S. L., tr., *De Motu Animalium*, in Barnes, Jonathan, ed., *The Complete Works of Aristotle*. Princeton: Princeton University Press, 1984.

Frankena, William, *Ethics*, 2nd ed. Englewood Cliffs, N.J., Prentice-Hall, 1973.

Hampton, Jean, "Does Hume Have an Instrumental Conception of Practical Reason?" Paper delivered at the Twenty-First Hume Society Conference, Rome, Italy, 1994.

Hardie, W. F. R., *Aristotle's Ethical Theory*. Oxford: Clarendon Press, 1968.

Homiak, Marcia L., "Virtue and Self-Love in Aristotle's Ethics," *The Canadian Journal of Philosophy*, 11 (1981): 633–51.

"The Pleasure of Virtue in Aristotle's Moral Theory," *Pacific Philosophical Quarterly*, 66 (1985): 93–110.

"Politics as Soul-Making: Aristotle on Becoming Good," *Philosophia*, 20 (1990): 167–93.

"Does Hume Have an Ethics of Virtue? Some Observations on Character and Deliberation in Hume and Aristotle." Paper delivered at the Twenty-First Hume Society Conference, Rome, Italy, 1994.

Hursthouse, Rosalind, "Virtue Theory and Abortion," *Philosophy & Public Affairs*, 20 (1991): 223–46.

Irwin, Terence, *Plato's Moral Theory*. Oxford: Oxford University Press, 1977.

Aristotle's Nicomachean Ethics, trans. and notes. Indianapolis: Hackett, 1985.

"Some Rational Aspects of Incontinence," *The Southern Journal of Philosophy*, 27 (supplement, 1988): 49–88.

Classical Thought. Oxford: Oxford University Press, 1989.

Joachim, H. H., *The Nicomachean Ethics*. Oxford: Clarendon Press, 1951.

Joint Association of Classical Teachers, *The World of Athens*. Cambridge University Press, 1984.

Kant, Immanuel, *The Metaphysical Principles of Virtue*, trans. James Ellington, Indianapolis: Bobbs-Merrill, 1964.

Kenny, Anthony, "The Practical Syllogism and Incontinence," *Phronesis*, 11 (1966): 163–84.

Aristotle's Theory of the Will, New Haven: Yale University Press, 1979.

Korsgaard, Christine, "Does Hume Believe in the Hypothetical Imperative?" Paper delivered at the Twenty-First Hume Society Conference, Rome, Italy, 1994.

Kraut, Richard, *Aristotle on the Human Good*. Princeton: Princeton University Press, 1989.

Louden, Robert, "On Some Vices of Virtue Ethics," *American Philosophical Quarterly*, 21 (1984): 227–36.

MacIntyre, Alasdair, "Virtue Ethics," in Becker, Lawrence C., and Becker, Charlotte B., eds., *Encyclopedia of Ethics*, Vol. 2. New York: Garland Publishing, 1992, pp. 1276–82.

McDowell, John, "Comments on T. H. Irwin's 'Some Rational Aspects of Incontinence,'" *The Southern Journal of Philosophy*, 27 (supplement, 1988): 89–102.

McIntyre, Alison, "Is Akratic Action Always Irrational?" in Flanagan, Owen, and Rorty, Amélie, eds., *Identity, Character, and Morality: Essays in Moral Psychology*, Cambridge: MIT Press, 1990, pp. 379–400.

Mele, Alfred, "Aristotle on *Akrasia* and Knowledge," *The Modern Schoolman*, 58 (1981): 137–57.

Nussbaum, Martha, *Aristotle's De Motu Animalium*, Princeton: Princeton University Press, 1978.

"The Discernment of Perception: An Aristotelian Conception of Private and Public Rationality," in Cleary, John, ed., *The Proceedings of the Boston Area Colloquium on Ancient Philosophy*. Lanham, MD: University Press of America, 1985, pp. 151–201.

Ross, David, ed., *Aristotle's Prior and Posterior Analytics*. Oxford: Clarendon Press, 1949.

Santas, Gerasimos, "Aristotle on Practical Inference, the Explanation of Action, and *Akrasia*," *Phronesis*, 14 (1969): 162–89.

Sherman, Nancy, *The Fabric of Character*. Oxford: Clarendon Press, 1989.

Trianosky, Gregory, "What Is Virtue Ethics All About?" *American Philosophical Quarterly*, 27 (1990): 335–43.

Wiggins, David, "Deliberation and Practical Reason," in Rorty, Amélie, ed., *Essays on Aristotle's Ethics*. Berkeley: University of California Press, 1980.

NOTES

More years ago than I care to acknowledge, John Rawls served as second examiner at my dissertation defense. I claimed then in writing, and do so now for a second time, that my greatest philosophical debt is to him. Because he does not consider himself expert in Greek ethics, my testament then, I know, must have puzzled him. I meant that I had learned from him that important elements of a philosopher's view often emerge from passages that are traditionally thought to be subordinate discussions or merely interesting asides. Rawls's lectures on moral and political philosophy served as a model to me of how to ask questions of a philosophical text and of where to look to find the right questions to ask. At the time I wrote my dissertation, I was working on topics that most writers on Aristotle considered peripheral and hence left untouched. Rawls may remember that he seemed most intrigued by my inchoate musings about the effects of character on practical deliberation. I thought it fitting here to show him how these views have developed.

I am grateful to the National Humanities Center, Research Triangle Park, NC, for a fellowship year in 1988–9, during which the strategy and direction of this essay were first developed, and to John Cooper, Burton Dreben, Janet Levin, Charles Young, and the editors of this volume for challenging and constructive comments on subsequent versions.

1. As most writers on this topic do. See, for example, Anscombe (1958) and MacIntyre (1992).
2. In addition to an early statement of this contrast in Anscombe (1958), see Trianosky (1990) and Hursthouse (1991). In my description of the contrast, I am most influenced by Hursthouse, though I depart from her exposition to clarify the place of virtue in a modern theory.
3. By "practical reason," I mean noninstrumental reasoning about the ends of action or about which actions are right or are to be done. Successful practical reasoning will, then, often involve the development of related capacities, such as the capacity to grasp relevant particulars and means. In this sense, both Aristotle and Kant employ practical reason, whereas Hume, on the canonical reading, does not. For insightful discussions of Hume's views on nondemonstrative reasoning, see Hampton (1994) and Korsgaard (1994).
4. Kant seems to be suggesting a secondary practical role for the virtues when he writes in (1964) that the development of sympathetic feeling can make following the moral law easier, since sympathy "is one of the impulses placed in us by nature for effecting what the representation of duty might not accomplish by itself" (AK. 457).
5. In this essay all references to Aristotle are to the *Nicomachean Ethics* (hereafter *EN*), unless otherwise signaled. I follow the translation of Irwin (1985) except where noted.
6. In (a) her rejection of what she calls the "grand-end" view of Aristotle's ethics (ch. 4), according to which the virtuous person's decisions rest on deliberation about an ultimate good, and in (b) her defense of the inexact nature of Aristotelian ethics (e.g., at pp. 242–60), Broadie (1991) emphasizes some of the elements of Aristotle's views that appeal to expositors of virtue ethics.
7. For a discussion of this difficulty, see Frankena (1973). For a general discussion of some important problems facing virtue ethics, see Louden (1984), and for a response to some major criticisms, see Hursthouse (1991).
8. See, for example, Annas (1993), who describes virtue ethics as agent-centered in the sense that the virtuous agent is "primary for understanding" what we ought to do, "because if we want to know what the point is of avoiding cowardly acts, we shall understand this best if we look closely at the agent, and what it would be for him to be brave or cowardly" (p. 113).
9. Though Annas (1993), for example, stresses that virtue involves an affective as well as an intellectual side, it is not clear to me how the affective side plays more than a supporting role to the agent's recognition of what gives point to her actions, since Annas allows for the possibility that "one might have a badly developed character and yet still become virtuous, perhaps by being converted by Aristotle's arguments" (p. 54).
10. There are some ethical theories in which character does not seem to play a derivative role. If Hume, for example, is correct to think that "reason is, and ought only to be, the slave of the passions and can never pretend to any other office than to serve and obey them" (*Treatise*, III, i), then the emotional

attitudes and feelings that, on his view, constitute virtue are not subordinate to practical reason, because there is no practical reason. For a brief discussion of these issues, see Homiak (1994).

11. The first three articles in this series are Homiak (1981), (1985), and (1990).
12. Although Aristotle sometimes writes as though morally vicious people are also single-minded about what to do (as in his discussions of the particular moral vices in *EN* III and IV), he describes them as conflicted at *EN* IX.4, 1166b7ff. Some interpreters regard these later passages as anomalous. See, for example, Annas (1977). For a response to Annas, see Broadie (1991, p. 161).
13. Cf. Irwin's (1977) discussion of *thumos* in the *Republic*, pp. 192–5.
14. Following Irwin and reading *boulēsin*, rational desire, rather than *bouleusin*, deliberation.
15. The agent's *prohairesis* is itself the combination of his rational desire, *boulēsis*, about what he deems best overall (*EN* 1152a17, 1146b22–23) and his deliberation about how to achieve the end(s) of his desire (*EN* 1139a21–b5).
16. For Aristotle, incontinence is thus a special kind of internal conflict. First, the presence of contrary appetitive desires separates incontinence from moral and practical dilemmas. The incontinent is not the person who thinks that, whatever choice he makes, he will be transgressing some moral principle or producing overall bad results. Even a morally virtuous person can find himself in these situations. (See, for example, Aristotle's discussion of "mixed actions" at *EN* 1110a19–23.) For Aristotle, however, the morally virtuous person cannot be incontinent (or continent) (*EN* 1146a8).

   Second, not any contrary desire will mark a case of conflict as simple, or canonical, incontinence (or continence). For simple incontinence, the contrary desire must be for the objects of the bodily pleasures (*EN* 1148a5–11). Hence other cases, in which, for example, an agent may allow sympathy or compassion to prevent him from acting according to his judgment of what is best, will not count as incontinence for Aristotle, although they may be related to it. In what follows I shall be primarily concerned with Aristotle's canonical cases of incontinence, but I shall indicate in Section VI how the canonical case can be extended to psychic conflict in regard to fear.

   Finally, the incontinent agent is importantly different from the intemperate person, who acts on his (incorrect) *prohairesis*, "thinking it is right in every case to pursue the pleasant thing at hand" (*EN* 1146b22–23).
17. For Socrates' views on *akrasia*, see *Protagoras* 352a–360d. Both the general direction and the particular details of Aristotle's discussion favor an argument in support of Socrates, to the extent that Aristotle agrees with Socrates that straightforward "knowing" incontinence does not occur. In emphasizing that Aristotle has a Socratic conclusion, I follow the majority of commentators on Aristotle's ethical writings. See, for example, Burnet (1904), Joachim (1951), Hardie (1968), Santas (1969), and Cooper (1975). Commentators who argue for a nontraditional interpretation, in which Aristotle accepts the existence of straightforward *akrasia*, include Kenny (1966, 1979), Mele (1981), Dahl (1984), and Broadie (1991).
18. So interpreters have come to call the inference described here (and, more generally, at 1147a25–28). For thorough discussions of the practical syllogism, see Cooper (1975), Nussbaum (1978, Essay 4), and Charles (1984).

19. For a summary of the interpretive difficulties, see Charlton (1988), p. 46.
20. For the view that *protasis* is best translated "premise," see Ross (1949), p. 288, and Hardie (1968), p. 278.
21. See Dahl (1984) and Charles (1984) for two different arguments in favor of the view that *protasis* in 1147b9 is best taken as "proposition."
22. Irwin proposes this strategy in (1988).
23. See Note 17. For Plato's view of incontinence, see *Republic* IV, 437–end.
24. Although not so labeled, the most detailed defense of this view known to me is in Irwin (1988).
25. This is Irwin's suggestion in (1988).
26. I do not mean to suggest here that Aristotle's texts clearly indicate whether the best human life is more a matter of contemplation or more a matter of the social goods. The literature on this question is vast. For a compelling recent defense of contemplation as the best life, see Kraut (1989).
27. So Broadie seems to argue in (1991), pp. 248–9.
28. For an insightful discussion of Homeric ethics, see Irwin (1989), ch. 2. For a discussion of the differences between Homeric and Aristotelian virtues, see Homiak (1985).
29. This seems to be Davidson's suggestion in (1969). Davidson thinks his interpretation of incontinence is close to Aristotle's (p. 111, n. 2). For a discussion of the weaknesses of such an approach, see McIntyre (1990).
30. This characterization seems broad enough to accommodate both those who view the major premise as the statement of a rule and those who view it as the specification of an end to be achieved. For skepticism about whether Aristotle has a systematic account of the practical syllogism, and of practical reasoning in general, see Annas (1993), pp. 87–94.
31. See, for example, Cooper (1975), p. 48, n. 61; Nussbaum (1978), p. 204; and Sherman (1989), pp. 58–60.
32. Here I am assuming that the earlier difficulties noted with the incontinent's ignorance of the minor premise have been resolved according to the suggestion in Section I that we can distinguish between what the incontinent knows prior to, and what he knows at, the time of action.
33. See Cooper (1975), p. 53.
34. As translated by Farquharson (1984).
35. Wiggins (1981), p. 233. Wiggins emphasizes what he calls "situational appreciation," the ability to recognize the features of a situation most relevant to an agent's practical concerns. The minor premise of a practical syllogism, according to Wiggins, records such recognition (or lack of it). Although Wiggins suggests that the practically wise person has a high order of situational appreciation, Wiggins does not attempt to explain the relationship between excellence at situational appreciation and excellence of character.
36. This reading of Aristotle's description of incontinence thus supports the prevailing view that the incontinent has two practical syllogisms. His second syllogism (of appetite) displaces his first syllogism (of reason).
37. In (1980), Wiggins calls "most salient" those features of practical situations agents deem most relevant and in response to which they act. Some commentators have used a notion of salience to detail the complexity and multileveled nature of practical reasoning. See, for example, Nussbaum (1985), McDowell (1988), and Sherman (1989), chs. 2–3. Yet none of these philosophers (including Wiggins himself) has developed a view of the rela-

tionship between character and practical salience. In this essay I try to rectify that deficiency. If there is no systematic relationship between different types of character and different perceptual tendencies, then Aristotle's doctrine of the mean lacks content. We are left with the formal recognition that "what determines which concern a virtuous person acts on . . . is that one rather than another of the potentially practically relevant features of the situation strikes such a person – rightly – as salient, as what matters about the situation" (McDowell, 1988, p. 93).

38. This example (and the later comparison of Paris to Odysseus) is inspired by and in part derived from Charlton's discussion in (1988), pp. 47–50. Although Charlton believes that the incontinent has a distorted perception of his practical situation, Charlton fails, I think, to characterize correctly the cause of the incontinent's misperception.

39. For a general discussion of Greek cultural values, including the importance of following the conventions governing hospitality, see Joint Association of Classical Teachers (1984), ch. 3.

40. Aristotle recognizes cases of incontinence in regard to sexual desire at 1149b15.

41. This is Charlton's suggestion in (1988), p. 50.

42. I do not mean to suggest that Paris *must* view his actions as exceptional. His attraction to Helen's beauty and his desire for the associated pleasure *might* simply obscure her other features. But it makes sense to think that Paris will find a way to view his actions as exceptional, because they are in such flagrant opposition to the aristocratic norms he accepts and which constitute his sense of who he is. But in other cases where the threat to one's self-image is weaker, there may be less need to view one's actions as exceptional.

43. For a discussion of these criteria, see Irwin (1989), ch. 2.

44. This is not to say that material possessions are unimportant to the Homeric hero. But they must come to him in the proper manner as a reward for heroism or for his ability to care for his people, which would ultimately involve heroism.

45. I do not mean to be suggesting here that the virtuous person will take pleasure from every exercise of rational activity, whether his own or others'. There is, after all, only so much that one person can appreciate. More important, some rational activity (such as that involved in morally vicious activities) will not appeal to the virtuous person.

46. For an insightful discussion of the ways friends can identify with each other's activities, see Cooper (1980).

47. For more detailed arguments in support of these connections, see Homiak (1981) on courage, temperance, and their associated vices and Homiak (1985) on the virtues and vices of social life as described in *EN* IV, 6–8.

Coercion, Ideology, and Education in Hobbes's *Leviathan*

S. A. LLOYD

Some years ago while studying Rawls's Dewey Lectures I came across a footnote to Lecture II that forced a conceptual shift in my understanding of Hobbes's political philosophy as dramatic as a duck-rabbit. The note was not about Hobbes. It was appended to Rawls's discussion of the full publicity condition of Justice as Fairness, and in it Rawls observed that a well-ordered society does not require an ideology (in Marx's sense) in order to achieve stability. Full publicity requires a transparency of the real terms of social cooperation, which citizens can then measure against their fundamental interests and their self-conceptions. Marx, I ruminated, must have been right in holding that a state not founded on subjects' real interests will require ideology for its stability over time, because force alone cannot maintain stability forever. The latent assumption that force alone cannot ensure stability struck me as obviously correct,[1] and I found myself at a loss to understand how Hobbes, the forefather of our social contract tradition and undeniably a formidable and savvy philosopher, could have failed to realize it. The philosophical interpretations of Hobbes I was acquainted with all urged that he sought to secure a perpetual order based on absolute obedience by means of credible threats of physical force against subjects. If that long-run strategy was so obviously hopeless, what must Hobbes actually have been trying to do?

The product of my struggle with that question was an interpretation of *Leviathan* as an attempt to persuade subjects to accept an absolutist principle of political obligation by arguing that it was a corollary of their deepest religious interests, when properly understood, as well as an implication of their primary moral duty, and a dictate of prudence in most cases.[2] The idea was that Hobbes understood disorder to be primarily the result of people's action, not on their narrow interest in self-preservation, but rather on interests for which they were willing to fight and perhaps die. Their interests in fulfilling their duties to God, achieving salvation, doing their moral duties, or protecting the interests of their children – the sorts of potentially *transcendent* interests that could motivate defying threats to one's bodily preservation or comfort – were what both moved and enabled people to rebel. If this were the problem, force alone could not be expected to solve it. Attention to people's potentially transcendent interests would be required.

Hobbes's attempt to gain support for his (allegedly) maximally stable principle of political obligation through rational argumentation from sources which subjects *themselves* insisted were authoritative in moral and religious matters required, as I argued, extensive redescription and rationalization of religious interests, as well as an aggressive system of education to reproduce over time the conclusions of Hobbes's conceptual arguments. In this interpretation, force or the threat of it played no significant role in Hobbes's account except as a necessary aid in reforming the universities of his day, the bastions, as he saw it, of disruptively erroneous conceptions of religious and moral duty.[3] It was in the last analysis a kind of *education*, and not might, as I came to think, that made for order in Hobbes's system.

Supposing one suspends disbelief about this interpretation, one might say that it is fine as far as it goes, but that it doesn't address the whole challenge posed by Rawls's footnote. Even if Hobbes doesn't make the patent error of relying on force alone to maintain social stability, he might still be relying on *ideology* to shore up a political system that is against the true interests of its subjects. Whether a system that relies on ideological indoctrination is an improvement over one based on physical coercion is surely an open question. Depending upon the specifics, we might find an effective system of mind control, socialization, propagandization, or ideological indoctrination *more* objectionable than the most draconian physical penalties so long as these were for voluntary infractions of justified and well publicized laws. So to acquit Hobbes of the charge of naively assuming that mere force secures order is not yet enough to show that his system is not every bit as morally objectionable for other reasons.

That is the question I wish to address in this essay. Is Hobbes's solution to social disorder ideological, or in some other way objectionably intellectually coercive? Answering this question requires separating out a number of considerations. What sort of education does Hobbes have in mind: what is to be taught, and how is it to be taught? Are people to be taught falsehoods and, if so, are the falsehoods contrary to their interests? Does their acceptance of the teaching depend on illusion or delusion? Are subjects asked to believe conclusions without having the grounds of those conclusions divulged? Is dissent allowed and, if not, is that in itself objectionable? Is it independently problematic that it is the state that is doing the teaching, rather than, say, parents or lesser associations within society? And is the mandatory character of the education objectionable? This complex of questions, which bears on our own attempts to delimit a justifiable system of public education, will be my focus.

My approach will be to attend to the formal features of Hobbes's educational system, rather than to its peculiar content. In particular, I'll set aside the question whether the doctrines offered in political education are *true*. The reason is this. Any educational program that contains false doctrines will for that reason be objectionable, and its falsehoods should be excised, or the system rejected. But acknowledging this doesn't tell us anything *systematically* interesting about *types* or *kinds* of educational systems. When we point to the objectionableness of, say, a physically coercive system, we are interested in why and how its being coercive makes it objectionable, and determining this requires that we consider how we would judge such a type of system even were it to impart only true doctrines. If we consider a system of subliminal education, our interest is in seeing whether its subliminal mode of operation is distinctively problematic, but to determine this we must abstract from its content. Similarly, if we are interested in evaluating the Hobbesian system of mandatory political education, we do best to consider it in isolation from our judgment of whether its content is true, and concentrate instead on its virtues or defects *under an appropriate formal description*.

Some examples may help to clarify what is meant by a formal description of an educational system. A liberal society might describe its educational system as "teaching all children of the society, by means of a mandatory system of publicly funded education, those attitudes, skills and true (or at least reasonable) views necessary for them to develop into independent citizens able and willing to engage in fair social cooperation." Here the description picks out the aims of the teaching, its means and scope, and our intention that it convey true/reasonable views. Contrast this with the sort of educational system depicted in the John Carpenter film *They Live*. In that science fiction world, aliens have gained control of the earth's population, unbeknownst to most humans, by means of what is best described as "a system of social saturation by subliminal messages to induce in the population a sense of private contentment and political apathy." Here there is no suggestion that the doctrines conveyed are intended as either true or consonant with the satisfaction of true human interests. To compare these as educational systems, it makes sense to set aside the question of whether the specific doctrines they teach are true and focus instead on the methods, aim, and scope of the educational systems. Further on I isolate what I take to be a defensible formal description of Hobbes's educational system, as well as a third contrasting case, roughly characterized as Machiavellian. Both of these cases have a (similar) particular content that we may dismiss as involving false claims about how basic human interests are best served, but merit very different degrees of condemnation reflecting their quite different formal descriptions. I hope these four differing cases will make sufficiently clear this distinction between a formal description of a system and its more particular content.

Once this distinction is in place, we can consider how to rank systems along the dimensions of desirability of formal features and truth of content. Though we should most prefer a good formal system with true content and least prefer a system defective in both respects, how to order the intermediate possibilities is subject to disagreement. I will suggest that Hobbes's educational system is properly characterized, from the point of view of liberal political philosophers, as having acceptable formal features but defective content, and that this characterization should not render it anathema to liberals, since at least one founder of their own tradition, J. S. Mill, held that a system with acceptable form but defective content is superior to one with defective form though its content be true.[4] My first task will be to isolate the proper formal description of Hobbes's educational system. But since we can't get started without some idea of the specifics of Hobbes's educational system, I'll begin with a thumbnail sketch of the aim and content of Hobbes's proposed teaching.

I. Aim and Content

The broad aim of Hobbes's political theory is to show people that they have what they can see in their own terms to be good and sufficient reasons for obeying their effective sovereign except in extremely rare circumstances. The kinds of reasons Hobbes recognizes people to have are narrowly prudential interests in one's physical survival and flourishing; moral interests (including reasons from both obligation and natural duty); affectionate interests in the wellbeing of loved ones; and religious interests, both in fulfilling one's duties to God and in achieving one's own salvation (what I have called elsewhere "special prudential interest"). Hobbes aims at a confluence of reasons from these distinct interests, for adhering to his principle of political obligation, and accordingly mounts arguments for that principle on each of these grounds.[5] Hobbes's principle of political obligation, stated at *Leviathan* 395 [186], is this: "subjects owe to soveraigns simple obedience in all things wherein their obedience is not repugnant to the lawes of God."[6]

The prudential argument urges that it is in our interest to live in a stable state that can increase our prospects for security and a commodious life, and the best candidate for a principle that ensures stability across the relevant range of circumstances is Hobbes's. The moral argument holds that we have a natural duty not to act in a way that we would be unwilling to have others act, and that since our prudential interests dictate that we should want *others* to adhere to Hobbes's principle (because it promises maximal stability), natural duty requires us to do likewise. Moreover, if we have either explicitly undertaken to obey our sovereign (through, say, one of the oaths of allegiance common in Hobbes's day) or tacitly done so (by openly receiving the protection of the commonwealth),[7] then we have as well a moral obligation to obey in all of the conditions that Hobbes's principle specifies.[8]

Most importantly, Hobbes offers two religious arguments for his principle: the primary one from religious duty, and a supplemental one from special prudence. Our only available sources of religious knowledge – namely natural reason, personal revelation, and Scripture – all show that our primary duty to God is to obey our civil sovereign. They show further that a good faith effort to obey the civil sovereign (where God takes the will for the deed) is a necessary condition of salvation. If these and his earlier arguments are accepted, and their conclusions and essential implications taught, Hobbes imagines that it may be possible to convert his "truth of speculation, into the utility of practice" (408 [195]).

Although bringing subjects to accept these *conclusions* is central to Hobbes's strategy for addressing social disorder, teaching all subjects the central *arguments* of *Leviathan* would be, for every venue but the universities, overly ambitious and potentially self-defeating. But rather than proposing such an educational program, Hobbes offers a small number of specifics to be taught to the general public: (1) the content and grounds of "the essential rights of sovereignty," (2) the Laws of Nature, (3) the sovereign's positive laws (whatever they may be), and (4) the Scriptual grounds for the sovereign's virtually absolute authority. (Hobbes assumes that in addition subjects will continue to receive ordinary religious instruction from their local pastors.) Hobbes's teaching does not include rules as to the specific characteristics that government, or governors, or positive laws, must have to merit obedience, nor stipulations concerning the content of the religious doctrines to be taught. These may be (according to both natural law and Scripture) as the sovereign would have them.

Mechanisms of Education

How is this education to be accomplished? The specifics are to be taught publicly, to the common man at regular intervals from the pulpit, and to the educated in the universities. The common folk will receive most of their education from preachers.[9] Parents will also be responsible for some of the teaching.[10]

But because preachers are educated in the universities, as are parliamentarians and others who might by their poor leadership or example corrupt the people's education, the universities must be especially carefully monitored:

the greatest part of Man-kind . . . receive the notions of their duty chiefly from divines in the pulpit. . . . And the divines, and such others as make shew of learning, derive their knowledge from the universities, and from the schooles of law, or from the books which by men eminent in those schooles and universities have been published. It is therefore manifest, that *the instruction of the people dependeth wholly, on the right teaching of youth in the universities.* (384 [179–80], emphasis added.)

It would be difficult to stress sufficiently how important Hobbes takes the influence of the universities to be: in fact he repeatedly blames them for the English Civil War and regards their reformation as a necessary condition for the maintenance of peace.[11]

In addition to controlling the education of the educators such as preachers and teachers, the books they use and the actual doctrines they teach are also subject to the sovereign's direct prescreening and approval:

It is annexed to the soveraignty, to be judge of what opinions and doctrines are averse, and what conducing to peace; and consequently, on what occasions, how farre, and what men are to be trusted withall, in speaking to multitudes of people; and who shall examine the doctrines of all bookes before they be published. (233 [91])

When potentially seditious works are used, like the classical republican texts, they are to be used under the supervision of state-authorized teachers.[12] And the sovereign may select his public teachers using a litmus test, or even a catalog of what is to be taught:

It is true, that the civill magistrate, intending to employ a minister in the charge of teaching, may enquire of him, if hee bee content to preach such and such doctrines; and in case of refusall, may deny him the employment. . . . (700 [378])

It would appear, then, that the state possesses a thoroughgoing control over a system of mandatory education acknowledged, if not actually designed, to maintain the state's stability.

II. Truth, Transparency, and Dissent

At this point, things look pretty bleak for Hobbes. Subjects are to be regularly taught what conduces to the state's stability by state-approved teachers using state-screened books, and this is worrisome. But why, exactly? We'll consider first whether the problem is with the content (under a description) of the teachings, with what they include or exclude. The problem might be, for example, that subjects are being taught known falsehoods, or that the true grounds of the doctrines taught are not being divulged. Or perhaps what is objectionable is that no competing doctrines are taught or that dissent is not allowed. We consider Hobbes's position on each of these issues in turn.

Ideology

This sort of state teaching might be objectionable if the doctrines taught were known or with reason thought to be false, especially if they were needed to maintain a political regime that was against people's true interests and so could be accepted only if people were mistaken or deluded about the grounds of those doctrines. An educational system with those features would be providing ideological support for a defective regime. It may seem on its face a crazy question even to *ask* whether Hobbes's educational system is a mere ideological tool – isn't it obvious that it *must* be, given that Hobbes endorsed Absolutism? How could any educational system that helps to make stable a bad political regime be anything but objectionably ideological?

Let us grant at the outset that the political regime Hobbes favors is in fact defective, and let us assume that his educational system would in fact support it. It is still sensible to ask whether Hobbes's educational system is objectionably ideological. If it is proper to describe that system as distorting half-truths into lending support for institutional arrangements whose actual operations are, contrary to appearances, against true human interests, then we should conclude that it is objectionably ideological. But what if its proper description is quite different? Imagine, for instance, that its support for absolutist conclusions is the result of faulty internal logic or faulty causal inferences concerning the best means of satisfying basic interests, rather than of any misidentification of true human interests, dependence on half-truths, or deceptive methodology. We must allow room for some distinction between merely mistaken systems and objectionably ideological ones. The fact that the educational system conveys falsehoods is not enough to establish that it is objectionably ideological. The issue then, is a complicated one that requires a closer examination of the formal features of Hobbes's system.

The first point to consider is, again, not whether the views Hobbes wants taught *are* true, but whether Hobbes intends his educational system to be properly describable as "disseminating only true doctrines." The textual evidence on this point is wholly unambiguous. Hobbes takes his educational system to be teaching (by a perfectly transparent mechanism), not only *true* doctrines, but doctrines whose truth is *evident* – that is to say, readily perceived – and whose recognition is *necessary* for the satisfaction of genuine human interests. Political education is to teach "the science of just and unjust," and to teach a science is to "demonstrate the truth thereof perspicuously to another" (117 [22]). "Why," Hobbes asks rhetorically in his *Behemoth*,

> may not men be taught their duty, that is, the science of just and unjust, as divers other sciences have been taught, *from true principles and evident demonstration*; and much more easily than any of those preachers and democratical gentlemen [during the civil war] could teach rebellion and treason? (*B* 39, emphasis added)

Hobbes sees the views he is promoting as not only true, but as *evidently* true. People are gullible and *could* be made to believe almost anything; but what Hobbes wants taught are doctrines whose truth is so evident that it will be readily perceived by any unbiased listener. In a passage where he addresses the objection that the vulgar are incapable of learning the "principles of reason" that compose the essential rights of sovereignty, Hobbes insists:

> the common-peoples's minds, unlesse they be tainted with dependance on the potent, or scribbled over with the opinions of their doctors, are like clean paper, fit to receive whatsoever by publique authority shall be imprinted in them. Shall whole nations be brought to acquiesce in the great mysteries of Christian religion, which are above reason; and millons of men be made believe that the same body may be in innumerable places at one and the same time, which is against reason; and shall not men be able, by their teaching and preaching, protected by the law, to make that received *which is so consonant to reason that any unprejudicated man needs no more to learn it than to hear it?* I conclude therefore, that in the instruction of the people in the essentiall rights (which are the naturall and fundamentall lawes) of soveraignty, there is no difficulty . . . (379 [176–7], emphasis added)

So the doctrines advanced by education are taken to be both true and evident. But doesn't Hobbes famously endorse an idiosyncratic view of religious (and moral) truth that makes impossible any divergence between teaching what is really true and teaching what the state judges to be true?[13] According to a widely received interpretation of Hobbes, those religious doctrines are true which the sovereign propounds, because the sovereign's pronouncements *define* true doctrine. If this interpretation were correct, the formal feature of Hobbes's educational system that it is to convey true doctrines (including relevant religious doctrines) could not do any justificatory work. This "voluntarist" interpretation in essence collapses any distinction between this structural feature of an educational system and its content: it would be properly formally described as "conveying true doctrines" only because whatever doctrines it conveys are said to be true by definition.

The voluntarist interpretation misunderstands Hobbes's position, which is not that the sovereign's pronouncing something true makes it so, but is rather that Scripture requires us to regard the sovereign's judgments in matters of religion as *authoritative, whether or not they are true.* (In this way the sovereign's judgment is like that of the Supreme Court, or an umpire in a baseball game: authoritative even if "cosmically" incorrect.) True religion (the plain parts of Christian Scripture as interpreted by Hobbes) and true morality (the self-evident laws of nature) direct us to subordinate our judgment to that of the sovereign, even when his judgment is erroneous. This corrected reading is confirmed by Hobbes's acknowledgment that sovereigns may be *mistaken* in their religious conclusions, which would be strictly impossible if their judgments defined truth:

Suppose that a Christian king should from this foundation *Jesus is the Christ*, draw some false consequences, that is to say, make some superstructions of hay, or stubble, and command the teaching of the same. . . . *Christian kings may erre in deducing a consequence*, but who shall judge? Shall a private man judge, when the question is of his own obedience? (624–5 [330], emphasis added)

The same goes for moral judgment. If the sovereign's moral judgments may be mistaken, then his judgment cannot be what defines moral truth, yet

There is no judge subordinate, *nor sovereign*, but may erre in a judgement of equity. . . . (323 [144], emphasis added)

Thus Hobbes does maintain the distinction between true religious doctrine and the sovereign's pronouncements on religious doctrine, allowing that when Hobbes characterizes his educational system as teaching truths, he is saying something more than simply that it teaches what it teaches.

Perhaps most important is Hobbes's insistence that true doctrines cannot urge action against humanity's general interests. Humans fundamentally need peace as a condition of the realization of most of their other interests. Hobbes argues that "it is annexed to the soveraignty to be judge of what opinions and doctrines are averse, and what conducing to peace, . . ."

And though in matter of doctrine, nothing ought to be regarded but the truth; yet this is not repugnant to regulating of the same by peace. *For doctrine repugnant to peace, can no more be true, than peace and concord can be against the law of nature.* (233 [91], emphasis added)

So doctrine against humans' fundamental interest in peace must be false. This view is a part of what I have elsewhere called Hobbes's doctrine of the unity of reason,[14] and it resurfaces in his defense of Galileo:

[As an instance of vain philosophy] with the introduction of false, we may joyn also the suppression of true philosophy, by such men as neither by lawfull authority, nor sufficient study, are competent judges of the truth. . . . But what reason is there for it? Is it because such opinions are contrary to true religion? *that cannot be, if they be true.* (703 [380], emphasis added)

True doctrines, Hobbes maintains, cannot be contrary to the basic human interests in peace, preservation, flourishing, and piety, and all truths hang together in a perfectly coherent way. This is a consequence of God's activity in constructing the world. And so Hobbes criticizes the "vain and false philosophy" of Aristotle and the schoolmen who succeeded him on the grounds that it is "not onely vain, but also pernicious to the publique state" (697 [376]). This means that Hobbes *cannot* see the truths disseminated by his educational system as incompatible with the realization of our true human interests, for that would imply that they were not true.

What Hobbes apparently intends, then, is a system of education under the description "education in *evidently true doctrines that conduce to the satisfaction of basic human interests.*" Furthermore, this education is to be carried out by exposing the *true grounds* of the doctrines taught. Hobbes intends his education to be transparent, requiring that not just the doctrines, but also their grounds or reasons, be taught:

It is against [the sovereign's] duty to let the people be ignorant or misinformed of the *grounds and reasons* of those his essentiall rights; because thereby men are easie to be seduced, and drawn to resist him, when the commonwealth shall require their use and exercise. *And the grounds of these rights, have the rather need to be diligently and truly taught;* because they cannot be maintained by any civill law, or terrour of legal punishment . . . (377 [175], emphasis added)

and

Common people know nothing of right or wrong by their own meditation; *they must therefore be taught the grounds of their duty, and the reasons why calamities ever follow disobedience to their lawful sovereigns*. But to the contrary, our rebels were publicly taught rebellion in the pulpits. (*B*, 144, emphasis added)

Even our obvious religious duties are better grasped once their true justifying grounds have been laid out:

All that is required, both in faith and manners, for man's salvation is (I confess) set down in Scripture as plainly as can be. . . . *Let all men be subject to the higher powers whether it be the King or those that are sent by him* [etc.] . . . are words of the Scripture, which are well enough understood; but neither children, nor the greatest part of men, do *understand why it is their duty* to do so. (*B*, 54, latter emphasis added)

On the basis of these passages it seems, then, that Hobbes believes that subjects' attachment to the doctrines will be strengthened rather than undermined if their true grounds are understood.

What all of these considerations taken together allow us to say is that Hobbes's educational system, under its proper formal description, is not obviously a mere ideological support for a defective political regime. Let us say, with Rawls, that a political system depends on ideology for its stability if it would not be stable unless people held views that they could affirm only if they were under illusions or delusions concerning the facts about the operation of the system, or its grounds, or their own interests. For Hobbes's educational system to be condemnable as simply the ideological prop for such a political regime, it would have to reliably create the necessary illusions or delusions, and in the right sort of way. But in Hobbes's system, the doctrines taught are advanced in good faith as true, and overtly argued to be doctrines squarely in line with people's interests in peace, security, flourishing, and piety, which are plausible candidates for fundamental interests. The political mechanisms that advance these interests are transparent and fully revealed by the education, and, moreover, the grounds for the doctrines are fully revealed. For this reason their acknowledgment seems not to be dependent on illusion or delusion (though of course they may depend on faulty inferences and thus prove mistaken). As far as Hobbes is concerned, one who sees her basic interests as they really are, can in cognizance of the actual grounds of the claims on her political obedience and the actual operation of political institutions, affirm those claims as both true and proper. No illusion or delusion is needed.

Constrast this with a system that appears to be quite willing to rely on ideology. Consider the view suggested by Machiavelli's remarks in *The Discourses*:

it is the duty of the rulers of a republic or of a kingdom to maintain the foundations of the religion that sustains them; and if this is done it will be easy for them to keep their republic religious and, as a consequence, good and united. And they must favor and encourage all those things which arise in favor of religion, even if they judge them to be false.[15]

And

If one desires or intends to reform the government of a city so that the reform will be acceptable and will be able to maintain itself to everyone's satisfaction, he should retain at least the shadow of ancient customs so that it will not seem to the people that they have changed institutions, whereas in actual fact the new institutions may be completely different from those of the past; for the majority of men delude themselves with what seems to be rather than with what actually is; indeed, they are more often moved by things that seem to be rather than by things that are.[16]

These passages suggest a view that is happy to disseminate doctrines that its author knows or believes to be false and to welcome people's erroneous assumptions about the actual character of their political institutions, all to preserve the state, and without any mention of the interests of the people. The proper formal description of such a system would seem to be as one to "create the illusion that whatever doctrines conduce to the state's own particular interest are true, whether or not we actually think them so." But in this respect, it is quite unlike Hobbes's system, under the appropriate formal description.

To be sure, we cannot acquit an educational system of the charge of providing ideological support for a defective regime simply by pointing to the sincerity of the belief that it is teaching evident truths, since an ideological view may be held as sincerely as any other. But *in*sincerity of the sort that Machiavelli evidences bodes ill. What then *would* acquit a system of the charge of ideology? It would be too much to require a demonstration that what the system teaches *actually* is true; for one thing, we cannot agree on which doctrines are true, and so requiring this would deprive the term "objectionably ideological" of any instructive application.

What we might reasonably require of a view as security against ideology is that the interests it advances be at least plausible candidates for true human goods, and that the means it uses be fairly transparent to those on whom they work, so that no wholesale illusion or delusion is needed for their successful operation. And we can require that it not take merely partial truths, and distort them to create the appearance that ends inimical to human good are in fact worth pursuing. If these are the tests, Hobbes's proposed educational system appears to pass them.[17] So, unless we are to say that all educations endorsing (for whatever reason) views we believe false are objectionably ideological, we must recognize that the

burden of proof lies with Hobbes's critic. The proper question is not
what it takes to *acquit* a view of the charge of being a tool of ideology, but
rather when it is reasonable to *suspect* a view of being one; and on any
plausible account of grounds for suspicion, our own educational system
will be no less suspect than Hobbes's. What is objectionable in Hobbes's
system must lie elsewhere than in its being ideological.

Dissent

What may be objectionable is that people need not be taught competing
doctrines and, more strongly still, that dissenting teachings need not be
countenanced. Mill famously argues that the squelching of dissent or
even the failure to encourage a lively debate among diverse doctrines has
undesirable effects ranging from people's becoming unable to discover
the truth, or to make the truth once gained a vibrant force in their lives,
to confining people to a merely imitative apelike existence unfit for
progressive beings. To the extent that we accept these or other arguments to the same conclusion, we will object to Hobbes's educational
methods.

Two of the passages quoted earlier may suggest that Hobbes does not
forbid all unorthodox teaching. In the first, Hobbes says that when the
erroneous doctrines of the ancients are publicly read, they should be
taught by a judicious teacher who can correct those authors' errors. This
suggests that contrary views may permissibly be taught so long as they
are simultaneously subjected to critical examination by someone versed
in the correct view. That subjection to examination need not itself be
objectionable, so long as it involves no intellectual manipulation; indeed
Millian considerations might persuade us to view it as a good thing. Still,
the only likely "public" reading (i.e., institutional reading, or reading
outside of persons' private libraries) of these texts would be in the
universities, and so Hobbes's remarks here might not extend to public
preaching. The reforming effects on state doctrine of consideration in the
universities of contrary views may trickle down to the masses, but the
masses themselves would not, it seems, be presented with alternative
views for their consideration.

The second passage, concerning the suppression of Galileo's heliocen-
tric view, suggests that Hobbes welcomes an open examination of non-
conforming doctrines to determine the truth (which is then to be taught).
The remark continues: "Let therefore the truth be first examined by
competent judges, or confuted by them that pretend to know the contrary" (703 [379]). Again, however, this sort of examination might be

confined to dissent prior to public dissemination of doctrines and not allowed for subsequent disagreements.

These passages introduce some uncertainty about whether or not Hobbes intends to illegalize the teaching of dissenting doctrines. I am not aware of any passage in *Leviathan* that says that dissent should be made illegal, nor any in which this question is explicitly treated. We know that Hobbes intends some of the needed education to be carried out by parents, and this allows room for some discussion within families concerning the doctrines taught. But there is a passage in Hobbes's *Historical Narration Concerning Heresy* that as much as says that dissenting teachings are subject to prohibition and punishment:

It is absolutely necessary, both in kingdoms and in republics, to take care lest disorders and civil wars occur. And since these are most often generated by differences of doctrine and intellectual wrangling, there must be some restraint, in the form of punishment, on those who teach, in books or sermons, things whose teaching the laws of the prince or republic prohibit.[18]

This passage tells us that if subjects teach doctrines the sovereign has made it illegal to teach, they must be punished. But it doesn't assert that the sovereign must make the teaching of some doctrines illegal, since he may refrain from issuing any laws proscribing what is to be taught. But let us assume the worst case, and ask how objectionable Hobbes's educational system would be if it were illegal to teach dissenting doctrines.

How objectionable controls on teaching are may depend on what they affect. Is their purpose to censor our thoughts – to make sure that we think only correct things – or are they intended merely to constrain our behavior in acting on our views? The latter, though involving more alienation of practice from idea, still is less personally invasive, and may for that reason be less objectionable.

Throughout *Leviathan* Hobbes drives a wedge between belief and action, insisting that the state is concerned only with external obedience – that is, behavior. What subjects believe is their own business, and cannot help but be so, for

By the captivity of our understanding is not meant a submission of the intellectuall faculty to the opinion of any other man; but of the will to obedience, where obedience is due. For sense, memory, understanding, reason, and opinion are not in our power to change; but alwaies, and necessarily such, as the things we see, hear, and consider suggest unto us; and therefore are not effects of our will, but our will of them. (410 [196])

And so forbidding a belief "is of no effect, because beleef, and unbeleef never follow mens commands." Though the state wishes to affect belief through education, it may *require* only obedience, and not the belief it hopes for. Hobbes is fully explicit about this in his attack on the practice of inquisition: It is an "error"

to extend the power of the law, which is the rule of actions onely, to the very thoughts, and consciences of men, by examination, and inquisition of what they hold, notwithstanding the conformity of their speech and actions. (700 [378])

And this is true even when the doctrines held are false, for,

shall the law, which requires nothing but obedience, take vengeance on faulty reasoning? (*Heresy*, p. 533)

Nonetheless, we might hope to say more in Hobbes's defense than that his scheme does not allow inquisition. A more promising tack is to take seriously the status of the dissenting teacher on Hobbes's view. Someone who teaches a view in opposition to the demonstrable implications of, say, the Laws of Nature is simply mistaken. His view is not partially true nor a reasonable conjecture concerning an unsolved problem, etc., but merely in error. Hobbes argues further that to permit the teaching of such errors is usually dangerous, because subjects' acting on false conceptions of political duty threatens the grave evil of social disorder. If we take seriously this trio of ideas – that teachers of dissenting doctrines are *dangerously merely mistaken* – it becomes an open question whether Hobbes would do wrong to silence them, since the stakes are very high. Would *we* allow the teaching of, for example, demonstrably false mathematics in engineering schools if its result were collapsed bridges? And what if its result were worse, say, collapsed nations?[19]

The suggestion here is that even liberal societies, which incorporate the values Mill emphasizes in the form of protections on dissent, do nonetheless put limits on what views may be publicly acted upon, ruling out some uses of unreasonable or illiberal or intolerant views, and sometimes also of merely false ones.[20] They do not, for example, allow the teaching of racist or sectarian religious doctrine in the public schools, let alone of numerology or astrology or phlogiston theory. Part of the justification for this regulation is that liberal democracies require a threshold level of tolerance and civility if they are to survive; the liberal society does not insist on securing conditions for its own annihilation. Neither does Hobbes's. So if the liberal society's regulation in public teaching of dissenting doctrines (qua unreasonable, false, or dangerous) is judged unobjectionable while Hobbes's similar regulation is judged problematic, the problem with Hobbes's system must lie in something other than its readiness to regulate public teaching. Perhaps it is independently objectionable that in Hobbes's system it is primarily the state, rather than parents, private associations, or smaller communities, that is doing the educating, or that the state's education is inescapable.

III. State-Administered Education

We might worry that for the state rather than private persons or associations to administer this education lessens people's sense of autonomy or self-determination. Even if we would in due course come to the same conclusions as those the state would teach us, our sense of self-determination is enhanced when we come to them through contact with our voluntary, or at least intimate, associations.

It is difficult to assess the force of this worry. If the underlying concern is about pressuring or coercing subjects to accept the proffered doctrine (where we imagine, perhaps implausibly, that the state, but not any lesser association, imposes such pressure), then we may from the point of view of Hobbes's theory be unable even to make sense of this worry. From Mill onward our liberal tradition has recognized the subtle armtwisting that social opinion imposes upon individuals, though only Mill's view seeks to counter the effects of more broadly social, as opposed to strictly political, pressures to uniformity of opinion. But Hobbes's theoretical apparatus does not enable him to take up this worry, because he argues that teaching is always an activity only of *persuasion* and never of *coercion*. That is, teaching *by its nature* seeks to attract, persuade, invite, or even lure individuals to belief, but it does not (nor could it) compel them to belief. Hobbes has to hold this position in order to undermine the Roman Catholic Church's claim to have indirect sovereignty (which necessarily involves coercive power) over Christians in virtue of its authority to teach and preach. Indeed, grants Hobbes, ecclesiastical power does include authority to teach and preach, but these activities are

compared by our Saviour, to fishing; that is, to winning men to obedience, not by coercion, and punishing; but by perswasion: and therefore he said not to his Apostles, hee would make them so many Nimrods, *hunters of men*; *but fishers of men*. It is compared also to leaven; to sowing of seed, and to the multiplication of a grain of mustard-seed; by all which *compulsion is excluded* . . . the office of Christ's ministers in this world, is to make men beleeve, and have faith in Christ: But faith hath no relation to, nor dependence at all upon compulsion, or commandment; but onely upon certainty, or probability of arguments drawn from reason, or from something men beleeve already. (525–6 [270], last emphasis added)

The state's power over teaching, then, cannot by its nature be coercive. This, combined with Hobbes's express distinction between conformity in

belief and obedience in action, implies that if our worry is that subjects
are *more* coerced by the sovereign's teachings than they would be by
those of their parents, or parish, or any lesser association, it is simply
misplaced.

But the self-determination worry might be rather that self-persuasion
is morally preferable to state-persuasion. I assume that there is something to this preference, although I won't attempt here to say what it is.
But even taking self-persuasion to be of value, whether Hobbes's system
is objectionable on this point cannot be settled without considering
whether some greater good can be achieved only by a system involving
state-persuasion. On Hobbes's behalf one might argue the reasonable
position that state education, because uniform, provides subjects with
greater confidence that others share (or at least have been exposed to
and considered) their views, and so induces a greater sense of social
cohesion than would be possible in a more fragmented educational system. We, in our practice of public education in civics, seek to induce
allegiance to democratic ideals and decision procedures, whose widespread acceptance seems itself to be one of the most desirable outcomes
of the education. Even Rawls, a political rather than comprehensive
liberal, stresses the importance of publicity in the well-ordered society:
the public acceptance of both principles of justice and their grounds, and
of uniform education in the essential rights and ideals of citizenship to
encourage development of the political virtues of tolerance, civility, and
a sense of fair play. So it is at least possible that the value of the social
cement provided by uniform state teaching of basic truths outweighs the
good of subjects' independent discovery of them.

If there are such reasons supporting a uniform education for subjects,
Hobbes wants to argue that to permit any entity other than the state to
determine the content of education would be both harmful[21] and *unfair*.[22]
In a commonwealth, no private person is subject to the authority of any
other private person, and so to impose on others an educational program
dictated by any merely private person would be arbitrary and hence
unfair. On this point Hobbes's view is quite compatible with that of his
liberal critic Mill, who writes: "Unless we are willing to adopt the logic of
persecutors, and to say that we may persecute others because we are
right, and that they must not persecute us because they are wrong, we
must beware of admitting a principle of which we should resent as a gross
injustice the application to ourselves" (*OL*, 106). Hobbes's own peculiar
twist on the logic of persecutors (and here, obviously, he departs from
Mill) is to argue that the only mutually acceptable principle is one of
submission to arbitration:

And therefore, as when there is a controversy in an account, the parties must by their own accord set up for right reason, the reason of some arbitrator or judge, to whose sentence they will both stand, or their controversie must either come to blowes, or be undecided, for want of a right reason constituted by nature; so it is in all debates of what kind soever: And when men that think themselves wiser than all others, clamor and demand right reason for judge, yet seek no more, but that things should be determined by no other mens reason but their own, it is as intolerable in the society of men, as it is in play after trump is turned, to use for trump on every occasion that suite whereof they have most in their hand. (111–12 [18–19])

To put Hobbes's and Mill's worry in contemporary terms, there is no *naturally given publicly available perspective* that can distinguish true views from untrue ones. And so, from the point of view of others who disagree with him, a citizen's insistence that his doctrine should be enforced because true cannot be seen as anything more than an insistence on his own opinion. In Rawls's words,

those who insist, when fundamental political questions are at stake, on what they take as true but others do not, seem to others simply to insist on their own beliefs when they have the political power to do so. Of course, those who do insist on their beliefs also insist that their beliefs alone are true: they impose their beliefs because, they say, their beliefs are true and not because they are their beliefs. But this is a claim that all equally could make; it is also a claim that cannot be made good to citizens generally. So when we make such claims others, who are themselves reasonable, must count us unreasonable. And indeed we are, ...[23]

This pretty well captures Hobbes's position.[24] Since everyone is in the same boat, the problem, as Mill suggests, is to find a principle that subjects should not resent as unjust when applied to themselves. No grounds for preferring one private opinion over another can be justified to subjects generally. Hobbes concludes that the only fair course is to submit all controversies (including those over what subjects are to be taught) to the judgment of an impartial arbitrator, and this arbitrator must be the (universally authorized) state. Without such an arbitrator, we could not ground a commonly acceptable policy. So *if* a uniform core education is good, it is most fair for the state (as the authorized representative of each subject) to determine its content in line with its judgments of truth and the requirements of peace.

With further argument, we might bring ourselves to agree with Hobbes that it is permissible for a society to institute a system of educating subjects in those basic truths that are necessary for the maintenance of conditions for human survival and flourishing; and the state, if it is the authorized representative of the people, is to carry out this education uniformly, so that subjects may enjoy the benefits of social unity that come from the confidence that they are affirming a common set of social principles. Still, even if we conclude that the state may offer an education with a permissible content, we might object to the non-optional character of state education in Hobbes's scheme. The next step then, is to see whether it is objectionable that Hobbes's state education is compulsory.

IV. Compulsory Education

First, we should ask, is the education Hobbes envisions effectively mandatory, or can it be avoided by those who do not wish to receive it? Obviously Hobbes could not have viewed university education as mandatory. If the state does not require attendance at the church events where the common man's education is to be carried out, then the education might be merely pervasive rather than mandatory. (If the state's educational efforts were as pervasive, but avoidable, as government public service announcements on television are today – really hard to avoid if one watches television, but one needn't watch television – we might think them permissible.) Even so, the social or personal costs of declining church attendance might be so grave that opting out was, practically speaking, impossible. And Hobbes holds that it is a sovereign's duty to see to it that his subjects actually receive the desirable instruction, so he might rush to fill any gap we could exploit between the merely pervasive and the mandatory. I have not been able to determine the answer to these questions on the basis of Hobbes's text, and so will proceed on the worst-case assumption that state education is inescapable.

State-mandated compulsory education with a particular content is certainly not unique to Hobbes, so if this practice is objectionable, many systems will be similarly suspect. Rawls's *Political Liberalism* insists on fairly extensive mandatory education in the essentials for maintaining one's status as a free and equal citizen.[25] But liberal systems generally confine the imposition of education to children, and limit its scope to the essentials for reproducing a society of their distinctive character. Hobbes, we must assume, extends education to adults, whether they desire it or not, and this may strike us as unacceptable.

Arguably, if the content of education is acceptable, its being mandatory would not be objectionable if those educated were children, or relevantly like children.[26] What is interesting and not easy to see in Hobbes (usually touted as the theorist of individual rationality) is that, for Hobbes, subjects *are* relevantly like children, and this is partly what justifies the sovereign's educational measures. Their own judgment cannot be relied upon to inform them about how to avoid seriously harming themselves and others. To see how this works, we need to attend to a difficult puzzle in Hobbes interpretation.

The Hobbesian Responsibility Puzzle

Hobbes scholars have long noted Hobbes's insistence in Chapters 16 and 17 of *Leviathan* that subjects "own and authorize" all of the actions of their sovereign, and hence (in Chapter 18) that subjects are responsible for all that the sovereign does and so cannot reasonably accuse his actions.[27] More recently, as they have scrutinized Parts 3 and 4 of that work, they have identified what some philosophers believe to be a contradictory doctrine in Hobbes's theory of passive obedience.[28] The relevant passage is

a Christian, holding firmly in his heart the faith of Christ, hath the same liberty which the prophet Elisha allowed to Naaman the Syrian . . . that whatsoever a subject, as Naaman was, is compelled to in obedience to his sovraign, and doth it not in order to his own mind, but in order to the laws of his country, that action is not his, but his sovraigns; nor is it he that in this case denyeth Christ before men, but his governour, and the law of his countrey. (528 [271])

Hobbes seems to hold both that subjects are and are not to be held responsible for the sovereign's commands and their actions in obedience to them.

The solution to this apparent inconsistency is what allows us to see the degree to which Hobbes views subjects as relevantly like children. It employs a hierarchical ordering of authority most plausibly explained by the hypothesis that subjects' judgments are (like children's) importantly unreliable. First, Hobbes lays out a hierarchical ordering. God, who desires the preservation and flourishing of his human creation, directs men (via his Laws of Nature and revealed positive laws) to submit themselves to a sovereign; God doesn't care whom they select, but once they have chosen a sovereign, their first duty to God is to obey that sovereign in all that it should command.[29] God lays down this system because it better conduces to men's well-being than one in which they exercise their private judgments about how to act. So *subjects* are accountable to God for their *obedience to the sovereign. Sovereigns*, in contrast, are accountable to God for the content of their *commands*, and should they command subjects to do something wrong, God will hold them responsible for the resulting actions.

We find textual evidence that Hobbes intends a hierarchy of responsibility in this passage:

[A Christian King] cannot oblige men to beleeve, though as a civill soveraign he may make laws suitable to his doctrine which may oblige men to certain actions, and sometimes to such as they would not otherwise do, *and which he ought not to command; and yet when they are commanded, they are laws*; and the external actions done in obedience to them, without the inward approbation, are the actions of the soveraign, and not of the subject, *which is in that case but as an instrument, without any motion of his owne at all, because God hath commanded to obey them.* (591 [309], emphasis added)

Once subjects bind themselves to obey a sovereign, the sovereign becomes the author of its commands, and the obedient (if unwilling) subject a mere actor. Reading "subject" for "actor" and "sovereign" for "author," we see a categorical statement of Hobbes's hierarchical picture of responsibility in his systematic discussion of authorization in Chapter 16:[30]

When the [subject] does any thing against the Law of Nature by command of the [sovereign], if he be obliged by former covenant to obey him, not he, but the [sovereign] breaketh the Law of Nature: for though the action be against the Law of Nature; yet it is not his: but contrarily, to refuse to do it, is against the Law of Nature, that forbiddeth breach of covenant. (218–19 [81])

And what Hobbes proposes for our relationship to the sovereign's commands generally would apply to the subcase of the sovereign's commands concerning doctrine and education. The precise sense in which the sovereign's command is to be thought of as the subjects' own lies in Hobbes's distinction between public and private conscience:

the conscience being nothing else but a man's settled judgment and opinion, when he hath once transferred his *right of judging* to another, that which shall be commanded, is no less his judgment, than [it is] the judgment of that other; so that in obedience to laws, a man doth still according to his own conscience, *but not his private conscience.* And whatsoever is done contrary to private conscience, is then a sin, when the laws have left him to his own liberty, *and never else.*[31]

Action against one's private conscience is blameworthy only when one's authorized public conscience (the sovereign) has issued no command concerning that action. To follow a *sovereign command* I believe to be wrongful is no sin, because of the hierarchy of responsibility just explained; to do what I believe wrong *absent* any sovereign command to do so, is indeed wrong, and my own responsibility. Thus it makes sense to say that my sovereign's erroneous command both is and isn't mine, as it both accords with my public conscience and fails to accord with my private conscience. Hobbes's view here is no more inconsistent than our own view that the will of the majority is (in one sense) our will even though we willed (in another sense, by our vote for the minority position) a defeated course. And if it is said that *we* subordinate our private will to the public will on grounds of principle, the same can be said of Hobbesian subjects, whose ordering of duties is grounded on religious principle, since it is understood to be God who requires them so to order the claims of their consciences.[32]

So the solution to the Hobbesian Responsibility Puzzle identifies a hierarchical structure of responsibility.[33] But the interesting question for our purpose is *why* such a structure is justified. One obvious possibility would be by analogy with military discipline: a hierarchical authority structure suits the military because they pursue an end (victory in war) best achieved by the kind of disciplined, decisive judgment these hierarchical authority structures yield. But this justification by appeal to some unified end to be pursued by the society as a whole seems quite implausible for most political societies.[34] Though societies may have the sorts of common goals Hobbes recognized – for example, peace, prosperity, and the advancement of true religion – these alone would not justify a hierarchical internal ordering of authority unless we further assumed that subjects' individual judgments could not be relied upon to yield the correct conclusions.

A hierarchical system of responsibility might be justified if, for example, it conformed to the model of parents' directives to their children. Parents, who recognize that their children's own judgment will be inadequate to keep them from harming themselves or others, direct them first and foremost to obey a responsible (though of course fallible) adult – their teacher, for example. The child is responsible for obeying the teacher, and is to be faulted for failing to do so; but the teacher is responsible for the content of her directives and is to be faulted for issuing a wrongful directive. The alternative of letting the child decide whether the teacher is to be obeyed (and hence how to act) is rejected as more dangerous than subjecting the child to even an acknowledgedly imperfect authority figure, because this is a child, whose judgment is immature. For children, this hierarchy of responsibility makes sense.

But are subjects generally of unreliable judgment, as if they were immature? We might doubt that Hobbes thought so, because he insists that subjects are to be taught the *grounds* of their political obligations, and why would one offer reasons to the immature? But we do think it right to offer to our immature charges reasons as full and accurate as they are capable of understanding, in part to better dispose them to accept our judgment.[35] And passages abound in *Leviathan* in which Hobbes speaks of subjects as needing guidance for their own good. The clearest occurs in his discussion of what makes laws necessary for the good of the people, and so good laws:

For the use of Lawes . . . is not to bind the people from all voluntary actions; but to direct and keep them in such a motion, as not to hurt themselves by their own impetuous desires, rashnesse, or indiscretion, as hedges are set, not to stop travellers, but to keep them in the way. (388 [182])

That people need guidance in avoiding harm justifies God's adoption of the hierarchical authority structure Hobbes describes.[36] So in order to resolve the responsibility puzzle and to reconcile Hobbes's remarks on authorization, we have appealed to a picture of subjects as of unreliable judgment and thus subject to authoritarian measures if needed to secure their good. If we accepted the picture, it would go part of the way toward justifying Hobbes's readiness to inculcate salutary doctrines. But it would not go all of the way, because we further require evidence that such education is necessary for either subjects' own protection or protection of the serious interests of others.

What Harm in Error?

Even supposing that we reject Hobbes's conception of adults as lacking in judgment, we may be willing to impose education where we judge the significant interests of others to be at stake.[37] Mandatory education might be judged acceptable if people posed a grave threat to one another avoided only by an awareness and self-restraint that education could encourage.

This is precisely what Hobbes believes. The evil averted when subjects act on the proper political principles, namely bloody civil war, is a horrifying evil. Indeed, Hobbes famously argues that civil war and its accompanying anarchy are such "horrible calamities" that in comparison the incommodities of political subjection "are scarce sensible" (238 [94]). Barring special assumptions (attributing, say, unsavory personal motives to particular individuals), Hobbes seems to believe that civil wars are the undesired, unforeseen effects of people's acting on false beliefs. Take, for example, this passage from *De Corpore*:

The utility of moral and civil philosophy is to be estimated . . . by the calamities we receive from not knowing them. Now, all such calamities as may be avoided by human industry, arise from war, but chiefly from civil war. . . . But the cause of war is not that men are willing to have it; for the will has nothing for object but good, at least that which seemeth good. Nor is it from this, that men know not that the effects of war are evil; for who is there that thinks not poverty and loss of life to be great evils? *The cause, therefore, of civil war, is that men know not the causes neither of war nor peace*, there being but few in the world that have learned those duties which unite and keep men in peace. . . .[38]

Were the general population not ignorant of the causes of civil wars, troublemakers could not attract sufficient support to upset the prevailing peace. In this sense, education can effectively forestall subjects' *unwittingly* eliciting the horrible evil of civil war, and is, moreover, the least coercive method of forestalling it. This completes Hobbes's justification for his system of education.

Hobbes's attitude toward his system of mandatory education might be similar to the one we have toward public service announcements that attempt to stem the spread of contagious diseases, or toward mandatory driver's education. The harms to others avoided by these sorts of compulsory education are so great that they outweigh whatever may weigh against them. The avoidance of accidental civil war is at least as great a good as either the containment of disease or road safety. So, if either of these dangers warrants prophylactic education, the danger of inadvertent civil war does.

We conclude, then, that the mandatory character of Hobbes's education will be unobjectionable to the extent that it really is the least invasive effective method of averting a very great evil, especially if subjects are rightly viewed as lacking the judgment necessary to restrain themselves from harming others. It would thus seem to follow that Hobbes's system of education is not to be rejected as objectionably ideological, or as a coercive program of mind control, at least not under its formal description as a system of education in evident truths consonant with basic human interests by means of reasoned argument exposing their true grounds; nor, under Hobbes's descriptions of the circumstances and psychology of subjects, is it to be rejected as unfair to subjects or unnecessarily invasive. Under these formal descriptions of the educational system and its background psychological and social assumptions, this looks like a system that even philosophical liberals could accept. And so, if it is correct to see Hobbes's solution to the problem of recurrent social disorder as solely dependent on such an educational system, we must conclude that there is nothing *structurally* objectionable about Hobbes's political solution.

Of course it does not follow from this that there is nothing objectionable about Hobbes's political solution. We would object to being subject to a Hobbesian system of political education, not because it is state-sponsored or mandatory, but rather because we object to the substantive views Hobbes proposes to teach.[39] This in itself is an interesting result, and suggests that the acceptability of Hobbes's solution to social disorder may depend on historically specific, and hence contingent, beliefs. How great a cause for condemnation of a political–philosophical theory such historical specificity is remains a disputed matter. Some even think that it is a virtue, and that it is no coincidence that Rawls's solution to the problem of social justice is historically specific in the very same way.

NOTES

I owe a debt of thanks for helpful criticism of earlier versions of this essay to Zlatan Damnjanovic, Peter deMarneffe, Barbara Herman, Chris Korsgaard, Nick Pappas, Andy Reath, Larry Solum, and Paul Weithman.

1. And familiar. Jean-Jacques Rousseau had famously acknowledged that "the strongest is never strong enough to be master all the time, unless he transforms force into right and obedience into duty" (*Social Contract*, I.3.1, in *The Basic Political Writings of Jean-Jacques Rousseau*, Donald A. Cress, trans. and ed. [Indianapolis/Cambridge: Hackett Publishing Company, 1987], p. 143), though of course Rousseau denied that this implies any "right of the strongest."

2. S. A. Lloyd, *Ideals as Interests in Hobbes's Leviathan* (Cambridge University Press, 1992; hereafter cited as *IAI*).

3. Threat of force could play the further role of deterring ordinary crimes, but this was of no special significance for understanding the central problem of social disorder as a result, not of ordinary crime, but of rebellion. If credible threats of physical force could prevent rebellion, established states should not relapse into disorder. But frequently they do, and Hobbes's explanation of this is that rebellion is largely the result of subjects' action on transcendent interests, which override their narrowly prudential interests in temporal survival and commodious living. So, for example, when people rebel because they believe that their eternal salvation requires it, even the sovereign's threat of capital punishment cannot compete. Only the elimination, or reconceptualization, of transcendent interests that renders them compatible with civil obedience will end recurrent social disorder. This is the work of education.

4. Mill's allegiance to proper procedure over substantive truth is a continuing theme of *On Liberty*, suggested by these remarks:

   Assuming that the true opinion abides in the mind, but abides as a prejudice, a belief independent of, and proof against, argument – this is not the way in which truth ought to be held by a rational being. (John Gray, ed., *John Stuart Mill On Liberty and Other Essays* [Oxford/New York: Oxford University Press, 1991; hereafter cited as *OL*], p. 41)

   and

   No one can be a great thinker who does not recognize, that as a thinker it is his first duty to follow his intellect to *whatever* conclusions it may lead. . . . Freedom of thinking is . . . even more indispensable, to enable average human beings to attain the mental stature which they are capable of. (*OL*, 43, emphasis added)

   Mill is after the satisfaction that comes with the development of human potential, and he holds that the free thinking necessary for self-development is to be institutionally protected even if it results in adherence to false doctrines. I assume here that Mill's attitude toward social systems in general gives us insight into what would be his attitude toward educational systems in particular.

5. This is what accounts for the difficulty of extracting "the" argument Hobbes gives for political obedience. "The" argument has appeared to many to be self-contradictory or elliptical, but this sense is diminished once we see Hobbes as offering a number of different, though intertwined, arguments to the same conclusion. See *IAI*, pp. 88–94, 155–6, and 266–8.

6. C. B. Macpherson, ed., *Hobbes Leviathan* (Harmondsworth: Penguin, 1968). The first number given is the page reference to this edition; the numbers in square brackets refer to the original Head edition page numbers as these are indicated (also in square brackets) in Macpherson's edition.

   Hobbes continues: "There wants onely, for the entire knowledge of civill duty, to know what are those laws of God. For without that, a man knows not, when he is commanded any thing by the civill power, whether it be contrary to the Law of God, or not. . . ."

   Discovering this is the task of Parts 3 and 4 of *Leviathan*, in which Hobbes concludes that "the Laws of God therefore are none but the Lawes of Nature, whereof the principall is . . . a commandement to obey our Civill Soveraigns . . ." (612 [322]).

   Our primary religious duty is to obey our civil sovereign in all things, because that is what God requires of us.

7. According to Hobbes, the promise of obedience that issues in political obligation "may be either expresse or tacite." See 720–1 [391].

8. This obligation arising from subjects' own acts is underwritten by the natural duties to keep our promises and not "to weaken that power, the protection whereof he hath himself demanded, or wittingly received against others" (320 [142]).

9. Seeing people cannot be taught [their duty], nor when 'tis taught, remember it, nor after one generation past, so much as know in whom the sovereign power is placed, without setting a part from their ordinary labor some certain times in which they may attend those that are appointed to instruct them; It is necessary that some such times be determined, wherein they may assemble together, and (after prayers and praises given to God, the soveraign of soveraigns) hear those their duties told them, and the positive lawes, such as generally concern them all, read and expounded, and be put in mind of the authority that maketh them lawes (318 [178]).

10. Hobbes seems to approve of Old Testament practice in teaching civil duty:

    And for the law Moses gave to the people of Israel at the renewing of the covenant, he biddeth them to teach it their children, by discoursing of it both at home, and upon the way; at going to bed, and at rising from bed; and to write it upon the posts and dores of their houses; and to assemble the people, man, woman, and child, to heare it read. (319 [141])

    Cf. also 614 [324] where Hobbes says the ordinary cause of belief in the Scriptures is the teaching of "those that are by law allowed and appointed to teach us, as our parents in their houses, and our pastors in the churches."

11. The most striking passages on this point occur in *Behemoth*. See, for example, Ferdinand Tönnies, ed., with an introduction by Stephen Holmes, *Behemoth* (Chicago: The University of Chicago Press, 1990; hereafter cited as *B*), pp. 58–9, where Hobbes insists that England will never have a lasting

peace until the universities have been reformed, and p. 71, where Hobbes's discussants have this exchange:

B. For aught I see, all the states of Christendom will be subject to these fits of rebellion, as long as the world lasteth.
A. Like enough; and yet the fault, as I have said, may be easily mended, by mending the Universities.

12. Hobbes writes:

I cannot imagine, how anything can be more prejudiciall to a monarchy, than the allowing of such books to be publikely read, without present applying such correctives of discreet masters, as are fit to take away their venime. (369–70 [171])

Discretion is needed, not only in university instruction, but also in the preachers who teach common folk from the pulpit:

Considering what harm may proceed from a liberty that men have, upon every Sunday and oftener, to harangue all the people of a nation at one time, whilst the state is ignorant of what they will say; and that there is no such thing permitted in all the world out of Christendom, nor therefore any civil wars about religion; I have thought much preaching an inconvenience. Nevertheless, I cannot think that preaching to the people the points of their duty, both to God and man, can be too frequent; *so it be done by grave, discreet, and ancient men.* . . . (*B*, 63–4, emphasis added)

13. I am indebted to Paul Weithman for correspondence on this important point.
14. See *IAI*, pp. 278–80.
15. In *The Portable Machiavelli*, Peter Bondanella and Mark Musa, eds. and trans. (New York: Viking Books, Penguin, 1979), p. 211.
16. Ibid., p. 231.
17. Whereas, if, e.g., Marx's description of capitalism as a mode of production is correct, then its operations are neither transparent nor contributory to the satisfaction of true human interests, and so educational systems functional to the maintenance of that mode of production do fail even these weak tests.
18. *Historical Narration Concerning Heresy*, in Edwin Curley, ed., *Leviathan* (Indianapolis/Cambridge: Hackett Publishing Company, 1994), p. 526; hereafter cited as *Heresy*.
19. Of course (as we noted earlier) sovereigns can also be mistaken – but not, Hobbes thinks, dangerously so. What threatens social order is *disagreement* in judgment and the resultant *factional* infighting, whereas sovereign judgment, effectively authoritative, determines the content of a uniform education that conditions consensus in judgment. The mistakes of dissenting teachers engender faction; the mistakes of sovereigns concerning education do not.
20. Sometimes even of true ones. See, for example, Scanlon's argument that the Millian Principle properly endorsed by liberal states may prohibit even true expression if it is sufficiently harmful, by, for example, illegalizing the publication of a (true) recipe for nerve gas. T. M. Scanlon, "A Theory of Freedom of Expression," *Philosophy and Public Affairs*, 1(2) (1972): 204–26.
21. The argument that it would be harmful is contained in Hobbes's broader argument against dividing the essential rights of sovereignty. For the details of this argument, see *IAI*, pp. 81–8.

22. It is contrary to the Law of Nature (the tenth, against arrogance) to reserve to oneself any rights one would be unwilling to have extended to others, because we are required to acknowledge the equality of others (by the ninth law, against pride). "Equity" thus requires that "if one be admitted to be judge, the other is to be admitted also" (seventeenth law). Hence it is unfair to others to subject them to one's own merely private judgment, which Hobbes likens to cheating at cards. See *Leviathan*, 211–14 [77–8], and 111–12 [18–19], which I quote next. Cf. *IAI*, pp. 93–4.
23. John Rawls, *Political Liberalism* (New York: Columbia University Press, 1993; paperback edition with new material, 1996), p. 61; hereafter cited as *PL*.
24. Cf. *Leviathan*, p. 132 [31].
25. The sort of education Rawls must require is more extensive than might at first be imagined, especially since it does include far less than comprehensive liberalisms would. Still,

    It will ask that children's education include such things as knowledge of their constitutional and civic rights so that, for example, they know that liberty of conscience exists in their society and that apostasy is not a legal crime, all this to insure that their continued membership when they come of age is not based simply on ignorance of their basic rights or fear of punishment for offenses that do not exist. Moreover, *their education should also prepare them to be self-supporting; it should also encourage the political virtues* so that they want to honor the fair terms of social cooperation in their relations with the rest of society. (*PL* 199, emphasis added)

    When we think carefully about how intrusive this education might be judged by adherents to, say, a separatist religious community which affirms a strict sexual division of labor, we can see that this education is not as unobjectionable as those affirming comprehensive doctrines, or those aiming to operate "neutrally" between them, might desire. This decreases the contrast with Hobbes.
26. I include the case of those who are relevantly like children, because even liberal views countenance such dealings with persons who lack the judgment required to look after themselves and to avoid harming others. It was after all Mill, and not Hobbes, who famously wrote that

    those who are still in a state to require being taken care of by others, must be protected against their own actions as well as against external injury. . . . *Despotism is a legitimate mode of government in dealing with barbarians, provided the end be their improvement, and the means justified by actually effecting that end.* (*OL*, 15–16, emphasis added)

27. See *Leviathan*, p. 232 [90].
28. This apparent tension within Hobbes's view is noted by Elizabeth Anderson in her review of *IAI*, in *International Studies in Philosophy*, 27(2) (1995): 123–4, and also by Edwin Curley in a note to his edition of *Leviathan*, p. 339, n. 12.
29. It is important to the palatability of the argument that follows to remember that, for Hobbes, the sovereign need not be a monarch, and may even be a democratically elected representative assembly subject to constitutional constraints. See *IAI*, pp. 291–6, and Chapter 2.
30. We can confirm the correctness of these substitutions by noting that because Hobbes insists that subjects are bound to obey the sovereign by covenant

with one another, whereas sovereigns have made no covenant at all, the quoted phrase "if he be obliged by former covenant to obey" must refer to the subject, there identified as the actor. Notice also that it is the author who is doing the "commanding," and only sovereigns command.

31. Hobbes, *The Elements of Law*, Ferdinand Tönnies, ed. (London: Frank Case, 1969), 2.6.12; emphasis added.

32. Hobbes was worried about the claims of private conscience because various parties in the English Civil War and its surrounding struggles made appeal to conscience to justify their disruptive actions, and Hobbes thought history showed that people's actions on their own private judgments under the "reverenced name of conscience, as if they would have it seem unlawfull to change or speak against them" (132 [31]) were a common thread among many disastrous civil conflicts. Hobbes noted that religious fanatics and others prone to prideful self-deception set great store in the claims of private conscience, on this point anticipating Rousseau's complaint that "fanaticism dares to counterfeit [conscience] and to dictate crime in its name" (*Emile*, in J. B. Schneewind, ed., *Moral Philosophy from Montaigne to Kant*, Volume II [Cambridge University Press, 1990], p. 627).

33. This hierarchical structure is complicated by the apparent exceptions for disobedience under what Hobbes terms "the true liberties of subjects," but these liberties turn out not to cause any problem for the hierarchical author- ity picture, and it would carry us way beyond our topic to discuss them here.

34. It is interesting to note, though, that Aristotle took the state to have a common end, and thought that it was this common end which justified a mandatory system of public education:

> The whole of a state [i.e., the whole body of its members] has one common End. Evidently, therefore, the system of education in a state must also be one and the same for all, and the provision of this system must be a matter of public action. . . . Training for an end which is common should also itself be common. (*Politics*, Book VIII, Ch. 1, §3, from Ernest Barker, ed., *The Politics of Aristotle* (New York: Oxford University Press, 1982), pp. 332–3.)

35. Also in part to prepare them for self-government upon maturity. But recall that for Hobbes the sovereign may be a democratic assembly, so education that also prepares subjects for self-rule is desirable. What is essential is that private judgment be subordinated to public judgment, and this is what the hierarchy of responsibility accommodates.

36. It may also be justified by Hobbes's (perhaps less offensive) parallel argu- ment that submission to public judgment is necessary because *disagreement* in private judgment is *ineliminable*, and for reasons other than subjects' immaturity (much like the reasons Rawls terms "burdens of judgment"). For discussion, see *IAI*, pp. 260–5.

37. We may agree with Mill's condemnation of paternalism that

> As soon as mankind have attained the capacity of being guided to their own improve- ment by conviction or persuasion (a period long since reached in all nations with whom we need here concern ourselves), compulsion either in the direct form or in that of pains and penalties for non-compliance, is no longer admissible as a means to their own good, and *justifiable only for the security of others*. (*OL*, p. 16, emphasis added)

38. *De Cive*, in *The English Works of Thomas Hobbes*, Vol. I; Molesworth edition in nine volumes (London: John Bohn, 1839), p. 8; emphasis added.
39. For instance, we may not believe that we have a religious duty of civil obedience, or we may not recognize the Bible as an authoritative source from which to argue for our political duties. Nor, it seems, do we believe that political stability requires that the ordinary power of governments be undivided, and we see nothing incoherent in the idea that the people may retain constitutive power.

The Hobbesian Side of Hume

JEAN HAMPTON

For years after the publication of *Leviathan* in 1651, there was enormous interest in Thomas Hobbes's project of defining and justifying the virtues as dispositions that (in the right circumstances) advance self-interest. One theorist who was strongly influenced by this approach a century later was David Hume (a philosopher who tends to be incorrectly classed with the Benthamite utilitarians who followed him),[1] insofar as he relies on self-interest to defend what he calls the "artificial" virtues (such as being just, respecting others' property rights, keeping one's promises, and being chaste). But Hume's moral theory also has a non-Hobbesian side, which credits people with substantial other-regarding sentiments that are the source of what he calls the "natural" virtues (such as being benevolent or generous or humble). These two sides of Hume's moral theory reflect his desire to join together the Hobbesian moral approach and the sentiment-based approaches of Scottish moralists, such as Hutcheson and Shaftesbury.[2]

In this essay I have two objectives: First, I want to show just how considerable Hume's "Hobbesian side" is. I argue not only that Hume's theory of the artificial virtues is developed along Hobbesian lines, but also that his theory of the natural virtues uses Hobbesian ideas to explain the process by which these virtues are generated.[3] Second, I want to show that Hume's attempt to join a morality of sentiment to a Hobbesian morality is full of problems so severe that philosophers who wish to develop a sentiment-based moral theory should be wary of using Humean models to do so. In the end, Hume's Hobbesian side turns out to be virtually all of the Humean theory, leaving sentiment with virtually nothing to do.

I. Hobbes's Moral Theory

I begin by sketching the major outlines of the Hobbesian approach to morality, which we can then use in assessing Hume's moral theory.

---

* Jean Hampton died, suddenly and tragically, at the age of 41, while this volume was in production. We mourn the loss of a valued friend and gifted colleague.

Because this is a sketch, it must, of necessity, ignore certain nuances in the Hobbesian approach. Space constraints also force me to resist the temptation to consider passages that suggest another, more deontological moral theory than the one I sketch here. Suffice it to say that such passages do not supplant the many passages that (as I will discuss) develop a type of moral theory I call "consequentialist contractarianism," although they may well be signs of a certain Hobbesian ambivalence about the plausibility of his genuinely revolutionary moral theory.[4]

Because the terms "consequentialist" and "contractarian" are not normally conjoined, I want to spend some time explaining how both apply to Hobbes's moral theory. First, Hobbes's theory is consequentialist because it evaluates actions (and, for that matter, motives, character traits, and social institutions) solely in terms of their consequences. But his conception of what counts as good consequences is very different from the conception usually accepted today. Consider, for example, Samuel Scheffler's definition of consequentialism as the position that "the right act in any situation is the one that will produce the best overall outcome, as judged from an impersonal point of view."[5] Scheffler's definition builds in the assumption that a consequentialist theory must rest on an account of good consequences that is *impersonal*. Modern consequentialists give different accounts of what these impersonal good consequences are: candidates include welfare, pleasure, and preference satisfaction. But they all agree that the pursuit of any of these things – no matter who experiences it – is good; I am not supposed to think that only *my* (or my friends' or family's) pleasure, or preference satisfaction, or welfare, is good, and hence the basis of act-evaluation.

However, for a Hobbesian contractarian, there is no such thing as an impersonal good, but only what particular human beings regard as good:

> whatsoever is the object of any mans Appetite or Desire; that is it, which he for his part calleth *Good*: And the object of his Hate, and Aversion, *Evill*; And of his Contempt, *Vile* and *Inconsiderable*. For these words of Good, Evill, and Contemptible, are ever used with relation to the person that useth them: There being nothing simply and absolutely so; nor any common Rule of Good and Evill, to be taken from the nature of the objects themselves. . . . (*Lev*, 6, 7, 24)[6]

So the Hobbesian conception of good consequences is personal rather than impersonal, and thus relativized to each agent, meaning that the consequentialism Hobbes endorses is interestingly different from modern impersonal forms of consequentialism. Note that Hobbes does not explicitly put forward here a projection theory of value, which contemporary historians of philosophy (such as Stroud and Mackie[7]) have found in Hume's writings, that is, a theory that says that positive or negative evaluations are projected onto objects in the form of properties, by virtue of our perception of them as objects that satisfy or impede desire (and which are therefore experienced as pleasure-producing or pain-producing). But his remarks are certainly suggestive of, and consistent with, such a theory (and may have had an influence on Hume).

This subjectivism is, in essence, a position on value that eschews the metaphysical "nonsense" that, in Hobbes's view, plagues other theories of morality. Thus, for example, it is an anti-Aristotelian position because it starts from the assumption that there is no "naturally good" object in the world which moral action serves and which people ought to pursue. Hobbes dismissed the existence of any Aristotelian *Summum Bonum*, the prescriptive entity that his academic contemporaries were most likely to embrace, considering it an imaginary object, unrecognized by science. That which is responsible for our evaluations and which moves us to act is not some kind of mysterious intrinsic good "out there," but our desires, whose satisfaction is accomplished by securing objects that, in virtue of their power to satisfy desires, we call good. This position on value also repudiates the conception of reason associated with the natural law tradition. In particular, note that in the quoted passage Hobbes recognizes no forms of action that are supposed to be valuable solely because reason tells us so. We value things – objects, states of affairs, or actions – only insofar as our desires approve them, not because there is anything about them (of which reason informs us) that makes them valuable in and of themselves.

Finally, it is a position on value that is in opposition to any theory, such as utilitarianism, that accepts an impersonal account of good consequences. For Hobbes, the idea that, say, some conception of welfare is good no matter who experiences it is just as metaphysically fantastic as the idea that there is a *summum bonum*. Accordingly, something is not wanted because it is valuable, but valuable because it is wanted. Hence Hobbes would reject the impersonal conception of value normally conjoined with contemporary consequentialist views.

Nonetheless, Hobbes's thesis of value is under-developed. Even if desires or passions are the "source" of value (so that all value is personal and subject-relative), there are a number of ways they could be a source. It is doubtful that *everything* we want could be said to be of value to us, insofar as some of our wants are informed by false information. Were we supplied with true information, our wants would presumably change. Moreover some of our desires are ill-considered or ill-defined; reflection could cause us to modify or even lose these desires altogether. So we seem to recognize a difference between what we desire and what we value. A well-developed Hobbesian theory would have to explain how desires are the foundation for, but not identical with, our values.[8]

It is important to appreciate that any development of Hobbes's view of value need not be "egoistic" as that term is usually understood. Whether or not a person's values are self-regarding, on this theory, depends on what the contents of his desires are: self-regarding desires produce self-regarding evaluations (e.g., the desire for pistachio ice cream produces the evaluation that pistachio ice cream is good), and other-regarding desires produce other-regarding evaluations (e.g., the desire that one's sick child become well produces the evaluation that the medicine that will cure the sick child is good). Notoriously, Hobbes happens to think that the content of human desires is primarily self-regarding in nature, where self-preservation is the self-regarding object that he believes is most important to us. But that position is not built into a subjective definition of good consequences, and instead is imported by Hobbes's psychological assumptions about human beings. Moreover, Hobbes *does* recognize that there are *some* other-regarding desires and sentiments in human beings – he just discounts their power and extensiveness. For example, in *Leviathan* he recognizes the existence of pity, understood as "Griefe, for the calamity of another" (*Lev*, 6, 26, 27) as an animating passion of human beings. And, as I discuss in the next section, he suggests that there is something analogous to Hume's operation of sympathy that produces in us concern for others. Thus, he says that pity arises in a person "from the imagination that the like may befall himself" (*Lev*, 6, 26, 27). But he does not think that passions such as pity are significant or frequent motivators of human action.

All of this is important in understanding Hobbes's approach to morality: if our desires were cooperative or primarily other-regarding in nature, it seems we could explain and justify moral behavior simply by saying that it was straightforwardly desired by human beings by virtue of the content of their desires. But because Hobbes maintains that human desires are not, for the most part, other-regarding, he must come up with a theory that will *convince* people who are otherwise not disposed to act in an other-regarding way, to act that way nonetheless. But if there is nothing, apart from desires, that we can use to establish what counts as valuable, and if our desires are primarily self-regarding, how can we convince people to engage in moral activity that is other-regarding? It would seem to be neither behavior that we value in itself nor behavior that is in service of what we value. Hobbes's conception of good consequences does not seem to be the proper foundation for a (genuine) *moral* theory (which is probably why consequentialists such as Scheffler define consequentialism in a way that doesn't even include the theory).

However, Hobbes insists that even though our desires are primarily self-regarding, certain kinds of other-regarding behavior that have traditionally been called "moral" can serve our self-regarding purposes, where the efficacy of this behavior is discovered by reason understood, not as a natural law theorist or an Aristotelian understands it, but as a wholly instrumental faculty. Insofar as reason is specifically excluded as the *source* of what we take to be our good (since our good is defined only by what we desire), it becomes a faculty that counsels us how to attain what we desire as good. So in order for us to find moral action rational on this view, such action must be instrumentally valuable for us; that is, it must enable us to achieve or maximize the satisfaction of our desires, where these desires are primarily self-regarding in content. And indeed, Hobbes defends the authority of the nineteen "Laws of Nature" that constitute his Science of Moral Philosophy by calling them "Conclusions, or Theoremes concerning what conduceth to the conservation and defence" of people (*Lev*, 15, 41, 80). The argument for this contention begins with a psychological characterization of human desires. Although men differ greatly in what they desire, Hobbes insists that "all men agree on this, that Peace is good" (*Lev*, 15, 40, 80). But what is not so manifest to all men is that, if peace is good, then also

the way, or means of Peace, which (as I have shewed before) are *Justice*, *Gratitude*, *Modesty*, *Equity*, *Mercy*, and the rest of the Laws of Nature, are good; that is to say *Moral Vertues*; and their contrarie *Vices*, Evill. (*Lev*, 15, 40, 80)

So for Hobbes, morality is a science that gives us a certain kind of causal knowledge: it tells us how to behave in order to effect peace in a human community, where these causal theorems are interesting to us, and rational for us to follow, because they tell us how to get an object that virtually all of us want (and that is in perfect joint supply) in view of the fact that it is a means to what we desire most – namely, our self-preservation. Cooperation is instrumentally valuable according to Hobbes because he believes that human beings are not self-sufficient and that they are roughly equal in strength and mental ability, so that none of us is so strong as to find cooperation with others unnecessary, nor so powerful as to be able to succeed for very long in coercing from others that help each requires. Hence, Hobbes says these actions are ones we "could agree to": "all men agree on this, that Peace is good, and therefore also the way or means of Peace" (*Lev*, 15, 40, 80).

Now we see one way in which this consequentialist theory is also "contractarian": it represents moral actions as rational (and thus defensible) because they tend to produce mutually agreeable – meaning mutually advantageous – consequences. One might say that for Hobbes, even though good consequences are personally (rather than impersonally) defined, we can nonetheless identify and justify moral actions from an "interpersonal" standpoint, by virtue of the fact that (virtually) all of us find that moral actions lead to consequences that, in the right circumstances, each of us regards as good.[9]

However, the way in which moral actions are "mutually agreeable" for Hobbes is more complicated than these remarks make it appear. Hobbes is adamant that it is *not* rational (i.e., in one's self-interest) to engage in moral behavior *unilaterally* (*Lev*, 15, 36, 79). If self-preservation is what one pursues, then it is not pursued effectively if one, say, keeps one's part of a contract in situations where one's contractual partner is not disposed to do so. In order for it to be rational to keep one's contract, one must live in a world where others are disposed to do likewise. But this essentially means that *moral conventions* must exist in a human community in order for it to be rational for individual members of that community to perform moral actions. Peace-producing action is individually rational to perform (hence moral action) only when there is a convention in the community that people perform such action (so that I know that if I behave cooperatively, then others will do so too, and vice versa). So, if morality is to be not only a body of causal knowledge but also an institution in society that has power over people's lives and in which they participate, the theorems of the moral science must be made into conventional rules.

It is an interesting exercise, one which I have pursued at length elsewhere, to explore the kinds of game-theoretic situations that precipitate the need for coordination in Hobbes's state of nature, and that define the problem of generating conventions to achieve this coordination.[10] These game-theoretic situations are such that Hobbesian people require the help of a sovereign to get these conventions generated, so that Hobbes follows his discussion of the laws of nature with a detailed account of how and why people would create a sovereign in his state of nature in order to achieve a state of affairs in which cooperative action is rational. For Hobbes, the institution of morality presupposes polity, and not the other way around.

Once these conventions exist (presumably with the sovereign's help), does Hobbes believe each of us should comply with them in order to produce peace *even when doing so is not expected to be individually rational for us* (e.g., when we can "free-ride" on the compliance of others with impunity)? Some interpreters, for example Kavka,[11] would argue that as long as an action was peace-producing and one that others were disposed to perform, Hobbes would commend it as moral, even if performing it were not expected to be individually rational for the agent, so that he should be understood as a kind of "rule egoist." However, I would argue that Hobbes would not want to commend the cooperative actions in these situations because acting cooperatively and thereby bringing harm to yourself is "contrary to the ground of the Laws of Nature, which tend to Nature's preservation" (*Lev*, 15, 36, 79). So an action's being peace-producing is a necessary but not a sufficient condition of its being right to perform; it must also be expected to be productive of peace in a way that *will not cost* the agent more than the benefits it will bring to him. Hence I would argue that, on Hobbes's theory, in order to be moral, an action must be not only peace-producing and performed in the knowledge that others are willing to do the same, but also an action that involves no net loss for the agent.

If this is right, Hobbes has a very controversial answer to the question "Why be moral?" His answer asserts that I am right to perform a cooperative action only when I can be satisfied, after I look at all the implications of it, that doing so is not costly for me. Of course, this kind of "act egoism" is consistent with a commitment to rules (e.g., the rule to cooperate in iterated prisoners' dilemmas) that will be advantageous in the long run; but it is not consistent with a commitment to rules in circumstances (e.g., a single-play prisoners' dilemma) where no individual benefit would be forthcoming by following them – such a commitment would, I believe, strike Hobbes as inexplicable (and psychologically impossible) rule-worship. So Hobbes's theory puts limits on the rationality of morality; there is no way a Hobbesian can rationally recommend moral behavior when that behavior is contrary to the desire-defined interests of the agent.

There is one final way in which Hobbes's theory is contractarian: it suggests the idea that the content of some kinds of moral behavior, and in particular the content of *justice*, can be determined by thinking about a hypothetical bargaining procedure. Consider what he says in the following passage:

If *a man be trusted to judge between man and man*, it is a precept of the Law of Nature, *that he deale Equally between them*. For without that, the controversies of men cannot be determined but by War. He therefore that is partial in judgment, doth what in him lies, to deter men from the use of Judges, and Arbitrators; and consequently (against the fundamental Law of Nature) is the cause of War. (*Lev*, 15, 23–24, 77)

Although not explicitly presented in this passage, the following (surprising) strategy for how to resolve a conflict is naturally suggested by it (although whether or not this resolution is really "fair" is, as we'll see, debatable).[12] Hobbes says that an arbitrator in a dispute must beware not to be "partial." The sanction for being partial is having the parties ignore one's resolution and go to war to resolve their dispute. But the knowledge that warfare may be deemed rational by the parties if the outcome is not to their liking will affect *how* the arbitrator resolves the conflict. He must try, as far as possible, to mimic the distribution of the goods or the resolution of the conflict which the parties believe warfare between them would likely effect (assuming that each would stop short of attempting to kill the other). To do otherwise would be to risk one party deciding, "I won't accept this resolution; I can get more if I go to war." Of course there are costs to going to war that are not involved in accepting an arbitrator's resolution of the conflict, so that even if the arbitrator got the resolution wrong, he might be close enough to the division each thinks warfare would effect that no party would feel it was worth the cost of warfare to try to get more. On the other hand, one or both of them may be vainglorious and believe (falsely) that he can win a fight over the other and wrest away everything that he wants. In this situation there is no way that the arbitrator can resolve their dispute which both will find acceptable.

Now Hobbes believes it is a fact we are roughly equal in strength and mental ability, and thus he thinks that in a situation where all parties have a realistic assessment of their powers, arbitration should dictate equal division of goods, and/or an even-handed resolution of a conflict, and this would be acceptable to nonvainglorious people. Hence the resolution Hobbes believes a good arbitrator would recommend is an equal division, which strikes us intuitively as just or fair. But if the disputants are not equal, then the impartial arbitrator would be correct to grant a larger portion to the stronger, more powerful party. So Hobbes's argument establishes that arbitrators should decide according to the maxim, "To each according to his threat advantage in a conflict between them." A "just" or "equitable" or "fair" bargain on this theory is a resolution in which each party receives a share that is roughly commensurate with his strength. Modern readers are unlikely to think that this maxim captures the nature of justice, but Hobbes would insist that it is the only conception of justice that fits with the (naturalistically acceptable) conception of good consequences as personally defined.

Thus we have the outlines of a Hobbesian consequentialist contractarian theory of morality. It is consequentialist because it maintains that what it is right to do is what will maximize good consequences, where those consequences are personally defined by desires that are, by and large, self-regarding. And it is contractarian in three respects: First it is committed to the idea that morality is a *human-made institution*, which is justified to the extent that it effectively furthers human interests. Just as a social contract theory of the state presents political institutions as a human product (and thus as neither God-made nor inherent in nature), this kind of contractarian moral theory takes morality to be a human creation, designed to benefit the individuals who participate in it. Thus, Hobbes seeks to explain the *existence* of morality in society (solely) by appealing to the convention-creating activities of human beings. Second, Hobbes uses the contract device to justify and critique existing moral conventions. By using what is called a "hypothetical contract device" in which we imagine what each of us *"could* agree to" given our self-interested concerns if we had the chance to reappraise and redo the cooperative conventions in our society, we are able to determine the extent to which our present conventions are "mutually agreeable" and so (instrumentally) rational for us to accept and act on. Third, Hobbes suggests that the content of justice and equitable distribution can be defined using the device of a hypothetical contract. Disputed goods should be distributed, on Hobbes's theory, by thinking about what each party could agree to, where this contractarian thought experiment is filled out using each party's perceived threat advantage in war. What each person could agree to is that distribution which yields as much as or more than war would be likely to give to each of them if they resorted to war in order to settle the dispute (factoring in the costs of war).

However, note that the justificational force of Hobbes's moral theory is derived *not* from the appeal to agreement per se, but from the good consequences of the actions being assessed by that theory. One might say that the notion of "contract" is a device in Hobbes's theory that in various ways enables us to assess the consequences that are relevant to making certain cooperative behavior rationally justified.

II. How Hobbesian Is Hume?

Of all the precepts of Hobbes's moral theory, the ones most associated with Hume are surely the subjective conception of value and the instrumental conception of reason. Not only does Hume argue (in *Treatise*, II, iii, 3 and III, i, 1) that our actions have their source in human passion rather than reason – particularly our moral passions – but he is also adamant that reason's only role is theoretical. It can inform us about matters of fact and it can be used to relate ideas (as in mathematical and logical reasoning), but it *cannot* be the sole source of a distinction between what is good and what is evil. " 'Tis not contrary to reason to prefer the destruction of the whole world to the scratching of my little finger. 'Tis not contrary to reason for me to chuse my total ruin, to prevent the least uneasiness of an *Indian*, or person wholly unknown to me" (*Treatise*, II, iii, 3, 416).[13] So Hume's judgment of the rationality of a moral action must be contingent on how well that action effects the satisfaction of the agent's desires and passions – and this is all that Hobbes's theory says. I believe, however, that Hume and Hobbes have different conceptions of the normativity of instrumental reasoning; this issue is complicated, so I leave it aside here.[14]

Of course, Hume is much more inclined than Hobbes to recognize that some of those desires and passions will be other-regarding passions. In speaking about human selfishness, Hume writes:

> I am sensible, that, generally speaking, the representations of [selfishness] have been carried too far. . . . So far from thinking, that men have no affection for any thing beyond themselves, I am of the opinion, that tho' it be rare to meet with one, who loves any single person better than himself; yet 'tis as rare to meet with one, in whom all the kind affections, taken together, do not over-balance all the selfish. (*Treatise*, III, ii, 2, 486)

But Hume does go on to admit that our generosity and benevolence toward others is strongest for friends and relatives, and has little power to move us to act in beneficent fashion toward strangers (*Treatise*, III, ii, 2, 488). And he asserts without reservation that "each person loves himself better than any other single person," a fact that, in his view, can produce conflict among people which "cannot but be dangerous" to any human society (*Treatise*, III, ii, 2, 487). Remember also that Hobbes himself admitted that human beings were capable of being animated by other-regarding passions, although he took these passions to be narrow in scope and relatively weak in power. So Hume differs from Hobbes only in the degree to which he is willing to recognize the extent and force of these other-regarding passions. That we have both sorts of passions, and that the self-regarding ones are a particular obstacle to the establishment of a harmonious social union, are beliefs they both share.

In circumstances where human beings have little or no beneficent concern for those whom they do not know (or do not like), Hume must rely on the same motivation as Hobbes to explain the possibility of cooperation, namely, self-interest:

> Men being naturally selfish, or endow'd only with a confin'd generosity, they are not easily induc'd to perform any action for the interest of strangers, except with a view to some reciprocal advantage which they had no hope of obtaining but by such a performance. (*Treatise*, III, ii, 5, 519)[15]

Moreover, although they differ about the ultimate reasons for remedying conflict, Hobbes and Hume agree that human society is only possible once such conflict is remedied. And they agree roughly on the kind of remedy for conflict – namely, the creation of behavioral conventions that are peace-producing. Hume considers justice to be the most important of these conventions, and the fact that it is a construction of mankind makes it, for him, an "artificial" virtue. Being just is necessitated by the "circumstances of justice," that is, the confined generosity of human beings and the moderate scarcity of objects useful in the satisfaction of their desires, which precipitate conflict that is difficult to resolve amicably. The remedy for the conflict is the creation of a set of rules defining, first, the ownership of objects; second, the methods by which objects can be legitimately transferred (e.g., via contracts); and third, the promise-keeping signs upon which transferrers can rely when they are carrying out their parts of any bargain (see *Treatise*, III, ii, 1–6).[16] Hume follows Hobbes in using the phrase "laws of nature" to refer to his rules of justice (e.g., see *Treatise*, III, ii, 1, 484) and he insists that the motive to obey them is self-interest.[17] So Hume regards the imperatives associated with the artificial virtues as hypothetical imperatives for the achievement of human harmony, recommending action that is agreeable (insofar as it is advantageous) to all.

One of the most important, and least appreciated, aspects of Hobbes's moral theory is its analysis of moral rules as kinds of conventions. But Hume is even more clear in recognizing that the game-theoretic situation underlying cooperative proposals (such as contracts) is really a kind of coordination game, whose solution is the generation of mutually agreeable and mutually agreed-upon conventions. Hume also states quite explicitly that the motive to performing peace-producing actions, such as keeping promises or being just, is self-interest – as long as there is a convention in the society to do so (see *Treatise*, III, ii, 2, 490). For Hume, justice and promise-keeping are "artificial" virtues because of their basis in conventions that secure the self-interested concerns of all (and his discussion of how conventions grow out of our self-interested concerns in coordination games has been influential in the twentieth century).[18] But whereas Hobbes perceived such conventions as comprising *all* of morality, Hume sees them as comprising only one part – what he calls the "artificial" part – of morality, and he is also more optimistic than Hobbes about the possibility of some of these conventions emerging prior to the creation of a political society.

So we see that, at least as far as the artificial virtues go, Hume's theory, like that of Hobbes, is a consequentialist contractarian theory. It is consequentialist because it understands human rules, policies and institutions as conventionally created in order to maximize good consequences (where "good" is subjectively determined), and it is contractarian because it represents morality as a human-made institution, which we can evaluate by asking "is it mutually agreeable?" – a question that considers the extent to which it is operating effectively to further the interests of those who have created it.

There is a third contractarian element in Hobbes's theory: Hobbes suggests the idea of using a hypothetical agreement procedure to define just treatment in situations of conflict by considering what resolution the people involved "could agree to," and he suggests that the principle that would animate this hypothetical agreement is "to each according to his threat advantage." Does Hume embrace this idea?

He certainly regards systems of property that define justice in a society as conventionally generated, and thus the collective invention of human beings, because they appreciate that it is mutually advantageous for them to have a set of rules defining property and property transfer in order to facilitate their cooperation. He writes:

> The possession of all external goods is changeable and uncertain; which is one of the most considerable impediments to the establishment of society, and is the reason why, *by universal agreement*, express or tacite, men restrain themselves by what we now call the rules of justice and equity. (*Treatise*, III, ii, 3, 505, emphasis added)

Conventional agreements specifying these property rules can be "express or tacite," and their mutually advantageous nature is one sense in which we can take them to be rules that we "could agree to."

This position implies that the *details* of property rules, on Hume's view, can be criticized by appealing to a hypothetical contract defining what could *reasonably* be agreed to by people acting out of self-regarding interests. (Remember that Hume takes it that other-regarding interests are irrelevant to the concerns of justice.) Some systems of property rules would, it seems, be more advantageous than others, and an existing system might not be advantageous enough, given available alternatives. But does Hume think about mutual advantage in a Hobbesian way, by appealing to the idea of each party's threat advantage?

Initially it might seem that he does not. Consider that in the second *Enquiry*, where he rails against any meritorious distribution of property, he notes that some systems of property have transformed women into being property themselves.[19] Now clearly this system would be rejected as unreasonable by women were such a system proposed for the group's agreement. Hume also admits that in many existing systems of property, the inequality of holdings is extreme and places the poor at a severe disadvantage.[20] And once again, surely such people would object to any system of distribution that would threaten them with severe impoverish-ment. So these arrangements would be rejected, it would seem, in a Rawls-style hypothetical social contract aimed at securing the mutual advantage of the parties.[21]

Yet Hume himself recommends that conventionally generated rules of property should recognize present possession as being the most salient solution to the problem of defining ownership, supplemented by the principles of occupation, prescription, accession, and succession (*Trea-tise*, III, ii, 3, 505). Clearly this solution could allow some human beings to be possessed as slaves or chattel, and could allow or even encourage the severe impoverishment of others. If those who agreed upon the system of property-holdings were in a position to bargain with each other *on an equal footing*, these schemes of distribution would be rejected in favor of a more egalitarian and non-slave-owning system. The fact that Hume did not see this latter system as a "salient" solution to people's coordination problem in the state of nature suggests that his vision of the process of generating a convention defining property was more Hobbesian than he might have cared to admit; for a system that starts by recognizing present possessions as property makes sense in a world where the convention-creators are prepared to use all the advantages of war at their disposal to hang on to what they already have. The "present possession" rule is one reasonable implementation of the Hobbesian principle of distributive justice: "to each according to his threat advantage."

So although Hume never endorsed such a principle explicitly and says things that, at least on the surface, are hostile to the implementation of such a principle, the details of the system of distributive justice that he actually recommended seem animated by it nonetheless. To those who are granted little by the system, Hume might say that the state of nature he envisages, where warfare is relatively intermittent, is still bad enough in terms of conflict and inconvenience to make such a system better than none at all, since without any system at all human beings would find themselves in "that savage and solitary condition, which is infinitely worse than the worst situation that can possibly be suppos'd in society" (*Treatise*, III, ii, 2, 497). Those human beings who have been severely impoverished by systems of property distribution, or who have also been turned into property themselves, have considerable reason to reject such an assertion – and regard it as irrelevant to defining and instituting *justice* (which, they will insist, cannot be instantiated by just *any* system of property). But pursuing this last thought would mean rejecting alto-gether the Hobbesian/Humean approach to justice.

III. How unHobbesian Is Hume?

The preceding review of Hume's theory seems to establish that, at least with respect to the artificial virtues, Hume has the same type of theory as Hobbes. It is consequentialist, insofar as it recommends behavior that will have good consequences as judged by the (subjectively determined) interests of the agents, and it is contractarian, insofar as it relies on the idea that moral behavior is and must be mutually advantageous, and conventionally established, in order for it to be rational for any agent to perform. However, Hume's belief in the strength and extensiveness of our other-regarding passions, along with his theory of the natural virtues, would seem to be significantly different from the Hobbesian approach, and what transforms it into a genuine *moral* theory.

Indeed, there are good reasons to worry that a Hobbesian-style theory fails to qualify as a moral theory at all. It is supposed to be a moral theory because it defines moral behavior as instrumentally valuable and mutually advantageous other-regarding behavior, insofar as the consequences of such behavior (in the right circumstances) lead to peace, which furthers people's survival and comfort. Nonetheless, Hobbes is committed by his position to accepting that when moral behavior is not advantageous to the individual, then it is not rational to engage in it. This is an inevitable feature of his consequentialism: morality is justified for as long as, and no longer than, the consequences of that behavior are desirable, and those consequences are measured by each person's largely self-regarding desires. But how can a theory successfully model our moral life when it is unable to justify moral action that is opposed by self-interest? Doesn't a person's moral integrity consist in the ability to do the moral thing even when one's own self-interest opposes it? Hobbes's theory also seems to lose the caring and the distinctive moral motivation that are hallmarks of our moral life, and because his conception of justice permits favoring the strong over the weak, it violates our intuitions of fairness.

Such criticisms of Hobbes's theory have inspired philosophers enamored of Hobbes's general approach to see how they could revise or supplement the Hobbesian framework to escape them. In our time, such philosophers as David Gauthier and Edward McClennen have tried to argue that Hobbesian reasoning permits, even requires, a certain kind of commitment to cooperative behavior, even in circumstances where exploitative opportunities from noncooperative behavior exist.[22] Before them, however, Hume tried a different way to supplement the Hobbesian framework so as to make it "more moral," which involved adding to it ideas drawn from the moral sentimentalists of his day. What rationality cannot handle, maybe sentiment can.

For one thing, the inclusion of sentiment into the theory seems to enable Hume to enrich the stock of good consequences that justify action, and thereby make it easier for him to argue that a person's subjectively defined good consequences are such that, in many circumstances, other-regarding behavior is rational. Thus he can explain why people would be able (and think it right) to cooperate in situations where doing so does not advance their self-regarding desires. It also allows him to develop a theory of our moral judgments that seems to accord more successfully with our actual moral practices than does Hobbes's account. According to Hume, we approve of people's characters according to how they please us, either by being agreeable or by being useful, and we disapprove of those traits that we find disagreeable or have disutility. Among those traits we find "agreeable" are wit, gentlemanliness, and cleanliness, and among those we find "useful" insofar as they serve the public interest are benevolence, compassion, and gratitude. The latter are the sort of natural virtues that tend to be considered "moral."

Yet in what follows I argue that Hume's addition of other-regarding sentiments into his theory does not help to "moralize" it in any substantial way. The argument has two parts: First, I argue that the Humean conception of sympathy, on which the theory of natural virtues and vices is based, is much more Hobbesian, and much less effective as a theory of the generation of other-regarding passions, than many have thought. Second, I examine the natural virtues and vices themselves, and argue that both in how they are defined and in how they motivate us to action, they are substantially similar to the artificial virtues, despite the fact that Hume tries mightily to suggest otherwise.

A. Sympathy

Hume insists that his principle of sympathy is quite different from any form of imaginative identification endorsed by Hobbes, insofar as it is not a form of psychological egoism:

An Epicurean or a Hobbist readily allows, that there is such a thing as friendship in the world, without hypocrisy or disguise; though he may attempt, by a philosophical chymistry, to resolve the elements of this passion, if I may so speak, into those of another, and explain every affection to be self-love, twisted and moulded, by a particular turn of imagination, into a variety of appearances. (*Enq*, 296–7)

But Hume does Hobbes an injustice here, for a careful reading of Hobbes's texts shows that Hobbes is not a psychological egoist (*Lev*, 6,

26, 27). Recall that Hobbes explicitly says that when a person feels pity for someone who is suffering, he is concerned with that suffering person, not with himself. The cause, however, of that other-regarding concern is an imaginative identification with the suffering person. So for Hobbes, when I feel pity for another, I am not feeling pity for *myself* imagined in these circumstances; instead, I am feeling pity for this other person, where that emotion has been created in me by imagining myself in his shoes. Hobbes's position requires that we distinguish between the *causal process* producing someone's sentiments for others, and the *object* of those sentiments. The reason any of us might experience compassion for another may have to do with the way in which our imaginative identification with the other's plight plays a causal role in the origination of this emotion in us, but the emotion itself is about the other person, not ourselves.

This Hobbesian process of imaginative identification sounds exactly like Hume's psychological principle of sympathy, which he considers part of our imagination (see *Treatise*, II, ii, 7, 371; II, ii, 9, 385–6):

'Tis evident, that the idea, or rather impression of ourselves is always intimately present with us, and that our consciousness gives us so lively a conception of our own person, that 'tis not possible to imagine, that any thing can in this particular go beyond it. Whatever object, therefore, is related to ourselves must be perceived with a like vivacity of conception, according to the foregoing principles; . . .

Now 'tis obvious, that nature has preserv'd a great resemblance among all human creatures, and that we never remark any passion or principle in others, of which, in some degree or other, we may not find a parallel in ourselves. . . . There is a very remarkable resemblance, which preserves itself amidst all their variety; and this resemblance must very much contribute to make us enter into the sentiments of others, and embrace them with facility and pleasure. (*Treatise*, II, i, 11, 317–18)

So, like Hobbes, Hume explains the origination of certain kinds of sentiments within us by appeal to a psychological process in which we "enter into the sentiments of others" and, as a result, develop certain desires and feelings with respect to them.[23] Hume and Hobbes agree that self-regarding concerns are the (mere) *source* of certain other-regarding passions and sentiments; they are involved in explaining how they are generated within us. But both philosophers believe that, once the other-regarding passions are generated, they are really *for* and *about* others. However much Hume may want to distance himself from "Hobbism," if that position is represented fairly, he himself must be regarded as holding it.

But doesn't Hobbes's insistence that we are always motivated to act in order to achieve pleasure and minimize pain (see *Lev*, 6, 1, 23) make him a kind of psychological egoist, and therefore different from Hume? If each of us always acts to secure as much pleasure as possible, doesn't this mean that the ultimate end of human action is self-regarding, so that any other-regarding action must be undertaken by us as a mere means to the satisfaction of our ultimate self-regarding end?

This is a misrepresentation of Hobbes's position, encouraged in the modern mind, I suspect, by Bentham's remarks on pleasure and pain. Bentham does seem to believe that the maximization of pleasure is indeed the *object* of all our desires. But unlike Bentham, Hobbes distinguishes the causes of desires from the objects of a desire. Pleasure-pursuit explains, for Hobbes, the cause of the origination of desires in us, but it does not constitute the object of those desires. So we can want to help a dying man because we genuinely care about him, although the cause of our concern for him will make reference to the way in which our desire to alleviate his suffering is caused within us because of the pain we experience at the thought of his suffering. What we want, and the cause of what we want, are two different things. And Hume must agree with the Hobbesian (and not the Benthamite) position on these matters insofar as he, too, considers human desires to be created in us by our biological propensity to seek pleasure and avoid pain, as demonstrated in the following passage from the *Treatise*:

The chief spring or actuating principle of the human mind is pleasure or pain; and when these sensations are removed, both from our thought and feeling, we are, in great measure, incapable of desire or volition. The most immediate effects of pleasure and pain are the propense and averse motions of the mind; which are diversified into volition, into desire and aversion, grief and glory, hope and fear, according as the pleasure or pain changes its situation. (*Treatise*, III, iii, 1, 574)

So in the end Hume agrees with Hobbes that these "springs" of human action are the causes, but not the objects, of our desires.

The fact that Hume accepts the basic outlines of a Hobbesian account of sympathy – which turns out not to be "Hobbist" at all – has serious implications for the rest of his theory, because in that theory, sympathy is important for the definition of natural virtues and vices. And as I shall now show, the operation of sympathy, as Hume understands it, is simply insufficient to perform that task.

According to Hume, judgments of natural virtue and vice are the result of a rather complicated mental process. When we contemplate a person's character trait, Hume says that we experience certain pleasures or displeasures as a result of appreciating how that person is disposed to affect others by virtue of having that trait, where these feelings are reflective of certain desires in us, many of which are other-regarding. These feelings are projected onto the person's character, and we call some of those projected responses judgments of moral approbation and disapprobation when the pleasure or displeasure experienced by us is a function of the way in which the character trait being contemplated is, or is not, useful to the public good.

Note that in this process sympathy performs two different tasks. First, sympathy produces certain other-regarding passions, such as benevolence, that are central to the feelings of pleasure or displeasure (particularly with respect to the public good). Second, sympathy is the process by which each of us comes to identify with those individuals affected by a person's character trait, such that we experience a feeling of pleasure or displeasure at those effects by virtue of having the sympathy-produced other-regarding passions. When sympathy plays the first task and produces other-regarding passions, I will call it "motive-sympathy." When it plays the second task and produces feelings of pleasure and pain related to these passions after the contemplation of someone's character, I will call it "feeling-sympathy." (The motivational efficacy of the products of feeling-sympathy is an issue I take up later in this section.) So when examining Hume's theory of the natural virtues, our first concern is understanding how sympathy performs these two tasks.

Conventional wisdom has it that there is nothing problematic about understanding the first task. I know of no one who has challenged the idea that Humean sympathy can produce other-regarding passions. However, Hume gives us no account of how it can do so, and there is, I think, reason to worry that it cannot. To see this, suppose that a human being, with no regard for anyone but himself, employs the Humean (and Hobbesian) operation of sympathy and gets a (lively) idea of the suffering of a person in great pain. How – why – does that lively idea turn into a caring passion, for example, pity or compassion? Hume himself admits that it *need not* do so. Sometimes he admits we feel, not concern for the other, but relief that we ourselves are not in his shoes, and he calls the process by which such self-regarding concerns are generated "comparison" rather than sympathy (*Treatise*, III, iii, 2, 593). But this admission only compounds the puzzle, for now it is clear that there is no inevitable passage from the lively idea of another's suffering to an other-regarding sentiment. So what is the explanation of when and why this passage occurs?

To show that Hume (or, for that matter, Hobbes) never gives any explanation of it, let me go slowly through one particularly clear text setting out how sympathy produces benevolent sentiments:

When the present misery of another has any strong influence upon me, the vivacity of the conception is not confin'd merely to its immediate object, but diffuses its influence over all the related ideas, and gives me a lively notion of all the circumstances of that person. . . . By means of this lively notion, I am interested in them; take part with them and feel a sympathetic motion in my breast, conformable to whatever I imagine in his. (*Treatise*, III, ii, 9, 386)

Notice that, by the end of this passage, Hume has *not* explained the origination of the benevolent feeling I have toward this person. I imaginatively identify with this person, and feel what he feels. So? I "take an interest in him" – that is, I am interested in what he is feeling, and imagine myself feeling it too. This "interest" is not the same as *concern for him*. All that Hume has established is that, through my imagination, I can come to have an impression of his pleasure or pain. But vicariously experiencing what he is going through is not to have other-regarding sentiments with respect to him or his experiences.

   Modern scholars (including, in the past, me) have invariably missed the puzzle;[24] for usually they are content to say that sympathy works by giving me the thought of another's suffering, which is then converted into an impression of pain (analogous to her suffering) in me. This operation explains only the process by which I go from the idea of what she is feeling to the impression of that experience in me. But that impression is still not the same as a feeling of *care for her*. To go from the idea:

"She is suffering pain"

to the following impression, via the operation of sympathy:

"If I were in her position I would be feeling *this*, so she must be feeling *this*"

is still not to experience any concern for *her*, that is, it is still not the same as:

"In virtue of the fact that she is feeling this, I pity her, and wish to alleviate her suffering."

Indeed, as I noted above, Hume says that putting myself in another's shoes can result in "comparison," in which I experience *pleasure* at my own more favorable circumstances compared to my lively idea of what the other is suffering.[25] So the most one can say about the operation of sympathy as Hume has described it is that it can give me a certain kind of information: it can lead me to understand another's experience as pleasant or unpleasant, welcome or distasteful, and thus something I should either wish or never wish to experience. But there is nothing in Hume's description of this operation that could explain how the concern for another is generated. Of course, if I already care about one whom I realized (via the operation of sympathy) was suffering something un-pleasant, the fact that I could perform this operation and achieve this realization could lead me to seek to relieve her suffering. But here my benevolent actions presuppose the existence of this caring posture *prior to* the operation of sympathy; the operation of sympathy does not create or induce that caring.

The same point can be made using a passage from the *Treatise* in which Hume elaborates upon the operation of sympathy:

> As in strings equally wound up, the motion of one communicates itself to the rest; so all the affections readily pass from one person to another, and beget corre-spondent movements in every human creature. When I see the *effects* of passion in the voice and gesture of any person, my mind immediately passes from these effects to their causes, and forms such a lively idea of the passion, as is presently converted into the passion itself. (*Treatise*, III, iii, 1, 576)

Notice, however, what Hume *does not* explain in this passage. He sets out how I could come to feel what another is feeling, but to feel what another feels is not the same as caring about *her* in virtue of what she is feeling. What is missing from Hume's (and also Hobbes's) account is something that would explain the generation of other-regarding care – indeed, the care that Hume had thought the operation of sympathy was sufficient to explain.

Suppose we try arguing that sympathy produces other-regarding pas-sions in the following way: Sympathy generates in me the impression of the experience of another – suppose it's great pain; this experience produces pain in me, which I desire to alleviate; hence I desire to help the person in pain. The problem with this explanation is that it is the "Hobbist" theory – but not, as I've discussed, Hobbes's theory – of the nature of other-regarding concern, of the sort Hume standardly dis-misses. To see this, recall that we have distinguished between the physi-ological causes of desire and the objects of desire – that which desires are *about*. Let us further distinguish between an object of a desire that is wanted because it is a means to the satisfaction of some other desire, and an object of a desire that is wanted for its own sake, and is not wanted as a means to anything. Now the account just given assumes that pleasure and pain are the causes of desire, and it explains the generation in me of a desire whose object is to help another person in distress. But note that the object of this desire is itself a means to the satisfaction of another desire, namely the alleviation of my own pain. So the account explains the origination of a desire to help the other, but it does *not* do so by positing a concern *for the other* that renders helping her desirable. In-stead it is because the object of the desire is a concern for *myself* that I help the other; it is not because I am concerned for *her* and desire to help her because of that concern. Indeed, to quote Hume, this account posits that "even unknown to ourselves we seek only our own gratification, while we appear the most deeply engaged in schemes for liberty and happiness of mankind" (*Enq*, 296).

So how does genuine concern for the *other person* come about? Perhaps Hume could invent some additional psychological mechanism to explain it; but offhand it is hard to see what it might be. Alternatively, he might regard sympathy (merely) as a process supplying us with information about others that, in conjunction with a pre-existing concern for them, triggers certain other-regarding passions. But what is this pre-existing concern? As discussed above, Hume rejects the idea that there is some sort of universal love of mankind as such, having nothing to do with specific character traits. And his tendency in Book III of the *Treatise* is to explain other-regarding concerns as derivative from sympathy, not as something that sympathy actually presupposes. To say that there is some sort of intrinsic other-regarding sentiment in human beings, upon which the principle of sympathy rests in order to generate other-regarding passions, is to presuppose at least some of the sentiments that the mechanism of sympathy, coupled with self-interest, was supposed to explain.

A modern follower of Hume may be able to develop ways of understanding sympathy such that it can produce other-regarding passions that genuinely incorporate not just other-regarding action but other-regarding concern. We await such an account.[26]

B. The Natural Virtues

For the sake of argument, suppose we have such an account in hand so that we can assume that human beings experience other-regarding passions, such as benevolence, that are necessary for the generation of judgments of natural virtue and vice. How successful is the rest of Hume's story of their generation? That account says that after experiencing certain feelings associated with these desires when contemplating a person's character, then "we tend to project these sentiments onto the actions or characters that arouse them, or read some sort of image of these sentiments into them, so that we think of those actions and characters as possessing, objectively and intrinsically, certain distinctive moral features."[27] So (what I have called) "feeling-sympathy" operates as a kind of emotional triggering mechanism, producing feelings that are then projected onto the people we are judging. To quote Hume, "We do not infer a character to be virtuous, because it pleases: But in feeling that it pleases after such a particular manner, we in effect feel that it is virtuous" (*Treatise*, III, i, 2, 471). However, natural sentiments are not, on Hume's view, straightforwardly projected as properties onto the characters, events, or actions for, if they were, our judgements of the virtues and vices of people would vary according to our capacity to sympathetically identify with them – which they manifestly do not do.

They would vary along two dimensions. First, they would vary *among* different people, whose natures would make them develop different sentimental responses to different people:

every particular man has a peculiar position with regard to others; and 'tis impossible we cou'd ever converse together on any reasonable terms, were each of us to consider characters and persons, only as they appear from his peculiar point of view. (*Treatise*, III, iii, 1, 581)

Second, they would vary *within* any one of us. This is, in part, because a person's evaluations will naturally change over time as his physical constitution changes. But they will also vary, at any given time, by virtue of how close or far we were to the person(s) with whom we sympathetically identified. That is, because our other-regarding sentiments are stronger toward those near us and weaker toward those distant from us, as Hume notes, if our sentiments were straightforwardly projected onto people, our evaluations of them would reflect their proximity to us – in a way that our judgments of virtue do not:

Now 'tis evident, that those sentiments, whence-ever they are deriv'd, must vary according to the distance or contiguity of the objects; nor can I feel the same lively pleasure from the virtues of a person, who liv'd in *Greece* two thousand years ago, that I feel from the virtues of a familiar friend and acquaintance. (*Treatise*, III, iii, 1, 581–2)

But, as Hume goes on to note, although our sympathy induced evaluations vary in this way, "yet I do not say, that I esteem the one more than the other" (*Treatise*, III, iii, 1, 581). Hence he realizes that he must explain how our sympathy-induced evaluations are "corrected" so as to become impartial, stable, and commonly accepted judgements of virtue and vice.

His explanation invokes the idea of a "general point of view," from which each of us, when judging others, arrives at the same (impartial and impersonal) assessments of others:

In order, therefore, to prevent those continual *contradictions*, and arrive at a more *stable* judgment of things, we fix on some *steady* and *general* points of view; and always, in our thoughts, place ourselves in them, whatever may be our present situation. In like manner, external beauty is determin'd merely by pleasure; and 'tis evident, a beautiful countenance cannot give so much pleasure, when seen at the distance of twenty paces, as when it is brought nearer us. We say not, however, that it appears in such a position, and by that reflexion we correct its momentary appearance. (*Treatise*, III, iii, 1, 582)

It is not exactly clear from this passage whether Hume thinks we are correcting what we naturally *feel*, or only what we judge about what we feel. However, he goes on to suggest it is the latter when he says, "Experience soon teaches us this method of correcting our sentiments, or at least, of correcting our language, where the sentiments are stubborn and unalterable" (*Treatise*, III, iii, 1, 582). But mere linguistic correction doesn't seem to be enough. Surely we need to correct not only what we say but also how we judge or evaluate a situation that engages our other-regarding sentiments. Hume indicates that this correction involves making new judgments from the "general point of view," which any common moral language will reflect. Henceforth I shall speak of these as "corrected judgments."

Before I proceed further, let us note that this account of the natural virtues invokes Hobbesian theoretical strategies in three respects. First, Hume is essentially saying that human beings have a coordination problem to solve with respect to other-regarding sentiments: because none of us is the same as any other person, nor the same over time, our community will enjoy no stability or commonality of judgment unless there is some uniform system of moral judgment used by all, no matter the nature or strength of the feelings that any person happens to experience because of sympathy. A Hobbesian fear of conflict based upon conflicting and changeable evaluations seems to be behind Hume's remarks in these passages. As one Hume scholar has put it, "Hume's worry is basically a civilized version of Hobbes's more nightmarish vision of unregulated self-interest leading to destructive interaction."[28]

Second, although the general point of view is not itself something that Hume considers to be conventionally constructed (he seems to think it as "natural" as the point of view we use to correct perspectival judgments), nonetheless he does accept that it must be conventionally established, such that it will be common knowledge that all will use it. But this means, as J. L. Mackie appreciated, that the resulting "natural" judgments have an important artificial (convention-based) component:

Although we may have some instinctive tendencies to develop those dispositions and actions (namely those that are close to us), the precise way in which we approve of them (namely interpersonally and impartially) must, like the rules of justice, be understood as a system which flourishes because *as a system* it serves a social function, helping human beings who are made pretty competitive both by their genetic make-up and by their situation to live together fairly peacefully and with a certain amount of mutual aid and cooperation. Though the psychology of sympathy may play some part, the natural virtues themselves and the fully developed form of the recognition of them as virtues will owe a good deal to conventions and reciprocal pressure.[29]

So our judgments of virtue and vice are a function not only of other-regarding sentiments, but also of the conventionally constructed corrections of these sentiments. The "natural" virtues, despite their foundation in sympathy-created other-regarding sentiments, are indebted to convention for their existence, giving them an important "artificial" component.[30]

Third, this account of the natural virtues is Hobbesian because of the way it relies on reason to construct the corrected judgments associated with the natural virtues. Hume's remarks suggest that human reason sees the danger of not controlling the raw evaluations of other-regarding sentiments and that human reason figures out how to control them. The convention that is established not only controls the use of moral language, but, more fundamentally, also establishes the point of view that judgments using such language must reflect. The reasoning involved in its establishment solves the problems of coordination and conflict associated with other-regarding sentiments, in just the way it does when it constructs conventions creating the artificial virtues.[31]

Hume's discussion of the general point of view raises many questions, chief of which concerns what that point of view actually *is*.[32] But I want to put aside that question here and pursue certain motivational issues raised by these passages.

There are two such issues. First, what motivates us to make corrected impartial judgments from the general point of view, rather than partial judgements from uncorrected sentiments? As I noted above, Hume suggests that it is the judgment and the language with which that judgment is expressed that are conventionally "corrected," in a way that may (perhaps usually) leave the original partial sentiment remaining in the mind of the evaluator. If this happens, the evaluator has two (potentially competing) responses to the person being evaluated: the evaluation from partial sentiment, and the judgment made from the general point of view. So how can we explain why someone would be motivated strongly enough to evaluate another using the impartial judgment? A person might be aware of both ways of judging but be more strongly motivated (indeed, find it inescapable) to "see" the person in the way directed by the partial, uncorrected sentiment.

One way to explain the motivation to judge impartially is to invoke the passions that mandate the correction of raw sentimental responses to others' characters. Hume does not expressly tell us what these passions are (indeed, he sometimes even suggests that there are no such passions; see *Treatise* III, iii, 1, 583). However, as I noted above, Hume does make Hobbesian remarks about the inconvenience and confusion caused by conflicting and varying judgments. This suggests that self-interested passions are largely responsible for wanting the end of this inconvenience and confusion. Although concern for family and friends might also play a role in one's desiring stability and uniformity of judgment, certainly concern for self and one's own well-being and comfort is a powerful reason for rejecting the chaos. Moreover, if Hume is right about the inconveniences and problems associated with variation in judgment, even a person devoid of all other-regarding sentiment would have reason to want uniformity and stability of judgment (although even if he could use this common language to express such feelings, whether he could actually understand their content is questionable if he did not have the feelings that the general point of view is supposed to correct).[33]

If this is right, the next question is whether the passions supporting conventional correction of judgment are always or usually strong enough to motivate a person to make those corrections and judge according to them. If not, she will persist in her uncorrected judgments. So, for example, an impartial judgment that someone else's child has performed just as admirably as one's own child in a school contest ought to be accompanied by equal praise for both, and yet one's greater love for one's own child will lead one to want to give higher praise for her. How do we explain why the self-interested passions that motivate establishing a general point of view to correct partial judgments are strong enough to motivate one to praise both children equally, in the face of one's strong love for one's own child? It would seem that the vague and long-term benefits that come from a common system of judgment would be unable to compete against an immediate and strongly felt parental love. There is evidence that in the *Treatise* Hume is worried that they are not when he says that the principles of correcting partial sentiment "are not altogether efficacious, nor do our passions often correspond to the present theory. 'Tis seldom men heartily love what lies at a distance from them" (*Treatise*, III, iii, 1, 583). The problem with any such concession, however, is that it amounts to an admission that the Humean approach cannot explain the fact of impartial judgment in the face of partial sentiment, nor the conviction we are under that we *should* make impartial judgments even in the face of strong partial passions.

Indeed, since the costs of partial, unregulated judgments will be borne only if *everyone* departs from the general point of view, then even if the costs are considerable, such that you have a strong desire to avoid them, still you won't actually pay them if *you alone* depart from the system of common judgment while everyone else continues to use it. So why isn't there a free rider problem involved in maintaining the convention to judge impartially, so that even if it is collectively rational for each person to persist in using a common system of impartial judging, it is individually rational to judge partially (and individually irrational to judge impartially)?

Consider the following possible answer to this problem:[34] Perhaps a considerable part of the rationality of judging impartially comes from the fact that doing so is prized by the rest of society, whose good opinion we value so much that to run afoul of it is to experience not only the pain of their contempt for us, but also the pain of self-hatred. Asks Hume, "Would you have your company coveted, admired, followed; rather than hated, despised, avoided? Can anyone seriously deliberate in the case?" (*Enq*, 280–1). However, the problem with this strategy is that it presupposes that other people's good opinion of your character will track (almost exclusively) the extent to which your behavior is collectively useful. Now it is certainly true that if any of them has feelings of benevolence, they will experience pleasure if they see you judging others in a way that is useful to the public good and pain if they see you not doing so. But why shouldn't more partial passions trigger other pleasures and pains at the same action? Wouldn't the father of the child in our example be inclined to approve of the mother's partial judgment? Wouldn't one anti-Semite be inclined to approve of the partial evaluations of another anti-Semite? Don't our own partial passions incline us to approve of the judgments of people who are similarly prejudiced? Isn't it common for people to be irritated by, even resent, someone who tries to be a relentlessly impartial judge? (Indeed, isn't it common for them to disagree, because of their partial passions, about who counts as such a judge?) A Humean appeal to the opinions of others to give us reason to judge impartially is a risky business, given the way others' opinions often, maybe even usually, respond to partial passions of their own. And, indeed, isn't that the problem? If I am having trouble finding it rational to judge impartially, won't everyone else have trouble as well? Even though virtually all of us are responsive to the public interest given our feelings of benevolence, won't we (mustn't we) also be responsive to other passions, many of which incline us to judge people in partial and prejudicial ways? And how can Hume explain the extent to which we do, and believe we ought to, prefer impartiality in the face of these competing and often very strong competing passions?

Suppose Hume tried to explain the fact and rationality of impartial judgment in the face of what seem to be the stronger motives to judge partially by invoking the idea of socialization. Because it is collectively desirable to judge impartially, he might argue, society rears us such that we do so inevitably and without thinking, just as we correct our perspectival judgments inevitably and without thinking. There are, however, two problems with this argument, leaving aside any worry we might have about the extent to which Hume's theory can accommodate a substantial socialization process. First, when perspectival judgments are corrected, their correction is unopposed by any motives encouraging one to persist in the uncorrected judgments. But there are motives that oppose impartial judgments of character. It isn't easy for a mother to judge two children impartially when one of them is her own child; hence Hume's theory must acknowledge this difficulty even while explaining how socialization can generate a motive to judge impartially that is strong enough to overcome powerful opposing passions to do otherwise. Those Kantians who believe that human beings possess a motivationally efficacious and reason-based conception of "fairness" mandating impartial judgment believe they can explain the reality and rationality of impartial judgment in the face of a considerable partial sentiment pressing for a different response. But certainly Hume cannot appeal to any such thing, and the idea that socialization can make impartial judgment irresistible in the face of such sentiments seems very implausible.

Still, for the sake of argument, let us grant Hume this possibility: now he can explain the fact of impartial judgment, but it seems he can no longer explain its rationality. Were people to reflect on the rationality of using the general point of view to correct their partial judgments, it seems they would be correct to decide that it was often (maybe even usually) not rational to do so, either because of the free rider problem I mentioned earlier, or because of the greater strength of the partial sentiments opposing its use, or both. It would seem that such "reflective endorsement"[35] is extremely important in ensuring that a moral theory, if made public, does not undermine people's commitment to moral judgment and action. If my arguments above are correct, then even if Hume can argue that socialization explains why people make impartial judgments, his theory is just as unstable upon critical reflection because it cannot establish that moral judgment from the general point of view is always, or even usually, rational.

The best chance that supporters of Hume have to allay these concerns is to stop handwaving about those "contradictions and confusions," define them precisely so as to identify the game-theoretic problems they pose for people, and try to argue that they are serious enough that people would desire and find it rational to establish and *use* a general point of view to solve them, even in the face of most opposing passions, where there is no unsolvable free rider problem preventing them from doing so. I take this to be a tall order, and maybe an impossible one (if the game-theoretic facts are other than those Hume requires to get his theory off the ground).

But even if Hume's followers succeed in filling this tall order, that is not sufficient to establish the soundness of Hume's theory of the natural virtues. The second motivational problem raised by Hume's discussion of the general point of view concerns why we would be motivated to act *from* impartial judgments. Morality is not simply a matter of judging but also of acting. Even if self-interested passions motivate us to *make* corrections of our sentiments from the general point of view and so judge impartially, why should they motivate us to try to *act* morally, in a way described by the natural virtues? Such is Hume's concern when he says, at the end of the *Enquiry*:

Having explained the moral *approbation* attending merit or virtue, there remains nothing but briefly to consider our interested *obligation* to it, and to inquire whether every man, who has any regard to his own happiness and welfare, will not best find his account in the practice of every moral duty. (*Enq*, p. 278)

To pursue this concern, consider the example of a cool-headed assessment by a nurse that of two sick patients, one is in greater pain, and deserving of more attention from her than the other: this judgment ought to motivate her to focus her attentions on the patient she judges to be sicker. Yet if the less sick patient is her friend, she would be motivated by her partial sentiments for this friend to focus on him instead. So how do we explain why she could – and should – be motivated to serve the sicker patient anyway?[36] That is, even if the nurse corrects the partiality produced by sympathy-induced sentiments by taking the conventionally defined "general point of view" so that she arrives at the judgment "Patient A is more deserving of my care than patient B," why should she feel any motivation to act from that judgment?

One might believe that because these judgments are "based on" other-regarding sentiment, they are sentiments themselves, and thus motivationally efficacious.[37] Yet the preponderance of textual evidence indicates that Hume himself did not believe this. This is, in large part, because the corrected judgments are products of a process of reflection that produces a different *judgment* but not a different sentiment. He suggests this in the passage I quoted above, which admits that it is not the sentiment but the language (and presumably the judgment it expresses) that is corrected, and he also suggests it in such passages as these:

The passions do not always follow our corrections; but these corrections are sufficient to regulate our abstract notions, and are alone regarded, when we pronounce in general concerning the degrees of virtue and vice. (*Treatise*, III, iii, 1, 585)

The judgement corrects or endeavours to correct the appearance: But it is not able entirely to prevail over sentiment. (*Enq*, 228, n. 1)

The heart takes not part entirely with those general notions, nor regulates all its love and hatred, by the universal abstract differences of virtue and vice, without regard to self, or the persons with whom we are more intimately connected; yet, have these moral differences a considerable influence, and *being sufficient at least for discourse*, serve all our purposes in company, in the pulpit, on the theatre and in the schools. (*Enq*, 229; emphasis added)

Note that the last passage insists on the "influence" of these judgments, but only explicitly recognizes their role in discourse, not in action. So although Hume's rhetoric sometimes suggests that the motivational force of the original, partial sentiment will somehow stick around and be infused into the impartial judgment, these passages show that even he thought the process of correction was too reflective and "abstract" to affect feeling. So what motivational effects can come from such (unsentimental) abstract judgments?

Even if Hume admits there are no such effects, he can still motivate action from them in certain ways. For example he can (and in fact does) argue that morally virtuous action is instrumentally valuable for the satisfaction of self-interested passions: "That the virtues which are immediately *useful* or *agreeable* to the person possessed of them, are desirable in a view to self-interest, it would be surely superfluous to prove" (*Enq*, p. 280). Recall that this is the Hobbesian strategy for commending the virtues. But if this is *all* that Hume can say to motivate us to behave morally, he has explained moral action as motivated (solely) by a concern for self. Nor can this argument work in all situations, since sometimes vicious behavior is individually rational (as all knaves understand).

Suppose Hume argues that we are motivated to act morally by virtue of a desire to be well thought of (a desire that is, arguably, akin to Hobbes's desire for glory).[38] Yet we have already reviewed the problems that such reputation arguments have when we discussed the use of such an argument to explain the motivation to make moral judgments. First, this argument is only as strong as the sentiments that produce pleasure at the contemplation of moral traits. Not only might these sentiments not be particularly efficacious as motives; more worryingly, they might be opposed by sentiments that produce pleasure at the contemplation of nonvirtuous action. (I once overheard an undergraduate telling a friend about a person she knew: "She was so cool – totally out for herself. I really want to be like her.") Moreover, people such as the nurse in our example, who are not evil, nonetheless have powerful sentiments motivating partial action that might well outweigh desires to curry the good opinion of others. Second, this type of argument presupposes what it is supposed to explain: that is, it assumes that other people will approve of you only if you act from your impartial moral judgments. But why should that be true? Why shouldn't their approval track their partial judgments, so that impartial action on your part would be less likely, or at least no more likely, to secure your good reputation than partial action? Third and finally, the desire to secure a good reputation is still a self-regarding desire, and hence a motive that fails to ensure that moral action arises from a concern for another. Hence it is the wrong type of explanation to use in order to capture genuinely moral motivation.

This last problem also plagues any argument that says that the same passions directing us to create a general point of view also move us to act from its impartial judgements. Now, how it could be that passions motivating the creation of a point of view with respect to judgment should have any motivational efficacy whatsoever with respect to action is a question to which I do not have an answer. Moreover, the same problems we faced before, concerning the strength of the motivational efficacy of these passions and the possibility of free rider problems undercutting the individual rationality of adhering to conventions motivating them, must be solved if this argument is going to work. However, the more fundamental problem with the argument is this: Given that the passions motivating the creation of the general point of view are primarily self-regarding, an implication of this position is that people are moved to act morally because they are concerned with themselves – indeed the passions defining this self-concern are the same passions that mandate the construction of the artificial virtues. But now we seem to have lost the whole reason for incorporating other-regarding sentiment into our moral theory in the first place, namely, our interest in explaining how moral people act morally because they *care* about other people – including ones they do not know – such that they seek to cooperate with, and benefit, them in an impartial way! What is the point of trying to incorporate other-regarding sentiment into one's moral theory if it can be done only in a way that precludes one from locating such sentiments as a motive for moral behavior?

Only if Hume claims that not just our moral language but our original sentiments are transformed by taking the "general point of view," so that we now not only judge but *feel* in impartial ways (such that the original partial sentiments are expunged), can he explain how we could be motivated to act on these impartial judgments. But Hume's remarks cited above show that he doubted that such transformations occurred, and many would go further and question whether such transformations are even possible, much less common.

Suppose, however, that Hume's followers (I'll call them "neo-Humeans") decided to take seriously the possibility that this transformation of feeling commonly occurs (contra Hume's own views in the text): the problem is that this way of understanding the Humean view is now only inches away from the traditional view that impartial reason corrects partial sentiment in a way that accords reason a non-instrumental role! These neo-Humeans and Hume's traditional opponents would now agree both that partial sentiments need correction, and that reasoning generates the correction. They would disagree only about how to categorize the product of reasoning that produces the correction: whereas the neo-Humeans would call it a sentiment, his opponents would consider it some sort of (non-sentimental) moral judgment with motivational force. Not only will Hume's critics insist that their categorization is psychologically the more plausible, but they will also question whether Humeans can, consistent with their other philosophical commitments, claim that (*bona fide*) *sentiments* (even impartial ones) could be produced by a kind of *reasoning*, and they would query how reason could do so if it is only, as Hume says, instrumental. It is a nice bit of irony that Hume's followers may only be able to establish the motivational efficacy of Hume's moral judgments if they are forced to recognize a non-instrumental role for reason.

Conclusion

Those who wish to defend successfully a moral theory that captures both moral feelings and (impartial) moral judgments must figure out a way of handling Hume's problems, but I suspect they will likely have to do so using a framework of moral theorizing that is very different from the Hobbesian framework that I have argued Hume continually relies upon (even when he says he is not). They also need to reflect on questions that the problems of Hume's theory raise for anyone interested in a sentiment-based moral theory. In particular: Why must other-regarding sentiments be derived from anything? Why can't they be considered as "natural" as self-regarding desires? If they can, will they be strong enough to compete with self-regarding desires, at least sometimes? Moreover, since other-regarding sentiments seem too changeable, transitory, and partial to be considered "moral responses" in their raw form, can we generate an account of how they can be refashioned into the kind of impartial responses we consider "moral"? And can we do so in a way that will assume a plausible account of the reasoning that performs the refashioning, even while explaining the motivation to make them and establish why the motivation to act from them persists in the refashioned responses? Will an account of this refashioning rely heavily on a conception of reason operating non-instrumentally? And if that is so, why won't it be the reasoning, rather than the sentiment, that gives the resulting moral judgements their authority over our beliefs and actions? At the deepest level, Hume's problems developing the theory of natural virtues suggest that our sentiments merely assist, but do not define, motivate, or constitute, the moral point of view.

NOTES

I am very grateful to Paul Hurley, Gregory Loeben, Ken O'Day, David Owen, and Andrews Reath for very helpful discussions of certain aspects of this essay. Portions of this essay were read at the University of Utah and Brigham Young University; I thank the audiences at both places for their helpful discussions of its ideas. I also want to thank John Rawls; although I never discussed this paper with him, it was he who got me interested in contractarian thinking, and who encouraged my interest in Hobbes, when I was a graduate student. This and many other publications on these topics have been the result. To say that I am deeply grateful to him is an understatement; to be able to say "thank you" to him is a great pleasure.

1. For a good discussion of why this classification is mistaken, see David Gauthier, "David Hume: Contractarian," *Philosophical Review*, 88(1) (1979): 3–38.
2. Stephen Darwall discusses the influence of Hutcheson on Hume in *The British Moralist and the Internal "Ought": 1640–1740* (Cambridge University Press, 1994) and in "Motive and Obligation in Hume's Ethics," *Nous*, 27(4) (1993): 415–48.
3. There is a sense in which this article follows up ideas about interpreting Hume suggested by John Rawls in *A Theory of Justice* (Cambridge: Harvard University Press, 1971); see especially pp. 32 and 184ff.
4. I discuss these passages, and the ambivalence they suggest, in *Hobbes and the Social Contract Tradition* (Cambridge University Press, 1986) and in "Hobbes and Ethical Naturalism," in *Philosophical Perspectives, Volume 6: Ethics*, ed. James Tomberlin (Atascadero, CA: Ridgeview, 1992), pp. 333–53.
5. Samuel Scheffler, "Prerogatives Without Restrictions," in *Philosophical Perspectives, Volume 6: Ethics*, ed. James Tomberlin, pp. 375–97.
6. References to Hobbes's *Leviathan*, hereafter cited as *Lev*, are to the edition by C. B. MacPherson (Harmondsworth, England: Penguin, 1968). References appear in the text and cite the chapter number, followed by the number of the paragraph in the chapter, followed by the page number of the original Head edition of 1651.
7. See J. L. Mackie, *Hume's Moral Theory* (London: Routledge, 1980), pp. 71–5; Barry Stroud, *Hume* (London: Routledge, 1977), pp. 86–7.
8. Hobbes recognizes this at least somewhat, distinguishing in his later book *De*

Homine between goods that are "real" and goods that are only "apparent." For a discussion of the possible divergence of desires and values, see Peter Railton, "Naturalism and Prescriptivity," *Social Philosophy and Policy*, 7(1) (1989): 155–7.

9. For discussions of interpersonal as opposed to impersonal standpoints in moral theory, I am indebted to Paul Hurley.

10. See my *Hobbes and the Social Contract Tradition*, especially chapter 6.

11. See Gregory Kavka, *Hobbesian Moral and Political Thought* (Princeton: Princeton University Press, 1986).

12. I am indebted to Brian Barry for the kind of strategy I am using to interpret this passage, and Buchanan also suggests it in his Hobbesian reconstruction of deliberation in the state of nature in *Limits of Liberty* (Chicago: University of Chicago Press, 1975), e.g., pp. 23–5.

13. All references to Hume's *Treatise of Human Nature* are to the edition of L. A. Selby-Bigge, revised by P. H. Nidditch (Oxford: Clarendon Press, 1978). References appear in the text as follows: (*Treatise*, Book number, Part number, section number, page number in Selby-Bigge edition).

14. I discuss the way Hume (unlike Hobbes) tries to drain away all normativity with respect to action from instrumental reasoning in "Does Hume Have an Instrumental Conception of Reasoning?" in *Hume Studies*, April 1995, and in "On Instrumental Reasoning," *Essays in Honor of Kurt Baier*, ed. J. Schneewind (La Salle, IL: Open Court, 1996).

15. But Hobbes and Hume disagree somewhat about why human cooperation is valuable. Like Hobbes, Hume prescribes the creation of a social union to deal with the "inconveniences" created by the lack of human self-sufficiency. We require a social union to increase each individual's power, ability, and security. But unlike Hobbes, Hume does not see conflict among men as an additional reason for the creation of a social union. For Hume, society is not a solution for conflict; it is a solution for human weakness, and conflict is merely the impediment to its creation. Annette Baier has an interesting discussion of this point in *A Progress of Sentiments: Reflections on Hume's Treatise* (Cambridge: Harvard University Press, 1991), chapter 10.

16. Note that, like Hobbes, Hume regards the reasons for the establishment of rules of cooperation as the elimination of conflict, and he sees the elimination of conflict as obviously in each person's self-interest. However, unlike Hobbes, Hume does not believe that self-interest is dominated by the desire for self-preservation, nor does he believe that conflict prior to the creation of these rules is as severe or as extensive as does Hobbes. These differences are discussed by Baier at some length (*A Progress of Sentiments*, pp. 222–3).

17. Self-interest must also constrain itself: "For whether the passion of self-interest be esteemed vicious or virtuous, 'tis all a case; since itself alone restrains it" by creating and motivating conformity with these moral conventions (*Treatise*, III, ii, 2, 492).

18. For example, it influenced David Lewis's *Convention: A Philosophical Study* (Cambridge: Harvard University Press, 1969).

19. David Hume, *Enquiry Concerning the Principles of Morals*, ed. L. A. Selby-Bigge, revised by P. H. Nidditch (Oxford: Clarendon Press, 1975), p. 191. Henceforth all references to this work appear as: (*Enq*, page number).

20. See *Enq*, 194.

21. Baier agrees; see *A Progress of Sentiments*, chapter 10.
22. See David Gauthier, *Morals by Agreement* (Oxford: Clarendon Press, 1986); and Edward McClennen, *Rationality and Dynamic Choice* (Cambridge University Press, 1990).
23. But it may be that the details of those accounts are not exactly the same. Both philosophers are far too sketchy about how the operation of sympathy works, and we can imagine a number of different ways to cash out those details. Consider one way: Via the operation of sympathy we imagine ourselves in the position of others, form an idea of the passions they are experiencing by imagining what we would experience in that situation, and that idea is then converted into the impression of the passions of the other. Consider a second way (suggested to me by Andrews Reath): We form an idea of the passions of the other insofar as we see the other as resembling us (where the mechanism precipitating this reaction, given the resemblance, might be taken to be virtually inevitable), and these ideas are then converted into the passions of the other. Both accounts generate the passions of self-regard, but in completely different ways: The first makes my self-concern the *cause* of my acquiring the ideas (and eventually the impressions) of the others' experience; the second makes the acquiring of those ideas and impressions simply the result of a mechanism that is not motivated by self-concern but only the other's resemblance to me. Hobbes certainly suggests the former account; Hume may have meant the latter. (But note that the two accounts are not inconsistent, and could be held together.) I do not have space here to explore which of these accounts is really the Humean one, but for my purposes it doesn't really matter which of them is correct. Because both accounts take other-regarding passions to be created by a mechanism having to do with the self, where that causal story of their creation does not affect the object of these passions (which have to do with the other), both accounts preserve the other-regarding nature of the passions in question. Thus, even if Hobbes held the former view and Hume (only) the latter view, Hume would still be accepting an explanation of the origination of other-regarding passions with the same basic structure as the Hobbesian account.
24. And I plead as guilty of doing this as anyone else in *Hobbes and the Social Contract Tradition*, chapter 1.
25. In *Treatise* (III, iii, 2, 593–5), Hume tells a story that tries to explain the difference between sympathy and comparison, but it is both implausible and incomplete. He says, "Sympathy being the conversion of an idea into an impression, demands a greater force and vivacity to the idea than is requisite to comparison." Again, Hume is hoping that he can somehow generate other-regarding concern from the mere *force* of the impression that another's experience makes upon us after we sympathetically identify with them. But mere force doesn't tell us *how* the impression is converted into a form of care for the other. Moreover, even weak ideas can generate in us sympathy, and strong ideas can generate comparison.
26. Note that this problem occurs in John Rawls's account of a Humean-style ideal observer theory in *A Theory of Justice*, pp. 185–6. Rawls argues that an ideal observer would use sympathy to experience the pleasures and pains of each person affected by a social system, and then experiences pleasure in contemplating that social system in proportion to the net sum of pleasure felt

by those affected by it. He implies that this overall feeling of pleasure is what, on the theory, would constitute the extent to which the ideal observer morally approved of the system. But even if the ideal observer's aggregation of personal pleasures and pains matches a utilitarian calculation, why should that fact tell us anything about whether or not the ideal observer approves or disapproves of it? It tells us how he gets information about and calculates net pleasure in the system; we have no knowledge that his sentiments of approval or disapproval track this calculation, nor is the calculation itself a form of approval or disapproval.

27. J. L. Mackie, *Hume's Moral Theory*, p. 71.
28. Geoffrey Sayre-McCord, "On Why Hume's 'General Point of View' Isn't Ideal – and Shouldn't Be," *Social Philosophy and Policy*, 11(1) (Winter 1994): 217.
29. Mackie, p. 123.
30. This is not to say that the two kinds of virtue are the same. For a discussion of the difference, see Ken O'Day, "Hume's Distinction between the Natural and the Artificial Virtues," *Hume Studies*, 20(1) (April 1994): pp. 121–41; see also Sayre-McCord, "On Why Hume's 'General Point of View' Isn't Ideal."
31. However, it has also struck people as a proto-utilitarian idea, suggesting that morality requires assuming the standpoint of an ideal observer. See, for example, Rawls, *A Theory of Justice*, pp. 184–7; and see a discussion of this interpretation in both Sayre-McCord, "On Why Hume's 'General Point of View' Isn't Ideal," pp. 203–13, and Elizabeth Radcliffe, "Hume on Motivating Sentiments, the General Point of View, and the Inculcation of Morality," *Hume Studies*, 20(1) (April 1994): 39–48.
32. These questions are discussed by Sayre-McCord, "On Why Hume's 'General Point of View' Isn't Ideal," and Radcliffe, "Hume on Motivating Sentiments."
33. Hume himself suggests this point in *Enq*, 20. Radcliffe notes this passage in "Hume on Motivating Sentiments," p. 51.
34. It is suggested by Christine Korsgaard (albeit with reference to the motivation to act morally, rather than the motivation to judge morally) in *The Sources of Normativity: The Tanner Lectures on Human Values* (Cambridge University Press, 1996), Lecture 2: "Reflective Endorsement", §§2.2.1–2.2.7, pp. 51–66.
35. This is Korsgaard's term; see *The Sources of Normativity*, §§2.1.1–2.1.2, pp. 49–51. For the importance of stability under reflection, see Bernard Williams, *Ethics and the Limits of Philosophy* (Cambridge: Harvard University Press, 1985), especially chaps. 8 and 9 and p. 148; and J. L. Mackie, *Ethics: Inventing Right and Wrong* (Harmondsworth: Penguin, 1977). For evidence that Hume took it to be important, see *Enq*, 279.
36. The fact that there may be moral reasons for questioning the unrelenting impartiality of judgment that Hume is recommending is an issue that I leave aside for now.
37. Elizabeth Radcliffe suggests this line, e.g., "Hume on Motivating Sentiments," pp. 51–3, but argues for it using examples of divergence of partial and impartial judgment that are not flatly contradictory, and do not generate opposing courses of action. It is precisely because the corrected judgment can oppose the original sentimental response in content and implication for

action that the divergence between the two becomes a serious problem for Hume.

38. Such an argument is suggested by Korsgaard on Hume's behalf in *The Sources of Normativity*, §2.2.3, especially pp. 58–9.

The Natural Goodness of Humanity

JOSHUA COHEN

> Men are wicked; a sad and constant experience makes proof unnecessary.
>
> Jean-Jacques Rousseau[1]

> Despite the depressing sight, not so much of ills that oppress mankind from natural causes as of those men inflict upon each other, the mind is cheered by the prospect that things may be better in future.... Empirical arguments against the success of these resolves, which rest on hope, are insufficient here. The argument that what has not succeeded so far never will succeed, does not even justify the abandonment of a pragmatic or technological intention ... much less than abandonment of a moral intention that becomes a duty unless its accomplishment is demonstrably impossible.
>
> Immanuel Kant[2]

> Let us ... begin by setting aside all the facts, for they do not affect the question.
>
> Jean-Jacques Rousseau[3]

Introduction

As Rousseau tells the story, he was walking along the road from Paris to Vincennes in 1749 (on his way to visit Diderot, then imprisoned in the château of Vincennes), contemplating a question from the Academy of Dijon – "Has the restoration of the sciences and the arts helped to purify morals?" – when he was overtaken by a flood of ideas, "a thousand lights." Lying at the heart of this "sudden inspiration" was the thought that dominated his subsequent writing: "that man is naturally good, and that it is solely by [our] institutions that men become wicked" (*M*, 1136).[4]

The conception of natural human goodness is not uniquely Rousseau's. Egalitarian and radical democratic political views commonly hold that human motivations supporting unjust institutions are not intrinsic to our nature, but explained by those institutions themselves. Such views, however, often accompany this claim with implausible assertions about human plasticity, and denials that human beings have a nature (or claims about its complete social determination or construction).[5] Rousseau's account of natural goodness separates it from this undesirable company. Human beings have a complex natural endowment, including self-love, a sense of self-worth and an associated concern to be treated with respect, compassion (*pitié*), a power of choice, and a range of cognitive powers. To be sure, this endowment is, in a way, *abstract*: self-love, for example, can take many forms, depending on how a person thinks about herself; similarly with a sense of self-worth and compassion. And social-institutional environments account for the determinate expressions of the endowment. But the endowment itself is fixed and provides an underlying structure that helps explain the variety of human motivations: thus Kant's description of Rousseau as the Newton of human nature.[6]

The idea of natural human goodness, then, gives Rousseau's moral and political views their bearings, and is important in its own right. But it is also obscure.[7] How can we combine the view that human beings have a nature with the claim that current expressions of it – indeed virtually all its observed expressions – are distorted? And if all our evidence involves such distortion, how can we acquire knowledge of our nature? More fundamentally, is it reasonable in the face of observable patterns of motivation and conduct to endorse a hopeful conception of human nature, or is such endorsement simply a matter of wishful thinking – of projecting moral and political preferences into our nature?

In this essay, I present an interpretation of Rousseau's account of natural goodness with a view to addressing these questions. In Section I, I briefly sketch Rousseau's ideal of a political society in which citizens achieve full autonomy by cooperating as equals for the common good, and present an objection to this ideal: that it is incapable of engaging human affections and therefore objectionably unrealistic.[8] The idea of natural goodness provides the basis for Rousseau's response to this charge. In Section II, I present the foundations of natural goodness in human nature, emphasizing Rousseau's distinction between the *abstract potentialities* intrinsic to human nature and the *determinate expression* of those potentialities as a result of social circumstances. Chomsky has argued that a distinction of this kind was central to the Cartesian tradition in linguistics: though language acquisition is of course triggered by circumstance, and the particular language a speaker acquires depends on the social environment, certain fundamental features of the acquired state reflect intrinsic features of human nature.[9] A parallel idea guides my discussion of the formation of human motivations in Section II:

though the acquisition of motives is of course triggered by circumstance, certain fundamental features of the acquired state reflect intrinsic features of human nature. In Sections III–V, I present the two main elements of the conception of natural goodness itself: that we are originally innocent, in that all the vices can all be explained without attributing them to "the human heart" (*E*, 92; *B*, 936), and that the same properties of human nature – in particular, concerns about self-worth – that are now expressed in vice can also be expressed in ways that support the political ideal of free association among equals. In Section VI, I conclude by explaining why Rousseau might have thought that an affirmation of the idea of natural goodness is reasonable, notwithstanding all the evidence of human vice. Rousseau believes that his own view of human nature can explain that evidence, and that this explanation permits us to affirm the natural goodness of humanity for moral-practical reasons, without offending against theoretical reason.

My aims are principally interpretive, and I will not be defending the details of Rousseau's view. Still, I think the main outlines have considerable force, and my interpretation undoubtedly emphasizes elements that strike me as most plausible: in particular, the central role in our psychology of the sense of self-worth, the view that our natural endowment consists of a set of abstract powers capable of diverse forms of expression, and the idea that moral considerations provide good reasons for endorsing a hopeful conception of human nature.

I. The Possibility of Free Association

The *fundamental problem* of Rousseau's political philosophy is "to find a form of association that defends and protects the person and goods of each associate with all the common force, and by means of which each one uniting with all, nevertheless obeys only himself and remains as free as before" (*SC*, 1.6.4).[10] Rousseau wants to know how there can be a stable form of human association that ensures protection and security to its members and at the same time enables them to be self-governing.

The importance of this problem reflects the central role of self-love and freedom in Rousseau's conception of our nature.[11] Because self-love is an essential aspect of our nature, we cannot be indifferent to the protection of our person and goods. But not just any form of protection will do. We are "born free," with the capacity to choose and to regulate our own conduct. Moreover, this capacity is the source of our special worth and the basis of our standing as responsible agents with rights and duties: "renouncing one's liberty is renouncing one's dignity as a man, the rights of humanity and even its duties" (*SC*, 1.4.6; *D2*, 148, 189–90).

We need, then, to find a form of security that does not require us to alienate our freedom.

Perhaps Rousseau's fundamental problem cannot be solved. Assuming conditions of social interdependence, personal security arguably requires authoritatively imposed constraints on freedom. And if such constraints are necessary, how *could* we associate in a way that accommodates concerns rooted in self-love – "defends and protects the person and goods of each associate" – and also enables each to achieve "moral freedom" – the full political autonomy that consists in "obedience to the law one has prescribed for oneself" (*SC*, 1.8.3; *LM*, 807)?

According to one natural line of thought – Hobbes provides its classical formulation – we cannot. Security and the pursuit of happiness depend on peace. But, given the "known natural inclinations of mankind"[12] and de facto conditions of human interdependence, peace requires an agreement that proceeds "as if every man should say to every man *I authorise and give up my right of governing myself to this man, or to this assembly of men, on this condition, that thou give up thy right to him, and authorize all his actions in like manner.*"[13] In short: to ensure physical security and provide hope for felicity, we must trade in self-government. Hobbes's absolutism exaggerates the terms of trade. But even if an authority short of absolute suffices for achieving peaceful order, we still may wonder how each citizen could possibly achieve *full* political autonomy – each giving the law to him- or herself – within an organized political society.

But whereas Hobbes aims "to set before men's eyes the mutual relation between protection and obedience,"[14] Rousseau locates "the essence of the body politic" precisely in "the harmony of obedience and freedom" (*SC*, 3.13.5) – a harmony that ensures protection, without imposing a morally unacceptable subordination of will.[15] This proposed harmony is puzzling. How could each "unite with all" for security, while obeying only him- or herself and so remaining "as free as before"? Rousseau needs to explain how it is possible to combine the social union that provides protection with individual autonomy – with the "moral freedom" that consists in giving the law to oneself (*SC*, 1.8.3). And that explanation needs two components, corresponding to two kinds of doubt about possibility: doubts about *content* and *motivation*.[16]

The Content Problem

Accepting authority appears to be a matter of letting oneself be ruled by the decisions of others (perhaps the majority). Explaining how self-government can be reconciled with the chains of social connection and

bonds of political authority requires some way to dispel this appearance
– to show that the idea of such reconciliation is even coherent.

Rousseau's conception of a society guided by a *general will* addresses
this problem.[17] In such a society, the political obligations of citizens are
fixed by laws, those laws reflect a shared understanding of the common
good, and that understanding expresses an equal concern for the good of
each citizen (*SC*, 2.1.1, 2.4.5, 2.11.2). Because the content of the conception of the common good reflects an equal concern with each citizen's
well-being, the society provides security for person and goods; because
citizens, as members of the sovereign people, share the conception, and
the laws emerge from it, each citizen remains free in fulfilling his legal
obligations.[18] In short, the society solves the fundamental problem. I will
not expand here on the terms of this solution; my present concern is only
to say enough about content to set the stage for introducing the problem
of motivation, which is where the idea of natural goodness enters. The
essential point about content, then, is that Rousseau's solution to the
fundamental problem requires that the parties to the social compact
treat one another as equals, both in the institution of equal citizenship
and in their agreement to regulate conduct by reference to reasons of the
common good.

The Motivation Problem

Even if we have available an account of the content of the proposed
reconciliation, however, we may still wonder whether human beings
could live as it requires. The society of the general will may solve the
fundamental problem, but we also need some reason to think that people
could be *motivated* to cooperate according to the terms of that ideal. The
resolution of the first problem of possibility underscores the force of this
second issue. The reconciliation of autonomy and social connection requires a shared understanding of and allegiance to the common good. In
the face of widespread vice – selfishness, pride, jealousy, envy – we may
wonder whether that ideal is humanly possible, consistent with human
motivations.

Hobbes would doubtless have raised this objection. His case for the
alienation of rights of self-government rested on a philosophical anthropology that makes Rousseau's solution psychologically unrealistic, however coherent and attractive it may seem as a political ideal. Surveying
the "known natural inclinations of mankind,"[19] Hobbes found desires for
individual preservation and happiness; he noted the strength of human
fears about violent death; he observed (in at least some people) passions
of pride, envy, and greed rooted in a sense of natural differences of worth

and a concern that *relative social standing* mirror those presumptively natural differences; and he found that people are often blinded by passions – prompted by them to act for near-term advantages and against their own longer-term interests in preservation and happiness.[20] Departing from these observations, he concluded that we need a sovereign with unconditional authority. Only a sovereign with unbounded authority would have power sufficient to overawe subjects, tame their pride (and other passions) with fear, and ensure the peace required for preservation and felicity.[21]

Hobbes's argument for political submission is driven, then, by a general pessimism about human capacities for self-regulation, whether for the common good or any other long-term good.[22] But he was also dubious in particular about the motivational power of reasons of the common good because he did not see human beings as moved by the thought that our conduct treats others as equals, or is part of a system of conduct that ensures such treatment. Concerned with preservation and happiness, we have only instrumental reasons for endorsing equality (if we have any reasons at all); and insofar as we are prone to pride, we will reject equality as inconsistent with our naturally superior worth and an insult to our dignity.[23]

Rousseau would have had a simpler case for the motivational possibility of a general will and the political autonomy it makes possible had he rejected Hobbes's psychological observations. But Rousseau largely endorsed Hobbes's dismal description: "Men are wicked; a sad and constant experience makes proof unnecessary" (*D2*, 208). We see widespread vice – selfishness, pride, jealousy, envy – and underlying that vice a "frenzy to distinguish ourselves" (*D2*, 195), an "ardent desire to raise one's relative fortune less out of genuine need than in order to place oneself above others" (*D2*, 181). This frenzy and desire in turn have roots in the inflated, false sense of self-worth that drove Hobbes's absolutism. In principle, a sense of duty, itself tied to the common good, could override these tendencies to vice, thus taking care of the problem of motivation. But Rousseau was skeptical about the strength of a sense of duty, when opposed by other motivations (see below, pp. 125–6). So he did not put much weight on this possibility.

This description naturally prompts the thought that the society of the general will is incompatible with human motivations, that the commitment to equality required for political autonomy has no basis in human psychology. And if we could directly infer intrinsic properties of human nature from the observed motivations – if, for example, the "ardent desire" for relative advantage were a direct expression of an original predisposition – that thought would be true, and would drive us to pessimistic conclusions about the possibility of a stable order in which citizens give the law to themselves. But we have no reason for confidence in any such direct inference, and so no reason to endorse the thought or its pessimistic implication. That, in a nutshell, is the point of Rousseau's idea of natural goodness: to defeat an argument that starts from "sad and constant experience" and ends by rejecting an ideal of free cooperation among equals. In response to the problem of motivational possibility, Rousseau advances an account of human nature organized around the contention that human beings are *naturally good*, "but that society depraves him and makes him miserable" (*RJ*, 213). This natural goodness underwrites the possibility of our being motivated to associate according to terms of an ideal that reconciles association and autonomy.

II. Human Nature

The central tenet of the idea of natural goodness is that "There is no original perversity in the human heart. There is not a single vice to be found in it of which it cannot be said how and whence it entered" (*E*, 92; *B*, 935; *RJ*, 23).[24] More particularly, the explanation of "how and whence" is "that society depraves [human beings] and makes [them] miserable" (*RJ*, 213).

To understand the content and force of these claims, we need to interpret them in light of a distinction, fundamental to Rousseau's conception of human nature, between the abstract potentialities intrinsic to human nature and the determinate expressions of those potentialities.[25] *Determinate* motivations are not themselves original elements of our nature but instead reflect the way our nature is expressed, given our circumstances and the self-conceptions that arise from those circumstances. Depending on these circumstances, the expression of the intrinsic properties of human nature will take quite different forms.

This distinction provides, as we will see, the basis of Rousseau's answer to the motivation problem. Though depressing experience suggests that the society of the general will is not in the human cards, such experience does not provide a direct window on our nature. Our observations are confined to the expression of human powers within institutional forms, and nothing in those observations excludes the possibility that we could, under suitable conditions, express the very features of our nature that are now manifested in vice in quite different ways – in particular, by regarding one another as equals and being moved to comply with regulations because they advance the common good of members thus conceived.

This rough sketch of the idea of natural goodness must suffice for now.

A fuller and more precise statement awaits an account of Rousseau's conception of human nature.

Three Properties of Human Nature

According to Rousseau, human beings are naturally endowed with self-love, compassion, and a set of cognitive powers. Let's consider each in turn, bearing in mind that we want eventually to understand more complex motivations in terms of these essential elements.

Self-Love. Each human being has a natural concern for his or her own welfare – *amour de soi*, or self-love. Self-love is itself not a simple idea, in part because what we love in loving ourselves depends in part on how we conceive of ourselves. But whatever else it involves, self-love includes concerns to preserve ourselves and to protect the means of that preservation. Moreover, self-love, like love of other people, is a matter of valuation as well as affection.[26] However I think and feel about myself, among the things I value is myself. We each have a sense of our own worth that animates our more specific concerns and aims.[27]

This self-love need have no relative or comparative aspect; it need not be a matter of loving oneself more than others. But when I develop relations with others, self-love, understood to include a sense of self-worth, naturally extends to include a concern for the relations in which I stand to others and for the regard of those others for me – a concern that they affirm my worth. The extension is natural because my sense of self-worth includes the thought of myself as valuable. Because self-love is not simply a matter of affection for myself or wishing myself well, but of regarding myself as valuable, I suppose that others ought to recognize my value as well. "*Amour propre,*" generically speaking, names this concern for my standing in the eyes of others – the abstract concern that they value me as I value myself (*E*, 213–15).

Amour propre comes in two forms, corresponding to two ways I might value myself. On the one hand, I might regard my worth as equal to that of others. If I do, then I will think that others ought to take my well-being equally into account, to treat my concerns and theirs as on a par. This form of self-regard is reasonable, in two ways. It conforms to a correct understanding of human beings, of our "true relations" as equals in virtue of our common human nature. Rousseau summarizes the "whole of human wisdom" about the development of the passions this way: "(1) To have a sense of the true relations of man, with respect to the species as well as the individual. (2) To order all the affections of the soul according to these relations" (*E*, 219). To order affections according to

true relations is to have affections rooted in true beliefs about the relations of human beings – in particular, about the "identity of our natures"
with the natures of other people, despite differences of social station (*E*,
221):

Man is the same in all stations. . . . To the man who thinks, all the civil distinctions disappear. He sees the same passions, the same sentiments in the hod-
carrier and the illustrious man. He discerns there only a difference in language,
only a more or less affected tone. (*E*, 225; also 194, 222)

An egalitarian sense of worth is reasonable in a second way: unlike the
view of oneself as of greater worth, it can genuinely (without affectation)
be upheld by others, and so need not be a source of discontent and
misery. This possibility reflects a further psychological premise: that it is
"impossible" that "each person should prefer us to all else and to himself" (*RJ*, 113),[28] but not impossible that each should regard himself as
our equal. If our sense of self-worth takes the egalitarian form, then we
are not led to make the psychologically impossible demand on others
that they think better of us than they think of themselves. By contrast, if
we "[prefer] ourselves to others," then we also "[demand] others to
prefer us to themselves, which is impossible" (*E*, 213–14).[29]

The second, inegalitarian form of self-regard is to think oneself more
worthy of regard than others, and find it insulting if they reject this
elevated conception. A point of terminology before proceeding:
Rousseau often uses "*amour propre*" exclusively for the prideful form of
self-regard (*D2*, 226). But in *Emile* in particular, the generic use – which
covers both forms – is more clearly in evidence (*E*, 92, 215, 235), and one
passage suggests the phrase "inflamed *amour propre*" for the prideful
form (*E*, 247). I will follow the latter usage here.[30]

A person with an inflamed sense of self-worth "set[s] greater store by
himself than by anyone else" (*D2*, 226); he assigns himself "the first and
better place" (*RJ*, 112). This inegalitarian form of *amour propre* conflicts
with a correct understanding of human beings: naturalizing status inequalities, it treats them as outward expressions of inner differences of
nature and natural worth.[31]

If as a consequence of my care Emile prefers his ways of being, of seeing, and of
feeling to that of other men, Emile is right. But if he thus believes himself to be
of a *more excellent nature* and more happily *born* than other men, Emile is wrong.
He is deceived. (*E*, 245, emphases added)

In addition to resting on error, the inegalitarian form of *amour propre*
provokes inner discontent and anxiety and interpersonal conflict because
it demands the impossible self-abasement of others.

Although self-regard is intrinsic to our nature, then, its particular form of expression – whether reasonable or inflamed – depends on circumstances. Describing Emile's entry into the "moral order," Rousseau says that the point at which he begins to make comparisons with others

is the point where love of self turns into *amour propre* and where begin to arise all the passions which depend on this one. But to decide whether among these passions the dominant ones in his character will be humane and gentle or cruel and malignant, whether they will be passions of beneficence and of commiseration or of envy and covetousness, we must know what position he will feel he has among men. (*E*, 235; also 243)

In Section IV, I explore the connections between circumstances – "position among men" – and the different forms of self-regard. Suffice to say here that these connections play a central role in Rousseau's answer to the problem of motivational possibility. Such vices as jealousy, selfish indifference, greed, cruelty, envy, and cowardice are all fueled by inflamed *amour propre*; they are not original to human nature, nor do their roots lie in egoistic hedonism or in an insatiable desire to accumulate goods. Instead they reflect a conception of one's relative worth that issues in a desire – indeed a demand, a sense of entitlement – to live a better life than others. And this sets the central question for an explanation of vice: *How does a generic, not-intrinsically-inegalitarian concern to be treated with respect come to be particularized as a desire and demand to be treated as a better?* If Rousseau can answer this question – and explain how the concern to "assign oneself the first and better place" (*RJ*, 112) might be forestalled – then he will have accounted for the origin of vice without supposing it to be an original predisposition, whether express or latent.

Compassion (Pitié). Each person is moved by compassion, a non-derivative predisposition to respond with aversion to the suffering of others (*D2*, 160–3; *E*, 221ff.). To say that this predisposition is natural is not to attribute a determinate kind of compassion to human beings quite generally. On the contrary, the natural predisposition to compassion – like the concern about self-worth – can be expressed in various forms, and the form of expression depends on circumstances.

With self-regard the important dimension of variation was rank ordering; here the dimension of variation is extent. In particular, the compassion we tend naturally to experience when we understand the sufferings of others can be generalized to cover wider groups of people; suitably extended, compassion provides the foundation for a concern with the welfare of human beings quite generally (*E*, 253), and so provides the affective soil for genuine virtue: "from this single attribute flow all the social virtues that he [Mandeville] wants to deny men. Indeed what are generosity, clemency, humanity, if not pity applied to the weak, the guilty or the species in general" (D2, 161; E, 253)?[32]

As vanity provides the foundations for the vices – though it is not itself an original sentiment – compassion provides the basis for the virtues. Whereas compassion itself is original to human nature, however, its extended expression is not, and depends on how we regard others. In Section V we will explore the conditions that encourage this extension.

Cognitive Powers/Perfectibility. Along with these basic affective powers, we are endowed with a set of cognitive capacities, including capacities for memory, imagination, abstraction, conceptualization, self-reflection, and reason. These powers develop from their form as unrealized capacities into realized abilities only under the pressure of circumstances. "Superfluous faculties," they are put "as it were, in reserve in the depth of his soul, to be developed there when needed" (E, 81). Indeed, apart from sensory powers (D2, 149), all forms of cognition involved in representing and thinking about actual and possible states of the world and of the self are triggered by circumstances: "It was by a very wise providence that the faculties he had in potentiality were to develop only with the opportunities to exercise them" (D2, 158; B, 951).

There is much to be said about the details of these powers, and how they are activated by social setting. But for the purposes of understanding the idea of natural goodness, further discussion of these points is best pursued by considering how these basic powers combine to generate more complex forms of motivation.

Social Bases of Motivations

These three properties of human nature provide the foundation of the doctrine of natural goodness. To defend this doctrine, Rousseau must show how these three properties suffice to explain the "sad observations" about human motivations and conduct. Even if they do, we may of course still wonder whether they are part of the correct account of our nature; but it would be irrational to believe that they are unless we can show that they meet a threshold condition of consistency with the available evidence.

To see how this consistency requirement might be met, we need first to see how these three elements of our nature work in combination.

Cognition and Motivation. The evolution of the cognitive powers (enlightenment) – "the successive developments of the human mind" (*D2*, 168) – enables people to think more complex thoughts and engage in more complex forms of reasoning and deliberation, and, more to the point here, gives more complex shape to the fundamental motivations. Combining with the basic affective aspects of human beings – self-love and compassion – the development of cognitive powers generates the full range of human desires and passions.

More specifically, motivations fall into two broad types. First, we have a restricted class of natural desires – for food, sex, and sleep. These desires correspond to natural needs – the needs associated with preservation of self and species – and pursuing them is an aspect of self-love.[33] These desires – really instinctual urges – reflect "the simple impulsion of nature" (*D2*, 116).[34]

All other desires depend on beliefs: "for one can desire or fear things only through the ideas one can have of them or by the simple impulsion of nature; and savage man, deprived of every kind of enlightenment, feels only the passions of this last kind" (*D2*, 150, 220–1; *LD*, 65–75). By contrast with hunger or primitive sexual appetites or the desire for sleep, all other desires are concept- and belief-dependent. They depend in particular on opinions and judgments, and require that the subject have a conception of the desired object: that the subject be able to represent the particular object of desire as an individual with certain general properties.

Consider, for example, the distinction between natural and extended forms of compassion. The development of more complex forms of compassion – the generalization of compassion to the weak (generosity), the guilty (clemency), and the species (humanity) – requires enlightenment because those forms require thoughts about the weak, the guilty, or the species as objects of concern.[35] Similarly, the development of *amour propre* requires a capacity for representing oneself in relation to others, and that, too, is possible only with the realization of cognitive powers initially latent in human nature.

The same is true for the sentiment of love, understood as an "ardent, impetuous . . . terrible passion that braves all dangers, overcomes all obstacles, and in its frenzy seems liable to destroy mankind" (*D2*, 163).[36] Although love has a natural or physical aspect – the sexual desires associated with species reproduction – the sentiment as we know it also has a "moral aspect" that directs love to particular individuals. This aspect depends, for example, on ideas of "merit and beauty," and thus on comparisons. Fixed on an individual – a "preferred object" (*D2*, 164) – it

rests in part on understanding and appreciating that individual's distinguishing features. In particular, it requires a grasp of "abstract ideas of
regularity and of proportion" (*D2*, 164). By contrast, the physical aspect
knows no "preferences." Absent a realized capacity for certain complex
thoughts, then, a person cannot be moved by love, or any of the emotions
or motivations associated with love – for example, jealousy, despondency
following rejection, heartbreak.

Social Bases of Cognition. Social practices explain beliefs, in particular
the socially shared beliefs that Rousseau calls "public opinion" and that
figure centrally in shaping the determinate content of motivations. This
explanation works in two ways. First, as a general matter the ability to
conceptualize can be realized only with the evolution of social interdependence. For conceptualization depends on the ability to judge and on
a grasp of definitions (*D2*, 156); these are tied in turn to the mastery of
language; and the existence of language depends on social cooperation
(*D2*, 158).

   Why Rousseau supposes that language requires social cooperation is
not clear, but the dependence of thought on the mastery of a language
seems more plausible. Rightly emphasizing that images are always particular – that mastering the concept *tree*, for example, cannot be a matter
of having tree-images – Rousseau holds that "general ideas can enter the
mind only with the help of words, and the understanding grasps them
only by means of propositions" (*D2*, 156). That is, having a concept is a
matter of having the ability to use a sign (e.g., a word) that is part of a
system of signs that can enter into combination with one another in
various ways. Thus, "one has to state propositions, hence one has to
speak in order to have general ideas: for as soon as the imagination stops,
the mind can proceed only by means of discourse" (*D2*, 156).

   Second, the specific concepts and beliefs that people have depend on
specific features of their form of association. Rousseau's views about the
mechanisms of their formation are obscure. But, for example, acquiring
the idea of property – that is, having thoughts about things belonging to
people – appears to depend on interacting with others in circumstances
in which people in fact have some form of independent existence, some
real ability to control things on their own (*D2*, 179). Furthermore, the
mastery of such abstract ideas as *person* – a mastery exhibited in such
thoughts as that *I am a person, one among many* – depends on regular
connections with other human beings under conditions that enable me to
see similarities. And the conception of myself and others as equals
requires some substantial echo in our social relations.

   Putting aside the detailed mechanisms that figure in the formation of concepts and beliefs, the central point is that social practices and political institutions figure centrally in the explanation of shared beliefs, including the ideas that people have about themselves: "A people's opinions arise from its constitution" (*SC*, 4.7.4; *LD*, 73–4). An important consequence of this view is that opinion – including the motivation-forming self-understandings – can be shaped by altering institutions. Because "a people's opinions" depend on "its constitution," part of the work of institutional design is to devise constitutions in light of this dependence.

Social Bases of Motivations. It follows from the social bases of cognition, together with the cognitive bases of motivations, that motivations – other than the purely natural urges – have social roots. In short, social arrangements explain motivations by explaining the ideas that make the motivations possible.

Rousseau, for example, famously rejects Hobbes's "naturalistic" explanation of the state of war because Hobbes "improperly included in savage man's care for his preservation the need to satisfy a multitude of passions that are the product of society" (*D2*, 160). But what accounts for Rousseau's conviction that the Hobbesian passions are not natural? Certainly not a sustained case drawn from empirical anthropology, a discovery of pre-social individuals, or the "uncertain testimonies of history" (*D2*, 150). Rousseau's case rests more fundamentally on the observation that the motivations relevant to Hobbes's account of human conflict are *cognitively complex*; the desire for long-term happiness, the insatiable desire for "power after power ceasing only in death," and a concern for personal honor are possible only for people who are also capable of having certain ideas. The desire for future happiness requires a representation of myself as the subject of future desires; selfishness and pride (inflamed *amour propre*) require an understanding of myself as one person among others and an estimate of my relative value. But cognitively complex passions require "enlightenment," and enlightenment is a result of social interdependence. Outside of social interdependence, abstracting from the self-conceptions it engenders, we experience neither pride, nor hatred, nor a desire for vengeance.

Pride, for example, requires that I compare my circumstances to those of others. And such comparisons depend on conceptions of oneself and one's relations to others that are beyond the competence of separate, asocial individuals. So "in the genuine state of nature, vanity [*amour propre*] does not exist" (*D2*, 226), because

it is not possible that a sentiment which *originates in comparisons he is not capable of making*, could spring up in his soul: for the same reason, this man could have neither hatred nor desire for vengeance, passions that can *arise from the opinion* of having received some offense; and since it is contempt or the intent to harm and not the harm itself, that constitutes the offense, men who are unable to appreciate one another or to compare themselves with one another, can do each other much violence when there is some advantage in it for them, without ever offending one another. (*D2*, 226–7, emphases added)

Similarly, because the moral aspect of love depends on ideas – of beauty and merit, for example – that lie beyond the natural individual's competence, such love cannot be part of our initial constitution. And absent the particular intensity of feeling that surrounds love, we would see "fewer and less cruel quarrels" among men. So it would be wrong to regard a state of war consequent on conflicts of the heart as a consequence of human nature's original constitution.

III. Innocence and Virtue

With the conception of human nature as background, we are now in a position to state more formally the idea of natural goodness. The statement is complicated and its complexity reflects three features of the view of human nature: the cognitive powers that are part of our natural endowment are initially present only as a potentiality; that potentiality is realized only under certain social conditions; and the realization of the potentiality produces important changes in the determinate content of the basic motivations. The consequence of these features is that the idea of natural goodness includes claims both about what we are like *antecedent to* the development of the potentialities (considered in abstraction from the "successive developments of the human mind" (*D2*, 168)), and what is possible for us *given the development* of our potentialities.

Thus consider three proposed statements of the idea of natural goodness:

Innocence/Vice Thesis: Antecedent to the development of the cognitive potentialities, human beings are innocent of vice, but the development of those potentialities must lead to vice.

Brutishness/Virtue Thesis: Antecedent to the realization of our cognitive powers, human beings are brutish, but with that development, they can become virtuous.

Innocence/Virtue Thesis: Human beings are antecedently innocent and, while our potentialities may be realized in a vicious way, it is possible for them to be expressed in a virtuous form, even after the development of human powers has initially taken a vice-ridden form.

We know that Rousseau rejects *Brutishness/Virtue*: the idea that civilization corrects natural tendencies to human brutality and cruelty. And although it is not clear that accepting it would cause trouble for his political philosophy, I will put it to the side, and concentrate on the *Innocence/Vice* and *Innocence/Virtue* interpretations.

Of these two, *Innocence/Virtue* seems clearly right. Without the possibility of virtue, the doctrine of natural goodness would reduce to the idea that our nature in its undeveloped form is not evil. Natural innocence, however, is compatible with the view that vice necessarily accompanies the development of our latent cognitive powers. And indeed this possibility is suggested in Rousseau's remark that "the state of reflection is a state against nature, and the man who meditates a depraved animal" (*D2*, 145). But, putting aside interpretive concerns that arise from Rousseau's penchant for dramatic statement, note how Rousseau begins the sentence from which this passage is taken: "If it [nature] destined us to be healthy then, *I almost dare assert . . .*" [emphasis added]. So Rousseau does not make the daring assertion.

Similarly, in the *Discourse on Inequality*: "It is reason that engenders vanity, and reflection that reinforces it" (*D2*, 162). This remark suggests that the distinction-drawing powers of reason and reflection make us evil by separating our own fate from the welfare of others. And in the *First Discourse* Rousseau claims that virtue has ebbed in proportion to enlightenment, and that "luxury, licentiousness, and slavery have in all periods been punishment for the arrogant attempts we have made to emerge from the happy ignorance in which eternal wisdom placed us" (*D1*, 11).

Both passages sharply underscore the historical correlation of enlightenment and vice. But that correlation is not in dispute between *Innocence/Vice* and *Innocence/Virtue*; so these passages provide no evidence for *Innocence/Vice*. The correlation of enlightenment and vice provides the point of departure and sets the problem for the doctrine of natural goodness; it does not exhaust the substance of that doctrine. On the contrary, the point is to show that the expression of originally latent human powers need not lead to vice, despite the evidence provided by the correlation.[37]

Moreover, *Innocence/Vice* is badly captured by the slogan "There is no original perversity in the human heart" (*E*, 92), or by claims about how our social arrangements are the source of evil and vice. After all, if *Innocence/Vice* is right – if the realization of human powers must lead to vice – then the tendency to evil does lie in latent human powers themselves; there is a fundamental conflict between culture and nature; and civilization must be accompanied by all its familiar discontents. Furthermore, the last parts of *Emile*, which sketch the conditions for goodness without innocence, would have at best an uncertain role in a work that is "nothing but a treatise on the original goodness of man" (*RJ*, 213), and at worst would refute one of the central elements of the doctrine it sets out to defend.

The theory of natural goodness is, then, captured by *Innocence/Virtue*, which affirms that *unsuitable* social arrangements, not society itself, explain the unhappy path taken by the development of our natural potentialities.[38] Put more constructively, *Innocence/Virtue* holds that essential human powers *can be realized* without taking the vice-ridden form that they have in fact taken. But such realization requires, inter alia, that we develop a sense of duty and motivational supports for it, thus enabling us to resist the many temptations to vice that are ingredient in social interdependence (see Section V for details).

Because it states that the development of virtue is merely possible, this account may seem too weak to capture the idea of natural *goodness*. After all, if virtue is possible, so, too, is vice; in the absence of some asymmetry between vice and virtue, however, it may be thought misleading to say that human beings are naturally good. Something stronger seems necessary: for example, that our natural endowment is aimed at the good, or tends to the good, or would achieve the good were it not for distorted circumstances.[39]

This point may have some force as an objection to Rousseau's terminology, though it must be stressed that he affirms our *natural goodness*, not our *natural virtue*. More fundamentally, I do not think that his principal statements of the conception of natural goodness do affirm more than that people are naturally innocent and that virtue is compatible with our human nature – nor, in view of the Hobbesian background, is such affirmation trivial. Furthermore, Rousseau's attention to the degenerative tendencies of even well-ordered societies (*SC*, 3.10–11, 4.1) indicates his strong reluctance to affirm a tighter connection between our nature and a virtuous life – say, a general tendency to virtue, manifest under normal conditions. If there is an asymmetry, it is only this: that under conditions of social interdependence, we can express our nature as free and thus achieve moral freedom only if we have a general will, and having such a will constitutes civic virtue. And that is to say that virtue, which is possible for us, is also required for realizing our nature.

IV. A Genealogy of Vice

"Sad and constant experience" makes it unnecessary to show that "men are wicked." But experience does not explain that wickedness; indeed, experience may misleadingly suggest that wickedness belongs to our nature. To correct this misleading suggestion, the *Discourse on Inequality* presents a "genealogy" of vice (*B*, 936; *DI*, 48). Officially about the origins of inequality, Rousseau's essay offers support to the idea of natural goodness by explaining the origins of vanity, greed, hate, jealousy, envy, covetousness, and misery, without postulating an original, non-derivative predisposition to vice.[40]

The explanation is historical in form, and proceeds through six stages: three stages of equality, three of inequality (the inequality of rich and poor, powerful and weak, master and slave). At each stage we find characteristic forms of association, modes of cognition, and types of motivation; the circumstances shape the development of the cognitive powers, which in turn shape motivation. Evolution between stages is driven by motivations generated at one stage that eventually alter the circumstances that produced those motivations, and, by altering the circumstances, eventually transform the dominant ideas and passions, too.

Rousseau's explanation provides (and is designed to provide) an alternative to Hobbes's theory of human nature and the Augustinian doctrine of original sin.[41] Rejecting Hobbes's view, Rousseau aims to explain how the vices arose, without attributing them to human nature itself; rejecting the idea of a choice of evil associated with original sin, Rousseau thinks that their emergence can be explained as consequent on social arrangements that tend to channel motivations in certain directions: "The scorn which J. J. had displayed for that entire pretended social order, which in fact hides the most cruel disorders, fell much more on the constitution of the different estates than the subjects filling them and who, by this very constitution, must of necessity be what they are" (*RJ*, 176–7).

The doctrine of original sin – whether it has the choice of evil occurring in each generation, or inherited across generations – requires some assumption of an original predisposition to evil, even if choice is also needed to express this predisposition. Rousseau thinks he can do without that assumption, and without thinking that God is unjust for making us so predisposed (*B*, 937–8). Where Archbishop Beaumont believes that the source of evil is the corruption of human nature, Rousseau wants to discover the cause of this corruption (*B*, 940). To explain the patterns of motivation and conduct described by Augustine and Hobbes, "it is not necessary to suppose that man is evil by his nature," because the conflict between "our social order" and our nature "explains by itself all the vices of men and all the evils of society" (*B*, 967).

Structural Interpretation of Vice

Rousseau is concerned principally to account for vices that involve indifference or hostility to the welfare of others, an interest in their well-being only insofar as advancing it also advances one's own: "No one wants the public good unless it accords with his own" (*B*, 937; *SC*, 4.1.6). He traces the foundations of such vice to a concern for one's standing relative to others. Vice does not arise simply from a desire to do well, or from an original insatiability of human appetite, but from the thought that doing well requires (perhaps consists in) doing better, a thought rooted in the sense that affirming my worth requires acknowledging me as a better, in short, in the inflamed form of *amour propre*: "The gentle and affectionate passions are born of self-love, . . . the hateful and irascible passions are born of *amour propre*" (*E*, 214; *RJ*, 112). Once pride is in place, unhappiness follows, too. For with the desire to have more than others comes an insatiable desire to accumulate powers – the "perpetual and restless desire of power after power, that ceaseth only in death."[42] Once that desire is in place, we are bound to be dissatisfied, because our finite powers can never be sufficient to meet its demands (*D2*, 209). But with Rousseau, this insatiability is not original, nor – as Hobbes suggests – a response to such general features of human circumstance as uncertainty and a desire to protect one's current means.[43] It derives instead from the desire for relative advantage.

Premising, then, that the vices are modifications of *amour propre*, Rousseau's genealogy of vice needs principally to explain this heated concern for relative advantage. More precisely, his central question, as I indicated earlier, is: *How is the generic concern to be treated with respect particularized as a demand and desire to be treated as a better?*

The roots of the demand and desire lie in social inequality. That much seems clear. What are less clear are the particular aspects of inequality that create troubles and the precise mechanism through which they work their psychological effects. Rousseau sometimes emphasizes that inequality produces a conflict of interests, and that such conflict makes it impossible to resist putting one's own advantage first (*D2*, 208). But this account is not satisfying. It is not obvious why inequality produces a conflict of interest rather than a willingness to explore mutual gains, albeit from unequal starting positions. To be sure, if inequality leads people to "value the things they enjoy only to the extent that others are deprived of them," or "to find our advantage in what harms our kind" (*D2*, 208), then it is easy to see how inequality turns interactions into zero-sum conflicts. But these assertions beg the question. We are trying to understand why inequality leads to a concern with relative position –

to a link between enjoyment and deprivation, advantage and harm – and this explanation simply assumes the link.

Moreover, Rousseau does not condemn all inequality. His *Letter to D'Alembert* suggests that a certain measure of material inequality "can have its advantages" (*LD*, 115). And even when he emphasizes the importance of limiting inequalities of wealth and power among citizens – ensuring that no one must "sell himself" to secure basic necessities – he nevertheless permits some socioeconomic inequalities (*SC*, 1.9.8n., 2.11; *PE*, 221; *LM*, 890; *P*, 963, 1002). Understanding the connection between inequality and inflamed self-love requires, then, an account of why certain types of inequality, or inequalities under certain conditions, have troubling psychological effects.

The explanation is that certain forms of inequality lead us to identify the affirmation by others of our worth with our securing advantage over them, for this good reason: that under the relevant conditions gaining advantage is the only stable, socially recognized way to secure our natural aspiration to such affirmation. Consider two idealized social worlds. In the first, there is some socioeconomic inequality, but people have equal standing as citizens. By ensuring equal rights, the political institutions in effect announce the equal worth of citizens. And given this background equality, the social–economic inequality need not undercut the role of political institutions in affirming our equality, upholding our worth as equals, and so establishing the conditions of free association.[44] In the second social world, there is socioeconomic inequality, but no institutionally acknowledged equality of worth running parallel to the inequalities. Under such circumstances, the natural strategy for winning recognition from others – even for those who might be prepared to accept the egalitarian conception of worth – is to win advantage.

I will call the interpretation of vice I have just sketched "the structural interpretation," and will elaborate on it by sketching Rousseau's quasi-historical genealogy.[45]

Troubles in Paradise

The story begins with human beings in conditions of independence. Because the realization of latent cognitive powers traces to social cooperation, human beings in the initial state lack the ability to conceptualize, and so are moved only by desires that arise immediately from natural needs (for hunger, sex, sleep). Such individuals lack the conceptual resources for desiring to live in a better world, wishing to be treated as equals, acting strategically, or having a conception of honor and a passionate attachment to protecting it. Given these motivational limits, themselves rooted in the limited realization of cognitive powers, we have sufficient bodily powers to satisfy our desires – no need to compensate for a shortfall of natural powers by subordinating the powers of others – and live in a state of innocence.

This equilibrium is disrupted by "difficulties" in satisfying the natural desires, and those difficulties lead to the formation of temporary associations to facilitate such satisfaction. Temporary cooperation for specific purposes – catching deer, for example – triggers the realization of latent cognitive powers, in particular the power to represent future states of myself and of the world. It is not clear how temporary associations could form antecedent to this triggering, or why the change of circumstances prompts the expression of precisely the latent powers that are functional for the circumstances. But I do not think that these problems raise fundamental troubles, and so do not propose to dwell on them here. In any case, the new "enlightenment," itself elicited by altered conditions, stimulates a desire for continued cooperation, if only as a way to satisfy the basic desires.

Eventually, then, we arrive at more settled forms of association – families and associations of families. More settled conditions prompt ideas about one's relations to others and thoughts about relative social positions, and those thoughts generate a shift from a natural concern for well-being to a concern about one's situation relative to others – in particular, a concern to have *advantage* over others (*D2*, 175). But although association engenders the desire for esteem – giving rise to vanity, contempt, shame, and envy – that desire and the pursuit of it are limited by the absence of specialization, a division of labor, and private property. Absent a form of social interdependence that enables individuals to gain and to maintain great advantages over others, individuals lack a conception of such advantages. Their sense of their own worth, and of the conditions necessary for affirming it, therefore do not depend on such advantages; nor do they believe that a failure to provide relative advantages would be a denial of their worth, or that they merit such advantages, deserve them, or in any other way could claim them as a matter of right. Stating the point at the level of the emotions, people are not insulted, injured, or made resentful if they are not relatively advantaged.

Here we have the final stage of equality, the happiest and most durable period because of its balance between our desires and our powers. Desires remain limited because people do not desire more than others and so are not driven to endlessly desire more for themselves: they are not egoists, because egoists are people who "pay more attention to others than to themselves" (*RJ*, 148). Because people under these conditions are not plagued by expansive desires that they cannot satisfy, they are relatively happy, and are not impelled to transform the conditions of their association.

Against this background of limited social cooperation and nascent *amour propre*, the advent of metallurgy and agriculture prompt specialization and private property. This change of circumstance expands the range of opportunities for pursuing the desire for advantage that is already in place. Moreover, the expanded opportunities increase the temptation to pursue the desire for advantage by increasing the benefits that can be expected from such pursuit. In particular, the settlement of individual property gives rise to inequality, in part because of the inequalities of "talents" (*D2*, 179) that people put to work on their property.

So long as property remained common, talents could have only a limited effect on inequality because each person would share in the fruits of the benefits – for example, improvements in the land – created by the talented. But private ownership eliminates this constraint on the social effects of differences of talent: "That is how natural inequality insensibly unfolds together with the inequality of associations, and how the differences among men, developed by their different circumstances, become more perceptible, more permanent in their effects, and begin to exercise a corresponding influence on the fate of individuals" (*D2*, 180).

It is this system of private property and specialization, and the growing inequality resulting from it, that stimulates inflated *amour propre* and vice. The reason – here we come to the structural interpretation – is that circumstances lead people to identify achieving their own aims with achieving relative advantage, and that puts the interests of individuals at odds; the identification turns conflict zero-sum: "if one sees a handful of powerful and rich men at the pinnacle of greatness and fortune while the mass crawls in obscurity and misery, it is because *the former value the things they enjoy only to the extent that others are deprived of them*, and they would cease to be happy if, without any change in their own state, the people ceased to be miserable" (*D2*, 195, emphasis added). But why is the natural concern with self-worth expressed as inflamed self-love? Because inequalities emerge under conditions in which recognition can only be ensured by establishing advantage – because, for example, there is no institutional form analogous to equal citizenship that enables individuals to be treated as equals irrespective of their differences. Socially speaking, there are only the differences: perceptible, permanent in their effects, and exercising a profound influence on the fate of individuals. Furthermore, differences among people (say, differences in their talents) play such a fundamental role in determining their fate that they regard those differences of fate as reflecting intrinsic differences of worth. And this of course reinforces the identification of the natural desire for an affirmation of worth with the demand that others treat one as a better.

At the same time, enlightenment enables the formation of more expansive desires: "imagination . . . extends for us the measure of the possible, whether for good or bad, and . . . consequently excites and nourishes the desires by the hope of satisfying them" (*E*, 81). This conjunction of vanity and enlightenment generates the more familiar vices: given a desire for relative advantage, there are benefits to appearing different from the way one really is; hypocrisy, deceit, and other forms of dissimulation are now rational (*D2*, 180–1). Relative advantage being essentially a scarce resource, antagonisms intensify, are moralized, and tend to break out into open conflict. "Nascent society gave way to the most horrible state of war" (*D2*, 182) – a Hobbesian war of all against all, now understood as the effect of circumstances of inequality rather than an immediate expression of our nature.

Nature, then, endows us with desires that correspond to our needs, and powers sufficient to satisfy those desires: it provides a basis for an innocent freedom without unhappiness or vice (*E*, 80). Inequality encourages a concern for relative advantage and a sense of deep insult – of being wronged – if it is not achieved. Working together with the enlightenment engendered by social association, this concern expands our desires without triggering a commensurate expansion of our capacity to satisfy them. So we are finally beset by desires that we can pursue only through social association, in particular through subordinating the powers of others to our own, although we also recognize that participation in such association implicates us in a system of mutual abuse, manipulation, hypocrisy, and deceit.

If this explanation is right, then inflamed self-love and the vices flowing from it create no troubles for the doctrine of natural goodness. The social explanation implies that inflamed content is not intrinsic to the abstract desire for the social affirmation of worth. The very same feature of our nature that is expressed in the form of vice could, as a matter of its intrinsic character, be expressed in other ways. Under alternative conditions, treatment as an equal could suffice for the affirmation of worth. And if it did, then the worth of each could in principle be affirmed, whereas the prideful form of self-worth makes such mutual affirmation impossible. How might the affections take this more attractive path?

V. Complementary Motivations

According to the doctrine of natural goodness, we are naturally innocent and capable of virtue. I have discussed the idea of natural innocence and the etiology of vice, and want now to sketch the ways in which the conception of human nature underwrites the possibility of virtue and so provides the basis for addressing the problem of motivational possibility. Premising that compassion and concerns about self-worth are intrinsic to our nature, and that their determinate expression depends on social–institutional setting, how might these properties be expressed in a virtuous form?

Why Duty Is Not Enough

Answering this question requires some initial clarification of the "virtuous form" of expression. To provide that clarification I will start with some schematic observations about Rousseau's account of the sense of duty:

1. Social cooperation inevitably encourages the development of various human attachments and affections – for example, loves for particular individuals. Rejecting the Stoic ideal of extirpating the passions, Rousseau thinks that such attachments are unavoidable (see note 41).
2. Attachments and affections are not reliable guides to correct conduct: "A man is not guilty for loving another's wife if he keep this unhappy passion enslaved to the law of duty. He is guilty for loving his own wife to the point of sacrificing everything to that love" (*E*, 445).
3. In a world of passions and attachments, the only reliable guide to right conduct is a sense of duty (the "law of duty"). In this world, "Goodness is broken and perishes under the impact of the human passions. . . . Who, then, is the virtuous man? It is he who knows how to conquer his affections; for then he follows his reason and his conscience; he does his duty" (*E*, 444–5).[46]
4. The capacity for a sense of duty, awakened by social cooperation,[47] is part of our native endowment. Speaking through the Savoyard Vicar, Rousseau explains: "There is in the depth of our souls . . . an innate principle of justice and virtue according to which, in spite of our own maxims, we judge our actions and those of others good or bad" (*E*, 289; also *E*, 66, 267, 290). And "Rousseau" in *Rousseau*,

Judge of Jean-Jacques puts the point still more strongly: "The voice of conscience can no more be stifled in the human heart than that of reason can be stifled in the understanding; and moral insensitivity is as unnatural as madness" (*RJ*, 242).

5. Though a sense of right is part of our natural endowment, the content of that sense is not similarly fixed by nature. In particular, its content in the society of the general will is given by laws issuing from the shared sense of the common good that defines the general will.

6. We cannot have much confidence in the motivational strength of the sense of duty. In political society, citizens face constant temptations to subordinate their concern for the common good to other interests; the larger the temptation, the more likely the subordination.[48] Indeed, the "great lesson of morality" is that we should avoid "situations that put our duties in opposition with our interests, and show us our good in the evil of others: certain that in such situations, however sincere our love of virtue, sooner or later it will imperceptibly give way and we shall become unjust and wicked in fact, however upright in our intentions" (*C*, 56).

Taking these points together, then, the problem is to find *motivational complements* to the sense of duty – motives that are distinct from the sense of duty, but that, as a general matter, support our efforts to comply with our duties, as those duties are specified by the general will, rather than strengthening our disposition to subordinate the general will to our particular interests. My earlier discussion of the *content problem* indicates the kinds of motivational complements that are needed: because the general will is oriented to the common good, the problem is to find possible sources of motivation for treating others as equals – to show that and how the demands of the general will can engage our affections. The earlier discussion of the theory of human nature suggests two such sources of engagement, and I will add a third.

Self-Worth, Reciprocity, Generalized Compassion

The desire for relative advantage associated with an inflamed sense of self-worth is plainly the enemy of the general will; it is an especially important enemy because the sense of self-worth is psychologically fundamental and resistant to change: a sense of one's greater worth "is the error most to be feared, because it is the most difficult to destroy" (*E*, 245). So the requirements for achieving a sense of self-worth must not by and large conflict with the demands of duty as specified by the general will. One way to build psychological support for the sense of duty, then, is to discourage the inflamed form of self-love and foster instead an understanding of others as equals – of "the identity of our natures with theirs" (*E*, 221) – and a correspondingly egalitarian conception of self-worth as requiring treatment as an equal.[49]

Although the sense of self-worth is not intrinsically egalitarian, its intrinsic features can be developed along these lines. Its content depends on our beliefs about our worth, which depend in turn on circumstances. When social arrangements are such that our "true relations" as equals are manifest in social experience, and differences are neither so perceptible, nor permanent, nor influential – say, when individuals have the public status of equal citizen in the society of the general will – individuals can reasonably be expected to acquire an understanding of one another as equals. And if we do regard each other as equals, then those same arrangements will – for example, by establishing citizenship rights, and taking the interests of each into account – confirm our sense of our own worth.[50] The sense of duty has motivational support from the sense of self-worth, then, when the latter is informed by an understanding of equality.

To strengthen this point about compatibility, let's add Rousseau's idea that reciprocity is important to the formation of our motivations: "those from whom one expects good or ill by their inner disposition, by their will – those we see acting freely for us or against us – inspire in us sentiments similar to those they manifest toward us" (*E*, 213). In this way – through reciprocation – "the gentle and affectionate passions are born of self-love" (*E*, 214). Assume, then, a society with a general will, which encourages the more egalitarian conception of self-worth. If others comply with the requirements of the general will, they uphold my sense of self-worth, generating a disposition to reply in kind and uphold their sense of their own worth. And that disposition binds us by affection to the common good, the source of obligations in the society of the general will.

If reciprocity leads to attachments to others as *agents* who act for our well-being, compassion leads us to concern for others as *sufferers*, "fellow-passengers to the grave": "we are attached to our fellows less by the sentiment of their pleasures than by the sentiment of their pains, for we see far better in the latter the identity of our natures with theirs and the guarantees of their attachment to us. If our common needs unite us by interest, our common miseries unite us by affection" (*E*, 221–3). Despite its importance, compassion – as all passions – is not an entirely dependable guide to conduct. To ensure that it conforms to duty, it must be "generalized and extended to the whole of mankind. Then one yields to it only insofar as it accords with justice" (*E*, 253). When it does so accord,

its presence strengthens the motivations to comply with the requirements of justice. In a striking passage in *The Metaphysics of Morals*, Kant
perfectly captures Rousseau's thought about the potential for compassion to serve as a motivational complement to the sense of duty: "compassion [*mitgefühl*] . . . is one of the impulses that nature has implanted
in us to do what the representation of duty alone would not
accomplish."[51]

But the extension and generalization of compassion – a sense of our
common miseries – is not intrinsic to compassion, or at all automatic. It,
too, requires a sense of others as equals, and that depends, again, on
circumstances:

Why are kings without pity for their subjects? Because they never count on being
mere men. Why are the rich so hard toward the poor? It is because they have no
fear of becoming poor. Why does the nobility have so great a contempt for the
people? It is because a noble will never be a commoner. . . . Do not, therefore,
accustom your pupil to regard the sufferings of the unfortunate and the labors of
the poor from the height of his glory; and do not hope to teach him to pity them
if he considers them alien to him. Make him understand well that the fate of these
unhappy men can be his, that all their ills are there in the ground beneath his feet,
that countless unforeseen and inevitable events can plunge him into them from
one moment to the next. Teach him to count on neither birth, nor health, nor
riches. Show him all the vicissitudes of fortune. (*E*, 224)

Here we have the kernel of a program of individual instruction aimed at
giving emotional immediacy to the thought "there but for the grace of
God go I" – at encouraging a self-understanding in which equality plays
a fundamental role, and extending compassion to all humankind.

More broadly, the path of moral development in Book 4 of *Emile* (esp.
E, 221–55) directs our "nascent passions" to goodness and humanity in
three stages: we first direct our compassion on those who suffer, focusing
on those forms of suffering to which we are susceptible ourselves; next,
we consider people in society, studying how they – particularly the more
powerful – mask their suffering and weakness; finally, we confront our
own weakness, and see ourselves as objects of compassion, not merely its
subjects. At each stage, the confirmation of the sense of equality gener-
alizes and reinforces compassion, ensuring that it takes the common
good as its object. Here, an "ordered development of the primitive
affections" (*E*, 235) attaches our affections to the source of duty.

The political problem is to transform this program of individual
instruction into proposals about institutional design. Social–political
circumstances must foster the experience of others as equals, thus
discouraging inflamed *amour propre* and the forms of vice and conflict
that follow on it, generating – through reciprocity and extended compas-

sion – motivational complements to the general will, and so establishing a stable political order that answers to the concerns of self-love and in which citizens give the law to themselves.

Rousseau's answer is to establish the position of equal citizen in an association guided by a conception of the common good. Given public conditions of equality – both in the rights associated with the status of equal citizen and in the content of the general will – I come to see myself as an equal; others, therefore, affirm my worth when they treat me as an equal. Because of that affirmation, the society of the general will discourages the inflamed form of self-love. But when there is a supreme general will, each person is in fact treated by others as an equal. So the existence of a general will ordering the terms of social association not only assigns equal weight in settling the laws to each citizen's security and liberty interests. It also provides a way to affirm the equal worth of each even in the face of the inevitable differences in the social and economic circumstances of different citizens.

Here, too, we find Rousseau's strongest case for a "participatory" politics that brings citizens together under manifestly equal conditions: "the person of the humblest citizen is as sacred and inviolable as that of the first magistrate; because where the represented person is, there is no longer any representative" (*SC*, 3.14.1). Public deliberation proceeding among equals visibly guided by reasons of the common good provides institutional expression for the egalitarian form of self-regard and helps to extend compassion, thus discouraging inflated forms of *amour propre*. To be sure, a background of public deliberation among citizens is most likely to support the formation of a general will if citizens can assume that their decisions – and not those of wealthy and powerful factions – settle the terms of their political order. The institutional picture must, then, include various restrictions on inequality. But I have said enough to make the essential story about compassion clear: appropriate institutional design encourages "an ordered development of the primitive affections," leading to a generalization of compassion; compassion, suitably generalized, prompts us to act for the common good, thus complementing – though never substituting for – the motivations that arise from the sense of duty itself.

VI. Conclusions

This completes my sketch of the content of the conception of human nature and natural goodness. Thus far, however, I have not mentioned any reason for endorsing these views.[52] Each person may be, as Rousseau says, "naturally moved to believe what he wishes" (*RJ*, 239). But does an attraction to the doctrine of natural goodness merely reflect this natural disposition to wishful thinking? To show that it does not, we need responses to two concerns: that there may be decisive evidence against the doctrine (for example, evidence provided by our experience of human vice); and that even if we can explain away that evidence, there may simply be no positive reason for affirming it. To conclude, I consider these objections in turn.

Recall Rousseau's injunction that we "begin by setting aside all the facts, for they do not affect the question" (*D2*, 139). Aiming to clarify "the question," Rousseau says that "inquiries that may be pursued regarding this subject [the foundations of society] ought not to be taken for historical truths, but only for hypothetical and conditional reasonings" (*D2*, 139). And he concludes the *Second Discourse* by restating that he has provided "an account of the origin and progress of inequality, the establishment and abuse of political societies, insofar as these things can be deduced from the nature of man by the light of reason alone" (*D2*, 199). Although his argument is historical in form, then, it is plainly not intended as genuine history. This observation, however, simply shifts the question: setting aside the facts may be acceptable in a hypothetical history, but what is the point of hypothetical history?

The answer lies in the problem of motivational possibility. Rousseau's ideal of free association is possible for human beings only if the vices are not part of human nature. But "sad and constant experience" suggests that they are. So that evidence must be explained away: Rousseau must give us an account of our nature and explain why the facts of vice do not undermine it. He does so by using his conception of our nature – which supports the society of the general will – to explain the evolution of vice, to indicate "for each one [vice], how and whence it entered" the human soul (*E*, 92). I emphasize that he must show that the basic properties of our nature *could*, working in combination, generate the phenomena. Even if the details are wrong, we can see that the facts of experience themselves do not drive us to a pessimistic outlook on human possibilities. Of course, that leaves the possibility that the vices *are*, after all, intrinsic to our nature: Rousseau has, I believe, no compelling argument against this possibility. But he does have a plausible case that the principal reason for believing that they are part of our nature – the reason provided by dismal experience – is not so compelling as we might have thought.

The genealogy of vice, then, provides part of the support for the theory of human nature that underwrites the doctrine of natural goodness. Our observations about the ubiquity of vice do not compel rejection of the idea that people are naturally good: it is "not necessary to suppose man evil by nature" (*B*, 967). And so nothing forces us to reject the political ideal as humanly unrealizable because motivationally impossible.

But the genealogy only supports the claim that endorsement of the theory of natural goodness is not incompatible with our observations about human motivations and conduct. It does not itself provide a positive reason for endorsing it. Are there such reasons?

The answer lies in the Profession of Faith that Rousseau attributes in *Emile* to the Vicar of Savoy (*E*, 266–94).[53] After describing the inability of traditional metaphysical theorizing to resolve fundamental questions about, for example, the nature of the self, the Vicar offers an alternative to a Cartesian "clear and distinct ideas" test for knowledge: he will "accept as evident all knowledge [*connoissances*] to which in the sincerity of my heart I cannot refuse my consent" (*E*, 270). A heart, however sincere, may strike us as an unpromising place to look for knowledge. But Rousseau attaches a moral force to the phrase "sincerity of my heart." He explains, for example, that a belief in the immortality of the soul passes his test because if the soul were mortal, then the wicked would triumph – and "that alone" suffices to establish the case for immortality (*E*, 283). Similarly, the Vicar links his faith that human beings are free to the experience of remorse and self-reproach for succumbing to temptations to vice (*E*, 280–1).

The Vicar's line of thought, then, is perhaps that we have reason to accept beliefs required by our moral convictions, on the assumption – suggested by the Vicar's own criticisms of metaphysics – that those beliefs are not inconsistent with our (possible) theoretical knowledge. And this provides a rationale for endorsing the theory of natural goodness. The ideal of free social cooperation is compatible with our nature only if we are naturally good. Experience of human motivations suggests that we are not. The genealogy of vice provides a way to explain that sad experience while endorsing the doctrine of natural goodness. Moreover, we must endorse the doctrine of natural goodness – or something like it – if we are to hold out the prospect of realizing the society of the general will: if, in particular, we are to address the problem of motivational possibility. Endorsement of the doctrine of natural goodness – Rousseau's defense of human nature – is recommended, then, on moral–practical grounds. And that defense is not contradicted by the facts and so is acceptable to theoretical reason. We may, therefore, use it to address the problem of motivational possibility. And that address permits us to hope, with reason, for a society that answers to the demands of self-love and freedom. Of course, "constant and sad experience" must limit our optimism. But hope is not optimism. And experience can only overturn moral hopes whose achievement is, in Kant's words, "demonstrably impossible."[54]

NOTES

I am grateful to Andrews Reath, Uday Mehta, Amélie Rorty, Victor Gourevitch, Annabelle Lever, and Martha Nussbaum for instructive comments on earlier drafts. My reading of Rousseau is guided by a desire to understand Kant's enthusiasm for Rousseau. And my understanding of Kant is substantially shaped by a spring 1974 seminar on moral philosophy with John Rawls. In that seminar Rawls distinguished Manichean and Augustinian strands in Kant's moral psychology; he emphasized the importance of the former in Kant's *Groundwork* and *Critique of Practical Reason*, and the latter in his *Religion Within the Limits of Reason Alone*. The Manichean, dualist strand presents human conduct as the product of a struggle between reason and passion, and makes no place for emotions in a virtuous person's psychology. The Augustinian strand attaches central importance to the capacity to choose (Kant's *Willkür*), and provides a place for human emotions – especially for an appropriately generalized sympathy – in supporting the demands of morality. Rousseau, as I interpret him, anticipates much of what Rawls called the "Augustinian" strand.

References to Rousseau's work are included parenthetically in the text, using the following abbreviations and editions:

B: *Lettre à Christophe de Beaumont*, in J.-J. Rousseau, *Oeuvres complètes*, Vol. 4, ed. Bernard Gagnebin et Marcel Raymond (Paris: Pléiade, 1969).

C: *Les Confessions*, in J.-J. Rousseau, *Oeuvres complètes*, Vol. 1, ed. Bernard Gagnebin et Marcel Raymond (Paris: Pléiade, 1959).

D1:   *Discourse on the Sciences and the Arts (First Discourse) and Polemics*, ed. Roger D. Masters and Christopher Kelly, trans. Roger D. Masters, Judith Bush, and Christopher Kelley (Hanover: University Press of New England, 1992).

D2:   *Second Discourse* in *The First and Second Discourses, Together with the Replies to Critics, and Essay on the Origin of Languages*, trans. Victor Gourevitch (New York: Harper and Row, 1986).

E: *Emile*, trans. Allan Bloom (New York: Basic Books, 1979).

LD: *Politics and the Arts, Letter to M. D'Alembert on the Theatre*, trans. Allan Bloom (Ithaca: Cornell University Press, 1960).

LM: *Lettres Écrites de la Montagne*, in J.-J. Rousseau, *Oeuvres complètes*, Vol. 3, ed. Bernard Gagnebin et Marcel Raymond (Paris: Pléiade, 1964).

M: *Lettres à Malesherbes*, in J.-J. Rousseau, *Oeuvres complètes*, Vol. 1, ed. Bernard Gagnebin et Marcel Raymond (Paris: Pléiade, 1959).

OL: *Essay on the Origin of Languages*, in *On the Origin of Language, Two Essays by Jean-Jacques Rousseau and Johann Gottfried Herder*, trans. John H. Moran and Alexander Gode (New York: Ungar, 1966).

P: *Considérations sur le Gouvernement de Pologne et sur la Réformation Projetée*, in J.-J. Rousseau, *Oeuvres complètes*, Vol. 3.

PE: *Discourse on Political Economy*, in *On the Social Contract, with Geneva Manuscript and Political Economy*, ed. Roger D. Masters, trans. Judith R. Masters (New York: St. Martins, 1978).

RJ: *Rousseau, Judge of Jean-Jacques: Dialogues*, ed. Roger D. Masters and Christopher Kelley, trans. Judith R. Bush, Roger D. Masters, and Christopher Kelley (Hanover: University Press of New England, 1992).

SC: *Social Contract*, in *On the Social Contract, with Geneva Manuscript and Political Economy*, ed. Roger D. Masters, trans. Judith R. Masters (New York: St. Martin's, 1978). References are given by book, chapter, and paragraph number.

1. *D2*, 208.
2. Immanuel Kant, *On the Old Saw: That May Be Right In Theory but It Won't Work In Practice*, trans. E. B. Ashton (Philadelphia: University of Pennsylvania Press, 1974), pp. 77–8.
3. *D2*, 139.
4. In his letter to Archbishop Beaumont (1762), Rousseau says that the idea of natural goodness is the "fundamental principle of all morals," and the basis of "all my writings" (*B*, 935; *RJ*, 213).
5. For critcism of this claim and its role in some strands of leftist thought, see Noam Chomsky, *Reflections on Language* (New York: Pantheon, 1975), pp. 128–34.
6. See Ernst Cassirer, *Kant's Life and Thought*, trans. James Haden (New Haven and London: Yale University Press, 1981), p. 89.
7. Starobinski raises an important variant of this question: "How does one reconcile the assertion that 'man is naturally good' with the assertion that 'everything degenerates at the hands of man?'" See Jean Starobinski, *Jean-Jacques Rousseau: Transparency and Obstruction*, trans. Arthur Goldhammer (Chicago: University of Chicago Press, 1988), p. 20.
8. Did Rousseau have a utopian's indifference to charges about the lack of realism? In *Rousseau: Judge of Jean-Jacques*, he has Rousseau say of Jean-Jacques: "Deluded by the ridiculous hope of *making reason and truth triumph at last over prejudice and lies*, and of making men wise by showing them their true interest, his heart – *excited by the idea of the future happiness of the human race and by the honor of contributing to it* – dictated to him a language worthy of such a great undertaking." *RJ*, 131, emphases added.
9. *Cartesian Linguistics* (New York: Harper and Row, 1966), pp. 59–72.
10. According to *Emile*, "one is more free under the social pact than in the state of nature" (*E*, 461).
11. Among the other central ideas: that we are naturally endowed with conscience and compassion, and that our cognitive powers are originally present as potentialities whose use is triggered by circumstances. For discussion, see Section II below.
12. Thomas Hobbes, *Leviathan*, ed. Edwin Curley (Indianapolis: Hackett, 1994), p. 495.
13. Hobbes, *Leviathan*, p. 109.
14. Hobbes, *Leviathan*, p. 497.

15. "In the relations between man and man, the worst that can happen to one is to find himself at the other's discretion." *D2*, 186.
16. A third possibility problem that I do not discuss in this essay arises from doubts about "accessibility": is there any route leading from current circumstances to the society of the general will? Corresponding to the three problems of possibility, we can distinguish three ways that political thought might be utopian: it might rest on values that simply cannot be jointly realized under any conditions; it might endorse values whose realization is incompatible with human nature; and it might embrace an ideal that cannot be realized by a social trajectory that begins from current conditions (barring some catastrophe that "wipes the slate clean"). Judith Shklar argues that Rousseau was, at least in this third sense, a utopian theorist: he aimed "to show that the ills of actuality were as irreparable as they were unnecessary." See *Men and Citizens: A Study of Rousseau's Social Theory* (Cambridge University Press, 1985), p. 7. Rousseau certainly focused less on the problem of accessibility than on the other problems. But his proposed constitution for Poland suggests serious – which is not to say successful – engagement with it. See for example *P*, 1020–9; see also the discussion of the right of representation and the importance of periodic meetings of the Council in *LM*, 850–68.
17. This paragraph draws on my "Reflections on Rousseau: Autonomy and Democracy," *Philosophy and Public Affairs*, 15(3) (Summer 1986): 276–9.
18. To say that the conception of the common good is shared is not to say that citizens agree that existing laws are the best ways to advance that conception. See *SC*, 4.2 on why citizens who comply with laws they disagree with are nevertheless obeying themselves.
19. *Leviathan*, p. 495.
20. See generally *Leviathan*, chaps. 10, 11, 13, 17. On the passions as sources of irrational conduct, see Hobbes's distinction between "multiplying glasses" and "prospective glasses," *Leviathan*, p. 118; also, *De Homine*, chap. 12, sec. 1, in *Man and Citizen: Thomas Hobbes's "De Homine" and "De Cive,"* ed. Bernard Gert (New York: Anchor Books, 1972).
21. *Leviathan*, chap. 17.
22. Thus Hobbes's emphasis on fear of punishment, which serves to "tame pride" – to "bridle men's ambition, avarice, anger, and other passions" (*Leviathan*, p. 196) – and not principally to concentrate the mind or elicit an "extraordinary use of reason" (p. 195), or in some other way psychically transform natural individuals into self-disciplined subjects who are able to control their "perpetually incumbent and pressing" passions (p. 195).
23. See Hobbes's derivation of the eighth to twelfth laws of nature in *Leviathan*, pp. 96–7. The ninth law, proscribing prideful conduct, is especially important.
24. Kant's *Religion within the Limits of Reason Alone* (trans. Theodore M. Green and Hoyt H. Hudson [New York: Harper and Row, 1960]; hereafter cited as *Religion*) offers an account of evil with broadly Rousseauean contours, though Kant differs from Rousseau in his views about the possibility of *explaining* moral evil. According to Kant, we are naturally endowed with a "predisposition to humanity" (*Religion*, pp. 21–2), a form of self-love that leads us to "mak[e] comparisons with others" and from which "springs the inclination *to acquire worth in the opinion of others*" (p. 22). "Originally a desire merely for equality" (p. 22), this inclination is corrupted by social cooperation (pp. 85–6), which changes it from a concern to be on an equal

footing to "an unjustified craving to win it [superiority] for oneself over others" (p. 22). And this desire for advantage leads in turn to the "vices of culture" – for example, envy, greed, spitefulness, and the lust for power. So far Kant has simply borrowed from Rousseau. But Rousseau sometimes appears to think that an explanation of this corruption – of the emergence of what I will be calling the inflamed form of *amour propre* – also suffices to explain vice, perhaps because he supposes that conscience is simply motivationally "weaker than" [*plus faible que*] the inflamed passions (*B*, 937); given a corrupt social order, then, people in it "must of necessity be what they are" (*RJ*, 176–77). To be sure, Rousseau thinks it possible to take special measures both to diminish the unjustified craving to win superiority and strengthen the sense of duty associated with conscience, enabling a person better to resist the passions. *Emile* and *Social Contract* describe two ways to encourage such strength, and both underscore (with Kant) that a clear sense of duty is the only way to avoid vice, once human powers are developed. But despite Rousseau's emphasis elsewhere on the importance of choice, his distinction between choice and natural mechanisms, and his insistence on our capacity to choose to resist inclinations (*D2*, 149; *E*, 280–2, 293), his explanation of vice is more naturalistic than Kant's, and does not develop the claim that choice underlies human corruption. Here Kant disagrees. To be sure, he accepts that the weakness or "frailty of human nature" (*Religion*, p. 24) is the first phase of vice, that the corruption of self-love makes it more difficult to throw off "the sovereignty of evil," and that "as far as we can see" the only path to avoiding such corruption and so to establishing the "sovereignty of the good principle" is to construct an "ethical commonwealth" (pp. 85–6). Still, Kant emphasizes that a person with corrupted predispositions can resist their demands: we can only regard a greedy man, for example, as responsible for his conduct if we believe that such resistance is possible. In short, Kant distinguishes sharply between the corruption of our natural predispositions and the emergence of moral evil; the corruption of self-love has social causes, but does not suffice to explain evil; instead, moral evil requires a choice (ultimately mysterious) to subordinate moral considerations to self-love.

25. I take this distinction from Rousseau's account of "perfectibility" (*D2*, 149).
26. On love of others, and the role of valuations in such love, see *D2*, 164.
27. The remarks that follow draw on Kant's remarks on the predisposition to humanity in *Religion*, pp. 22, 85–6; John Rawls's discussion of self-respect and envy in *A Theory of Justice* (Cambridge: Harvard University Press, 1971), secs. 67, 81; and especially N. J. Dent's *Rousseau* (Oxford: Blackwell, 1988), chaps. 2, 4. Dent's book is easily the best available discussion of Rousseau's psychological views, and I have drawn heavily on his compelling treatment of the different forms of *amour propre*.
28. The plausibility of this assumption is a matter of longstanding controversy in historical sociology. To what extent do people in socially subordinate positions internalize the regnant conceptions of their "inferior" nature (or people in socially dominant positions embrace the regnant view of their "superior" nature)? For skeptical views about such internalization, see, for example, Orlando Patterson, *Slavery and Social Death* (Cambridge: Harvard University Press, 1982); James Scott, *Domination and the Arts of Resistance: Hidden Transcripts* (New Haven: Yale University Press, 1990), esp. chap. 4.

29. Hegel's account of master and slave suggests a further problem for inflated *amour propre*: that it is directly self-defeating to depend for my sense of self on the recognition of others whom I denigrate. I do not find a view of this kind in Rousseau, but see Dent, *Rousseau*, pp. 63–4.

30. This is all discussed, in convincing detail, by Dent. See *Rousseau*, pp. 52–6.

31. The trouble comes from differences presumed to be natural. Rousseau has no objection to taking pride in one's virtues, because virtues are achievements, not endowments: "The good man can be proud of his virtue because it is his. But of what is the intelligent man proud?" (*E*, 245).

32. Rousseau's view of compassion and its diverse forms may be obscured by the discussion of compassion in the *Discourse on Inequality*. There, he associates natural compassion with a more or less mechanical aversion to suffering – the "pure movement of nature *prior to all reflection*" (*D2*, 161, emphasis added). But his *Essay on the Origin of Languages* and *Emile* present a different and more plausible picture: "Although pity is native to the human heart, it would remain eternally quiescent unless it were activated by imagination. How are we moved to pity? By getting outside ourselves and identifying with a being who suffers." But, he continues, "It is clear that such transport supposes a great deal of acquired knowledge." And because it does, "he who has never been reflective is incapable of being merciful or just or pitying" (*OL*, 32). *Emile* states the cognitive preconditions of pity in similar language (*E*, 222–3). There, too, he recognizes that compassion – like reciprocity, or the concern to be treated with respect – can be part of our natural endowment, even if its expression is triggered only by circumstances.

33. In the *Second Discourse*, Rousseau adds to these the natural aversion to the suffering of others.

34. It is not obvious why the natural desires should be so closely tied to needs. Of course, we could not survive as a species if we did not desire what we need. But there is no parallel problem with natural desires for goods that, while unnecessary for survival, are not detrimental to it – say, natural curiosity, or a natural desire for companionship. Rousseau offers this reason in *Emile* for tying natural desires to natural needs: "nature, which does everything for the best . . . gives him with immediacy only the desires necessary to his preservation and the faculties sufficient to supply them" (*E*, 80). If we were endowed with desires that outstripped our natural powers, that would have been for the worse, since it would have been a source of unhappiness. But why suppose that nature does everything for the best? The doctrine of natural goodness does not require such a strong assumption.

35. This condition is necessary, not sufficient; that is, it is possible to develop the cognitive powers without the extension of compassion following on that development.

36. It is clear from the context that Rousseau is concerned with the "impetuous ardor" that men direct to women. See *D2*, 164.

37. See Kant's discussion of how to reconcile the apparently conflicting strands of Rousseau's view in his "Speculative Beginning of Human History," in *Perpetual Peace and Other Essays*, trans. Ted Humphrey (Indianapolis: Hackett, 1983), pp. 54–5.

38. Starobinski suggests that Rousseau was simply torn between *Innocence/Vice* and *Innocence/Virtue* – between "an optimistic and a pessimistic version of the myth of origin" (*Transparency and Obstruction*, p. 15).

39. See, for example, Seneca, *On Anger*, in *Seneca, in Ten Volumes*, Vol. 1 (*Moral Essays*) (Cambridge: Harvard University Press, 1928), p. 119.

40. As a general matter, I will focus on the vice rather than the unhappiness. But the two are closely connected. True happiness consists in an equilibrium of desires and capacities (*E*, 80). The vices are rooted in a desire for advantage over others, and an insistence that others acknowledge us as their betters. They make us miserable – irritated or discontent – because desires rooted in vice necessarily outrun our capacities.

41. On Hobbes, see *D2*, 159–60; on the Augustinian view, see *B*, 937–38. Arthur Melzer contrasts Rousseau's views with Platonist as well as Hobbesian and Augustinian conceptions. See his *The Natural Goodness of Man: The System of Rousseau's Thought* (Chicago: University of Chicago Press, 1990), pp. 17–23. According to Melzer, Platonism endorses a dualistic conception of the soul, with one part fixed as "selfish" and "irrational." Human virtue, then, requires a constant struggle against part of our own nature. And he claims that Rousseau rejected this dualism and "inaugurated the great moral revolution" that emphasizes the unity of the soul and proposes to replace "wisdom and self-control with the new ethic of sincerity and spontaneity" (p. 22). This revolution represents a continuation of the Stoic tradition, "carrying on their argument against Plato and others in support of the natural unity of the soul" (p. 21). Starobinski, too, suggests Rousseau's affiliation with Stoicism. See *Transparency and Obstruction*, pp. 28, 37. This association strikes me as very much exaggerated. The role of the sense of duty in the final stages of Emile's education reveals Rousseau's distance from Stoicism. In explaining why Emile must leave Sophie, Emile's teacher rejects the Stoic ideal of extirpating the passions: "It is not within our control to have or not to have passions" (*E*, 445). Moreover, once the passions have been awakened, goodness demands virtue, which depends in turn on a sense of duty and strength of will.

I have made you good rather than virtuous. But he who is only good remains so only as long as he takes pleasure in being so. Goodness is broken and perishes under the impact of the human passions. . . . Who, then, is the virtuous man? It is he who knows how to conquer his affections; for then he follows his reason and his conscience; he does his duty.

He continues: "Now be really free. Learn to become your own master. Command your heart, Emile, and you will be virtuous." Elaborating the conception of command, the teacher says:

It is an error to distinguish permitted passions from forbidden ones in order to yield to the former and deny oneself the latter. All passions are good when one remains their master; all are bad when one lets oneself be subjected to them. . . . What is forbidden to us by conscience is not temptations but rather letting ourselves be conquered by temptations. It is not within our control to have or not to have passions. But it is within our control to reign over them. All the sentiments we dominate are legitimate; all those which dominate us are criminal. (*E*, 444–5; see also 446, 473; *RJ*, 158)

And in the continuation of this passage, he explains that to "dominate" our sentiments is to follow "the law of duty." Rousseau's motto for *Emile* comes from Seneca's *De Ira*, but we find nothing in Seneca's treatise corresponding to Rousseau's account of "reigning over passions" and resisting temptations by following the law of duty. See Seneca, *On Anger*, pp. 106–356. Cassirer is more nearly right when he says that "Rousseau's ethics is not an ethics of feeling but the most categorical form of a pure ethics of obligation (*Gesetzes-Ethik*) before Kant." See Ernst Cassirer, *The Question of Jean-Jacques Rousseau*, trans. and edited by Peter Gay (Bloomington: University of Indiana Press, 1963), p. 96. But Cassirer neglects issues of motivational strength, and so omits any account of the complexities (explored in Section V below) of ensuring a fit between the general will and our affections. On the Stoic idea of extirpating the passions, see Martha C. Nussbaum, *The Therapy of Desire: Theory and Practice in Hellenistic Ethics* (Princeton: Princeton University Press, 1994), chaps. 10, 11. I am grateful to Martha Nussbaum for discussion of the themes in this note.

42. *Leviathan*, p. 58.
43. Ibid.
44. How much inequality, and of what sort? Rousseau's scattered remarks do not add up to a sustained answer.
45. The structural interpretation is suggested in the Preface to Rousseau's *Narcissus*:

   In Europe, government, laws, customs, self-interest, all put individuals in the necessity of deceiving each other mutually and incessantly; everything makes vice a duty; it is necessary to be wicked in order to be wise, for there is no greater folly than to create the happiness of cheaters at the expense of one's own. Among the savages, personal interest speaks as strongly as among us, but it doesn't say the same things, . . . nothing carries them to deceive one another. (*DI*, 194n)

46. The person who does what is right without having to resist inclinations is at best "good without merit." Genuine virtue depends on following the sense of duty in the face of conflicting temptations. See *E*, 473; *SC*, 1.8.1; *RJ*, 158.
47. More particularly, by the existence of a legal order and legal obligation, even if that order is a mere pretext. See *E*, 473.
48. On the importance of this idea in Rousseau's institutional views, see the discussion of temptation and assurance in Cohen, "Reflections on Rousseau," pp. 294–5.
49. Recall that the "whole of human wisdom in the use of the passions" is to keep a "sense of the true relations of man" and then to "order all the affections of the soul according to these relations" (*E*, 219).
50. Rousseau's point is not simply about what Rawls calls the social bases of self-respect. The idea of such bases is, roughly, that self-respect typically depends on having the respect of others. See Rawls, *Theory of Justice*, pp. 178–9, 440–6. Rousseau agrees, but is making a further point about how individuals acquire an understanding of their true relations as equals and so come to see the requirements of mutual respect in egalitarian terms, and not in the hierarchical terms associated with the inflamed sense of self-worth. Rousseau's point is about the formation of a particular conception of self-worth, and not only about the achievement of a sense of self-worth, given such a conception.
51. Immanuel Kant, *The Metaphysics of Morals*, trans. Mary Gregor (Cambridge University Press, 1991), p. 251.
52. Melzer presents an illuminating discussion of four arguments for the doctrine

of natural goodness – introspective, psychological, social, and historical – and mentions in passing (page 30, note 1) a fifth, metaphysical argument. My rationale for the doctrine is specifically moral, and thus seems different from any of these five. Melzer, *Natural Goodness*, Part 2.

53. I interpret the Profession of Faith as anticipating Kant's conception of reasonable faith, as presented, for example, in the "Dialectic of Pure Practical Reason," in *Critique of Practical Reason*, trans. Lewis White Beck (Indianapolis: Bobbs-Merrill, 1956), Book 2. For a moving statement of the animating moral idea behind the doctrine of reasonable faith – a statement that reveals the deep affinity of Kant and Rousseau – see the concluding paragraph in "The Canon of Pure Reason," in the *Critique of Pure Reason*, trans. Norman Kemp Smith (London: Macmillan, 1929), A831/B859. On the connections between the Vicar's Profession of Faith and Kant's idea of moral religion, see Dieter Henrich, "The Moral Image of the World," in *Aesthetic Judgment and the Moral Image of the World: Studies in Kant* (Stanford: Stanford University Press, 1992), pp. 3–28.

54. See the quotations from Rousseau and Kant placed at the beginning of this essay.

Metaphysics, Philosophy:
Rousseau on the Problem of Evil

SUSAN NEIMAN

The desire to become the "Newton of the mind" was an understandable eighteenth-century aspiration. It may be less understandable that Kant awarded the honor to the philosopher whose writings seem closest to literature, and even more surprising that he does so because of Rousseau's response to a problem that seems closest to theology.

Newton was the first to see order and regularity combined with great simplicity, where disorder and ill-matched variety had reigned before. Since then comets have been moving in geometric orbits. Rousseau was the first to discover in the variety of shapes that men assume the deeply concealed nature of man and to observe the hidden law that justifies Providence. Before them, the objections of Alfonso and the Manicheans were valid. After Newton and Rousseau, God is justified, and Pope's thesis is henceforth true.[1]

The present essay seeks to understand just what Kant meant in this unpublished note. Initial study of Rousseau's writings on the subject will raise more questions than it answers. For where Rousseau seems to be addressing the traditional problem of evil, he is conventional, even reactionary; where his work is interesting, and revolutionary, he seems to be addressing different questions altogether. Thus it may be unsurprising that this extraordinary note is seldom quoted in full, and that requests to explain it rarely produce more than the apologetic suggestion that the remark is, after all, pre-Critical.[2] In trying to appreciate Kant's claim, I examine Rousseau's discussion of the problem of evil[3] and his role in transforming that problem in several directions.

For contemporary readers, Rousseau's work proves particularly remarkable because it forms a bridge between at least two kinds of problem which can be called the problem of evil. The first, which I shall call the cosmological problem, is the question of why a benevolent and omnipotent God created a world that contains instances of terrible evil. In classical discussions of this problem, moral and physical evils were often distinguished only to be connected again. So one sort of solution argues that moral evils exist because of the great gift of free will, while physical evils exist because of the abuse we have made of that gift. The second, moral problem of evil, is the question of why rational beings would choose to do moral evil, given even minimal assumptions about the connections between freedom and morality. For twentieth-century readers, at least in the English-speaking world, these problems appear to be completely distinct. In particular, it is possible for an atheist to care about the second problem while finding the first arcane and remote. (Indeed, the intransigence of the first problem has often been viewed as the most conclusive argument in favor of atheism.)

During the Enlightenment, however, the two were almost invariably entwined. The importance of the problem for most eighteenth-century thinkers is part of the reason for Kant's suggestion that anyone who solved it would be a second Newton. Yet despite its centrality, it would not be until Kant's last decade that anyone stated clearly the several strands and problems involved. The equivocation between the two kinds of problem is not, however, accidental. It is easy to see how an earlier reader would have held an answer to the second, moral problem of evil to be necessary for responding to the first, cosmological one. For without an account of how rational beings could freely choose to do evil, the free will defense – on which most attempts to solve the first problem depend – simply collapses. If physical evils result from moral evils, which in turn result from our misuse of freedom, the latter must be made comprehensible before God's original plan can be vindicated. So for Leibniz, who holds such an Augustinian view, it is only the existence of moral evils that raises a cosmological problem.[4] Although this connection between the two problems is crucial, there are others that are even more direct. Though many eighteenth-century thinkers did so, one need not hold the strongest version of the assumption that humankind is the final end of the universe to view the moral and cosmological problems of evil to be intimately related. For even if humankind is not viewed as the ultimate purpose of creation, its role is more central, its iniquity more apparent and jarring, than that of other elements of creation. One need not share Leibniz's views about the relations between moral and physical evils to believe that moral evils are those that raise the cosmological problem of evil in its starkest form; conversely, to attempt any resolution of the cosmological problem without addressing the nature of moral evils would seem to leave the hardest questions untouched.

Like his predecessors, Rousseau neither adequately distinguished nor made clear the connections between these kinds of problem of evil. More than others, however, his work is interesting precisely because in addressing both, often ambiguously, he changes the form of the problem itself. Some readers may be inclined to take seriously only his contribution to the moral problem of evil, as most clearly relevant to contemporary concerns, and to dismiss the cosmological concerns with which he begins as a historical curiosity. In discussing both together I wish not only to exhibit the complexity of the problem of evil itself, but to show something about the transformation of philosophical problems in general. The essay is divided into three parts: first, a discussion of the historical background informing Rousseau's work on this subject; second, a sketch of Rousseau's account of the development of evil; and finally, an examination of what, exactly, that account accomplishes within the demands of a Kantian philosophical framework.

I

Let's begin the explication of Kant's note by exploring its most obscure reference. The thirteenth-century Castilian king Alfonso X had a distinctive place in eighteenth-century philosophy. His influence derived from an instance of blasphemy: after devoting years of study to Ptolemaic astronomy he declared "that, if he had been of God's counsel at the creation, certain things would be in better order than they are."[5] At the end of the seventeenth century, Bayle's *Dictionary* devoted some space to discussing the various punishments that may have been the result of divine wrath at this piece of hubris, but the first philosophical use of the figure was made by Leibniz. Alfonso proved a perfect foil in Leibniz's polemic against Bayle. Although the *Theodicy* contains a number of arguments against Bayle's assertion that Manicheism is the theory that best accounts for experience, all depend on an assertion of the limits of our knowledge. Could we but know the universe as a whole, Leibniz tells us, we would see that it is the most perfect one which could have been created; appearances to the contrary result from our simple lack of knowledge of the larger contexts and connections.

Most of his discussions in support of this claim are disturbingly hypothetical. He writes, for example, that it may be the case that the inhabitants of other planets are much happier and more blessed than we are, so that humankind's lot is to bear the majority of evils which the universe had to contain. It seems hard not to reply that it is equally possible that the inhabitants of other galaxies are even more miserable and wicked than we are. Similarly, in trying to defend the most difficult of theological claims for his account – the idea that the number of the eternally damned is far greater than the number of the saved – Leibniz proposes that there *may* be incomparably more good in the glory of all the saved than there is evil in the torments of the damned. On the face of things, one possibility seems just as likely as the other; in the latter case, it is difficult even to know how the alternatives should be clearly stated.

While Leibniz's use of King Alfonso may be equally hypothetical, the ad hominem example lends plausibility to his claim as little else does. For Alfonso's blasphemy was based on the miserable state of thirteenth-century astronomy: had the world been created as Ptolemy supposed, the Creator could indeed have used advice in design. Modern science, however, has proven Alfonso wrong: the universe could not possibly have been created with more structure, order, and harmony. Objections to the contrary are as dependent on our lack of knowledge as was the Castilian king's dependent on the mistaken belief that the Ptolemaic system was true. Future discoveries, Leibniz assures us, will show the moral order of the world to be as marvelous and transparent as we now know the physical order to be. To those of us latter-day Alfonsos who believe we could advise God about designing a world with fewer evils in it, Leibniz replies:

You have known the world only since the day before yesterday, you scarce see farther than your nose, and you carp at the world. Wait until you know more of the world . . . and you will find therein a contrivance and a beauty transcending all imagination. Let us thence draw conclusions as to the wisdom and the goodness of the author of the world, even in things that we know not.[6]

It is easy to see how the example would have seemed compelling in 1710. An era still dizzy with the success of seventeenth-century scientific discovery, which had yet to distinguish between "natural" and "moral" sciences, allowing many to aspire to be the Newton of the mind, could have drawn hope and patience from the story of Alfonso. But while the later eighteenth-century did not draw the distinction between physics and psychology as we do, they did begin to raise a contemporary question. Leibniz's optimism may have seemed justified by the increasing amount of order discovered in natural phenomena (though even this would be questioned with the Lisbon earthquake), but human affairs seemed to present as great a mass of unintelligible barbarism as ever. Although the question may have been implicit in such writers as Voltaire and Hume, it is urgent, and explicit, in Rousseau and Kant. Newton alone was not enough to answer Alfonso; to do this, someone also needed to provide an account of the structure and order in human nature.[7]

By the mid-eighteenth century it no longer suffices to claim, as Leibniz had done, that the order of the universe is intelligible in principle, subject to the laws of reason, while lamenting the fact that the human intellect is not, or not yet, capable of telling us how.[8] Those wanting to maintain that intelligibility must do more than assert it: they must do some work to show it, by giving details. The hardest case against the claim that the universe is thoroughly ordered is the existence of moral evil; that case must be tackled directly. This just means that the debate about the problem of evil turns from a formal to a substantive one. For Leibniz, as indeed for any rationalist, the goodness of God and the comprehensibility of the laws by which He structured Creation stand or fall together. God must not, he tells us, be compared to a ruler like Caligula, "who has his edicts written in so small a hand and has them placarded in so high a place that it is not possible to read them."[9] After Leibniz, those wanting to maintain conviction in the existence of universal order must make legible the laws underlying moral evil. It is this that Kant took to be Rousseau's project, in the very broadest sense.

Note that it is rationalism, not theism, that is immediately threatened by the problem of evil. Initially, it may seem that only the latter is jeopardized by the absence of an adequate explanation of the existence of evil. One might conclude that the incomprehensibility of evil should lead us only to reject the belief that the universe was created by an omnipotent and benevolent God. We may still be left with the moral problem of evil, which has its own form of unintelligibility, the mystery of a free rational being's choice to engage in evil actions. But we could simply conclude that this is one piece of the world that resists explanation; and, without the pressure of theocentric assumptions implying a universal order, be less inclined to be troubled by the unintelligibility of one phenomenon, however practically significant. That such a conclusion is not, even today, as easy to maintain as it looks can be seen in the work of certain twentieth-century European philosophers whose atheism was as decided as their engagement with the cosmological problem of evil.[10] For the eighteenth century, the terms of debate were not set by the alternatives between atheism and a theology embedded in the argument from design, but between the latter and fideism.[11] Fideism was the alternative chosen by Bayle, whose discussion of the problem of evil opened and informed debate on the subject throughout the century. Bayle's attacks on traditional attempts to defend Providence in the face of radical and pervasive evil were quite similar to Hume's, who acknowledged his debt to Bayle. Yet Bayle uses those arguments to provoke skepticism not about God's existence but about philosophy and science in general. The skeptical arguments shared by Hume and Bayle may be as easily followed by a leap of faith to positive religion as by a rejection of all religious belief. What could not be maintained, unless those arguments were answered, is a belief in human reason's capacity to find or make the world intelligible.[12]

Although the problem of evil runs through all of Rousseau's writings, his explicit discussions of the subject hardly seem to contain the force that Kant attributed to them. Though he directly attacks Leibniz's position, much of his writing seems a curious throwback to the views of the *Theodicy*, bereft even of the latter's optimism about the possibility of progressive, scientific understanding. Rousseau's initial reference to the question appears in a reply to objections to his own first publication. There he expands on the first *Discourse* claim that the study of philosophy leads to little but vanity. A contrast between the philosopher and the ploughman shows the former imagining himself to fathom God's secrets, and having the right to judge them, while the ploughman

does not censure God's works, nor challenge his master in order to display his self-importance. Never will the impious remark of Alfonse X occur to one of the vulgar; that blasphemy was reserved for a learned mouth.[13]

Here Rousseau does not even suggest, like Leibniz, that Alfonso would have done better to study modern science; he would have done better not to study at all. His next, more sustained set of remarks on the subject seem replete with an appeal to the primitivism that his contemporaries loathed.[14] They occur in a long letter to Voltaire concerning the latter's poem "The Lisbon Earthquake."

Voltaire's poem had provided one of the strongest expressions of the shock felt by European intellectuals in 1755. Subtitled "An Inquiry into the Maxim, 'Whatever is, is right,'"[15] the poem takes the disaster at Lisbon to undermine not only the work of the philosophical poet whom Voltaire had loved and translated, but philosophy in general as well. "The Lisbon Earthquake" begins with a description of the destruction of the city in a matter of minutes. Though he would go on to attack in detail Pope's and Leibniz's arguments on behalf of optimism, Voltaire suggests that the simple description of experience refutes all the theories that attempt to explain it. The "babies shattered on their mothers' breasts" defy every previous philosophical discussion; sheer decency, Voltaire thinks, requires us to abandon the latter, for only a mad and distant vision could maintain a belief in eternal law while looking directly at the former. Leibniz and Pope had attacked "seditious, reasoning pride" as the source of our skepticism about Providence, and Rousseau would initially follow them: could we but know ourselves and our place in the world with appropriate humility, we would accept the apparent evils that befall us as part of a larger, natural order. Voltaire is never more convincing than when attacking this set of claims, to which he makes two kinds of response. Not pride but compassion, not presumption but a sense of justice, are the source of our outrage at events like the Lisbon disaster. It is just the finest sorts of emotion of which human beings are capable that move us to question divine justice at moments like these;

the optimists' attack on our motivation in doing so is at best an ad hominem diversion from the problem at hand. Second, Voltaire argues that Pope's view increases our pain not only by denying its legitimacy, but by urging its necessity. If evil is unalterable, all the more reason for despair.

Despair and consolation are questions at issue in the long-winded letter Rousseau sent to Voltaire on 18 August 1756,[16] but for once in their long, complex, and hostile relationship, Voltaire appears not only the more serious but the more compassionate thinker. Although the letter is interesting, even unwittingly funny, its force is finally almost sinister. Rousseau is concerned to argue, as elsewhere, that not only moral but most physical evils are of human origin. Had the inhabitants of Portugal not insisted on building large houses, but stayed scattered in the country where nature had put them, the damage caused by the earthquake would have been minimal. Moreover, Rousseau asks, "How many miserable creatures perished in this disaster for wanting one of them to take his clothes, another his papers, another still his money?" The question fully ignores Voltaire's suggestion that the notion of blame is indecent in view of babies dying in their mothers' arms, and comes close to reviving the traditional responses most theologians made to the earthquake. Natural evils are divine punishments for moral evils; at issue was only the nature of the crimes of the people of Lisbon that had provoked a wrath of such proportions.

Voltaire's poem, Rousseau continues, succeeds merely in increasing the misery suffered by humankind by describing it in desperate detail. "Where Pope's poem eases my suffering, and brings me patience, yours aggravates it, leads me to murmur, and undermines my hope." Voltaire, claims Rousseau, has failed in his task as a writer, that of providing the public with hope. Here Rousseau's position seems no better than that of a government official urging another not to reveal the scope of the misfunctioning surrounding them, for fear of driving the public to despair (or rebellion). But Rousseau, of course, is everything but cynical. The conclusion of the letter is, if anything, merely pathetic: unlike the well-situated Voltaire, Rousseau has "suffered too much in this life not to await another." He is therefore prepared to ignore "the subtleties of metaphysics" (not to mention the brute force of experience, Voltaire's real focus) in favor of the faith in Providence, which he feels as much as he desires. Much of this line of thinking remains in Rousseau's longest explicit discussion of Providence, the "Creed of the Savoyard Vicar."[17]

Nothing in these discussions seems to justify Kant's enthusiastic, even *schwärmerisch* note. Where Rousseau discusses the traditional problem of evil, his remarks seem inferior to the classical responses that were perceived to be sorely wanting by, at the latest, 1755. Kant's excitement can be understood only by looking at the account given in the second *Discourse* and the body of *Emile* (without the "Creed," which, despite the furor it aroused, is probably the least radical part of the book). Though the letter to Voltaire, in particular, suggests an approach to the problem verging on the Panglossian, Rousseau's actual position is far deeper. Indeed, one might say that though the eighteenth century is dominated by discussions of the issue, he is the first to truly treat the problem of evil as a philosophical problem. Let me explain. Earlier accounts, I believe, are forced to one of two positions. In arguing that this is the best of all possible worlds, or that whatever is, is right, one must effectively deny the existence of evil: things that we view to be evils are merely necessary elements in a greater, unknown plan. There is thus no genuine, only an apparent problem, because there is no genuine, only apparent evil. In various versions, this has been called the doctrine of optimism, and if quietism is its most disturbing consequence, sheer blindness seems its most appealing cause. That Rousseau is concerned to avoid both these perils is made explicit in his letter to "Philopolis," the pseudonym used by the Leibnizian Charles Bonnet in an article criticizing Rousseau's second *Discourse*. Rousseau's reply runs, in part:

To deny the existence of evil is a most convenient way of excusing the author of that evil; the stoics formerly made themselves a laughing-stock for less. . . . If everything is as best it can be, then you must blame any action whatsoever . . . and the most absolute quietism is the only virtue left to man.[18]

But those who acknowledge, and enumerate, the existence of genuine evils, seem forced into the opposite position. The problem of evil is so vast and extensive that it seems not only to resist philosophical solution, but to rebuke philosophy itself. If there are evils in the world that nothing can explain or justify, this suggests – as Hume would argue most cogently – not only that human reason cannot help us in making the world intelligible; it seems to put us constantly at odds with it. Taking evil seriously requires denying philosophy: not analysis or resolution but description is all we have left. (A parallel to this can be seen in certain forms of Christian theology, which acknowledge, even emphasize, the existence of moral evil in the form of original sin. Here the genuineness of evil is asserted, but only a non-rational approach to the problem is possible: things are so bad that only a miracle, the passion of Jesus, can save us.) Before Rousseau, one might say, either there is no problem of evil, or there is no answer.

All of Rousseau's writings reflect an attempt to take both sides of this dilemma seriously. Unwilling to view evils as merely apparent, Rousseau annoyed most of his contemporaries by arguing that things are even worse than they seem. Equally annoying, perhaps, was his repeated insistence that "of all those evils that could be blamed on Providence, not one has not its source rather in the misuse that man has made of his faculties than in Nature itself."[19] Like traditional theologians, he thereby vindicates God, but unlike them, he will do it without damning human-kind. If evil is of our own doing, we could also undo it; not grace but, he will argue, a particular sort of knowledge is all that is required. There is, for Rousseau, both a problem and a solution: both are contained in the idea that evil has a development, because we do. Thus we get the first, radical claim of the second *Discourse*: human nature has been altered. Earlier thinkers had assumed the fundamental similarity of human nature across time; indeed, one might say that the doctrine of original sin is just the claim that human nature changed, and could change, only once: at the time of the Fall. Secular eighteenth-century thinkers, oddly enough, often maintained a similar view about the invariance of human nature across space; Voltaire was not the only writer to use the extensive interest in comparative culture opened up by the possibility of travel to argue that Europe and the Orient, savage and citizen, offered a depressingly familiar picture of fundamentally barbarous natures.[20] For Rousseau, by contrast, human nature is not fixed at any point; we are essentially different than we used to be, because society has changed us. Between necessity and accident there is a third alternative: call it history. The implication Rousseau draws is, of course, more hopeful than anything provided by optimism. History is fundamentally dynamic, and if change was possible once, it may be possible again. But in addition to the pragmatic consequences of his view, Rousseau's account offers the possibility of conceptual satisfaction that none of the alternatives provide. A historical explanation offers the right sort of comprehensibility. If the introduction of evil was necessary, we face a conflict between theoretical and practical reason that seems intolerable. If it was simply accidental, we must conclude that the world, at a crucial point, makes no sense. The introduction of history, by contrast, does justice to all of reason's interests. We need not ignore practical reason's demand to change the world, nor theoretical reason's need to interpret it. The exploration of evil as a historical phenomenon becomes rather *part of* our efforts to make the world intelligible, in both these ways.

The very possibility of a statement of the problem of evil that allows for a philosophical account – as much as the details of the account itself – must have impressed Kant as Newtonian. The form of Rousseau's account would look very different from every earlier discussion of the problem of evil, but this was precisely because the debate had reached a point at which a substantive account was demanded – if philosophical discussion not simply of this problem, but of many others, was to continue at all. As Kant could see, the new discussion was very much an answer to the traditional questions represented by Alfonso, even as Rousseau opened up not only new modes of response but also entirely new areas of inquiry.[21]

The possibility of a philosophical account must be distinguished from what I will call a metaphysical one. We must pause to consider the question: How might the author of the Critical Philosophy take Alfonso for a threat so great that a second Newton would be required to overcome it? As the quickest reading of Kant's mature work will tell us, God, hence God's intentions and purposes, are excluded from the domain of knowledge. Even more generally, if the traditional movement of theodicy is to seek an explanation in terms of the unity of the whole, integrating all our experience, including the experience of evil, into a meaningful and purposive system, the very project should have come to seem pointless once we have grasped the basic tenets of Kant's work. Were we in any doubt about the implications of Kant's general position for the questions at issue, he makes them explicit in the essay "On the Failure of All Philosophical Attempts at Theodicy," published in 1791 in the *Berliner Monatsschrift*.

Yet while Kant tells us that every attempt at theodicy is doomed to failure, the same essay represents his own work as responding – he suggests, uniquely – to the Book of Job, which he called "the most philosophical book of the Bible." Kant may dismiss the claims of metaphysics, but he is unwilling to dismiss the claims of Job, whose fate might be said to form the focus of discussion of the "Dialectic" of the second *Critique*.[22] Indeed, the arguments offered in "On the Failure . . ." show that theodicy is rejected not only on systematic grounds. Kant suggests two sorts of reasons that fuel the impulse to theodicy. The first is the honest doubt of Job, awakened by the experience of particular evils. If those evils drop out of any metaphysical theodicy, the very project can provide no response to the experience that leads us to seek it in the first place. The alternative motivation for undertaking such a project is, Kant tells us, at best disingenous. Job's friends, like other theodicy-makers, speak in the hope that God may be eavesdropping. Only Job, as God Himself will tell us, speaks in truth.

Moral sense demands from philosophy more acknowledgment than Job received from his friends. God cannot, Kant has Job tell us, be defended with injustice. This means that sheer rejection of theodicy, in the form of a claim that "God in His infinite wisdom has reasons which our weak and feeble minds cannot hope to comprehend" is no solution at

all. Though something like this might seem to follow from Kant's general
account of metaphysics, he views this claim itself to be a form of
theodicy, and one of the worst. Indeed, he calls it an apology that requires no refutation but the abhorrence of anyone with the least feeling
for morality.[23] This passage relies on Kant's view of the infinite worth of
practical reason: in questions of justice, God has no more insight than we
do.[24] Thus we cannot vindicate God by appealing to His superior wisdom, against which the judgment of our own practical reason has no
claim. When a man of perfect integrity questions the justice of Creation,
he speaks on equal footing with God. But if God Himself deemed Job's
questions to be worthy of an answer, philosophy cannot simply deny
them.

II

Like Newton, Rousseau would undertake to explain a vast array of
phenomena using a very small set of tools. Newton had shown that, given
a description of the initial conditions and properties of all parts, one can
derive the state of the system of the universe at any given time. No
hypothesis of intention is required to explain occurrences; once the
system is set in motion, it runs on its own.[25] Starobinski is clearly right to
describe the second *Discourse* as a substitute for sacred history, in which
Rousseau recasts the story of the Fall.[26] Yet Kant must have also read it
as Rousseau's attempt to recreate elements of a Newtonian explanation:
giving a statement of the initial conditions of the bodies involved, ascribing to them a small set of properties, and showing how the present state
of affairs follows naturally from these. So the second *Discourse* begins by
positing a fairly minimalist conception of human nature, and goes on
to show how all the vices that currently plague us could have evolved
from the original condition through a few developmental principles.[27]
Rousseau's account of the origin of evil is naturalistic in several senses.
First, it makes no reference to supernatural forces, divine or demonic;
once we have left "the hands of the Author of Nature" we are entirely on
our own. Any explanation of our condition will have to be made without
reference to God. This is revisionary enough, but Rousseau goes
further: his Fall involves no notion of sin, original or otherwise. Not only
divine, but also human intention thus drop out of the picture entirely.
Fundamental evil does not occur at the level of individual intention, but
emerges as a collective process. This is not to suggest that Rousseau's
assumptions are mechanistic: in introducing both history and psychology
to the discussion of the problem of evil, Rousseau means to argue
that evil arose through a process that was understandable but not

necessary. If Rousseau could show how we became wicked without willing it, through a series of particular historical events, he could show that the course of tendencies within human nature is not inevitable.[28] The second *Discourse* shows how certain processes, once begun, gain compelling momentum, but they could, at each point, have been otherwise.

This, and not rhetorical confusion, is, I believe, the source of one of the more frustrating features of the second *Discourse*, its apparent and dramatically authoritative location of the turning point in civilization in not one but several events. Were we ruined by the introduction of iron and wheat? Private property? The desire for the other's desire which took place when early savages built groups of huts and danced around common fires? The search for a decisive moment may itself be an error; in introducing several of them Rousseau may be warning us against the inclination to determine one moment as decisive. At several points in time, we might have turned the course of history. The goal is to show that once certain mechanisms begin, the move to the next stage of civilization – and misery – is not a surprising one, but history as a whole isn't necessary.

Rousseau's account of evil, then, originally involves neither theological nor moral categories. It is also naturalistic in the sense that evil is something that is fully external. The Fall in Rousseau's story occurs when the first man refused to heed, not some incomprehensible prohibitions of the Lord, but the voice of his own true nature. Evil arises not from obstinacy but from weakness, the savage's inability to recognize his own true needs, or indeed his self at all, unreflected in the eyes of others. Here Rousseau introduces the idea of alienation: social man lives in and through the reflection of others. We no longer know our true needs, but allow false needs to be imposed on us externally, because we no longer know ourselves, but only the ways in which we appear to others. Rousseau tells us that the seeds of this process occurred in the era he clearly views as the golden age, the point at which groups joined together to build rudimentary villages, while land was still held in common. As soon as people gathered together on a permanent basis, public esteem acquired value, if only through sexual competition: each hoped to sing or dance better than the others in order to rouse the desire of the opposite sex. Still, he suggests, this sort of alienation could have been contained, and might yet be transformed. At each step of our downfall, it is the further disconnection of need and gratification that leads us astray. Rousseau's discussion of alienation attempts to show that evil has no *depth*. Moral evil is the externalization of the self, not the realization of it. Starobinski emphasizes this as follows:

Evil can be identified with man's passion for what is external to himself: prestige, appearances, possession of material wealth. Evil is external, and it is the passion for the external . . . Rousseau, unlike most previous moralists, is not content merely to criticize external things; he incriminates the external in his very definition of evil.[29]

Of course, the force of Rousseau's account depends on the fact that the temptation to this sort of externality is a part of our own constitution. Humans are creatures who are vulnerable to *amour propre*. This vulnerability is an internal and essential feature of our nature, yet its outcome is undetermined.[30]

What follows from this is a final sense in which Rousseau's account can be described as naturalistic. The result of evil is immediate misery – not in the world to come, but in our own. As did Adam, we bring evil upon ourselves, but as the direct consequence of our errors rather than as punishment.[31] Most importantly, there is nothing seductive about sinning. As Rousseau paints it, civilization is not even tempting. His analysis of the effects of false needs produced by this process is precise:

Not only did they continue to weaken body and mind, but since these conveniences, by becoming habitual, had almost entirely ceased to be enjoyable, and at the same time had degenerated into true needs, it became much more cruel to be deprived of them than to possess them was sweet, and men were unhappy to lose them without being happy to possess them.[32]

False needs engender, and are in turn reinforced by, the relations of domination and submission that constitute inequality and are the basis of evil. They create a double slavery, subjecting us to people as well as to things. Not only does each new thing soon become a need rather than a source of pleasure; it forces us into permanent conflict with the rest of our species. For (assuming conditions of even moderate scarcity) ownership of anything requires denying others' claims to it. For the rich, this leads to isolation, uncertainty, fear, and misery; for those less clever or violent, the consequences are the same, with the addition of poverty as well. Misery, then, is the result from any standpoint, soon leading to the Hobbesian state of war which all will seek to escape at any cost. A more traditional picture views evil as an expression of something in our (usually called "animal") nature, bringing us immediate gratification if at the expense of long-term satisfaction, earthly or otherwise. For Rousseau it is just the opposite: there is nothing appealing about the acts that make up evil. On the contrary: he assures us that Emile, raised to know only his true needs and desires, will always reject the temptations of civilization on sheer sensual grounds. When Rousseau indulges, in Book 4 of *Emile*, in a fantasy of vast wealth, he maintains that pure natural inclination would lead him to the simple life he now enjoys.

To call Rousseau's account of evil naturalistic is not to say, as some have suggested, that Rousseau replaces moral categories with psychological ones. His aim is not to reduce moral categories to other kinds, but to enable us to realize them. The exquisite sense of understanding, even sympathy, which allows him to accurately describe the ways in which rich people suffer from self-perpetuated enslavement, is not a suspension of moral judgment. The point is to bring home, from many directions, the idea that evil actions are not natural ones: if they were, something in our nature would be deeply satisfied by them. Not satisfaction but constant frustration is the result of evil; from this we must learn that it is fundamentally distortion. Now if evil is the result of a distortion that developed historically, it is also something that could be deconstructed. Showing this will be the goal of *Emile*. If the state of things we recognize as evil can be shown to have been brought about by a natural and comprehensible set of processes, a natural and comprehensible set of processes could produce the opposite. Moral categories are not to be set aside, but provided with a developmental, scientific basis. Rousseau's attempt to do this was presumably one source of Kant's excitement about *Emile*.[33]

The second *Discourse* contains no prescriptions: it is a work of diagnosis or, as Rousseau suggested more darkly, even autopsy.[34] Though he displays a clear sense of nostalgia for the state of nature, he sees no possibility of a return to it; nor, I suggest, does he hold such a return to be desireable. The Fall he describes there is as final and irrevocable as that of Genesis.[35] By 1762, with the publication of *Emile*, however, something like salvation is conceivable. In *Emile* the isolated savage of the second *Discourse* is given another chance. This time he will not be left on his own. Rousseau's insistence that the child be left to develop needs and interests naturally should not obscure the fact that Emile's is the most consciously controlled upbringing ever imagined. Nor should that control be viewed as a tension in the text, as is occasionally suggested. The balance between control and independence, between the artificial and the natural, is just the point of the method by which Emile is to be raised. In receiving an education that will allow him to become a man without the fetters of civilization, Emile must be forced to be free.[36]

A reading of *Emile* would be required to defend these claims in any detail. Rather than providing such a reading here I wish to point out another of its elements that might have led Kant to the Newtonian analogy. As Newton had united apparently diverse phenomena in one single and simple order, Rousseau would link behavior where no-one before him had suspected connection. His description of our lives in civil society as a continual process of adaptation to slavery, from swaddling clothes to the coffin, is not merely a display of rhetorical talent.[37] To connect the state of perpetual war at the end of the second *Discourse* with the savage's development of *amour propre*, and these with the social institutions of eighteenth-century arts and sciences, was feat enough. To connect the teaching of a La Fontaine fable and the prattling of an incompetent nurse with the mechanisms through which tyrants accommodate us to unjust authority, may have seemed no less astonishing than the explanation of terrestrial and celestial motion by the same laws. It will be difficult for post-Rousseaueans to be *surprised* by such connections, and we may well be inclined to dispute any particular set of them. I submit, however, that few of us can better appreciate the force of Pope's verse: "Nature and nature's laws lay hid in night / God said, 'Let Newton be,' and all was light."[38]

Recall that the premise which allows Rousseau both to formulate the problem of evil and a solution to it is a simple one: if we are "the authors of all our misfortunes," we ourselves must be able to remove them.[39] A natural, though not strictly necessary precision of this claim, is the idea that the very forces that led to our downfall could be the sources of salvation.[40] Important here is not merely the idea that a natural cure is the only sort that will be effective, but the only kind in keeping with the most general aim of Rousseau's writing on this score – namely, vindicating the goodness of creation as God made it by demonstrating the goodness of its most problematic element. A God who allowed our natural faculties to lead us into disaster, then required a miracle to get us out of it, is just not as good as one who gave us the means to repair what we have damaged. For Rousseau God is not only blameless, but all the more praiseworthy, for having given us faculties that allow us to undo the corruption just as naturally as to cause it – and indeed, he suggests at several points, provide us with a firmer foundation for virtue than the original innocence with which we began.[41]

Now at least as early as Augustine, traditional theology had an argument to absolve God of the responsibility of the moral evil rampant in His creation. Loving humankind so deeply that He chose to give us the dignity of a free will, He cannot be blamed if we chose to abuse it. Here one may wonder: just what does Rousseau contribute to the discussion of the problem of evil that was unavailable in the classic free will defense? Metaphysically speaking, the answer is: nothing at all. Rousseau loves the free will defense, and appeals to it often in the "Creed."

Providence does not will the evil a man does in abusing the freedom it gives him. . . . To complain about God's not preventing man from doing evil is to complain about His having given him an excellent nature, about His having put in man's actions the morality which ennobles them, about His having given him the right to virtue.[42]

Formally, we might say, Rousseau's entire position is built on the free will defense. His contribution is not a metaphysical one, but can provide some response to metaphysics – if indirectly, by shifting ground – because the details of his position leave it less open to the trenchant objections raised against earlier ones.[43]

Classically, the free will defense was coupled with a notion of original sin: moral evil was introduced into a world created by a benevolent God through one wrong free choice (which then, on most accounts, also introduced physical evil – pain and death – as its consequence). Of the many problems which this account may raise, one should concern us here: its explanatory power is limited to that available to myth. Like any myth, it may illuminate something crucial in our experience – indeed Voltaire, despite a strong anti-Christian bias, found the myth of the Fall more revealing than accounts that tried to do without it. Yet like any myth, it gives us no clear directions for how to go on. The light it may throw on pieces of our experience is diffuse, leaving us without guidelines for interpretation. The detail given by Rousseau, by contrast, is that of both experiment and manual. Evil was introduced into a good world through processes easy to follow, and it can be abolished by anyone willing to study "nature's language."[44] *Emile* is, notoriously, a work which conflates – or transcends – genres. In addition to the clear poetic strands of the work, it can also be read as an instance of the procedure on which modern science was based, namely, the investigation of general processes by performing single experiments on particular cases which are used to display universal laws.[45] (Here Rousseau's repeated emphasis that Emile is an ordinary, "average" boy is crucial.) Without *Emile*, it might be argued that despite a difference in amount of detail, the account of the Fall in the second *Discourse* is just as mythic as that in Genesis. But we do have *Emile*, which contains not just repeated assertion of the natural goodness of our faculties, but explicit instruction in how to cultivate them.

It is fruitless to seek in Rousseau the sort of systematic account of human faculties that Kant would develop, but he does offer insightful discussion of two faculties which develop relatively late in human history: human reason and, important but less centrally, human sexuality. To summarize, most briefly: both are natural faculties subject to the distortion that leads to the worst sorts of abuse described in both *Dis-*

courses. Both can be used to reverse those evils, and Rousseau suggests they must be, if we are to become, individually and collectively, self-determining adults.

Reason gives us the capacity for self-knowledge, the importance and difficulty of which is stressed as early as the second *Discourse*, and runs throughout Rousseau's work. It is crucial for understanding Rousseau's answer to the problem of evil. For although it is reason that engenders vanity[46] it is the inability to see oneself without the representation of others which perpetuates it. Self-knowledge, therefore, is the only thing that can save us. Knowledge of the species, of what is essential to the nature which has been altered, is required of us as a group; knowledge of our own true needs, a task demanding constant vigilance, is required to resist the development of vanity, which undermines all individual efforts toward virtue. Here Rousseau provides his own answer to the first *Discourse*. There he had concluded that one had to be a Socrates in order to avoid the corruptions of the sciences; now one need only be an Emile. Of all human faculties, Rousseau believes reason to develop latest, and with most difficulty.[47] Its cultivation, therefore, should follow nature's course. Emile will be given no books at all until he is 12, but by the age of 18 he will have become a philosopher.[48] At issue in education is whether a process collaborates with or disfigures nature;[49] never are we told simply to let it be. Left on his own, the child will recapitulate the savage's history, for the savage's innocence is as vulnerable as his isolation. Emile's ultimate goal is not independence from other people, but from their reflection as constitutive of his sense of self-worth. To make this distinction, however, a degree of self-knowledge is required that cannot be acquired without reflection. What is learned, thereby, is our own true nature; but few knew better than Rousseau how much effort this is to learn.[50]

Like reason, sexuality is a natural force which, left unguided, can lead to disaster, but rightly cultivated, can be a means of redemption. The birth of sexuality is the point at which everything becomes precarious, because it requires other human beings as nothing else does. The possibilities for domination and submission it contains are so great that it could be the downfall of everything, and at one point in the *Discourse* Rousseau suggests that it was. Humankind faltered at its adolescence; Emile must be carefully guided through his. Rousseau holds the transition to be so crucial that he describes adolescence as a second birth: "We are, so to speak, born twice: once to exist and once to live; once for our species and once for our sex."[51]

In the second *Discourse*, sexual desire provides the original motive for entering society and the urge to distinguish oneself that leads to initial inequality. But consider the alternative to the birth of vanity that takes place in the first society he there describes. Without the attempt to distinguish himself from his rivals in the search to obtain the desire of the one he himself prefers, the savage's sexual behavior is but animal caprice. In the transition from animal to human sexuality is a structure of desire that implies preference, distinction, and thereby struggle. Rousseau's goal is not to eliminate that struggle but to direct it: by using the desire to be preferred by his beloved that Emile will experience, he can realize ideals that no other object could produce. Moreover, Rousseau holds sexual desire to provide the connection between self-interest and morality that could form the surest ties of civil society. The bonds between men and women are more natural than the sociability posited by the *philosophes*, deeper than the mutual self-interest offered by earlier social contract theories. Rousseau's discussion focuses on the importance of developing the natural through the ideal. Emile's transition to manhood will be accompanied by every sort of reflection on this score. No longer self-sufficient, he needs poetry, history, religion, and philosophy.[52] With these, he can safely seek the woman with whom he will become a free adult, and found a civil society.

Having shown us the conditions of the possibility of natural goodness in the first three books of *Emile*, Rousseau can return to the traditional problem of evil in the fourth. The progress of the reader mirrors that which Emile himself undergoes: having been safely brought to an independent sense of self, he can consider philosophical and religious questions; having seen that this is possible, so can we.

III

How does the account sketched thus far answer the objections of Alfonso, as Kant was convinced it did? Recall that Rousseau needs to fulfill, at the outset, two very different sorts of tasks. First, he confirms that there is a genuine problem that traditional theodicy fails to address.[53] The evils described by the *philosophes* satirizing or excoriating the optimists are not imaginary: indeed, the *philosophes* themselves are corrupt in ways they cannot yet fathom, miserable in ways they do not yet sense. Human life, in society, is indeed solitary, poor, nasty, brutish, and short.

Yet acknowledgment of those evils does not require the sort of intellectual abnegation that commonly accompanied it, from Bayle to Voltaire. Here Kant was surely right to see beyond Rousseau's disappointment with social practices of science and the paeans to sentiment a deep-seated rationalism that, curiously enough, put him at odds both with traditional orthodoxy and the *philosophes* who opposed it. Forced to confront head-on the problem of evil, both threw up their hands: the one for miracles, the other for the cold comforts of general skepticism and, perhaps, limited improvements to a circumscribed garden. Against them Rousseau will insist that acknowledging just how far this world is from the best of all possible ones is not the end but the beginning of inquiry.

Now the inquiry undertaken by Rousseau can be described as psychological and political, in the very broadest of senses. As such, it can seem to miss the very question posed by the problem of evil: how can we understand the existence of terrible suffering in a world created by a benevolent and omnipotent God? Rather than addressing this question directly, except in conventional terms, Rousseau devotes his attention to explaining one particular sort of suffering, the fact that innocent beings are often at the mercy of their crueler fellow creatures. And this may seem to be not only an evasion of the issue at hand, but a gross confusion of the domains of the metaphysical and the empirical. I will not speculate on the degree to which Rousseau may have suffered from what we should here call creative confusion; but Kant most certainly did not. As so often in the history of philosophy, he made a series of extremely helpful distinctions that had been lacking in earlier discussions of the problem.

His essay on theodicy identifies three kinds of *Zweckwidrigkeit*.[54] The first, moral evil, is *Zweckwidrigkeit schlechthin*, which no wisdom could possibly will either as means or as end; the second, conditional *Zweckwidrigkeit*, physical suffering, is explainable, under certain circumstances, as a means. (Here the standard examples about pain serving as a means to self-preservation will suffice.) Now all discussions of the subject had made the distinction between moral and physical evils, and seen the need for offering wholly different kinds of response to account for the existence of each.[55] They failed, however, to distinguish between these and what Kant would call the third kind of *Zweckwidrigkeit*, namely, the disproportion between the first two. The fact that moral and physical evils have no intelligible connection – that it is, very often, wicked people who thrive while righteous people suffer – is the intractable question. (The Leibnizian form of failure to make this distinction is simply to deny the existence of the third form of *Zweckwidrigkeit* and to maintain that all physical evils are punishments for moral evils, whether or not we can understand the connections in any detail. God knows what offense Job committed, if we do not.)

The demand to understand the third form of *Zweckwidrigkeit* is a metaphysical demand, one whose fulfillment would require a complete explanation of the world as a whole. (Although no attempt at theodicy ever assumes that we are actually in a position to give such an explanation, all seem to rely on the conceptual coherence of the possibility thereof. Like the demand for certain kinds of epistemological grounding that tacitly rely on a notion of intellectual intuition, theodicy fails to state the conditions of its own possibility.) It finds its fullest expression in Hegel, who would reinterpret the assertion of Providence as the claim that "reason governs the world," and describe his own investigation as a continuation of Leibniz's theodicy (using categories less "abstract and indeterminate" than those of Leibniz, of course). Hegel describes the goal of his philosophy of world history as

a knowledge of the affirmative side of history, in which the negative is reduced to a subordinate position and transcended altogether. In other words, we must first of all know what the ultimate design of the world really is, and secondly, we must see that this design has been realized and that evil has not been able to maintain a position of equality beside it.[56]

I will return to those consequences of such a view that must be unacceptable to Rousseau or Kant. For the moment, it should be clear that, from a Kantian viewpoint, the very project of theoretical comprehension of the third sort of *Zweckwidrigkeit* would require an external perspective on the world that is available, at most, to God.

Yet the other kinds of *Zweckwidrigkeit* may prove less intransigent. Conditional *Zweckwidrigkeit* may be explained by the standard appeal to the need for continuity in natural law. We don't want a world in which the law of gravity may be suddenly suspended to spare the owner of a fragile vase chagrin, and meteorological predictions overthrown to prevent rain on the picnic of the person who prayed the hardest.[57] As human understanding progresses to uncover more of the order existing in the world, we may well find that the genuine cause for wonder is the scope and extent of natural law. Something like Kant's own essays on the Lisbon earthquake could be enough to account for the existence of conditional evils.[58] Leibnizian arguments cannot answer the question of why an altruistic traveler, rather than an intransigent thug, happens to die in a particular earthquake.[59] This, as Kant rightly saw later, belongs to the third sort of *Zweckwidrigkeit*, and both Leibnizians and their accusers were mistaken in confusing this sort with the other two. Yet Leibnizian kinds of argument may well be enough to satisfy our demands to understand why earthquakes happen at all. Here Newton, standing in for all the achievement and promise of natural science, does rebuke Alfonso.

What about the first sort of *Zweckwidrigkeit*, unconditional or moral evil? It is just this sort of evil that most demands a philosophical account. Because it is suited to no purpose whatsoever, thwarting all other purposes, unexplained moral evil seems to leave an abyss in the heart of Creation itself.[60] Insofar as Rousseau has provided such an account, he has given a description of the order in human nature comparable to the description Newton provided of the order in the physical world. By showing that the moral evils we experience arise through a set of comprehensible processes, he not only shows them to be malleable, but stills a part of the despair and confusion that may arise from acknowledging them. As we come to accept certain forms of physical evil as following from the laws of natural science, and use the laws of science themselves to mitigate their worst effects, so we can understand moral evils as the products of particular historical developments and use the laws of social psychology to undo them. As the progress of science gives us protection against the unpredictability of nature, the capacity for reflection on our own history allows us to resist evil by protecting ourselves against what seemed hitherto random manifestations. As crucial as these features of Rousseau's account are, they are less important than another one: through that account, our commitment to rationality itself is strengthened. It is no longer the case that the sheer existence of moral and physical evils threatens the notion of a benevolent and powerful God and the comprehensibility of His Creation. An account can be given of each. After this account is completed, there is still something left unexplained – as indeed there should be, if philosophy is not to become mere apology. But it is no longer the basic stuff of Creation that threatens to remain fundamentally mysterious. Though this does not give us the statement of a thoroughgoing universal order that would be provided by a successful theodicy, it does show us the intelligibility of the components of such an order. There remains an unresolved and unresolvable question about the relations among the elements of Creation, but the elements themselves are basically sound. In this way Kant could view Rousseau's discussion of the moral problem of evil to be a direct contribution to the cosmological one.

If God is justified after Newton and Rousseau, it will not be in a form that traditional theodicies had expected – whether or not this was clear to the pre-Critical author of these lines. The general marks of Kant's critical method should be familiar here. Having defined a problem precisely, he shows which pieces of it are accessible to theoretical reason and assigns those to the domain of empirical science. Demarcating the limits of reason may allow us to understand more than we thought: if, for example, Rousseau is correct, we can provide an account of the existence of moral evil where none existed before. It will also, invariably, show that certain things are beyond our own understanding; in particular, we cannot explain the relationship between physical and moral evils. Here Leibniz's use of the figure of Alfonso confused the perspectives of science and metaphysics. Although the extension of knowledge may enlighten us in many ways, nothing Newton could have taught Alfonso will help on this score. But traditional philosophy was wholly mistaken in attempting to treat the third form of *Zweckwidrigkeit* as a theoretical problem: not only is it resolvable only from a perspective that is necessarily unavailable to us; the impulse that leads us to address this relationship cannot appropriately be stilled by metaphysics.

Our inability to understand the relationship between moral and physical evils can be taken as an instance of the claim that there is a gap between reason and nature. But this, for Kant, is simply a statement of fact (we might call it *the* metaphysical fact of the Critical Philosophy) and one that requires precise acknowledgment.[61] Here a practical, not theoretical, solution is the only appropriate one, and we begin to near what I take to be the most conceptually difficult aspect of the problem of evil itself, namely, a form so peculiar that it threatens its very right to be called a problem at all. For formulated in one way it isn't an intellectual problem at all but a simple statement of fact: the world contains instances of terrible evil. Alternatively, it can be given the form of a problem, but then it seems to have no possible answer that adequately acknowledges the facts it was meant to explain. We can best see this, again, by returning to Hegel, whose discussion of philosophy as theodicy entails two conclusions that must be unacceptable to any Kantian. The two fit together, if not quite by implication: "Reason cannot stop to consider the injuries sustained by single individuals, for particular ends are submerged in the universal end."[62] "To return to the true Ideal, the Ideal of Reason itself, philosophy should help us to understand that the actual world is as it ought to be."[63] For Leibniz as for Hegel, particular sufferings are more than irrelevant; if part of a whole that is as it ought to be, they too are not only justifiable but – in some never to be explicated sense – right as well. For Kant as for Rousseau, particular sufferings are crucial, reminding us of the ever-present gap between what is actual and what ought to be. *We should not even try to solve the problem of evil*, if solving it means eliminating that gap through the brute force of denial. After Rousseau and Newton, something is missing, but the urge to supply it cannot be satisfied by any of the forms available to metaphysics.

The denial implicit in traditional theodicy seems to trade on an ambivalence between the claims that (1) there is no genuine evil and (2) certain evils are necessary for the good of the universe as a whole.[64] In rejecting both these claims Rousseau, like Kant, would make others which appear initially similar. The teleological history provided in the *Discourse*, and its counterpart in *Emile*, show that the development through evil was more or less inevitable in the process of development to stable, self-reflected moral maturity. (In a parallel story in his "Conjectural Beginning of Human History," Kant tells us that reason was born with the expulsion from Eden.) Clearly, there are traces here of the classical attempt to find a meaning in the existence of evil, but Rousseau's second type of response makes the relevant difference clear. This response would also be adopted and refined by Kant: if evil is knowable while God is not, the only morally legitimate response to the problem of evil is to reject attempts at theodicy and devote our efforts to the practical task of abolishing what evil is within our reach. Rousseau connects these responses in a way that illuminates their distinction from classical theodicy. The first, teleological response is required to sustain our hope that the practical response is viable. If history is, as Bayle put it, simply an unbroken record of the "crimes and misfortunes of the human race," attempts to halt the decline will seem merely quixotic. Without some assumptions about the natural goodness of humankind, and the ways in which it (at least potentially) may have developed through a series of painful historical processes to a more free and reasonable state, we cannot have confidence in our efforts to contribute to that development. Thus Rousseau's teleological account can be seen to ground his practical one. But here it is crucial that Rousseau's teleological history, unlike that of a traditional theodicy, does not purport to give us knowledge of a universal and harmonious plan, but rather a discussion of possibility.[65] In so doing, Rousseau seeks to provide the basis for hope; the aim of theodicy, by contrast, is patience.

Thus it is not surprising that Rousseau's position could seem unsatisfactory – and may even have run counter to some of his own aims. Paradoxically, though Rousseau's desire to justify Providence against writers like Voltaire was clearly genuine, those traditional powers that finally banned his work were not wholly mistaken in accusing him of irreligion. Naturalism has consequences. The Creator, having formed us, is as absent in the *Emile* as he is in the second *Discourse*. God is benevolent, but we do not need Him. For both Newton and Rousseau, mapping the order of the universe may have been intended as a demonstration of God's glory, but this turns out not to be the point at issue. In the end, it is less God that Rousseau has vindicated than the practice of philosophy – and philosophically informed politics.

But does Rousseau in fact provide an answer to Voltaire's charge that the Lisbon earthquake subverts philosophical discussion? Everything depends on what we mean by philosophy. Recall that Voltaire's most damning claim against philosophical optimism concerned its most pessimistic implications: its demonstration that evils are necessary violates the sense of justice that produced the questions it was meant to answer. The consequence, for Voltaire, is that any philosophical explanation is worse than none at all. For if explanation proceeds with the goal of displaying that "reason rules the world" it seems to require us, with Hegel, to ignore "the injuries sustained by particular individuals" in the race to show that "the actual world is as it ought to be." Forced to choose between understanding and justice, some of us will prefer to remain in the dark. We may not go as far as Voltaire in concluding, by contrast, that "the world exists to drive us mad,"[66] but it is not through philosophy that we will seek a resolution between the claims of morality and those of nature.

Rousseau's attempt to show that some kinds of evil are both understandable and avoidable is a demonstration that philosophical explanation need not issue in the claims of necessity and the denials of justice that Voltaire rightly shuns. Even further: what Rousseau offers is not simply the possibility of an account; embedded in that account is a defense of philosophy itself as a process of acquiring the self-knowledge that will thwart the development of that vanity through which moral evils arise. Prior to becoming a man, Emile will become a philosopher.[67] Of course, in offering such a demonstration Rousseau offers no direct response to Lisbon.[68] Voltaire's attack on philosophy works on the conflation between the three kinds of *Zweckwidrigkeit* that characterized pre-Kantian discussions of the problem. The defense provided by Kant and Rousseau proceeds not only by clarification: through this clarification, the framework of the questions themselves will be changed. Progress in philosophy, as in history itself, is not always straightforward.

NOTES

My debt to John Rawls is greater than I can adequately acknowledge. Perhaps most importantly, he provides an example of the ways in which ideas and ideals can be kept alive through the study of the history of philosophy. I am immeasurably grateful for his continuing encouragement. For extremely helpful comments on an earlier draft of this paper I am indebted to Gideon Freudenthal, Eli Friedlander, Irad Kimhi, Christine Korsgaard, and Andrews Reath.

1. I. Kant, *Gesammelte Schriften* (Berlin: de Gruyter, 1902), XX: 58.12–59.3. References to Kant will be to volume and page number in the Akademie-Ausgabe of *Kants Gesammelte Schriften*, followed by the page in translation if the translation does not include the Akademie paging. References to Rousseau are to the following editions:

The First and Second Discourses together with the Replies to Critics, trans. and ed. Victor Gourevitch (New York: Harper and Row, 1986); this volume will be referred to as *Discourses*

Emile or: On Education, trans. and ed. Allan Bloom (New York: Basic Books, 1979)

The Confessions, trans. J. M. Cohen (Harmondsworth: Penguin, 1953)

2. Cassirer's discussion of the note in his *The Question of Jean-Jacques Rousseau* (Bloomington: Indiana University Press, 1975) is the most important exception to this claim, and I follow his account of it on many points. The note is dated at 1763 and is therefore, of course, pre-Critical. Much contemporary Kant scholarship is devoted to exploring the relations between the Critical and pre-Critical writings and to questioning the traditional belief in a sharp division between Kant's early and mature work. Two texts that examine those relations in questions related to the present topic are Richard Velkley's *Freedom and the Ends of Reason* (Chicago: University of Chicago Press, 1989) and Christoph Schulte's "Zweckwidriges in der Erfahrung," *Kant-Studien* 82(4) (1991): 371–96. In one form or another, the problem of evil was a focus of Kant's attention through all three *Critiques* as well as in popular writings from, at least, the three essays on earthquakes (1756) to "Über das Misslingen aller philosophischen Versuche in der Theodicee" (1791) and "Das Ende aller Dinge" (1794). It would be silly to deny a development in Kant's views during the forty years he devoted to these questions, but my purpose in this essay is not to trace it. Rather, in trying to understand how he read Rousseau – whose work concerned Kant throughout his life – I draw upon all of Kant's work in order to present the most philosophically coherent position.

3. Here it should be noted that the eighteenth century refers to a set of topics as, variously, the problem of evil, the problem of optimism, the question of Providence, and the problem of theodicy. While these names reflect differences of emphasis, I will, for the purposes of this paper, take the complex of problems thus referred to as the same.

4. *Theodicy*, trans. E. M. Huggard, ed. Austin Farrar (Lasalle, Ill.: Open Court, 1985), p. 276.

5. Pierre Bayle, *Historical and Critical Dictionary*, ed. Burton Feldman (New York: Garland, 1984), "Castile."

6. *Theodicy*, p. 248.

7. See, for example, *Emile*, p. 278, and Kant, "Idee zu einer allgemeinen Geschichte in Weltbürgerliche Absicht," VIII: 30.

8. Leibniz seemed to deny the legitimacy of a request for more than this in writing:

> But it appears that M. Bayle asks a little too much: he wishes for a detailed exposition of how evil is connected with the best possible scheme for the universe. That would be a complete explanation of the phenomena, but I do not undertake to give it, nor am I bound to do so, for there is no obligation to do that which is impossible for us in our existing state. It is sufficient for me to point out that there is nothing to prevent the connection of a certain individual evil with what is the best on the whole. This incomplete explanation, leaving something to be discovered in the life to come, is sufficient for answering the objections, though not for a comprehension of the matter. (*Theodicy*, p. 214)

9. *Theodicy*, p. 227.
10. Most interesting among these is the Viennese philosopher Jean Améry; see especially his *Jenseits von Schuld und Sühne* (Stuttgart: Klett-Cotta, 1980) and *Über das Altern* (Stuttgart: Klett-Cotta, 1979). But see also Theodor Adorno, *Dialektik der Aufklärung* (Frankfurt-am-Main: Fischer Verlag, 1969) and *Negative Dialektik* (Frankfurt-am-Main: Suhrkamp, 1966), and Hannah Arendt, *The Life of the Mind* (New York: Harcourt, Brace, Jovanovitch, 1976).
11. It is of interest to note that even at the end of the eighteenth century, the most radical treatment of the problem of evil, that given by Sade, does not simply reject the argument from design but inverts it, taking the pervasiveness of evil in nature to be a cosmological argument for the existence of a malevolent God. See his *Juliette*, trans. Austryn Wainhouse (New York: Grove Weidenfeld, 1968).
12. Although I cannot argue for these claims at length in the present space, this essay is part of a longer study in progress that will explore the idea that the cosmological problem of evil is less directly theological than it appears, and examine the transformation of the various aspects of the problem of evil in modern philosophy.
13. "Observations by Jean-Jacques Rousseau of Geneva on the Answer to His Discourse," in *Discourses*, p. 36.
14. Although Rousseau was unfairly accused of primitivism by many people, including Voltaire, who wrongly understood his state of nature as a place we ought to return to, I take the following passages, among others, to show that there is something nevertheless right about the accusation.
15. In *The Portable Voltaire*, ed. Ben Ray Redman (New York: Viking Press, 1949).
16. *Correspondance complète de Jean-Jacques Rousseau*, vol. 4, ed. R. A. Leigh (Genève: Institut et Musée Voltaire, 1976) (unpublished translation by Trip McCrossin).
17. See, in particular, *Emile*, pp. 281–94.
18. "Letter to Philopolis," in *Discourses*, pp. 233–4.
19. *Confessions*, p. 399.
20. For a particularly biting example, see Kant's discussion in *Religion within the Limits of Reason Alone*, trans. T. M. Greene and H. H. Hudson (New York: Harper and Row, 1960) VI: 33/28. For Rousseau's critique of what he takes to have become an unscientific cliché, see the "Preface to *Narcissus*," *Discourses*, p. 106, and the second *Discourse*, Note 11.
21. It should be noted that both the *Discourse* and *Emile* are texts rich enough to be not simply open to a number of readings; each is clearly performing a variety of tasks as well. For a discussion of the way in which their accounts provide the groundwork for the political goals of the *Social Contract*, see Joshua Cohen, "The Natural Goodness of Humanity," this volume. My goal here is merely to show how they provide what Kant took to be an answer to the problem of evil.
22. See Neiman, *The Unity of Reason* (New York/Oxford: Oxford University Press, 1994), chap. 4, for further discussion of this claim and a general account of Kant's notion of practical faith.
23. "Über das Misslingen aller philosophischen Versuche in der Theodicee," VIII: 258.
24. See, for example, the claim that "Even the Holy One of the Gospel must first

be compared with our ideal of moral perfection before we can recognize him to be such" (*Groundwork of the Metaphysics of Morals*, IV: 409).

25. The exception to this is, of course, Newton's hypothesis that God's intervention is required to replace the quantity of momentum lost in the universe, but as early as Leibniz, this was criticized as an ad hoc explanation unbefitting the scientific character of the Newtonian system. I am indebted to Gideon Freudenthal for discussion of Kant's reading of Newton; see also his *Atom and Individual in the Age of Newton* (Dordrecht: Reidel, 1986), chapter 3.

26. Jean Starobinski, "The Discourse on Inequality," in *Jean-Jacques Rousseau: Transparency and Obstruction*, trans. Arthur Goldhammer (Chicago and London: University of Chicago Press, 1988), p. 290.

27. For a thorough account of that development, see Cohen, "The Natural Goodness of Humanity."

28. By contrast, the Holbachian materialism to which most of the Encyclopedists subscribed leads to fatalistic political consequences that Rousseau was concerned to avoid; so he noted that his religious principles were much more threatening to the Jesuit hierarchy than the atheism of his Parisian contemporaries. See Friedrich Tomberg, "Rousseaus Streit mit den Enzyklopädisten," unpublished manuscript, pp. 14–15.

29. *Jean-Jacques Rousseau: Transparency and Obstruction*, p. 20.

30. I am indebted to Irad Kimhi for clarifying this point.

31. In this context it is important that Rousseau insists that children's punishment should be arranged so as to follow this natural order. The only permissible punishment is that which occurs as a natural consequence of their wrong actions, though as always, the tutor is allowed to manage the natural order. ("Thus you will not declaim against lying; you will not precisely punish them for having lied; but you will arrange it so that all the bad effects of lying – such as not being believed when one tells the truth, of being accused of the evil that one did not do although one denies it – come in league against them when they have lied" [*Emile*, p. 101].)

32. *Discourse on the Origins of Inequality*, in *Discourses*, p. 174.

33. That the goal of Rousseau's work as a whole is a moral one seems incontestable; but the relationship between Rousseau's naturalism and his interpretation of moral categories requires further explication not provided in Rousseau nor, more surprisingly, in Kant. I do not know how far these relationships were simply left unexplored, and how much they reflect a real difference in Kant's and Rousseau's views on the development of evil – in particular, on the issue of the relationship between our capacity to choose evil, as described in *Religion within the Limits of Reason Alone*, and the social conditions that affect those powers of choice. One interesting way of exploring this question would be to examine, in detail, Kant's practical philosophy against the background of *Emile* – just as the theoretical philosophy has been fruitfully read as an attempt to provide the metaphysical foundations for Newtonian science.

34. As he answered in a reply to an objection that he had provided no suggestions for remedying the conditions he had described: "I am not unaware of the fact that once a man is dead one does not call the doctor" (*Discourses*, p. 30).

35. Even there, however, he denies that the force of the work is pessimistic: "I am always the monster who maintains that man is naturally good, and my adversaries are always the honest folk who, for the sake of public edification,

try to prove that nature made only scoundrels" ("Letter to Philopolis," in *Discourses*, p. 237).

36. Note Rousseau's claim that "one is more free under the social pact than in the state of nature" (*Emile*, p. 461). The text suggests that neither the savage nor the child can be genuinely free because neither has acquired a full self.

37. *Emile*, p. 42.

38. "Epigraph Intended for Sir Isaac Newton," *Poems of Alexander Pope*, Vol. 6: *Minor Poems*, ed. Normal Ault and John Butt (London: Methuen, 1954), p. 317.

39. Here, as is usual in Rousseau, the use of the plural is intentional. The responsible agent is a collective one; Rousseau does not mean to suggest the voluntaristic position that the individual could fully determine the world anew in the absence of the appropriate social conditions. Even Emile, of course, for all his isolation, is the product of a most precisely constructed social environment.

40. Starobinski calls this the idea of the antidote in the poison. See his *Blessings in Disguise; or, the Morality of Evil* (Cambridge: Harvard University Press, 1993), chap. 5.

41. Of course, the theological implications of this view proved responsible for the public burning of *Emile* and the exile of its author; for it follows that neither the Church nor even Christianity is required for salvation.

42. *Emile*, p. 281.

43. Of which Bayle's complaint that this defense left God's benevolence in doubt may be the most disturbing:

> If you join with those who come closest to exonerating providence, by saying that God did not at all foresee the Fall of Adam, you will gain very little; for at the very least he certainly knew that the first man ran the risk of losing his innocence and introducing into the world all the evils of punishment and guilt that followed his revolt. Neither his goodness, nor his holiness, nor his wisdom could allow that he risked these events; for our reason convinces us in a most evident manner that a mother, who would allow her daughters to go to a ball when she knew with certainty that they ran a great risk of losing their honor there, would show that she loved neither her daughters nor chastity. (Bayle, *Historical and Critical Dictionary*, "Paulicians")

44. *Emile*, p. 291.

45. This suggestion is made most explicit in the *Confessions*. For this question, and a discussion of different views on the relations between the *Confessions* and the *Emile*, see Christopher Kelly, *Rousseau's Exemplary Life: The "Confessions" as Political Philosophy* (Ithaca: Cornell University Press, 1987). The question is also discussed by Tomberg, "Rousseaus Streit mit den Enzyklopädisten."

46. *Discourses*, p. 162.

47. *Discourses*, p. 158; *Emile*, p. 89.

48. *Emile*, p. 315.

49. Ibid., pp. 254, 314.

50. In addition to the discussion of the question in the preface to the second *Discourse*, the *Confessions* stresses the difficulty often.

51. *Emile*, p. 211.

52. Rousseau often notes, but does not explicate, the relationship between the development of morality and that of sexuality: "If this were the place for it,

I would try to show how the first voices of conscience arise out of the first movements of the heart, and how the first notions of good and bad are born of the sentiments of love and hate. . . . It is sufficient for me to mark out the order and progress of our sentiments and our knowledge relative to our constitution. Others will perhaps demonstrate what I only indicate here" (*Emile*, p. 235). In this context, given the importance of the timing of Emile's growth to reflective maturity, it can hardly be accidental that Rousseau chose the name "Sophie" to designate Emile's beloved.

53. It could be argued that Rousseau too dismisses the problem, in leaving no room for radical, demonic evil. I cannot discuss here the adequacy of Rousseau's account of evil, which was challenged, at the latest, by Sade. It should be pointed out, however, that the insistence that evil is demonic is just the insistence that it remain fundamentally inexplicable – and this, of course, is what Rousseau is most concerned to deny.

54. According to Schulte, the word was coined by Kant, and it is extremely difficult to translate. The dictionary gives us "inappropriateness" and "unsuitableness." "Anti-purposiveness" would probably capture the sense of the term, which depends on the importance of purpose, or end, in Kant's work.

55. But on the instability of the distinction between moral and physical evils, see Shklar, *The Faces of Injustice* (New Haven: Yale University Press, 1990), chaps. 1 and 2.

56. G. W. F. Hegel, *Introduction to the Lectures on the Philosophy of World History*, trans. H. B. Nisbet (Cambridge University Press, 1975, 1980), p. 43.

57. *Theodicy*, p. 256.

58. In addition to appealing to the need for continuity of natural law and making several attempts to discover what laws underlie earthquakes in general, and their occurrence at particular times, Kant offers us the suggestion that earthquakes teach us that the human being "has no right to expect merely comfortable consequences from the natural laws that God has ordered, and he learns perhaps in this way the insight, that this *Tummelplatz* of his desires does not contain the goal of all his intentions." ("Geschichte und Naturbeschreibung der merkwürdigsten Vorfälle des Erdbebens, welche an dem Ende des 1755sten Jahres einen grossen Teil der Erde erschüttert hat," I: 430.)

59. Voltaire, *Candide*, trans. and ed. R. M. Adams (New York: Norton, 1991), chapter 4.

60. Kant's claim that radical evil rests on freedom and is, therefore, inscrutable, is not a claim that evil resists accountability in this sense (*Religion within the Limits of Reason Alone*, VI: 21–2/17, 25/20–1). Indeed, Rousseau could be viewed as providing Kant with a naturalistic account of freedom itself, in describing the conditions under which a child can grow to become a free man. That all acts which rest on freedom are not subject to *some* conditions of theoretical knowledge is, of course, a fundamental tenet of the Critical Philosophy. In this sense, the choice to do good is as mysterious as the choice to do evil. But for a different view, see Schmidt-Biggemann, "Geschichte der Erbsünde in der Aufklärung" in his *Theodizee und Tatsachen* (Frankfurt-am-Main: Suhrkamp, 1988).

61. See Neiman, "Understanding the Unconditioned," in *Proceedings of the Eighth International Kant Congress* (Milwaukee: Marquette University Press, 1995) for further discussion.

62. Hegel, *Introduction to the Lectures on the Philosophy of World History*, p. 43.
63. Ibid., p. 66.
64. This does turn God into a utilitarian, which would make such a solution unacceptable to Kant, and probably to Rousseau, even if nothing else did. I am grateful to Christine Korsgaard for pointing this out, and for helping me to clarify the questions in the following paragraph.
65. For further discussion see Neiman, *The Unity of Reason*, chapter 5, and Cohen, "The Natural Goodness of Humanity."
66. *Candide*, chapter 21.
67. I cannot resist asking which philosopher he will become. In the chapter following this reference, Rousseau tells us: "His aim is not to write books, and if he ever does, it will not be in order to pay court to the powers that be, but *to establish the rights of humanity*" (*Emile*, p. 458, emphasis added). The coincidence with Kant's most famous reference to Rousseau is hard to ignore.
68. At least by the time of *Emile*, Rousseau would acknowledge that no such response is possible; insofar as the question can be addressed, it will be in those parts of the "Creed" that foreshadow Kant's notion of rational faith.

Within the Limits of Reason

ONORA O'NEILL

The title of Kant's *Religion within the Limits of Reason Alone*[1] often seems at odds with the work itself. Hardly anything else that he wrote is so full of specificity, colour, and variety. It ranges across comparative religion, Scriptural exegesis, the nature of evil, the destiny of mankind, and church governance; it is full of wry comments on sects and superstitions, on religious follies and excesses. And yet it is never dismissive about the claims of popular religion. How can this exuberant work be thought to lie "within the limits of reason"? The title might seem appropriate to the restrained tone of the passages on the Postulates of Pure Practical Reason towards the end of the *Critique of Practical Reason*, but not to the baroque structure and texture of the *Religion*.

On reflection, I believe that a large part of the difficulty in making sense of Kant's choice of title for this work is that we remain surprisingly unclear about his conception of reason. This is surprising because the theme of reason is surely at the centre of Kant's work. Yet many discussions of his work investigate the role of reason in cognition or in morality, or even in the task of connecting the two, but seem to avoid direct questions about what reason is and how its authority may be vindicated, and even relatively guarded questions about what Kant's account of reason is and how he thinks it can be vindicated.

There are good reasons for this caution. We are all familiar with the problem that a vindication of reason – surely the fundamental task of a critique of reason – seems to be in principle impossible. Any supposed vindication must, it seems, either presuppose principles of reason or rely on principles that are avowedly not those of reason: in either case it fails. As a poor third option an attempted vindication of reason might lead into an unending regress, in which case failure would be postponed, but so too would vindication. On a certain foundationalist conception of what it would be to vindicate reason, the task is surely impossible.

However, Kant does not shirk the task of providing an account of the authority of reason. Rather he offers a vindication of reason that is, as I read it, definitively anti-foundationalist. I believe that an account of this conception of reason can be helpful in understanding the sense in which his conception of religion may be said to be "within the limits of reason". In this essay I offer no more than a compressed account of the Kantian vindication of reason, and will then use this to try to shed light on some aspects of *Religion within the Limits of Reason Alone*. There is much more to be said both about Kant's account of reason and about its authority than I can say here; I have tried to say some of it elsewhere.[2] I believe that there is also much more to be said about the implications of Kant's conception of reason for his views on religion and specifically on reasoned hope: this essay is only a beginning.

I. Kant's Vindication of Reason

In the Prefaces of the *Critique of Pure Reason* Kant offers an account not of the *principles* but of the *predicaments* of human reasoners. The capacities for organizing our thinking and acting which lie to hand prove unreliable:

[Reason] begins from principles whose use in the course of experience is unavoidable and thereby well established . . . and yet through this it falls into darkness and contradiction. (*KrV*, AK 3 and 4: Avii–viii)

There is no prospect of discerning the principles of reason by a Cartesian *inspectio mentis*; reason does not lie "whole and complete in each of us".[3] Still worse, the iterated use of even the most ordinary procedures of what we take to be reason leads us into the cognitive shipwreck of the antinomies. It seems both that we need and that we cannot find a vindication of reason: it would hardly be an exaggeration to say that the *frustrations* of reason are the keynote of the prefaces of the *Critique of Pure Reason*.

Nevertheless we have to begin with these inadequate capacities. Since we cannot expect to intuit or discover the principles of reason, either we must forego reasoning or we must see establishing principles of reason as a *task*, as something that those who begin with inadequate capacities to reason must *construct* or *plan*.

Although Kant often speaks of the "task of reason", or "plan of reason" in the Prefaces of the *Critique of Pure Reason*, he does not undertake the task systematically until far on in the text, at the beginning of the *Doctrine* of *Method*. In its remarkable opening passage he suggests (after 700 taxing pages!) that the task of critique of reason remains far from complete:

it can be said that in the *Transcendental Doctrine of Elements* we have made an estimate of the materials, and have determined for what sort, height and strength of building they will suffice. Although we had in mind a tower that would reach the heavens, it turned out that the stock of materials was only enough for a house [*Wohnhaus*], – one just roomy enough for our tasks on the plain of experience and just high enough for us to look across the plain. The bold undertaking had to come to nothing for lack of materials, let alone the babel of tongues that unavoidably set workers against one another and scattered them across the earth, each to build separately following his own design. Our problem is not just to do with materials, but even more to do with the plan. Since we have been warned not to risk everything on a favourite but senseless project, which could perhaps exceed our entire resources, yet we need to erect a solid house, so must build taking due account of the supplies that we have been given and of our needs. (*KrV*, 3 and 4: A707/B735)

The task then is to identify the "plan of reason". Yet just this is what seems initially impossible if foundationalist strategies cannot be used. How could one plan, rather than another, acquire the unrestricted authority that anything that can count as the "plan of reason" must have? Yet if nothing at all could be said about the plan of reason, then, as the passage quoted makes very clear, the whole gigantic labour of the *Doctrine of Elements* has supplied no more than an "inventory of materials" and has established no definite conclusions.

In the immediately following short section, titled simply *The Discipline of Pure Reason*, Kant maintains that the unruly and inadequate capacities with which human reasoners set out need disciplining:

But where, as in the case of pure reason, we find a whole system of deceptions and illusions, which are interconnected and united under shared principles [cf. the antinomies], then it seems that a wholly underivative and specifically negative law-giving is required [*da scheint eine ganz eigene und zwar negative Gesetzgebung erforderlich zu sein*] which in the name of a discipline erects a system of precautions and self-examination out of the nature of reason and of the objects of its pure use. (*KrV*, 3 and 4: A711/B739)

Apparently the discipline of reason is simply a matter of adhering to "*eine ganz eigene und zwar negative Gesetzgebung.*"

What Kant characterizes in one metaphor as a *plan* that can be followed by workers who would otherwise lack coordination, and in another as a *law-giving* (*legislation* in many translations) that is "wholly underivative and yet negative" – that is, neither derived from some other "authority" nor having determinate content – is simply the well known demand that thinking and acting be guided by principles that have the *form* of law, yet are not heteronomous – that is, do not presuppose some other, "alien" authority. In effect the discipline of reason is to reject as arbitrary any principle that could not be adopted by all. This demand is *wholly underivative* because it does not derive its authority from any supposed but unvindicated authority, such as a creed or dogma, a tradition or a consensus. It is correspondingly *negative* because it enjoins the rejection of any content that might be derived from such spurious authorities. Nevertheless this discipline is not trivial because it is a *law-giving*: it demands that action be on principles, and specifically on principles that could be adopted by all.

In the familiar formulation that Kant offers of this meagre supreme principle of reason for the domain of action, practical reason demands simply: *"act only on that maxim through which you can at the same time will that it be a universal law"* (*G*, AK IV: 421). The same meagre demand for lawfulness without a law-giver is presented as the basic principle for the theoretical use of reason in *What Is Orientation in Thinking?*, where Kant asserts:

To employ one's own reason means simply to ask oneself, whenever one is urged to accept something, whether one finds it possible to transform the reason for accepting it, or the rule which follows from what is accepted, into a universal principle governing the use of one's reason. (*WH*, VIII: 146–7n; 249n)

A great deal of further evidence can be given to show that this modest principle is *all* that Kant offers as the *supreme* principle of reason. A great many further questions can be asked about its relation to *subordinate* principles of reason, such as the Categories of the Understanding, the Ideas of Reason, and the Postulates of Pure Practical Reason and the various principles of logic, of duty, or of reasoned hope and the extent to which reason determines or underdetermines what can be known, what ought to be done, or what may be hoped. For present purposes, however, it is only the *constructive* rather than *foundational* character of the vindication of reason that is of concern. On this I offer four rather general comments.

First, it is clear that this vindication of reason is anti-foundationalist. Kant does not seek – let alone find – axioms of reason. We know from *The Discipline of Pure Reason in its Dogmatic Use* that he thinks that philosophy lacks definitions and axioms, that it cannot be done *more geometrico*, and moreover that geometry and mathematics in general cannot be done *more analytico*. Kant's starting point is rather the unsatisfactory character of daily attempts at reasoning: for him the starting point of inquiry is the *problem*, and not any *foundation* or *axioms* for its solution.

Second, Kant's vindication of reason is avowedly circular, in the sense that he quite deliberately identifies the vindication of reason with a *reflexive* process. Reasoners begin with whatever unreliable capacities for organizing thinking and action they find to hand (which they proleptically speak of as capacities to reason), but they can then use these capacities reflexively to identify less treacherous principles for orienting thought and action. This reflexive process can be used to construct the supreme principle of relying only on those principles which others too can adopt. Reasoning once disciplined in this way will have the twin Kantian hallmarks of rejecting any "alien" authority, yet insisting on lawfulness (more strictly translated *lawlikeness*; compare *eine Gesetzgebung*). Put more abstractly, it will neither assume arbitrary starting points nor jump to arbitrary conclusions.

Third, this process of emergence of more reliable capacities to reason has begun and is continuing among a plurality of incipiently reasoning beings, in whom no fully adequate principles of reasoning have been preinscribed. Since more adequate standards of reason emerge through this process gradually, reason has a *history*, which it does not for foundationalists. Moreover, the reflexive process in which reason is best developed is best embodied in *public* discussion, and the private use of reason is to be seen as a limited rather than as the central case – contrary to the view that we might expect from foundationalists, and find in Descartes.[4]

Fourth, there are no reasons to think that this vindication of reason will fully determine the final shape of some edifice of knowledge, will provide a fully determinate guide to action, or will determine a unique configuration of what we may reasonably hope. The emergence of standards of reason may yield algorithms neither for knowledge nor for morality – nor for their connection. Rather it may yield constraints upon all three.

II. Reasoned Religion

When we turn to the text of *Religion within the Limits of Reason Alone* the most obvious strategy for interpreting the claim that this is a work "within the limits of reason" would be this. We could first emphasize Kant's claims to give an account of "moral religion", and then we could use an account of the vindication of reason, such as that just given, to explain why in Kant's view the supreme principle of morality is indeed a principle of reason, and conclude that an account of moral religion stays within the "limits of reason". I do not think this account would be mistaken, but it seems to me that there is a great deal that it leaves unexplained about the strategy, let alone the details, of the text.

In *Religion within the Limits of Reason Alone* Kant adheres to this view, but he does not explicitly discuss the place of religion within the critical enterprise which he had presented in earlier works. On that account religion is to bridge the gap between the critical accounts of nature and of freedom, and is to do so by offering an account of a possible future.[5] This account of the future is guided by Kant's third question – "What may I hope?" – and so is quite different from conceptions of reasoned religion which are based on claims about knowledge. For Deists, and for certain other rational theologians, we may hope for the best of all possible futures because we have a cognitive demonstration that this is the best of all possible worlds, created by a beneficent Deity. In those conceptions, the claims of rational religion and specifically about human destiny are cognitive claims. For Kant they are claims – Postulates – that link cognition and morality. Kant understands a Postulate of reasoned hope as "a theoretical but not theoretically provable proposition . . . in so far as it is indissolubly dependent on an a priori unconditionally valid practical law" (*KpV*, AK 5: 122).

These thoughts carry us towards an understanding of a sense in which the Postulates of Pure Practical Reason in the *Critique of Practical Reason* might be thought to constitute a religion "within the limits of reason". However, quite apart from the question of the validity of the arguments for the postulates, the discussion of the Postulates in the *Critique of Practical Reason* seems in one central respect simply illdesigned to provide an answer to the question "What may I hope?". For although the question is framed as *permissive*, the postulates are formulated as *requirements* on reasoned hope: the argument for the existence of God ends with the words "it is morally necessary to assume the existence of God" (*KpV*, AK 5: 125).[6] Both the postulate of immortality and that of the existence of God appear to offer answers not to the question "What may I hope?" but to the narrower and more demanding question "What must I hope?"

It may be that reflection on the modalities of these claims can shed some light on the connections, and the differences, between the *Critique of Practical Reason* and *Religion within the Limits of Reason Alone*. An answer to the question "What must I hope?" would presumably restrict, but not fully determine, an answer to the question "What may I hope?" For it may be the case that a number of different answers to the second question will all fall within the constraints set by an answer to the first.[7] If this is the case, then the austere – if highly controversial – claims of the *Critique of Practical Reason* can provide at most the beginnings of an answer to the question "What may I hope?" The difference between the tone and texture of argument of the two works may perhaps be clarified by the hypothesis that in *Religion within the Limits of Reason Alone* Kant hopes to articulate not only what we *must* but also more ambitiously what we *may* hope, and that he will show how and why a work that claims to investigate religion "within the limits of reason" can be so largely preoccupied with a specifically Christian inflection of reasoned hope.

III. The Authority to Interpret Scripture

At various points in *Religion within the Limits of Reason Alone* Kant repudiates claims to be undertaking Scriptural exegesis. For example, at the end of the First Book, just after extensive commentary on the Adamic myths, and just before his discussion of the life of Christ, he insists rather surprisingly that

what is written here must not be read as though intended for Scriptural exegesis, which lies beyond the limits of the domain of bare reason. (*R*, AK 6, V: 47n, 39n)

The remark has to be taken in context, and that context is made clear not only in later sections of *Religion within the Limits of Reason Alone* but above all in Kant's discussion of the competences of the several university faculties in his almost contemporary *Conflict of the Faculties*. Here Kant emphasizes the radical division of labour between the "higher" faculties of theology, law, and medicine and the "lower" faculty of philosophy:

So the biblical theologian . . . draws his teaching not from reason but from the *Bible*; . . . As soon as one of these faculties presumes to mix with its teachings something it treats as derived from reason, it offends against the authority of the government that issues orders through it. (*SF*, AK 7: 23; 35)

Kant's remarks in the immediately following section on the *Distinctive Characteristic of the Theology Faculty* (*SF*, AK 7: 23–4; 35–36) restrict rather than extend its competence. The biblical theologian cannot demonstrate that the Bible is the word of God, cannot claim that any human interpretation has divine authority, and may not appeal to reason, which challenges all authorities and so would end by bringing down Church authority on which theology itself depends. The biblical theologian is left appealing not to divine but to ecclesiastical authority. In the later section on the conflict between the theological and philosophical faculties (*SF*, AK 7: 36ff.; 61ff.) Kant quite explicitly consigns the biblical theologian to the task of interpreting Scripture under the authority of ecclesiastical statutes, and hence as bound to offer only a *doctrinal* interpretation (cf. *R*, AK 6, V: 166, 105) and contrasts this task with that of the "lower" philosophical faculty, which abjures authority and thereby acquires a unique competence to expound not ecclesiastical faith but reasoned religion. These very strong claims merit fuller quotation:

A biblical theologian is, properly speaking, one *versed in the Scriptures* with regard to *ecclesiastical faith*, which is based on statutes – that is, on laws proceeding from another person's act of choice. A rational theologian, on the other hand, is one *versed in reason* with regard to *religious* faith, which is based on inner laws that can be developed from every man's own reason. The very concept of religion shows that it can never be based on decrees (no matter how high their source); for religion is not the sum of certain teachings regarded as divine revelations (that is called theology), but the sum of all our duties regarded as divine *commands* (and, on the subject's part, the maxim of fulfilling them as such). As far as its matter or object is concerned, religion does not differ in any point from morality, for it is concerned with duties as such. Its distinction from morality is a merely formal one. . . . This is why there is only one religion. (*SF*, AK 7: 36; 61)

In the same passage *religious faith* and *ecclesiastical faith* are specifically presented as comprising respectively the *canon* and an *organon* of belief. A canon of belief would establish reasoned constraints on belief; an organon for Christian or another "statutory" faith would present one possible and permissible way of filling out the sparse framework of the canon of reasoned religion. This passage therefore fits well with the picture of religion "within the limits of reason alone" as answering (as do the passages on the Postulates in the *Critique of Practical Reason*) to "What must I hope?" while ecclesiastical faith provides varied possible answers to Kant's more encompassing question "What may I hope?"

However, this contrast between ecclesiastical faith and religion "within the limits of reason" will not explain why the text of *Religion within the Limits of Reason Alone* is in fact crammed with a distinctive sort of Scriptural exegesis. To understand what Kant intends by "religion within the limits of reason alone", it is not enough to point out that for Kant morality is reasoned, or that he insists on a strict division of labour between the theologian and the philosopher. We must also understand how his account of a distinctive way of interpreting Scripture, which does not appeal to ecclesiastical faith, is linked to the task of elucidating religion "within the limits of reason". On Kant's view the philosopher as well as the biblical theologian has something to say in answer to the question "What may I hope?" and the philosopher as well as the biblical theologian has something to say about interpreting Scripture.

IV. Hermeneutics without Authority?

Kant's scattered comments on Scriptural exegesis within *Religion within the Limits of Reason Alone* present a quite definite and very ambitious view of the aims of exegesis "within the limits of reason". Unlike earlier attempts to characterize rational religion, Kant does not confine himself to the more abstract propositions of faith. He takes on a very wide range of Scriptural passages, including, for example, passages dealing with the Fall of Man, the virgin birth, and prophecies of the Kingdom of God. In each case he offers not so much an interpretation of the texts discussed as *comments on the constraints on their interpretation*. Very often these comments are *permissive*: a certain passage *may* be taken in a certain way, or we are *permitted* to read it along certain lines. Consider the following passage on the incarnation, where I have underlined the modal emphasis Kant places on his interpretative comments:

just because we are not the authors of this idea [of moral perfection], and because it has established itself in man without our comprehending how human nature could have been capable of receiving it, it is more appropriate to say [kann *man hier besser sagen*] that this archetype has *come down* to us from heaven and has assumed our humanity.... Such union with us may therefore be regarded [kann ... *angesehen werden*] as a state of *humiliation* of the Son of God. (*R*, AK 6: V 74; 54–5); my underlining of modal terms)

Alternatively, consider the oblique endorsement of Scriptural claims made in passages such as the discussion of evil at the beginning of Book Two:

So it is not surprising [literally: it *may not* be taken as alien: "*es* darf *also nicht befremden*"] that an Apostle represents this *invisible* enemy, who is known only through his operations upon us and who destroys basic principles, as being outside us and, indeed, as an evil *spirit*. (*R*, AK 6: V 71–2, 52; my underlining of modal terms)

There are scores of analogous passages in which Kant comments on ways in which Scripture may be read from the perspective of religious faith.

Although these passages fit well with the thought that Kant's wider aim in *Religion within the Limits of Reason Alone* is to contribute to an answer to the question "what may I hope?" it seems clear that what he intends must be more than a matter of *mere permission*. If the point were only to assert that since reason leaves matters open here, we *may* take Scripture in this way, then presumably it would be open to us to point out that equally we *may* take it in some radically different way, say in the way in which it is taken by one or another preferred group of biblical theologians.

Kant rejects this minimalist approach. He points out that a hermeneutics that invokes no spurious authority might have either of two forms. The first would ascribe no authority to any specific principles or strategies of interpretation, and would lead to a postmodern interpretive frolic – which we have no reason to think need remain playful. Such a hermeneutics would hardly have appealed to Kant. He would have termed interpretation that drifts with feeling or inspiration, or with mere, sheer choice or preference, *lawless*, and thought that in religion such interpretations would lead only to *Schwärmerei* (enthusiasm; fanaticism; zealotry) (cf. *WH*, AK 8: 146–7; 248–9; *R*, AK 6: V 164–5; 104–5). Alternatively, a hermeneutics that appeals to no spurious, ungrounded authority, yet is not "lawless", would have to appeal to principles that have the *form* of law, but do not groundlessly invoke the force or the content of any particular authority, tradition or creed. It is only this way of interpreting Scripture that would, on Kant's account, lie "within the limits of reason".

There is plenty of evidence that Kant is not proposing a merely permissive hermeneutics that could lead indifferently to edifying or depressing, to historicizing or to mythicizing, to literal or to spiritual readings of Scripture. If that were what he were doing he could surely simply make the point that reason leaves the interpretation of Scripture open. He would not need to propose or defend specific types of exegesis; indeed exegesis would not play *any* part in religion "within the limits of reason alone", which – if it were possible at all on such assumptions – would be as austere as Deism.[8]

However, Kant's vision of the importance of Scripture is radically different. He is never dismissive. He takes it that the various established faiths of mankind can all be read as pointing to religion "within the limits of reason", and that they serve and have served as historically vital *vehicles* for the introduction of reasoned religion (*R*, AK 6: V 167ff; 105ff).[9] Indeed, he takes it that they *ought* to be read in this way. Even the most bizarre of religious myths may be interpreted as pointing to reasoned religion.

A clue to this picture of interpretation is given early on, in Book I of the *Religion*, in the discussion of *Genesis*, where Kant quotes a line from Horace: "*mutato nomine de te fabula narratur*" (*R*, AK 6: V 45; 37). The context of this line in Horace[10] is a reproof to those who foolishly scoff at ludicrous tales about the gods, not seeing that "under another name the tale is told of you". No doubt Kant thought it more discreet to make this point by invoking a pagan author, since ludicrous tales about pagan gods were safe territory. But his attitude to exegesis remains the same when he comes to biblical interpretation: nothing in Scripture is to be derided or discarded; rather it is to be interpreted in a certain way.

The crucial question is, of course, *how* it is to be interpreted. Adherents of established faiths are experts in *doctrinal* interpretation. Kant takes issue with them not by denying their beliefs, but by casting doubt on the status of their interpretive claims outside the circles of established faith. Unlike those Enlightenment critics of established faith who sought to extirpate superstition and to read miracles out of Scripture, Kant is content to leave doctrinal faith its place. He seeks only to argue that the tenets of doctrinal orthodoxy cannot claim unrestricted currency. Since such interpreters presuppose the authority of Church or creed or tradition, their claims will hold only where those authorities are presupposed. *Doctrinal* interpreters cannot circumvent this restriction by assuming the backing of Divine revelation. For claims that particular sacred texts are the very word of God are themselves historically transmitted and doctrinally interpreted, hence presuppose the authority of that transmission (*SF*, AK 7: 36ff.; 61ff.). A holy book commands esteem, but it is not itself divine revelation (*R*, AK 6: V 152–3; 97–8). In this negative move Kant has much company and I will not discuss the point any further. If reason requires the rejection of "alien" authorities, rejection of *doctrinal* interpretation must surely be part of any religion "within the limits of reason".

However, the rejection of doctrinal interpretation is both less controversial and less puzzling than the positive moves by which Kant seeks to establish an account of what he terms *authentic* interpretation. Authentic is distinguished from doctrinal interpretation at various points both in *Religion within the Limits of Reason Alone* and in *The Conflict of the Faculties*, and more generally.[11] Interpretation is authentic not because it appeals to some "authentic tradition" or "authentic experience". Those are the strategies of doctrinal interpretation (cf. the biblical theologian) and of the enthusiast (cf. the religious mystic or zealot or alternatively the postmodernist). Kant regards interpretation as authentic only if it appeals to nothing derivative – borrows nothing from "alien" authorities – and yet is based on principles. Only if it meets both standards does it rely on "*eine ganz eigene und zwar negative Gesetzgebung*". The reference to that which is "*ganz eigen*" excludes anything which derives its laws from elsewhere (for then they would be derivative), and the reference to "*eine Gesetzgebung*" excludes anything that is radically particular or individual (for that would not be any sort of law-giving). As we have seen, meeting these two conditions is all that there is to the basic principle of reason. Authentic interpretation takes reason, and specifically practical reason, as "the highest interpreter of Scripture": it is because the supreme principle of reason is the basis of authentic interpretation that "only a moral interpretation is really an authentic one" (*SF*, AK 7: 48; 85; *R*, AK 6: V 157ff.; 100ff.).[12]

This position is most succinctly summarized by the title of the longest consecutive discussion of interpretation in *Religion within the Limits of Reason Alone*, which asserts that "*Ecclesiastical Faith has Pure Religious*

Faith as its Highest Interpreter" (*R*, AK 6: V 157; 100). In the text this is expanded by the claim that

If such an empirical faith, which chance, it would seem, has tossed into our hands, is to be united with the basis of a moral faith . . . an exposition of the revelation which has come into our possession is required, that is, a thorough-going interpretation of it in a sense agreeing with the universal practical rules of a religion of pure reason. (*R*, AK 6: V 158; 100; cf. *SF*, AK 7: 41; 71)

In the footnote to this paragraph Kant elucidates the point by posing the question:

whether morality should be expounded according to the Bible or whether the Bible should not rather be expounded according to morality. (*R*, AK 6: V 158–9n; 101n)

It is easy to miss how radical this disjunction is. *Doctrinal* interpretation too links Scripture and morality, as every sermon that draws a moral lesson from sacred texts attests. However, in this case the authority of the text is presupposed, the moral lessons are seen as backed by that authority, and the principles of interpretation are derivative rather than nonderivative. Kant's strategy of interpretation reverses this order: no antecedent authority can be assigned to sacred texts, including the Scriptures, since they are only "a book, [that has] fallen into men's hands"[13] (*R*, AK 6: V 153; 98). The only source of authentic authority is reason, and specifically those formulations of the fundamental principle of reason that bear on action. The *only* religion within the limits of reason is therefore moral religion.

The strategy of authentic interpretation permits a "philosophical theology [which] remains within the limits of reason alone" (*R*, AK 6, V xv–xviii; 8). In Kant's view, authentic interpretation may properly be used to impose apparently far-fetched readings:

Frequently this interpretation may, in the light of the text (of the revelation), appear forced – it may often really be forced; and yet if the text can possibly support it, it must be preferred to a literal interpretation which either contains nothing at all [helpful] to morality or else works counter to all moral incentives. (*R*, AK 6, V 158; 100–1)

On the surface this is an endorsement of hermeneutic violence. Sacred texts are apparently to be expounded according to the fundamental principle of morality even where this means doing violence to the text. The strategy of authentic as opposed to doctrinal interpretation is a strategy of understanding sacred texts (and traditions of faith) in the light of the meagre constraints of mere (practical) reason. This strategy of interpretation does not seek authenticity in the sense of recovering a lost or original meaning from sacred texts – that conception of authenticity has to be rejected with the dismissal of authors' intentions as standards of interpretation. Authentic interpretation is rather a matter of determining an understanding of Scripture or other sacred texts without at any stage deriving it from other, supposed authorities and without engaging in the sort of hermeneutic arbitrariness which would make the interpretation inaccessible to others.

Kant's resolute engagement with the religious tradition he knew well, and his brief comments on others, reflect the second demand: religion "within the limits of reason" can no more neglect popular faith than it can accept the claims to authority of doctrinal interpreters. As Kant sees it, a transition from doctrinal to authentic modes of interpretation has long been practiced. The moral philosophers of Greece and Rome reinterpreted their established tradition in this way:

They were able in the end to interpret the grossest polytheism as mere symbolic representation of the attributes of the single divine being. (R, AK 6: V 159–60; 101)

So too for Judaism, Christianity, Islam, and Hinduism (R, AK 6: V 159–60; 102). For each faith, progress towards religion "within the limits of reason" has been a matter of coming to understand the elements of sacred texts as *symbols* that form part of the popular faith, but point towards deeper moral truths, and so ultimately to the demands of reason.[14] Religion "within the limits of reason" on this view is the recognition of "all our duties as divine commands" (R, AK 6, V 229–30; 142).

Kant is well aware that the guardians of ecclesiastic faith, let alone the faithful multitudes, may feel uncomfortable with, indeed threatened by, such moral (re)interpretation of their sacred texts. He retreats from the dangers of confrontation with the rather evasive assertion that moral interpretation of texts does not claim to be authoritative interpretation of claims about the *origins* of those texts:

Nor can we charge such interpretations with dishonesty, provided we are not disposed to assert that the meaning which we ascribe to the symbols of the popular faith, even to the holy books, is exactly as intended by them, but rather allow this question to be left undecided and merely admit the *possibility* that their authors may be so understood. (R, AK 6, V 161; 111; Kant's italics)

Avoiding the intentionalist fallacy in interpretation may be enough to avoid outright contradiction of others' claims that their interpretations have divine origins or inspiration. But it will hardly satisfy the defenders of doctrinal interpretation, for several reasons. First, in construing sacred texts as symbols of moral truth, Kant avoids the question whether all established faiths can be interpreted as falling within the constraints defined by the demands of morality and of reasoned hope for human destiny. (He occasionally suggests that Christian ecclesiastical faith has got further towards reasoned religion than other statutory faiths.) Some doctrinal interpreters have deep convictions that not all established faiths are on an equal footing here. Further, the adherents of some faiths may feel that *authentic* interpretation undermines their tradition and makes it unrecognizable to them, while other doctrinal interpreters may insist on realist and foundationalist conceptions of cognition and of reason on which they purportedly rest their case. They may view Kant's cautious constructive accounts of reason, cognition, morality, and hope as mere and inadequate substitutes. However, unless the defenders of doctrinal orthodoxies are prepared to make the latter decisive move, and also to provide the arguments that will establish a realist metaphysics and with it a realist vindication of reason, they will have to counter the claims of authentic interpretation by showing why a constructivist vindication of reason cannot be extended into an account of authentic interpretation which constitutes, strange as this may sound, a *hermeneutics of reason*.

NOTES

In thinking about these themes I have become more and more aware that part of my good fortune in attending John Rawls's seminars at Harvard some thirty years ago was that he took the history of ethics seriously. Many of my contemporaries were less fortunate. They were taught by a generation who, although themselves versed in the traditional scholarship of the subject, often focussed their writing and teaching of philosophy on detached arguments rather than on systems of thought or on texts, let alone on the historical contexts within which those texts were written and received. John Rawls always took the thinking of his predecessors seriously, and in doing so showed us that appropriating decontextualized arguments so that they can appear and be criticized in their naked glory is not always philosophically fruitful, and that serious attention to earlier thinkers matters. Since then I have often disregarded the supposed chasm that separates philosophy from history of philosophy, and sometimes been criticized for trespassing across this important intellectual boundary. I thank John Rawls for his enlightened and then unfashionable example. Here I have continued my trespassing, and remain unrepentant.

An earlier and less developed version of this article appeared in German with the title "Innerhalb der Grenzen der bloßen Vernunft" in *Kant Über Religion*, ed. Friedo Ricken and François Marty (Kohlhammer, Stuttgart, 1992), pp. 101–11, and appears here with permission.

1. Perhaps more aptly translated as *Religion within the Limits of Mere Reason*: cf. the standard French rendering of the title as *La Religion dans les Limites de la simple Raison*. The suggestion that reason makes *minimal* demands is significant.

References to Kant's writings are given parenthetically in the text. They include an abbreviation of the title, the number of the volume of the Prussian Academy edition in which the work appears, followed by page numbers for the Prussian Academy or other German edition used, and for the English translation listed, if any. Page numbers for the English and German texts when different are separated by a semi-colon; where the listed translation includes the page numbers of the German edition a single page number is given.

KrV: *Die Kritik der reinen Vernunft*: (1st ed. 1781; 2nd ed. 1787; AK 3 and 4), German text edited by Karl Vorländer (Hamburg: Felix Meiner Verlag, 1971 and 1990).

Critique of Pure Reason: Here I have used my own translations. Although deeply indebted to the translation by Norman Kemp Smith (London: Macmillan, 1933), there are aspects of the passages of interest here which are overly abstract in his renderings. The page numbers are those of the first and second editions, which are included in the margins both of the Vorländer and of the Kemp Smith texts.

KpV: *Die Kritik der praktischen Vernunft* (1788; AK 5).

Critique of Practical Reason: trans. L. W. Beck (Indianapolis: Bobbs Merrill, Library of Liberal Arts, 1977). The page numbers are those of the Prussian Academy edition, which the translation includes in the margins.

R: *Die Religion innerhalb der Grenzen der bloßen Vernunft* (1793 and 1794; AK 6): In this case I have used the edition by Karl Vorländer (Hamburg: Felix Meiner Verlag, 1990). Page references are prefixed with a V, and refer to the marginal pagination, which is that of the 1794 edition, and is used in the very useful index to the Vorländer edition.

Religion within the Limits of Reason Alone: trans. Theodore M. Green and Hoyt H. Hudson (New York: Harper and Row, 1960).

G: *Grundlegung zur Metaphysik der Sitten* (1785; AK 4).

Groundwork of the Metaphysic of Morals: trans. H. J. Paton (New York: Harper Torchbooks, 1964). The page numbers are those of the Prussian Academy edition, which the translation includes in the margins.

WH: *Was Heisst: Sich im Denken Orientieren?* (1786; AK 8): The page numbers are those of the Prussian Academy edition.

What Is Orientation in Thinking?: trans. Barry Nisbet, in Hans Reiss, ed., *Kant: Political Writings*, 2nd ed. (Cambridge University Press, 1991), pp. 237–49.

SF: *Der Streit der Fakultäten* (1798; AK 7).

The Conflict of the Faculties: trans. M. Gregor (with R. Anchor) (New York: Abaris Books, 1979). The text includes a facsimile of the Prussian Academy edition, with page numbers preserved at the top of the page and the translation facing.

2. For example, in the papers titled "Reason and Politics in the Kantian Enterprise" and "The Public Use of Reason" in Onora O'Neill, *Constructions of Reason: Explorations of Kant's Practical Philosophy* (Cambridge University Press, 1989), pp. 3–27 and 28–50 respectively; in "Vindicating Reason" in *The Cambridge Companion to Kant*, ed. Paul Guyer (Cambridge University Press, 1992), pp. 280–308 and in "Four Models of Practical Reason", forth-

coming in my *Bounds of Justice* (Cambridge University Press), published in German as "Vier Modelle der praktischen Vernunft" in *Vernunftbegriffe in der Moderne*, ed. Hans Friedrich Fulda and Rolf-Peter Horstmann (Stuttgart: Klett-Cotta, 1993), pp. 586–606.

3. René Descartes, *Discourse on the Method of Rightly Conducting One's Mind and Seeking the Truth in the Sciences*, trans. John Cottingham, Robert Stoothof, and David Murdoch (Cambridge University Press, 1985), Vol. 1, p. 112.

4. Cf. "The Public Use of Reason" in O'Neill, *Constructions of Reason*, pp. 28–50. Kant's conception of reason is not, however, discursive in the sense of thinking that the principles of reason will be constituted by actual processes of public discourse among some socially defined group. His conception of the public use of reason is modal: public reasoning is a matter of adhering to principles and standards which at least could be adopted by all, and correspondingly of rejecting those which could not.

5. Arguably Kant leaves it open whether an account of the future for which we must hope is to be articulated in political, cultural, or religious terms, or whether these are differing ways of articulating a single vision.

6. Elsewhere Kant is less sure whether there is anything that we *must* hope: see, for example, *R.* AK 6: V 229–30n; 142n. The issue is discussed by Allen Wood in "Rational Theology, Moral Faith, and Religion" in *The Cambridge Companion to Kant*, ed. Paul Guyer (Cambridge University Press, 1992), pp. 394–416.

7. Cf. the Preface to the second edition of 1794, where Kant depicts the larger sphere of ecclesiastical faith as including the narrower sphere of reasoned religion (*R*, AK 6: V xxi–xxii; 11).

8. Some writers have construed Kant as endorsing a form of Deism. For a recent and sophisticated version see Allen Wood, "Kant's Deism", in *Kant's Philosophy of Religion Reconsidered*, ed. Philip J. Rossi and Michael Wreen (Bloomington and Indianapolis: Indiana University Press, 1991), pp. 1–21.

9. Whether Kant is right to think that the "historical vehicle" which ecclesiastical faith provides for religious faith will be superseded and ultimately become redundant (*R*, AK 6: V 228–9; 140), indeed whether such a view is coherent is a more complex matter. See Michael Baumgarten, "Das 'Ethische Gemeine Wesen' und die Kirche in Kants 'Religionsschrift'" and Friedo Ricken, "Kanon und Organon: Religion und Offenbarung im Streit der Fakultäten", both in *Kant Über Religion*, ed. Friedo Ricken and François Marty (Stuttgart: Kohlhammer, 1992), pp. 156–67 and 181–94 respectively.

10. Horace, *Satires*, in *O. Horati Flacci Opera*, ed. E. C. Wickham, revised H. W. Garrod, Oxford Classical Texts (Oxford: Oxford University Press, 1984), Book I, i, line 69, p. 135.

11. For a discussion of some broader uses of the distinction see Rudolf Makkreel, *Imagination and Interpretation in Kant: The Hermeneutical Import of the Critique of Judgement* (Chicago: University of Chicago Press, 1990), chap. 7.

12. There is much more to be said about Kant's conception of interpretation; in particular I am leaving aside his comments on the role of Scriptural scholarship. See *R*, AK 6: V 162; 103.

13. The German phrase "ein solches den Menschen zu Händen gekommenes Buch" displays a robust view of the Bible's contingency. Cf. the next page,

"mit einem solchen empirischen Glaube der uns dem Ansehen nach ein Ungeführ in die Hände gespielt hat" (such an empirical faith, which chance, it would seem, has tossed into our hands) (*R*, AK 6: V 157–8; 100).

14. See also *R*, AK 6: V 202–6; 125, 126 for a vivid discussion of passages of biblical narrative and elements of ecclesiastical faith that may be authentically interpreted as a symbolic representation of morality and reasoned hope.

A Cosmopolitan Kingdom of Ends

BARBARA HERMAN

There is an often unspoken assumption at work in modern moral philosophy that morality is in important ways independent of social and political institutions. The intuitive idea is that whatever morality requires of us as individuals, it will be something that we are, as individuals, able to do, or able to do to the degree that we are virtuous or good. The assumed moral effect on us of political and social institutions is either, positively, to provide us with a set of benefits and burdens, the enjoyment and discharge of which may give us occasion for moral action, or negatively, if we hold political office or have some role with special responsibilities, to sometimes call for compromise with moral principle in order to do what is politically or institutionally necessary.

Kant's ethics has often seemed the exemplar of such a "separate spheres" conception of ethics and politics. Social and political institutions are presumed to arise as the necessary strategy for negotiating the natural lawlessness of collective life. Morality, by contrast, has its source in the a priori requirements of practical reason. It is thus both independent of and prior to politics. Moral action, accordingly, is a matter of bringing the will into conformity with a priori principles of practical reason. What calls for philosophy is the demonstration that this is possible.

The complement to this view of morality is a conception of the moral person as an autonomous individual acting under the burden of practical reason (in particular, the necessitation of the categorical imperative). Much of the attractiveness of traditional Kantian ethics derives from the dignity it accords the individual person because of her capacity to act both freely and as reason requires, as well as from the moral equality of persons that follows from locating the basis of moral status in each agent's own practical reason.

Unhappily, these same attractive features present serious obstacles to the perceived adequacy of the theory – both as an account of what morality is, and as the basis of an adequate account of moral agency. For instance: if autonomy is a source of dignity, it seems equally to be the source of a kind of autarchic individualism, supporting a conception of persons as radically separate from one another. Social connections appear to be morally contingent, if not arbitrary; at most they are the result, not the condition, of obligation. The paradigm moral encounter or relationship looks to be the one between strangers – persons who cannot assume common interests but who are rationally compelled to acknowledge limits on their mutually affecting actions in virtue of their common humanity. One might say that it is the moral theory fit for the modern city, and not the town, or village, or extended family. In those locales, the pervasiveness of local knowledge and the bonds of shared life make the austerity of a morality for autonomous individuals appear sterile and unresponsive to salient particularity. Kantian moral autonomy, so understood, is in general incompatible with conceptions of morality or virtue or the moral life that depend on excellence at a social role. One is therefore likely to be drawn to applaud Kantian morality where it rejects those hierarchical or excluding social connections we abhor, and then to condemn it for heavy-handedly refusing moral standing to connection per se, since there are areas, like the community or the family, where we find it attractive.

My purpose here is not to argue directly for or against the merits of such sweeping assertions. The point of rehearsing them is to bring to mind a sense of familiarity about these or analogous descriptions of the power and the limits of the Kantian account of morality and moral agency. I think such views have been accepted as almost uncontroversially true by friends and critics of Kantian ethics alike. The former prize its securing moral relationship between persons as such; the latter fault the theory for its eschewal of the moral importance of attachment and place. The conditions on morality that each supports are surely correct. That it does not seem possible to have both autonomy and deep social connection within Kantian ethics is to be explained by the fact that *both* camps endorse what I believe is a mistaken view of Kantian moral agency and judgment.[1]

There is a different place one might begin. The Kantian rational agent need not and should not be conceived as an isolated individual whose autonomous self-legislation is to bridge the gap from her own concerns to a regard for others as equal, rational, and autonomous. The "other" is not by conceptual necessity alien: a burden, a limit to be negotiated by reason. Some would even argue that, for Kant, to be a human rational agent is to be one among others in relations of rational colloquy.[2] It is not morality that compels us to acknowledge other persons as equal and authoritative sources of reasons; insofar as we are rational, the other is integral to – even partly defining of – our rational activity. And if we cannot conceive of the individual rational agent qua rational agent without other persons, there is no gap that starts a skeptical argument, requiring some special reason to take other agents' reasons into account. No principle I offer on rational grounds requires a further step in order to secure the assent of the other as a condition of rational justification. Nonetheless, this deep fact of sociality does not by itself secure the principles of rational coordination necessary for rational agency. It is not just that we lack instincts for rational coordination, though that is true.[3] The difficulty is that the necessity of the project does not translate into a determinate solution. There is a task of construction for normative principles that can command rational assent. So understood, the social basis of agency and judgment is no threat to our autonomous rationality (a condition that as rational beings we must, or must wish to, overcome), but the natural and inescapable arena for its expression.[4]

Nothing in this alternative conception of rational agency alters the primary task of moral philosophy: namely, giving an account of the nature and possibility of obligation. What does change is our sense of the primary task of Kantian moral *theory*: it is more plausibly seen as elaborating the practical consequences of the fact that the basic norms of rationality for autonomous agents are social. In what follows, I want to think about the kingdom of ends as a small piece of the moral theory project so understood. It would seem to be the obvious place to look if one wants to consider the place of the social as constitutive of the conditions and constraints on moral agency and judgment.[5] The kingdom of ends appears to represent persons qua moral agents as (legislative) members of a possible social order. We are, in some sense, to consider our maxims as possible principles of an order of co-legislating beings. It is surely significant, and should be more puzzling than it is usually taken to be, that the representation of the principle of moral agency – the Categorical Imperative (CI) – has the form of a social order.

Within the *Groundwork*, the kingdom of ends is given several roles: as an ideal, as a further formula for representing the CI (and therefore as a distinct or complementary route to moral judgment), and as a component of the "complete determination of all maxims" that "brings an idea of reason closer to intuition (in accordance with a certain analogy) and thereby closer to feeling",[6] useful "to secure acceptance for the moral law" (*G*437). The kingdom of ends also provides the framework for the discussion of price and dignity that precedes the so-called summary of the argument. It would be nice to have an account of the kingdom of ends that explains the unity of these roles (if they are distinct) as well as explaining why the social dimension the kingdom of ends introduces is important to them. My plans for this essay, however, are more modest. I want to consider some basic questions about the idea of a kingdom of ends, and then, with some preliminary answers in hand, to begin exploring the sort of resource it provides for moral judgment, particularly in circumstances of social pluralism. This is an important focus for obvious moral reasons, but also because the effort to accommodate social pluralism brings to center stage the role that social institutions play in moral judgment in general.

I

If the idea of a kingdom of ends plainly gives expression to some sort of social element in Kant's account of moral judgment and obligation, it is not clear what the dimensions of the sociality might be or, therefore, what the significance of this social dimension is in our understanding of the nature and obligations of the autonomous rational agent. I want to approach this issue indirectly, by way of a set of more immediate, text-related questions. There is reason to be puzzled about the kingdom of ends as a formulation of the CI (if it is one) and about its relations to the other formulations; there are intriguing questions about the representation of persons in the kingdom of ends; it is not at all clear why or in what sense the kingdom of ends is an "ideal"; and there are, as I noted above, questions about the "strategy" of introducing a social dimension – what it means, what role it plays – that will affect our understanding of both persons in the kingdom of ends and the kingdom of ends itself as or as part of a formula of the categorical imperative.

The plan for this section is, first, to situate the kingdom of ends in the *Groundwork* argument, and then to begin an interpretation of it by raising and discussing two basic issues: whether the kingdom of ends is or contains the idea of a union of good wills, and the related matter of what is to be included as an end in the kingdom of ends. Since some of what I wish to do is to make some things puzzling that are not generally thought to be so, the discussion proceeds through a series of interpretive forays that set some constraints on further interpretation and raise more questions than they answer.

Consider the moment of introduction of the idea of a kingdom of ends (at *G*433). It occurs immediately after the generation of the three formulae of the one categorical imperative, and so at a point when we know quite a lot about Kant's moral project. We know that there can be only one CI and that what it requires is the conformity of maxims to the principle of universal law-giving. We also know that it in some way supports a derivation of ordinary duties (although the reasons that support these duties may not be so ordinary). Left to be shown is that the CI is a necessary law for all rational beings – indeed that it is even possibly such a law. This possibility hinges, Kant argues next, on the existence of an objective end: that is, an end that depends on motives valid for every rational being *and* that determines the will to act in conformity to the principle of universal law-giving. "Rational nature as an end in itself" is offered as the unique candidate for this role. However, rational nature can be an objective end – have standing as a regulative reason independent of agents' contingent and merely subjective interests – only if the rational will is, and conceives of itself as, an autonomous source of reasons. As beings with an autonomous will, we must be able to regard ourselves as subject to an objective norm whose authority is in no other place than "the idea of the will of every rational being as a will that legislates universal law" (*G*431).

With this, Kant completes the stage-setting for the metaphysical arguments of *Groundwork* III. The possibility of a categorical imperative has been shown to depend on proving that the will of a rational agent is autonomous: capable of determining itself to action through a principle whose authority is independent of contingent interest.[7] But before taking up the metaphysical argument, Kant introduces "the very fruitful concept" of a kingdom of ends (*G*433). I want to think about why he does this.

It has been said that with the formula of the kingdom of ends we can see a completion of the "perspective set" of the CI, of the agent in the formula of universal law, of the recipient in the formula of humanity, and of a citizen in a cooperative social order (a legislative perspective) in the formula of the kingdom of ends. The last shift tells us that morality, through the CI, directs us to act on maxims whose principles could constitute the public rules of a possible social order of autonomous (human) beings.

The difficulty here is not that these ideas are somehow objectionable or un-Kantian. On the contrary, they are plausible, compelling, useful, and plainly expressive of central Kantian themes. The difficulty is in understanding how they could arise from the argument of the *Groundwork*. For if we have not correctly understood the point and place of the kingdom of ends in the argument of *Groundwork* II, despite the power of the ideas, we may doubt whether this interpretation gives us adequate access to the concept's intended fruitfulness.

The problem, as I see it, is this. *Starting* with the thought that the kingdom of ends represents morality in terms of an ideal social order is misleading, just in the way that taking "respect for persons" to be a first-order interpretation of treating humanity in persons as an end in itself is. There are surely connections and resonances between the two notions in both pairs, but using the ordinary notion to interpret the Kantian idea not only begs the interpretive question, it draws us away from core features of Kant's argument. Take the formula of humanity pair. If it seems that the formula of humanity is Kant's representation of respect for persons – an idea with moral content – it can be tempting to think that respect for persons as ends in themselves can operate in moral judgment independently of the formula of universal law (that the formula of humanity is a distinct principle of judgment). Certainly many of the canonically immoral actions are not respectful of persons in any sense. But the *Kantian* idea behind the deployment of the concept of respect is that it is the appropriate practical regard for beings who are end-setters of a certain sort, and whose status as rational beings is a limiting condition on what we can (rationally) will. It is this fact that sets the requirement to act only on maxims and for ends that others, as ends in themselves, can share or hold. And what that means, I believe, is that we are to act only on maxims that have the form of universal law (or law-giving). That is, when the Kantian argument is spelled out, we come to understand what respect for persons is: we respect persons *as ends in themselves* when our maxims of action satisfy the constraints of the categorical imperative (in its first formulation). It is thus not inappropriate to talk of respect for persons as what the formula of humanity is about. But to use the notion of respect to interpret the Kantian argument gets the order of concepts reversed.

The situation is the same with the kingdom of ends. If it is a notion that has something to do with rational natures in a social system, the order of explanation must not be *from* the idea of a social union of rational beings *to* the kingdom of ends. Rather, since the kingdom of ends, as it bears on judgment, must be formally equivalent to the formula of universal law, the only thing that can make a principle a possible principle of an order of rational beings (that is expressive of their rational natures) is that it has the form of universal law-giving. What it signifies about us – whether we (might possibly) belong to such an order – is what needs to be worked out.

The merit of this order of explanation will be manifest in sorting out many of the difficulties encountered in producing a satisfactory reading of the *Groundwork* presentation of the kingdom of ends. Whatever new element the kingdom of ends brings to the moral story will be visible only after we fix the connections with the argument that has come before. It is time to look at the text.

A kingdom (*Reich*) is "a systematic union of different rational beings through common laws" (*G*433). Since, as Kant points out, ends are of two kinds, "rational beings as ends in themselves and . . . the particular ends which each may set for himself" (*G*433)), we get to a kingdom of ends this way:

Now laws determine ends as regards their universal validity; therefore, if one abstracts from the personal differences of rational beings and also from all content of their private ends, then it will be possible to think of a whole of all ends in systematic connection; . . . that is, one can think of a kingdom of ends that is possible on the aforesaid principles. (*G*433)

Assuming that "the aforesaid principles" are the three formulations of the one categorical imperative, one might suppose that the kingdom of ends is the law-governed union of rational beings that would follow just in case they all acted in conformity with the CI (made the CI the principle of their willing).[8] This looks like a union of good wills. It is worth walking through the reasons why this cannot be right.

It is true that a set of persons with good wills would, in that respect, be persons under one law. They would act in a single, lawful way with respect to all ends (other persons and particular ends). Would they thereby constitute "a systematic union of different rational beings through common laws"? Surely, yes, if "systematic union" just means "under one law." But why, we might ask, is this worth saying? What question might it answer?

The idea of the end-in-itself is brought in to answer the question of the end of maxims for agents for whom the moral law is the determining ground of their willing. Autonomy responds to the worry that this end might be given "externally," through some contingent interest; that the moral imperative might not be categorical. There is no comparable gap that the good wills interpretation of the kingdom of ends fills. Moreover, the "aforesaid principles" are principles of *all* rational wills, not just good ones. It is the rational will that is autonomous, not just the good will. And rational nature as an end in itself "is the supreme limiting condition of *every* man's freedom of action" (*G*431, emphasis added). Indeed, immediately after the introduction of the concept of a kingdom of ends (in the passage I quoted), Kant sounds this same inclusive theme. He says:

For *all* rational beings stand under the law that each of them should treat himself and all others never merely as a means but always at the same time as an end in himself. *Hereby* arises a systematic union of rational beings through common objective laws. (*G*433, emphasis added)

The sense in which *the law* constitutes a social union "of rational beings through common objective laws" remains to be worked out.

Some puzzles: Why would Kant have us "abstract from personal differences" in order to think of rational beings in systematic union? And what are we to make of the fact that the kingdom is a kingdom of *ends*, not just of rational beings? The law that is constitutive of the kingdom brings ends of both sorts – the ends of agents and agents as ends (in themselves) – into systematic union. Why are private ends included at all? And in what sense if we must abstract from their content?

We need to be wary of the ease with which we now accept the idea that the appropriate representation of persons, especially for purposes of moral deliberation, requires abstraction from differences. If the kingdom of ends is supposed to extend our understanding of the categorical imperative, the potential members of the kingdom of ends ought to be particular agents with maxims. The CI does not address abstract persons.[9] Abstraction from personal differences more reasonably marks the condition of *membership* in a kingdom of ends: a union of persons qua rational beings whose personal differences are not relevant to their status as members. This fits a general procedure for regarding classes of things under law, as when we abstract from the particulars of size and shape in giving an account of which objects are brought into systematic union by the law of gravity. However, not all conditions of membership indicate the defining character of members: though birthplace or naturalization can be the conditions of citizenship – for a union of persons under law – the conditions do not specify what it is to be a citizen, and surely not what it is to be a good citizen. If we are *members* of a kingdom of ends just insofar as we are rational beings, the particular facts about what we will must be irrelevant, just as our size or gender or nationality would be. But it does not follow from the fact that abstraction from personal differences reveals our membership qualification that the representation of persons within the kingdom of ends is as abstract persons.

Next there is the puzzling matter of private ends. Why are private ends (in abstract form) given equal play as constituent ends of the kingdom of ends? It would seem that if you abstract from the content of private ends, you get the mere concept of a private end: a state of affairs valued as a possible effect of willing. But since under such abstraction all private ends are the same, in what non-trivial sense can they be in systematic union?

There are other ways to abstract from the content of private ends. We might take the lawful union of private ends-as-such to be a system of (all?) possible permissible ends, or perhaps as the somewhat stronger notion of a system of permissible compossible ends (permissible ends whose joint satisfaction is possible). There are problems with both options. The set of all permissible ends – all ends that are neither obligatory nor forbidden – surely offers too minimal a conception of order to fit an idea of systematic union. Think of the jumble of things persons might do or bring about, all on maxims that satisfy the CI. (Part of the practical necessity that supports a coercive system of *Recht* is precisely the need to secure order among permissible ends.) Although a standard of compossibility gives a more robust sense of system, it seems arbitrarily restrictive to privilege only ends that can be jointly satisfied.[10] There may be an argument that shows why ends that are inherently or even contingently conflictual are morally problematic, but nothing like that is in place at this stage of the *Groundwork*.

One might think that, given a Kantian account of value, a more reasonable interpretation of the system requirement on private ends would be compossible permissible *willings* of ends. (If not everyone can satisfy the end of winning X, everyone can will – as in try or attempt – to win X.) This picks up the essential fact that, for Kant, an end is not a state of affairs, but that which serves the will as the "ground of its determination" (*G*427): that is, a rational agent's conception of what is choiceworthy (possibly, a representation of a possible state of affairs). Private ends are grounds of the will's determination that are not valid for all rational beings (what Kant calls "merely subjective ends"). Their abstracted-from-content inclusion further elaborates the membership condition of the kingdom of ends: it is a systematic union of ends-willing-ends. If this is right, abstraction from personal differences and from the content of private ends makes it possible "to think of a whole of ends in systematic union" only in an entirely formal sense. That is, when we think of persons qua rational agents and ends qua ends of their willing, we can say that both agents and their ends are under – in the sense of "governed by" – a single universal law (the CI): the law that determines universal validity for ends of both sorts.

Now to say that material objects are governed by the law of gravity or that cows are governed by the laws of their bovine nature is to say that there is a law that describes what they do qua object or cow. Material objects are subject to certain forces; cows to certain principles of growth and change. Neither law wholly determines behavior, for neither law works alone. Similarly with rational wills. There is a law describing the activity of such a will qua rational will, but it is not a law that wholly determines behavior. There are other influences. And there is an important difference, because the law of the rational will is a different kind of law. Cows cannot grow into horses, but humans can act like beasts. It is no less true, when they do, however, that their wills are law-governed (and by the law of rational wills). It is rather that it is the nature of the human will to be both law-governed and free. Whether or not an agent wills well, the moral law *is* the law of her rational nature. It is the basis of her dignity (a status she does not lose on occasions of willing badly).

The basic idea here is this. Just as our wills are autonomous when we act contrary to the moral law, so we will remain members of the kingdom of ends, however "irrational" our willing is. The kingdom of ends, like autonomy, is not something to be realized through the excellent activity of rational agents. We belong to a kingdom of ends just insofar as we are rational agents. But unlike autonomy, which is an essential property of a rational will, the kingdom of ends is a way of thinking about rational agents under law. We will have to see whether the formal idea of "systematic connection" that it introduces is rich enough to do any work.[11]

II

The kingdom of ends is not the only lawful order to which we belong. Insofar as we are rational beings, we are subject to the law that is expressed by the categorical imperative. Insofar as we are material beings, we are also subject to the empirical laws of the natural world. But toward one of the realms to which we belong – the realm of ends – we are said to stand as both subject and legislator. ("The concept of every rational being as one who must regard himself as legislating universal law by all his will's maxims" [*G*433].) That is, belonging to the concept of rational agency is the idea of an agent subject to a law (the CI) that applies to her because she legislates it for herself. This complicates the story about membership conditions in the kingdom of ends. Here is what Kant says:

A rational being belongs to the kingdom of ends as a member when he legislates in it universal laws while also being subject himself to these laws. He belongs to it as sovereign, when as legislator he is himself subject to the will of no other.

A rational being must always regard himself as a legislator in a kingdom of ends rendered possible by freedom of the will, whether as a member or as sovereign. The position of the latter can be maintained not merely through the maxims of his will but only if he is a completely independent being without needs and with unlimited power adequate to his will. (*G*433–4)

Although all rational beings must regard themselves as legislators in a kingdom of ends, rational beings like ourselves are dependent beings and so mere members (*Glieden*). An independent being (*unabhängiges Wesen*) is sovereign (*Oberhaupt*), because he is as legislator "subject to the will of no other." The implication is strange: how could we, as legislators, be subject to the will of *any* others consistent with our autonomy?[12]

Kant says that for a sovereign member of a kingdom of ends, it is not enough that he legislate universal law through his maxims; he must also be "a completely independent being without needs and with unlimited power adequate to his will" (*G*434). I take the fact that the sovereign member is without needs to imply that he cannot have private ends – his ends follow from his rational nature (they are necessary ends).[13] Further, he has the power to realize these ends without dependence on either contingent material conditions or the support of other rational agents. By contrast, we are dependent beings: we have needs (and so private ends) and lack power adequate to our will. But how does it follow that we are subject to the wills of others? Certainly one of the reasons why our power is not adequate to our wills is that others may interfere with us. So perhaps we are subject to the wills of others in the sense that our ability to will effectively is conditional on some degree of noninterference. But if independent wills are *not* subject to the wills of others in the sense of "subject to" in which all rational beings are subject to the laws of a kingdom of ends, the permanent possibility of interference does not seem to be what makes us subject to the wills of others.

Just before the member–sovereign distinction is made, Kant remarks that the systematic union of rational beings may be called a kingdom of ends because the common law that constitutes the kingdom has in view "the relation of such beings to one another as ends and means." That is: beyond external non-interference, the moral law regulates the conditions and terms of human cooperation. We may not subject others to our will in certain ways: we may not enslave others, act to control or manipulate their willings for our purposes, and so on. But this sense of "subject to" does not explain why we remain "subject to" the will of others when our use of them as means is constrained by our conception of them as ends in themselves, nor does it explain the sense in which we are "subject to" the will of others when we are treated as an end.

We are subject to the wills of others when we are subject to their authority: as citizen, institutional subordinate, and the like. This is a condition we are in, one might suppose, because we are beings with needs for whom hierarchical social roles provide useful, even necessary, means.[14] On similar grounds the *Groundwork* argument for a duty of mutual aid holds that the help of others is a condition of our successful agency that we cannot rationally reject. In both cases, our limited powers lead to compromised empirical autonomy (independence). Because we have needs and only limited power, we are not, even as legislators, independent of the wills of others.

We can take this idea another step. We are, in an extended sense, dependent on the wills of others insofar as the conditions of our agency are social. As our needs determine private ends, so also the particular and social conditions of our agency partly determine what we can will.[15] This is a social fact beyond the requirements of cooperation or non-interference. Thus although the principle of our willing is the self-legislated principle of autonomy, because we have needs that are mediated by social structures, what we will – the content of our maxims – is not.[16] On this interpretation, a being would be "subject to" the will of no other if and only if there was never sufficient reason to have the content of its willing determined by the content of the willings of others. We are not and cannot be in that position.

One final aspect of sovereignty needs attention: the sense in which the sovereign is a sovereign. This is the question of power. We know the sovereign's negative power: he is subject to the will of no other. But what can he bring about? If we are already legislating members of a kingdom of ends in virtue of our autonomous wills, what remains to be "realized" is precisely a kingdom of good wills and, beyond that, the highest good (the general condition in which virtue prevails and happiness is exactly proportioned to virtue, in direct response to it). Each of *us* lacks two relevant powers: to bring it about through our own good willing that others will also act well, and to make it the case that our virtue is rewarded (even, that our willings be effective: that we accomplish what we will). Even the "best" sovereign lacks the former power (concurrent good willing is a necessary condition for a union of good wills). Of course a *community* of sovereigns would have no need of either power: their maxims "necessarily conform with this objective principle of rational beings as legislating universal laws" (*G*434), and they have no needs.[17] Our condition might be compared to that of a government in exile: possessing a constitution and legitimacy, but lacking the power "to realize" just rule. What a supreme being could do is bring the kingdom of nature into harmony with a kingdom of ends (make nature friendly to virtue). But it could alter neither the conditions of the objective reality of a kingdom of good wills (that each act according to self-legislated universal law) nor the conditions of "worth" of its members. The kingdom of ends is a kingdom of limited sovereignty.

III

If, then, the kingdom of ends is just a way of representing an order of beings falling under the moral law, it remains to be seen what it contributes to the moral story. Does the order it represents bring to the practice of judgment any robust, normative sense of the social? Or does it merely represent the metaphysical fact that *as rational beings*, we are under self-given common law: the law of our autonomous rational natures?

Indeed, we might ask, what *could* follow from the mere fact of thinking of ourselves and all rational beings as under common law? Not that we are therefore to reject maxims that are not possible public rules of a *single* social order of rational persons. For if the principle of order just is the moral law – the principle of the CI – *any* maxim that has the form of universal law is consistent with the constitutive principle of a kingdom of ends. The set of all permissible maxims does not have the form of a social order, much less a unique order.[18]

Alternatively, one might suppose that the role of the kingdom of ends is to extend the reach of the CI to public rules, doing the work (on the moral side) of a principle or conception of justice. Only those laws or practices that could be laws for an order of rational beings (that is, consistent with the principle of their rational nature) are morally legitimate. I have no substantive objection to this extension; many have made good use of it. But I don't see where in the *Groundwork* discussion of the kingdom of ends there is support for this application.

Along these lines, one might think there is a prior question. Is it the case that, insofar as rational natures constitute a realm under a law of autonomy, it must therefore be possible for any group of rational natures to exist as a real social order according to principles consistent with their status as rational natures? That is, the idea of a kingdom of ends is the solution to the possibility question of a moral social order. But why should it be? Why should the fact that there is order of one kind when you abstract from differences imply that order of a different kind is possible when you do not? And recall that, for Kant, the state is a solution to the problem of order for a race of intelligent devils.[19]

The general form of the difficulty is this. If one sees the kingdom of ends as just another way of representing the moral law, then it is hard to see how it supports the idea of morality as a principle for a *social* order of rational persons (as opposed to an order of persons under law *simpliciter* – each acting permissibly, violating no duty). But if one thinks of Kantian morality as inherently social, that is, if we start by thinking that the moral order must be a social order, it is hard to see what the idea of a kingdom of ends adds. What we want is an account of how the kingdom of ends – as it bears on judgment, though formally equivalent to the formula of universal law – explains what it means to think of persons as in a social union that is, as such, expressive of their rational natures.

I think we can make progress here if we follow a lead John Rawls

offers in his unpublished lectures on Kant's ethics. Wanting to understand how the kingdom of ends is supposed to bring the moral law (as an
idea of reason) closer to intuition, Rawls focuses on Kant's remark that
the kingdom of ends is an ideal (G436).[20] Rawls's interpretation looks to
the technical notion of the *Ideal* in the *Critique of Pure Reason*: a kind of
individual thing that has a special role in judgment. The first feature, that
it is a kind of particular, serves Rawls's stated purpose; the second, its
role in judgment, serves mine – providing a way of thinking about the
nature of the order the kingdom of ends introduces.[21]

The relevant section of the first *Critique* is "The Ideal in General,"
Kant's prefatory remarks to the discussion of the Transcendental Ideal.[22]
The topic is the representation in thought of the concepts (loosely speaking) of reason. The general concept of the ideal is introduced this way.
"No objects can be represented through pure concepts of the understanding apart from the conditions of sensibility." When applied to appearances, the pure concepts of the understanding – the categories –
"can be exhibited *in concreto*." *Ideas* are farther removed from objective
reality than are categories, for "no appearance can be found in which
they can be represented *in concreto*." This is so because ideas "contain a
certain completeness to which no possible empirical knowledge ever
attains." The moral law is such an idea. The idea provides a conception
of systematic unity that reason tries to find, if only approximately, in
what is empirically possible. The *ideal* is yet further removed from objective reality. Kant says, "By the ideal I understand the idea, not merely *in
concreto*, but *in individuo*, that is, as an individual thing, determinable or
even determined by the idea alone."

The ideal as it figures in morality provides an example:

Virtue, and therewith human wisdom in its complete purity, are ideas. The wise
man (of the Stoics) is, however, an ideal, that is, a man existing in thought only,
but in complete conformity with the idea of wisdom. As the idea gives the *rule*,
so the ideal in such cases serves as the *archetype* for the complete determination
of the copy; and we have no other standard for our actions than the conduct of
this divine man within us, with which we compare and judge ourselves, and so
reform ourselves, although we can never attain to the perfection thereby
prescribed.

Kant warns that we cannot concede objective reality (existence) to the
ideal. We are further warned not to try to represent the ideal in an
example – as when one might depict the wise man in a story or romance.
As a product of imagination and not reason, such depiction necessarily
introduces arbitrary elements and limitations. Reason, rather, "thinks
for itself an object which it regards as being completely determinable in
accordance with principles." Although the ideal cannot exist, even in

example, it is not "a figment of the brain." The ideal supplies reason with a standard of judgment. Kant compares the ideal with Platonic "ideas of the divine understanding." Ideals of reason are like Platonic ideas insofar as they are the basis for realizing or approximating a kind of perfection. But unlike Platonic ideas, which have creative power in themselves (to bring into being copies), the ideal of reason has "practical power." As an object of reason it contains regulative principles that "form the basis of the possible perfection of certain *actions*."

Although the idea gives complete content to the ideal, it is the ideal as individual thing that plays the role in judgment – the role one would have expected moral rules or regulative principles to play. The idea gives the rule; the ideal serves as the archetype: the rule given the form of a human life. We do not, because we cannot, use the idea in judgment. Principle (the rule of reason) is nonetheless available to judgment in the shape of an exemplary human life. Judgment, using the archetype, depends on a kind of modeling.[23]

How would it work? In what way could we use the wise man of the Stoics as an ideal: a man existing in thought only, but in complete conformity with the idea of wisdom? To think of the wise man of the Stoics is to think of a person, mature and knowledgeable, in control of his desiring, who acts on certain principles (e.g., of studied detachment from material objects, personal relationships). There is *this kind* of abstraction: we do not know what he looks like, how old he is, or what he does. We do not know how his life goes. Yet the wise man remains a standard in the sense that we can intelligibly ask: How would he behave here? But that is because *he is* a set of principles, principles that are animated in a particular way, given a certain form. The ideal is a formal *embodiment* of regulative principle. The animation is not trivial; it is necessary in order to represent the Stoic principles as ones that can be the principles of *a human life*. This is the difference between thinking of Stoic principles as such, and acting with respect to judgment based on the Stoic ideal. If we cannot instantiate Stoic principles as such (they are principles of a kind of perfection that is outside empirical possibility), we can model our actions on that of the "divine man within us." The wise man eats, marries, negotiates the obligations of citizenship, raises children, and the rest. These are the things that a human person must do; they are the settings in which virtue can be shown.[24] Though I am unable to act on a principle of forming no attachments, when faced with loss, I have a model for how to behave: a way to think about what to do.

If the kingdom of ends is an ideal in this sense, it is a representation of an idea of reason (the moral law) as an individual thing, "determinable or even determined by the idea alone." The unrepresentable perfection of the moral law *as a law* is not that of the perfection of the individual will, but of the systematic unity, or order, of rational beings under a law of autonomy. The kingdom of ends cannot then be the bare formal idea of "ends under universal law." It would not then be an individual thing. As an archetype, available in thought as a standard of judgment, it has to be an order of persons – a social order – under common law. Not persons with any particular characteristics or with any specific ends. There is *that kind* of abstraction. But the kingdom of ends is not persons *in abstraction* from particularity and specificity: not abstract persons. Because the ideal represents the idea of the moral law in the form of a human social order, we are to think of finite beings, in a place, with possessions, attachments, histories, and the rest. So, the kingdom of ends exists, in thought only, as an *individual* order of human beings under a law of autonomy: an archetype of human order, against which we can "compare and judge ourselves, and so reform ourselves." We cannot know ahead of time just what kind of order judgment in terms of the kingdom of ends will yield. That remains a function of the actual circumstances of living together. Though we cannot instantiate the law as a principle of order, faced with hard choices, we have a model we can interrogate about what to do.

IV

Let us suppose that the kingdom of ends is an archetype, a representation of the moral law as an individual thing. Would it make any real difference to moral judgment to have the moral law so represented? The rule of the archetype is: "act in accordance with the maxims of a member legislating universal laws for a merely possible kingdom of ends" (*G*439). It contains the "complete determination of all maxims" by the moral law, combining the idea of legislating universal law through one's maxims and the idea that one is legislating law *for* a system of ends (persons who are ends in themselves).

This representation of the moral law must be identical in its requirement to the other formulations of the categorical imperative. It can be distinct only in the *way* it represents the moral. However, to say that the idea of a kingdom of ends cannot be the source of a normatively distinct principle of judgment is not to say that it adds no practical content to moral judgment. *Each* formulation of the categorical imperative not only sets out a stage in the chain of conditions that must be satisfied if a categorical imperative is to be possible, it also offers what I have elsewhere called an "interpretation" of the categorical imperative's universalization requirement.[25] Moral judgment requires the interpretations that the subsequent formulations of the CI provide. If the formula of universal law tells us *that* a given maxim is impermissible, the full account of *why* it is comes only with the richer representations of the moral law provided by the subsequent formulations.

Suppose we have shown that a maxim of deceit cannot be a universal law for rational agents. We still need to determine what it is about deceit that is wrong-making in order to know, for example, whether or when we are to classify telling partial truths with deceitful utterances.[26] If the wrong-making characteristic of the maxim of deceit were in the intentional falsehood, we would not. If, however, it is in the treatment of an agent's reason-giving capacity as a manipulable thing, this gives us reason to put "partial truths offered with manipulative intent or expectation" in the same category as deceit. Without the formula of humanity's interpretation of maxims that fail universalization *as* maxims whose principles do not accept rational nature as a final end, this would not be possible.[27]

Now if each level of interpretation of the CI further explains the wrong-making characteristics of impermissible actions and maxims, we should find ourselves able to use the idea of a kingdom of ends to expand the casuistical power of Kantian moral judgment. What we want is an example or class of examples where there is a maxim whose rejection by the CI procedure lacks didactic import without the kingdom of ends interpretation. Moral judgment, enhanced by the resources of the archetype, should expose their dependence on principles that oppose or subvert the conditions of lawful union for autonomous agents, and for us in particular, the lawful union of autonomous agents with private ends.

Let us consider again the status of private ends in the kingdom of ends. I earlier rejected a compossibility requirement – that only those private ends are permissible that can be jointly acted on successfully – on the grounds that a success condition for ends was not consistent with the Kantian account of permissibility. But (some) failures of compossibility look to be just the kind of thing a universalization test rejects: not everyone can win the game, the prize, the place. I believe that the kingdom of ends interpretation can explain why some of these failures (and not others) are morally significant. For example, maxims of unqualified competition *should be* rejected; it is when competitors have unadorned maxims of winning that competition tends to breed excess, cheating, and violence. We can say: their principles fall short of the archetype of possible laws for an order of autonomous co-legislating persons (dependent rational beings with private ends). There are other possible conceptions of a competitive end. All competitors can do their best, all can try to win, and the like. And all such maxims are com-possible. But what makes this morally significant is not the possibility of joint success, but that the principle of these maxims can be understood to support a lawful social order of autonomous agents.

We can trace the significance of this sort of result in two ways. First of all it guides casuistry, allowing us to distinguish cases of agents who act on permissible maxims in circumstances where, as it happens, not all can succeed from cases of agents with maxims whose principles are incon-sistent with possible principles of an order of rational agents. Extra-polating, we can use this result to distinguish among maxims of pursuit of different categories of scarce resources. It can explain why a maxim with a "first come, first served" principle could be morally permissible for concert tickets but not for scarce medical resources. If persons have an in principle equal claim on aid, but not music, the system constraints of the kingdom of ends require (something like) the complex principles of triage for medical need, while they can permit a more laissez-faire reso-lution to competition for tickets.[28]

Second, the interpretation provides agents with a fuller understanding of their permissible and obligatory actions *as* moral actions. The agent who acts well – who makes the moral law her principle – acts from maxims that express the full conditions of choiceworthiness as elabo-rated in the interpretations of the categorical imperative. So, in the trivial case, I head off early in the day to get tickets with an understanding that interest and willingness to queue are morally reasonable conditions of success here. Such a conception of action would be morally inappro-priate, however, where the good in question is necessary to sustain lives. (Thus the fact that I went to a concert yesterday need have no bearing on my going again today, whereas among a group of starving persons, those who have eaten recently may have less claim on remaining resources. Analogous reasoning would show the impermissibility of hoarding.)

As an interpretation of the CI, the kingdom of ends casts as morally relevant facts those features of social life that impinge on the conditions of rational agency. It is not discretionary, then, whether such facts are reflected in agents' maxims. Thus in circumstances of scarcity, when my action would have an impact on vital resources, I may not consider it as "merely an economic venture." In this way the kingdom of ends contrib-utes categories of moral salience necessary for moral judgment. Just as the formula of humanity informs us that to act in conformity with the moral law we must acknowledge others in our maxims as autonomous end-setters, so the kingdom of ends directs us to regard others as possible co-legislators in a lawful order. By adding the *form* of the social to our conception of autonomous rational beings, the kingdom of ends both sets conditions on a social order that require consistency with autonomous rational nature, and, insofar as the kingdom of ends is a representation of the moral law (or of willing according to the moral law), it introduces the idea of the moral order as itself a social order. It is not an order imposed on agents, but an order of agents whose rationality is essentially expressed as much through social as through natural-physical means. The full deliberative constraint derived from the kingdom of ends – of a moral order as a social order – requires a degree and depth of adjustment to others, to their ways of life and values, that transforms the very conception of self that is the foundation of the moral enterprise.[29]

Individuals act from and with a complex sense of themselves, their projects, and their actions. The details of this complexity can be essential to accurate moral assessment. For example, we can see that the adequacy of a maxim of beneficence turns not only on whether one is acting to meet a claim of need, but also on the attitude of respect with which one acts.[30] The moral requirement is not that we do two things – give aid and act respectfully – but that the aid given should be conceived of and expressed in a respectful way. The requirement of respect can then complicate the moral story, given possible social facts about agents' actions.

Let us now take this a step further. Suppose I view my level of wealth as a contingent feature of class and good fortune, and have a conception of wealth as joint social product. I then act as beneficence requires, fully acknowledging the claim of need, with a conception of giving shaped by the idea of trusteeship. There are two things to note here. The first is about action–description: much of moral importance would be lost if moral judgment could not distinguish this maxim from one of giving *as charity*. If wealth is regarded as deserved private possession, providing aid may be more personal (giving what is one's own) than if one views possessions as common goods held in trust for all (giving as a required redistribution). Second, it may be that the further requirement on beneficence – that the giving be respectful – gives reasons to favor an institution with a conception of property as trusteeship insofar as it supports a moral climate of ownership that avoids both arrogance and servility. This is a way of taking fuller deliberative account of the fact that morality is a social order of rational persons, and it discloses a finer grain of moral requirement. In light of this, we might find that morality requires (or tolerates) different ways of responding to need at a distance than to need at home, and this fact may reach much deeper than what first appears to be involved in having a respectful attitude.[31]

It would appear to follow from such a "complete determination" of maxims that certain institutions of property are morally suspect because of the attitudes toward wealth and possessions they invite. And I think this is right. We should note, however, that such a conclusion transforms the way we think about the results of moral judgment in that the moral failure identified here is not one that the individual agent can remedy. Nonetheless, the uncovering of such "global" moral failure affects how the individual agent acts. Although one may not be able to transform or fully escape institutions that encourage moral arrogance, one can become attentive to an institution's effects and work to resist the way it would shape responses to others. We might think about the various ways it is difficult to respond in a respectful way to homeless panhandlers – the mix of dirt, aggression, discomfort, moral exhaustion. There can be substantial salutary effect in acknowledging the ways social institutions encourage a culture of street poverty. In addition to gaining reasons to support institutional change where that is possible, one comes to recognize the circumstances of poverty as a structural assault on the conditions of human choice and agency. Such recognition can, and should, affect one's response to "victims."[32]

This enhanced conception of judgment also alters the way we think about the general conditions of moral judgment and action. Given the complex social bases of *normal* action, there is reason to be cautious about projecting descriptions of others' actions, needs, and so on, based on an understanding of our own circumstances. My maxims of action must be formed on the basis of some knowledge of how others act and react. If I had no idea about another agent – how she understands or reacts – the possible maxims of interaction I could responsibly adopt would be minimal. Much of this we take for granted because we assume that the other is like us: needing food when hungry and help when injured, being susceptible to guilt and shame, responsive to disrespect, and so on. And to a very large extent we are warranted in this assumption: others *are* pretty much like us. Because we tend to live among others whose similarities to ourselves we take for granted, and because patterns of action become routine, most of us are rarely challenged – in our private lives, anyway – to acknowledge differences that are deep or make us uncomfortable.

Recent lessons about gender and race in the workplace warn of ways this ordinary fact may support culpable complacency. When apparently sincere and decent people infer from the elimination of formal institutional discrimination that the barriers to the advancement of women and persons of color have been removed, it becomes easy for them to regard remaining complaints of discrimination as matters of unintentional insensitivity or excessively delicate feelings, residues to be dissolved over time, aided by the accumulated effects of good intentions. There is a moral fault in such attitudes. They miss the ways facts about institutions that favor white males, as well as facts about women and racial minorities that make them especially vulnerable to informal barriers, need to be acknowledged as morally relevant conditions of action, *given* the elimination of formal barriers.

The possibility of such moral complexity enjoins agents to develop a morally tuned sensitivity to the effects of their sincerely intended actions and to the interplay between what they intend and the social or institutional contexts in which they act. These burdens of moral judgment are present when social circumstances are such that first-order sincerity is morally insufficient. They are therefore especially acute in circumstances of social pluralism, where there are present, not just in society, but in one's normal range of activity, persons whose moral circumstances and claims reflect distinct traditions and ways of life or different distributions of power.

The extreme condition shows something about the normal one. Even ordinary moral judgment takes place within a community of judgment: a conceptual space constructed by rules of salience that identify the features of our circumstances that require moral attention, as well as regulative principles that shape agents' deliberations. These include social rules acquired through participation in a moral community. Even the most basic moral facts – what counts as a harm that sets a moral claim, what counts as a valid agreement – are functions of social practice. The fact that neither agents' moral circumstances nor their obligations can be understood without locating them within a social setting is neither an aberration nor something ideal moral theory might avoid (by abstraction, say). It is what follows from the fact, recognized in the kingdom of ends, that autonomous moral agency is social. That is why failure to acknowledge the social conditions of agency – to actively identify and include them in maxims – is a moral failure.

The idea of a kingdom of ends tells us that even if the social world of persons with private ends is immensely varied, moral order is possible. This does not mean that there is any unique set of ideal social relations or institution – not for rational beings in general, and certainly not for human beings. What the kingdom of ends as an ideal (an archetype) demonstrates is simply that a world of moral full-compliance will be an ordered world.[33] Certain sorts of moral disorder are therefore problematic.

What kind of order is morally possible for us? There are different ways to picture it, connected to different views about the fit of ends in the kingdom of ends. One sort of order involves agents acting for their diverse ends, accepting full "side-constraints" of permissibility, and satisfying whatever positive moral obligations apply. It is a minimal, mostly negative ideal of order, capturing the sense of a stable, principle-based community. In this kingdom of ends, no one acts on maxims of deceit, no one denies a claim of need for reasons of mere self-interest, and so on.

But suppose one asked: How many languages are spoken in the king-dom of ends? How many local systems of custom and practice? We need to pay attention to the presumption of homogeneity in our picture of the kingdom of ends. There is a moral point to the first *Critique*'s injunction not to try to represent the ideal in an example (a political story or romance). Thus maxims can fail if they do not acknowledge differences that arise from specific histories that affect the ways individuals understand their lives. Consider the ease of unintended insult in socially complex circumstances, the disparities in what counts as threat or advantage. Actions I judge to be harassing are often not performed according to maxims of harassment, and yet I may not be wrong about what has happened. Sincerity is often a virtue; sometimes it is a mask. If such facts bear directly on the morality of maxims, minimal order is not enough.

One source of resistance to this line of argument might be the thought that such problems are merely variants of a more general problem for Kantian ethics: its inability to move beyond an agent's conception of her action, however parochial, to a neutral conception or description suitable to action assessment. Because maxims are the objects of moral assess-ment, agents' subjective limitations are passed on. If I do not know that what I am saying is false, I cannot deceive; if I have forgotten an obliga-tion, the maxim I do act on does not contain an impermissible principle; if I offer what I believe is a suitable gift, I am not insulting the recipient who, for cultural reasons, finds it offensive.

Kantian theory can deal with many normal errors through an exten-sion of the context of assessment to maxims that agents adopt before and after acting. Where the risk of advantage is high, "innocent" falsehood caused by lack of effort to acquire knowledge is a moral failure. Obliga-tions impose requirements of preparation that allow us to condemn routine causes of omission; failures of reasonable preparation ground subsequent obligations of response. Likewise, in circumstances in which one knows or should know that divergent cultural facts affect the mean-ing of social gestures, one is under obligation to make one's maxims responsive to these facts. This is in part determined by the normal conditions of practical efficacy – a sincere agent wants her actions to express her volitions. I am arguing here that it is also a condition set by the deeper practical demands of the kingdom of ends.

To the extent that one assumes social homogeneity, the social bases of moral judgment remain in the background, encouraging a reasonable but mistaken expectation of uniformity in the domain of morally correct actions. But if social pluralism is deep, the set of permissible actions – taken one by one – is not likely to be well-ordered. When sincere moral agents act on parochial maxims – maxims that make essential reference to a local community of judgment – that can defeat the possibility for mutual moral understanding and engagement, leaving us unable to recognize the moral content of another's action or incapable of understanding how our own sincere actions could be other than morally benign. This is a condition we are under obligation to overcome. We might say: in circumstances of social pluralism, the kingdom of ends supports an obligation to extend the community of moral judgment. Good willing is not a standard of solipsistic or parochial virtue. The obligation to act as law-making members of a kingdom of ends thus amplifies the normative content of the categorical imperative: it is a cosmopolitan ideal.

The task of constructing a more inclusive community of moral judgment is not one of accepting reasonable principles for adjudicating conflict; the moral problem that comes with any deep social pluralism is prior to that in the mutual opacity of local value concepts. If we accept that there is more than one permissible way to order the social world (different institutions of property, marriage, etc.; different patterns of child-rearing, schedules of autonomy, conceptions of illness, injury, offense), then we will often not be able to tell whether someone's maxims are permissible, their practices acceptable, without undertaking the more practically freighted task of coming to moral terms with their ways of life.

The kingdom of ends thus offers a cosmopolitan ideal that undercuts parochialism, though not without potential cost. The mutual adjustment of concepts necessary to secure the conditions of successful moral understanding and colloquy may challenge local values. Some local values will survive in changed form; others may be incompatible with the conditions of extended moral order. Certainly, immoral values have no claim on our support. But some of the values that may not survive exposure to "foreign" ways of life might be permissible in their own space. The fact that a community would not survive the loss or change of a value may be an occasion for profound regret; it is not in itself a sufficient reason to resist change. Communities as such do not have rights of survival. How to work out the moral pragmatics for such costs – who should bear them? on whose terms is the more extended community to be built? – requires its own discussion. My claim here is only that such a project is necessary.

The practical guidance provided by the kingdom of ends as an ideal is not, then, to be found in abstractions from particulars, or in the image of an ideal order, but in directions for the deliberative accommodation to particular differences. Its cosmopolitanism is a standard of deliberation, a way of getting to order from the bottom up. We do not fail to live in a kingdom of ends because we are imperfectly rational beings, our propensity to rational order interfered with by compulsions originating in our systems of desire. If that were the case, the solution would be found in coordination rules for permissible sets of ends: a political solution in the narrow sense, suitable for a race of devils. Nor is it an ideal in the sense of a community of good wills; that would have no bearing on our condition. The kingdom of ends is an ideal because it is (perhaps impossibly) hard even to imagine the full import of the requirement to regard ourselves and one another as co-legislating members of a moral order: potential members, as I would put it, of a community of moral judgment. If the homogeneity of values is not a human goal, then the idea of a kingdom of ends marks a permanent practical vocation.

V

The kingdom of ends as an ideal allows us to reflect on our actions as a whole and on the institutions and practices that provide the background for action and judgment. It therefore fills two serious gaps in standard Kantian accounts of moral judgment. But must one interpret the kingdom of ends the way I have here? I think it is enough to argue that one can. The rest should be decided by the fruitfulness of the concept.

NOTES

For many years I did not write about Kant's kingdom of ends, not because I thought there was nothing to say, but because it seemed to me in too many ways mysterious. When at last I made some progress, it was because I did something I have often done when I am similarly puzzled: I read John Rawls's lectures on Kant's ethics. The benefits go well beyond the specifics of interpretation. The questions he asks, the connections he makes, the texts he brings to bear – these cumulatively urge a patient, philosophical seriousness towards the problem and towards Kant. They enable one to see familiar things in deeper and more interesting ways. Twenty-eight years ago I took my first class with John Rawls. I learned a great deal from him then; it is no surprise that I am learning from him still.

1. That they do not seem to be possible co-conditions for any possible ethical theory I believe comes from misunderstanding both the demands of rational cosmopolitanism – what it means to regard another as a rational agent per se – and the constraints of the local – how it is that particular values have standing in a general moral framework.

2. See Onora O'Neill, *Constructions of Reason* (Cambridge University Press, 1989), especially chap. 1, and Christine Korsgaard, *The Sources of Normativity* (Cambridge University Press, 1996), Lecture IV.

3. This is O'Neill's point (ibid).

4. Nietzsche seems to have understood Kant this way. To go beyond good and evil is to act on principles others cannot endorse.

5. That the expression of rational nature as in some way social is part of the idea of a kingdom of ends is not exactly news. Interesting elaborations of this idea figure in the work of Onora O'Neill and Christine Korsgaard, and especially of Thomas Hill, who has used the kingdom of ends as the centerpiece of what he calls a "constructivist" interpretation of Kantian ethics; see his *Dignity and Practical Reason* (Ithaca: Cornell University Press, 1992). This body of work makes a convincing case for the importance and usefulness of the notion of a kingdom of ends. It certainly shows that the role of the kingdom of ends in the *Groundwork* argument had to be more than a conclusory high-toned moral ideal. However, it does not satisfactorily resolve the role the kingdom of ends is supposed to have, either as an element in the *Groundwork* argument, or as an idea with practical import connected to the main line of Kantian deliberation and judgment.

6. Immanuel Kant, *Grounding for the Metaphysics of Morals*, trans. James W. Ellington (Indianapolis: Hackett Publishing Co., 1981), AK. 436 (hereafter cited in the text as "*G*", page numbers following the Akademie edition).

7. It is the object of Groundwork II to argue that this principle is "the principle that every human will is one which legislates law in all its maxims" (*G*432).

8. Could the "principles" be the principles of the three kinds of imperative: assertoric, apodeictic, and categorical? This does not seem possible. Only the principle of the categorical imperative is a law.

9. If the model for a kingdom of ends is some kind of social order, then you do not want to abstract from all differences in picturing the union of persons under law. You want an idea of the differences that are morally compossible. Some differences matter, and it is an important moral question what they are. (Some rational beings are children; others are materially dependent; and so forth.)

10. Even in the natural world, order is measured by system and subsystem, not by the success of any given organism or activity.

11. At three points, Kant says things that might seem to run counter to this line of argument. When he says that "morality consists in the relation of all action to that legislation whereby a kingdom of ends is possible" (*G*434), one might read this as a claim that morality (moral action or good willing) is the means whereby a kingdom of ends may be brought about. I don't think it is. "Morality" names the authoritative relation of the CI to all willed actions of rational beings. It is the legislation that makes beings like us members of a possible kingdom of ends: a systematic union of rational wills under law. That is why in acting according to the moral law (in making the CI the principle of our actions) we can think of ourselves as giving expression to a "higher law" than the law that governs the realm of things. Failure to act lawfully, however, does not constitute freedom from the law. Kant also describes the kingdom of ends as "an ideal" (*G*433), which suggests a concept of moral perfection: the way things would be if only we acted well (with a good will). Again, I think this is not correct. The sense of "ideal" that Kant

has in mind is nothing so simple. "Ideal" is a technical term in the vocabulary of critical philosophy. It is a particular way of representing a concept of which we can have no experience. There are connections with notions of perfection, but they are epistemic, not utopic. (This notion of the ideal is examined in Section III.) And last, when Kant says that "a kingdom of ends would actually be realized through maxims whose rule is prescribed to all rational beings by the categorical imperative, if these maxims were universally obeyed" (*G*438), he seems to be describing how the kingdom of ends comes about: through good willing. But in the context of the passage, I think it is plain that we should take "realized" (*vorschreibt*) to mean "instantiated" or "inscribed" in *this* world, the "kingdom of nature." We are, he says, already members of "a world of rational beings" (*mundus intelligibilis*) as a kingdom of ends, because of the legislation belonging to all persons as members (ibid).

12. There is no shifting of terms here: *unterworfen* is the term for being subject to the law and subject to the will of another.

13. Since needs individuate empirical selves, no sovereign could have reason to adopt ends that were not a function of his rational nature.

14. The *Rechtslehre* can be seen as finding its moral place here in what is for us a non-contingent need.

15. So the desires for sexual gratification, stable intimacy, and procreation are channeled by social institutions into a need for a spouse. Neither the conjunction nor the heterosexual demand are necessary.

16. Perhaps this tracks part of the elusive difference between the holy will and the merely good will.

17. They would also, I assume, have no virtue that calls for reward.

18. If we say that it rules out maxims that could not be public rules of any social order of (co-)legislating rational beings, we deploy the concept "social," but do not give it any work to do.

19. Immanuel Kant, "Perpetual Peace," in *Kant On History*, ed. Lewis White Beck (Indianapolis: Bobbs-Merrill, 1963), p. 112. Kant does not think that a requirement of moral social order follows from the mere possibility of order among rational beings. Attempts at world government invite "soulless despotism."

20. John Rawls, *Kant Lectures* (Harvard University, 1987), pp. 45–50.

21. In the *Kant Lectures*, Rawls is puzzled about the point of abstraction ("from personal differences between persons and from the content of their private ends") in the idea of a kingdom of ends (p. 46). As I hope to show, further reflection on Kant's notion of the *Ideal* helps make sense of this.

22. All quotations in this section are from the *Critique of Pure Reason*, trans. N. K. Smith (London: St. Martins, 1970), A567/B596–A571/B599.

23. The analogous move is made in the *Groundwork* use of the formula of the law of nature to represent, for purposes of judgment, the formula of universal law. The explanation of this limit of judgment in using the ideas of reason is the subject of the Typic of the second *Critique* and the Schematism of the first.

24. "Remember that you ought to behave in life as you would at a banquet. As something is being passed around it comes to you; stretch out your hand and take a portion of it politely. It passes on; do not detain it. Or it has not come to you yet; do not project your desire to meet it, but wait until it comes in

front of you." Epictetus, *The Encheridion*, §15 in *The Discourses*, Vol. II, trans. W. A. Oldfather (Cambridge: Harvard University Press, 1979).

25. This interpretation is set out in my "Leaving Deontology Behind," in *The Practice of Moral Judgment* (Cambridge: Harvard University Press, 1993).

26. *Pace* the tradition, moral judgment is not possible if we bring every maxim to judgment without a prior understanding of its morally salient features.

27. It is also the formula of humanity that directs us to regard maxims that fail the CI procedure's universalization test as containing a principle that disregards the conditions of rational agency as limits on discretionary willing. The interpretation thus also allows us to see how such diverse needs as life support, education, physical integrity, and even the social conditions of self-worth have the same ground of moral claim, based on the idea of taking the "subject who is an end in himself" as far as possible as one's own end (*G*430).

28. Of course, a different view of music would challenge this permissiveness.

29. This way of understanding the place of the social in moral judgment distinguishes the view offered here from what has been called a "constructivist" interpretation of the kingdom of ends. A constructivist interpretation regards the kingdom of ends as a device of representation in which the idea of a possible social union of autonomous, co-legislating agents provides a standard of judgment independent of the formula of universal law. Legitimate principles of action are those that can be endorsed as public laws or rules of a social union through which all members can conceive of themselves and each other as ends in themselves. By contrast, what I have been exploring is the idea of the kingdom of ends as the "complete determination" of the moral law: a way of coming to see what is involved in a fully amplified (interpreted) conception of moral judgment based on the formula of universal law. The two interpretations therefore differ regarding the scope of judgment: not all actions with moral significance can be correctly represented as involving principles of a possible social order. A constructivist interpretation locates the social external to the conception of rational agency: that we require acceptable principles of a social order is a contingent problem practical reason has to solve.

30. Immanuel Kant, *Doctrine of Virtue*, in *The Metaphysics of Morals*, trans. Mary J. Gregor (Cambridge University Press, 1991), p. 247.

31. Some of the material here and in the rest of this section is drawn from a more extended discussion of these issues in my "Pluralism and the Community of Moral Judgment," in *Toleration: An Elusive Virtue*, ed. D. Heyd (Princeton: Princeton University Press, 1996).

32. The beginning of such a transformation might be found, for example, in the acknowledgment of the "battered wife syndrome" as part of a legitimate legal claim of self-defense. It is not a stable understanding of the problem because legal change works by taking old concepts into new contexts. One can nonetheless understand the tension caused by enlarging "self-defense" as a stage toward a conceptually deeper response that, on the one hand, does not diminish the agency of the battered wife, and, on the other, is open to understanding the constraint on choice as constructed by morally unacceptable social roles.

33. It will be a kingdom "realized through maxims whose rule is prescribed to all rational beings by the categorical imperative, if these maxims were universally obeyed" (*G*439).

Legislating for a Realm of Ends:
The Social Dimension of Autonomy

ANDREWS REATH

I

Shortly after Kant claims autonomy for the moral agent, the argument of the *Groundwork* takes a turn that leads one to question what this autonomy amounts to. In attributing autonomy to rational agents, Kant regards them as a kind of sovereign legislator with authority over the use of their rational capacities. He holds that they have (in some sense) the power to enact law through their wills, without being bound to any external authority, and are subject only to their own legislation. Kant also says that this conception of the moral agent leads to the concept of a "realm of ends":

> The concept of every rational being as one who must regard himself as legislating universal law by all his will's maxims, so that he may judge himself and all his actions from this point of view, leads to another very fruitful concept, which depends on the aforementioned one, viz., that of a realm of ends. (*G*, IV: 433)[1]

The subsequent discussion makes it clear that Kant believes that autonomy is exercised by enacting principles that could serve as law for a community of agents, each of whom possesses the same legislative capacities as oneself (*G*, IV: 433–40). It would then seem that the laws enacted by such an agent must be able to gain the agreement of all members of this community of ends. But how is one autonomous if the laws that one wills are subject to the constraint that they can be accepted by, or justified to, all members of a realm of ends? This question is an instance of the general problem of how Kant can combine the universal validity of moral requirements with the autonomy of moral agents. Kant ties moral autonomy to the capacity to act from reasons, or to will practical principles, that are universally valid. But why isn't the condition that one's willing be universally valid a limitation on an agent's sovereign authority and a restriction of autonomy?

This essay uses the connection between Kant's conception of autonomy and his concept of a realm of ends as the occasion to explore a number of issues about the nature of autonomy. The core of Kant's conception of autonomy is that rational agents are sovereign over the employment of their rational capacities. One's exercise of one's reason is not subject to the governance of any external authority, or to any standards other than those generated by one's reason. Kant explicitly views moral agents as a kind of sovereign legislator who are autonomous in both a negative and a positive sense: they are not bound to any higher external authority, and have the power to give law through their wills.[2] He believes that moral agents exercise or fully express their autonomy by guiding their willing by certain kinds of principles and norms. We can see why this is a conception of autonomy if agents choose these principles themselves, and if governance by these principles creates the control over external and subjective influences that is needed for self-determination. But Kant also holds that one's adoption of particular norms is constrained by a higher-order norm of universal validity, which agents do not choose. So it is natural to ask how Kant can attribute autonomy to the moral agent while holding that its exercise must meet this condition of universal validity.

The idea that one exercises moral autonomy by legislating for a realm of ends leads to further complications. Kant defines a realm of ends as a "systematic union of rational beings through common objective laws," and it is his ideal of a social order in which relations between agents are governed by moral principles (*G*, IV: 433). Situating the autonomous agent in a community of agents who share the same legislative capacities appears to introduce a dependence on the judgments of other agents, whose potential responses may constrain what one can will. One does not decide in isolation whether one's willing is universally valid, since that is a question of whether one's principles can gain the acceptance of other rational agents. Either one is bound to exercise one's autonomy by willing principles acceptable to the members of a realm of ends, or the measure of whether this capacity is fully exercised is that one's volition has this general acceptability. Either way, the willing of an autonomous agent appears subject to socially applied norms not chosen by the agent, including the general norm that one's willing be acceptable to the members of a realm of ends. Again, one may wonder why that does not limit autonomy.

A standard approach to these issues is to note that Kant's thought contains conflicting strains. While roughly the first half of the *Groundwork* stresses the necessity and universality of moral requirements, Kant introduces the notion of autonomy at a crucial transition in the text and thereafter views moral agents as a kind of sovereign legislator bound only to self-given laws. The interpretive question is how to fit these strains together. The approach that takes these concepts to need reconciliation sees them as separate and self-standing ideas, whose consistency is problematic. Clearly there are difficulties here, but they are more easily resolved if, instead of initially assuming an inherent opposition between autonomy and universal validity, we look for ways in which they are mutually dependent. Accordingly, I want to explore ways in which the exercise of autonomy is made possible by the capacity to think, act, and judge in ways that can make claims to universal validity, or as Kant might put it, in ways that can gain "the agreement of free citizens, each of whom must be permitted to express, without let or hindrance, his objections or even his veto" (*KrV* B767). Kant calls such agreement the "verdict" of reason, and it has an obvious tie to the ideal of consensus implicit in the idea of a Realm of Ends. I will approach this issue by asking how Kant's conception of autonomy leads to the notion of a realm of ends. Reflection about the connection between these concepts reveals that the autonomous agent is neither unbound by rules, or free from all socially applied constraints. Autonomy (in individuals) is made possible by certain kinds of laws, norms, and standards that guide an agent's willing, and it presupposes, and is only exercised among, a community of rational agents with equal capacity to give law. In sum, the introduction of the concept of a realm of ends makes explicit the social dimension to Kant's conception of autonomy.

This puzzle – how could one have autonomy if one's willing must be acceptable to all members of a realm of ends (i.e., meet a condition of universal validity)? – arises from our expectation that autonomy and constraint by socially applied rules and standards are incompatible. Why do we expect an inconsistency here? One answer is that, for Kant, autonomy involves (the capacity for) independence from certain kinds of external influence on the use of one's reason, specifiable in different ways. Autonomy requires the capacity to reason and act independently of inclinations – that is, to arrive at conclusions and to act from reasons and principles that are not based on inclination and private conditions in oneself. It also requires the capacity for independence from certain kinds of social influence (e.g., custom, tradition, social convention, or established political and religious authorities, etc.) in the formation of beliefs, desires, values, and general principles of conduct.[3] It may in addition require freedom from subjection to external authority in the use of one's reason – for instance, in the judgment of what one has reason to do, or in the choice of ends, principles of action, or higher-order values. Since focusing on this aspect of autonomy leads one to detail the kinds of influence and authority from which the autonomous agent is free, it tempts one to think that autonomy insulates the agent from all unchosen constraints and social influence. One is led to view the autonomous agent

as a sovereign law-giver, unbound by tradition, convention, and authority, who legislates for himself (boldly and proudly!). But while agents
with autonomy must be able to abstract from certain kinds of psychological and social influence, they do not for that reason think and act in
isolation. Autonomy has a positive aspect, and without specifying the
kind of meaningful activity that the agent is free to engage in, it remains
an empty concept. The positive specification of autonomy is likely to do
two things: it will introduce rules that structure and make possible the
activity that the agent is free to engage in, and it will introduce interaction with other agents. The activities providing the positive specification
of autonomy will be rule-governed activities that require the participation of others, and presuppose social practices sustained by a community
of agents.

One element in my proposal for dissolving the tension between
autonomy and subjection to rules and social constraint is to approach
autonomy through the triadic analysis of liberty. We should begin by
viewing autonomy schematically as the freedom of a rational agent from
certain kinds of constraint and authority to engage in certain kinds of
meaningful and creative activity.[4] While the negative component of the
schema (the "independence condition") removes the agent from certain
kinds of social influence, its positive specification will make it clear that
autonomy is only a possibility for agents located within sets of practices
that structure their activity and interaction with other agents. This is not
for the psychological reason that it is only under certain social conditions
that one can develop the capacity for independent and critical thought.
Rather it is because the kinds of activities that provide the positive
specification of autonomy presuppose systems of constitutive rules and
the participation of other rational agents. As the rules that define various
kinds of rational activity, they are the rules that one must follow in order
to exercise the capacity with which autonomy is identified. In addition,
this capacity is exercised in relation to other agents, who can recognize
that the constitutive rules have been followed and can respond in appropriate ways. Thus, the exercise of autonomy presupposes a community of
agents with the capacity to follow a system of rules, judge their correct
application, and respond as called for.

I pursue these issues in different stages. Before going into the connection between Kant's substantive conception of autonomy and the notion
of a realm of ends, I develop some general observations about how
freedom and autonomy may be related to governance by rules and
standards. We tend to think that rules restrict free activity, but there are
also rules that make meaningful and creative activities possible. Attention to the different functions that rules serve, specifically to their consti-

tutive role, supplies another key element in dissolving the conflict between autonomy and governance by rules. In the next section I look at
instances where the freedom to engage in certain activities and governance by rules are not in tension. The point I make requires the introduction of rules with a special (non-restrictive) function, but there is no
thought that these rules are self-imposed or self-chosen. In Sections III
and IV, I apply this framework to Kant's conception of the autonomy of
the moral agent.

II

Are speakers "bound" by linguistic rules in a way that limits their freedom? Do the rules of a language restrict my ability to express my
thoughts and communicate them to others? Clearly not, since they make
expression and communication possible in the first place. When I follow
the rules of a language, I have accomplished something that is recognizable by others. I have said something, made sense, conveyed a thought.
The possibilities are more elaborate when further rules and standards
are in place. By conforming to the relevant rules, one can say something
that is recognizable as an apology or a reproach, an act of encouragement or consolation. One can make a true statement, construct a valid
argument, develop an analysis, or write a poem; and by meeting further
standards covering that activity, one can do it well or insightfully, in a
way that gains the appreciation or respect of others. Presumably the
same rules and standards that the speaker follows are employed by
others in the linguistic community to recognize, interpret, and evaluate
his or her activity. Thus they must share, and the speaker must presuppose that they share, the same basic understanding of and ability to apply
these rules. The responses of others can indicate the extent to which one
has conformed to these rules, and can measure one's success in the
intended activity. Others finding you unintelligible, or reflecting back a
meaning that you did not intend, may be a sign that you failed to conform
to the rules. To the extent that one can communicate a thought only by
following the relevant rules, they limit what one can intelligibly do. But
when one does conform to the rules, one has accomplished something
and has the right to certain responses from others who share the system
of norms – for instance, that they interpret one's act in a certain way, that
they acknowledge one's achievement, or where appropriate, that they
respond as prescribed by a further rule of the practice (accept the apology, either acknowledge the validity of a reproach or defend against it,
show gratitude for the encouragement, etc.).

The general point that I wish to make draws on an important insight of

H. L. A. Hart. One of Hart's concerns in *The Concept of Law* is to demonstrate the flaws in the "imperative theory of law," whose model of law is that of "general orders backed by threats given by one generally obeyed."[5] The imperative theory attempts to fit all laws to the model of coercive rules requiring individuals to perform or omit certain types of action. Hart observes that although this model may be adequate for criminal law and for certain features of tort law, it fails as a general theory because it ignores the variety of functions that laws can serve. Many laws are not coercive and do not play the role of social control. In particular, Hart points to what he calls "power-conferring" laws, whose function is to enable individuals to enter into and create legal arrangements, to modify existing legal relations, or to introduce new legal rules. Hart writes:

But there are important classes of law where this analogy with orders backed by threats altogether fails, since they perform a quite different social function. Legal rules defining the ways in which valid contracts or wills or marriages are made do not require persons to act in certain ways whether they wish to or not. Such laws do not impose duties or obligations. Instead they provide individuals with facilities for realizing their wishes, by conferring legal powers upon them to create, by certain specified procedures and subject to certain conditions, structures of rights and duties within the coercive framework of law.[6]

Hart distinguishes laws conferring "private powers," such as those governing the creation of contracts, trusts, or wills, from laws conferring "public powers," which include laws that set out the procedure by which a legislature enacts or repeals laws or that determine the adjudication of laws in the courts. A common feature of each is that they are rules by which individuals (in either a private or a public capacity) can create rights and duties.[7]

The rules defining the practice of promising or the rules of a game are obvious examples of power-conferring rules found outside the law. Let us rehearse some of their principal structural features. First, power-conferring rules are *constitutive* of the activity that they govern. They define certain kinds of activities (such as promising, scoring, or making an exchange), as well as relationships, moves that one can make, or roles that one can occupy within a practice, none of which can exist apart from these rules.[8] Rather than restricting action, they *enable* individuals to engage in certain activities and arrangements by setting out the procedure to follow, broadly construed to include the actions that must be performed and qualifications or other conditions that one must satisfy, in order to make a promise, enact a law, score a goal, etc. They determine what counts as performing any of these activities. But though power-conferring rules are not primarily restrictive, they limit the exercise of the powers that they define. As rules that can be applied correctly or incorrectly, they introduce the notion of *validity*. One can perform the act in question only when one properly follows the relevant procedure and meets its qualifications. But as Hart points out, the consequence of not following the rule is not that one is liable to a sanction, but simply that one has failed to perform the intended act.[9] In addition, a set of constitutive rules may contain substantive limitations on the exercise of a power, failure to conform to which nullifies an attempted use of the power. For example, a constitution may authorize a legislature to enact laws only on certain subjects, or may contain a bill of rights invalidating certain kinds of laws. A body of contract law may not allow individuals to enter into certain kinds of contracts – which is to say that it will not view certain (purported) agreements as binding contracts.

Finally, by conferring important powers and capacities on agents, power-conferring rules give one a social stature that one could not otherwise have. Restrictive rules also give agents a social status, since, in addition to imposing duties, they give individuals rights and entitle them to consideration by others. But power-conferring rules give one an active role in shaping the progress of social life, over and above the passive role of bearer of rights and duties.[10] They enable individuals to make moves, to create arrangements, relationships, and structures whose validity others must acknowledge. The rules, for example, constitutive of promising and private legal powers give one a capacity to create rights and duties and, by enabling one to create reasons binding others, give one a kind of authority in relation to others. Other such rules create the framework within which one can perform meaningful activities that others can acknowledge and – if one's performance satisfies further standards – admire. Both confer a distinct kind of social status on an agent. They make one an active participant in a public life and open up possibilities for various kinds of recognition and respect from others.

In short, power-conferring rules make one a player in social life. And obviously one cannot play on one's own: anyone's ability to exercise these capacities is made possible by general understanding of and adherence to complex systems of rules and standards, and one's success on any particular occasion depends on other agents recognizing that one has properly exercised the capacity in question (properly followed the rules, met the standards, and so on).

This notion of a power-conferring rule is most readily applied to social practices with a fairly explicit (formalizable) structure – law, language, and logic come to mind. But it is applicable to many other areas of social life. Indeed, the real question is whether one can find an important range of human activities that are not structured by something like constitutive rules. Most intelligible and meaningful conduct is guided by rules that sort actions into socially significant categories. These norms and standards govern the production of meaningful actions and are used by others to recognize and interpret what an agent has done. Systems of rules and practices of this sort are the framework within which individual agents form their aims and intentions, as well as their responses, evaluative and otherwise, to the actions of others. Without them, a human agent could do little that is meaningful and significant. Claiming that such rules render an action intelligible is not to claim that they render an action rational in the sense of cohering with an agent's beliefs and desires; they may not. The point is that there is a kind of conformity to rule that seems prior to this kind of rationality, which has to be established before one knows how to assess the coherence of an action with an agent's beliefs and desires, or even to know that it is a candidate for this kind of assessment.[11]

Though this topic is too complex for adequate treatment here, a few examples are in order. Consider the background of rules and practices that is presupposed for an action to count as a gift, insult, expression of gratitude, gesture of hospitality, act of religious devotion, assertion of authority, or piece of performance art. Actions with a communicative or expressive dimension provide another kind of example. Think about the role of social convention in determining what counts as the expression of certain attitudes and emotions such as deference, contempt, sympathy, humility, or indignation. Both sorts of action presuppose some shared constitutive rules that determine what counts as engaging in that activity or expressing that attitude. These rules are embedded in a larger complex that includes standards for the situations in which such actions are appropriate, who can (sensibly) perform them, appropriate responses from others, and so on. It is the existence of such systems of rules and of a community that can apply them which makes it possible to do any of these things.

The concept of a power-conferring rule suggests a strategy for dissolving the appearance of inconsistency between autonomy and governance by rules, by reminding us that not all governance by rules is restrictive. Certain kinds of rules are constitutive of the possibility of free, creative human activity. Their primary function is not to constrain, since there is no independently describable activity that they prevent one from doing. The alternative to conforming to these rules is not doing something else that one prefers, but random activity, failing to do anything at all. Governance by some kind of rule is presupposed by most intelligible human activity.[12]

In closing this section, let me note a further structural feature of power-conferring (constitutive) rules, which might be termed their *recip-rocal* character. We have seen that they govern the exercise of the power or activity that they create by setting out standards of validity; but they also govern proper responses from members of the community that shares these rules. (This is part of what it is for such rules to confer powers.) When an agent properly follows a constitutive rule, other agents are bound to interpret the act, and to acknowledge its validity, as an instance of a particular category (as a promise, gift, expression of sympathy, argument, legislative act) and, in the case of communicative and expressive acts, to interpret it as carrying a particular meaning. Some acts will oblige others to perform further actions (keep an agreement, show gratitude for a gift, accept the conclusion of an argument, obey a law). And an agent who satisfies further evaluative standards may be entitled to various kinds of admiration and respect. An agent who exercises a power is bound by its constitutive rules, and whether one has validly exercised the power may require confirmation by the judgments of others. But the rules that govern the agent and bind one to the community also bind the community to recognize the validity of one's activity and to respond accordingly. Rules of this sort play a mediating role in social interaction. They are the laws of interaction of a community of rational agents, the laws governing the mutual and reciprocal influence that we exert on each other, that make action and coexistence in a shared world possible.[13]

III

Can moral rules and principles that initially strike us as restrictive also be regarded as rules that enable rational agents to engage in certain kinds of meaningful and creative activities? I believe that this shift in perspective is possible, and that it offers a way to understand certain aspects of Kant's view that a will with autonomy is subject to the moral law, or to the principle of willing in ways that can gain the agreement of the members of a realm of ends. I will argue that the Categorical Imperative is, and is understood by Kant to be, a principle that is constitutive of a certain kind of rational activity and that creates and confers on rational agents certain powers. To put the point paradoxically, an "imperative theory of imperatives" presents too narrow a view of moral imperatives, as Kant understands them. Moral imperatives are restrictive in their capacity of limiting permissible conduct through requirements and pro-hibitions, but that dose not exhaust their practical role.

This point requires some attention to the distinction between particular categorical imperatives and the Categorical Imperative, and some clarification of the practical or social role of both. The distinction between particular categorical imperatives and the Categorical Imperative marks a difference between two levels of principle. Particular categorical imperatives are best understood as the substantive results of moral deliberation. They could include either substantive moral principles that determine duties, rights, and permissions, or conclusions about how agents ought to, or may, act in a specific situation. Kant's tendency to depict moral principles as yielding "commands" carrying absolute necessity, along with his choice of the term "imperative," suggests that their social role is to control conduct.[14] Certainly that is one of their functions, but there are grounds for viewing their primary social role more broadly as that of justification. They are principles used to resolve normative questions in an authoritative way, by which agents can justify their conduct to each other and live on terms of mutual respect.[15] They are the principles underlying the things that we say to each other in our (conscientious) attempts to achieve reasoned consensus on normative questions.

The Categorical Imperative is the general moral principle by which one arrives at particular imperatives, and thus the principle that, at the highest level, guides and makes possible the activity of justification. As the general criterion of moral acceptability, its application establishes the norms that create duties, rights, and permissions. What determines the normative status of an action or principle is whether the relevant maxim can be willed as universal law in accordance with the procedure set out by the Categorical Imperative. Kant regards the Categorical Imperative as a principle to be applied by agents already in the business of acting from considerations that they take to be good reasons, and to have some kind of justificatory force for others as well as themselves. The primary question of moral evaluation is whether the reasons for action expressed in one's maxim are in fact reasons that anyone can regard as sufficient. In this respect moral deliberation aims at determining whether an agent's underlying principle of action is suited to play a certain social role: can it be made into a principle that yields authoritative justifications and can settle questions about the normative status of an action? That is to say, can it be made into a practical law? So understood, the Categorical Imperative is a "norm for norms": it is the higher-order norm by which one can assess the substantive norms that underlie particular choices and that might be cited in their justification.

Since the Categorical Imperative is a higher-order requirement of acting only from reasons that anyone can regard as sufficient, it limits permissible conduct, as do categorical imperatives. But because it sets out and structures the activity of justification, the Categorical Imperative

also confers a capacity to engage in a meaningful and creative activity. It
is the deliberative procedure that determines whether a maxim can serve
as a practical law, and by properly employing this procedure, one makes
one's maxim available as a principle that can resolve questions of justification. That is to say, one gives it the status of a practical law.[16] It is thus
a kind of legislative procedure that any rational agent can employ to
arrive at first-order norms for conduct, whose authority others must
acknowledge and which can settle questions of justification.

We have seen that autonomy may be understood schematically as the
freedom of a rational agent from certain kinds of constraints to engage in
certain kinds of rational activity. The power-conferring aspect of the
Categorical Imperative can be clarified further by saying more about the
kinds of activity that it enables a rational agent to engage in, and this will
help show why autonomy is exercised by willing principles that can gain
the agreement of other rational agents with the same legislative capacities as oneself. In Kant's conception of autonomy, the negative component, or independence condition, is that one is not bound to any
standards or authority external to one's reason. Put another way, the
autonomous agent's activity is guided by a process of reasoning in which
what count as reasons is not settled by (is independent of) facts about
one's desires or other private features of one's condition, or by what
social convention, tradition, or any uncritically accepted external authority (civil, ecclesiastical, familial, etc.) regard as reasons.[17] The three main
versions of the Categorical Imperative suggest the following positive
specifications of autonomy:[18]

(1) the capacity to formulate and act from reasons and principles that
    can justify one's actions to other rational agents;
(2) the capacity to confer a value on objects, activities, and states of
    affairs that other agents must acknowledge, by adopting them as
    the ends of one's rational choice;
(3) the power to adopt principles that can serve as practical laws – that
    is, principles to which one can appeal to resolve questions of
    justification, or questions about the normative status of an action.

To combine these with the independence condition, the agent with
autonomy is free from constraint by any standards or authority external
to one's reason to engage in the relevant rational activity. When the
reasoning that guides his or her activity satisfies the independence condition, the validity of its results is not conditioned by private or subjective
facts about the reasoner, nor conditional upon taking social convention,
tradition, or the will of an external authority by itself as a source of
reasons. That is to say, one has not arrived at one's conclusions simply in

virtue of factors such as beliefs, desires, or values peculiar to oneself; nor is the acceptability of one's conclusions contingent upon taking approval by social convention, tradition, or an external authority as a reason in its favor. The validity of the conclusions does not depend on accepting any source of authority external to reason, or which cannot be shared by all potential reasoners.[19] Kant thinks that a form of reasoning that satisfies the independence condition is unconditionally valid, and that its authority extends to all reasoners. Thus autonomy will be interpreted, roughly, as the capacity to construct and act from justifications, or the capacity to confer value, or the capacity to adopt justifying principles – in each case, whose validity and authority are unconditional and can be acknowledged by any rational agent.

A common feature of these activities is that they are deliberative procedures by which one can create reasons that bind other agents. They are procedures through which a deliberating agent can establish principles that determine the normative status of an action and affect normative relations between agents – that is, principles that create permissions, rights and duties, or that confer value, which others must acknowledge. As such, they interpret autonomy as a capacity to create reasons and value. For example, through moral deliberation that establishes the permissibility of an action, one shows that one may rightfully perform the action, and gives others reasons to accept or endorse one's choice. One uses the deliberative procedure that is the final criterion of validity to confer a normative status on an action, and one's employment of this procedure gives others reasons to adopt various evaluative attitudes, and may lead to reasons for action (e.g., not to interfere, to give aid, etc.) One confers a value on an object when one adopts it as one's end through a rational process in which the value of humanity limits acceptable ends or choices. Rational deliberation that is constrained by respect for humanity leads one to regard the object as choiceworthy, and by making it one's end, one singles it out for a consideration that it would not have apart from one's choice. When one shows that a maxim can be willed as law for a realm of ends, one establishes it as a practical law (normative principle) that other agents must acknowledge. In each case, the Categorical Imperative may be viewed as the principle constitutive of this activity, which confers a power on the agent. By enabling one to create permissions, rights, and duties, or to confer value, or to establish authoritative practical principles, it enables one to create reasons that other agents must acknowledge. It thus renders that agent a kind of sovereign authority.

When autonomy is understood in any of these ways, it is a power exercised in relation to others, made possible by their responses and requiring their participation. The construction of justifications, the conferral of value, or the adoption of authoritative normative principles are not the kind of activity that one can do on one's own, and would make no sense for an agent not engaged in ongoing social interaction. This dependence on the participation and responses of other agents can be elaborated in various ways.

First, when autonomy is specified as a capacity to engage in deliberation through which one creates reasons for others, it presupposes as the locus of its exercise a community of agents with the ability to guide their conduct by what they regard as good reasons. They must be able to recognize when one has carried out a reason-creating procedure, and to take one's doing so as giving them authoritative reasons for action.

Second, when one exercises a power in relation to others, those agents must be disposed to display the appropriate responses – in this case, to take one's employment of the deliberative procedure as giving them reasons. Since autonomy (as interpreted here) is a power to move other agents through their rationality by one's employment of one's own, the responses of others provide a partial measure of whether an agent has successfully exercised this capacity. For example, an aim of moral justification is to move other agents to share an evaluation of an action by presenting them with sufficient reasons. Since justification succeeds when it moves other agents through their own reason to take up the intended evaluative attitude, one who engages in this activity must advance normative claims with which others can be expected to concur. The failure to gain the agreement of others can be prima facie evidence that the force of a claim depends upon a private condition in the agent, or on accepting a source of authority that need not be generally shared. While it is not decisive indication that one's normative claim cannot play the intended role in justification, it does give the agent a reason to reconsider the grounds of his claim and to continue his deliberations. Similar points may be made about conferring value on the end of one's rational choice. Value presupposes the possibility of shared evaluative attitudes. In viewing one's end as having value and as a source of reasons for others, one supposes that other agents can come to endorse one's evaluative attitude toward the end and regard one's pursuit of it as good. The capacity to confer value thus presupposes a community of agents with the same basic evaluative capacities as oneself, whose (potential) agreement with one's use of this capacity confirms its successful exercise. In each case, the failure of others to share one's evaluative conclusions can indicate that the capacity for autonomy has not been properly exercised, while their concurrence can confirm that it has.

Third, since one's capacity to construct justifications and to confer value depends on the dispositions of other agents to take one's deliberations as giving them reasons, its exercise is limited by the possibility of their sharing one's conclusions. But that is to say that the ability of others to accept one's conclusions is constitutive of autonomy, and that nothing could count as a proper exercise of this deliberative procedure which other agents could not regard as giving them reasons for action. (This point can be extended to any use of authority: since authority is only effectively exercised when other agents respond in a certain way, the limits of what they can regard as reasons for acting will set the limits to the exercise of authority.)

Such considerations show why the identification of autonomy with the capacity to create authoritative reasons for others makes its exercise subject to the condition that it can gain the agreement of other rational agents. The underlying regulative principle of the agent with autonomy will be that of exercising his or her reason in ways that other rational agents can freely agree with. As one might say, the possibility of such agreement is a condition of the possibility of exercising autonomy.

IV

In this section I address in more detail the question of why the concept of the moral agent as autonomous legislator leads to "another very fruitful concept, which depends on the aforementioned one, viz. that of a realm of ends" (*G*, IV: 433). I explore the mutual dependence between these concepts by arguing that autonomy, as Kant understands it, presupposes and can only be exercised among a community of rational agents, each of whom possesses the same basic rational capacities and the same sovereign status. We have seen that there is no difficulty in understanding how autonomy is consistent with governance by socially applied rules once it is viewed in substantive terms as the ability to engage in certain kinds of activities. This framework can be used to explain why one exercises autonomy by using one's reason in ways that can gain the agreement of the members of a community of ends. Kant's conception of autonomy has been characterized as the freedom of a rational agent from constraint by external authority to engage in certain kinds of rational activities. The principle of willing in ways that can gain the agreement of the members of a realm of ends is the fundamental principle that is constitutive of these activities, and thus of the exercise of autonomy. I now wish to take these suggestions a step further by viewing autonomy more narrowly in terms of what Kant regards as its central feature: the capacity to give law through one's will.

The concept of autonomy first appears in the *Groundwork* with Kant's argument that the moral agent is not just subject to the moral law, but is also a law-giver. His claim is that agents subject to moral principles are bound in such a way that they must be regarded as their legislators.[20] The basis of this claim is that the reasons for an agent to comply with such principles are given by the reasoning that explains their validity and would lead a sovereign legislator to enact them as law. Thus agents bound to such principles must possess the same rational capacities as would be required of a legislator, and go through the same deliberative process in complying with the principle (display the same volitional state) as a legislator would use in enacting it. This conception of the moral agent is supported by a corresponding view of the Categorical Imperative as a kind of legislative procedure that any rational agent can employ to confer on a practical principle the status of practical law.[21]

When autonomy is viewed as a capacity to give law, questions about autonomy become questions about the nature of authority. In the political realm, the mark of legislative authority is the ability to create reasons for others through the exercise of one's will. The fact that a legislator wills, or duly enacts, a rule or principle makes it a law, and gives the subjects a reason to perform certain kinds of action that they did not have prior to the legislator's act. These reasons are generally viewed as final in the sense that the legislator's enactment precludes the need for further deliberation on the part of those subject to the law about how to act.[22] In the same way, an agent with autonomy has the capacity to will principles that have unconditional authority for others. That is to say, one has the capacity, through the (proper) exercise of one's will, to create reasons that are binding on other agents, which those agents did not have prior to the exercise of one's will.

How might this conception of the moral agent as autonomous lead to the concept of a realm of ends? In a rather uninteresting way, this concept results from generalization. Kant's arguments show that any agent bound to moral principles may be regarded as a sovereign legislator who should be accorded dignity, and one cannot apply this conception to oneself without also applying it to all other rational agents. But more to the point, some social notions are implicit in this conception of the moral agent. It makes no sense to conceive of the moral agent as legislator without bringing in a community to whom law is being given, as well as a conception of the social role of these laws within that community. Laws are norms that regulate the interaction of rational agents with the ability to guide their conduct by the application of such norms. As I indicated earlier, in Kant's view moral principles are principles by which agents can justify their conduct to each other, and which make possible social relationships based on mutual respect. In addition, legislative authority is a power exercised in relation to other agents and presupposes a certain kind of relationship between sovereign and subject. A sovereign has the power to move other rational agents to action through their rational capacities in specific ways. It thus presupposes a community of agents who can recognize exercises of authority and can take the fact that an agent in a position of authority has duly enacted a law as a reason to comply with it. Moreover, for the exercise of authority to be effective, the subjects must be disposed to do what the legislator wills for non-accidental reasons: because they regard the legislator's will as a source of sufficient reasons, and not, for example, out of self-interest or fear. Thus, authority is exercised over agents who possess certain normative capacities, and who acknowledge and respond to uses of authority as a result of their exercise of these capacities.

At this point the original puzzle reappears, now cast as a problem about the nature of legislative authority. An agent with autonomy is not bound to any external authority and has the power to give law through the exercise of her will. But such an agent must also be regarded as giving law to a community of agents, each of whom is as much a sovereign legislator as she. Since one is addressing agents with the same basic capacity to propose and evaluate normative principles, it would be unreasonable to will legislation that one knows could not withstand the critical scrutiny of other members of the community of ends. So it seems that one must guide one's legislative powers by the higher-order principle of willing principles that can gain the assent of all members of a community of ends. The question then is why that higher-order principle does not limit the agent's legislative authority. How is such an agent free from external authority to give law through her will? The answer must be that the principle of willing in ways that can gain the agreement of all members of a community of ends is constitutive of sovereign authority; it is the principle that confers authority on the agent, through which one gives law through one's will.

To develop this claim, let us take the central element of legislative authority to be the power of a legislator to create law through the exercise of his or her will, and ask how that is possible. How can a legislator's willing (enacting) a principle as law create reasons that bind other agents? One might approach this question through the following schematic model of legislative authority: law is created when an agent in a position of authority enacts a regulative principle addressed to some group of rational agents, which that agent sees reason to and is authorized to enact, and backs it with sanctions. One must then develop the elements of the model to explain how an authorized agent's carrying out a legislative procedure creates reasons for other agents to conform to its results.

If the legislator's *willing* of a principle is to create reasons, it must carry immediate authority in itself, without depending on anything outside the legislator's will to give the "subjects" reasons to acknowledge its normative force. This is clearly not the case if the account of legislative authority bases the reasons for accepting the law in sanctions or other consequences attached to the law, or in any contingent connections between the legislator's will and desires which the subjects happen to have. If one takes the reasons for adherence to come from sanctions, then it is the imposition of sanctions rather than the legislator's willing, or enacting, the law that creates reasons for the subjects. They then act from self-interest, rather than from a recognition of the legislator's authority. This would also be true if one based the reasons for compliance on such motives as a desire for certain goods provided by a law, habits of obedience to, or a desire to please the legislator. In each of these cases, the reasons for adhering to the law are conditional on the existence of certain interests in the subjects, or on a fortuitous convergence of the interests of subjects and legislator. Thus, when the model of authority is developed in this way, the legislator's willing of the law would not carry its authority in itself and does not by itself create reasons for the subjects. The legislator may control or manipulate the behavior of his subjects, but he does not move them to act in the way that is characteristic of pure exercises of authority, by giving them binding reasons for action simply through the exercise of his will.

A different elaboration of the above schema would hold that the reasons to conform to the law come from the fact that it is enacted by an agent in a position of authority – roughly, that the authority of the law comes from the authority of the legislator's office. But even on this account, the legislator's will is not the ultimate source of reasons. The authority of the legislator's enactments will be explained by whatever puts that agent in a position of authority – say, from whatever gives the legislator the right to enact law, or from a prior duty of the subject to take the legislator's will as a reason for acting. In this sense, authority is conferred on his enactments by a source external to his will. Within this model, the legislator may have free rein to specify the content of the subjects' obligations; his enactments determine *what* they have reason to do. But the legislator's enacting a law creates reasons only against the background of his occupying a position of authority (e.g., in conjunction with a general obligation on the part of the subjects to take the sovereign's will as a reason). What creates reasons for the subjects to obey, and ultimately does the work of explaining their obligation, is the fact that he occupies a position of authority, rather than his particular acts of willing.

How then, can a legislator's act of will carry authority in itself? Kant's answer must be that a legislator creates authoritative reasons for others when her willing is guided by reasoning that any rational agent can recognize as authoritative. The reasoning underlying the legislator's adoption of a law must be sufficient to lead anyone to regard it as a good law to enact. But that is to say that the reasoning leading to the adoption of the law does not depend for its validity on any private or subjective conditions in the reasoner; the underlying reasoning must be valid un-conditionally, and thus renders the principle valid without condition. What indicates that the legislator's willing is unconditionally valid is that it is able to gain the agreement of the members of a community of rational agents. Thus, if a legislator is to give law through her will – that is to say, if she is to act as a sovereign legislator – she must guide her legislative activity by the principle of willing in ways that can gain the agreement of all members of a community of ends.

To put the point another way, one gives law through one's will when one's willing a principle is sufficient by itself to give other agents authori-tative reasons for actions. This will only be the case when the legislator's willing is guided by reasoning that any rational agent can acknowledge as valid and authoritative. Only then will other rational agents be moved to action in the way that is characteristic of the relationship of authority: by their taking the legislator's enactment of a principle as giving them binding reasons for conforming to it.

The analysis just outlined proceeds by asking what is presupposed for a legislator to give law through the exercise of his or her will, and argues that one gives law through one's will only when the reasoning underlying one's willing is unconditionally valid. When a model of legislative authority bases the authority of a legislative act either on the sanctions or desirable consequences attached to it, or by appealing to the sovereign's legislative position, one cannot claim that the legislator creates law through his or her will. In such cases, the normative force of a legislative enactment depends either on the consequences of the law or on an external principle that confers authority on the legislator. Moreover, the subjects do not respond to the legislator in the appropriate way, since the normative force of the law comes from a source external to the legislator's will. The analysis to which I believe Kant is committed lo-cates the authority of a law in the deliberative procedure that the legis-lator follows in adopting it – that is to say, in the reasoning that goes into willing the law. Moreover, the deliberative procedure that a legislator must follow to create law through his or her will has its basis in the concept of authority. One "enacts valid law" when one guides one's deliberation by the higher-order principle of willing principles that are supported by reasoning sufficient to lead any rational agent to accept them. When a legislator follows this basic principle, she gives law through her will, since her willing of a principle contains within itself reasons for any rational agent to accept it. She has given them reasons for action in the way that is characteristic of the relation of authority, since they can take her willing a principle as a reason to accept it.

In this way one can argue that the higher-order principle of willing principles that can gain the agreement of the members of a community of ends is constitutive of sovereign authority. It is the principle implicit in the concept of sovereignty, which, as we might say, states the "form of law-giving." Think of it as the legislative procedure that an agent with autonomy must follow in order to create valid law. Since proper execution of this deliberative procedure confers validity on the resulting principle, it enables any agent with the capacity to employ this procedure to give law through his or her will.

This line of thought supports a conclusion about the deliberative procedure that a rational agent must employ in order to act as a sovereign. What does it tell us about the agents to whom law is given, or the community in which this power of sovereignty is exercised? We have seen that a sovereign legislator will give laws that are supported by reasoning that is unconditionally valid. But for the exercise of his sovereign powers to be effective, the subjects must recognize his willing of a principle as giving them reasons to accept it. If they are to accord immediate authority to the sovereign's willing, they must be moved to accept the sovereign's enactments through their understanding of the reasoning that goes into them. But then they must possess the same basic capacities to reason and to evaluate normative principles as the sovereign, and must also be able to carry out, and be motivated by, the deliberative process that guided the sovereign's enactment. Moreover, since the reasoning involved is valid without condition, they must have the ability to engage in, and be moved by, reasoning that is independent of private conditions in themselves. Thus, agents who are moved by their recognition of the authority of a sovereign's will must go through the same deliberative process in complying with his laws as he employed in enacting them. The law-following subject and the law-giving sovereign will display the same volitional state.

The further conclusion to which we are led is that sovereign authority, as understood by Kant, is exercised among rational agents with the same basic capacities as the sovereign. The exercise of sovereignty presupposes agents who can respond in appropriate ways. In a word, one can only give law to, and exercise sovereign authority among, fellow sovereigns; a sovereign agent needs autonomous subjects and legislates to a community of equals.

As we also saw in the previous section, regarding authority as a specific kind of social relationship brings out the extent to which the exercise of sovereignty depends on the existence of agents with certain rational capacities, who respond to the sovereign in specific ways. Since sovereignty is the power to move other agents through their rational capacities by one's use of one's own, its successful exercise is measured by the responses of other agents. In order to create law through the exercise of one's will, a sovereign's willing must be guided by reasoning that is unconditionally valid. The indication that this standard is satisfied is that one's underlying reasoning is sufficient to lead the other members of a community of rational agents to accept one's principles. One moves other agents through one's willing when they freely accept the principles that one wills on the basis of their understanding of one's underlying reasoning. In these respects a sovereign is bound to exercise this power in ways that can gain the agreement of all members of a community of ends. Their ability to agree with one's use of one's rational powers and to accept one's underlying reasoning is constitutive of sovereignty, establishing both the possibility of sovereign power and the limits within which it is exercised.

To forestall the complaint that this dependence of the sovereign on the agreement of other rational agents deprives the sovereign of independence, it is worth citing (again) the power-conferring features of this principle. First, the sovereign agent remains free from constraint by any external standard or authority because the only limitations on the exercise of sovereignty are those implied by the principle that is constitutive of law-giving. Second, guiding one's will by the principle of willing principles that can gain the agreement of a community of ends enables one to give law through one's will. It makes it possible to frame principles whose authority others must recognize, and to move them through one's willing. Thus, it gives one a power in relation to other agents, and a social status that entitles one to respect and dignity. These points illustrate the reciprocal nature of this constitutive principle. It is the common bond, the mediating principle that simultaneously binds the sovereign to his subjects, and obligates them to recognize his authority when he has followed its prescribed procedure.

This connection between autonomy and the idea of a realm of ends brings out the deeply egalitarian aspect of Kant's conception of the form that authority must take among agents with autonomy. True exercises of authority, and more generally, claims made in the name of reason, are not imposed from above, and cannot require blind submission or uncritical acceptance without an understanding of their underlying basis. Authority is exercised among equals, who are able to take a critical attitude toward any purported exercise of authority, and to acknowledge only those that they are led to accept by their own powers of reason. This authority, of course, that Kant hears in the claims of morality is the non-dogmatic authority of reason. Reason may be pictured as an ongoing process of thought and discussion whose only constraints are those provided by its guiding regulative principle of the universal agreement of agents with autonomy. The final standards of rational thought and volition are not fixed substantive principles, but rather are rooted in the possibility of acceptance by rational agents who are bound by no constraints other than those constitutive of their rational powers, which enable them to be active participants in an ongoing process of critical thought and discussion, and to arrive at conclusions that can command the agreement of other sovereign agents like themselves.[23] A remark from the first *Critique* is worth quoting here again:

For reason has no dictatorial authority; its verdict is always simply the agreement of free citizens, of whom each must be permitted to express, without let or hindrance, his objections or even his veto. (*KrV* B767)

This remark indicates that the realm of ends is not simply Kant's ideal of a moral community: insofar as reason must be understood as an ongoing and open-ended critical process, in which any rational agent may participate and which preserves the autonomy of its participants, agreement among the members of a realm of ends is emblematic of the nature and authority of reason.

V

A principal aim of this essay has been to explore how autonomy is made possible by the capacity to think, act, and judge in ways that can make claims to universal validity. In particular, it has tried to show why the principle of willing in ways that can gain the agreement of other rational agents should be constitutive of autonomy, and its underlying regulative principle. Let us review how these aims have been accomplished.

The first step was to articulate Kant's substantive conception of autonomy as the freedom from constraint by external authority to engage in certain kinds of rational activities. The last section focused on Kant's understanding of autonomy as the capacity to give law through one's will (independently of external constraint). Kant adopts this conception of autonomy because he views reason as a law-giving faculty. It is neither a body of given substantive principles for the regulation of thought and action nor the capacity to discover such principles. Reason is, rather, in the first instance, the critical process by which authoritative normative principles are generated and established. What confers the authority of reason on any principle or conclusion is that it can be derived from, or supported by (or can survive) this critical process. Individual reasoners may be viewed as legislators, as opposed to discoverers or seers, because of their capacity to employ the procedure by which authoritative conclusions may be derived; they are able to carry out the process of critical thought and reflection that confers on its results the authority of reason. To make the parallel with legislation explicit, what makes a principle a law is that it has been enacted by the appropriate procedure; a legislator is an agent authorized to carry out this procedure. Similarly, what confers rational authority on a principle is that it can be established by the right process of critical deliberation.

Once autonomy is interpreted as a legislative capacity, certain things follow. Law-giving is an activity that occurs in a community of agents, and a law-giver is someone who exercises a certain kind of power, and occupies a certain status, in that community. A law-giver has the capacity to move other rational agents through their reason by his use of his reason. One moves other agents in this way by engaging in reasoning (willing principles, judging, etc.) whose validity and authority does not depend on any private condition in the reasoner, and is thus general and unconditional. Reasoning that satisfies this standard is able to gain the agreement of the other members of a community of rational agents. One can thus hold that the higher-order principle of willing principles that can gain the agreement of a community of rational agents is constitutive of sovereign authority – in other words, that it is constitutive of autonomy. But as the principle that makes autonomy possible, it cannot be construed as a limitation on it. We have also seen that sovereignty, so understood, can only be exercised among sovereign agents with the same rational capacities as oneself. As a power to move other agents through one's reasoning, it must be exercised in relation to agents who can be moved by their understanding of the reasoning that goes into one's willing. Such agents must have the ability to engage in forms of reasoning that are unconditionally valid, and that ability confers on those who possess it the status of sovereign legislator.

This essay proposes changes in the way in which we think about autonomy – both in the context of Kant's moral theory and more generally. First, I have suggested that we need a substantive conception of autonomy that interprets it as a creative capacity of a certain kind. Kant, I have argued, understands it as the ability of a rational agent to create reasons and values that can have authority for other rational agents, through one's employment of the deliberative procedures inherent in our shared rational capacities. Second, I have tried to show that autonomy, as much as agency itself, has an essential social dimension. We tend to think that autonomy renders agents independent of all uncritically accepted social influence and externally imposed standards; and it does. But that does not mean that the autonomous agent is an isolated atomic unit. Autonomy is meaningfully exercised among other autonomous agents whose rational capacities serve as a constraint on, and confirmation of, its exercise. It presupposes a background of rules and social practices, or better, a system of reasoners able to exercise the same capacities, and limited only by the principle of using their reason in ways that other agents can accept while at the same time continuing to view themselves as autonomous.

This interpretation of autonomy also has implications for the shape that one might give to the Kantian account of the authority of morality. The main idea behind Kant's account of why moral requirements are demands of reason is, roughly, that conforming to moral demands makes one free, or autonomous, or the originator of one's actions; it makes one an agent in the fullest sense. The framework developed in this essay suggests a way to enrich this answer: having this status as an individual is inseparable from the ability to play an active role in a certain kind of public life. Kant's claim that the moral law is the law of a free will may be interpreted as the claim that it is the constitutive principle of an autonomous, or sovereign, will. It is the principle through which one occupies the status of sovereign legislator, bound to no external authority and with the power to give law to other rational agents through one's will. By conforming to this principle one overcomes private conditions in oneself and thinks from a universal point of view, in ways to which others can give authority. It thereby makes one an active participant in a public life, and as such entitled to the recognition and respect of other legislating members of a realm of ends.

NOTES

This essay was drafted in the Spring of 1992 at the National Humanities Center under a grant from the National Endowment for the Humanities. I am grateful to both the Center and to the NEH for their support. I would also like to thank Tom Hill, Jerry Postema, Chris Korsgaard, and Dan Brudney for their comments on earlier drafts of this paper.

This is an occasion on which I would like to express a very special sort of gratitude. In the spring of 1977, during my second year of graduate school, John Rawls was lecturing on Kant's moral philosophy. My interests in epistemology had led me to Kant's *Critique of Pure Reason*, in which I had immersed myself during the previous fall. Thinking that it might be useful to broaden my knowledge of Kant through some familiarity with his ethics, I decided to sit in on Rawls's lectures. There was also some talk around the department that Rawls might know something about this area of Kant's thought. The rumors were correct, and the lectures proved to be more than an interesting diversion. Reading Kant's moral philosophy reminded me of the reasons I had gone into philosophy in the first place, and Rawls's lectures showed me how to read Kant. More generally, these lectures were a model of how to approach any figure or text in the history of philosophy. I don't recall missing many of his lectures on Kant or any other subject in the years that followed. Rawls's lectures on Kant's moral philosophy set me on a path on which I continue to travel.

1. References to Kant are given in the text of the paper. Citations to the *Groundwork of the Metaphysic of Morals* are to the volume and pagination in the Prussian Academy edition of Kant's *Gesammelte Schriften*, while citations to the *Critique of Pure Reason* use paging in the B edition. Abbreviations and translations used are as follows:

   G   *Grounding for the Metaphysics of Morals*, trans. James W. Ellington, in *Kant's Ethical Philosophy* (Indianapolis: Hackett Publishing, 1983)

   KrV   *Critique of Pure Reason*, trans. Norman Kemp Smith (New York: St. Martin's Press, 1965)

2. I discuss this issue in more detail in "Legislating the Moral Law," *Nous* 27(4) (1994), and in "Autonomy of the Will as the Foundation of Morality" (unpublished).

3. For Kant's views on these aspects of autonomy, see his discussions of freedom of thought and criticism. Cf., e.g., *KrV* B766–B 785; "An Answer to the Question: What Is Enlightenment?" and "What Is Orientation in Thinking?" in *Kant: Political Writings*, ed. Hans Reiss, 2nd ed. (Cambridge University Press, 1991), in the latter, especially pp. 246–9; and *The Critique of Judgment*, §40. For important discussions of these passages, to which I am indebted at several points, see a series of essays by Onora O'Neill: "Reason and Politics in the Kantian Enterprise" and "The Public Use of Reason," in her *Constructions of Reason* (Cambridge University Press, 1989); "Enlightenment as Autonomy: Kant's Vindication of Reason" in *The Enlightenment and Its Shadows*, ed. Peter Hulme and Ludmilla Jordanova (London: Routledge, 1990); and "Vindicating Reason," in *The Cambridge Companion to Kant*, ed. Paul Guyer (Cambridge University Press, 1992). An overview of Kant's account of the authority of reason is included in her essay in this volume, "Within the Limits of Reason." For further discussion of autonomy in Kant, see also Thomas E. Hill, Jr., *Dignity and Practical Reason* (Ithaca: Cornell University Press, 1992), pp. 83–8, 138–43, especially p. 141.

4. For discussion of the now standard triadic analysis of political liberty, see John Rawls, *A Theory of Justice* (Cambridge: Harvard University Press, 1971), pp. 201–4; and Joel Feinberg, *Social Philosophy* (Englewood Cliffs, NJ: Prentice-Hall, 1973), pp. 4–14.

5. *The Concept of Law* (Oxford: Clarendon Press, 1961), p. 24. See also his

"Positivism, Law and Morals," reprinted in Hart's *Essays in Jurisprudence and Philosophy* (Oxford: Clarendon Press, 1983) pp. 57–62.

6. *The Concept of Law*, p. 27. For a more recent discussion by Hart of the concept of a power-conferring rule, see his "Legal Powers" in his *Essays on Bentham* (Oxford: Clarendon Press, 1982).

7. Hart views power-conferring rules as "secondary rules," which he distinguishes from "primary rules" as follows. Under primary rules

> human beings are required to do or abstain from certain actions, whether they wish to or not. Rules of the other type are in a sense parasitic upon or secondary to the first; for they provide that human beings may by doing or saying certain things introduce new rules of the primary type, extinguish or modify old ones, or in various ways determine their incidence or control their operations. Rules of the first type impose duties; rules of the second type confer powers, public or private. (Ibid., p. 79)

8. For a classic discussion of constitutive rules, see John Rawls, "Two Concepts of Rules," section III, *The Philosophical Review* 64(1) (1955).

9. *The Concept of Law*, p. 28.

10. Again, this point is made by Hart:

> possession of these [private] legal powers makes of the private citizen, who if there were no such rules, would be a mere duty-bearer, a private legislator. He is made competent to determine the course of the law within the sphere of his contracts, trusts, wills and other structures of rights and duties which he is enabled to build. (Ibid., pp. 40–1)

11. Just as linguistic rules govern the production of utterances and enable others to parse and interpret these utterances, there are cultural and social rules that both govern the production of meaningful actions and which other agents use to "parse" and categorize these actions. Their application is prior to assessment in terms of norms of rationality, morality, various kinds of social propriety, etc., in that actions must meet these base level standards of intelligibility before they are candidates for further evaluation.

12. For another discussion of these issues, see Robert Brandom, "Freedom and Constraint by Norms," *American Philosophical Quarterly*, 16(3) (1979), pp. 187–96, especially pp. 192–6. I thank Lynne Tirrell for bringing this article to my attention.

13. Kantians seeking structural parallels between theoretical and practical reason should compare the progression of *form, matter*, and *community* found in the Analogies of Experience with that found in the formulas of the Categorical Imperative. The Analogies take up the permanence of substance (the underlying ground that remains the same during change), the law of causality (the form of alteration or of interaction between substances), and the principle of coexistence in accordance with the law of reciprocity (mutual interaction between objects that is presupposed by coexistence in a world). One might think of the Formula of Humanity as concerned with the substance that is the subject matter of morality, the Formula of Universal Law as the law of interaction between such substances, and the Formula of the Realm of Ends as spelling out the principle of reciprocity presupposed by moral substances inhabiting a shared world.

14. See, e.g., *G*, IV: 416–20. The command model is appropriate for requirements and prohibitions, though less so for permissions. However Kant's

examples suggest that the Categorical Imperative is used principally to determine the permissibility of proposed intentions or actions.

15. For examples of this approach to the social role of moral principles see Rawls, *A Theory of Justice*, §40; "Kantian Constructivism in Moral Theory: Rational and Full Autonomy," in *The Journal of Philosophy*, 77(9) (1980), especially pp. 516–19; and Lecture 2 of *Political Liberalism* (New York: Columbia University Press, 1993/1996); and see also T. M. Scanlon, "Contractualism and Utilitarianism," in *Utilitarianism and Beyond*, ed. Amartya Sen and Bernard Williams (Cambridge University Press, 1982). For a recent discussion of this theme, see Samuel Freeman's discussion of "public reasons" in "Reason and Agreement in Social Contract Views," *Philosophy and Public Affairs*, 19(2) (1990): 122–57, and "Contractualism, Moral Motivation, and Practical Reason," *The Journal of Philosophy*, 88(6) (1991): 281–303.
16. I develop this view of the Categorical Imperative in more detail in "Legislating the Moral Law," especially Section V.
17. Here I elaborate on Thomas E. Hill, Jr.'s explanation of the sense in which practical reasoning for agents with autonomy is independent of inclination. See "Kant's Theory of Practical Reason" (especially Section III) in his *Dignity and Practical Reason in Kant's Moral Theory*.
18. I associate (1) with the Formula of Universal Law, (2) with the Formula of Humanity, and (3) with the Formula of the Realm of Ends (act only from maxims that one could at the same time will as law for a realm of ends). Despite surface differences, I assume in this essay that (1) and (3) are at least extensionally equivalent.
19. It is worth noting that judgments that depend on an authority that is accepted uncritically, or without rational grounding, are conditionally valid in precisely the same way that hypothetical imperatives are. Take, for example, a belief whose acceptability depends on treating the pronouncements of a certain religious figure as authoritative, and a practical principle that states a desire-based reason. The normative force of the first will be restricted to those who regard the religious figure as an authority, that of the second to those who have the relevant desire. In each case acceptability depends on some condition in an individual that need not be shared by all others qua rational. I draw this point from Onora O'Neill; see *Constructions of Reason*, pp. 34–6 and 58–9.
20. See *G*, IV: 431: "The will is thus not merely subject to the law but is subject to the law in such a way that it must also be regarded as legislating for itself and only on this account as being subject to the law (of which it can regard itself as author)."
21. Here I summarize arguments that I have developed elsewhere. See "Legislating the Moral Law" and "Autonomy of the Will as the Foundation of Morality."
22. Cf. Joseph Raz, *The Authority of Law* (Oxford: Clarendon Press, 1983), pp. 16–19.
23. Though I cannot argue the point here, I suspect that Kant replaces the substantive first principles that provided the content for earlier dogmatic conceptions of reason with the idea of a plurality of reasoners whose primary resource is their own ability to reason and whose only restriction is the autonomy of others.

Kant on the Objectivity of the Moral Law

ADRIAN M. S. PIPER

In 1951 John Rawls expressed these convictions about the fundamental issues in metaethics:

The objectivity or the subjectivity of moral knowledge turns, not on the question whether ideal value entities exist or whether moral judgments are caused by emotions or whether there is a variety of moral codes the world over, but simply on the question: does there exist a reasonable method for validating and invalidating given or proposed moral rules and those decisions made on the basis of them? For to say of scientific knowledge that it is objective is to say that the propositions expressed therein may be evidenced to be true by a reasonable and reliable method, that is, by the rules and procedures of what we may call "inductive logic"; and, similarly, to establish the objectivity of moral rules, and the decisions based upon them, we must exhibit the decision procedure, which can be shown to be both reasonable and reliable, at least in some cases, for deciding between moral rules and lines of conduct consequent to them.[1]

In this passage Rawls reconfigured the issue of moral objectivity and so reoriented the practice of metaethics from linguistic analysis to rational methodology. In so doing, his work has provided inspiration to philosophers as disparate in normative views as Thomas Nagel,[2] Richard Brandt,[3] Alan Gewirth,[4] and David Gauthier.[5] Rawls replaced the Moorean question, Do moral terms refer? with the Rawlsian question, Can moral judgments be the outcome of a rational and reliable procedure? He later gave a resoundingly positive answer to this question[6] and later still, a more tentative one.[7] Rawls's considered qualification of his earlier enthusiasm about the extent to which moral philosophy could be "part of the theory of rational choice"[8] is a tribute to the seriousness with which he took his critics' objections.

The above passage, and the article from which it is excerpted, make clear that Rawls took his original inspiration from a carefully worked out analogy with inductive logic in scientific procedure. But a fellow traveler among rational methodologists in metaethics – namely

Kant – risked defending an even closer and more controversial relationship between scientific and moral objectivity. I argue here that Kant's thesis that the moral law is objectively necessary[9] relies on the same type and degree of objectivity he earlier claimed for scientific knowledge. Thus Rawls's early impatience with "speculative" metaethics, and the boldness of his claiming for ethics the same sort of procedural rigor to be found in the natural sciences, puts him in the best possible philosophical company: of those whose ambitions for moral philosophy – and the philosophical powers by which they serve it – are greatest.

In the *Groundwork* Kant characterizes the moral law as an objective principle that compels imperfectly rational human beings with objective necessity (AK. 412–13). Kant establishes the metaethical foundations and technical terminology of his conception of moral objectivity in the Analytic and Dialectic of the *Critique of Pure Reason*.[10] Although many of Kant's views undergo revision or development from the first *Critique* to the *Groundwork* to the second *Critique*,[11] we will see that the conceptual foundations Kant establishes early on for addressing the issue of moral objectivity remain firmly in place.

I. Understanding

A. Synthesis

A *representation*, for Kant, is any mental content. Representations can be either intuitional or nonintuitional. *Intuitional* representations "get directly to"[12] an object that is given to us in sensibility (A 19/B 34). An intuitional representation organizes the data of sense in space and time, which Kant calls the *forms of intuition*. So only intuitional representations are directly of given objects. All nonintuitional representations are themselves of representations rather than directly of objects (A 68/ B 93). Since intuitional representations are by definition of objects and not of other representations, and since empirical objects are themselves representations, the objects intuitional representations represent cannot be, in turn, empirical objects. Rather, they are objects in themselves apart from their representations.[13]

A *concept* "orders various representations under one common representation" (A 68/B 93). We do this *spontaneously* in that this mental act is not a reaction to some external cause, as is sensation (A 50/B 74, *passim*). Conceptualizing representations is something we initiate rather than something that is imposed upon us. This, Kant thinks, is what it means to be an intelligence (B 158n). And to conceive ourselves in this way as active, spontaneously reasoning and thinking agents is to conceive ourselves as *persons*.[14]

The representations we conceptualize can be either intuitional or nonintuitional. They have in common what is expressed by the representation that subsumes them. The common representation is the concept that unifies the various representations under it. A concept, then, is a rule of selection for collecting mental contents similar in a certain respect under the rubric of that concept; or, as Kant also puts, it, a *function* (A 79/B 105). "Since," Kant tells us, "no representation other than intuition gets directly to the object, a concept is never in unmediated relation to an object, but rather to some other representation of it (be it an intuition, or itself a concept)" (A 68/B 93). Concepts, therefore, mediate and qualify our relation to externally given objects.

Synthesis is Kant's technical term for the process by which different, specifically intuitional representations are collected under one concept. Synthesis is collection when applied specifically to intuitional representations. It is, Kant tells, us, "the act of adding different representations together, and of grasping their manifoldness in one cognition" (A 77/B 103). Synthesis supplies order and continuity to our moment-to-moment sense experience (A 99–102). It also unites intuitional representations into a particular, identifiable content (A 78/B 103). This content is what the concept that unites them expresses. So intuitional representations are synthesized according to a particular rule of selection, and this rule can be inferred from the content of the concept under which they are subsumed.

What determines the content of that rule of selection? That is, what determines which similarities among intuitional representations are relevant to their synthetic grouping under concepts? Kant uses the term "synthesis" specifically in connection with intuitional representations, and intuitional representations are direct and unmediated representations of externally given objects in themselves. So it would be tempting to think that the similarities represented were similarly given by those objects; and therefore that the basis for our grouping of representations was to be traced to attributes of those objects themselves. But Kant thinks that the similarities most salient to us, and therefore the best candidates for conceptual synthesis, are those which most closely conform to the innate conceptual preconceptions we bring to the act of cognitive discrimination.

The concepts that select and group intuitional representations are what Kant calls the *pure transcendental concepts of the understanding*, or *categories*. These include substance and attribute, and cause and effect. These pairs are not *analytic*, that is, conjoined by definition – as are such concepts as a bachelor and an unmarried man. Rather, they are conjoined in the spatiotemporal form of our intuitional representations. And since, according to Kant, they are innate, logically necessary[15] and universal concepts, they are cognitive preconditions for experiencing something as a coherent and unified object at all.

B. Judgment

Kant thinks that "the understanding can make no other use of these concepts than to judge by means of them" (A 68/B 93). A *judgment* – more specifically, a categorical judgment that ascribes predicate to subject – does exactly what concepts do, only at a more abstract level: it collects relevantly similar representations that are already subsumed under a less abstract concept under a more abstract concept (A 79/B 105). A *synthetic a priori judgment*, then, is an innate, logically necessary and universal judgment that collects intuitional representations under the pure concepts of the understanding listed in the Table of Categories (A 80/B 106).

Kant tells us that by abstracting from the content of any such judgment and "attending only to the mere form of [our] understanding" (A 70/B 95), we can cull the formal rules of selection among representations. These are the *logical forms of judgment* set out by Kant in their entirety in the Table of Judgments (A 70/B 95). So whereas the categories of the understanding listed in the Table of Categories combine the innate, logically necessary, and universal rules for collecting representations with specifically intuitional representations, the logical forms of judgment listed in the Table of Judgments abstract from both intuitional and nonintuitional representations. Subtract representations themselves from the conceptual rules for collecting them and you get the logical forms of those rules.

Among the representations subsumed by a judgment under any concept, whether transcendental or empirical, there will be at least one which is intuitional, that is, in direct relation to a given object. "All judgments," Kant says, "are functions of unity among our representations, since instead of an unmediated representation, a higher one, which comprises this and more, is used in knowing the object, and thereby many possible cognitions are gathered into one" (A 69/B 94). Thus, the underlying structure of the categorical judgment, "All bodies are divisible," might look something like this:

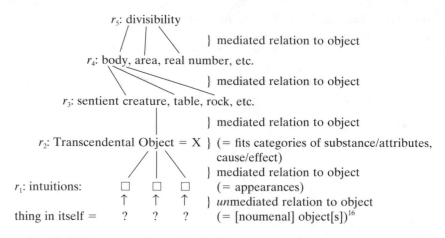

r_5: divisibility
} mediated relation to object
r_4: body, area, real number, etc.
} mediated relation to object
r_3: sentient creature, table, rock, etc.
} mediated relation to object
r_2: Transcendental Object = X } (= fits categories of substance/attributes, cause/effect)
} mediated relation to object
r_1: intuitions: □   □   □   (= appearances)
} unmediated relation to object
thing in itself =   ?   ?   ?   (= [noumenal] object[s])[16]

In this judgment, relevantly similar intuitional representations of (a) given noumenal object(s) r_1 are synthesized under the transcendental concept of an object r_2, to which certain categories apply, such as substance/accident and cause/effect. These situate the appearance of the object in space and time. They also define what it is for something to be an object of our experience. We must represent it as a discrete substance with attributes. We must also represent it as both having and being susceptible to causal force. Once we become aware of something as satisfying the cognitive criteria for being an object, we are in the realm of empirical objects of experience. Here we next try to ascertain what kind of object it is. We collect observational representations under higher-level empirical attributes. Representations of the relevantly similar empirical attributes of that object are in turn collected under a more abstract empirical concept r_3, that of a sentient creature; that representation, in turn, along with representations of other relevantly similar three-dimensional entities under a yet more abstract concept r_4, that of a body; and that representation, finally, along with representations of other similarly individuated but non-three-dimensional entities under the even more abstract concept r_5, divisibility.

So on the one hand, all higher concepts or representations implicitly embed externally given objects in the judgments we make, no matter how tenuous or distanced our conceptual connection to those objects. On the other, any nonintuitional representation distances us from the object to some extent, including the representations "I," "I think," or "is my experience." All of our experience is theory-laden in this way. This is what Kant means when he says that "judgment is . . . the mediate knowledge of an object, that is, the representation of a representation of it" (A 68/B 93). Any cognition that I can recognize and represent as mine is thereby distanced from sensibility and mediated by that judgment itself. On Kant's view, being "detached" from my "feelings" is the necessary price of unified selfhood.

C. Categorical Indicatives

The two logical forms of judgment of interest for this discussion are the first two under Section III, "Relation," in the Table of Judgments of the first *Critique*, the categorical and the hypothetical. *Relational judgments* generally connect a priori concepts that have already synthesized intuitional representations. *Categorical judgments* – more specifically, categorical *indicative* judgments – have the form, "All (or some) A is B." Categorical indicatives relate the predicate concept to the subject concept by way of the representations subsumed under each. An example would be the judgment, "The human soul is immortal." A second example would be "All bodies are divisible." Both examples relate predicate to subject, but only the second relates attributes to substances because the first is true by definition of the concept of a soul, whereas the second connects intuitional (as well as nonintuitional) representations of objects.

Hypothetical judgments have the form, "If P then Q." Hypothetical judgments relate two categorical indicative judgments as antecedent (or, to use Kant's technical term, *ground*) to consequent. For example, the hypothetical judgment, "If there is a perfect justice, the obstinately wicked are punished," relates the two categorical indicatives, "There is a perfect justice," and "The obstinately wicked are punished" (A 73/B 98). Another example of a hypothetical judgment would be, "If one answers the telephone, it ceases ringing." This one relates the two categorical indicatives, "One answers the telephone," and "The telephone ceases ringing." Both examples relate antecedent to consequent, but only the second relates cause to effect, and again the reason is the same. The first is true by definition of the concept of perfect justice, whereas the second connects intuitional representations of objects.

At B 141n and A 73/B 98–A 74/B 99 Kant inveighs against the reduction of hypothetical and disjunctive judgment forms to the categorical.[17] Nevertheless he is wrong. Disjunctive judgments can be translated into hypothetical ones, and any hypothetical judgment can be replaced by a categorical one that ascribes to the subject a complex property, such as that of being an antecedent to the consequent or a cause of the effect. For example, the above two hypothetical judgments can instead be rendered as "Perfect justice requires punishing the wicked," and "Answering the telephone stops its ringing." By reducing the number of judgment forms Kant claims to be transcendentally necessary to the categorical and extending its scope to cover antecedental and causal predicates, Kant's argument for the objectivity of empirical knowledge is strengthened, not weakened as he seems to think. The reason is that categorical indicatives have a special status in Kant's theory; and in the B Deduction Kant explains what it is:

> [A categorical indicative] judgment is nothing other than the way to bring given cognitions to the objective unity of apperception. This is what the relational term "is" aims at: to distinguish the objective unity of given representations from the subjective. It denotes their relation to original apperception, and its necessary unity, even if the judgment itself is empirical, and therefore contingent, as for example, in the judgment, "Bodies are heavy." I . . . here assert that these representations . . . belong to one another in virtue of the necessary unity of apperception in the synthesis of intuitions. . . . Only thus does there arise from this relation a judgment, that is, a relation which is objectively valid, and so can be adequately distinguished from a relation of the same representations that would have only subjective validity, for example according to laws of association. In the latter case, I would only be able to say, "When I carry a body, I feel an impression of weight"; but not, "It, the body, is heavy"; which is as much as to say that these two representations are bound together in the object, that is, without regard to the state of the subject, and not merely in perception (as often as that perception may be repeated). (B 142)

Kant's point is that the relational term that connects predicate with subject in a categorical indicative judgment – and it is a point that would apply as well to "has the attribute of" as it does to "is" – *objectifies* that connection as being in the object rather than in the subject. To recognize the connection of representations as being in the object is to recognize the representations that constitute that object as epistemically distinct from those that constitute the subject.

Now the logical function of judgment, Kant tells us, is to collect all such representations, whether intuitional or conceptual, in one consciousness, or *apperception*; that is, to finally subsume all of them under the concept "I think" (B 143). This means that, necessarily, I must be able to conceive of any such representation, concept, or judgment, no matter how abstract or removed from sensibility, as mine in order for it to be part of my consciousness. But the representations that collectively comprise the representation of a unified object presuppose a unified conscious subject – *the transcendental unity of apperception* – in which those representations are ordered and collected according to innate, logically necessary, and universal concepts. Therefore, a categorical indicative asserts a connection among representations that is as objective as anything can be for us.

Kant's doctrine of transcendental idealism clearly rejects any concept of empirical objectivity as consisting in the ontological independence of the object. And the Analogies demonstrate Kant's attempts to ground the objectivity of objects and causally related events in an analysis of temporally sequential representations. Objectivity, for Kant, is objectivity of knowledge, not the ontological independence of the object from the knowing subject. On Kant's view, objectivity just is the conceptual a priority, logical necessity, and universality *of judgment about* the object.[18]

Even if we concede Kant his insistence on the essential difference between categorical, hypothetical, and disjunctive judgments, however, hypothetical and disjunctive judgments both still embed categorical indicatives that implicitly assert objective relations between subject and predicate. Therefore, all such relational judgments implicitly presuppose the objectivity of these relations. Whether the telephone ceases ringing because I answer it or not may be open to question; that I answer it, and that it ceases ringing, is not.

But all such empirical hypothetical judgments presuppose the transcendental forms of judgment that unify a priori intuitional representations. Kant describes all of the synthetic a priori judgments that comprise the Table of Categories as universal rules of unity in the synthesis of appearances that have objective reality as necessary conditions of experience (A 157/B 196). He means that the relational judgment forms (inter alia) that we find in the Table of Judgments, when applied to the synthesis of intuitional representations, further objectify those representations by linking them in the form of discriminable events and entities. These empirical events and entities are, from the point of view of my experience, fully objective and veridical. *A fortiori*, the hypothetical judgment form synthesizes intuitional representations already objectified by their categorical indicative form into a causal relation that, from the point of view of experience, objectifies them even further.[19]

II. Reason

A. Ideas

In the Analytic of the first *Critique*, Kant has tried to show that the logical forms of relational judgment listed in the Table of Judgments, when combined with intuitional representations, yield objective knowledge. In the Dialectic he tries to show that these same three logical functions, when extended beyond intuitional representations, yield increasingly abstract, comprehensive concepts and theories that encompass all lower-level representations; and finally yield transcendent and transcendental *ideas of reason*. Kant defines an idea or concept of reason as "a concept formed from [pure concepts of the understanding] that transcends the possibility of experience" (A 320/B 377). Ideas are highly abstract concepts that unify less abstract concepts of a certain kind under a single, comprehensive concept. An idea can be a theoretical entity (such as a perfectly rational being or a quark), a theoretical law (such as that of freedom or relativity), or a concept strictly speaking (such as immortality or the unified field). Ideas deal only indirectly with experience (B 359), since "an object that would be adequate to the transcendental idea can never be found within experience" (A 327/B 384).

However, these most sweepingly universal concepts do not abstract from intuitional representations, but instead embed them in more abstract and general judgments. Thus, when Kant characterizes reason as the faculty of principles, and knowledge from principles as "that knowledge in which I cognize the particular in the universal through concepts" (A 299/B 356–A 300/B 357), he is making the same point about the theory-ladenness of experience he made at A 68/B 93–A 69/B 94 discussed in Section I.B, but at a higher level of abstraction. Reason, he says, is the faculty of judging mediately (A 330/B 386).

There are many ideas of reason.[20] But Kant claims that the three most abstract, comprehensive, and universal ones are engendered by the three relational judgment forms themselves. We have seen in Section I.A that when these judgment forms apply to the intuitional data of sense they yield the categories. But when their scope of application is extended sufficiently far beyond the data of sense they yield the higher-level concepts that Kant calls ideas (A 323/B 380). First, there is the idea of immortality, which he argues is engendered by universalizing the categorical judgment form: the search for completeness and comprehensiveness of predication yields the concept of a subject that is never a predicate. Since ideas of reason must unify intuitional as well as nonintuitional representations and lower-level principles, this, in turn, according to Kant, becomes the idea of "the absolute unity of the thinking subject" (A 335/B 392), which itself undergoes no change.[21]

Second, there is the idea of freedom, which is engendered by universalizing the hypothetical judgment form: in hypothetical reasoning, the search for completeness and comprehensiveness in the series of antecedents of a consequent yields the concept of the original antecedent without antecedents – the groundless ground. Because it, too, must unify intuitional as well as nonintuitional representations, it, in turn, yields the idea of freedom as the first or uncaused cause of everything, the "absolute totality of the series of conditions for any given appearance" (A 340/B 398). Of course a judgment characterizing a groundless ground or first cause could also be rendered as a categorical indicative that predicates the consequent as a property of the antecedent *qua* subject that cannot be predicated of any further subject. A judgment ascribing an action to a free agent would, for example, satisfy this criterion.

Finally, there is the idea of God, which is engendered by universalizing the disjunctive judgment form: Here the search for completeness and comprehensiveness in the set of disjuncts that jointly exhaust the scope of a concept (A 73/B 99) yields the concept of the aggregate of all disjuncts of the most complete concept; and this becomes the idea of God as the totality of all parts of the system, the "being of all beings" (A 336/B 393).

In the Dialectic Kant tries to show how all of these ideas of reason naturally develop as higher-level universal principles from the conceptual presuppositions or *Grund* of objective empirical knowledge, namely the logically necessary functions of thought. He characterizes these ideas, and the reasoning by which we arrive at them, in the same indicative mood as he did the concepts of the understanding and the synthetic process of judgment by which we unify and objectify our experience. Kant argues that, being committed to the objectivity of our empirical experience, we then must be committed to the regulative authority of the abstract theories and universal principles it engenders. Since they transcend the empirically verifiable, we cannot experientially confirm their truth. But since they naturally arise out of it, we cannot easily reject them either.

B. *Vernunftschlüsse*[22]

Kant's account of the way in which ideas of reason are engendered from objective knowledge is based on his conception of cognitive functions as fundamentally spontaneous – that is, active rather than reactive – and synthetic – that is, unifying rather than particularizing. We saw in Section I.A that concepts collect representations, and in Section I.B that relational judgments collect concepts. Similarly, syllogisms, or inferences of reason – *Vernunftschlüsse* – collect relational judgments (A 301/B 358). Therefore inferences of reason indirectly collect representations and concepts.[23] Whereas the understanding collects intuitional representations under lawlike concepts, reason collects what we've conceptualized under yet more abstract and universal explanatory principles that organize and unify them in relation to each other (A 302/B 359). Kant thinks we are so constituted cognitively as to strive naturally to reduce, simplify, and extend the explanatory scope of theoretical principles to cover the greatest variety of intuitional and nonintuitional representations. Reason embeds the particulars of experience in universal judgments that define the broadest possible theoretical framework because to universalize over the particulars of experience is a natural and necessary expression of the self's striving for rational coherence.[24]

According to Kant, the forms a *Vernunftschluß* can take depend on the logical form of judgment employed. Again the categorical and hypothetical forms are most important for our purposes, and the categorical form is the foundation from which the others are constructed:

	categorical (indicative):	hypothetical (indicative):
Major Premise:	All A are B.	If D is E then F is G.
Minor Premise:	All/Some C are A.	D is E.
Conclusion:	All/Some C are B.	F is G.

In each case the major premise is a given judgment stating a universal rule that ascribes a predicate to all subjects of a certain kind (A 322/B 379). The minor premise is a judgment that subsumes a second subject, or condition, under the concept of the first. And the conclusion yields a further judgment by applying the universal rule of the major premise to the subsumed condition of the minor premise. A *condition*, for Kant, is a certain kind of state of affairs. In a categorical indicative judgment that functions as a premise in a categorical *Vernunftschluß*, it is the referent of the subject to which predicates are ascribed. In a hypothetical *Vernunftschluß*, it is the referent of the subject of the antecedent in the major premise (and, of course, of the subject of the minor premise).[25] Thus a condition functions as does the premise whose subject refers to it, as an antecedent from which some consequent or conclusion can be inferred (this is why Kant sometimes uses the terms "condition" and "premise" interchangeably). The conclusion then describes the *conditioned* (A 330/B 386–A 331/B 387), and the major premise *conditions* the conclusion: that is, it explains the condition or subject described in the conclusion by subsuming it under a general rule. Reason seeks to subsume that kind of subject under more and more abstract and universal kinds in a series of increasingly general judgments.

Take the categorical indicative *Vernunftschluß*,

(1)	Major Premise:	All humans are mortal.
	Minor Premise:	Caius is human.
	Conclusion:	Caius is mortal.

The major premise of (1) may be in turn the conclusion of even more general and abstract ones, such as

(2)	Major Premise:	All sentient creatures are mortal.
	Minor Premise:	All humans are sentient creatures.
	Conclusion:	All humans are mortal.

And the minor premise of (1) also may be conditioned by prior *Vernunftschlüsse*, such as

(3) Major Premise: All featherless bipeds are human.
     Minor Premise: Caius is a featherless biped.

     Conclusion: Caius is human.

In both cases reason seeks more general and abstract principles under which a judgment can be subsumed, and from which it can be derived. For any *Vernunftschluß*, both of its premises can be regarded as conditioned by the more general *Vernunftschluß* from which they are derived as conclusions.

The principle of reason in general, according to Kant, is "to find for the conditioned knowledge of the understanding the unconditioned whereby its unity is completed" (A 307/B 364). This then becomes a regulative principle of pure reason on the presupposition that "if the conditioned is given, the whole series of conditions subordinated to one another, which itself is therefore unconditioned – is also given." A *regulative principle* is one that guides and directs our innate patterns of reasoning in a way that enables us to extend it past the empirical limits of experience (A 509/B 537). It contrasts with a *constitutive* principle that defines and determines objectively the existence of some object or state of affairs. The regulative principle of pure reason, then, leads us to seek that most abstract, universal and all-inclusive first principle or *Grund* from which everything else can be deduced.[26]

Thus, in order to generalize over such principles to increasing degrees of abstraction, Kant argues, we must assume a totality of such conditions (or premises) for any given conditioned (or subject to which those predicates are ascribed in the conclusion). The complete series of conditions contained in prior universal judgments that determine a conclusion about some object or state of affairs is what Kant calls *the unconditioned* (A 322/B 379). The unconditioned, then, is the idea of a first and most abstract, universal idea or descriptive principle that functions as a premise subsuming all lower-level descriptive principles or premises under itself. This idea of the unconditioned leads us to try to generate a series of *Vernunftschlüsse* whose major premises increase in generality and comprehensiveness relative to the particular facts (or "empirical conditions") with which it began – what Kant describes as the *ascending* or *regressive* series (A 331/B 388).

The transcendental ideas of God, freedom, and immortality are unconditioned in that they express the most abstract and universal principles under which all lower-level disjunctive, hypothetical, and categorical *Vernunftschlüsse* respectively must finally be subsumed (A 336/B 393–A 337/B 395). According to Kant, we know that these are the most comprehensive and universal principles there are because, as we have already seen above, they are derived by universalizing the forms of principles in which reasoning itself occurs. Beyond these most fundamental explanatory principles, Kant thinks, there are no further principles that might subsume them. Just as experience defines the limits of understanding, the ideas of God, freedom, and immortality define the limits of reason.

C. Hypothesis Construction

According to Kant, we embark on the ascending series of *Vernunftschlüsse* in our search for eventual theoretical completeness by formulating and testing general hypotheses that are intended to explain an increasing variety of particular events. This process of theory-building, the prototype of Hempel's covering-law theory of scientific explanation,[27] Kant describes as the *hypothetical employment* of reason:

> If reason is a faculty of deducing the particular from the universal, then either the universal is already certain in itself and given, and so requires only judgment for subsumption, and the particular is thereby necessarily determined; . . . or else the universal is given only problematically, and is a mere idea. Here the particular is certain, but the universality of the rule from which it follows is still a problem. Then more particular instances, each of which are certain, try on the rule for size to see whether they follow from it. In this case, if it appears that all particular instances assigned do follow from it, then we conclude to the universality of the rule, and thence to all instances, even those not themselves given. (A 646/B 674)

The procedure is clear. We begin with a universalization we rationally suppose to be true, and a firmly established particular case we rationally suppose might instantiate it. We scrutinize several relevantly similar particular cases in order to ascertain whether they do, indeed, instantiate the universalization, such that the formulation of the universalization allows the derivation of the particular instances from it: Does universalizing over the particular instances yield the universal from which they are supposed to be derived? Does the resulting rule apply not only to these cases, but to all relevantly similar ones? If the relevant instances, and other citable ones, can be derived from the universalization, we are then justified in regarding it as a valid universal principle that will predict and subsume future instances of that kind.[28]

The example Kant offers combines the ideas of God, freedom, and immortality in the idea of rational personhood as a substance with causal power (also see A 672/B 700–A 673/B 701). This is a particularly apt example in light of Kant's project of establishing metaethical foundations in the first *Critique* for the substantive moral theory he first invokes to illustrate moral reasoning in the *Groundwork*. There he argues that "because moral laws should be valid for every rational being as such, to derive them from the universal concept of a rational being in general is thereby to explicate all moral philosophy, which needs anthropology for its application to human beings, first independently from this as pure philosophy, that is, entirely as metaphysics (which can very well be done in this kind of wholly abstract knowledge)" (AK 412). The concept of a rational being in general is thus both the highest-level idea of reason that unifies the ideas of God, freedom, and immortality, and also the most fundamental concept of morality.

Beginning with various established mental dispositions – "sensation, consciousness, memory, wit, power of discrimination, inclination (*Lust*), desire, etc.," (A 649/B 677) – Kant directs us to employ the "logical maxim through which we reduce, so far as possible, this seeming diversity, so that through comparison one might discover hidden identity." By sorting them into nonredundant groups and universalizing over them we collect them under higher-level principles such as imagination plus consciousness; then under the more general headings of understanding and reason; then under the yet more general explanatory principle of a fundamental power, that is, a substance with causality, which each such disposition instantiates. Notice that this is one example of the reduction of a hypothetical judgment to a categorical one, that is, through the ascription of causal properties to substances. But this is a very particular kind of causal substance, namely one that has mental powers with causal efficacy.

Finally, Kant says, we may subsume all such causally powerful substances under the principle of an absolutely fundamental power that underlies all relative ones (A 649/B 677). But he cautions us, "This unity of reason is merely hypothetical. It is not claimed that such[29] must in fact be encountered, but that we seek it for the benefit of reason, that is, of establishing certain principles for the many rules which experience may offer us" (A 649/B 676–A 650/B 678; see also A 682/B 710). The concept of the soul as a self-identical and unchanging entity with the causal powers of understanding and reason can be invoked to explain the diverse manifestations of consciousness. And the concept of God can be invoked to explain the existence of such causally powerful substances. But these are only *concepts* (or ideas), not empirical experiences. Therefore they are not themselves susceptible to empirical confirmation. They are merely regulative ideas of reason that unify the diversity of our particular experiences.

On the one hand, this employment of reason itself remains hypothetical because the ideas of God, freedom, and immortality are merely hypotheses that explain our experience rather than statements of fact about our experience. As Kant later remarks about the idea of immortality, "one posits (*sich setzen*) an idea merely as the one and only *point of view* from which one can extend that unity which is so essential to reason and so beneficial to the understanding" (A 681/B 709; italics added). To say, however, that ideas of reason are regulative hypotheses is not thereby to underestimate their foundational necessity in human thought. Kant makes it quite clear that the validity of any such regulative hypothesis turns on its ability to unify our experience, our thought, and finally our selves in accordance with the demands of logical necessity.[30] So to the formula for Kant's account of objectivity earlier adduced – conceptual a priority, logical necessity, and universality of judgment – reason adds something more, namely, theoretical coherence. A higher-level theoretical principle of reason is objectively valid if it subsumes its lower-level principles, concepts, and representations, both intuitional and non-intuitional, under it, such that it allows the systematic inference of those lower-level principles, concepts, and representations as logically necessary syllogistic conclusions. Only then can the self be fully unified and the rules of understanding be true.

III. Action

In this section I apply the conclusions of the preceding account of Kant's models of understanding and reason to the special case of action, following Kant's claim in the Preface to the *Groundwork* that

the unity of practical with speculative reason simultaneously in a common principle must be able to be delineated, since *in the end there can be only one and the same reason, which must be differentiated solely in its application*. (AK 391; italics added)

A. Maxims

Earlier, in Section I.C, we saw that intuitional representations are synthesized by the categories of the understanding first and foremost into categorical indicatives that claim a certain degree of objectivity in virtue of their form. We also saw that these are then further synthesized into hypothetical indicatives, that is, descriptive causal judgments that are, from the perspective of one's own experience, even more objective. The objectivity of this causal relation holds as much for human actions and consequences as it does for other causally linked events. Action and passion, according to Kant, are *pure derivative concepts*, or *predicables* of the pure understanding, derived from the category of cause and effect (A 82/B 108). Since action and passion are transcendental concepts, they, too, synthesize intuitional representations into objects and events.[31] This means that as agents and patients of action, we experience ourselves as genuine empirical causes and effects, and our actions as causally effective events in the world. To me, the causal link between my action and its consequences is as objective and lawlike as any other causal regularity I perceive.

The descriptions by which we encode our actions conceptually are no different in form than those by which we encode other causally linked events. They are reducible to categorical indicatives that ascribe causal properties, namely actions, to agents.[32] The "accordion effect"[33] of action-descriptions makes it possible to ascribe a range of such properties, depending on the causal scope of the action the description is intended to capture. So, for example, "I (will) answer the telephone" captures a more restricted causal scope than "I (will) stop the ringing of the telephone."[34] Each expresses a different intention but both may describe the same physical action. Kant's primary concern is with action-descriptions that capture a more restricted causal scope – and so a narrower intention, for two reasons. First, he is concerned primarily with our immediate intentions, regardless of their further actual causal consequences, because our intentions are for him the primary locus of moral value. On Kant's view, the rightness or wrongness of actions are derivative from the goodness or badness of our intentions.[35] And second, he thinks that only the immediate objects of our intentions, and certain basic actions[36] (i.e., the "exerting of every means so far as they are in our power" [AK 394]), are under our direct control (AK 401).[37]

A *maxim* is a first-person categorical indicative judgment that ascribes a causal property, namely an act, to the subject. It thus both expresses an intention and describes an action. For this reason it may function as a resolution or as a prediction respectively – or both simultaneously. It may also describe a mental or a physical act. Kant derives the term "maxim" from the notion of a *maximum* as the rational idea of what is "greatest and absolutely complete . . . in the division and unification of the knowledge of the understanding under one principle" (A 665/B 693). We have already seen in Sections II.B and II.C that the role of reason is to unify the knowledge of understanding under fewer, increasingly abstract and comprehensive higher-level principles. We have also seen above that Kant includes among the objects of knowledge of the understanding knowledge of our actions and of ourselves as agents. Kant defines *maxims of reason* as all subjective principles which are derived, not from the constitution of the object but from the [speculative] interest of reason in respect of a certain possible perfection of the knowledge of the object. (A 666/B 694)

Maxims may include principles of thought (such as "I will gather as much relevant information as possible before drawing any conclusions") as well as of action. All maxims have in common that they are guided by reason's interest in theoretical completeness. In the case of action, then, we seek an idea of reason – a highest-level comprehensive explanatory principle – that enables us to understand all of our intentions and resolutions as theoretically coherent principles of action derivable from it – and therefore, as we have seen in Section II.C, as objectively valid in light of it.

When Kant moves from a formal analysis of how reason operates in general to the content of a particular idea of reason, he moves from rational procedure in general to its application to a substantive theory. In the Canon of Pure Reason Kant describes the idea of reason that guides the formulation of maxims. It is the idea of a world ruled by moral law – a necessary idea of reason (A 812/B 840) that has objective reality (A 808/B 836) "in the concept of which we abstract from all the hindrances to morality (the inclinations)" (A 809/B 837). Kant's idea of a moral world comprises two elements: an entire world as a theoretical entity; and a system of operative principles – moral law – that is universally binding on it. Since in this world moral law is fully operative in the behavior of its inhabitants, it explains and describes their behavior. And since it consciously guides their actions as well, it also prescribes it. Finally, since the moral law is authored by those inhabitants themselves, it describes and prescribes action that is rationally self-determining.

The concept of rationally self-determining action, uncoerced by empirical antecedents, is an application of the principle of self-caused causation, that is, of transcendental freedom, to the special case of rational agency.[38] Kant's conception of unconditioned moral freedom, that is, as freedom to act in accordance with moral self-determination, is not different or separate from the highest-level unconditioned idea of freedom, but instead an instantiation of it in a particular kind of cause. Between the Resolution of the Third Antinomy and the *Groundwork* Kant preserves the consistency of his conception of unconditioned moral freedom with his accounts of God, freedom, and immortality as furnishing highest-level regulative ideas that govern and unify our patterns of thought. *All* lower-level principles describing causally connected experience of any kind, whether action, desire, free association, or external events, must terminate in the unconditioned idea of freedom. So the criteria of objectivity remain the same for all of them.

The unconditioned speculative idea of freedom as autonomous and operative moral law in turn provides the practical foundation for moral conduct. For from the interest of reason in the idea of a perfect world governed by moral law (which for Kant is also "a mere idea" (A 813/B 841); also see *Groundwork*, AK 407, 409, 412, 433, 434, 436n, 439), we then derive the subjective principles that actually govern our moral agency:

Practical laws, in so far as they become at the same time subjective grounds of actions, that is, subjective principles, are entitled maxims. The judgment of morality, regarding its purity and consequences, happens in accordance with ideas, the adherence to its laws in accordance with maxims. (A 812/B 840)

So we evaluate moral law as a speculative idea of reason; and we follow moral law by deriving practicable maxims from it. To the extent that moral laws are antecedents of a subject's actions, they are maxims; and the entire course of our lives is necessarily subject to them (A 812/B 840). Maxims of action such as "I (will) answer the telephone" or "I (will) return borrowed books" are lower-level conceptualized intentions, derivable as conclusions from higher-level moral principles, and finally from the highest-level unconditioned idea of a world governed by autonomous moral law, that is, from the idea of freedom. The relationship between maxims and moral ideas, then, is the relationship between particular intentional action-descriptions and the more universal and comprehensive principles that explain them.

B. Universalization

By now it should be clear how we get from one to the other. To move from practicable maxims to the highest-level theoretical principle of operative, universal moral law from which those maxims are derived, we enact exactly the same procedure we use in any rational inquiry – namely, hypothesis-construction of the sort described in Section II.C and exemplified in the idea of a causally powerful substance. In the case of action, we begin with both a prereflective rational idea of moral law (AK 402–3) and also an established particular intention to act. In light of this prereflective conception, we consider several such relevantly similar intentions. These are *ex hypothesi* certain, whereas "the universal is admitted as . . . a mere idea, . . . [and] the universality of the rule of which [the intention's maxim] is a consequence is still a problem" (A 646/B 674). So we scrutinize these intentions in order to ascertain whether they do, indeed, instantiate the moral law, such that the formulation of the moral law allows the derivation of the particular intentions from it. Again we deploy the "logical maxim through which to reduce, so far as possible, this seeming diversity, so that through comparison one might discover hidden identity" (A 649/B 677). That is, *we ascertain whether universalizing over the maxims yields the rule from which they are to be derived, such that the resulting rule applies not only to these established cases, but to all relevantly similar ones.* If the relevant intentions, and other citable ones, can be derived from this formulation of the moral law, we are then justified in regarding it as a universal principle that may predict and subsume future instances of that kind. Kant's remarks about hypothesis-construction in the first *Critique* provide a more complete account of his universalization procedure for moral maxims than is to be found anywhere in the *Groundwork*.

As we have already seen in Section II.B, universalizing a principle that functions as a major premise in a *Vernunftschluß* results in a categorical indicative that ascribes a predicate to all subjects of a certain kind. And we have also seen in Section II.C that in the *Groundwork*, Kant tells us to ascend in the series to the most universal and comprehensive principle of action from which lower-level maxims can be derived, namely to "the universal concept of a rational being in general" (AK 412). So, for example, I might begin by universalizing over the maxims,

(1) (a) I (will) return borrowed books,
    (b) I (will) pay my bills, and
    (c) I (will) keep my appointments.

This results in the principle

(2) (a) I (will) keep my promises.[39]

because (1.a–c) are all instances of promise-keeping. In the next step up in the ascending series of *Vernunftschlüsse*, we universalize over (2.a) to get

(3) (a) Rational beings (will) keep their promises, (AK 422, passim)

since I identify myself generically as (among other things) a rational being and suppose trustworthiness to be a characteristic of rationality. Next, we universalize over (3.a) plus other, relevantly similar *Vernunftschlüsse* such as

   (b) Rational beings refrain from acting on the opportunity and desire to commit suicide, (AK 422, passim)
   (c) Rational beings sometimes cultivate some of whatever their natural talents, (AK 423, passim) and
   (d) Rational beings sometimes help some of the individuals in need whom they encounter. (AK 423, passim)

Principles (3.a–d) have in common, first, that they result from having universalized over more localized *Vernunftschlüsse* and maxims; and second, that they themselves, according to Kant, can be further universalized without theoretical incoherence. Like the ideas of God and immortality, the unconditioned idea of operative moral law can be derived by universalizing the form of principles in which reasoning itself, specifically about action, occurs:

nothing remains but the universal conformity to law of actions in general, which alone should serve the will as its principle. (AK 402)

Since actions are simply a species of cause, the universal law to which actions should conform has exactly the same form as any other law of nature to which other events must conform, namely the universalized categorical indicative that predicates effects as properties of their causes – here, universalizable actions as properties of rational beings. And since the unconditioned idea of a moral world includes the idea of moral law as universally binding on and operative for all its inhabitants, we must regard such universal laws as objective laws of nature in such a world (A 808/B 836, A 815/B 843). So (3.a–d) are, according to Kant, derivable from the higher-level *Vernunftschluß*,

> (4) (a) Rational beings perform only those acts that can be universalized as laws of nature. (AK 402, passim)[40]

C. Kant's Explanatory Moral Theory

We have seen in Section II.C that, according to Kant, a higher-level principle of reason – any principle – is objectively valid if it subsumes its lower-level principles, concepts, and representations, both intuitional and nonintuitional, under it, such that it allows their systematic inference as logically necessary syllogistic conclusions; and this degree of rational coherence simultaneously secures both the unity of the self and the objectivity of experience. So if Kant's account of moral reasoning is as integral to his more general account of reason and understanding as I have argued, the same formal criteria he develops for the latter – of objectivity and subjective rational coherence – will apply without revision to the former. And indeed we have also seen in Section III.B that Kant's proto-Hempelian procedure of rational hypothesis-construction developed for reasoning in general applies without revision to moral reasoning.

But is Kant's substantive moral theory entirely susceptible to these formal criteria? Is it a genuine theory, the hypotheses of which follow from its higher-level principles, can be objectively tested, and at least in many cases confirmed? And is it internally rationally coherent to the extent of securing unity of thought and experience for the self that accepts it? In what follows I address the first question only; I defer the second to another occasion, for reasons of space.[41] Given Kant's special interest in moral theory, it is not surprising that the resources he developed for constructing Hempelian explanatory theories – of the cosmos, or of the human psyche – are, in fact, sufficient for a genuinely explanatory theory of moral freedom as well.[42] Here, then, are some further explanatory principles to be found in the text of the *Groundwork*:

(4) (b) Rational beings perform only those actions that treat humanity as an end in itself. (AK 427, passim)

(5) (a) Rational beings are motivated by *Achtung*[43] for the moral law. (AK 400, passim)

(b) Rational beings will universal law through their actions. (AK 431, passim)

(c) Rational beings legislate autonomously for a kingdom of ends through their actions. (AK 433, passim)

(d) Rational beings are noumenally free and phenomenally determined in their actions. (AK 451, passim)[44]

(6) (a) The causality of the will of rational beings is expressed in action performed out of *Achtung* for the moral law. (AK 453, passim)

(b) The freedom of rational beings as noumenal subjects is expressed in such moral action. (AK 454, passim)

Principles (3.a) through (6.b) are categorical indicative judgments about the behavior of certain sorts of phenomena, namely rational beings. The concept of a rational being can be similarly rendered by ascribing to it theoretical and practical rationality. So (3.a) through (6.b) contain no prescriptive terms. They also satisfy the basic Hempelian criteria that identify a set of principles as a genuine theory.

A theory begins with *hypotheses* – that is, proposed lawlike explanations of phenomena that are accepted conditionally on confirmation of their experimental regularities, and from which we should be able to infer causal regularities that can be experimentally tested. The more confirmable predictions we can make, the more credibility accrues to the hypothesis. We have already seen in Section II.C that Kant's concept of the hypothetical use of reason enables us to do just this; and principles (1.a–c) and (3.a) suggest how this might work in the case of action. Principle (3.a), together with the suppressed premise that you are a rational being, implies that you will return this borrowed book (1.a). If you do, then you have confirmed at least one experimental prediction of

(3.a). A second prediction of (3.a) might be (1.b). If you do, indeed, pay your bills, then you have further confirmation of (3.a). Notice that all the principles in group (3) are susceptible to the same sort of experimental testing, on oneself as easily as on others.

As Kant has already instructed us, the more confirming instances accrue to (3.a), the more we are entitled to regard (3.a) not just as a hypothesis but as a *law*, that is, a true hypothesis stated in the form of a generalization that ascribes causal properties to subjects. Like all the principles in group (3), (3.a) satisfies the *nomological* requirement that it support counterfactual conditionals: Rational beings would keep any promises they made, and would have kept any promises they had made. Thus (3.a) ranges over not only the actual past, present, and future, but over possible pasts, presents, and futures as well. It has universal rather than merely spatiotemporally limited application. Thus (3.a) contrasts with a mere accidental generalization such as

(7) (a) Anyone who keeps her promises is a rational being,

since someone could conceivably keep her promises – say, because she had been hypnotized into doing so, without being a rational being.

Explanatory theories contain both *lower-* and *higher-level laws*. The latter are laws that satisfy the same criteria just discussed, but that generalize over lower-level laws with respect to more abstract features of the phenomena described. We have already seen in Section II.B that Kant's account of reason supplies us with plenty of those. Principles (4.a) and (4.b) above are higher-level laws from which (3.a–d) can be deduced as experimental predictions: For example, because a rational being performs only those acts that treat humanity as an end in itself, she will keep her promises (because keeping one's promises treats humanity as an end in itself). Since Hempel's own covering law schema

(covering laws) $L_1, L_2, \ldots, L_n$	} Explanans
(particular circumstances) $C_1, C_2, \ldots, C_m$	
(phenomenon to be explained) E	} Explanandum

is a modern elaboration of Kant's ascending series of *Vernunftschlüsse*, it naturally organizes some of the principles to be found in Kant's moral theory quite well:

(1) (L_1, L_2) Rational beings keep their promises (3.a); and rational beings sometimes help some of the individuals in need whom they encounter (3.d);
(C_1, C_2) Your colleague borrowed your textbook, and promised to return it in time for you to prepare your lecture;

(E_1) Your colleague returns your textbook in time for you to prepare your lecture.

(2) (L_3, L_4) Rational beings perform only those acts that can be universalized (4.a) and that treat humanity as an end in itself (4.b);

(C_3, C_4) Keeping one's promises and sometimes helping some of the needy can be universalized (4.a), and also treat humanity as an end in itself (4.b);

$(E_2)(=(L_1, L_2))$ Rational beings keep their promises (3.a); and sometimes help some of the individuals in need they encounter (3.d).

Just as Kant's higher-level *Vernunftschlüsse* finally terminate in unconditioned ideas of reason, Hempelian higher-level covering laws finally terminate in a theory's *theoretical constructs* and the principles governing it. The theory is a higher-level hypothesis that is accepted as true because it successfully explains lower-level, law-governed uniformities as manifestations of "deeper" unobservable entities and processes that are themselves governed by theoretical laws and principles. Examples of such constructs from Kant's moral theory appear with increasing frequency as the level of abstraction of the principles increases: "Reason," "will," "law," "humanity," and "end" are theoretical constructs in (4), according to this description, as are "kingdom of ends," "freedom," and "noumena" in (5). All are abstractions that combine to form an ideal type whose behavior explains the uniformities of behavior of rational beings as described in (3).

These theoretical constructs are, like scientific theoretical constructs, governed by two kinds of principles. First, there are *internal principles* that describe their behavior. Applied to maxims of action, Kant's account of the hypothetical use of reason describes the operation of the rational will as legislating moral law; his account of the ideas of reason explain how the concepts of humanity as an end in itself and of the kingdom of ends function for us; and in the Resolution of the Third Antinomy and third chapter of the *Groundwork* he explains in what freedom, autonomy, and the noumena–phenomena distinction consist. These accounts provide internal principles that describe and explain the behavior of these theoretical constructs.

In addition to internal principles, Kant's explanatory moral theory also contains *bridge principles* that connect these constructs with the familiar empirical phenomena of moral action; (6.a) and (6.b) are bridge principles. Both contain what we might describe as "double connections." First, there is the *causal* double connection in (6.a), between

(i) the causality of the will and the feeling of *Achtung*, and
(ii) the feeling of *Achtung* and the resulting moral action.

Rational principles of action command *Achtung*, which in turn motivates moral action. Second, there is the *evidential* double connection in (6.b), between

(i) freedom and the noumenal subject, and
(ii) the noumenal subject and the moral action.

Freedom is manifested by a subject whose behavior is not determined by empirical inclinations – that is, a noumenal subject, and noumenal subjecthood is evinced by moral action. In both cases, these principles link the moral actions we observe with the theoretical constructs that ultimately explain them. Thus Kant's moral theory does satisfy the basic requirements of a genuine theory, and so is fully congruent with his account of reason and theory-construction more generally.

I have argued that Kant's moral theory explicates substantive ethical principles in terms of the "universal concept of a rational being in general . . . i.e. entirely as metaphysics" (AK 412), and so as categorical principles in the indicative mood. I have not mentioned Kant's famed categorical imperative at all. One reason for this is that, as a purely exegetical matter, Kant himself does not make much use of it. Out of thirty-two formulations of the fundamental principle of morality in the *Groundwork*, only four are in the imperative mood.[45] The remainder are in the form either of laws,[46] or of commands,[47] neither of which express the imperative.[48] This bias toward the categorical indicative is, as we have already seen, consistent with his metaethical conception of freedom as a highest-level explanatory idea of reason in the first *Critique*; and he reiterates this bias consistently throughout the *Groundwork* and second *Critique*.

But more importantly, Kant does not think imperatives apply to rational beings as such.[49] In the *Groundwork* Kant denies repeatedly that the "ought" (*sollen*) is to be found in the *intelligible world*, that is, the viewpoint of reason and conceptualization that furnishes the cognitive foundation (or *Grund*) for the viewpoint of understanding and empirical experience. If we were solely members of the intelligible world, he says, all our actions just *would* conform to moral law (AK 454). Because reason would be motivationally effective without any hindrance in such a being, the expression of moral intention would be not "I ought" but "I will" (AK 449). "The moral 'I ought'," Kant says, "is thus an 'I will' for us as members of the intelligible world" (AK 455). A rational and perfectly good or holy will, he tells us, would be governed by objective moral law; but it would not be necessitated or compelled to conform to it, as we are. Instead, such a will would conform to the moral law naturally, in accordance with its subjective constitution (AK 414). Its maxims of action would necessarily conform to moral law, but unlike us, it would have no obligation or duty to do so (AK 439), since, as Kant reminds us in the second *Critique*, such a being would be incapable of any maxims that conflicted with the moral law – a model to which we as sensuous beings must (albeit in vain) aspire (AK V, 32; also cf. 84–5).

So as is true for Kant's metaphysics more generally, his moral theory is fashioned primarily with an eye to its application to rational beings in general.[50] The categorical imperative enters in only as a problem of the application of this theory to imperfectly rational instances. How this might affect human beings in particular is a different question for a different essay.

NOTES

This discussion is excerpted from my "Rationality and the Structure of the Self, Volume II: Kant's Metaethics" (unpublished manuscript, 1994). It has benefited from criticisms of earlier drafts by Henry Allison, Gordon Brittan, Kenneth Winkler, Guenter Zoeller, and the Wellesley Philosophy Department Faculty Seminar.

Unfortunately, editorial restrictions on space necessitate deferring many issues raised in this essay to a fuller treatment in the larger project. Thus interpretations and arguments are often summarized rather than developed in depth, and extended exposition is replaced by the presupposition of a familiarity with all parts of Kant's *Kritik der Reinen Vernunft* (I use the edition herausg. von Raymund Schmidt [Hamburg: Felix Meiner Verlag, 1976]), the standard commentaries to that work (e.g., Allison, Bennett, Brittan, Ewing, Guyer, Kemp Smith, Melnick, Paton, Strawson, Vaihinger, Wolff), and German idiom. Nor is there any examination of relevant competing views, such as Allison's *Kant's Theory of Freedom* (Cambridge University Press, 1990), Susan Nieman's *The Unity of Reason* (New York: Oxford University Press, 1994), Onora O'Neill's *Acting on Principle* (New York: Columbia University Press, 1975) and her *Constructions of Reason* (Cambridge University Press, 1989). These, too, are to be found in *Kant's Metaethics*.

1. John Rawls, "Outline of a Decision Procedure for Ethics," *Philosophical Review* 60(2) (1951): 177–97; reprinted in *Ethics*, ed. Judith J. Thomson and Gerald Dworkin (New York: Harper and Row, 1968), 48–70.
2. *The Possibility of Altruism* (Princeton: Princeton University Press, 1978).
3. *A Theory of the Good and the Right* (New York: Oxford University Press, 1980).
4. *Reason and Morality* (Chicago: University of Chicago Press, 1979).
5. *Morals by Agreement* (Cambridge University Press, 1984).
6. *A Theory of Justice* (Cambridge: Harvard University Press, 1971).

7. "Justice as Fairness: Political not Metaphysical," *Philosophy and Public Affairs* 14(3) (1985): 223–51.
8. *A Theory of Justice*, pp. 16, 47, 172.
9. *Grundlegung zur Metaphysik der Sitten*, herausg. von Karl Vorländer (Hamburg: Felix Meiner Verlag, 1965), AK 413. Translations from the German texts are my own unless otherwise indicated. My renderings are generally more literal and attentive to Kant's fondness for colloquialisms – and so, I think, truer to Kant's thought – than the standard ones.
10. Op. cit.
11. *Kritik der Praktischen Vernunft*, herausg. von Karl Vorländer (Hamburg: Felix Meiner Verlag, 1974).
12. I reject Kemp Smith's translation of *unmittelbar* as "immediately" because of the latter's temporal connotations, which are inappropriate to Kant's meaning. Instead I substitute "direct" or "unmediated," depending on context.
13. Of course this is not to claim that the intuitional representations of those objects are veridical, or even *about* those objects, but merely, as it were, *from* them. I discuss at length the textual evidence for the thesis that sensible representations are caused by things in themselves, and the case for this unorthodox use of the term "cause," in footnote 17 of "Xenophobia and Kantian Rationalism," *The Philosophical Forum* 24(1–3) (Fall-Spring 1992–93): 188–232. The term *appearance* (*Erscheinung*) raises more questions than it answers, so I'm going to disregard it for purposes of this discussion.
14. See ibid., Sections III, "The Concept of Personhood," and IV, "Self-Knowledge," for an extended discussion.
15. That is, "logically necessary" in Kant's anachronistic and overly rich sense of comprising all of the constraints on thought imposed by the forms of judgment enumerated in the Table of Judgments (A 70/B 95).
16. I think Kant was wrong to drop the useful notion of the Transcendental Object = x from the B Edition, since it captures the case of recognizing something as an object independently of knowing what kind of object it is.
17. Also see Kant's *Logic*, trans. Robert Hartmann and Wolfgang Schwartz (New York: Bobbs-Merrill, 1974), paragraphs 24–9, 60 n. 2; and *Lectures on Logic*, trans. J. Michael Young (Cambridge University Press, 1992), 374 and 601n.
18. Even synthetic a posteriori judgments about particular empirical objects or events owe their objectivity to the synthetic a priori judgments they necessarily presuppose. I discuss the relationship of transcendental to empirical concepts in "Xenophobia and Kantian Rationalism," Section II. Of course a judgment can be objective without being true.
19. If this is what objectivity is for Kant, how are mistaken judgments to be explained? See his pronouncements at B 70n, B 278, and A 297/B 353. I take up this question at greater length in *Kant's Metaethics*.
20. See, for example, his discussion of the ideas of virtue, a just constitution, the order of nature, and humanity at A 312/B 369–A 319/B 376.
21. As is so often true, Kant does not actually argue for these claims (or if he does, the arguments are not very good); he simply states them and relies on their intuitive philosophical plausibility. It is not impossible that they could be given a more rigorous, discursive form. But I will not attempt that here, since my primary concern is to establish what Kant thinks rather than whether he is justified in thinking it.

22. I use the term *Vernunftschluß* (inference of reason) instead of "syllogism" in order to emphasize its centrality to Kant's conception of how reason operates.

23. All our knowledge begins with the senses, goes from there to understanding, and ends with reason, beyond which there is no higher faculty to be found in us for fashioning the matter of intuition and bringing it under the highest unity of thought. (A 299/B 355) . . . In inference reason seeks to reduce the great manifoldness of knowledge from the understanding to the smallest number of principles (universal conditions) and thereby to produce in it the highest possible unity. (A 305/B 361; also see A 86/B 118–9)

24. See "Xenophobia and Kantian Rationalism," Sections I–III.

25. In the *Lectures on Logic* Kant defines a condition as that in the subject "that makes the predicate be attributed to it" (497). Despite the category mistake I will assume we know what he means, sort of.

26. That a certain systematic unity of all possible empirical concepts so far as they can be derived from higher and universal ones must be sought is elementary, a logical principle, without which no employment of reason would occur, since we can conclude from the universal to the particular only so far as universal properties of the thing are presupposed, under which the particulars stand. (A 652/B 680)

    Kant goes to some length to distinguish the unity of understanding from the unity of reason (see, for example, A 302/B 359, A 306–7/B 363, A 311/B 367, A 409/B 436, A 422/B 450), but only in order to establish how dependent the former is on the latter (see, for example, A 299/B 355, A 305/B 361–A 306/B 363, A 326/B 383, A 329/B 385, and especially A 647/B 675–A 651/B 679, quoted below in note 30).

27. The footnote to A 337/B 395 does not, in fact, disconfirm this reading. See my *Kant's Metaethics* for a fuller treatment.

28. Although Kant does not explicitly state this, we can assume that this procedure also requires us to take care to preserve the integrity of the universalization on the one hand, and of the firmly established instances on the other. Although we may tinker with the formulations of each, we may neither distort the referential scope of the universalization through rationalization, nor deny nor dissociate any of the instances it is intended to explain. (I discuss the concepts of rationalization, dissociation and denial at greater length in "Pseudorationality," in *Perspectives on Self-Deception*, ed. Amelie O. Rorty and Brian McLoughlin [Los Angeles: University of California Press, 1988], 297–323). Given the particular instances with which we began, the universalization is valid only if it subsumes all of them and all relevantly similar ones, and excludes those that are too dissimilar to have been grouped with them at the outset.

    In this procedure two interconnected elements – the universalization as expressing a rational idea that is in some degree fixed by innate, a priori concepts of experience, and the assured particular empirical experiences it is intended to explain – are mutually determining. Criteria of validity for the scope of the universalization depend on the lower-level instances it subsumes, and criteria of salience, similarity, and relevance of those instances depend on the rational idea the universalization attempts to express. It is because Kant presupposes the same innate conceptual structure both to the assured particular instances with which we start and to the inductive generalization we initially formulate to explain them that he is so sure this generalization will eventually prove to be a universal principle.

29. Kemp Smith gets this sentence wrong. «*Eine solche*» refers to the unity of reason. It is that and not the absolutely fundamental power that Kant wants to claim we must seek for the benefit of reason.

30. The hypothetical employment of reason therefore gets at the systematic unity of the knowledge of understanding, and this is the touchstone of the truth of its rules. (A 647/B 675) ... [This] systematic or rational unity is a logical principle for assisting the understanding by means of ideas where the understanding alone does not reach rules; and at the same time for systematically giving to the diversity of its rules uniformity and consistency under one principle, and thus for providing coherence as far as possible. (A 648/B 676) ... The law of reason directing us to seek this unity is necessary, because without it we would have no reason at all; without this no coherent employment of the understanding; and in the absence of this no sufficient criterion of empirical truth. (A 651/B 679)

31. In this case the given immediate object I intuitionally represent to myself is myself as I am in myself, i.e., as the *noumenal subject* to which I have no direct epistemic access. By acting I cause in myself intuitional representations that are, like other intuitional representations, passively received in sensibility.

32. In the *Groundwork* Kant often formulates his examples of maxims more complexly, in an "Out of ... [motive], I will ... [intention/resolution], in order to ... [purpose]" format. This is for the pedagogical purpose of contrasting morally valid with invalid motives, categorical with hypothetical imperatives, and of identifying what sorts of results of action are irrelevant to the assessment of moral worth.

33. See Joel Feinberg, "Action and Responsibility," in *Doing and Deserving* (Princeton: Princeton University Press, 1970).

34. Compare the flexible temporal range of the indicative in German with its comparatively restricted temporal range in English. My analysis covers both.

35. For a discussion of the implications of this for Kant's purported deontologism, see my "A Distinction Without a Difference," *Midwest Studies in Philosophy VII: Social and Political Philosophy*, ed. Peter A. French, Theodore E. Uehling, Jr., and Howard Wettstein (Minneapolis: University of Minnesota Press, 1982), pp. 403–35.

36. See Arthur Danto, "Basic Actions," in *Readings in the Theory of Action*, ed. Norman S. Care and Charles Landesman (Bloomington: Indiana University Press, 1968), pp. 93–112.

37. Actually, even if we interpret the immediate objects of our intentions and resolutions as narrowly as possible, as involving only "attempt" verbs such as *trying* or *moving* to answer the phone rather than "success" verbs such as *answering* the phone, the immediate objects of our intentions and resolutions could be brought about by causes other than our rational will, such as hypnosis or cortical stimulation.

38. Since the power of beginning a series in time entirely from itself is thereby proved, ... it is now also permissible for us to allow within the course of the world

different series as capable in accordance with their causality of beginning of themselves, and so to ascribe to substances themselves a power of acting from freedom.... For here we speak not of an absolutely first beginning in time, but rather in causality. If I now, for example, arise from my chair in full freedom and without the necessarily determining influence of natural causes, a new series thus begins simply in this event, together with all its natural consequences into infinity.... For this resolution and act do not lie in the succession of purely natural effects, and [are] not simply a continuation of them. (A 450/B 478)

39. Of course this requires us to conceive of the subject of (1) as a universalization over discrete occurrences of subjective agency. But this is consistent with Kant's infamous claim in the A Paralogisms that "the identity of the consciousness of myself at different times is therefore only a formal condition of my thoughts and their coherence but in no way proves the numerical identity of my subject" (A 363). See the rest of that paragraph for elaboration and also the Strawsonian fireworks in the footnote at A 364. In keeping with this doctrine we might indexicalize the "I" of act-token descriptions as follows: "I_1 (will) return this book," "I_2 (will) pay my bills," and so forth.

40. That Kant's account of moral reasoning is merely an application of his account of reasoning in general should not be surprising. It would be very odd if, given Kant's intellectual delight in architectonics and his preoccupation with it, his account of empirical human actions failed to conform to the category of causality; and odder still if they did but yet failed to conform to the higher-level theoretical principles all events that fall under that category engender. Oddest of all would be if Kant's account of action satisfied all of these requisites for cognitive objectivity, yet required a completely separate and unconnected treatment of moral objectivity. Given Kant's emphasis on theoretical coherence as the foundational lynchpin of the a priori, logical necessity, and universality that he claims give *any* judgment objective validity in the first place, this would be no account of objectivity at all. What has not been sufficiently appreciated, despite Kant's repeated reminders, is how important and constant all of these requisites are.

41. I address the second question in "The Meaning of 'Ought' and the Loss of Innocence," Invited Paper delivered to the American Philosophical Association Eastern Division Convention, 1989, and give it a fuller treatment in *Kant's Metaethics*.

42. At AK. V. 137 in the *Critique of Practical Reason*, Kant reiterates his warning from the Dialectic of the first *Critique*, that the ideas of God, freedom, and immortality are mere suppositions that reason must make for practical purposes, and not knowledge, in the following words:

[The predicates derived from our own nature we might be inclined to ascribe to God, the intelligible world, and immortality] can never be used in a theory of supersensuous beings and ... so on this side do not have the power to ground a speculative knowledge, but rather restrict their use solely to the practice of the moral law.

Astonishingly, Beck translates *spekulative* as "theoretical." But the original context makes clear that Kant means to warn us against confusing rational hypothesis-construction with knowledge in the technical, experiential sense he has defined in the first *Critique*: Although we need to suppose the validity of these ideas of reason in order to act morally, we cannot thereby infer that we know what God, freedom, or immortality is. Kant here inveighs against the same sins of speculative metaphysics to which he devoted the Dialectic of the first *Critique*. He is not attacking rational theorizing as such (since, as we have already seen, this is precisely how he claims reason operates).

43. Again I use the German term because I find the English translations inadequate. I discuss the correct translation of *Achtung* in *Kant's Metaethics*. Also see "The Obligations of Philosophical Performance," paper delivered to the Greater Philadelphia Philosophy Consortium, February 1994.

44. Here and below I make an unargued assumption about the semantic equivalence of Kant's use of the terms "noumenal" and "intelligible" on the one hand, and "phenomenal" and "sensible" on the other. To defend this assumption would require an essay of its own, but I have every faith that such a defense would succeed.

45. I.e., at AK 402, 433, 436, and 438.

46. I.e., at AK 424, 431, 432, 434, 436 (twice), 438, 439, 444, 447, 458 (twice), 461, 462.

47. I.e., at AK 421 (twice), 429, 432, 434–7, 437 (three times), 437–8, 438, 439, 440, 447. Note that what is widely considered the first, "universal law" formulation of the categorical imperative at AK 421 is mistranslated by Paton and in fact contains no "ought."

48. Many assume that imperatives and commands are interchangeable, and Kant himself sometimes speaks this way. But they are not, and Kant knows it (for example, compare his conflicting definitions of an imperative at AK 413 and AK 414). I discuss the distinctions among a law, a command, and an imperative at greater length in "The Form of Self-Knowledge in Kant's Metaethics," in *Diskursparadigma: Form*, ed. Georg Schöllhammer (Vienna: Springer Verlag, 1997).

49. Although he says they *can* (AK 425).

50. See, for example, AK 408, 410n, 413, 425, and 447.

Kantian Virtue:
Priggish or Passional?

NANCY SHERMAN

It has long bothered readers of Kant's *Groundwork* that Kant takes himself to be reconstructing ordinary morality and yet assigns no clear place to the emotions that support morality. Indeed, in the *Groundwork*, emotions often seem to be either enemies of morality or immediate and impulsive inclinations that have no reliable or noteworthy connection to moral practice.[1] Though on a friendly reading of the first chapter of the *Groundwork* the assignment of moral worth for the performance of a dutiful action does not entail that emotions cannot be present,[2] that same reading still leaves it unclear what substantive role emotions might have in a Kantian account of moral conduct. The worry is somewhat alleviated by the time we come to the later works. There Kant recognizes the duty to develop emotions as a part of our duties of virtue. We have a duty to habituate empirical character, including our passional natures. Our agency extends deeply to the cultivation of emotions. More specifically, according to *The Doctrine of Virtue*, our end-setting capacities (i.e., rational agency) are sustained and developed by the setting of obligatory ends and sub-ends. These require the cultivation of our natural powers and receptivities in ways that empower our agency. Included among these receptivities are emotions. Yet positing a duty to cultivate emotions as part of a general project of moral development again leaves open the question of what roles these emotions will play within a conception of moral character ultimately grounded in reason. In this essay I want to explore this issue in the context of revisiting some of Kant's texts.

Kant's overall discussion of the emotions and their relation to virtue is episodic, but still there is more to draw from than most commentators have noted. Some of the important treatments are in the later works: in *The Doctrine of Virtue* (1797), in *Religion within the Limits of Reason Alone* (1793), and in *Anthropology from a Pragmatic Point of View* (1798). But there is also a substantive discussion in the *Critique of Practical Reason* (1788), written only three years after the *Groundwork*.[3]

I. Cultivating Full Virtue
(*The Doctrine of Virtue*)

In *The Doctrine of Virtue*, Kant conceives of virtue as the strength of a person's commitment (maxim) in fulfilling one's duty. The commitment amounts to obedience to an internal sanction (i.e., the dictates of the Categorical Imperative) in the performance of ethical or juridical duties. Kant familiarly suggests that virtue may be most perspicuous in fortitude against contrary inclinations – in forbearing against temptations and the like.[4] But the power and mastery of a will governed by morality is also manifest, he argues, in the transformation of our sensuous natures by that will into states that positively support it. Realizing the full capacity of such a will involves transforming our animal nature in ways that align with morality. "Man has a duty of striving to raise himself from the crude state of his nature, from his animality, and to realize ever more fully in himself the humanity by which he alone is capable of setting ends."[5] Briefly put, our humanity is the capacity to set ends, or adopt reasons for action.[6] The perfection of our humanity (or a good will) involves choice guided by reason's own legislative principles, that is, the Categorical Imperative. But perfection also involves working up our natures to support that moral motive. Kant puts it as follows:

When we say that man has a duty to take as his end the perfection characteristic of man as such (of humanity, really), we must locate perfection in what man can bring into being by his actions, not in the mere gifts he receives from nature; for otherwise it would not be a duty to make perfection an end. This duty must therefore be the *cultivation* of one's powers (or natural capacities).... At the same time this duty includes the cultivation of one's *will* (moral attitude) to fulfill every duty as such.[7]

Here Kant is anticipating a bifurcation of the duty to one's own perfection into the duty of natural perfection and the duty of moral perfection. The duty of natural perfection, as we have been saying, involves not simply inhibitory control, but positive cultivation and transformation of powers. Kant has in mind primarily "powers of mind, soul, and body, as means to all possible ends." Powers of mind he specifies later as involving understanding and reasoning; powers of soul as involving capacities of "memory, and imagination and the like"; and powers of the body as involving our animal stuff whose maintenance is required for our "animal vigor."[8] Surprisingly, Kant does not list here emotional capacities as among the natural powers which subserve our duty to moral perfection. Whatever the reason for the absence,[9] it is quickly remedied. For we do find explicit and extended appeal to the notion of cultivated feelings as among the resources we need to rely on in fulfilling our other obligatory end, namely the promotion of the happiness of others. It becomes systematic in the discussion of that end that we have derivative duties to cultivate feelings, such as sympathetic joy and sorrow, as ways of realizing beneficence and other sub-ends of that general duty. As Kant says, "nature has already implanted in man the susceptibility for these feelings. But to use this as a means to promoting active and rational benevolence is still a particular, though only a conditioned duty."[10] Once we get this far, it is easy to see that the cultivation of such feelings becomes part of an underlying project of natural perfection that supports our moral perfection and our regard for others.

Kant adds to the above quoted text that as a human being one has a duty of cultivating one's will "to the *purest* attitude of virtue, in which the law is the motive as well as the norm for his actions and he obeys it from duty" (emphasis added). What stands out here is that at the same time as we are to develop our talents and emotional capacities as part of virtue (and so conceive of virtue along the ancient model of an empirical project of character habituation), we are nevertheless to develop a *purer* attitude of virtue which is grounded in and responds to the rational nature of persons as end setters and moral legislators. It is this moral interest, that is, interest in acting from moral principles for their own sake, that guides our will, as criterion and motive, in the performance of dutiful and permissible action. So we need to cultivate our natural receptivities and the like to support our legislative capacity, but the latter remains, in the purest sense, the source of morality. All this seems to diminish the role of emotions again. Does Kant's expansion of the notion of virtue, in the end, amount to little?

I don't think so. Kant can be seen as reiterating the claim that the ultimate ground of the moral project must rest in the *authority* of reason without denying that natural receptivities can be shaped by and respond to that authority. On this interpretation, it is more the authority of the moral law than its purity or sufficiency for full moral agency that is key. But Kant can go further. He might also be seen as arguing that this responsiveness to morality, as rooted in the rational nature of persons, flourishes best in someone who has cultivated and cooperative emotional capacities. The emphasis in *The Doctrine of Virtue* is on *who* will act in morally worthy ways from a pure attitude of virtue.[11] And the thought is that what we can do to increase our chances to be part of that pool is to cultivate emotions that don't battle with our duty motive and that positively promote it. Such emotions are not themselves expressive of the purest attitude of virtue in that they are not the ultimate source of adequate reasons for doing what is required or determining what is morally permissible. But they are a layer of character that can, nonetheless, best support moral motivation. The point is overlooked if we insist upon emotions as only expressions of self-interest.

As such, it becomes important to understand what this supportive structure could be like. Following Kant's broad suggestions, we can sketch several ways in which emotions serve supportive roles. First, emotions serve as *modes of attention* that help us to track what is morally salient in our circumstances, and thus locate possible moments for morally permissible and required actions.[12] Sympathy, for example, draws us to occasions of distress or need. We attend in a charged and alert way, taking in what detached reason or perception might miss. Like all feelings, these inclinations need to be cultivated to serve morality well. We have natural susceptibilities to feel others' pleasure and pain, Kant says.[13] We need to cultivate these – visit the debtor's prisons and sick beds[14] – in order to orient these sensitivities appropriately, in this case, toward circumstances of need and poverty that are potential occasions for beneficence. Untutored sympathy might not align with moral interest as well. The more general point is that the moral vision we commonly associate with moral character typically works through the medium of emotional sensitivities. Capacities for grief prime us to notice human mourning and loss, capacities for pity, to notice that others suffer in ways that often seem undeserving. In general, emotions help us track morally relevant "news," not in indefeasible ways, but in ways that are a start for morality. Moral agency is truncated if it begins with choice rather than in what we frame as the circumstances relevant for choice. And emotions play a role in what we record.

Second, not only do we read circumstances through the emotions, but we *respond* through them. Manifest affect is a vehicle or *mode for conveying* moral interest. Through emotions, we communicate or *signal* moral interest to others in ways tailored to particular circumstances and needs. I take it that this is implicit in Kant's claim that benevolent feelings are a means for fulfilling our duty of beneficence.[15] The interpretive emphasis is now not on locating moral salience through the emotions, but on doing what is right with the right sort of emotional attitude. Kant does not emphasize this claim in the way that Aristotle does, but there is more to his remarks than has typically met the commentator's eye. As Kant sometimes puts it, emotion is a "garment that dresses virtue to advantage." The general point comes across clearly in the following passage from the *Anthropology*:

No matter how insignificant these laws of refined humanity may seem, especially in comparison with pure moral laws, anything that promotes sociability, even if it consists only in pleasing maxims or manners, is a garment that dresses virtue to advantage, a garment to be recommended to virtue in more serious respects too.

The *cynic's purism* and the *anchorite's mortification of the flesh*, without social well-being, are distorted figures of virtue, which do not attract us to it. Forsaken by the graces, they can make no claim to humanity.[16]

Kant does not speak directly of the emotions here, though he is explicit in a parallel passage in *The Doctrine of Virtue*. "Pleasantness in our relations with others, good-naturedness, mutual love and respect" are ways in which "we associate virtue with the graces, and to effect this is in itself a duty of virtue."[17] Emotions of this sort *intensify and enhance* the content of moral principle, presenting virtue in a more palpable and agreeable way. They make more attractive a morality that in its purer form may gain few adherents. The educational dimension of this aesthetic is unmistakable.[18] Virtue has an educative role. What is to serve as a model of virtue must be practically and pedagogically sound. Virtuous character must be something we could admire and be encouraged to be like. An attractive aesthetic of virtue recommends the life of virtue to both agent and beneficiary, and stably reinforces its value within the community.[19]

This is the positive way of making the point. But Kant's remarks about the *aesthetic* of emotion betray a characteristic ambivalence. Indeed, in the above passage from *The Doctrine of Virtue*, he goes on to say that the emotions are "only small change" or literally, "mere fashion" that form the outer semblance of virtue. The point now seems to be that emotions are mere decorative flourish; they *enhance* morality, but only as ornamental trim. They are little more than window dressing, their absence leaving the core of morality unmarred. Elsewhere too he suggests that emotions provide only a *faute de mieux* morality. They constitute an early stage of moral development, a provisional morality, to be superseded when reason is mature enough ultimately to take the reins. "It was still wisdom on nature's part" Kant remarks in the *Anthropology*, "to implant in us the predisposition to sympathy, so that it could handle the reins *provisionally*, until reason has achieved the necessary strength."[20] One needn't look far for yet other remarks that marginalize the emotions. They are there in number, often side by side an acknowledgment of the moral benefit of emotions. This is part of Kant's familiar teeter-totter with the emotions. It is part of the highly rhetorical style he resorts to when discussing the emotions. But perhaps Kant's negative attitude toward the emotions can best be understood as part of a contrast in which he pits the conditional value of emotion against the unconditional goodness of the moral motive. On this Kantian view, affability, sympathy, and the like gain their moral value derivatively. In the person who constrains her actions and does what is dutiful in response to the requirements of the moral law, they provide attractive, indeed human, ways of expressing that interest. However, in and of themselves, apart from their role in a structured conception of character (grounded in legislative reason), they do not convey moral concern; for in and of themselves these emotions are not specifically responses to our rational agency and the claims that flow from that. Significantly, Kant recognizes that emotion *can* respond to this fact. He takes respect to be such an emotion, and we shall come to his discussion of it shortly. It is a feeling that registers and expresses the purest moral concern toward the person as a rational agent, and thereby author of the moral law. Still, other more context-specific emotions, though not morally "responsive" in the same, pure way, are nonetheless an indispensable part of moral practice by connecting us palpably with human circumstance and by giving us a medium for conveying that connection to others. They are responsive to the *conditions* of morality, if not to what *grounds* our morality.

Third, and finally, emotions play a motivational role. The question, of course, for the Kantian is, Do they play a role as *moral motive*? For we can regard emotions in their other two roles as merely supportive – as supporting the motive of duty – by helping us to locate what is morally salient and then helping us to express our morally required actions in a humanly engaged way, and we can do this without thereby claiming that the moral action is itself *done out of emotion*. Rather, duty, or acting on principle, remains the moral motive. That is, on the Kantian view, as a morally motivated agent, what grounds my reason (for not betraying the patriot to the tyrant for gain, say) is not compassion I happen to feel, but that such action is wrong, and wrong because it manipulates another's rational agency. Emotional motivation is non-moral. On some views, non-moral motivation may be present, but all the same, it is not the locus of the morality, or moral worth, of the action.[21]

But there seems to be something arbitrary about allowing emotions a role in virtue that nevertheless precludes a morally motivational role, especially once we come to view the emotions that are a part of virtue as cultivated emotions, responsive to the authority of reason as the ultimate source of moral values. Presumably the restriction has to do with Kant's claim that reasons based on emotion are only *accidentally* connected with the rightness of action. But suppose compassion could be cultivated so that to act from it involved a concern for the rightness of action and for the claims others make on one in virtue of their agency. And too, that in acting from compassion, we could distinguish needs that ought to be satisfied from those that ought not to be satisfied. On such a view, a maxim grounded in compassion would seem to have moral content, and moral worth. Compassion would no longer be merely accidentally connected with morality.[22] One might object here that it is reason that is still doing the discriminative work, and that compassion could never be so thoroughgoingly responsive to reason that it, so to speak, could fully internalize moral principle. There may be something to this point. Our compassion may extend to circumstances wider or narrower than our morally justified reasons for beneficence. *On its own*, it may not lead us to the moral import of the "news" it records or leads us to actions which are responsive to moral claims. But still, as something of a compromise point, we might want to hold that when acting from compassion is properly regulated by concerns for the rightness of action, then that fully emotionally embodied response is morally worthy.

Several implications follow from this Kantian conception of the moral significance of emotions. Though there is a tradition of viewing the feelings connected with virtue as primarily captured by the notion of the derivative pleasure of an unconflicted commitment to morality, the above discussion suggests that a conception of the emotions along these lines will be far too thin.[23] Effective moral agency requires cultivated *ordinary* emotional sensitivities *to record and express* the demands of morality in context-specific ways. The Stoic idea that Kant rehearses, that duty alone is sufficient for doing what is right (and that this, on the Kantian view, yields pleasure), may eliminate a role for emotions as moral motives, but it does not eliminate a role for emotion in the other functions we discussed. To fill in these functions, a broad band of emotions is required, far broader than a band that contains only the moral cheer of unbegrudgingly acting on moral principles. A stripped down notion of moral gladness or cheer simply does not convey the richness of full emotional engagement characteristic of virtue rooted in the epistemic and attitudinal supports of ordinary emotions. On my reading of *The Doctrine of Virtue*, it is cultivating this more diverse palette that is especially important to the project of virtue. And the graciousness that follows from acting from duty without resentment itself depends on having these specific ordinary emotions as a general part of the practice of morality. Though perhaps possible, it would be peculiar to think an individual could do what is right "gladly" merely in the absence of opposing inclination, and not in the presence of supportive emotions that alert one to moral occasions and that convey affectively, to oneself and others, one's moral concerns.

Along these lines, it is important to emphasize that in *The Doctrine of Virtue* Kant views the empirical supports of moral interest as not simply the natural consequences of a commitment to morality, but as ends we have a positive duty to promote.[24] This strengthens the view found in the earlier *Lectures on Ethics*. There, Kant says, somewhat paradoxically, duty *becomes* inclination:

the command to love our neighbor applies within limits both to love from obligation [practical love] and to love from inclination [pathological love]. For if I love others from obligation, I acquire in the course of time a taste for it, and my love, originally duty-born, becomes an inclination.[25]

The claim in this early writing is that duty becomes naturalized. In acting from duty, an agent comes to develop the positive, phenomenal supports that underlie duty, presumably both context-specific emotions, such as benevolence and love, and the overall sense of cheer – a *fröhliche Hertz* – that follows from an integrated moral character. *The Doctrine of Virtue* (written some twenty years later) appeals to these psychological principles of habituation but strengthens the claim. It is not enough that benevolence or love be conceived of as the natural consequence of duty-generated maxims of beneficence. In addition, we have a positive duty to cultivate these emotions. We have a duty to promote them actively as derivative duties of our general duty of beneficence.[26] In short, we have a moral duty to "naturalize" our duty.[27] This is no more and no less than the duty to perfect our nature as a sub-part of our duty of moral perfection. A program of morally habituating the emotions is something we must actively choose to engage in.

Thus, a central focus in *The Doctrine of Virtue* is on what we can do to become the sort of persons for whom moral interest is abiding. The Aristotelian notion of a stable and reliable character rooted in appropriate emotions re-emerges. But on the Kantian view, these emotions are regulated by an interest that looks beyond the narrow focus of ordinary emotions – beyond responses to need, loss, shared interests, attractiveness, and all the ordinary contexts to which we have emotional reactions. To be cultivated properly, emotions must ultimately be responsive to the demands of reason as the source of moral agency. So, for example, sympathy serves beneficence because recognizing others' frustrations or pain is a way of seeing how one can step in to support their sense of being an agent who can meaningfully set ends and bring them about. Sympathy helps to get us to the moral claims others make on us, but it doesn't, on its own, constitute a direct or complete moral response. (Though, on the somewhat unorthodox view entertained earlier, it may itself have moral content if thoroughly cultivated in a way in which it fully internalizes moral principles.) On the Aristotelian view, in contrast, responding to others through pity, friendliness, generous feelings, and so forth (in ways that are medial, i.e., properly delimited or "fine") just *is* to respond morally, for there are no other purer or more principled ways of grasping what makes action right. The emotions, when transformed through habituation in ways that harmonize with overall considerations of good living, themselves embody the moral response. Kant too recognizes that morality becomes efficacious and discriminating *via* the discernment of the emotions. But the values of the moral law and the fundamental notion of free practical agency shape and regulate ordinary emotions. In the Aristotelian scheme, in contrast, there is no comparable, higher order value to be appealed to, abstractable from the circumstanced person and an agent's ability to respond to a person in those circumstances.[28] There is no moral interest that takes us to a person as such, independent of a shared conception of the good or of context.

Before proceeding, I want to pause for a minute and take stock. What we have seen so far is that emotions are *necessary conditions* for acting from the motive of duty. In some cases, they serve instrumental (epistemic) roles indispensable for acting from moral interest; in other cases, they are intrinsically valued as ways in which we act and convey moral interest with a human face. In light of this last claim especially, I would argue that emotions are constitutive of virtue in its human embodiment. More generally, we might say Kantian virtue, on this view, is a hierarchically structured composite, whose primary constituent is the disposition to act from moral principles for their own sake and whose subordinate constituents include cultivated natural capacities, such as emotions, that support that disposition. To say that cultivated emotions are part of virtue is to expand upon Kant's own theme in *The Doctrine of Virtue* that emotions can become "practical" or "moral" and no longer merely "pathological."

II. Virtue as a Structured Composite
(*Religion within the Limits of Reason Alone*)

The notion of virtuous character as a hierarchically structured composite with cultivated emotions forming a constitutive part is supported by a central passage in the *Religion*.[29] The thrust here is that good character has a regulative structure; it is an ordered composite in which incentives from inclination are not denounced, but rather conditioned and transformed.[30] Briefly put, Kant distinguishes three *Anlage* or predispositions to good that characterize human nature: the predisposition to animality (as a mere living being), the predisposition to humanity (as a living *and* rational being), and the predisposition to personality (as a living and rational being who is *accountable*).[31] The predisposition to animality concerns self-love expressed in our impulses toward self-preservation, propagation of the species, and basic sociality. The predisposition to humanity is a form of self-love expressed in our cultural strivings and social dependence upon and rivalry with others. The predisposition to personality is the capacity to hold ourselves morally accountable, by justifying our actions in terms of the moral law and by acting from respect for its command. All of these predispositions are "original" parts of our human nature, which when properly transformed and ordered, are a part of a more inclusive, composite conception of good character.

All of these predispositions are not only *good* in negative fashion (in that they do not contradict the moral law); they are also predispositions *toward good* (they enjoin the observance of the law). They are *original*, for they are bound up with the possibility of human nature. Human beings can indeed use the first two contrary to their ends, but they can extirpate [*vertilgen*] none of these. By the predispositions of a being we understand not only its constituent elements which are necessary to it [*Bestandstücke, die dazu erforderlich sind*], but also the forms of their combination, by which the being is what it is.[32]

Here again we have essentially the ancient project of ordering and rendering harmonious the parts of the human psyche or soul. A well regulated soul is not simply a matter of the absence of counter-incentives. The goal is to transform our self-love so that it promotes and advances compliance with the moral law. Moreover, Kant's language makes clearer here than in other places that cultivated natural powers and capacities are not simply necessary, instrumental *conditions* of moral agency, but necessary, hierarchically structured *parts* (*Bestandstücke*) and "elements" (*Elemente*) of the overall character or fixed (original) disposition (*Bestimmung*) of a human being to achieve the moral good. They support moral personality within a wider, composite notion of what it is to be a morally good person. Natural powers and capacities which when untutored fall under principles of self-love, when properly habituated and ordered, can be supportive parts of moral character. This is not to eliminate conflicts or to claim that a transformation of the passions is anything but difficult. Ours is an "unsocial sociability," Kant says pithily elsewhere,[33] and a decision to reorder one's incentives (a "revolution in one's cast of mind") makes one merely "susceptible" to goodness. "Only in continuous labor and growth" does one become "a good person."[34]

This change can be regarded as a revolution. But in the judgment of human beings, who can appraise themselves and the strength of their maxims only by the ascendancy which they win over their sensuous nature in time, this change must be regarded as nothing but an ever-during struggle toward the better, hence as a gradual reformation.[35]

Virtue requires not simply choosing character, but choosing the course of habituation that goes with it, however suspicious Kant sometimes seems to be of the idea of virtue as an habituated state.[36]

But what now can we say about the praiseworthiness of this more composite conception of virtue? Are virtuous feelings, and more generally, the structured character that supports motivation from duty, candidates for moral worth, or is moral worth limited (as it is in the *Groundwork*) to dutiful action done from the motive of duty, irrespective of the presence of emotions, whether supportive or contrary? I don't think there is a clear textual answer here, in part because the notion of moral worth is not central to *The Doctrine of Virtue* or the *Religion* as it is to the first chapter of the *Groundwork*. In these later works the shift is to the psychological constitution of the person for whom acting from duty is itself not an accidental sort of thing, but an interest stably rooted in character and its supportive structure. The shift is to moral anthropology, to how we can practice morality, and not merely to how morality is possible. This is the shift to virtue. But once virtue becomes the focus, the notion of moral credit directed at pure agency or good will no longer has easy application. For virtuous character will include not only the effort and agency of virtue (i.e., strength and fortitude, in Kant's terms), but also the gifts that attitude must work with. Praise directed toward virtue can only address a composite: *cultivated nature*. Virtuous character is embodied, and thus, to some extent, always limited by step-mother nature's endowments.[37] In contrast, true moral merit or worth (however difficult to determine the actual conditions for its assignment) is, in principle, meant to zero in on the pure agency involved in acting from moral interest, independent of constitutional and external circumstances. Still, there is one passage worth calling attention to at the conclusion of *The Doctrine of Virtue*.[38] Here, Kant suggests, in language reminiscent of the opening of the *Groundwork*, that duty done without emotion has no inner worth (*keinen inneren Wert*), and only with emotion can it become meritorious and exemplary (*verdientslich und exemplarisch*). Kant specifically refers to the notion of a cheerful frame of mind (*fröhlichen Gemüt*) and does not mention the ordinary, context-specific emotions he emphasizes earlier. However, if we are guided by my earlier interpretation that a cheerful frame of mind is not just a matter of acting from duty in the absence of contrary inclination, but of acting in a way that is supported by context-specific emotions (in their various roles), then the presence of these emotions too might be required for the action to be truly "meritorious and exemplary." Granted, we are no longer working with the *Groundwork* notion of "moral worth." But even so, we have some conception of moral praiseworthiness that Kant is willing to put forth. And it is a notion that needn't be devoid of a connection with credit; for the moral agent with a structured conception of character *cultivates* emotions in a way that is responsive to the conditions of the moral law. His emotional alignment is not just a matter of luck. As such, dutiful action done from the motive of duty without the support of emotions that flow from a structured conception of character would, on this interpretation, simply not be, in the fullest sense, morally praiseworthy.[39] Here again, the emotional aesthetic of morality seems more than merely decorative.

III. In What Sense Are We Agents of Our Emotional Experience?
(*Anthropology from a Pragmatic Point of View*)

To some, the *Anthropology* may be a strange text to appeal to for evidence of Kant's positive evaluation of the emotions in the moral project. For here, Kant makes explicit the impulsive and obsessive nature of certain emotions (what is translated as "emotional agitation" and "passion"),[40] and the ways both can resist the dominion of reason. In the grip of tumultuous and sudden emotion, an agent sees with blinders, getting lost in the moment, missing the forest for the trees:

Generally speaking, what constitutes a state of emotional agitation is not the intensity of a certain feeling but rather the lack of reflection that would compare this feeling with the totality of all the feelings (of pleasure or displeasure) that go with our state. A rich man whose servant awkwardly breaks a beautiful and rare goblet while carrying it around at a banquet will think nothing of this accident if, at the same moment, he compares this loss of *one* pleasure with the multitude of all the pleasures that his fortunate position as a rich man offers him. But if he isolates this one feeling of pain and abandons himself to it (without quickly making that mental reckoning), no wonder he feels as if he had lost his happiness completely.[41]

Kant makes similar remarks about passion – that it dwarfs other inclinations, that "it sweep[s] them into the corner just to please one," that the folly of the person gripped in passion is that he makes a *part* of his end the *whole*.[42] Passion "is an enchantment that refuses to be corrected."[43] As he paints it colorfully, "emotional agitation works like water breaking through a dam: a passion, like a stream that burrows ever deeper in its bed."[44] Although "emotional agitation does a momentary damage to freedom and self-mastery; passion abandons them and finds its pleasure and satisfaction in slavery."[45] Each, in its own way, threatens our practical agency.

And yet these emotions are only part of a wider range of emotional experience that Kant is eager to detail in this work. They are some of the ways we experience emotions, but not the only way. Indeed, on his view, they are extremes, maladies that require therapy and spiritual doctors. Following the Stoics, he argues that an effective therapy will promote a sense of "apathy." But he insists that by "apathy" he means neither "lack of feeling" nor "subjective indifference regarding objects of choice." In the truly tranquil mind there will be emotions, but none that are abject or lacking the sovereignty of reason. In this sense, a "noble character" will be freed from both the turbulence of affect and the desperate edge of passion.[46] For Kant even more than the Stoics, *apatheia* really does become *eupatheia*, not the absence of emotion, but a state of good or wholesome emotions which support duty. These are the so called "practical" emotions.

What I wish to emphasize about the *Anthropology* is that despite much of the negative rhetoric about various emotions, here we see Kant struggling to redraw the battle line between reason and emotion (and agency and passivity) in a more discriminating way. As part of this orientation Kant stresses that maladaptive emotional states are often to be viewed not as permanent disabilities, but as malleable conditions that can be transformed through our practical agency. There are things that we can do, through our will and reason, to transform them. Though emotions are not states that can be directly willed, Kant insists in these lectures that emotions can often be affected by what we will and by how we understand the circumstances that surround us. Indeed, the general focus of the *Anthropology* is on psychological empowerment – how to heal mental weaknesses and how to enhance the scope and reach of effective practical agency. Setting out the spirit of this work, he states: "The ineradicable *passive* element in sensibility is really the source of all the evil things said about it. Man's inner perfection consists in his having control over the exercise of all his powers, so that he uses them *as he freely chooses*."[47] An underlying theme is that agency can extend into the domain of feelings as well.

The effect of practical agency on emotional experience emerges forcefully in a distinction Kant draws between "sensitivity" (*Empfindsamkeit*) and "sentimentality" (*Empfindelei*):

Sensitivity is a *power* and *strength* by which we grant or refuse permission for the state of pleasure or displeasure to enter our mind, so that it implies a choice. On the other hand, sentimentality is a weakness by which we can be affected, even against our will, by sympathy for another's plight; others, so to speak, can play as they will on the organ of the sentimentalist; sensitivity is virile; for the man who wants to spare his wife or children trouble or pain must have enough fine feeling to judge their sensibilities not by *his* own strength but by their *weakness* and his *delicacy* of feeling is essential to his generosity. On the other hand, to share ineffectually in others' feelings, to attune our feelings sympathetically to theirs and so let ourselves be affected in a merely passive way, is silly and childish.[48]

Embedded in this sexist passage is the important point that emotions needn't be impulsive or resist reform. They aren't only agitations and passions. Many are quite susceptible to the influence of reason. With effort and guidance, they can be trained to become more discerning and supportive of endorsed ends. In particular, Kant suggests here that, with effort, we can cultivate a sense of empathy that allows us to identify with those whose circumstances may be considerably different from our own. From this empathic perspective, we look at others not in terms of our own abilities or weakness, but in terms of theirs. We learn how to reach out to them in a way that doesn't merely project ourselves. Moreover, there is strength of will involved in this refined way of attending. In a perspicuous way, we cultivate *how* we will be affected. The emotion involves cognitive assent. As Kant says elliptically, perhaps in reference to the Stoic notion of emotion as involving an assent to belief, "it implies a choice."

Kant nicely illustrates in this passage the supportive roles emotions can play in the moral life. First, they record moral salience: The husband is able to make nuanced discriminations because of his emotional sensitivity. He sees what might otherwise go unnoticed, and sees with an alertness (and readiness to act) that a cooler registering of "the news" might not facilitate. Second, this sensitivity is a "delicacy of feeling," Kant says, essential to generosity. Conveying certain emotions (enhancing one's actions through accompanying emotions) may itself be a constitutive part of what it is to act generously in a virtuous way.[49]

As we have said, the above passage adverts to the idea that there is agency in how we stand toward our emotions. They don't merely happen to us. We assent to various ways of being affected, and to various forms of control. Some of this may involve taking actions that are conducive to certain emotional consequences rather than others. In homespun style, Kant says if one wants to soften one's anger, then sitting rather than standing when one is angry might help to dissipate the tension.[50] But changes in how we think about circumstances also affect our emotions. Shifts in the beliefs and construals that ground emotions can sometimes help to change those emotions. Relevant here is a discussion entitled, "On voluntary consciousness of our ideas." Here, Kant suggests that directing where and how one attends to sense representations, for example, consciously "turning away from an idea" "even when the senses urge it on us," is a "strength of mind" acquired by practice.[51] Applying these remarks to modes of attending through the emotions, we can say that what emotions pick up and record is itself not a passive process but subject to the influence of persuasion and discourse. Still, Kant suggests that this can be an uphill struggle when particularly strong emotions are on board. Kant makes the point in terms of love, and in his hands, the subject turns comical:

The suitor could make a good marriage if only he could disregard a wart on his beloved's face or a missing tooth. But our power of attention is guilty of particularly bad manners if it immediately fastens, even involuntarily, on others' shortcomings: to direct our eyes to a button missing from the coat of someone we are face to face with, or a gap between his teeth, or to fasten our attention on a habitual speech defect not only disconcerts him but also spoils our own chances of social success.[52]

What is comical here is Kant's wistful attempt to deny that an important value of the testimony of the emotions is precisely its rawness. Emotions let us see ourselves and others with a certain immediacy and candor. They record values with a bruteness that more studied reflection often misses. If there is something called "love at first sight," then it would seem to depend more on this candor of the emotions than on learning how to direct one's eyes. All the same, sustained and mature love surely depends not just on mood but on will, and on how we learn to see the world and correct for our shortsightedness. That too is a part of loving. If we pair this passage with the earlier one about sensitivity, Kant is suggesting that attending through the emotions often requires control and focus in the very way that the loving husband takes effort to see things without merely projecting onto his wife his own notions of virility and strength.

IV. Respect as a Distinctive Moral Emotion
(The Critique of Practical Reason)

Finally, we need to turn to the *Critique of Practical Reason* and the singling out of respect as *the* most fundamental practical or moral emotion. In the section entitled, "The Incentives of Pure Practical Reason," the explicit focus is on the effects of pure practical reason – that is, the source of the moral law – on our phenomenal nature: "what happens to the human faculty of desire as a consequence of the determining ground" of morality.[53] Kant's claim is that practical reason motivates us directly (that is, we take a direct interest in the principle of pure practical reason), but in addition, insofar as we are affective creatures, we experience that determination, affectively, as respect. Respect is not itself a separate sort of motivation. Rather, it is the effect of moral motivation on feeling.[54] More specifically it is the feeling of pleasure in appreciating oneself as author of the moral law and capable of reasons for action that meet the demands of the moral law, and yet of pain, in having one's reasons for action based on self-love judged untenable and in conflict with morality.

If anything checks our self-conceit in our own judgment, it humiliates. Therefore, the moral law inevitably humbles every man when he compares the sensuous propensity of his nature with the law. Now if the idea of something as the determining ground of the will humiliates us in our self-consciousness, it awakens respect for itself so far as it is positive and the ground of determination. . . . The effect is on the one side merely negative; but on the other, in respect to the restrictive practical ground of pure practical reason, it is positive.[55]

Kant goes on to claim that respect is a priori. His meaning is unclear, but one possible interpretation is something along the following lines: if there are a priori practical principles (by which rational agents, such as ourselves, are capable of being moved), and if in addition to being rational agents, we are also affective agents so constituted that we have desires that can always conflict with those principles, then there will always be present the ingredients for respect. There will always be present not only the conditions for the "painful" checking of reasons for action based on self-love, but also the conditions for the "pleasurable" feelings of mastery that come from appreciating our legislative status. Put more simply, respect is just the affective side of our ever-available capacity to be moved by practical reason.

But there is something else to notice in Kant's remarks above. And that is that respect seems to be an emotion that has clear connection with a cognitive content. The negative feeling, or pain associated with respect, arises when we *dwell on* the frustration of specific ends of self-interest (i.e., the striking down of self-conceit as one "*compares* the sensuous propensity of one's nature with the law" [italics added]); its pleasure is that stirred by *appreciating* our legislative authority and new found mastery in its regulative agency. It is not just that the emotion has pleasurable and painful "feels." Rather, the pleasure and pain are directed at certain thoughts or construals. To feel respect is to see ourselves *as* inhibited and *as* governed by a supreme law whose source is our own reason. The pain and pleasure of the emotion are directed at those judgings and are the causal effects of them. Respect is that emotion that has *that* specific evaluative content. There is no qualitative feel that we can identify as characteristic of respect that reliably sets it apart from other emotions. Rather, the emotion just is a particular intentional content and an affective feeling directed toward that content. Other emotions too will have a similar account. Benevolence, for example, becomes a feeling that has to do with pain at the sight or thought of another's suffering and pleasure at the thought of their joy. Such emotions can be said to become "practical" (or properly conditioned by and supportive of duty within a structured conception of character) when they embrace increasingly more adequate cognitions, such as when we take to heart new relevant information, for example, that this is not a worthy object of benevolence or love, or that this too is a case of need or distress and is a possible occasion for beneficence.

This is not Kant's official account, however.[56] In the case of ordinary emotions, he never develops the view that they are intentional – that is, about things that we judge to be good or bad. The view that emotions are intentional is, of course, Aristotle's view. Connecting emotion with cognition is at the heart of an Aristotelian account of the emotions and at the heart of an Aristotelian view that emotions can be transformed by revisions of those evaluations such that they come to embrace more adequately our judgments of what is overall good. I shall say something about this account later. But what is relevant here is that Kant's willingness to appreciate the moral significance of emotions – be it respect or more ordinary context-relative emotions – makes best sense when we adopt a theory of the emotions that is, in fact, not his own.

Kant's own view is that emotions are essentially sensations. They are a psychic quality of feeling. So consider the following remarks from the *Metaphysics of Morals*:[57]

We call the capacity for pleasure or pain at a representation *"feeling"* because both of these comprise what is *merely subjective* in the relation to our representation and contain no reference to an object which could give us knowledge of the object (or even knowledge of our own state). . . . Pleasure or pain . . . expresses nothing at all in the object, but simply a relation to the subject.[58]

As Kant puts it in the note that follows,

if the subjective aspect of our representation cannot become *part of our knowledge* because it is merely the reference of the representation to the *subject* and contains nothing that can be utilized for knowledge of the object, then this receptivity to the representation is called *feeling*.[59]

The claim is that feelings don't tell us much of anything about the world. They tell us that we have been affected, but give us no determinate news of those things or of our own state either. "Pleasure and displeasure do not belong to the cognitive power as it refers to objects; they are determinations of the subject and so cannot be ascribed to external objects."[60] All we get is a feeling – a feeling that, according to famous remarks in the *Critique of Practical Reason*, registers quantitative, not qualitative differences.[61] Of course, Kant might still hold that emotions are essentially sensations, and that cognitions nonetheless count among the typical causal antecedents. This may go some way to establishing a connection between cognition and emotions, but so long as emotions are essentially sensations, it is an inadequate position. For on such a view, the emotion is no more than contingently connected with a certain cognitive content. The emotion of respect could conceivably be caused by cognitions very different from the ones Kant lists or, again, could be caused by no cognition at all. For on the official account, emotion would just be a "characteristic feel."[62]

Now how damaging is this to Kant? For after all, he thinks the emotions do give us important information about the world and direct our attention to action that reason judges we ought to do. Is there still a point in visiting the debtor's prisons and sickbeds in order to cultivate a discerning sense of sympathy, if feelings of sympathy are not themselves representations of objective features of the world (though caused by them)? Is there a point to perfecting our affective susceptibilities as ways of tracking "the news" if they are themselves not cognitive or epistemic capacities, but rather, as Kant puts it in the *Critique of Practical Reason*, brute receptivities of commensurable pleasure or pain?

I think Kant's position on the emotions is unsatisfactory but that, nonetheless, his overall view of the importance of cultivating emotions can be salvaged.[63] In part, Kant seems to be relying on the idea that (a) though emotions themselves do not contain appraisals about the morally salient features of the world, nor (b) are themselves a source of determinative reasons for moral action, in both cases they play a role (and, with training, a more reliable role), in directing our attention to circumstances that are morally salient and to actions that are responsive to moral claims. So, for example, overcoming prejudice and understanding the neediness of a particular group of individuals can *evoke* or *cause* feelings of sympathy we previously didn't have. In this case, emotions would give us some news, though they would not themselves be constituted by that evaluative "news" nor determine its moral import, nor be a source of reasons for action, without supplementation from judgments of reason concerning the demands beneficence makes.

Even so, we shouldn't minimize a certain instability in Kant's views when it comes to the emotions. An intentional or evaluative view of the emotions would better cohere with his appreciation of their epistemic function, while still not disturbing his view that emotions may not themselves be the source of determinative reasons (or motives) for moral action. For to justify such choices, we may simply need additional and different information than emotions typically contain (e.g., information that helps us grasp the claims of individuals in terms of their rational agency). In a sense, there is a failure of systematization here. Kant's treatment of the emotions always, at a certain level, remains episodic, keyed to the interest at hand. Even when he talks head on about the role of emotions in the account of virtue – as he does in *The Metaphysics of Morals*, where he discusses natural and moral perfection, or in the second *Critique*, where the topic is the effects of duty on our phenomenal nature – the discussion is never fully brought round to a systematic treatment of emotion. His solutions remain ad hoc, unsupported by a theory of the emotions that does full justice to his own view of their utility. In addition, there is the challenge of Kant's rhetorical style when he takes on the emotions.

But to return to the notion of respect for the moment, there is nonetheless something terribly important that Kant captures in this notion. And this is the notion that a conception of morality must find room for a feeling that is responsive to persons simply as persons, independent of contingent circumstances or stations. So, whereas sympathy responds to need, affability to characteristics we find attractive in another, and pity to undeserving tragedy or misfortune, respect is different in that its focus is not local or context-specific. It can plausibly be singled out as *the* moral emotion, not so much because rational agency generates it spontaneously in everyone, but because it is a response to rational agency itself. More strictly, it is a response, in the first instance, to the moral law, and secondarily a response to persons, insofar as they have the capacity to act from that law. Its evaluative focus is legislative agency as such.

This survey of some of Kant's writings on the emotions has shown that Kant has considerably more to say about the moral benefit of emotions than is standardly acknowledged. Still, Kant's theory is unstable because his view of the emotions as sensations is implausible and tends to undercut the very roles he assigns to emotions in moral practice. It seems to me that Aristotle's theory of the emotions, with its focus on cognition, does better to explain the role of emotions in virtue, and perhaps it is not surprising that he, unlike Kant, accords emotions the unequivocal role he does in his moral theory. I want to turn to that briefly, noting some problems as well as indicating how Aristotle's eudaimonistic focus, while not an egoistic perspective, as Kant seems to think, nonetheless does not easily capture within its purview a Kantian-like notion of moral interest that goes beyond the contingency of shared boundary and context. But I warn that these remarks are meant only to point to Aristotle's theory, and are not themselves a full development of his views.[64]

V. Aristotelian Virtue, Very Briefly

Aristotle holds that fineness of virtue is expressed both in action and emotion. Both are subject to praise and blame, both are ways we fully actualize virtuous character in the world. As he puts it, hitting the mean is a matter of acting *and* feeling appropriately.[65] On one interpretive view, his claim is not simply that appropriate emotions are highly estimable states, but that, in addition, they are creditworthy in a way that presupposes some degree of moral responsibility and agency. On this view, when Aristotle claims that virtue is a state of character related to choice (*prohairesis*),[66] it is not only actions, but emotions constitutive of virtue, that are indirectly related to choice. For through a process of habituation, we choose how we will stand toward our pleasures and pains; we choose how we will effect our agency upon our *pathē*. Right pleasures and pains, or cultivated emotional states, are thus not accidentally connected with judgments of what is best for overall good living. Through education and a pattern of choices, our emotions come to express evaluations (judgings) that are endorsed by practical wisdom. Aristotle adds that, through such an education, the virtuous person becomes someone who is by and large beyond psychic conflict. She is not simply continent or in control of her wayward emotions (*enkratēs*), but temperate (*sōphrōn*). Her emotions have been transformed so that they are truly in harmony with judgments of practical wisdom.

Undoubtedly, there are problems with this view of eliminating psychic conflict, and Aristotle himself documents some of them in his account (in *Nicomachean Ethics* III.1) of the moral conflict involved in forced (or mixed) actions. But what interests me for the moment is Aristotle's own account of the way emotions can be transformed to become harmonious with the judgments of practical wisdom. As we said earlier, Aristotle, unlike Kant, puts forth an intentional theory of the emotions that goes some way toward explaining how emotions can come to support and express the overall endorsed ends of good living. But I want to suggest, somewhat sketchily, that Aristotle's theory of the transformation of emotions still cannot easily explain the type of psychic unity his theory of virtue requires.

In the second book of the *Rhetoric*,[67] Aristotle puts forth a theory of the emotions that supports his general understanding of the emotions in the *Nicomachean Ethics*. Emotion, according to the *Rhetoric*, is a complex of cognition, affective feeling, and – in some cases – desire. So anger is "a desire accompanied by pain toward revenge of what one regards as an unwarranted slight toward oneself or one's friends."[68] According to this definition, the feeling of pain characteristic of anger is directed toward a construal: *that* one has been slighted, unjustifiably; that construal or evaluative judgment often leads to a desire for action. The general force of Aristotle's view is that emotions are essentially connected with the evaluations that ground them, and that they develop or change as those evaluations do. The rhetorician can exploit this connection, changing emotions by changing evaluations.

Aristotle of course recognizes that emotions don't change as quickly as beliefs sometimes do. For one, the mental content of emotions isn't always evidentiarily warranted beliefs. And what we have good reason to believe often doesn't dislodge the more tenacious thoughts that inform our emotions. These often include musings and imaginings (*phantasmata*) which we dwell on and yet which may conflict with other more "appropriate" or "warranted" beliefs, or endorsed ends of good living. Ethical habituation is important precisely because it addresses the fact that time is required for the kind of change that takes root in character and that is more than either a manipulation of isolated behavior or belief.

Yet still, Aristotle does not really tell us how an internal transformation of emotion is to take place, though I believe his theory may have the tools for a more adequate explanation. The point is this: Aristotle often conceives of the habituation of the emotions as a top-down chastening of the emotions whereby the lower part of the soul "listens to" the wiser judgment of the higher part. Emotion, Aristotle suggests, must turn its ears upward and obey the higher part of the soul, as a child heeds the exhortations of a parent.[69] But it is not clear if through this process the effect on the emotions can be much more than control or inhibition. For without giving wayward emotions their own due (i.e., exposing and listening to them, though not necessarily allowing that they be *acted on*), they may not sufficiently change from within. What I want to suggest, rather tentatively, is that the notion of top-down chastening stands in the way of Aristotle's embracing the developmental implications of his own novel view: namely, that emotions have their own grounding reasons, and that as these change, emotions do too. As such, transformation requires first an exposing and acknowledging of those reasons, an engaging of them, if you like, from the bottom up, as part of the process of persuasion and discourse about their adequacy. The Stoics embrace this idea in their notion that an agent's exploration and acknowledgment of the "false" valuations upon which her emotions rest is an important start for a therapy of the emotions.[70] Freud's "talking therapy" expresses another version of the view that the articulation of disavowed desires is itself a step toward transformation and self-mastery.[71] Aristotle, clearly, does not push his theory in these directions. But nonetheless, I want to suggest that in his notion of emotions as constituted by reasons, and as transformed by a change in those reasons, lies a developmental account of emotions that may have far reaching implications for accounts of psychic harmony, including his own.

Finally, I want to say something briefly about Aristotelian *eudaimonia* and the moral perspective. The project of the *Nicomachean Ethics* is to show that the most defensible conception of *eudaimonia* or good living is that which is constituted by virtuous activity. The project, formally, is that of specifying *my good*; materially, the result is virtuous activity undertaken for its own sake, where to be committed to virtue in the requisite way involves a transformation of ordinary self-love into a love of what is fine or noble. To love what is fine or noble is, among other things, to express genuine altruism.[72] As such, Kant's critique of eudaimonism fails if it reduces the pursuit of *eudaimonia* to essentially a pursuit of self-love that ignores proper regard and respect for others. Yet, still, the sort of other regard proper to Aristotelian theory is limited in an important way. We can see this in the discussion of friendship in the ethical works. Aristotle makes clear in this discussion that friendship will be the most important forum for beneficence, because it is the most deeply connected with moral development and with the conditions for sustaining moral character.[73] There are forms of goodwill (*eunoia*) toward strangers and the like, but we do not realize ourselves as fully in these forms of virtue. For we do not, in addition, share a life or common good with these beneficiaries. Equally, it seems that on Aristotle's view, philanthropic feelings that go out to persons whom we do not know, such as in the case of pity, kindness, or goodwill, reach out to them on the basis of some shared context – that we could suffer similar fates – or that the beneficiaries are those who have a characteristic we admire or to which we can relate.[74] In a sense, our moral concern must connect with others whom we can appreciate from our own corner of the universe, who are part of our lives, relevant to our conception of good living, in a set of circumstances with which we can identify.[75] This, I take it, is at the heart of Kant's break with Aristotle. On the Kantian view, we must take a moral interest in persons as such, in virtue of a source of value (namely, rational agency) that is not dependent on circumstance or shared context. My claim in this paper is that this moral interest must be grounded within a conception of character that includes morally supportive emotions that *do* record the concerns of circumstance and context. Kant seems to have been arguing as much.

NOTES

1. See, for example, the famous sympathy passage at *Groundwork of the Metaphysics of Morals*, trans. H. J. Paton (New York: Harper and Row, 1956), 66/ IV: 398, hereafter abbreviated *G*. Where there are two sets of pages, the first set refers to the English edition, the second to the Prussian Academy edition. Other editions and abbreviations are as follows: *The Doctrine of Virtue*, trans. Mary Gregor (Philadelphia: University of Pennsylvania Press, 1964), abbreviated *MdS*; *Religion within the Limits of Reason Alone*, trans. T. M.

Greene and H. H. Hudson (New York: Harper and Row, 1960), abbreviated as *Rel.*; *Critique of Practical Reason*, trans. L. W. Beck (Indianapolis: Bobbs-Merrill, 1956), abbreviated as *KpV*; *Anthropology from a Pragmatic Point of View*, trans. Mary Gregor (The Hague: Martinus Nijhoff, 1974), abbreviated as *Anth.*

2. See Barbara Herman, "On the Value of Acting from the Motive of Duty," as it appears in revised form in her *The Practice of Moral Judgement* (Cambridge: Harvard University Press, 1993), p. 12. I refer to Herman's writings as they appear in that work.

3. Also the *Critique of Judgment*. The connection of Kant's aesthetic writings with the treatment of the emotions in the ethical texts has been discussed admirably by Paul Guyer in *Kant and the Experience of Freedom* (Cambridge University Press, 1993). The last chapter of his book focuses more exclusively on the treatment of emotions in the ethical works. For a discussion of his book, see my "Reasons and Feelings in Kantian Morality," *Philosophy and Phenomenological Research*, 55(2) (1995): 369–77.

4. *MdS* 37/VI: 380; 54/VI: 394.

5. *MdS* 45/VI: 387.

6. See *MdS* 51/VI: 392.

7. *MdS* 45/VI: 386–7.

8. *MdS* 111–12/VI: 445. Kant's division of powers of mind, soul, and body contrasts with the standard Aristotelian division of goods into goods of the soul, goods of the body, and external goods. Virtue has to do with the goods of the soul; health and strength would be bodily goods that promote virtue and may be intrinsically valuable but are not themselves a part of virtue. External goods would be such things as wealth, which also promote virtue, but which are not intrinsically valuable.

9. Guyer (p. 376) attributes this to Kant's borrowing of Wolffian categories of natural perfection.

10. *MdS* 125/VI: 456.

11. Herman (p. 13) too makes this point.

12. For suggestions of this view, see Herman, *The Practice of Moral Judgment*, chap. 4, and Onora O'Neill, "The Power of Example," in her *Constructions of Reason* (Cambridge University Press, 1989). I discuss the point in connection with Aristotelian ethics in *The Fabric of Character* (Oxford: Oxford University Press, 1989), chap. 2.

13. *MdS* 59–60/VI: 399; 125/VI: 456.

14. *MdS* 126/VI: 457.

15. *MdS* 125/VI: 456.

16. *Anth.* 147/VII: 282.

17. *MdS* 145/VI: 473.

18. For the notion of virtue as a moral ornament (a *moralische Zutat*), see *MdS* 134/VI: 463, though Kant does not specifically refer here to the affective element of the virtues.

19. See Kant's "Conjectural Beginning of Human History" in *Kant on History*, ed. L. W. Beck (Indianapolis: Bobbs-Merrill, 1963), 57/VIII: 113, for further suggestions of this view. Although Kant emphasizes the importance of aesthetics in conveying virtue toward others, he warns against settling for mere semblance in ourselves: "We must value even the semblance of good in others" but "the semblance of good *in ourselves* . . . we must ruthlessly wipe

away: we must tear off the veil with which self-love covers our moral defects" (*Anth.* 32/VII: 153; cf. *Anth.* 111–12/VII: 244–5). Also, note, the above remarks about the educative value of emotional aesthetics contrast with Kant's more austere remarks in the *Religion* and *Groundwork*, in which he emphasizes the educative importance of a "pure" example of virtue as a role model for children: *Rel.* 44; *G* 78n/IV: 411n; *G* 94n/IV: 427n. For an excellent contemporary, clinical discussion of the role of emotional commmunication in early moral development, see Stanley I. Greenspan, *The Development of the Ego* (Madison, CT: International Universities Press, 1988), esp. p. 36.

20. *Anth.* 104. The Stoic echoes here are clear. On the Stoic view, reason sets in late; the Stoics hold in addition, that we don't have genuine emotions until we have mature reason. Kant rejects the second part of the claim since he rejects the Stoics' cognitive account of the emotions.

21. See, for example, Herman, chap. 1.

22. I am grateful to Andy Reath for helping me formulate the point.

23. For Kant's own statement of this notion of pleasure or cheer, see his famous response to Schiller in *Rel.* 18n; also *MdS* 158–60/VI: 483–5.

24. Guyer emphasizes this point in his treatment of Kant.

25. *Lectures on Ethics*, trans. Louis Infield (Indianapolis: Hackett, 1963), p. 197.

26. See Guyer, p. 366; *MdS* 63/VI: 402.

27. Even the following *Groundwork* passage seems to be compatible with this line:

> Love out of inclination cannot be commanded; but kindness done from duty – although no inclination impels us, and even although natural and unconquerable disinclination stands in our way – is *practical*, and not *pathological*, love, residing in the will and not in the propensions of feeling, in principles of action and not of melting compassion; and it is this practical love alone which can be an object of command. (G67/IV: 399)

I take Kant to be repeating the familiar claim that we cannot be commanded to have certain natural advantages. That is a matter of external lottery. But we can be commanded to love out of inclination if this means, cultivate what by nature you already have.

28. Pity and goodwill, for example, are altruistic emotions. They are directed at another's benefit without ulterior motive. But they reach out to the person as one *I* can respond to. In the case of pity, I must to some degree think I too could suffer that sort of loss, and in the case of goodwill, that I admire or identify with that person (see *Rhetoric* II.9; *Nicomachean Ethics* [hereafter, *NE*] IX.5). The point is that the response does not go out to the person as such, but to the person in a local context to which I can connect. The point comes across most forcefully when we appreciate that civic friendship for Aristotle sets the boundary of those to whom we stand in relations of justice (see *Eudemian Ethics* 1242a21ff.). All works of Aristotle are cited from Jonathan Barnes, ed., *The Complete Works of Aristotle: The Revised Oxford Translation*, Vols. 1 and 2 (Princeton: Princeton University Press, 1984).

29. *Rel.* 21–3; 31.

30. See also *KpV* 92–3/V: 89–90.

31. *Rel.* 22.

32. *Rel.* 23.

33. In *Idea for a Universal History*, in *On History*, ed. L. W. Beck (Indianapolis: Bobbs-Merrill, 1963), p. 15.

34. *Rel.* 43.

35. *Rel.* 43.

36. Kant, in criticism of Aristotle, often seems to think of habituation as producing mindless states that will lack the intellectual structure necessary for sensitive moral judgment. So, for example, see Kant's remarks at *MdS* 42/VI: 383, where he clearly fails to appreciate Aristotle's view that reliable and stable habituated states of virtue are themselves informed by and expressed through practical reason. Kant's neglect of the Aristotelian notion of practical wisdom is also evident in his characterization of the principle of the mean at *MdS* 97/VI: 432. In the *Rel.* passage we have been considering, however, he seems far more appreciative of a general notion of habituation. And certainly, in *The Doctrine of Virtue*, despite his criticisms of Aristotle, he appeals to a project of virtue that implicitly relies on the steady transformation of character through choice, experience, and critical practice over time. For a discussion of Aristotelian habituation, see Sherman, chap. 5.

37. Perhaps the Stoics, more so than Kant, try to limit the notion of virtue to the activity of reason as inner skill. On this, see Julia Annas, *The Morality of Happiness* (New York: Oxford University Press, 1993).

38. *MdS* 158–60/VI: 483–5.

39. Note, my point is not simply that duty done without cheer is an indication that an agent has not truly internalized the demands of duty, and that her action lacks moral worth on that count. Rather, my point is that to internalize the demands of duty properly requires the positive and supportive presence of emotions in the work of morality. The result of cultivating this sort of unified moral character is a "cheerful" or "happy" heart.

40. Passion (*Leidenschaft*) falls under the general heading of inclination (*Neigung*) and inclination under the more general notion of appetite (*Begierde*). Emotional agitation (*Affekt*) is not an appetite but a reactive feeling of pleasure and pain (*Gefühl*).

41. *Anth.* 122/VII: 255; 133/VII: 266.

42. *Anth.* 134/VII: 267.

43. *Anth.* 133/VII: 265.

44. *Anth.* 120/VII: 252.

45. *Anth.* 134/VII: 267.

46. *MdS* 69/VI: 407.

47. *Anth.* 144/VII: 224.

48. *Anth.* 104/VII: 236; see also on the issue of training emotions through more behavioral methods *Anth.* 120/VII: 252 and *Anth.* 30/VII: 151.

49. Contrast the more qualified claim at *Anth.* 37/VII: 158 in which fine sensitivity is said to be important for well-being, but doesn't necessarily make an individual morally better (*nich eben moralisch-besser*).

50. *Anth.* 120/VII: 252.

51. *Anth.* 13/VII: 131; see also 10/VII: 128.

52. *Anth.* 13/VII: 132.

53. *KpV* 75/V: 72.

54. I am grateful to Andy Reath for correspondence on the Kantian idea of respect.

55. *KpV* 77/V: 74.

56. Though, as I have suggested above, in his account of respect, one sees faint glimmers of the notion that pleasure and pain are connected with cognitions we dwell on – in his terms, with what we dwell on when we "compare" the sensuous property of our nature with the view of ourselves as authors of the moral law.

57. I am grateful to Christine Korsgaard's discussion of this passage in her paper, "From Duty and For the Sake of the Noble: Kant and Aristotle on Morally Good Action," in *Aristotle, Kant, and the Stoics*, ed. Stephen Engstrom and Jennifer Whiting (Cambridge University Press, 1996).

58. *MdS* 7/VI: 211.

59. *MdS* 8/VI: 212n.

60. *Anth.* 107/VII: 240.

61. *KpV* 23–4/V: 24–5.

62. For a good discussion of a cognitive account of emotions, see Justin Oakley, *Morality and the Emotions* (London: Routledge, 1992).

63. I am grateful to Andy Reath for helping me moderate my view here.

64. For a fuller development of Aristotelian ethics, see my *The Fabric of Character* (Oxford: Oxford University Press, 1989).

65. *NE* 1106b18.

66. *NE* 1106a4.

67. The work is a popular handbook on forensics. Still, underlying the programmatics for persuasion is a view that has clear theoretical elements and important implications for his ethical writings.

68. *Rhetoric* 1378a31–2. For a more complete discussion of the moral significance of Aristotelian emotions, including an analysis of the different elements of an emotion, see my "The Role of Emotions in Aristotelian Virtue," *Proceedings of the Boston Area Colloquium in Ancient Philosophy*, Vol. 9 (Lanham, MD: University Press of America, 1994), 1–33.

69. See *NE* I.13.

70. This process is perspicuous in a work, such as Seneca's *De Ira*. For a discussion of Stoic transformation of emotions, see Martha Nussbaum, *The Therapy of Desire* (Princeton: Princeton University Press, 1993).

71. See Jonathan Lear, *Love and Its Place in Nature* (New York: Farrar, Straus, Giroux, 1990) for an interesting discussion of similar views. Also, see my "The Moral Perspective and the Psychoanalytic Quest," *The Journal of the American Academy of Psychoanalysis*, 23(2) (1995): 223–41, for the connection between traditional moral theories and Freud's account of character development.

72. See *NE* IX.8. For the connection of "the fine" or *to kalon* with a conception of morality and altruism, see *Rhetoric* I.9. For further discussion of the fine as a moral concept see T. Irwin, "Aristotle's Conception of Morality," with my commentary in *Proceedings of the Boston Area Colloquium in Ancient Philosophy*, Vol. 1 (Lanham, MD: University Press of America, 1985), pp. 115–50. For general discussion of Aristotelian *eudaimonia* as embodying a moral conception, see Annas, *The Morality of Happiness*, and Richard Kraut, *Aristotle on the Human Good* (Princeton: Princeton University Press, 1989).

73. For statements that friendship is the finest way of being beneficent, see *NE* 1154b9, 1169b12. For the connection of friendship with self-development, see the remarks on self-knowledge in IX.9 and the closing remark on friendship at 1172a10–12. For development of this view, see my chapter, "Shared

Voyage," in *Making a Necessity of Virtue: Aristotle and Kant on Virtue* (Cambridge University Press, 1997). Also, see Annas, ch. 12.

74. See note 29.

75. Michael Slote has raised to me the interesting question of whether some sort of identification is also required to respond to the rational agency in others. If so, Kant may have to give an account of the cultivation of respect much like the account he gives of cultivating the other emotions.

Taking the Law into Our Own Hands: Kant on the Right to Revolution

CHRISTINE M. KORSGAARD

> If we place ourselves at the end of this tremendous process, where
> the tree at last brings forth fruit, where society and the morality of
> custom at last reveal *what* they have simply been the means to: then
> we discover that the ripest fruit is the *sovereign individual*, like only
> to himself, liberated again from the morality of custom, autonomous
> and supramoral.
>
> Nietzsche[1]

I. Taking the Law into Our Own Hands

Morality is unconditional and overriding. Its demands are uncompromis-
ing and its claims take priority over all others. Yet we can all think of
situations in which, for reasons that seem to us honorable, unselfish, or
conscientious, we would do things which morality seems to forbid. I want
to ask how we can account for this fact.

There are two attempts to deal with the problem which, for obvious
reasons, I will call skepticism and dogmatism. The skeptic denies that
morality is unconditional and overriding. The dogmatist insists that it is,
and argues that either the actions in question are not wrong, or, if they
are, a good person just won't do them.[2]

Some skeptics and dogmatists are merely trying to domesticate the
phenomena. The skeptic may have pretensions to being worldly and
realistic, laughing at the ponderous claims of moralists. The dogmatist
may simply be a moralistic prig. But there are serious and attractive
versions of both views. The skeptic may think, as Bernard Williams does,
that a life in which moral considerations can always override love and the
cherished projects of a lifetime is not recognizably human.[3] The dogmatist may think that a suitably refined and sensitive moral theory will show
us that the actions in question are not wrong after all, but, in the complex
or terrible situations in which we are tempted to choose them, simply the
right things to do.

A Kantian's job is to find the path between skepticism and dogmatism.
In this essay, I try to construct an account of one category of cases in

which a good person will do a terrible thing: cases in which she judges that, for moral reasons, she must take the law into her own hands. There are many such cases, but the one I will examine is the standout in the category: the case of the conscientious revolutionary. From Kant I will derive an account of this case that, unlike skepticism and dogmatism, preserves at least something of both of the thoughts with which I began. Morality is unconditional and overriding, and revolution is always wrong. Yet sometimes the good person finds she must rebel.

I have another motive for examining this category of cases. It is that human beings seem to find them profoundly interesting and somehow attractive. Literature and the movies are full of them. We are shown a good person who, rather than violate his own standards, submits to the unjust treatment of himself and others. He holds out against solicitations to rebel long enough to convince us that his honor is real. And then a moment finally comes when, breaking the rules he has set for himself, he takes up his weapons and fights. Fletcher Christian finally mutinies against Captain Bligh. Ransom Stoddard, who came to the West to bring it law, picks up his gun and heads to the street for a shootout with Liberty Valance.[4] Instead of feeling disappointed at their defection, these are moments that we find *thrilling*.

Neither skepticism nor dogmatism can give an adequate account of this fact. The skeptic thinks that the hero has awakened to a more realistic view of the role of morality in human life. The dogmatist thinks that the hero has arrived at a more sensitive and refined conception of what morality demands. Both see these stories as what are sometimes called "coming of age" stories, in which the hero advances to maturity. This seems to me to be wrong in every way. Although the heroes of these stories have not previously taken the law into their own hands, they are not morally immature characters who have finally seen what they ought to do. And it is important to us that they do what they do with a sense not of rightness but of profound loss and pain. If Fletcher Christian rebelled any earlier, we wouldn't admire and sympathize with him nearly as much as we do. The moments when someone arrives at a more sensitive view of what morality demands, or of its role in human life, are no doubt important and deeply formative. But they are not thrilling, like the moment when the hero takes the law into his own hands.

II. Kant on Revolution

Kant's attitudes toward revolution, both in his work and in his life, are notoriously paradoxical. In many of his published works, revolution is roundly condemned. In the *Metaphysical Principles of Justice*, Kant argues that "there is no right of sedition, much less a right of revolution" and concludes that "it is the people's duty to endure even the most intolerable abuse of supreme authority" (*MPJ* 320).[5] In "On the Common Saying: 'This May Be True in Theory, but It Does not Apply in Practice,'" Kant says:

all resistance against the supreme legislative power, all incitement of the subjects to violent expressions of discontent, all defiance which breaks out into rebellion, is the greatest and most punishable crime in a commonwealth, for it destroys its very foundation. This prohibition is absolute. And even if the power of the state or its agent, the head of state, has violated the original contract by authorizing the government to act tyrannically, and has thereby, in the eyes of the subject, forfeited the right to legislate, the subject is still not entitled to offer counter-resistance. (*TP* 81)

And yet if a revolution succeeds, Kant thinks, the new government immediately becomes legitimate. In the *Metaphysical Principles of Justice* he writes:

if a revolution has succeeded and a new constitution has been established, the illegitimacy of its beginning and of its success cannot free the subjects from being bound to accept the new order of things as good citizens, and they cannot refuse to honor and obey the suzerain who now possesses the authority. (*MPJ* 323)

So even a regime newly established by an overthrow may not in turn be overthrown.

This may make it seem as if Kant were trying to defend quietism at any cost. And yet when Kant looked to history for a sign that would show whether the human race was making moral progress, he found encouragement in a phenomenon of his own day: the enthusiasm of the spectators of the French Revolution. In his essay "An Old Question Raised Again: Is the Human Race Constantly Progressing?" Kant writes:

The revolution of a gifted people which we have seen unfolding in our day may succeed or miscarry; it may be filled with misery and atrocities to the point that a sensible man, were he boldly to hope to execute it successfully the second time, would never resolve to make the experiment at such cost – this revolution, I say, nonetheless finds in the hearts of all spectators (who are not engaged in the game themselves) a wishful participation which borders on enthusiasm, the very expression of which is fraught with danger; this sympathy, therefore, can have no other cause than a moral disposition in the human race. (*OQ* 85)

Granted, it is the spectators, not the revolutionaries themselves, whose enthusiastic sympathy Kant thinks testifies to our moral nature. But if revolution is wrong, how can "wishful participation" in it be right? And we know that Kant himself was one of the most enthusiastic of these wishful participants. His personal obsession with both the French and the

American Revolutions, his constant eagerness for the latest news from France, his persistent championship of the French Revolution even in the face of the Terror, won him the nickname "the Old Jacobin." Indeed according to one report "he said that all the horrors in France were unimportant compared with the chronic evil of despotism from which France had suffered, and the Jacobins were probably right in all they were doing."[6] Kant not only could sympathize with those aroused to violence by injustice; he could even cheer for them.

So here we have Kant's three views: revolution is unconditionally wrong; yet if it succeeds the government it establishes is a legitimate authority to which citizens owe their obedience; and, finally, our enthusiasm for the French Revolution, even our wishful participation in it, is an outward sign of the presence of a moral disposition in our nature, from which we may derive hope for our own moral progress. In what follows, I try to show how this trio of views can make sense.

III. Justice and the Political State

Some background is necessary to my account. In the *Metaphysics of Morals*, Kant distinguishes two kinds of duties: duties of virtue and duties of justice (*MM* 218–21). Duties of justice are derived from the "Universal Principle of Justice" (*MPJ* 230), a restricted version of the categorical imperative. The Universal Principle of Justice tells us to act in a way that is compatible with the freedom of everyone according to a universal law (*MPJ* 231). Everyone is to have equal freedom of action, and the duties of justice are duties to avoid actions which violate that condition. According to Kant, the duties of justice are external duties. They are duties to perform or avoid certain outward acts. Insofar as a given action is regarded as a duty of justice, the duty is just to *do* it. The doctrine of right, in which the duties of justice are studied, is completely unconcerned about our motives. The sense in which the duties of justice are *duties* is cashed out entirely in terms of the fact that if you attempt to violate a duty of justice, others have the right to use force or coercion to stop you (*MPJ* 231). In the sphere of law and justice, "this is your duty" means "we have the right to demand this of you." This stands in sharp contrast to the sphere of ethics, which concerns the duties of virtue. There "this is your duty" means "insofar as you are autonomous, you demand this of yourself" (*MPV* 379–80).

Why is it permissible for others to force or coerce you to conform to the duties of justice? The Universal Principle of Justice in effect says that the *only* restriction on freedom is consistency with the freedom of everyone else. Anything that is consistent with universal freedom is just, and you therefore have a right to do it. If someone tries to interfere with that right, he is interfering with your freedom and so violating the Universal Principle of Justice. Violations of the Universal Principle of Justice may be opposed by coercion for the simple reason that anything that hinders a hindrance to freedom is consistent with freedom, and anything that is consistent with universal freedom is just. It follows that rights are coercively enforceable. Indeed, coercive enforceability is not something attached to rights; it is constitutive of their very nature (*MPJ* 232). To have a right just is to have the executive authority to enforce a certain claim. This in turn is the foundation of the executive or coercive authority of the political state.

Kant's political philosophy is a social contract theory, in obvious ways in the tradition of Locke. But the differences are important. In Locke's view, individuals have rights in the state of nature, and may enforce those rights. But when each person determines and enforces his own rights the result is social disorder. Since this disorder is contrary to our interests, people join together into a political state, transferring our executive authority to a government.[7]

Kant also believes that there is a sense in which we have rights in the state of nature. We have a natural right to our freedom (*MPJ* 237), and, Kant thinks, the Universal Principle of Justice allows us to claim rights in land and, more generally, in external objects, in property. Kant argues that it would be inconsistent with freedom to *deny* the possibility of property rights, on the grounds that unless we can claim rights to objects, those objects cannot be used (*MPJ* 246).[8] This would be a restriction on freedom not based in freedom itself, which we should therefore reject, and this leads us to postulate that objects may be owned. But unlike Locke, Kant argues that in the state of nature these rights are only "provisional" (*MPJ* 256). In this, Kant is partly following Rousseau. In contrast to Locke, Rousseau argues that rights are created by the social contract, and, in a sense, relative to it. My possessions become my property, so far as you and I are concerned, when you and I have given each other certain reciprocal guarantees: I will keep my hands off your possessions if you will keep your hands off mine.[9] Rights are not acquired by the metaphysical act of mixing one's labor with the land, but instead are constructed from the human relations among people who have made such agreements.[10] Kant adopts this idea, at least as far as the executive authority associated with a property right is concerned. I may indeed coercively enforce my rights. But if my doing so is to be consistent with the Universal Principle of Justice, it cannot be an act of *unilateral* coercion. To claim a right to a piece of property is to make a kind of law; for it is to lay it down that all others must refrain from using the object or land in question without my permission. But to view my claim as a *law* I must view it as the object of a contract between us, a contact in which we reciprocally commit ourselves to guaranteeing each other's rights. It is this fact that leads us to enter – or, more precisely, to view ourselves as already having entered – political society.

In making this argument, Kant evokes Rousseau's concept of the general will. He argues that a general will to the coercive enforcement of the rights of all concerned is *implicitly* involved in every property claim.

Now, with respect to an external and contingent possession, a unilateral Will cannot serve as a coercive law for everyone, since that would be a violation of freedom in accordance with universal laws. Therefore, only a Will binding every-one else – that is, a collective, universal (common), and powerful Will – is the kind of Will that can provide the guarantee required. The condition of being subject to general external (that is, public) legislation that is backed by power is the civil society. Accordingly, a thing can be externally yours or mine [that is, can be property] only in a civil society. (*MPJ* 256)

It is because the idea of the general will to the reciprocal enforcement of rights is implicit in any claim of right that Kant argues that rights in the state of nature are only provisional. They are provisional because this general will has not yet been *instituted* by setting up a common authority to enforce everyone's rights. The act that institutes the general will is the social contract.

Kant concludes from this argument that when the time comes to enforce your rights coercively, in the state of nature, the only legitimate way to do that is by joining in political society with those with whom you are in dispute. In fact, you enforce your right by first forcing them to join in political society with you so that the dispute can be settled by recipro-cal rather than unilateral coercion:

If it must be *de jure* possible to have an external object as one's own, then the subject must also be allowed to compel everyone else with whom he comes into conflict over the question of whether such an object is his to enter, together with him, a society under a civil constitution. (*MPJ* 256)

Suppose we are in the state of nature and we get into a dispute about rights. My goat has kids, and I take them to be mine because I was caring for the mother goat when they were born. However, one of them es-caped, and you found it wandering around apparently unowned in the state of nature, took possession of it, fed it, and cared for it for many years. Now we have discovered the matter, and each of us thinks she has a right to this particular goat. Since I think I have a right, I also think I may prosecute my right by coercive action. And you think the same. So what can we do? Perhaps I have a gun and you do not, so I can simply take the goat away from you. However, there are two ways to understand my action. One is: I am using unilateral force to take the goat away from you. Such an action would be illegitimate, a use of violence that interferes with your freedom. I cannot regard my action as an enforcement of my *right* without acknowledging that you have rights too, which also must be enforced. So if I am to claim that what I am doing is enforcing my right, I must understand my own action differently. The other way to understand the action is that I am forcing you to enter into political society with me. That gets us to the first step; the act of enforcing my right involves the establishment of a juridical condition (*rechtlicher Zustand*) between us and so establishes civil society. The second step, of course, is to settle the particular dispute in question in some lawful way.

This means that Kant's conception is different from Locke's in important ways. According to Kant a juridical condition – a condition in which human rights are upheld and enforced – can exist only in political society. And therefore existence in political society is not merely, as Locke had it, in our interest. It is a duty of justice to live in political society. That is to say, others have the right to require this of you, because that is the form that their authority to enforce their own rights takes. And you, reciprocally, have the right to require membership in political society of others with whom you might have such disputes. Since we will that our rights be enforced, reciprocal coercion, and therefore political society, can be seen as the object of a general will.

Kant does not take himself to be telling an historical story. He is answering a transcendental question: how is coercive political authority possible? His answer is that the idea of a general will to the reciprocal enforcement of rights is what makes coercive political authority possible. Governments are legitimate because human beings who live in proximity, who must therefore work out what their respective rights are, must form a general will. To put it another way, justice, which is the condition in which we have guaranteed one another our rights, exists only where there is government. Government, then, is founded on our presumptive general will to justice.

IV. All Governments Are Legitimate

Kant's account of the state, as I have just said, is transcendental: it is an account of how political authority is possible. But of course we need to know something more than that: we need to know when political authority is actual. Which regimes are legitimate governments, and which are mere Mafias ruling the people by main force? Kant's view is that *all* governments should be taken to be legitimate. That is, any regime's decisions are the voice of the general will of its people; and its procedures for making those decisions must be taken to be ones the people have agreed to.

Kant of course does not mean that all governments and all of their decisions are perfectly just. In fact, Kant thinks that his theory of the political state implies an ideal of the state that is not generally realized. The state must embody the general will of the people to the reciprocal enforcement of those rights that constitute the freedom of everyone. In order to do this, Kant argues, the state must be a republic, characterized by a constitution and by the separation of powers, in which legislation is carried on by representatives of the citizens. Although Kant has some negative things to say about "democratic" government, these must be understood in terms of his rather complex account of political authority. Kant asserts that "legislative authority can be attributed only to the united Will of the people" (*MPJ* 313). This authority is then invested in a sovereign authority or ruler, which may be constituted by all, some, or one of the people (*MPJ* 338–9; *PP* 352), making the form of sovereignty democratic, aristocratic, or autocratic, respectively. Members of the sovereign are citizens and must therefore be fit to vote (*MPJ* 314); Kant criticizes the autocratic form of sovereignty, which concentrates it in a single person's hands, because "none of the subjects are citizens" (*MPJ* 339). The sovereign is responsible for administering the government. If the sovereign "himself" carries out all three functions of government directly, the government is despotic; if, however, the sovereign adopts a constitution establishing legal and institutional forms through which it performs the three functions of government separately, then the government is republican.[11] A republican constitution, Kant says, is the "one and only legitimate constitution" (*MPJ* 340) since it is "the only enduring constitution in which the law is autonomous and not annexed to any particular person" and in which therefore "each person receives his due peremptorily" (*MPJ* 341). In a republican constitution, that is, every person is bound by the law and so one's rights do not depend on anyone's (not even the majority's) will. And therefore:

Every true republic is and can be nothing else than a representative system of the people if it is to protect the rights of its citizens in the name of the people. Under a representative system, these rights are protected by the citizens themselves, united and acting through their representatives (deputies). As soon, however, as the chief of state in person (whether it be a king, the nobility, or the whole population – the democratic union) allows himself to be represented, then the united people do not merely *represent* the sovereign, but they themselves *are* the sovereign. (*MPJ* 341)

Once such constitutional forms are established, the united people no longer have to invest the sovereignty in any other "person," not even the collectivity of the whole people themselves. Instead the people govern themselves *directly* through their constitutional forms. Outwardly, of course, somebody must administer the functions of government, but those who do so are now regarded as magistrates who work for the people, not as sovereign authorities. The magistrate who runs the government may still be a "monarch," and Kant sometimes suggests that he thinks this is the best arrangement (*PP* 352–3). Yet it seems clear enough that this ideal requires that the magistrates be responsive to the demands of the people. For instance Kant argues that the establishment of republican forms of government will bring war to an end, because a declaration of war will require "the consent of the citizens," who are unlikely to give it (*PP* 351). This result seems to depend on the idea that the citizens will have some actual influence on the political process. Thus Kant's ideal state appears to be most closely realized by our own modern constitutional "democracies." Legislation is to be carried on by more or less direct delegates of the citizens, while the other functions of government are to be separated from the legislative function and the magistrates who perform all three functions are to understand themselves as representing the united will of the people.[12]

Why then does Kant think we must treat every regime, and all of its decisions, as the voice of the general will? To understand this, we need to consider Kant's responses to two possible challenges to the legitimacy of a government, one based on its history – on the illegitimacy of its origins – and the other on its present imperfections, as measured by the ideal.

Start with the historical challenge. I have already said that Kant is not proposing that there was an actual contractarian origin to the state. His social contract is a hypothetical or, perhaps better, a transcendental one, which explains how such things as governments are possible. Kant signals this by grounding the state in what he calls a "postulate." Earlier in the *Metaphysical Principles of Justice*, Kant had also grounded the possibility of property in a postulate. The notion of a postulate is introduced in the *Critique of Practical Reason*, in connection with Kant's account of practical religious faith. Suppose we have some rational concept, but we do not have theoretical grounds for assigning it "objective reality" – that is, for asserting that it could apply to any actual object. In some cases, we may nevertheless have practical grounds for doing so, based on the considerations that (i) moral practice is intelligible or possible only if we assume that this concept has objective reality, and (ii) moral practice is absolutely obligatory. In the second *Critique*, this is our basis for assigning objective reality to God, Freedom, and Immortality, concepts that cannot be applied theoretically because their objects could not be part of the sensible world (*KpV* 119–46).[13] In the *Metaphysical Principles of Justice*, Kant argues that both "property" (or right) and "government" are moral or normative, and so intelligible or rational rather than sensible or empirical, concepts. Empirically, all we can identify is *possession* in the one case and *ruling power* in the other: people have certain objects in their possession, or under their control, and some people rule over others. Yet it is essential for moral practice, as we have seen, that we treat some of these empirical relations as having normative force: that we treat some possessions as rightful property, and some cases of ruling power as cases of legitimate political authority. For we cannot have freedom without property rights, and we cannot have rights without government. The "Juridical Postulate of Practical Reason" (*MPJ* 246) and the "Postulate of Public Law" (*MPJ* 307) establish the objective reality of rights and government respectively.

In contrast to the religious postulates, however, these postulates license us to assign their concepts to objects we encounter in the natural world. And in both cases, a problem springs from the fact that the concept invokes a kind of hypothetical history. Kant's account of the possibility of property follows the usual strategy of appealing to the legitimacy of an individual's taking first possession of some land in the state of nature, rightfully laying claim to an object hitherto unowned. The individual then of course has the right to transfer this property to others. This kind of story can make it seem as if the correctness of a property-claim depends on an object's entire history and ancestry. Ownership of an object must be the result of a series of legitimate transactions stretching all the way back to the beginning of human history, when someone took first possession of the land.

Suppose someone challenges my right to a book. I say it's mine, but he says it's not; it's stolen property. He doesn't mean that *I* stole it; but that there's an illegitimate move *somewhere* in its history. Imagine that a congress of Native Americans demands that immigrant Americans return all of the books made from paper made from American trees to them. They say: you stole the forests, and the forests were ours; so the paper is ours; and the books are ours. And of course they've got a point. If we traced the ancestry of the property each of us owns, it would be full of illegitimate transactions. No one would be found to be the legitimate owner of anything. The history of the human race is a history of war and looting and theft and violence, not a history of legitimate transactions. So here's what we do. We simply take it for granted that, generally speaking, what people now have is their property. And we try to ensure that, from here on in, transactions will be legitimate and just.[14]

Kant thinks that this is what we should do with governments too. We should take it for granted that the existing governments are legitimate representatives of the general will of the people who are ruled by them, as if they originated in social contracts. "One ought to obey the legislative authority that now exists regardless of its origin" (*MPJ* 319). Kant says in several places that it is criminal even to *research* the origin of a government if you do it with an eye to challenging its legitimacy (*MPJ* 318–19; 372). Now of course there is also an important difference between the two cases. Kant thinks that if a revolution succeeds, we should take it that the new government is legitimate. The policy of treating any extant political power as legitimate is an absolutely blanket one. But of course if a theft or a swindle succeeds, we do not take it that the new distribution of property is legitimate. We do trace ownership back in time, within limits. But there is also an obvious explanation of this disanalogy. When someone is accused of stealing property, there is a duly constituted authority, namely the state itself, to decide the case. So this kind of conflict can be handled in a just manner. But of course after a revolution, there is no duly constituted authority to settle the question whether the old government or the new government is legitimate. The question which one is legitimate just is the question what the general will of the people is. And that, of course, can be settled only by consulting the true government – the voice of the general will – which is exactly what is at issue here.

Now we come to the second possible kind of challenge. Even if we don't deem governments illegitimate because of their histories, we might challenge the legitimacy of those that fall short of the republican ideal to which the idea of government points us. Kant also argues against doing this. In an appendix attached to later editions of *The Metaphysical Principles of Justice*, Kant quotes a reviewer, Friedrich Bouterwek, who among other things called it "the most paradoxical of all paradoxes" that "the mere Idea of sovereignty should necessitate me to obey as my lord anyone who has imposed himself upon me as a lord, without my asking who has given him the right to command me" (*MPJ* 371).[15] And Kant replies:

Every matter of fact is an object that is an appearance (of sense); on the other hand, that which can be represented only through pure reason and which must be included among the Ideas – that is the thing in itself. *No object in experience can be given that adequately corresponds to an Idea.* A perfect juridical [just] constitution among men would be an example of such an Idea. (*MPJ* 370; my emphasis)

The claim is that no existing government adequately corresponds to the idea of a government. And yet:

When a people are united through laws under a suzerain, then the people are given as an object of experience conforming to the *Idea in general* of the unity of the people under a supreme powerful Will. Admittedly, this is only an appearance; that is, a juridical constitution in the most general sense of the term is present. Although the [actual] constitution may contain grave defects and gross errors and may need to be gradually improved in important respects, still, as such, it is absolutely unpermitted and culpable to oppose it. If the people were to hold that they were justified in using violence against a constitution, however defective it might be, and against the supreme authority, they would be supposing that they had a right to put violence as the supreme prescriptive act of legislation in the place of every right and Law. (*MPJ* 371–2)

There are two possible ways to understand this argument. One might read it, first, as a kind of slippery slope argument. Suppose that Kant is correct in saying that *no* extant government meets the ideal. If we then ask how close a government must come to the ideal before it counts as legitimate, there is no obvious place to draw the line. If we look for a minimum criterion of legitimacy, we find that the most natural one – universal adult suffrage – rules out nearly every "government" that has existed in the history of the world before the twentieth century.[16] So perhaps Kant thinks it is too dangerous to make such judgments.

This reading, however, does not sit well with the obviously Platonic character of the passage.[17] When Kant says that actual governments are only "appearances" he does not mean that they are not real. He means that they are imperfect participants, in the Platonic sense, in the form of justice, a form that is given by the ideal of the republic described earlier. When Kant contrasts autocracy, aristocracy, and democracy to the true form of government, he even calls them "those old . . . empirical forms of the state" in contradistinction to the "original (rational) form" that is the republic (*MPJ* 340). Kant is clearly confident that, despite their imperfections, we recognize these objects as governments, as imperfect approximations to a perfect form.[18]

In order to understand why, it helps to reflect that there is a kind of tension inherent in our very concept of justice: a tension between what I will call the procedural and the substantive elements of the concept. On the one hand, the idea of justice essentially involves the idea of following certain procedures. In the state, these are the procedures by which the three functions of government are carried out. In order to be just, any sort of decision, outcome, or verdict – any political judgment – must be the result of *actually following* these procedures. That is a *law* which has been passed in form by a duly constituted legislature; this law is *constitutional* if (say) the supreme court says that it is; a person is *innocent* of a certain crime when he has been deemed so by a jury; someone is *the president* if he meets the qualifications and has been duly voted in, and so forth. These are all normative judgments – the terms I have italicized imply the existence of certain reasons for action – and the normativity of these judgments *derives from* the procedures that have established them.

On the other hand, however, there are many cases in which we have an independent idea of how these procedures ought to turn out. These independent criteria form our more substantive judgments – in some cases, of what is just, in other cases, simply of what is right or best. Perhaps the law is unconstitutional, though the legislature has passed it; perhaps the defendant is guilty, though the jury has set him free; perhaps the candidate elected is not the best person for the job, or even the best of those available, or perhaps due to the accidents of voter turnout he does not really represent the majority will. As this last example shows, the distinction between the procedurally just and the substantively just, right, or best, is a rough and ready one, and relative to the case under consideration. Who should be elected? The best person for the job, the best of those who actually run, the one preferred by the majority of the citizens, the one preferred by majority of the registered voters, the one elected by the majority of those who actually turn out on election day. . . . As we go down the list, the answer to the question becomes increasingly procedural; the answer above it is, relatively, more substantive. We may try to design our procedures to secure the substantively right, best, or just outcome. But – and here is the important point – the normativity of these procedures nevertheless does not spring from the efficiency, goodness, *or even the substantive justice* of the outcomes they produce. The reverse is true: it is the procedures themselves that confer normativity on those results. The person who gets elected holds the office, no matter how far he is from being the best person for the job. The jury's acquittal stands, though we later discover new evidence that the defendant was guilty after all. And the normativity of the procedures themselves springs not from the quality of their outcomes but rather from the fact that we must have such procedures if we are going to form a general will. In order to act together – to make laws and policies, apply them, enforce them, in a way that represents, not some of us imposing our private wills on others, but all of us acting together from a collective general will – we must have certain procedures that make collective decision and action possible, and, normatively speaking, we must stand by their actual results.

This point has some weight in any collective decision – even when we make a decision, say, with a group of friends. But it applies most force-fully to cases of right and justice, to decisions backed by coercive authority. For if we reserve to ourselves the right to ignore the outcomes of such procedures when we believe them to be substantively wrong, then we are still in the state of nature. And this idea is reflected in our actual practice, leaving Kant aside, for it is a basic rule of citizenship, of living in accordance with the rule of law, that procedural judgments have a coercive normative force against which substantive ones have *no weight at all*. Your judgment that a law is stupid does not excuse disobedience; your conviction that the defendant is guilty does not justify a lynching; your belief that your candidate is the better man is no grounds whatever for a takeover.

When the substantive ideal that opposes the procedural outcome is also an ideal of justice itself, and not merely one, say, of efficiency or qualification, this gives rise to a tension. It's bad enough when the jury lets the guilty go free, but suppose you are sure they have convicted the innocent. The law passed by congress is not just stupid or inefficient or incoherent, but – you think – plainly unconstitutional; only the Supreme Court, called upon to decide the case, does not agree with you here. Where then does justice lie? When we are judging the very institutions of government themselves, this kind of tension can rise to the level of paradox, illustrated by a simple example. Suppose we are convinced that the idea that government should represent the general will of the people requires that some group of people, hitherto helplessly subjected to a powerful tyrant, be allowed to choose their own political institutions in a democratic election. And suppose that having been liberated from their tyrant and allowed to vote for their political institutions, they unanimously vote the democracy out, and their tyrant right back in again. Where now does justice lie? Shall we force upon these people a form of government they do not choose to have, in the *name* of respecting their general will?[19] We may be convinced, and for good reasons, that constitutional democracy is the best way for a people to express its general will. But the absence of democratic institutions cannot be taken as proof or even as evidence that a government does not represent the general will of its people.

"When a people are united through laws under a suzerain, then the people are given as an object of experience conforming to the Idea in general of the unity of the people under a supreme powerful Will" (*MPJ* 371–2). What makes a people unified is that there are procedures under which they are unified, procedures that make collective decision and action possible, and give them a general will. Kant's view is that wherever we see such an arrangement, we see an imperfect empirical realization of the form of justice, of the idea of a general will. If someone has enough authority to make and execute laws, and the people are living and acting and relating to one another under those laws, then that is their general will. The failure of their institutions to meet our more substantive ideals of justice is simply irrelevant.

It's worth pointing out that, in the international sphere, we accept this conclusion. Although we may agree with Kant that the modern constitutional democracy is the substantively best form of government, we do not think that this licenses us to impose it on other nations, or even to refuse recognition to those who neither have nor aspire to this ideal. It would, for the reasons just given, be not just wrong, but paradoxical, since the very idea embodied in the ideal of constitutional democracy is that government should be by the consent of the governed, or an expression of the general will. That idea demands that we recognize that the peoples of other nations must decide for themselves what kind of political institutions they will have.[20] If we are to recognize them as sovereign states at all, we must simply take it that their governments are expressions of their general wills.

To arrive at Kant's position you need only see that the individual subject, when considered only as a private individual with his own private ideas about what constitutes good government, is in exactly the same position as an outsider toward his *own* government.[21] He must acknowledge its procedures, as they stand, to be the expression of the general will, if he is to see his country as having a general will and so a government at all. And according to Kant he must see himself as living under a government because, as we saw earlier, it is our duty to live in political society.

V. Why There Is No Right to Revolution

Since Kant thinks that any government represents the general will of the people, his argument against the right to revolution is an immediate, simple, conceptual one. He says:

For in order for the people to be able to judge the supreme political authority with the force of law, they must already be viewed as united under a general legislative Will; hence they can and may not judge otherwise than the present chief of state wills. (*MPJ* 318)

The point is plain. The government is the representative of the general will. But if *it* represents the general will, whatever it says is the voice of the general will. To revolt, where that means to oppose the decisions of the government, is therefore to oppose the general will. And to oppose the general will is to dissolve the juridical condition among human beings, and so to return to the state of nature. Revolution "is not an alteration of the civil constitution, but the dissolution of it" (*MPJ* 340). This is wrong, for, as we have seen, Kant thinks that living in political society is not, as Locke thought, a mere remedy for inconvenience, but instead is a duty of justice.

However paradoxical it seems, this argument has real force. If government exists by the general will, a revolution could be legitimate only if it in turn were in accordance with the general will. Otherwise, it is just a few lawless individuals making war against the nation. But we should ask how it could be established that a revolution *is* in accordance with the general will. Kant's argument shows how serious this problem is. The government contains agencies for both determining and interpreting what the general will is. Of course the people may decide that the government is not doing a good job of this. But this judgment can be made only by someone who has the right to speak for the people, and that right belongs to the government itself.[22] Therefore, the government can reform itself, but the people *as subjects* cannot reform the government.

The problem arises because the will of the people must be represented. A people cannot literally speak with one voice. They must speak through a representative who has their mandate. What makes the problem of revolution so acute is that what is in question here *is* who represents the people. And the people cannot literally speak with one voice about *this* any more than they can about anything else. Until we settle the question who represents the people the general will has no voice to speak with. So we cannot start with the will of the people; to know what the will of the people is, we must start with someone taken to be their representative, their voice. This can make it seem strangely arbitrary who we take to represent them. Kant's solution to this problem is to say that the representative of the people *just is* the extant government, whatever it is.

If we accept Kant's solution, a revolution is necessarily opposed to the general will and so it is illegitimate. To see this, imagine the best possible case for revolution. Suppose we have a small nation ruled by a single tyrant and his army. The revolutionary, hoping to establish legitimacy, assembles the entire population and takes a vote. Everyone except the dictator and his army votes for a new regime. If the dictator does not bow out, do the people have the right to revolt? The answer is no. In this country, the procedure for determining the general will is to consult the dictator, not to take a vote. Votes can determine what the general will is only where they are the duly constituted procedure for determining the general will. So for these people to revolt on the basis of this vote would be a raw act of the tyranny of the majority over the minority. The majority only represents the general will where it has been established that they do; and in this case, it has not.

Kant's argument, as I've suggested, depends on a deeply procedural conception of the general will. Our general will, according to this argument, just is whatever follows from the procedures that make collective action possible, and so, in Rousseau's extravagant language, it can do no wrong.[23] Suppose we allow, instead, that there is such a thing as the general will, independently of our procedures, and that our procedures should be viewed as fallible devices for ascertaining it. Then we can allow, contrary to Kant, that the extant regime may not represent the will of the people and so may fail to be legitimate. Even so, we get the problem. It is still true that the people cannot speak as a people until they have a voice. A revolutionary who claims to be the representative of the people merely because of the spirit he senses among them or even because he has taken a favorable vote is misdescribing the situation. The people can give their mandate only through some duly constituted voice, through someone who has the right to represent them. If we admit the possibility that the extant regime does not represent the general will then there is *no way* to tell what the general will is. The general will has lost its voice, and there are only two ways to make it speak again. One is if the people arrive at actual unanimity – in which case, of course, there could be no need for revolution, since the people of a nation include its governors. The other is by the essentially arbitrary choice of a representative. So even if we grant the possibility that a government might be illegitimate, we can never say that the revolution is in accordance with the general will. Now all we have is a raw clash of arbitrary powers at war with each other in a world without justice. We have still not established that revolution is something to which there could be a *right*.

VI. What Follows from the Fact that There Is No Right to Revolution

Let's say Kant has made his case. There is no right to revolution. What follows?

It follows from the fact that there is no right to revolution that there is a duty not to revolt. This duty is a duty of justice. It is important now to recall what this means. A duty of justice is a duty in the sense that others may coercively require your performance. To say that something is a duty of justice is to say that its violation is punishable. So the first thing that follows is that if you participate in a revolution, it fails, and you are caught, you may be punished. As Kant says, revolution is the "most punishable crime in a commonwealth, for it destroys its very foundations" (*TP* 81). So far, this is unproblematic. It would be extraordinary to believe that people may not be punished for revolting. Of course if people get out their guns and shoot at others and make mayhem in society they may be punished. The fact that their motives were political rather than venal may make us judge them less harshly as human beings, but for all that they may be punished.[24] The whole point of a government is to enforce people's rights in a way that is orderly and grounded in reciprocal coercion, rather than in a disorderly and unilaterally coercive way. Executive authority is supposed to be concentrated in a government; and so the idea of a government which is not allowed to enforce its own decisions is incoherent. As Kant himself points out, a right to revolution would involve a kind of contradiction, rather like the Liar's Paradox: "the supreme legislation would have to contain a stipulation that it is not supreme" (*MPJ* 320).[25]

There is also a second consequence, which follows from Kant's views about responsibility for actions and their consequences. Kant argues that one must do what the moral law demands, let the consequences be what they may. If you do what is required of you, you are not responsible for the consequences. On the other hand, if you do something other than what the moral law demands, then you are responsible for the consequences. In the *Metaphysics of Morals*, Kant says:

The good or bad consequences of an action owed, as well as the consequences of omitting a meritorious action, cannot be imputed to the subject.
    The good consequences of a meritorious action as well as the bad consequences of an unlawful action can be imputed to the subject. (*MM* 228)

In other words, if you do your perfect duties, you are not responsible for the results; if you do an imperfect duty, such as helping someone, you count as the author of the good result; and if you violate perfect duty and the results are bad, the consequences are on your head. In the *Lectures on Ethics*, Kant puts the point more simply:

If we do either more or less than is required of us we can be held accountable for the consequences, but not otherwise – not if we only do what is required, neither more nor less. (*LE* 59)[26]

Now the duties of justice are all perfect duties, and so when you violate them, you are responsible for the results. Revolutionaries who are caught may be held legally liable not only for the crime of sedition but for the death, injury, and mayhem that result. But Kant makes it clear that this is not merely a legal point. He says that the consequences of violating a perfect duty should also be imputed to the agent "by his own conscience" (*MPV* 431). So someone who undertakes to start or participate in a revolution must regard himself as responsible for the results. A revolutionary must see himself as the author of the loss of life and limb, the social disorder, and the suspension of the juridical condition that results from revolution.

Although this is a more controversial point, this too, seems to me to be correct. Even those who are inclined to argue for a "right to revolution" cannot think that revolution is something to be undertaken lightly. Justice exists only where there is government; the revolutionary undertakes to destroy the government, and so undertakes to destroy justice. Of course his aim is to improve the juridical condition. He thinks that justice will rise revivified from its own ashes, like the Phoenix; he hopes to bring about a new and better system of justice, which will come closer to doing its job, which is guaranteeing freedom. As Kant says, revolutionaries undertake "to be unjust once and for all, in order thereafter to establish legal justice on a foundation that is so much more secure" (*MPJ* 353). But for however short a time, there will be a condition in which there is no justice. During this period, as a result of conditions the revolutionary himself has instigated or supported, lives will be lost, injuries sustained, property rights violated, careers interrupted and destroyed. During this period, the victims of these disasters will have neither recourse nor compensation. He may fail, and if he fails, all of this will have been for nothing. Surely the victims of social upheaval may rightly regard the revolutionaries as the authors of their injuries. And surely the revolutionary cannot just say: the consequences were not my fault, since I was doing what I had a right to do.

So far, we have two consequences. First, the conclusion that there is no right to revolution, in Kant's sense of a right, is unproblematic. Of course revolutionaries, if they fail or are caught on time, may be punished. The idea of a government that is not entitled to defend itself in this way makes no sense. But this is not merely a matter of what the law has to say, of whether there can be a legal right to revolution. Even from a purely moral point of view, a just revolution would have to be in accordance with the general will of the people, and we have seen that this is impossible. Either the government is the voice of the general will of the people, or there is no voice; in neither case can the revolutionary claim the mandate of the general will. So the revolutionary is doing something he has no right to do. And that means that all the consequences of the revolution are imputable to him. If he wins, his party becomes the legitimate government, and as such they are not legally answerable for their actions; and morally, then, he at least has an excuse. But if he loses, he is nothing more than a murderer and a thief. And this last should be not only in the government's eyes, but in his own.

But there is one consequence that does not follow. So far, I have said nothing that implies that there are no circumstances in which a good person would revolt.

VII. When the Virtuous Person Revolts

More than any other philosopher in the tradition, Kant gives us an agent-centered moral philosophy. His primary question is not who shall we praise or blame, or which actions are right and which wrong. He has things to say about these questions, but they fall out of the discussion of what he takes to be the central question of moral philosophy: what must I do? So far, we have remained on the territory of duties of justice, and have discussed what we must say *about* revolutionaries and revolution. But we have not yet addressed the main question: should *we* ever revolt? Nor could we address that question, so long as we kept the discussion to the duties of justice. To approach this question we must turn to the doctrine of virtue, to ethics.

Again we will need some background. Earlier I said that the duties of justice are external duties. The sense in which they are duties is that we may legitimately be forced to do them. The duties of virtue, by contrast, are internal duties. The sense in which they are duties is that morality requires them of us, which is to say that we require them of ourselves. Duties of virtue are concerned with our motives and attitudes. They arise from the command that we should not only do certain things, but do them for moral reasons: in Kantian language, they command us to make duty itself the incentive of our action. As the constitutive aim of the duties of justice is the achievement of external freedom, so the constitutive aim of the duties of virtue is internal freedom: for through the cultivation of virtue we achieve freedom of the will (*MPV* 379–384).[27]

Kant believes that all human action is purposive (*G* 427; *MPV* 381, 385; *R* 4, *R* 6–7n). This does not mean that we always act for the sake of some end in which we have taken a prior interest; but it does mean that we always act with some end in view. When we undertake an action, there is always some end to that action which we represent to ourselves as good. It does not have to be an end we are trying to bring about – it may be an end we wish not to act against, or wish to respect. In the moral case, for instance, we may simply see our action as expressing respect for humanity as an end in itself. Because morally good actions as well as others are purposive, Kant argues that the cultivation of virtue is achieved through the adoption of morally obligatory ends (*MPV* 380–1; 384–5).

Kant thinks that there are duties, and so ends, that belong specifically to the territory of virtue: the pursuit of the happiness of others, and the cultivation of our own talents, powers, and character (*MPV* 385–9). But ethics encompasses all of our duties. It is a duty of virtue to do the duties of justice from the motive of duty. In other words, justice itself is a virtue. And Kant says that the virtue of justice is possessed by one *who makes the rights of humanity his end* (*MPV* 390).

In ordinary circumstances, this is the end we have in view when we carry out the moral duty to obey the law. If you keep your hands off your neighbor's property, even thinking he has more than his fair share; if you refrain from stuffing ballot boxes, even when that means the better candidate will lose; if you pay your debts, even when you could get away with not doing so, this is because you care about the rights of others. The end you have in view is that their rights should be respected.

It is because justice is a virtue that there is an ethical duty, as well as a duty of justice, not to revolt. The just person respects the rights of humanity, and for this reason respects the government that enforces those rights, and the juridical condition that makes their enforcement possible. But it is by no means obvious that a person who makes the rights of humanity his end would never, under any circumstances, oppose the extant government. If this is correct, nothing in Kant's theory absolutely commits him to the view that a good person would *never* revolt. Nor, I believe, is this what he himself thought.[28]

Justice exists to preserve the rights and freedom of everyone: this is the idea, and the substantive ideal, of justice. But we all know that the procedures of justice may be used *against these very ends*. Apartheid South Africa horrified us more, perhaps, than more egregious despotisms, because of its outward forms of legality, its caricature of a modern Western democracy. The same is true of America before the Civil War. A master recapturing a runaway slave is brutal; but a court's ordering the slave's return is a mockery of justice. Women and children have often been returned to the legal custody of the very husbands and fathers who have abused them; Captain Bligh does not just beat his men, but does it with the King's authority. There is a special kind of horror associated with such cases. For in such cases the very language of rights, and the robes and wigs and forms and ceremonies with which we celebrate our will to form a general will, are used to corner the helpless. The agencies of justice are used to reinforce injustice; and what should be the recourse of the oppressed is the very tool of the oppressor. In such cases, justice is turned against itself, perverted; human rights need protection from the law itself.

Kant does not say this, of course, but he was keenly sensitive to the special kind of horror I am talking about here. This shows up, interestingly, in a footnote to the very section of the *Metaphysical Principles of Justice* in which Kant argues that revolution is always wrong. He says:

Of all the abominations involved in the overthrow of a state through revolution, the *murder* of the monarch is still not the worst, because it is possible to imagine that the people are motivated by the fear that, were he to remain alive, he might regain his power and give them the punishment they deserve; in that case, this deed would not be an act of penal justice, but only one of self-preservation. It is the *formal execution* of a monarch that fills the soul, conscious of the Ideas of human justice, with horror, and this horror returns whenever one thinks of scenes like those in which the fate of Charles I or Louis XVI was sealed. (*MPJ* 321n; my emphases)

Kant proceeds to examine the sources of this particular kind of horror. In the *Groundwork*, Kant had argued that since we cannot consistently will an evil maxim as a universal law, a person who acts wrongly cannot be doing *that*, but instead is making himself an exception to the law (*G* 424). Recalling these ideas, Kant argues here that to *get rid* of the ruler is to violate justice, and so to make yourself an exception to the law, but to *punish* the ruler (to execute the supreme executive) is to subvert justice – not just to make yourself an exception to the law, but actually to repudiate it, and so to make a kind of law of unlawfulness itself. In *Religion within the Limits of Reason Alone*, Kant distinguishes human evil, which consists in making yourself an exception to the law for the sake of satisfying some contingent interest, from the possession of a malevolent will, one that wills evil for its own sake, that wills evil as a law. Contrary to Augustine, Kant does not think that human beings choose evil for its own sake (*R* 30). Yet here Kant argues that the execution of the monarch is like an exhibition of a malevolent will, because it presents an evil act in the outward forms of a lawful one. This is why we find it so horrifying.

Revolutionaries who formally execute a monarch perform an unjust act while dressed in the robes and wigs of justice; in so doing, they seem not just to ignore justice, but to mock it. But in cases of the sort I have mentioned, the state may seem to do this too. And then the just subject may find herself locked in exactly the sort of horror that Kant describes. When the very institutions whose purpose is to realize human rights is used to trample them, when justice is turned against itself, the virtue of justice will be turned against itself too. Concern for human rights leads the virtuous person to accept the authority of the law, but in such circumstances adherence to the law will lead her to support institutions that systematically violate human rights.[29] The person with the virtue of justice, the lover of human rights, unable to turn to the actual laws for their enforcement, has nowhere else to turn. She may come to feel that there is nothing for it but for her to take human rights under her own protection, and so to take the law into her own hands.

The decision to revolt would be a hard one to make because a person who loves the rights of humanity necessarily places a high value on the actual procedures of justice as well as on the substantive ideal of protecting human rights. And as I argued earlier, the procedures of justice are important not just because they approximate our substantive ideals, but because without such procedures there is no justice at all. Nor, of course, will the achievement of more substantive ideals be the result of the sacrifice. At the very best, revolution will bring only a closer approximation to the ideal. At the very worst, the result will be an extended period in which there is no justice at all, the rights of humanity are trampled underfoot, and a new excuse for tyranny will have been created. Short of that, there may be only marginal improvements, not obviously worth the ruined and ended lives we paid for it. The revolutionary risks this, and knows that she does, when she decides to revolt.

Two things make this decision different from most of the decisions we make, at least as those are envisioned in Kantian ethics. The first is that the universalization test cannot serve as a guide when we make it. The imperfections of the actual state of affairs are no excuse for revolution – if they were, revolution would always be in order. It is the perversion of justice, not merely its imperfection, that turns the virtue of justice against itself. But the difference between imperfect justice and perverted justice is a matter of pure judgment. There is no criterion for deciding when imperfection has become perversion, when things have gone too far. If we turn for help to the Universal Principle of Justice, all it says is: Do not revolt. The revolutionary cannot claim he has a justification, in the sense of an account of his action that other reasonable people must accept. That consolation is denied him. It is as if a kind of gap opens up in the moral world in which the moral agent must stand alone.

The revolutionary's stance, in fact, is one of paternalism toward a whole society, when paternalism, which after all is a kind of despotism, is what he hates the most. And this reminds us that revolution is only one case, the most vivid perhaps, in which good people take the law into their own hands. Another, much more common and familiar sort of case, is when we paternalize an adult human being who is engaged in some sort of self-destructive behavior. Most of us, for instance, would take action to prevent a suicide (at least unless the person was hopelessly ill and in great pain) even if we didn't think the person had simply gone crazy, but was really acting from his own choice. And many of us would be prepared to take action to prevent a close friend from going too far with self-destructive activities like abusing drugs. The structure of the problem we face in these cases is exactly the same as that of the problem faced by the revolutionary. When we see someone perverting or destroying the humanity or autonomy in his own person, our respect for his humanity or autonomy is turned against itself. Respect for his autonomy demands that we respect his right to choose. But if we respect his autonomy we cannot stand quietly by and watch while he destroys it. Like justice in an unjust state, his autonomy requires protection against itself. And so like the revolutionary, the paternalist violates his respect for autonomy in order to save its object. Paternalists too take the law into their own hands. Here too, there is no way of deciding exactly when the moment has come, when things have gone too far. Morality cannot tell you when to leave the moral law behind, in order to make sure that the world remains a place where morality can flourish. In making this kind of decision, you are entirely on your own.

And this brings us to the second thing that makes this decision different from others. Since these decisions necessarily involve stepping outside of the law, they involve what Bernard Williams has called "moral luck." [30] For as Kant says, if you do more or less than the law requires, the consequences are on your head. The form of moral luck Williams describes exists in a case with these features: the agent does something that is, on the face of it, wrong, but may be justified by success. If the project fails, the agent will simply be wrong, and the consequences will be, in his own eyes and those of his victims, on his head. But if the project succeeds, he may at least be justified in his own eyes and in the eyes of outsiders, if not of those of his immediate victims. Williams thinks that the concept of moral luck is a notion inimical to Kantianism, but the case of the revolutionary has exactly this structure. Success makes the revolutionary, legally, the new voice of the general will, and, morally, one who has promoted the cause of justice on earth. In his own eyes and the eyes of the spectators this will justify him, though the victims of the revolution will still have a complaint. Failure, on the other hand, means that he has destroyed justice for nothing, that he is guilty of murder and treason, an assailant of the general will, and the enemy of everyone. Revolution may be justified, but only if you win.

Perhaps it will be doubted whether the view I have put forward could possibly be Kant's. Moral life in bad circumstances can be messy; Kant is often accused of denying this point. But I actually think it is a strength of his view that it allows us to see how one form of messiness arises – and that it does so without resorting to the pat explanation that we happen to be subject to an unsystematic plurality of duties that can of course conflict. [31] In the case of the conscientious revolutionary, the problem is not a conflict between different duties but rather the fact that a single duty – the duty to care for the rights of humanity – implodes when we try to act on it in an unjust world. But could Kant have recognized this? It is hard to know for sure, for the fact is that Kant never discusses the question whether the *ethical* duty not to revolt is always in place. His discussions of revolution are all concerned with the duty of justice, and it is, interestingly, the punishability of revolution that he always emphasizes. My view that he did recognize the possibility I've described here comes for the most part not from his published writings, but from what we know about his attitude toward the revolutions of his day. But there is one thing in the published writings that does support my claim. Listen again to part of the passage from "An Old Question Raised Again" where Kant praises the enthusiasm of the spectators of the French Revolution. Listen, in particular, to the way Kant imagines the deliberations of the would-be revolutionary himself:

The revolution of a gifted people which we have seen unfolding in our day may succeed or miscarry; it may be filled with misery and atrocities to the point that a sensible man, were he boldly to hope to execute it successfully the second time, would never resolve to make the experiment at such cost. (*OQ* 85)

Kant's revolutionary considers the prospects of success and views the costs of failure as his own. In this, he follows the pattern I have described.

VIII. Conclusion

The Kingdom of Ends is an ideal, not a goal. For the most part, our duty is to live as if it were real, not to bring it about that it is so. A Kantian doesn't paternalize every time a loved one makes a poor choice; a Kantian doesn't revolt every time the government makes a wrong decision. In the one case, respect for autonomy, in the other, respect for the rule of law, matter to her more than the content of the particular decisions which are made.

But in some cases, respect for autonomy, or respect for the rule of law, can be turned against themselves. When autonomy is used self-destructively, and law turns against the rights it is there to protect, morality ceases to give us clear guidance how to proceed. The claims of right remain clear, but the demands of virtue become ambiguous. In such cases, good people may do things that are, in one fairly clear sense, wrong.[32] A dogmatist may deny that a good person would ever do this; a skeptic may think such actions are unproblematic, showing only that morality is not unconditional after all. I believe that both views oversimplify our moral situation: the world is a less comfortable home for morality than they suppose. Skepticism and dogmatism are attempts to evade one of the most important facts about moral responsibility. The moral life can contain moments when responsibility is so deep that even a justification is denied us. The agent who can save morality only by violating its principles faces such a moment. At such moments the virtuous person may find that he must take morality itself under his own protection, and so take even the moral law into his own hands.

IX. Afterword: Why We Find Revolution Thrilling

Earlier I claimed that the moment of revolution, though hard and full of pain for the revolutionary himself, is thrilling to the spectator. I also claimed that neither skepticism nor dogmatism could give an adequate account of the thrill. How should a Kantian account for it?

Kant, as we have seen, had his own explanation, detailed in the essay "An Old Question Raised Again." There Kant argues that revolutionaries of his day sought republican forms of government, the only form under which Kant thought real justice and peace could possibly be secured. With peace and justice would come enlightenment. The nations would be able to guarantee civil liberties and spend money on education rather than on arms (*IUH* 26–28; *CBHH* 121). Enlightenment, the condition in which people think for themselves (*WE* 35), leads to morality, the condition in which people live by the laws of their own autonomy. Thus enthusiasm for the revolution can be understood as enthusiasm for the future of morality itself.

My explanation is different, though not incompatible with Kant's. If Kant is right, human freedom is autonomy and autonomy is morality. This makes human freedom a paradoxical thing. In everyday life, it consists to a surprising extent in having to do things. When we are dealing with evil, it consists to a tragic extent in having to put up with things. When faced with oppression, bullying, and heartbreaking unfairness, freedom can appear as helplessness; autonomy as a terrifying defenselessness. There's a real antinomy here, a natural dialectic that throws us into doubt about the nature and the value of our own moral capacity. Plato gave voice to this worry in the very earliest works of Western moral philosophy: Thrasymachus laughs at the just person as someone easily tricked into serving the interests of the stronger; Callicles argues that even self-government is merely a form of slavery.[33] Freud and Nietzsche recast the worry in more psychological terms. Morality is an expression of strength, the will to power, the aggressive instincts, turned inward. It is the magical transformation of masterfulness into self-mastery that makes us human. But morality is a form of weakness, for the will to power, the aggressive instincts, are eating us alive from the inside out, sapping our strength, making us herd animals, victims, sickly prey.[34] Autonomy gives life meaning, showing us that the world is ours to create; but autonomy is morality and morality leads to nihilism, for the good have no option but surrender.

The moment of revolution is a vindication of morality, and so of our humanity. We are the masters of our own self-mastery; in control of our self-control. Being human is not sapping our strength, for we still know when to fight. The revolutionary does not *become* strong and free when he picks up his gun. Instead, he proves to us that he's been free all along. It is because the laws of morality are his own laws that he is finally prepared to fight for them. The doubt created by the antinomy is dispelled. Revolution teaches us nothing but what we have known all along: that the good person and the free person are one and the same.

NOTES

Versions of this paper were delivered at the Central Division meeting of the American Philosophical Association in the spring of 1991, where I had the benefit of a helpful and sympathetic commentary by Andrews Reath; at the Kantian Ethics Workshop in Chapel Hill in the fall of 1991, where I received challenging comments from Simon Blackburn; and at the Political Philosophy Colloquium in Princeton in the fall of 1995. I am grateful to the audiences at all three occasions for many illuminating comments and useful objections; I would like especially to thank Stephen Engstrom, Avishai Margolit, and Arthur Ripstein. I have benefited from discussing the issues of the paper with Charlotte Brown, Daniel Brudney, Peter Hylton, Arthur Kuflik, Tamar Schapiro, and Jay Schleusenser, and from written comments sent to me by Kenneth Westphal. The paper was completed while I was a Laurence S. Rockefeller Visiting Fellow at the University Center for Human Values in Princeton in 1995–1996; I am deeply grateful both for the time the Center provided me to finish the paper, and for the useful discussions of it I had with the Fellows there. But my primary debt, here as in everything that I write, is to the example and inspiration of my teacher, John Rawls.

1. Friedrich Nietzsche, *On the Genealogy of Morals*, trans. Walter Kaufmann and R. J. Hollingdale. In *On the Genealogy of Morals and Ecce Homo*, ed. Walter Kaufmann (New York: Random House, 1967), p. 59.
2. This use of the terms dogmatism and skepticism is of course borrowed from Kant. Kant characterizes the dogmatist as one who assumes "that it is possible to make progress with pure knowledge, according to principles, from concepts alone" (*KrV* Bxxxv; see note 5 for an explanation of the system used for referring to Kant's works). Dogmatism itself produces skepticism when dogmatic claims are found to be defeasible, or, as in the case of antinomy, when dogmatic arguments can be made on both sides of a question. The alternative is criticism, which calls into question reason's jurisdiction over the matter at hand; and *sometimes* ends by establishing only a more

limited jurisdiction than reason had originally claimed. I leave the reader to judge for herself the extent to which these characterizations are apt for the work of this paper. Kant also characterizes dogmatism as despotic and suggests that skepticism, by contrast, is anarchic (*KrV* Aix). In these terms, it is apt to characterize the two views about the nature of morality's rule over us that I am discussing here as dogmatic and skeptical.

3. See, for instance, Williams's essays "Persons, Character, and Morality" and "Moral Luck" in *Moral Luck* (Cambridge University Press, 1981).

4. In the well-known story *Mutiny on the Bounty*, and in the movie, *The Man Who Shot Liberty Valance*, directed by John Ford. There are certain other popular characters whose appeal is certainly related to that of the good person who takes the law into his own hands. For example there is the hotdog cop, who uses irregular methods to catch bad guys. He doesn't take the law into his own hands on some particular occasion, but rather lives that way. Indeed, we are fascinated by the police in general, who, as Nietzsche points out, use all the same methods as criminals (*The Genealogy of Morals*, p. 82). Then there's the revenge film hero, who is, so to speak, *released* from the usual restraints of morality by a terrible crime committed against someone in his family. As we go down this list, a more deflationary account of the source of our pleasure becomes more plausible: the hero's plight serves merely to give us a kind of permission to enjoy the spectacle of violence wholeheartedly. But that's not what's going on in the cases mentioned in the text; and I think that an explanation of the phenomenon I discuss in the text should throw some light on the various pleasures we take in some of these stock figures.

5. References to and citations of Kant's works are given parenthetically in the text, using the abbreviations below, and for most works citing the page numbers of the relevant volume of *Kants gesammelte Schriften* (published by the Preussische Akademie der Wissenschaften, Berlin), which appear in the margins of most translations. The *Critique of Pure Reason*, however, is cited in its own standard way, by the page numbers of both the first (A) and second (B) editions. The *Lectures on Ethics* and the essay "On the Common Saying: 'This May Be True in Theory but It Does Not Apply in Practice'" are cited only by the page number of the translation. The translations of works from which I have quoted are also listed below.

KrV	*Critique of Pure Reason* (1st ed. 1781, 2d ed. 1787), trans. Norman Kemp Smith (New York: Macmillan, St. Martin's Press, 1965)
KpV	*Critique of Practical Reason* (1788)
CBHH	"Conjectural Beginning of Human History" (1786). Available in English translation in *Kant On History*, ed. Lewis White Beck (New York: Macmillan Library of Liberal Arts, 1963) or in *Kant's Political Writings*, 2d ed., trans. H. B. Nisbet, ed. Hans Reiss (Cambridge University Press, 1991).
G	*Groundwork of the Metaphysics of Morals* (1785)
IUH	"Idea for a Universal History from a Cosmopolitan Point of View" (1784). Available in English translation in *Kant On History*, ed. Lewis White Beck, cited above; or in *Kant's Political Writings*, 2d ed., trans. H. B. Nisbet, ed. Hans Reiss, cited above.

LE   *Lectures on Ethics* (1775–1780). Drawn from the lecture notes of Theodor Friedrich Brauer, Gottlieb Kutzner, and Chr. Mrongovious by Paul Menzer in 1924; trans. Louis Infeld (Indianapolis: Hackett Publishing, 1980).

MM   The General Introduction to *The Metaphysics of Morals* (1797), trans. James Ellington, in *Immanuel Kant: Ethical Philosophy* (Indianapolis: Hackett Publishing, 1983). The two main parts of the work are listed below.

MPJ   *The Metaphysical Principles of Justice* (1797), trans. John Ladd as *The Metaphysical Elements of Justice* (New York: Macmillan Library of Liberal Arts, 1965).

MPV   *The Metaphysical Principles of Virtue* (1797), trans. James Ellington, in *Immanuel Kant: Ethical Philosophy*, cited above.

OQ   "An Old Question Raised Again: Is the Human Race Constantly Progressing?" trans. Robert Anchor in *Kant On History*, ed. Lewis White Beck, cited above.

PP   *Perpetual Peace* (1795), trans. Lewis White Beck in *Kant On History*, ed. Lewis White Beck, cited above.

R   *Religion within the Limits of Reason Alone* (1793), trans. Theodore M. Greene and Hoyt H. Hudson (La Salle, IL: Open Court, 1934; rpt. New York: Harper Torchbooks, 1960).

TP   "On the Common Saying: 'This May Be True in Theory but It Does not Apply in Practice' " (1793), in *Kant's Political Writings*, 2d ed., trans. H. B. Nisbet, ed. Hans Reiss, cited above.

WE   "What is Enlightenment?" (1784) Available in English translation in *Kant On History*, ed. Lewis White Beck, cited above; or in *Kant's Political Writings*, 2d ed., trans. H. B. Nisbet, ed. Hans Reiss, cited above.

6. G. P. Gooch, *Germany and the French Revolution* (New York: Russell and Russell, 1966), p. 269.

7. Locke, *The Second Treatise of Government: An Essay Concerning the Original, Extent, and End of Civil Government*. For the discussion of rights in the state of nature, see Chapter II; for our reasons for leaving the state of nature, see Chapter IX.

8. Why must things be property in order for us to use them? In the case of immediate consumables, it is of course true that by using them we make them our own: we make them part of ourselves in the most literal way, so that interfering with our use of them becomes in the most literal way interfering with ourselves. If we could not make them our own in this way, we could not use them. In the case of "the means of production" a simpler and more practical argument can be made: we cannot make *effective* use of them without some guarantee that they will be reserved for us exclusively during the time of use, since, for example, I cannot effectively grow corn in the same field where you are trying, at the same time, to grow barley. It is worth pointing out that this argument, if it works, does not establish the necessity of "private property" in any controversial sense; it establishes only that the means of production and action must be reserved to the exclusive use of certain individuals in certain times and places. This applies even to things

owned communally – for instance, library books are reserved to particular patrons for specified amounts of time. Your right to the exclusive use of a book, for reading only, and for a certain length of time, still counts as a form of "property" in Kant's sense. In the same way, the means of production might be communally owned and "lent out" to particular users.

9. Rousseau, Jean-Jacques, *On the Social Contract*, Book I, Chapter IX.

10. Of course it may be argued that Lockean rights also depend on human relationships, because of the proviso that the laborer should leave "enough and as good" for others, which seems to substitute for making agreements with others. But Locke seems to take it for granted that this proviso not only can be but is met, whereas the relationships on which rights are built in the accounts of Kant and Rousseau are ones that people must actually enter into. See Locke's *Second Treatise*, Chapter V.

11. Following Rousseau, Kant argues that a republican constitution must provide for the separation of the three powers, since when they are united in one person the state is effectively despotic (*MPJ* 316–19; *PP* 352). Rousseau argues that legislation must be in couched in general terms, while it is the business of the executive to apply the law to particular cases (see *On the Social Contract*, Book II, Chapter IV). This makes it easy to see why unification of the powers leads to despotism. Suppose we legislate by majority vote, and suppose that the majority would like to institute a majority religion as the official church of the state. In their capacity as legislators, they cannot name a particular religion, but they could make a law that, say, everyone is to practice the one true faith. It will be left to the executive to determine which faith that is. Under these circumstances, it is plausible to suppose that individual citizens would have reason *not* to vote for such a law – the same sorts of reasons that the parties in Rawls's original position have for upholding freedom of conscience (see John Rawls, *Political Liberalism* [New York: Columbia University Press, 1993], pp. 310–15). But now suppose that the majority is also the executive, who will choose the one true faith. Then they can make the law in question with impunity. In this way the unification of the legislative and executive powers makes democracy degenerate into a form of despotism – the tyranny of the majority.

12. In reconstructing Kant's complex account of these matters, I have drawn on the discussion in Howard Williams, *Kant's Political Philosophy* (New York: St. Martin's Press, 1983), pp. 173–8.

13. Kant argues that morality requires us to make the "Highest Good" – a state of affairs in which we all attain a virtuous disposition and happiness proportionate to that disposition – the end of our moral practice, and that we cannot conceive how such a state could be brought about unless God exists and we are immortal. We are therefore licensed to postulate that these things are so.

14. Kant does not say this directly, but he appeals to considerations of exactly this kind in explaining why in civil society we take long possession to establish a property claim (*MPJ* 292–293) and how we deal with cases in which someone has come into possession of stolen property (*MPJ* 302–303).

15. According to Kant himself, the review appeared in the *Göttingen Journal*, Number 28, February 18, 1797.

16. This criterion seems called for by Kant's account of citizenship as fitness for voting. Kant himself attempted to argue that some adults – apprentices, servants, and "all women" – could still count as "passive citizens" even

though we are (rightly, according to Kant) not allowed to vote because of our "dependence" on others. But, in a textually rather unsteady moment, he also conceded that this is only legitimate if the laws chosen by the active citizens allow "everyone" to "work up" from a passive to an active status (*MPJ* 314–15).

17. Kant himself associates his use of the terms "Idea" and "Ideal" with Platonic forms at *KrV* A313/B370 ff., and A568–9/B596–7; and in the earlier discussion, he explicitly compares his own idea of a republic to Plato's (*KrV* A316/B373).

18. See Plato, *Phaedo*, lines 74a–76a, and *Republic*, especially books II–VII.

19. Kant himself says, "Even if the sovereign were to decide to transform himself into a democracy, he would still be doing the people an injustice, because the people themselves might abhor this kind of constitution and might find that one of the other two was more advantageous for them" (*MPJ* 340). Of course Kant is talking here not about whether the state should be a republic, but about which of the three "empirical" forms it should take. The remark raises odd problems about whether Kant thinks there is *any* legitimate way for a state to change its basic form of government, but I leave those aside here.

20. When thinking about the terms on which we interact with other nations, as when thinking about the terms on which we interact with other people, it is important to distinguish two different issues: one is whether you disapprove of the way they go on, and the other is whether the way they go on prevents you from interacting with them on terms that are honorable in your own eyes.

21. As a citizen, rather than merely as a subject, he is sometimes entitled to act on his own substantive views. For instance, they determine who and what he votes for. But the cases in which he is permitted in this way to act on his private views must be constitutionally defined.

22. Hobbes makes essentially the same argument in *Leviathan*, Chapter XVIII.

23. Rousseau, *On the Social Contract*, Book II, Chapter III.

24. For Kant's own reflections on this point, see note 28 below.

25. One standard response to this point is that it shows only that there cannot be a legal right to revolution, but not that there cannot be a moral right. Kant's system makes no use of any distinctive category of moral right; for him, a right is by definition the kind of moral claim that can legitimately be coercively enforced and so can be legalized. There are claims in Kant's system that it is tempting to identify with moral rights. Kant distinguishes duties of justice from duties of virtue on the grounds that the former are, and the latter are not, both legitimate and possible to enforce coercively. We *may not* force people to be virtuous because virtue is a matter of inner motives and attitudes, and your having a bad attitude toward me does not hinder my freedom. But we also *cannot* force people to do the duties of virtue, because we cannot control the motives from which they act. Yet one of the duties of virtue – the duty to respect others – seems to be a perfect duty and seems to establish a kind of claim, so that we might say that we have a moral right to the respect of others. This will not help us here, however. It is, though, related to what I take to be the most plausible grounds for claiming a "moral right" to revolution – namely, exclusion from full citizenship on arbitrary grounds. The most extreme case is that of slaves, but victims of apartheid,

and Kant's so-called passive citizens (see note 16 above) may also plausibly claim that the general will is not their will, that they have been left outside of the commonwealth. So let me just say that the case of the conscientious revolutionary that I will shortly examine, the one I think morally interesting, is not that of someone who himself can plausibly claim to be excluded from the commonwealth, but rather someone who is part of the commonwealth but objects to its actions. One obvious reason why he might object is that some others are arbitrarily excluded.

26. For a further explanation of the basis and meaning of this view, see my "The Right to Lie: Kant on Dealing with Evil" in Korsgaard, *Creating the Kingdom of Ends* (Cambridge University Press, 1996), pp. 141–3.

27. For discussion, see my "Morality as Freedom" in *Creating the Kingdom of Ends*, pp. 176–83.

28. Kant explicitly acknowledges the existence of conscientious revolutionaries in the course of a rather odd discussion of the morality of the death penalty at *MPJ* 333–4. People join rebellions both for honorable and for venal motives, Kant notices, and we might think that the former should be punished less severely than the latter. But applying the death penalty to all concerned achieves this, Kant argues, since "a man of honor would choose death and . . . the knave would choose servitude." The knave therefore *is* punished more severely.

29. I owe this formulation to Andrews Reath.

30. See Bernard Williams, "Moral Luck."

31. An account that, to my mind, makes sense of the complexity of morality at the expense of depriving morality itself of sense. I am indebted to Tamar Schapiro for illuminating discussions of this topic.

32. What fairly clear sense? Not universalizable, certainly; but the more important point is what that shows: that such an action relates us wrongly to others. Almost any moral philosopher would grant that wrong actions relate us wrongly to others, of course, but I mean something different. I don't regard that as an incidental feature of wrong actions, a mere effect of the fact that the actions are wrong and therefore others don't want us to do them. I regard the way it relates you to yourself and others as *of the essence* of the morality of an action. See my "The Reasons We Can Share" in *Creating the Kingdom of Ends*, pp. 275–6 and 300–2; and *The Sources of Normativity* (Cambridge University Press, 1996), p. 114 n. 26.

33. Plato, *Republic*, lines 338ff.; *Gorgias*, lines 491–2.

34. See Friedrich Nietzsche, *On the Genealogy of Morals* (cited in note 2 above), Essay 2, and Sigmund Freud, in, for example, *Civilization and Its Discontents*, trans. James Strachey (New York: W. W. Norton & Co., 1961), Chapter 7.

Kant on Aesthetic and Biological Purposiveness

HANNAH GINSBORG

One of the most problematic features of Kant's *Critique of Judgment* is its apparent lack of unity. Kant announces in the Preface that its topic is the faculty of judgment, which is one of the three higher faculties of the mind. But the two parts of which it is composed appear to have very little connection, either with each other or with the notion of judgment as such. Part One, the Critique of Aesthetic Judgment, is almost exclusively about aesthetics, focussing on the notions of the beautiful and the sublime as they apply to both nature and art. Part Two, the Critique of Teleological Judgment, is mostly about philosophical issues related to biology, dealing primarily with the role of teleology in the organic world. The long introduction preceding the two parts provides only obscure and fleeting hints of the relationship between them. Rather than lending coherence to the work, it increases the appearance of disunity by introducing a third and seemingly independent topic, that of nature's comprehensibility under a system of empirical concepts and laws.

The most inviting prospect for a unified reading of the *Critique of Judgment* is offered by the notion of purposiveness [*Zweckmäßigkeit*], which plays a central role in Kant's treatment of each of the main topics with which the *Critique of Judgment* is concerned. When we characterize living things and their organs in teleological terms, according to Kant, we regard them as purposive. By the same token, we ascribe purposiveness to the natural processes which produce living things and make possible their functioning and further reproduction. But we also attribute purposiveness to nature in general, both living and non-living, insofar as we regard empirical concepts and laws as amenable to systematization. And we ascribe a corresponding purposiveness to the activity of our own cognitive faculties in their activity of discovering and systematizing natural laws and kinds. Finally, aesthetic judgment too involves the ascription of purposiveness. In judging something to be beautiful, we perceive purposiveness both in the object of our judgment and in our mental activity of judging it. Thus the notion of purposiveness appears to be the common thread uniting Kant's otherwise disparate treatments of aesthetics, biological teleology, and the systematicity of nature.

Rather than solving the difficulty, however, the appeal to purposiveness merely refocusses it. For the issue of unity now arises for the concept of purposiveness itself. As we have just seen, Kant holds that we ascribe purposiveness to a wide variety of things: organisms and their parts, biological processes, nature as a whole, scientific theorizing, objects of aesthetic appreciation, and the activity of aesthetic judging. But it is by no means obvious that there is in fact a single concept of purposiveness which applies univocally in all these contexts. The difficulty emerges with particular sharpness when we compare the aesthetic context with that of biology. Intuitively, it is clear that the class of organisms is different from the class of those objects typically regarded as beautiful, and it is hard to see how a single concept of purposiveness could capture what is characteristic of both. Moreover, Kant himself emphasizes that there is a distinction between purposiveness as it applies in the biological realm, which he describes as objective and real, and purposiveness as it applies in aesthetics, which is subjective and formal. And although Kant clearly regards aesthetic and biological purposiveness as species of a more inclusive concept of purposiveness in general, they seem on the face of it to be related by only the most tenuous of connections.

This difficulty has led at least one influential commentator to claim that the term "purposiveness" has different senses in the two contexts.[1] More generally, it has encouraged the widely held view that there is no real connection between the two parts of the *Critique of Judgment*, and that Kant's juxtaposition of aesthetics and biological teleology represents what Schopenhauer calls a "baroque union" of two "heterogeneous objects."[2] My aim in this essay is to challenge these responses by arguing that aesthetic and biological purposiveness are applications of a single underlying concept, and that, correspondingly, the two parts of the *Critique of Judgment* represent aspects of a single project. The notion of purposiveness, I shall suggest, provides a common theme in terms of which the third Critique as a whole can be understood.[3]

The essay is divided into six sections. In Section I, I sketch what is apparently Kant's official account of purposiveness, and show how it applies in the biological context. In Section II, I discuss Kant's account of aesthetic purposiveness and the difficulties in relating it to his account of purposiveness in general. Sections III and IV present a new interpretation of the notion of purposiveness in general and of biological purposiveness in particular, and Section V extends this interpretation to the aesthetic context. Finally, Section VI addresses a question that arises for the line of interpretation presented in the preceding three sections.

I

A natural starting-point for an inquiry into Kant's notion of purposiveness is §10 of the *Critique of Judgment*, which is entitled "Of Purposiveness in General." Kant begins this section by defining a purpose as "the object of a concept, in so far as the latter is thought as the cause of the former (the real ground of its possibility)" (220).[4] He goes on to give a related definition of purposiveness as "the causality of a *concept* in respect of its *object*" (ibid.). The initial definition of a purpose is then elaborated:

Thus where not merely, say, the cognition of an object, but rather the object itself (its form or existence) as effect is thought as possible only through a concept of the latter, there we think a purpose. The representation of the effect is here the determining ground of the cause and precedes the cause. (ibid.)

This opening passage of §10 conveys the suggestion that the concept of a thing or of a state of affairs can play a causal role in bringing it about or endowing it with certain features. Concepts can thus make a contribution, not just to thought and cognition, but also to the processes by which change takes place in the spatio-temporal world. This happens whenever a thing or state of affairs is brought about by an intelligent agent in accordance with an intention or design. If a thing is intentionally produced, there is a concept of the thing in the mind of the agent which is antecedent to the thing's existence, and which governs or determines the agent's activity in producing it.

The most obvious example of this kind of causality is the production of artefacts by human beings. And passages elsewhere in the *Critique of Judgment* suggest that human artefacts, broadly construed, do indeed serve for Kant as central examples of purposes. Kant frequently alludes to artefacts as purposes, citing prehistoric tools (§17, 236n), a hexagon traced in the sand (§64, 370), and the regular arrangement of trees and flowers produced by the art of landscape gardening (§62, 364). Moreover, he claims that it is only in the case of artefacts that we are acquainted with the causality in question: "Only in *products of art* can we be conscious of the causality of reason of [sc. in respect of] objects which are hence called purposive or purposes" (*EE* IX, 234; cf. also 8:181).

The term "purpose" as defined in the opening passage of §10 can thus be understood as applying paradigmatically to human artefacts. Correspondingly, we may take purposiveness to be exemplified by the characteristic causality – namely that of human design – which is required for the production of artefacts. However, to avoid confusion, we should note two variations in Kant's use of these terms. First, Kant often uses the term "purpose" to refer, not to the object which is produced according to an antecedent concept or design, but to the concept or design itself. For example, in the published introduction he defines a purpose as "the concept of an object, in so far as it at the same time contains the ground of actuality of this object" (IV, 180; see also 8:181 and *EE* IX, 232). Second, the term "purposiveness" usually denotes the characteristic property of a designed object rather than the causality by which such an object is produced. In other words, purposiveness typically denotes the property of being a purpose, where "purpose" is understood according to Kant's original definition. This use is illustrated in the passage quoted above from the First Introduction, where Kant says that artefacts are called "purposive or purposes." These variations are terminological and do not indicate a departure from the general framework set by the initial definitions at §10.

So far we have seen only the first stage in Kant's development of the notion of purposiveness. Purposiveness, thus far defined, appears to be restricted to products of intentional causality, in contrast to natural things. But now Kant suggests that the term allows of a broader application:

An object or state of mind or also an action is called purposive, even if its possibility does not necessarily presuppose the representation of a purpose, merely because its possibility can be explained and conceived by us only in so far as we assume at its basis a causality according to purposes, i.e., a will, which ordered it in this way [*der sie . . . so angeordnet hätte*] according to the representation of a certain rule. The purposiveness can thus be without a purpose, in so far as we do not posit the causes of this form in the will, but still can make the explanation of its possibility conceivable to ourselves only in so far as we derive it from a will. (§10, 220)

Here Kant allows that we may assert that an object is purposive even if it is not the product of design. It is sufficient that we be unable to conceive how the object is possible without appealing to the assumption that it was designed. Briefly put, a thing may be called purposive on the grounds that it is "as if" designed or that it appears to be designed ("we call purposive that [*dasjenige*] whose existence appears to presuppose a representation of that same thing" [*EE* V, 216]).[5] However, it should be noted that the criterion for appearing to be designed in this context is a stringent one. It is not enough that a thing look as if it might have been designed while at the same time being comprehensible to us as the product of "blind" natural forces (as for example in the case of an interestingly shaped piece of driftwood). Rather, we must be unable to explain how the thing is possible except by invoking the notion of design.[6]

Thus extended, the concept of purposiveness applies to living things and their organs.[7] For, as Kant argues in the Critique of Teleological Judgment, we cannot understand the origin or functioning of living things unless we assume that they are produced by a causality working in accordance with concepts. The core of the argument is that, at least from the limited point of view of a human intellect, mechanical processes alone are insufficient to account for the unity of a living thing. From our point of view,

the construction of a bird, the hollowing in its bones, the situation of its wings for movement and of the tail for steering, etc. [are], . . . according to the mere *nexus effectivus* in nature and without appealing to a special kind of causality, namely that of purposes (*nexus finalis*), in the highest degree contingent [*zufällig*]. (§61, 360)

As far as we can tell, "nature, regarded as mere mechanism, could have formed itself in a thousand other ways, without hitting precisely upon the unity according to such a principle" (ibid.).

Kant elaborates on this line of argument by giving an account of the unity of a living thing. The parts of a living thing, he says, "connect themselves into the unity of a whole, by being reciprocally cause and effect of one another's form" (§65, 373). For example, the roots of a growing tree are causally necessary for the development and main-tenance of the leaves, since the leaves depend on the roots for water and other nutrients from the soil. Conversely, the leaves are causally neces-sary for the development and maintenance of the roots, since the roots depend on the leaves for energy. It is the unity conferred by this recipro-cal causal dependence which defies explanation in terms of mechanical laws alone. The organism's powers of growth, self-maintenance and reproduction cannot be reduced to the powers of unorganized matter, but must be referred to the organism as an irreducible whole. This can be done, Kant argues, only by regarding the organism as if it were produced in accordance with design. We can understand the mutually coordinated production of the parts only by thinking of it as if determined by an antecedent concept of the whole (*EE* IX, 236; §77, 407–8).

In ascribing purposiveness to living things, however, we do not assert that they are in fact the products of design. The purposiveness we ascribe is "without a purpose," in that we refrain from claiming that there is any actual concept or design that is responsible for the object's production. To claim that living things are designed – in particular, by God – would be illegitimate for two reasons. First, such a claim transcends the bounds of human experience (*EE* IX, 236–7; §74, 397). The fact that human beings can understand living things only on the assumption of design does not entail that no intellect could understand them on mechanical grounds alone. Second, to claim that living things are produced in accordance with a design would be to identify them with artefacts. It would remove living things from the sphere of nature, in that their origin and development would result, not from natural processes, but from divine art (§74, 397).

Kant's exposition at §10 has now indicated two uses of the term "purposiveness," one in application to artefacts and the other in application to natural things, specifically organisms and their parts. They are different in that only the former implies that the purposive object is in fact produced in accordance with a design, or, in other words, that the purposiveness has a purpose. Kant expresses this point elsewhere by qualifying the purposiveness we ascribe to artefacts as intentional purposiveness, while making clear that purposiveness as ascribed to an organism is indeterminate as to whether the relevant causality is intentional or not (*EE* IX, 236; §72, 390–1). This important difference aside, the concept of purposiveness in these two applications is the same. In both cases, it is qualified by Kant as "objective," "real," and "material" purposiveness.[8]

However, Kant concludes §10 by indicating a third sense of purposiveness which is in sharp contrast with the other two:

Now we do not always need to understand through reason (as regards its possibility) that which we observe. Thus we can at least observe and remark in objects, although only through reflection, a purposiveness according to form, also without laying at its basis a purpose (as the material of the *nexus finalis*). (§10, 220)

In the case of both artefacts and organisms, the ascription of purposiveness is based on the use of reason in considering the circumstances under which the object is and is not possible. Thus we ascribe purposiveness to a regular hexagon which we find traced in the sand because we cannot understand how such a thing could have come to be without the operation of an intentional causality (§64, 370). Similarly, we ascribe purposiveness to organisms because we cannot understand their possibility on the basis of mechanical laws alone. But Kant is now suggesting that there is a kind of purposiveness whose ascription does not depend on a consideration of the object's possibility. It is observed "only through reflection," that is, by reflective judgment alone without any use of reason. Rather than qualifying as real or material, it is "a purposiveness according to form," or, as Kant puts it later, "the mere form of purposiveness" (§11, 221) or "a merely formal purposiveness" (§12, 222; §15, 226).[9] And as the discussion following §10 makes clear, it is subjective rather than objective.

The purposiveness to which Kant is here alluding is the purposiveness involved in a judgment of beauty. To explore it further, we need to consider it in the context of Kant's aesthetic theory, specifically his theory of the beautiful. We turn to this in the next section.

II

The core of Kant's theory of the beautiful is to be found in the "Analytic of the Beautiful," which lays out the essential features of a judgment of beauty, or, as Kant also calls it, a judgment of taste. Kant's analysis is divided into four moments, each of which discusses one of four characteristics jointly distinguishing judgments of beauty from all other kinds of judgment. Purposiveness is the topic of the third moment; it will be helpful, before addressing it, to look at the other three. Kant begins his analysis in the first moment with the claim that a judgment of beauty is based on a feeling of disinterested pleasure [*Lust*] or liking [*Wohlgefallen*]. To judge an object to be beautiful I must like it, or feel pleasure in it. But my liking must be independent of any interest in the object, that is, it must not presuppose or otherwise entail any desire for the object. The pleasure I feel must not be based on the awareness that the object satisfies a need or fulfills an aim.

One important implication of this first feature is that a judgment of beauty is not objective. In this respect it is distinct both from a non-evaluative cognitive judgment and from a judgment that something is good. In contrast to what Kant calls "objective sensation," for example, the sensory awareness of a thing's color, a feeling of pleasure cannot serve on its own as the basis for ascribing an objective property to a thing (§3, 206; cf. also VII, 189). It makes the subject aware only of the way in which she herself is affected by, or responds to, the object. Thus judgments of beauty cannot be assimilated to those cognitive judgments – for example, secondary-quality judgments – that are immediately based on sensation.[10] Nor can they be assimilated to judgments of the good, which can be objective even though they involve a feeling of pleasure or approval. For pleasure in a thing's goodness is based on the recognition that it satisfies an aim, and it is in virtue of this recognition that a judgment of goodness can be objective. By contrast, the pleasure in a thing's beauty is disinterested and so cannot in the same way ground an objective claim.

However, in the second moment, Kant introduces a feature which is apparently at odds with that described in the first. Judgments of beauty, he says, are universally valid. When I judge that something is beautiful, I take my judgment to hold good not just for myself, but for everyone who judges the object. The significance of this feature becomes clear when we compare judgments of beauty with a third kind of judgment which involves pleasure, namely judgments of the agreeable. Judgments of the agreeable, for example about the pleasantness of food or drink, resemble judgments of beauty in respect of the first feature Kant identified. They do not ascribe an objective property but merely register the subject's response to the thing judged. However, unlike judgments of beauty, they do not claim to be universally valid. Someone who expresses liking for a particular kind of food makes no claim on the agreement of others. By contrast, someone who judges an object to be beautiful does claim that others should share his or her pleasure. He judges, Kant says, "not merely for himself, but for everyone" (§7, 212).

It should be noted here that the claim to universal validity in the judgment of beauty has normative force. I judge, not that other people will in fact share my pleasure, but that they ought to share it. This point is already implicit in the second moment: the person who judges that a thing is beautiful "does not count on the agreement of others . . . because he has often found them in agreement with his judgment, but rather *demands* [*fordern*] it from them" (§7, 212–213). But Kant emphasizes it in its own right in the fourth moment, where he characterizes judgments of beauty as having the feature of necessity. "The judgment of . . . [beauty] imputes agreement to everyone: and he who declares something to be beautiful insists that everyone *ought to* [*sollen*] approve of the object in question and likewise declare it to be beautiful" (§19, 237). We judge not "that everyone *will* agree with our judgment, but that everyone *ought* to agree with it" (§22, 239).

The combination of features so far identified sets up an apparent paradox. How can a judgment which is based on merely subjective grounds also be universally valid and necessary? Kant's answer is based on a more fine-grained characterization of aesthetic judgment, first introduced at §9. To judge an object to be beautiful is to engage in an activity of reflection which Kant calls the "free play" of the cognitive faculties. In this activity of reflection the two faculties of imagination and understanding are in a harmonious relation, just as they are in cognition. But rather than this relation being governed by determinate concepts, as it is in cognition, the faculties harmonize freely. As a result, rather than ascribing a determinate property to the object, we feel pleasure in it. Even though this pleasure has no objective basis, Kant argues, we can still claim that everyone ought to share it. For we have a right to claim universal validity for the workings of our own cognitive faculties. Thus the universal validity and necessity of a judgment of beauty derive from its origin in our cognitive faculties in spite of the fact that a judgment of beauty is not itself a cognitive judgment.

The notion of the "free play" provides the context for understanding how purposiveness fits into Kant's aesthetic theory. For the pleasure felt in this activity of aesthetic reflection is, Kant claims in the third moment, an awareness of purposiveness. In the first place, it is an awareness of purposiveness in the workings of our own cognitive faculties. The pleasure we feel is "the consciousness of merely formal purposiveness in the play of the subject's cognitive powers" (§12, 222). The aesthetic judgment, that is, "brings to our notice [*bemerken geben*] . . . the purposive form in the determination of the powers of representation which are engaged with it" (§15, 228). The "formal" character of the purposiveness is due to the absence of any cognitive content. Rather than being conscious of the activity as directed towards a specific cognition, we are aware of it as that activity of the faculties which is required for "cognition in general" (§9, 218, and 219).[11] Thus we do not perceive it as bound to the achievement of any particular cognitive purpose.

But this is not the only sense in which the pleasure in beauty is the awareness of formal purposiveness. For it is also the awareness of formal purposiveness in the object judged to be beautiful. Indeed Kant first introduces the idea of formal purposiveness by saying that we "remark it in objects" (§10, 220). And he sums up the third moment by identifying formal purposiveness with beauty itself: "*beauty* is the form of the *purposiveness* of an object, in so far as it is perceived in the object *without the representation of a purpose*" (236). Here the formal character of the purposiveness consists in the absence of any determinate concept under which the object must fall in order to be pleasing to us. Pleasure in an object's beauty, unlike pleasure in its goodness or in its perfection, does not depend on our recognition that it meets specific criteria which determine whether our approval is merited. We need not regard a given flower as falling under any particular concept (for example the concept of reproductive organ) in order to feel pleasure in its beauty (§16, 229), even though we need to invoke such concepts if we are to approve of it in other ways.

Pleasure in taste, then, appears to consist both in the ascription of formal purposiveness to one's own activity of judging and in the ascription of formal purposiveness to the object which is judged.[12] Kant sheds light on this double ascription when he suggests elsewhere that the pleasure makes us aware of a harmony or fit between the object and the activity of judging. In making an aesthetic judgment, he says, we represent the agreement of the object's form with the cognitive faculties (VIII, 192). The object is represented, in other words, not as purposive *überhaupt*, but as purposive in regard to the subject's cognitive faculties (VII, 190) or as purposive for judgment (VII, 190; *EE* VII, 221; §38, 289–90). This also indicates why aesthetic purposiveness is qualified as subjective rather than objective. Even when we view the aesthetic judgment as ascribing purposiveness to the object, the purposiveness is subjective because it applies only in relation to the faculties of the subject.

We can now raise the question with which this paper is centrally concerned. How is aesthetic purposiveness related to purposiveness in the context of biology? One approach has been to explain aesthetic purposiveness, like biological purposiveness, as the appearance of design. According to Donald Crawford, a beautiful object is "intelligible (explicable and conceivable) to us only in terms of purposes"; it has a "form and organization" which "leads us to say that it resulted from a concept."[13] But this approach, which in effect identifies the two kinds of purposiveness, fails to do justice to the specifically subjective character of aesthetic purposiveness. Moreover, it does not account for the fact that many objects which appear to be designed strike us as ugly or aesthetically neutral, and, conversely, that – as Kant himself emphasizes – beautiful objects can be intelligible without the assumption of design.[14]

In a contrasting approach, Paul Guyer has suggested that Kant employs different conceptions of purposiveness in the two contexts. While purposiveness in the context of organisms and artefacts is linked to the idea of design, something is purposive on the second conception if it satisfies an aim or objective, regardless of whether or not it is or appears designed to do so.[15] According to Guyer, beautiful objects are purposive on the second conception because, in giving rise to the free play of the faculties, they satisfy the "subjective aim of cognition." That is, they bring about a state of mind in which our manifolds of intuition are unified, where this unity corresponds to a basic cognitive aim of human beings. But this does not entail that they are purposive on the first conception. For they need not appear to be designed for the sake of this aim. Thus, according to Guyer, Kant's discussion of purposiveness at §10 is misleading. It develops a notion of purposiveness which is irrelevant to the aesthetic context, and thus "obscures [Kant's] fundamental idea."[16]

However, the implication that §10 is misleading should raise our suspicions. For this section, which occurs early in the Critique of Aesthetic Judgment, serves as the starting-point for Kant's detailed account of aesthetic purposiveness. It would be odd for Kant to begin this account by characterizing a separate notion of purposiveness which had no place in the aesthetic context. Moreover, although Guyer is right to challenge the unqualified identification of aesthetic and biological purposiveness, his denial that they have any substantive connection leads to disappointing consequences. For, as I suggested in the introduction, the notion of purposiveness seems to hold out the best hope for understanding how the two parts of the *Critique of Judgment* are related. If the notion of purposiveness cannot be univocally understood, then the prospects for a unified interpretation look bleak.[17]

III

So far, our discussion of the notion of purposiveness has been guided by Kant's account of "purposiveness in general" at §10. It was this account which led us to the view that a thing is purposive in virtue of being or appearing to be designed: a view which fits well in the case of biological purposiveness but does not seem to carry over to the aesthetic context. However, there are a number of passages in which Kant offers what is apparently an alternative characterization of purposiveness. In the First Introduction, he defines purposiveness as "a conformity to law [*Gesetzmäßigkeit*] of the contingent as such" (*EE* VI, 217), and alludes to it again, more elaborately, as "the conformity to law of an intrinsically [*an sich*] contingent connection of the manifold" (*EE* VIII, 228). In the published introduction, he characterizes purposiveness as "the lawlike [*gesetzlich*] unity in a connection, which we cognize . . . as contingent in itself" (V, 184). And in the Critique of Teleological Judgment he describes it simply as a "lawlikeness of the contingent" (§76, 404). These passages have received very little attention, but I believe that they point the way to a more satisfactory approach.

At first, there seems to be something paradoxical about this new characterization of purposiveness. To say that something is lawlike, or in conformity with law, seems to imply that it is necessary rather than contingent. When we say of the trajectory of a moving body that it conforms to the laws of mechanics, we are saying that the body is necessitated to move in the way that the laws dictate, and we rule out the possibility that it could have moved otherwise. However, the air of paradox is dispelled if we take the lawlikeness in question to be normative rather than natural. Something can be contingent with respect to natural laws and yet conform to a law which says how it ought to be. Indeed, it is plausible to suppose that conformity to normative law must involve contingency. For to say that something is as it ought to be implies that it could fail to be that way.

These considerations suggest that purposiveness, on Kant's alternative characterization, may be understood as conformity to normative law. This suggestion is borne out by several passages in which Kant describes objective purposiveness in explicitly normative terms. The most telling of these is from Section X of the First Introduction.[18] Kant is here discussing teleological judgments, which he has earlier defined as judgments on the objective purposiveness of nature (*EE* VII, 221; *EE* IX, 232).

A teleological judgment compares the concept of a product of nature, according to that which it is, with what it *ought to be* [*sollen*]. Here a concept (of the purpose) is laid at the basis of the judging of its possibility, which [concept] precedes a priori. In products of art, there is no difficulty in representing their possibility in such a way. But to think of a product of nature that there is something which it *ought to be*, and to judge it according to whether it indeed actually is that way, already contains the presupposition of a principle which cannot be drawn from experience (which teaches us only how things are). (*EE* X, 240)[19]

Kant's own concern in this passage is to argue that a judgment on the objective purposiveness of a natural thing is not licensed by experience alone, but rather requires a principle "which cannot be drawn from experience." What concerns us, however, is not the conclusion itself, but the basis on which Kant asserts it. A judgment of objective purposiveness involves a normative element. In making such a judgment, we judge that the object is as it ought to be, or, in other words, that it conforms to a normative constraint. Such a judgment (at any rate, in the case of a natural object) cannot be based on experience alone. For experience teaches us only "how things are" and not how they ought to be.

The conclusion I want to draw from this part of the passage is that objective purposiveness may be equated with conformity to normative law. Now Kant goes on to point out that we ascribe this normative lawlikeness to organic beings, in contrast to inorganic products of nature:

That we can see through the eye, we experience immediately, as we do its external and internal structure which contains the conditions of this its possible use, and thus its causality according to mechanical laws. But I can also make use of a stone, in order to smash something on it, or to build on it, etc., and these effects can also be referred as purposes to their causes; but I cannot on that account say that it ought to serve for building. Only of the eye do I judge that it *ought* to be suitable for seeing ... (*EE* X, 240)

We can learn from experience the characteristic capacities and potentialities of both organic and inorganic products of nature. We observe that eyes are capable of seeing and stones are suitable for building. Experience can also teach us the underlying mechanical or material grounds of these capacities. Eyes are capable of seeing because, among other things, they have a lens which refracts light. Stones are suitable for building because, among other things, their chemical composition renders them hard and durable. But in the case of organic beings, we take a step beyond experience to claim that these characteristic capacities, together with the material constitution which underlies them, exemplify how a being of that kind ought to be. Being capable of sight is not just a characteristic of eyes, but a normative requirement: an eye which cannot see may be judged, without qualification, to be defective. By contrast, there is nothing which a stone ought to be. We may judge a stone to be sound or defective with respect to some particular human purpose: it may conform to the requirements for a building-stone but fail as a knife-sharpener. But we cannot describe it – as we can an organic being – as sound or defective *tout court*.[20]

The continuation of the passage supports the present line of interpretation by showing that Kant thinks of conformity to normative law as a "lawlikeness of the contingent." For Kant now reminds us that, from the point of view of the human intellect, organisms and their parts are contingent with respect to the mechanism of nature. As we saw in Section I (and as Kant has just argued in the preceding section of the First Introduction) organisms have a unity which cannot be accounted for in terms of the laws governing unorganized matter. Our judgment that an organism or organ conforms to a normatively necessary constraint goes along with our recognition of its "physico-mechanical" contingency:

> ... and although [the eye's] shape and the constitution and composition of all its parts are, when judged by merely mechanical laws of nature, quite contingent for my judgment, nonetheless I think in its form and construction [*Bau*] a necessity to be formed in a certain way, namely according to a concept which precedes the formative causes of this organ, without which the possibility of this natural product is not comprehensible to me according to any mechanical natural law (which is not the case for the stone). Now this "ought" contains a necessity which is sharply distinguished from the physico-mechanical necessity according to which a thing is possible according to mere laws of ... efficient causes. (ibid., 240–1)

Implicit in this part of the passage is the idea that the necessity of the "ought" compensates for the absence of natural necessity in making the eye comprehensible. Kant indicates elsewhere that in order to understand a natural product we need to cognize it as, in some sense, necessary.[21] Here, while reminding us that we cannot grasp the eye's necessity according to physico-mechanical laws, he points out that we can grasp it as normatively necessary. While we cannot explain the formation of the lens as a consequence of mechanical laws, we can understand that an eye must have a lens if the eye is to be as it ought to be; more specifically, if it is to be capable of seeing. Briefly put, we can understand that having a lens is part of how an eye ought to be. In this way we can grasp the particular structure of the eye as a matter of normative, rather than natural necessity. We can recognize it as lawlike, and hence attain understanding of it, in spite of its contingency with respect to natural laws.

How does this account of biological purposiveness as normative lawlikeness square with the account we arrived at from our reading of §10, on which organisms count as purposive because they appear to be produced in accordance with an antecedent concept or design? I now want to propose that they are essentially the same. To see this, let us go back to the first stage in Kant's development of the notion of purposiveness in §10. We saw in Section I that Kant defines purposiveness as "the causality of a concept in respect of its object." We also saw that he typically treats the term "purposiveness" as applying, not to this causality itself, but rather to the objects produced by this causality. Thus an object counts as purposive if it is caused by an antecedent concept of that object.

Now it is clear that, by the "causality of a concept in respect of its object," Kant is alluding to the kind of causality at work when an intelligent being – paradigmatically a human being – produces an object in accordance with design. But we need to look more closely at what kind of causality this is. For a concept can play a causal role in producing a corresponding object, yet without the causality involved being that of design. Imagine a painter who is so obsessed with a certain woman that every portrait he paints ends up looking like her. Despite his most conscientious efforts to depict the features of his actual model, it is always the woman of his obsession who appears on the canvas. Here the concept of the woman is causally efficacious in producing her likeness. But this is not the kind of causality which Kant has in mind. For the characteristic causality of design it is needed, not just that the concept influence the painter's behaviour, but that it govern it normatively. The concept has to function as a rule which represents to the painter how the painting ought to be.

This suggests that the idea of normativity is already implicit in Kant's initial notion of purposiveness as applied to artefacts. To say that an artefact is purposive is to say that an intelligent being produced it in accordance with a concept of how it ought to be.[22] But let us now consider, in this light, what it means to say that an object is merely "as if" produced in accordance with design. Here, I suggest, we are making the same claim, but without the reference to an intelligent being. This leaves us simply with the claim that the object accords with a concept of how it ought to be, or, in other words, that the object conforms to a normative constraint. Thus, Kant's characterization of purposiveness as normative lawfulness does not represent a departure from his claim that we ascribe purposiveness to objects in so far as they appear to be produced in accordance with design. Rather, it spells out what we are ascribing to objects when they appear to us to be produced in accordance with design. To regard an object as if it had been designed, yet without committing ourselves to the claim that it was designed, is just to judge that the object conforms to a concept of how it ought to be.

IV

I argued in the previous section that purposiveness in the biological context may be interpreted as conformity to normative constraint, and that this interpretation is compatible with Kant's characterization of purposiveness as the appearance of design. But there is an unclarity in the interpretation which can be brought out by considering an objection to the second of these two points. The objection consists in pointing out that there is a difference between saying that something appears to be designed, and saying that it conforms to a normative constraint.[23] Something can appear to be designed and yet fail to be as it ought to be, that is, as it appears designed to be. Yet to say that something conforms to a normative constraint implies that it succeeds in being as it ought to be.

This objection is related to the following, more general issue. We can distinguish two kinds of judgments which invoke the idea of a normative constraint. The first kind of judgment says that the object is *subject* to a normative constraint: that it is the kind of thing with respect to which normative evaluation is appropriate. The second kind of judgment takes for granted that the object is subject to a normative constraint, and claims the object *satisfies* that constraint. Of which kind, according to Kant, is a judgment of objective purposiveness? On the first option, to judge that an object is purposive is equivalent to judging that it is, or appears to be, designed. We judge that it is or appears to be produced by an agent acting in accordance with a normative constraint, and we leave open the question of whether it successfully conforms to the constraint. But, on the second option, we may judge whether or not an object is purposive only once we have already recognized that it is or appears to be designed. Then, to say that the object is purposive is to evaluate it as successfully conforming to the way it is, or appears, designed to be.

Much of what Kant says about objective purposiveness appears to support the second option. He repeatedly identifies objective purposiveness with the obviously evaluative notion of perfection (§15, 226–7; §16, 229; *EE* VIII, 228).[24] Moreover, in at least two places he describes the judgment of objective purposiveness as presupposing a concept of what the object ought to be, and judging whether the object conforms to that concept. One is near the beginning of the passage from *EE* X which I cited in the preceding section: in a teleological judgment we "think of a product of nature that there is something which it *ought to be*, and . . . judge it according to whether it indeed actually is that way" (240). Another is at §15, shortly after Kant has explicitly identified objective purposiveness with perfection:

> In order to judge objective purposiveness, we always require the concept of a purpose . . . which contains the ground of the inner possibility of the object. Now since a purpose in general is that whose *concept* can be seen as the ground of the possibility of the object itself, the concept of this, *what sort of thing [was für ein Ding] it ought [sollen] to be*, will . . . precede; and the agreement of the manifold in the thing with this concept . . . is the *qualitative perfection* of a thing. (227)

We cannot judge whether or not a thing is objectively purposive unless we already have a concept of how it ought to be, which can serve as a criterion by which to evaluate it as perfect or imperfect.

But other passages point towards the first option instead. Among them are those on which we drew, in Section I, to reach our initial understanding of purposiveness in terms of design. To say that something is produced by "the causality of a concept in respect of its object" (§10, 220) is not, at least on the face of it, to make an evaluative claim. The judgment we make does not presuppose a concept of how the object ought to be: rather, it asserts that there is such a concept. This is borne out by Kant's related discussion of the idea of a "natural purpose" in the Analytic of Teleological Judgment. There is no suggestion here that to call an object a purpose is to mark it out as sound rather than defective.[25] We regard something as a purpose, or purposive, in so far as our conception of its possibility depends on the assumption that its cause is rational as opposed to merely mechanical (§64, 370). Further evidence is provided by Kant's parenthetical remark that "the stone implements sometimes excavated from ancient burial mounds, which have a hole as if for a handle . . . betray distinctly in their shape a purposiveness, for which the purpose is unknown" (§17, 236n). Here, since we do not know the purpose of the implements, there can be no question of recognizing that they are perfect rather than imperfect. We call them purposive simply on the grounds that they appear to result from design, rather than from purely mechanical causes.

A first step towards resolving the issue is to recognize that an object's purposiveness, on the account given at §10, entails not just that the object is or appears to be designed, but also that it conforms to the real or apparent design. For in the case of a defective artefact or organism, the object fails to qualify as purposive in that it neither is, nor appears to be, produced by a concept of that very object. The potter who produces a misshapen vase produces it with a concept in mind: but the concept is of a vase with a different shape. That concept does not have "causality in respect of its object" since its object is not in fact produced; conversely, the vase which is produced is not caused by a concept of that particular vase. This suggests that Kant's official view corresponds to a third option, one which apparently combines the two already mentioned. To say that an object is purposive is to say both that it is subject to a normative constraint, and that it conforms to that constraint. But this resolution appears unsatisfactory. For it makes it seem as though the judgment of purposiveness can be analysed as the conjunction of two separate claims. Thus the notion of purposiveness – even aside from the further complications arising from its application in the aesthetic context – comes to look hybrid or derivative. It loses its status as a fundamental philosophical concept.

We can overcome the difficulty by recognizing that a judgment of purposiveness, even when construed as implying both that the object is subject to a normative constraint and that it conforms to that constraint, can be understood in a way that is primitive. To see this, we need to recognize two different contexts in which an object given in experience may be judged to conform to normative law. The first context is that suggested in those passages in which Kant identifies purposiveness with perfection. Here we first grasp how the object ought to be, and then evaluate it as sound or defective. For example, we grasp that this vase ought to be symmetrical in shape: and then we determine that, since it is in fact symmetrical, it conforms (at least in that respect) with how it ought to be. Or we grasp that this horseshoe crab ought to have eight legs: and then we determine that, since it in fact has eight legs, it is (again, at least in that respect) well-formed rather than impaired. We can be construed here as judging that the vase and the horseshoe crab are purposive, in so far as our judgment implies both that they ought to be a certain way, and that they are as they ought to be. But our judgment of purposiveness is clearly not primitive. For it reduces to the conjunction of these two implications.

But now – as a way of approaching the second context – consider what enables us to claim that the vase ought to be symmetrical and that the horseshoe crab ought to have eight legs. In the case of the vase, we may be able to determine this by asking the potter what she intended in making the vase, or by drawing on our knowledge that, as a general rule, potters mean to make their vases symmetrical. In the case of the horseshoe crab, however, this route is not available to us. We know that a horseshoe crab ought to have eight legs only because previous examination of healthy and unmutilated horseshoe crabs has shown that they in fact have eight legs. But how can we get from the observation that certain previously examined horseshoe crabs have eight legs, to the claim that this particular horseshoe crab ought to have eight legs? We may do so only by way of the judgment that this feature of the previously examined horseshoe crabs exemplifies a norm or standard to which all members of the kind ought to conform. If the examination of how certain horseshoe crabs in fact are, is to provide a basis for judging whether or not other horseshoe crabs are as they ought to be, then we must be able to judge that the horseshoe crabs in the initial sample conform to – in the sense of exemplifying – a normative rule saying how horseshoe crabs in general ought to be.

Here we have the second context in which we judge that a thing conforms to normative law. As in the first context, we recognize that the way the object is, is the way it ought to be. Yet in this context the judgment is primitive. For we do not first judge that the horseshoe crabs in the initial sample ought to have eight legs, and then judge that they conform to that constraint. Rather, our judging that they are as they ought to be is a condition of our judging that horseshoe crabs ought to have eight legs in the first place. It is only because we can take healthy and well-functioning horseshoe crabs to serve as exemplars of how a horseshoe crab ought to be, that we can take their features to represent normative constraints to which horseshoe crabs in general are subject.

Once we recognize the difference between the two ways of judging purposiveness that are appropriate to these two contexts, we can drop the artificial distinction between the initial sample and the rest of the kind. Any properly constituted organic being, or indeed artefact, may be taken as a guide to the normative standards governing its kind. By the same token, any properly constituted organic being or artefact may be assessed by the standards of its kind and judged to conform to them. One and the same object, then, can at one time serve as a guide to the standards, and at another time be evaluated as meeting them. In both cases, the object is judged to be purposive. The difference is that in the former case the standards are not presupposed, whereas in the latter case they are.

Now, when Kant identifies objective purposiveness with perfection or soundness, he has in mind that way of judging purposiveness in which the standards are presupposed. But when he appears to identify it with a thing's merely being subject to normative evaluation, he has in mind the other, more fundamental, way of judging purposiveness. For even though a judgment of this kind can be made only about properly consti-tuted organic beings and artefacts, the point of the judgment is not to mark them out as sound rather than defective. Rather, it is to contrast them with inorganic products of nature, which are not subject to normative evaluation at all. To go back to Kant's example in *EE* X, we judge that the features of a healthy eye represent, not just how eyes generally are, but how an eye ought to be. But in the case of a stone, the parallel claim can be denied. We can raise the question of whether a stone is purposive and answer it in the negative: it does not qualify as purposive, not because it is defective, but because its features – unlike those of a healthy eye – do not represent normative standards governing its kind.

V

In the previous two sections I proposed an interpretation of purposiveness as conformity to normative law. In developing this interpretation, I left the aesthetic context out of account, considering purposiveness only as it applies to organic beings and artefacts. But we can now see a point of connection with Kant's theory of the beautiful. For, as we saw in Section II, the idea of normative lawfulness or necessity plays a prominent role in Kant's account of aesthetic judgment. Judgments of beauty have the feature of necessity, in that they make a normative claim about how the object should be judged. "He who declares something to be beautiful insists that everyone *ought to* [*sollen*] approve of the object in question and likewise declare it to be beautiful" (§19, 237).

Moreover, it is clear from *EE* X that Kant intends us to recognize just this connection. The point of the section as a whole is to argue that aesthetic and teleological judgment alike require an a priori principle of judgment, on the grounds that they both involve an "ought." Kant begins the section with a discussion of aesthetic judgments in which he emphasizes their normativity:

they make claim to necessity, and say, not that everyone does judge this way – in which case they would be a task for explanation by empirical psychology – but that we *ought* to judge this way. (239)

It is in this context that he raises the topic of teleological judgment, claiming, in the passage from *EE* X which I discussed in the previous section, that "a teleological judgment compares the concept of a product of nature, according to that which it is, with what it *ought to be*." At the end of that passage, after discussing the example of the eye and the stone, he turns again to the parallel with aesthetic judgment. To take up the passage again, this time going a few lines further:

this "ought" [in a teleological judgment] contains a necessity which is sharply distinguished from the physico-mechanical necessity according to which a thing is possible according to mere laws of . . . efficient causes, and we can no more determine this necessity through merely physical (empirical) laws, than we can determine the necessity of the aesthetic judgment through psychological laws. (*EE* X, 240)

To see the connection more clearly, we should note that an aesthetic judgment does not merely make a normative demand, but also – like a teleological judgment – claims conformity to normative law. For in judging that other people ought to judge the object as I do, I am judging that my own act of judging is as it ought to be with respect to the object. The necessity of an aesthetic judgment, Kant says, is "*exemplary* . . . that is, a necessity of *everyone's* agreement with a judgment, which is seen as the example of a universal rule which cannot be stated [*angeben*]" (§18, 237). In making the judgment, I take it to conform to, in the sense of exemplifying, a universal standard for how the object should be judged. Thus an aesthetic judgment is like the primitive judgment of biological purposiveness by which we judge a healthy organism to exemplify the normative standards governing its kind. The difference is that the purposiveness is ascribed, not to the object about which the judgment is made, but rather to the subject's act of judging in relation to the object. It is my activity of judging the object, rather than the object itself, which I regard as exemplifying a normative standard; and the standard applies, not to all objects of a given kind, but rather to all subjects who are judging a given object.

I am suggesting, then, that the purposiveness ascribed in an aesthetic judgment is to be understood in terms of the judgment's claim to universal agreement, a claim by which the subject takes that judgment to conform to normative law. How does this interpretation cohere with the more familiar account of aesthetic purposiveness which Kant presents in the Analytic of the Beautiful? As we saw in Section II, this account is tied to the notion of the free play of the faculties. When we engage in the free play we feel pleasure in the object; and this pleasure is, in turn, awareness of purposiveness both in the activity of our faculties and in the object. But this account may seem incompatible with the interpretation I am suggesting. For the free play of the faculties and its accompanying pleasure are often read as independent of, and prior to, the aesthetic judgment's claim to universal agreement. According to both Crawford and Guyer, the free play, although described by Kant as the "aesthetic judging" of the object (§9, 218), is to be distinguished from the aesthetic judgment proper. In Guyer's terms, the free play of the faculties and the accompanying pleasure in the object's purposiveness belong not to aesthetic judgment, but to aesthetic response: the judgment of beauty with its claim to universal agreement represents a subsequent and independent stage in which we reflect on our aesthetic response and judge it to be universally valid.

However, as I have argued elsewhere,[26] this reading is mistaken. There is no evidence that Kant distinguishes two separate acts of judging, one leading to the feeling of pleasure and the other claiming the universal validity of the pleasure. Rather, he takes there to be a single, reflexive act of aesthetic judging, in which the subject claims the universal validity of that very act of judging. To make an aesthetic judgment about an object, in other words, is to judge that one is, in that very judgment, judging the object as it ought to be judged. Now to make such a judgment is both to feel pleasure in the object and to claim the universal validity of that pleasure. This is because pleasure, according to Kant, is the conscious-ness that my present mental state is a cause or ground of my being in that very mental state.[27] Thus, when I judge reflexively that I am judging the object as I ought to, I feel pleasure; for I am conscious that I ought to be in my present mental state, and hence that my mental state causes or grounds itself by making me aware that I ought to be in it. But I am also judging that the pleasure is universally valid; for if my mental state in making the judgment is one of pleasure, then in judging my judgment to be universally valid I am also judging my pleasure to be universally valid.

When Kant speaks of the "free play of the faculties," it is this act of judging to which he is referring. The point of his characterizing it in this way is to draw out its similarity and dissimilarity with a cognitive judg-ment. Because it is an act of judging, which makes a claim to universal validity, it makes sense to characterize it as involving the same faculties that are required for cognitive judging. But unlike an act of cognitive judging, it does not invoke any determinate rule or concept that says how the object ought to be judged. For this reason, it makes sense to describe the activity of the faculties as "free." We can see this last point more clearly by returning to the passage where Kant describes the necessity of the judgment as exemplary: the judgment, he says, "is seen as the ex-ample of a universal rule *which cannot be stated [angeben]*" (§18, 237; emphasis mine). In making the cognitive judgment that an object is, say, red or square, I claim – as I do in an aesthetic judgment – that everyone ought to judge the object as I do. But in the cognitive case I claim, more specifically, that everyone ought to judge it *as red* or *as square*. I invoke a determinate concept which governs how the object ought to be judged, and I take my judging to be as it ought to be only in so far as I take it to conform, more specifically, to the concepts "red" or "square." In the aesthetic case, by contrast, I take my judging to be as it ought to be without it being possible to specify some determinate rule to which it conforms. I judge that everyone ought to judge the object just as I do, where the only way to indicate how the object ought to be judged is through the example of my judgment itself.

This analysis allows us to accommodate the proposed account of aesthetic purposiveness with Kant's own characterizations of purposiveness in the aesthetic context. Pleasure in taste is "the consciousness of . . . purposiveness in the play of the subject's cognitive powers" (§12, 222) because it is the feeling that my cognitive powers are functioning as they ought with respect to the object. And the purposiveness is "merely formal" (ibid.) for the same reason I invoked in the previous paragraph to explain why the play of the faculties is "free." I judge – and in so doing, feel – that my faculties are functioning as they ought, yet without taking there to be any determinate rule or concept which governs how they ought to function. But there is also a sense in which I perceive purposiveness "in the object" (§17, 236; cf. §10, 220). For in judging that my state of mind is as it ought to be in relation to the object, I am also judging that the object elicits from me the state of mind which it ought to elicit. I am conscious that the pleasure is not merely caused in me by the object – as in the case of pleasure in the agreeable – but also appropriate to the object. Accordingly, my pleasure represents not just how the object does in fact affect me, but how it should affect me. I thus perceive the object as "subjectively" purposive, or purposive "for my cognitive faculties"; I am aware, that is, of a relation of appropriateness or fit between the object and the state of mind which it brings about in me.

We can now summarize the differences between aesthetic and biological purposiveness. The first difference – corresponding to the subjective character of aesthetic purposiveness – is that a judgment of aesthetic purposiveness does not ascribe normative lawfulness to the object in and of itself. Rather, it ascribes it to the subject's act of judging in its relation to the object (and, correlatively, to the object in its relation to the subject's act of judging).

The second difference – corresponding to the formal character of aesthetic purposiveness – is that the normative lawfulness ascribed in an aesthetic judgment is independent of any determinate law or standard. In a judgment of biological purposiveness, as we saw at the end of Section IV, we either evaluate the object as conforming to an already recognized standard, or take the object to exemplify a standard that is as yet unspecified, with the aim of identifying the relevant standard for objects of that kind. The ascription of aesthetic purposiveness conforms to neither of these models. It is closer to the second model than to the first, in that it ascribes normative lawfulness to my act of judging without subsuming it under an antecedent rule specifying how the object in question ought to be judged. But it departs even from the second model in so far as I cannot then go on to specify any such rule for judging the object. Having judged that a given horseshoe crab exemplifies the standards governing its kind, I can go on to specify that a horseshoe crab ought to have eight legs, five pairs of gills, six sets of pincers, and so on. But the standard exemplified by my act of aesthetic judging "cannot be stated" (§18, 237): I can judge only that the object ought to be judged on the example of my present act of judging.

This last contrast aside, the second model for judging biological purposiveness is crucial for understanding how purposiveness, in both the aesthetic and the biological case, can be identified with conformity to normative law. For it shows how we can judge something to conform to normative law without first conceiving an antecedent law to which we take it to conform: namely, by taking it to exemplify the law. As we saw at the end of Section IV, the point of such a judgment in the biological context is not to evaluate the thing as sound rather than defective. Rather it is to contrast it with things that merely *are* a certain way, as opposed to exemplifying how they (and others of their kind) *ought to be*. The same is true in the aesthetic context. The point of judging that my state of mind is purposive with respect to the object is not to say that it is appropriate rather than inappropriate, but rather to distinguish it from my state of mind in, say, a judgment of agreeableness, where the issue of appropriateness does not even arise. It is to register that the relation between the object and my state of mind is not exhausted by its merely causal character, but has a normative aspect as well. What is common to organic beings and objects of aesthetic appreciation, then, is that they both call for recognition of a normative dimension: in the one case, to the way they are, and in the other, to their relation to our mental faculties. They both require us to go beyond the factual claim that this is how something is, to the normative claim that this is how it ought to be.

VI

This interpretation may seem to leave us with a puzzle concerning the character of the normativity involved in judging that an organic being, or my act of aesthetic judging, is as it ought to be. The "ought" here is clearly not a moral "ought": a horseshoe crab missing a pair of legs is not morally deficient, and I can claim that you ought to share my pleasure in a beautiful object without taking you to be morally required to do so.[28] But nor is it the cognitive "ought" associated with the claims of the understanding or theoretical reason. I can recognize that you fail to feel pleasure in an object which I regard as beautiful without believing that you are judging irrationally or making a cognitive mistake. Moreover, it is certainly not on pain of irrationality that a horseshoe crab ought to have eight legs.

One way to get clearer about this sense of "ought" is to consider the example of artefacts. As we saw in Section I, Kant initially invites us to understand the purposiveness of organisms on the model of that of artefacts.[29] So it seems reasonable to adopt the view, already plausible in its own right, that we are dealing with a kind of normativity which is also applicable to artefacts. This promises to be helpful because the example of artefacts appears to give us more purchase on the "ought" than we get from considering organic beings or aesthetic reflection alone. When we say that this vase is defective because there are cracks in the glaze, or that the green light on this machine ought to go on when the battery is running low, we are comparing the artefact in each case with the antecedent concept or design which guided its production. (We would be wrong if the potter had in fact intended to produce a crackled glaze, or if the manufacturer had intended that the green light should indicate that the machine was on.) But, as I briefly suggested in Section IV, the "ought" invoked in the concept applies not only to the artefact, but to the maker's activity. The concept of the artefact, in specifying how it ought to be, normatively governs the maker's behaviour in producing it.

This might lead us to think that the "ought" in question, while not necessarily a moral "ought," is still one of practical rationality. For we might assume that the concept, in so far as it governs the maker's actions in producing the object, represents to the maker what it is rational for him or her to do. In conforming her activity to an antecedent design, we might think, the maker is conforming to the rational requirement that she pursue the means to her ends. Consider a dressmaker who takes it that she ought to conform to the pattern agreed on with the client, because otherwise the client will be unhappy and may refuse to pay. Or consider a contractor who takes herself to be bound by the architect's plans on the grounds that failure to conform would compromise the safety of the building and perhaps result in someone's death. These examples suggest that the normativity invoked in saying how an artefact ought to be, is that of an imperative of practical reason.

Drawing on this understanding of the normativity of artefacts, we might then try to interpret the biological and aesthetic "ought" in terms of practical rationality also. We might suggest that what we mean by saying that an eye ought to be capable of seeing, or that a horseshoe crab ought to have eight legs, is that it is rational that an eye should be capable of seeing and that a horseshoe crab should have eight legs. But the rationality, on this suggestion, is not of course the rationality of the eye or the horseshoe crab, but rather of their hypothetical designer. To say that a horseshoe crab ought to have eight legs, on this suggestion, is to say that if a horseshoe crab were in fact the product of design, it would be rational for the designer to bring it about that it had eight legs. The same approach could be applied to the aesthetic case. In judging an object to be beautiful, I claim that my mental faculties ought to be working just as they are with respect to this particular object. But this is to say that there is something rational about the arrangement whereby my faculties respond as they do to this particular object. It is to say that if there were a creator responsible both for my existence and that of the object, that creator would have acted rationally in bringing it about that my mental faculties respond to the object in the way that they in fact do.

However, there is something implausible about this result. Intuitively, there does not seem to be anything irrational about a hypothetical creator who makes horseshoe crabs (or creatures resembling horseshoe crabs in every other respect) with three or five pairs of legs rather than four. Similarly it is not clear why such a creator would be rationally motivated to arrange that we find beauty in flowers as opposed to toads. We can recognize a degree of rationality in many organic arrangements, for example the hollow bones which make a bird suitable for flying (§61, 360). But, as illustrated by the example of the horseshoe crab's legs, the claim that certain features are normative for a given kind does not seem to rely on the belief that a creator would be rationally motivated to produce the kind accordingly.

This suggests that the "ought" with which we are concerned is not, after all, the ought of practical rationality. But this does not mean that it is different from the "ought" that applies to artefacts. For I now want to argue that it is a mistake to interpret the normativity associated with design as that of the imperatives of practical reason. While questions of practical rationality do indeed arise in the production of artefacts, the notion of design is tied to a thinner sense of normativity which does not derive from the demands of rationality. To produce something in accordance with design is to think of one's activity as guided by a rule whose normative force is independent of the value of the product and thus of the rationality of bringing it into existence.

The point may be illustrated by an example. Bored during a lecture, a student draws a chequerboard pattern in the margin of his notes by sketching a grid and then carefully filling in the alternating squares. Like that of the dressmaker or the contractor in our earlier examples, his activity is normatively guided by a concept of how the product ought to be. But the "ought" is not the ought of rationality, in that he does not take himself to have a reason for drawing that, or any other, pattern. He does not recognize the pattern, either as good in itself, or as a means to some further good. The rule he is following carries a normative force simply *qua* rule, and independently of the further question of whether it is rationally desirable for him to adopt that rule as governing his behaviour. I take this point to carry over to cases where questions of practical rationality do play a role. It may be rational, in the interests of safety, for a building contractor to adhere to the architect's plan. The contractor, recognizing this, may take it as a matter of practical rationality that she do what is required for the building to conform to the plan. But, quite independently of this, she recognizes the plan to have a normative force, simply in so far as she allows it to govern her activity. Even if she thinks the plan is a bad one, which would result in an unsafe and hence rationally undesirable building, she still recognizes it as specifying how the building ought – in the thin sense – to be.

Against this, it might be objected that my initial example is self-contradictory. I specified that the student who draws the chequerboard pattern does not recognize it as a good: he sees no value in it, either in itself or as a means to a further end. But it seems clear that his drawing the pattern is the result of a free choice. He does not produce the pattern passively, as if by instinct; rather, he brings it about through an exercise of will. And Kant indeed seems to be making just this point when he describes art (by which he means, not just fine art, but the production of human artefacts generally) as "production through freedom, that is through a will which lays reason at the basis of its actions" (§43, 303). Thus it is only by analogy that we can describe a honeycomb as made by the art of bees, because the bees "do not ground their work on any reflection of reason [*Vernunftüberlegung*]" (ibid.). Now, as Christine Korsgaard has persuasively argued, Kant holds that we recognize our ends to have a value simply in so far as they are the objects of our free and rational choice. "The fact that you will an end *is a reason* for the end . . . your willing the end in a sense makes it good."[30] But this makes it seem as though the bored student must ascribe at least some value to the pattern he has chosen to draw. He must regard it as good simply in so far as it is the object of his will.

The objector is right to point out that the production of the chequerboard pattern is an act of will rather than the mere effect of instinct. For on at least one possible definition, the will is a capacity "to produce objects corresponding to representations" (*Critique of Practical Reason*, 5:15); it is the "capacity of acting in accordance with purposes" (§64, 370), where a purpose, as we have seen, need be no more than a concept which is regarded as the ground of the actuality of its object. However, it is not clear that, simply by virtue of adopting such a concept as a guide to action, the agent regards the object of that concept as a good. There is a distinction to be made between setting oneself to act in accordance with a rule or concept generally, and setting oneself to act in accordance with the particular kind of rule or principle which Kant calls a maxim. And while it is plausible that, in adopting the maxim of an action, one recognizes the purpose of that action as a good, the same need not hold true for other kinds of rules, specifically for the kind of rule exemplified by a design or blueprint. The maxim of an action specifies both the action to be performed and the purpose of carrying out the action. It gives the agent's reason for performing the action, and hence explains why the agent sees the action as rationally desirable.[31] But in conforming my activity of drawing to a chequerboard pattern, I am not thereby adopting a maxim. For the rule simply specifies the outcome which I set myself to bring about; it does not give the reason which motivates me to bring about that outcome. So my adoption of the rule does not imply that I take the outcome of my activity to be rationally desirable.

Applying this to the example of the bored student, we must distinguish between the maxim which the student adopts in choosing to draw the chequerboard pattern rather than to listen to the lecture, and that rule in the following of which the student's action consists. A possible maxim might be: "I will draw a chequerboard pattern in my notes for the sake of avoiding boredom." But the action that the student thereby wills to perform consists in the deliberate following of a rule which is distinct from the maxim: namely the chequerboard pattern (or the representation of the chequerboard pattern) itself. Now in so far as the student wills to draw the chequerboard pattern, he regards the drawing of it as a good, since he recognizes it as a means to avoiding boredom. But this does not mean that he regards the outcome of his conformity to the pattern – that is to say the alternating black and white squares on the paper – as a good. He conforms to the maxim, and thereby achieves the good of avoiding boredom, even if he accidentally fills in two adjacent squares and thus fails to conform to the pattern.[32]

If this discussion is on the right lines, the case of artefacts reveals a sense of "ought" which is distinct from the "ought" of practical rationality in that we can recognize that something ought to be the case without ascribing any value to it. We might note, for further clarification, that this sense of "ought" is sometimes expressed in English by the expressions "meant to" or "supposed to." Thus if the contractor in our earlier example follows the architect's specifications even though they call for an unsafe building, we can represent her as thinking, say: "This building is supposed to have only two fire exits, but it really ought to have four." The "supposed to" here is normative: she is not merely describing the architect's intentions, but registering that they serve as a rule saying how the building should be. But it expresses a thin sense of normativity which is compatible with the idea that violation of the rule may be rationally desirable.

This should remove some of the puzzlement about the "ought" of aesthetic and biological purposiveness. Even though it is not the normativity of theoretical or practical reason, there is nothing mysterious about it. For in this respect it is just like the familiar normativity associated with design and with rule-following more generally. However, this conclusion raises another difficulty. What entitles us to invoke this normativity in the case of organisms and the workings of our own faculties, where we have no ground for asserting the existence of a designer? How can we speak of how an organism is "meant to" be if we have no evidence that an intelligent being meant for it to be that way?

This is a large and difficult question. But rather than seeing it as an obstacle to interpreting purposiveness in terms of normativity, we may understand it as one of the motivating questions of the *Critique of Judgment* as a whole. If I am right in understanding purposiveness as suggested here, Kant's claim that we ascribe purposiveness to nature and to our reflection on beautiful objects amounts to the claim that we are committed to an "ought" which, like that of design, belongs neither to theoretical nor to practical reason, but which, unlike that of design, has no empirical warrant. Our right to invoke this "ought" in these contexts thus requires an a priori justification: but it is a justification which falls outside the province both of the *Critique of Pure Reason* and of the *Critique of Practical Reason*. Answering the question of how this use of "ought" is legitimate, then, can be seen as one of the tasks for which a third Critique is needed.

NOTES

This essay expands on a shorter paper, "Purposiveness and Normativity," read at the Eighth International Kant Congress in 1995 and published in vol. II of *Proceedings of the Eighth International Kant Congress*, ed. Hoke Robinson (Milwaukee: Marquette University Press, 1995). Earlier versions were also read at Massachusetts Institute of Technology, New York University, and the Midwest Seminar in the History of Modern Philosophy. I am grateful to audiences on those occasions for helpful discussion, and to Christine Korsgaard and Andrews Reath for valuable written comments.

1. See Section II.
2. Schopenhauer, Appendix to Volume I of *Die Welt als Wille und Vorstellung*, in his *Sämtliche Werke* (Frankfurt am Main: Cotta-Insel, 1960), Vol. I, p. 711. A similar view is held by Konrad Marc-Wogau, who describes the connection

between aesthetic and teleological judgment as "in the highest degree forced" (*Vier Studien zu Kants Kritik der Urteilskraft* [Uppsala: Uppsala Universitets Årsskrift, 1938], 34n), and Lewis White Beck, who describes Kant's aesthetic theory as "forced into an alien mold" by its juxtaposition with Kant's teleological theory (*Early German Philosophy* [Cambridge: Harvard University Press, 1969], p. 497). This view is opposed, on grounds different from those presented here, in Richard Aquila, "Unity of Organism, Unity of Thought, and the Unity of the *Critique of Judgment*" in *The Southern Journal of Philosophy* 30, Supplement (1991): 139–55.

3. Unless otherwise noted, I use the expression "aesthetic purposiveness" as shorthand for the purposiveness ascribed in what Kant calls a pure judgment of taste or a judgment of free beauty. This is somewhat misleading, because the term "aesthetic" also applies to the agreeable, to the sublime, and to dependent beauty, and Kant sometimes describes these also as involving purposiveness. However, of the various possible kinds of purposiveness which are aesthetic in the broad sense, it is only the purposiveness associated with pure judgments of taste which plays a significant systematic role in the *Critique of Judgment* as a whole. Another qualification to be noted is that, in discussing purposiveness generally, I leave out of this account what Kant calls "outer" or "relative" purposiveness. This is because Kant's own characterizations of purposiveness *simpliciter* do not apply to outer purposiveness, and thus the notion of outer purposiveness appears to be peripheral to the sense of purposiveness with which Kant is primarily concerned and which is the focus of this essay.

4. References beginning with a Roman numeral or an Arabic numeral preceded by "§" are to the *Critique of Judgment* (Roman numerals refer to sections in the Introduction and arabic numerals preceded by "§" refer to sections in the main text); the number following indicates the page number according to the pagination of Volume 5 of the *Akademie* edition of Kant's collected writings (Berlin: De Gruyter, 1902–). References to the First Introduction ("Erste Einleitung") to the *Critique of Judgment* are abbreviated "*EE*" and include the section number and the page number according to the pagination of volume 20 of the *Akademie* edition. References to other works by Kant cite volume and page number of the *Akademie* edition. All translations are my own.

5. See also *EE* VI, 217. For the "as if" locution see *EE* I, 200; *EE* IX, 232; §64, 370.

6. This should be noted to forestall the criticism that the concept of being "as if designed" is so broadly applicable as to be vacuous. Marc Bedau raises this criticism in connection with C. D. Broad's use of the concept, pointing out, for example, that many stones are as if designed for use as paperweights ("Against Mentalism in Teleology," *American Philosophical Quarterly* 27[1] [1990]: 66–7). But on Kant's view such stones are not "as if designed" because we can understand them as a product of blind mechanical forces. Thus it should be clear that the criticism does not apply to Kant's view.

7. Purposiveness in this sense applies also, although with qualifications, to nature as a whole (§68, 380) and to organic nature as a system of living things (§82, 427). But my discussion of biological purposiveness will bear only on the purposiveness of living things and their organs.

8. Kant describes biological purposiveness as "objective" throughout. He de-

scribes it as "real" in the First Introduction (*EE* VI, 217; *EE* VII, 221; *EE* IX, 236) and also in the published introduction at VIII, 193; he describes it as "material" at *EE* VIII, 228; §63, 366. The purposiveness of artefacts is described as material at §48, 188, and as real at §62, 364.

9. Kant seems to use these expressions interchangeably. It might be thought that the identification of aesthetic purposiveness with "purposiveness according to form" commits Kant to a doctrine of aesthetic formalism. If this is so, then, as Paul Guyer argues (*Kant and the Claims of Taste*, Cambridge: Harvard University Press, 1979 [henceforth abbreviated *KCT*], ch. 6), Kant is not entitled to regard the form of purposiveness as equivalent to, or entailing, purposiveness according to form. Discussion of this issue lies beyond the scope of this essay.

10. This is discussed further in my "Kant on the Subjectivity of Taste," in *Kant's Aesthetics*, ed. Herman Parret (Berlin: Walter de Gruyter, 1996).

11. This is also the account given in the "Deduction of Taste" at §38. A somewhat different account is given at §22.

12. Kant also suggests that we ascribe purposiveness to the representation of the object (§11, 221). Since I do not think Kant makes a principled distinction between the representation of the object and the activity of representing it, I take this to be equivalent to saying that we ascribe purposiveness to the activity of our faculties in judging the object.

13. Donald Crawford, *Kant's Aesthetic Theory* (Madison: University of Wisconsin Press, 1974), pp. 93–4. Cf. also Clark Zumbach, *The Transcendent Science* (The Hague: Martinus Nijhoff Publishers, 1984), pp. 52–3, who suggests that works of art, for Kant, are analogous to organisms.

14. Cf. Kant's discussion of crystals at §58, 348–50. A variant of Crawford's approach is offered by Mary McCloskey, who identifies aesthetic purposiveness with the appearance, not of having been designed *tout court*, but of having been designed in order to please us. On her view, Kant "thinks of beautiful things 'as if' they had been designed in order to be reflected upon by us with pleasure" (*Kant's Aesthetic* [Albany: State University of New York Press, 1987], p. 67). Although this view appears to do better justice to the subjective character of aesthetic purposiveness, it remains subject to the same fundamental difficulty. Since we can understand the possibility of beautiful things without the assumption of design, we have no basis for saying that they are "as if" designed, whether for the sake of pleasing us or for any other purpose.

15. *KCT* 218; see also Guyer, *Kant and the Experience of Freedom* (Cambridge University Press, 1993 [henceforth abbreviated *KEF*]), 417n39. (I am simplifying Guyer's view by combining his account in *KCT*, which emphasizes a distinction between aesthetic purposiveness and the purposiveness of artefacts, with his account in *KEF*, which contrasts aesthetic purposiveness with the purposiveness of those things, presumably organisms, which are unintelligible except on the assumption of design.) Guyer motivates his approach with a useful criticism of the view that there is a "characteristic appearance of designed objects" (*KEF* 417; see also *KCT* 220–3).

16. *KEF* 417n39.

17. I believe that there are also some intrinsic difficulties in Guyer's account of aesthetic purposiveness, and in particular that it is incompatible with Kant's view that pleasure in beauty is independent of the recognition that the object

satisfies an aim. See my "On the Key to Kant's Critique of Taste," *Pacific Philosophical Quarterly*, 72(4) (1991): 293–4.

18. Other relevant passages are §15, 277; §16, 229; §48, 311.

19. My translation of the word *sollen* in this context as "ought to" may seem questionable. Although *sollen* is usually translated in this way, it seems more natural in this passage to use the locutions "is meant to" or "is supposed to." However, as we will see in Section V, *sollen* is used earlier in *EE* X in a context that unambiguously calls for translation as "ought to" or "should"; and it is clear from the overall line of argument in *EE* X that Kant is using the word in the same sense throughout the section. In any case, since "is meant to" and "is supposed to" carry a normative implication, their use to translate *sollen* would not invalidate the point I am making, although it would make it harder to express. There is more discussion of this point in Section VI.

20. As part of an argument against analysing sentences like "The horse is a four-legged animal" in normative terms, Michael Thompson denies that we can say of a horse that it ought *simpliciter* to have four legs. We have to specify the "ought" by saying, for example: "It ought *as far as its merely being a horse goes* to be four-legged" or "it is supposed *by its mere horse-nature* to be four-legged" ("The Representation of Life," in *Virtues and Reasons*, ed. Rosalind Hursthouse, Gavin Lawrence, and Warren Quinn, [Oxford: Clarendon Press, 1995], p. 290). On this point, I disagree with Thompson. It seems to me to be distinctive of organic beings, in contrast to inorganic natural things, that we can take it that they ought, without qualification, to have certain features. Consider a diseased eye that is used for teaching students of ophthalmology about a rare and interesting defect. We might say that this eye is just as it ought to be *qua* teaching aid. But this would not prevent us from also saying, this time without qualification, that it was defective. We would not need to specify that it was defective *qua* eye; indeed, this might carry the misleading suggestion that its soundness *qua* teaching tool and its defectiveness *qua* eye were somehow on a par.

21. I derive this from §64, 370: "reason ... must cognize ... the necessity in every form of a natural product, if it is indeed merely to understand [*wenn sie auch nur ... einsehen will*] the conditions connected with its production."

22. This point is suggested by a number of passages where Kant identifies the concept underlying the production of an object with the concept of how it ought to be. See the first two sentences of the passage from *EE* X, 240, quoted at the beginning of this section; see also §15, 277 (quoted later in this section), and §48, 311.

23. I am grateful to Kevin Thompson for helping me see the importance of this point.

24. More specifically, it is inner objective purposiveness which he identifies with perfection; outer objective purposiveness is identified with usefulness. But the notion of outer purposiveness lies beyond our present concerns.

25. It is true that Kant describes natural purposes as possessing "inner natural perfection" (§65, 370). But he is not suggesting that the point of calling them natural purposes is to say that they are perfect rather than imperfect.

26. "On the Key to Kant's Critique of Taste."

27. See for example §10, 220, where Kant defines pleasure as "the consciousness of the causality of a representation in respect of the subject's state *to maintain* the subject in the same state"; see also *EE* III, 206; *EE* VIII, 230–1.

These and other passages are discussed in my "On the Key to Kant's Critique of Taste." Note also that the definition of pleasure at §10 follows soon after the definition of purposiveness as the "causality of a concept in respect of its object." This indicates that the "causality" in the definition of pleasure may be understood, not only as natural causality according to psychological laws (in which case the pleasure is pleasure in the agreeable), but also as the causality invoked in the definition of purposiveness, namely the causality of a normative rule in bringing about an outcome which conforms to it (for this distinction see the example of the obsessed painter in Section IV). It is in this sense that my mental state in an aesthetic judgment "causes" me to be maintained in that state.

28. There is a connection between taste and morality, but it is too indirect to warrant identification of the "ought" in taste with the moral "ought."

29. Kant does emphasize that the analogy with artefacts has serious limitations (§65, 374). But these limitations do not affect the present point.

30. "The Normativity of Instrumental Reason," in *Ethics and Practical Reason*, ed. Garrett Cullity and Berys Gaut (Oxford: Oxford University Press, 1997). See also Korsgaard, "Kant's Argument for the Formula of Humanity," *Kant-Studien*, 77 (1986): 183–202, pp. 196–7.

31. I am here drawing again on Korsgaard's interpretation.

32. The point argued in the last five paragraphs is supported by Kant's distinction between an object's being a purpose and the existence of that object being a purpose (§67, 378; cf. also §63, 368 and §82, 425–6), a distinction which is connected with that between inner and outer purposiveness. Kant's aim is to distinguish between a natural thing's being purposive in virtue of having the kind of structure which is only intelligible on the assumption of an antecedent design, and its being purposive in virtue of being useful for some further purpose, or more generally, existing for a reason. Even though Kant concludes that we are inevitably led to regard things that are purposive in the first sense as purposive in the second sense also (§82, 425–6), he makes clear that there is a distinction in principle between the two senses. I take this to imply a corresponding distinction between an object's conforming to a rule or design, and its having a value: a distinction that is close to the one I have been trying to make in the text. Kant's distinctions in the First Introduction between technical and practical purposiveness (*EE* IX, 243), and in the published Introduction between the technically-practical and the morally-practical (I, 172) may provide further support. (I am grateful to Stephen Engstrom for helpful discussion of this issue.)

Kant on Ends and
the Meaning of Life

THOMAS W. POGGE

Around 1790, Kant thought intensively and movingly about the point of the universe and our role within it.[1] In this essay I try to bring these reflections to life by unifying and expanding them into a plausible account. This involves an exploration of Kant's diverse uses of the word "end" – as in "end in itself" and "final end."

I. Two Senses of *Zweck*

In the *Metaphysics of Morals*, Kant defines *end* (*Zweck*) as "an object of *Willkür* [of a rational being] through the representation of which it is determined to an action of producing this object" (*MdS* 6:381).[2] According to this definition, which fits most occurrences of the word throughout Kant's writings, ends are what we more commonly call aims or goals: namely states of affairs or events that one has in mind while acting and tries to attain through one's conduct.

In light of many other passages, it is appropriate to construe this definition broadly, by including goals that have one or more of the following four features: (1) *graduated* goals: whose attainment is a matter of degree (to become a top pianist); (2) *open-ended* goals: whose attainment is capable of indefinite augmentation (to become strong, wealthy, happy, secure); (3) *conservative* goals: to extend into the future a state of affairs that already obtains (to keep my weight below 140 lbs); and (4) *holistic* goals: to attain an overall pattern that includes elements of the past or present (that the Nazi crimes be punished). In all cases, an agent who sets herself a goal aims for some event or state of affairs of which she believes that it does not yet (fully) exist, that its coming to exist (fully) is not a matter of course, and that her efforts can contribute to its coming to exist (fully).

This broad construal of "end" fits many uses of the word in the *Groundwork*, but not all. For Kant also introduces, as one formulation of the categorical imperative, the command to "act so as to treat humanity, whether in your own person or that of any other, never merely as a means, but always also as an end" (*G* 4:429) and he often speaks of treating every person (or human being or rational being) never solely as a means but always also as an end or end in itself (*Zweck an sich*). Here ends are not states of affairs or events, which we might represent and then try to attain: The message of the categorical imperative is surely not that we are to treat persons or their humanity as aims or goals. Rather, ends in this sense are fully existing entities (or attributes), which we are to respect by restraining our conduct and adjusting our goals in appropriate ways. And Kant acknowledges this difference by defining *end*, in this context, more inclusively as "ground of [the will's] self-determination" (*G* 4:427).[3]

How does Kant come to use the word "end" in the second sense? The phrase "for the sake of" may give a clue. It can take on ends in both senses: We say of agents that they do, or ought to, act or hold back for the sake of achieving some outcome – and also for the sake of another person. Formulations of the first sort always leave room for further questions: When it is said that she organizes a party for the sake of making him happy, we can always ask whether she wants to make him happy for the sake of attaining some further goal. Formulations of the second sort leave no such room: When told that she organizes a party for his sake, we are thereby also told that there is no further link – his good is the ultimate point of the party (though one can still ask how the party is to contribute to his good). Kant may thus have thought of ends in themselves as beings for whose sake we sometimes do, or ought to, act or act differently than we would otherwise have wanted to.

These reflections fit well, I think, with Kant's thinking in the *Groundwork*. The *Critique of Judgment* suggests a further, related possibility (discussed below), which moves the two senses even closer together: Ends in themselves, though not beings whom *we* could make our aim or goal, can be conceived of as the aim of a hypothetical creator. As far as we can understand, such a creator must have created the whole world for the sake of creating us, that is, must have created the world for our sake. Ends in themselves are then beings worthy of being the end (goal) of creating the world, of being created for their own sakes.

There are then at least two senses of "end" at work in Kant's texts. In its first sense, the word refers to ends as goals (aims, targets, objectives): events or states of affairs to be brought about. In its second sense it refers to ends in themselves: beings "whose existence has in itself an absolute value" (*G* 4:428) and who therefore ought to be treated with respect.

Kant is not always fully aware that he is using "end" in these two senses. He does show through his fourth example (the maxim of never helping others in distress, *G* 4:430) that failing to treat another as an end in itself need not involve, and is therefore more inclusive than, treating another solely as means to one's own ends. He also speaks of a realm of ends as "a whole of all ends (both of rational beings as ends in themselves and also of the personal ends that each may set himself)" (*G* 4:433) and distinguishes between ends to be produced (*zu bewirkende*) and free-standing (*selbständige*) ends (*G* 4:437). But then he is also capable of conflating the distinction between ends as goals and ends in themselves with the quite different distinction between subjective and objective ends – distinguishing between "merely subjective ends, whose existence, as effect of our action, has a value *for us*; [and] *objective ends*, that is, things whose existence is in itself an end" (*G* 4:428, cf. 4:431).

This must be a slip. For Kant elsewhere applies the relevant subjec-tive–objective distinction *within* the domain of ends as goals, character-izing *subjective* goals as those a rational being actually has and *objective* goals as ones a rational being ought to have.[4] He says that objective goals "depend on motives valid for every rational being" (*G* 4:427). All rational beings have motives, inherent in their pure practical reason, for adopting certain abstract goals (e.g., to promote the welfare of others) and, in specific circumstances, more specific derivative goals (e.g., to make sure that Jim here gets a nutritious meal now). Though every rational being has a reason-based motive to pursue any goal that is obligatory for her, human beings are free to disregard such motives, free to adopt or not to adopt any obligatory goal.[5]

Let me stress two special features of this subjective–objective distinc-tion. First, "subjective" and "objective" do not stand in opposition here. A goal that qualifies, or fails to qualify, for one predicate can also qualify, or fail to qualify, for the other. All four combinations are possible: Obligatory goals one actually has (objective and subjective), obligatory goals one fails to have (objective and nonsubjective), nonobligatory goals one has (nonobjective and subjective), and nonobligatory goals one does not have (nonobjective and nonsubjective). Second, "subjec-tive" does not indicate a reference to the agent's perspective. An agent does (or at least can and should), within her own perspective, use both concepts, that is, distinguish not merely goals she does and those she does not have, but also goals that are and those that are not obligatory for her. Perhaps she can be mistaken about what goals she actually has (failure of self-knowledge) or about what goals she ought to have (moral error). If so, then her believed subjective goals could differ from her true subjective goals, or her believed objective goals from her true objective goals.

It is now clear that, contrary to Kant's confused passage (*G* 4:428), not only ends in themselves, but also goals, can be objective. Conversely, one might also (though Kant does not) speak of subjective ends in themselves. These would be any entities (or attributes) that an agent actually treats with respect (i.e., in the way ends in themselves ought to be treated). Objective ends in themselves, by contrast, are entities that ought to be treated with respect – by every rational being, since there is no relativity to circumstances here.

When applied to ends in themselves, "subjective" and "objective" again do not stand in opposition – an end in itself can be subjective or objective or both or neither. Interesting here is the possibility of subjective but nonobjective ends in themselves, exemplified by an agent who treats her dog with respect. The second special feature of the subjective–objective distinction also transfers from ends as goals to ends in themselves: Our dog lover can, within her own perspective, realize that her dog, though she is treating it with the respect due a being that has an absolute value, is not an (objective) end in itself (not something that ought to be treated with respect by every rational being). Or would her mere thought that the dog is not an objective end in itself show disrespect, entailing that she is not treating it as an end in itself? Be this as it may, one surely cannot dispute the converse: that it is possible for our dog lover to realize, within her own perspective, that her husband, though she is not treating him with the respect due a being who has an absolute value, is in fact such a being, that is, an objective end in itself. As before, perhaps an agent can be mistaken about what entities she actually treats with respect (failure of self-knowledge) or about what entities she ought to treat thus (moral error). If so, then her believed subjective ends in themselves could differ from her true subjective ends in themselves, or her believed objective ends in themselves from her true objective ends in themselves.

We might even extend this subjective–objective distinction to the word "means," which Kant uses in a novel sense in contrast to "end in itself": An objective means is anything that is not an objective end in itself and hence not to be treated with respect (cf. *G* 4:428). And something is a subjective means for a person just in case this person does not actually treat it with respect.

The two concept pairs of means/end differ importantly. The familiar means/goal pair expresses an asymmetrical relation: Every means is a means to, and thus (conceptually) presupposes, some goal, while goals do not (conceptually) presuppose means at all. The relation is also iterative: C may be a means to B, and B a means to A.[6] In this case, B is a means in one respect and an end in another. Kant uses the word "end" freely in reference to such goals that, in another respect, are merely means.

The other means/end pair expresses not a relation but a distinction: between entities that do and those that do not have an absolute value. Entities of the two kinds do not presuppose each other – the world might have contained entities of only one kind. The distinction is exhaustive in its domain: Every entity is either an end in itself or a mere means.[7] The means/goal distinction has no such exhaustiveness: What is not my goal need not therefore be my means.

The two pairs are conceptually related: Treating a person solely as a means to goals (i.e., making use of him without concern for his good and his goals) involves failing to treat him as an end in itself. But the converse does not hold. One can fail to treat someone as an end in itself without using him in an attempt to attain one's goals – for example, by simply ignoring him.[8] When Kant speaks of treating a person merely as a means, he may then have in mind either the narrower or the wider sense – or both.

II. Objective Ends and Objective Goals

How can Kant show that there are objective ends in themselves and objective goals, and how are they substantively related to each other? Kant offers the following account of objective (obligatory) goals (cf. *G* 4:413n, 4:460n; *KpV* 5:34). In the case of nonmoral conduct, an agent is motivated by a subjective goal to adopt a maxim (principle of action) that is designed to govern her effective pursuit of this goal. Someone who wants to run a profitable store, for example, may be motivated by this goal to adopt the maxim of giving correct change (*G* 4:397). In the case of moral conduct ("from duty"), an agent is motivated to adopt a maxim not by any goal, but by the categorical imperative.[9] Conduct on this maxim, however, is nevertheless directed toward some goal, as all action must be according to Kant (e.g., *KpV* 5:34; *Religion* 6:4; *MdS* 6:384f.). One difference between moral and nonmoral conduct is then that, with the former, the agent is committed to its goal for the sake of its maxim, whereas, with the latter, she is committed to its maxim for the sake of its goal. Objective goals are then, so to speak, byproducts of the adoption of maxims that the categorical imperative prescribes.[10] So we can say that (the recognition of) an objective goal presupposes (the recognition of) an obligatory maxim, which in turn presupposes (the recognition of) the bindingness on us of the categorical imperative.

Following this train of thought further, we find that (the recognition of) the bindingness of the categorical imperative presupposes (the recognition of) objective ends in themselves (*G* 4:428f.). The reason is this: The categorical imperative requires that one act only on maxims one can will to be universal laws. One must not arrogate to oneself a freedom of action that one could not will to be available to everyone (including oneself) at all times. This proposed thought experiment raises the obvious question of who is to be included in the scope of this "everyone," and on what grounds. Kant's answer here, in the discussion of the second formula, is that all and only persons (or rational beings) are to be included.[11] He reemphasizes this point in terms of his third formula: We must choose our maxims as if we were legislating for a realm of ends in which rational beings, and they alone, have membership. And he confirms it once more when he insists that any duties we have in regard to animals are derivative of duties to (human) persons: Cruel treatment of animals is wrong because it tends to destroy our natural sentiment of sympathy (*Mitgefühl*) for the suffering of human beings – a sentiment Kant considered "very serviceable to morality."[12]

The hypothetical universalization required by the categorical imperative is then universal only within a certain carefully stipulated domain; and its results crucially depend upon this stipulation: We are permitted to eat animals even if we cannot will a universal law permitting all sentient beings to eat one another. And we are not permitted to defraud Africans even if we can will a universal law permitting all Caucasians to do so. This point lends urgency to the second half of our question: On what grounds are all persons included, and on what grounds only they? The cited *Groundwork* passage (*G* 4:428f.) gives Kant's answer: Because persons, and only they, are objective ends in themselves. This answer leads to the next question: What renders persons, and only them, objective ends in themselves?

Kant replies that persons qualify by virtue of their pure practical reason, their capacity to recognize and to commit themselves to objective goals, prescribed by duties. This capacity involves a certain negative freedom of the will (that we can determine ourselves to action independently of our inclinations) and also a certain positive freedom of the will (that our practical reason, which identifies objective goals as such, has motivational force): "A person is any subject whose actions are capable of imputation. Therefore moral personality is nothing but the freedom of a rational being under moral laws."[13]

This answer is both weaker and stronger than it might have been. It is weak in that Kant requires, for the status of objective end in itself, merely the *capacity* to commit oneself to moral duties and obligatory goals.[14] It is strong in that it would exclude humans of the sort we all are according to Hume. It excludes, that is, beings who are quite intelligent as regards their understanding and theoretical as well as empirical practical reason, but in whom these faculties are practically subservient to their inclinations. Their reason would be the slave of their passions (Hume); they could, in Kant's terms, have only pathological but no practical interests (*G* 4:413n).[15] Such beings might be able to recognize a moral law in a cognitive way, and they might even follow it if they came to believe that doing so would best serve their inclinations in the long run.[16] But they could not be committed to it for its own sake, and hence would not qualify as ends in themselves. If there were such beings interspersed among us, and if we could reliably identify them,[17] then, according to Kant's mature philosophy, we would have the same moral freedom with regard to them as we have with regard to animals.[18]

This brings out a central Kantian claim: Moral concern is owed to all and only those who are themselves capable of moral concern.

There is an air of circularity about this train of thought: Objective goals presuppose obligatory maxims (duties), which presuppose the categorical imperative, which presupposes objective ends in themselves, which in turn are identified as beings who can recognize and commit themselves to moral duties and to the objective goals these stipulate. But there is nothing vicious about this circularity, as the capacity to recognize duties can exist even without there being any real duties waiting to be recognized.

III. Purposiveness

Kant broadens and deepens his thinking on ends in the *Critique of Judgment*. Judgment is our ability to link universals and particulars, to make judgments of the form *S is P*. Kant calls determinative judgment our capacity to subsume particulars under given universals, and reflective judgment our capacity to find suitable universals for existing particulars (*EE* 20:211; *KU* 5:179f.).[19] Only the latter requires a critical examination, because only it has an a priori principle of its own whose status and scope need to be determined. It is the a priori principle of reflective judgment to conceive particulars as manifestations of purposiveness, *as if* they had been produced by a mind: "We call purposive anything whose existence seems to presuppose a representation of that same thing" (*EE* 20:216); "through this concept [of purposiveness] we represent nature as if some understanding contained the ground of the unity of the diversity of its empirical laws" (*KU* 5:180f.).[20] This book presents then a critique really only of reflective judgment: an attempt to determine the meaning, status, and scope of the a priori principle of this capacity (*EE* 20:248; *KU* 5:186).

The central division of the work into two critiques – of aesthetic and of teleological judgment – is based on Kant's distinction of two main types of purposiveness (cf. *EE* 20:248f.; *KU* 5:193f.): *Subjective* (or formal) *purposiveness* is purposiveness in respect to our cognitive capacities – we approach things as if they had been made for (us to take pleasure in) their good fit with our cognitive capacities. We approach the world as subjectively purposive when we assume that "nature takes the shortest path; . . . yet it makes no leap, either in the sequence of its changes or in the juxtaposition of forms that differ in kind; . . . its great diversity in empirical laws is nonetheless a unity under few principles, . . . and so forth" (*KU* 5:182; cf. *EE* 20:210). Kant's critique of aesthetic judgments, his discussion of taste, of beauty and sublimity, yields little for our topic beyond the briefly sketched idea of beauty as a symbol of morality (*KU* 5:351–4).

Objective (or real) *purposiveness* is purposiveness irrespective of our cognitive capacities.[21] It comes in two subtypes (*KU* 5:367). We conceive a thing to have *extrinsic purposiveness* when we take it to exist for the sake of something else – for example, plants for the sake of animals, animals for the use of human beings, or wars for the sake of promoting human industry (cf. *Idea* 8:24–6). We conceive a thing to have *intrinsic purposiveness* when we take its various parts to be organized around a central purpose, when we take it to be "an *organized* and *self-organizing* being" (*KU* 5:374). We feel impelled to do this with plants and animals, whose various organs seem so perfectly attuned to one another, who can maintain themselves through severe environmental changes, and who can ingest alien materials and convert them into internal matter (such as blood or wood). The existence of such things, which Kant calls *natural ends* (*Naturzwecke*), suggests and supports the thought that nature as a whole is intrinsically purposive (*KU* 5:378f).

It is worthwhile to distinguish explicitly two variants of extrinsic purposiveness, although Kant does not do so. In the *dynamic* variant, something existing or happening at one time is conceived as existing or happening for the sake of bringing it about (or making it possible) that something else exists or happens later. Thus we might think that the Thirty Years' War existed for the sake of promoting religious toleration. In the *static* variant, something existing for some time is conceived as existing for the sake of contributing to the existence or thriving of something else during the same period. In this vein, we might conceive of gravity as existing to allow planets to maintain an atmosphere. An analogous distinction can be made for means and goals: I withdraw money in order to purchase food (dynamic); and I sit on my manuscript in order to keep it together in windy weather (static). Even in the static variant, the purposive relation is causal: P is the mechanical cause of Q,[22] while Q is conceived of as the final cause (*Endursache*) of P (cf. *KU* 5:372).

Kant holds that, without natural ends (intrinsic purposiveness), we would have no ground to view nature as purposive at all (*KU* 5:425f). His reason seems to be that viewing A as having the purpose to bring about or sustain B means thinking of A *as if* intentionally produced so as to bring about or sustain B. But this thought requires more than the mere fact that A brings about or sustains B. It also requires the idea that B is intended. And there is no ground for this thought when B is a simple inorganic substance or process, such as the rhythm of the tides, for example, as sustained by the moon's revolutions. In such a case, an explanation in terms of mechanical causation alone seems fully satisfactory.[23] To be an extrinsic purpose, something must then, directly or indirectly, contribute to bringing about or sustaining a natural end, something that has its purpose in itself (*KU* 5:425).

Is every natural end to be viewed as an intrinsic purpose and as something in which extrinsic purposive relations can terminate? Here Kant's thoughts go in two directions, giving rise, respectively, to a *physical* and a *moral* teleology.[24] Within the former, our inability to explain organized and self-organizing beings in purely mechanical terms is a sufficient ground to conceive of them as intrinsic purposes. Moral teleology, on the other hand, is more demanding:

> Judging a thing to be a natural end on account of its inner form is something quite different from considering the existence of that thing to be an end of nature. To make the latter claim, we need not merely the concept of a possible end, but knowledge of the final end (*scopus*) of nature. This involves a relation of nature to something supersensible which far transcends all our teleological knowledge of nature; for the end of the existence of nature itself must be sought beyond nature. (*KU* 5:378)

To judge something to be an end of nature, we must judge that a hypothetical creator could have valued its existence. And this may well be doubtful in the case of some self-organizing beings.[25]

Oddly, the substance of the two teleologies is discussed only in an appendix on methodology at the very end of the *Critique of Judgment*. Kant holds that, within both teleologies, we strive not merely to identify purposive objects and relations, but also to organize these into a systematic whole. In thinking of the world as if produced by a creative mind, we look for one central idea that pervades and explains all purposive objects and relations – we look for a highest end or purpose to which all others are, directly or indirectly, purposively subordinate (i.e., to whose existence or thriving it is their purpose to contribute). This quest instantiates a general tendency of our reason to strive for unification and systematization in all our intellectual endeavors – a tendency Kant asserts and expounds throughout his critical period.

IV. Physical Teleology

Physical teleology is constructed by reason in its theoretical employment. Because some parts of nature, especially plants and animals, display a high degree of internal organization (as in the various organs of an animal) and external symbiosis (as in relations among species), we find it unavoidable to conceive of them as purposeful and intended; and because this way of approaching nature proves to be an indispensable cognitive guide, we apply it in the study of nature generally (*KU* 5:398) – seeking to explain some things by reference to others, to whose existence or thriving they contribute, and also some earlier events by reference to later ones they help bring about. Thus, Kant speaks about plants and animals serving the needs of human beings (*KU* 5:426) and, in an intriguing passage (*KU* 5:419f), at least entertains the thought of a gradual evolution from lower to higher species.[26] He also provides a sketch of a teleological explanation of world history (*Idea* 8:15–31).

Reason in its theoretical employment works from the bottom up, seeking to systematize the diverse data of experience as far as possible toward complete unity:

Reason is impelled by a tendency of its own nature to go beyond [its] empirical employment, to venture by way of a pure employment and through mere ideas to the utmost limits of all knowledge, and not to rest until its course is completed in a self-subsistent systematic whole.[27]

Physical teleology therefore seeks a unity in nature by connecting purposeful objects and relations into chains and hierarchies, ideally relating them all to a single highest end to which everything in nature can be seen to be directed and causally contributing. This unified hierarchy of ends has static aspects (e.g., a plurality of species all teleologically directed toward sustaining the highest one: humankind), but Kant conceives it as essentially dynamic. He speaks of the highest end of physical teleology as the *ultimate* (*letzter* – literally, "last") end and thinks of it as a state of the world which we conceive nature as destined to attain or asymptotically to approximate.

In seeking and sketching such teleological explanations and teleological laws of nature,[28] Kant follows a long philosophical tradition. But he also departs from this tradition by moderating the claims made on behalf of physical teleology in two ways. He stresses that teleological and mechanical explanations are not on a par: It is pursuant to a constitutive principle of reason that we assume that every event has an efficient cause and hence is susceptible to a mechanical explanation. Our quest to understand some thing or event in terms of a purpose, by contrast, is guided by a merely regulative principle, whose application moreover is triggered a posteriori: by the encounter with things whose structure defeats analysis in mechanical terms.[29] He even holds that explanations in terms of intentions do not extend our knowledge (*EE* 20:234). It is merely for us an indispensable heuristic principle to approach things in nature *as if* they were the product of intentional design, on the "mere maxim": "that [to account] for the very manifest connection of things in terms of final causes we must think a causality distinct from mechanism – namely the causality of an (intelligent) world cause that acts according to purposes" (*KU* 5:389).

The second respect in which Kant's claims on behalf of physical teleology are modest is this: While the identification of purposive objects and relations is an empirical enterprise, it is not possible to single out the ultimate end, the focal point of a hierarchical system of purposes, on empirical grounds alone. Competing static and dynamic systematizations may be equally compatible with all empirical facts – for example, one that presents plants as existing to be food for animals versus one that presents animals as existing to produce carbon dioxide for plants (cf. *KU* 5:427), or one that presents world history as meant fully to develop humankind's native potential versus one that presents it as destined to evolve super-resilient roaches. If we single out one systematization nevertheless, holding that the ultimate end of nature lies in the full development of human capacities (culture), we can do so only by appeal to moral teleology, that is, by relating "both nature and [ourselves] to an end that can be independent of nature, self-sufficient, and hence a final end."[30]

V. Moral Teleology

Beyond its indeterminacy, physical teleology leaves us unsatisfied in another way as well. Located within nature, within space and time, the ultimate end of nature cannot achieve the completion sought by reason. Even the fullest understanding of how each thing in nature makes its contribution, in harmony with those of every other, to nature's ultimate end leaves nature as a whole unexplained and quite possibly pointless. It leaves us impelled to ask further: What is the point or purpose of this nature working over time toward its ultimate end? This question, too, shows the need for a moral teleology; and Kant frames it as the quest for the *final end* (*Endzweck*) of creation. He means by "creation" not what exists (the created), but the ground of its existence (the creating), and he conceives of this ground without religious presuppositions (*KU* 5:449n). The idea is that if we are to think of nature as a whole as having a point or purpose, then we must be able to think of the ground of its existence *as if* it were the act of a creative mind. Our thinking on what reasons might move such a mind is to some extent constrained by what we know about the world. But it is, nevertheless, as befits reason in its practical employment, chiefly top-down in that the main constraints on moral teleology are a priori – originating in the structure of our practical reason. Kant asks, in effect: If we could create a whole universe, what purpose could move us to do so and what sort of world would we then create (*Religion* 6:5)?

Kant defines a final end as one that contains the necessary and sufficient condition of all other ends (*Religion* 6:6n) and requires no other end as condition of its possibility (*KU* 5:434). This definition would seem to imply that there can be at most one final end. Kant's moral teleology, however, postulates two: the final end of creation and the final end of humankind. This is not problematic, because these two final ends preside over separate domains and are also suitably unified with each other. The final end of creation is the point of the universe, for the sake of which (as far as we can conceive) it would be worth creating and through an appreciation of which we can come to understand everything in it: freedom, nature, and their specific interconnection. The final end of humankind is (what, for now, I will call) our supreme goal, which can unify all human actions with their myriad particular goals. The duality of final ends harks back, as we will see more fully, to the two senses of "end" from which we started out: The final end of creation is a freestanding end, while the final end of humankind, like the ultimate end of nature, is an end to be promoted or achieved.

This duality of final ends also fits with what we tend to want when we ask the question of the meaning of life. We are not asking a merely practical question, seeking a supreme goal for ourselves, nor a merely metaphysical one, seeking an explanation of the structure and point of the universe. What we need is some *unified* combination of both: some idea of the structure and point of the universe that illuminates our role and project within it.

Kant provides this unity, but he gives it the inverse structure: It is only through understanding our moral task that we can understand the point of the universe – in fact, without this moral task, the universe would have no point: "the final end of creation is that constitution of the world which harmonizes with . . . the final end of our pure practical reason."[31]

Kant's moving thought here is that a supreme human goal can be the centerpiece of the fullest possible systematic unification. This means, in particular, that it should have the following four features. *First*, I should be able to think of this goal as the final end to which all my conduct on obligatory and permissible maxims contributes and is ultimately directed. *Second*, one should be able to think of it as the final end of all the moral conduct of every other rational being. This second desideratum is not a trivial generalization of the first. It would not be satisfied if the supreme goal were specified in agent-relative terms – as suggested by the categorical imperative, which commands you to focus upon your duties and me upon mine. A merely agent-relative supreme goal could render our ends and conduct mutually coherent; but only a supreme goal that has agent-neutral universality can fully unite all of our moral endeavors by directing them toward the very same state of affairs as a common goal.

Third, we should be able to think of our supreme goal as the purpose of nature and the point of (and pointer to) nature's ultimate end. Attainment of our supreme goal, it is true, crucially depends on our free decisions, which nature is in principle incapable of producing. But nature can be seen as providing all the materials necessary for our success: If nature had been much more complicated or more opaque to our cognitive faculties, we could not have learned to systematize it, to interrogate it so as to discover its laws, and to master it; and we would then also not have learned to understand our own faculties through their successful employment on materials suitable to them. If nature had not given us needs and the capacity for harm and suffering and had not exposed us to scarcity and harsh conditions, then our lives would lack a moral dimension, which alone makes it possible for us to transcend what is nature within ourselves: to become conscious of the moral law within us and, through it, of our freedom, and freely to impose this moral law upon our conduct. If nature had made us more kind-hearted and less inclined toward power and survival, we might never have begun the giant edifice of civilization and culture and we would then neither have arrived at any awareness of our supreme goal nor have had the skill and discipline necessary to pursue it. If nature had made us immortal, we might not have felt the same urgency to think and to communicate our thoughts to one another. If nature had made our life much harsher than it is, those stepping back from the daily struggle for survival to lift their eyes up to the starry heavens above or to raise their will toward the moral law within might never have survived to leave any traces in history. And we can then say that nature, by working toward its ultimate end, is also contributing what, consistent with human freedom, it can contribute toward our supreme goal. In fact, we identify the ultimate end of nature by asking "what nature can do in order to prepare man for what he himself must do in order to be the final end" (*KU* 5:431).

Fourth, we should be able to think of our supreme goal as the point of (and pointer to) the final end of creation as well. By regarding the universe as a whole as if it were the result of a creative act, we raise the question what could possibly have motivated the creating of it, and of it the way it is. This question includes all the issues of physical teleology raised above. But it includes more radical questions, too, such as: For what did human beings have to exist? (*KU* 5:436n) and: What is the end, which must lie in us, that is to be promoted through our connection [*Verknüpfung*] with nature? (*KU* 5:429). These questions cannot be answered by any speculative theology or theodicy, but only through our own practical reason, "which can be viewed as the immediate explanation and voice of God through which He gives a meaning to the letters of His creation" (*Failure* 8:264; cf. *KU* 5:454f). Thus I must ask myself what could have moved me to create a world and, in particular, a world consistent with what I know about ours:

Imagine someone who reveres the moral law and to whom occurs the thought (which he can hardly avoid) which world he would *create*, guided by practical reason, if it were in his power [to do this] so that he would place himself into it as a member. He would not only choose in accordance with that idea of the highest good, . . . but he would also will that there be a world at all, because the moral law requires that the highest good possible through us be brought about. (*Religion* 6:5)

The act of creating this world has then (as far as we can conceive) as its final end the existence of free rational beings who, thanks to being connected with a sufficiently cooperative nature (which includes our own physical and sensuous nature), can recognize and pursue and attain their common supreme goal as specified by practical reason: "without man all of creation would be a mere wasteland, in vain and without final end."[32]

Our reason thus discloses to us not merely our moral task and supreme goal, but also the structure and point of the universe. It shows our supreme goal to be the end of all ends – not just the final end of all human ends, but also the point of nature's ultimate end and even of the final end of creation itself. Nature aims at the full development of human capacities as its ultimate end. It cannot aim higher than that, and yet the point of this aim lies higher, namely in bringing forth human beings under moral laws (*KU* 5:448), who can emancipate themselves from their native desires and freely pursue their supreme moral goal. The existence of such beings is, as far as we can conceive, the purpose of (creating) the world. Yet the point of this purpose lies higher still, namely in our exercising our freedom so that we realize our supreme moral goal. This is an amazing thought:

Reason tells [human beings] that the duration of the world has a value only insofar as the rational beings within it accord with the final end of their existence;

should this however not be attained, then creation itself seems pointless [*zwecklos*] to them: like a play that has no conclusion and reveals no rational [*vernünftige*] intention. (*End* 8:330f.)

This thought gives rise to a further reflection about ends. When Kant insists that the final end of creation is man *under* moral laws – not man acting *pursuant to* moral laws – he does so on the ground that "with the latter expression we would be saying more than we know, namely that it lies within the power of a creator of the world to ensure that man will always behave pursuant to moral laws" (*KU* 5:448n). Thus, he assumes it to be a conceptual truth about ends that one can make one's end only something one takes to lie within one's power. But, seeing how the word is actually used (in German and in English), this requirement seems overly strict. It would force us to say that my end in buying a lottery ticket is to have a chance at winning a prize. But my real end, speaking more loosely, surely is to win; I care nothing about the mere chance as such. Kant formulates his teleology in terms of the strict sense of "end," thus assigning different highest ends to nature, creation, and humankind. I have shown how one can reformulate it in terms of the looser sense of "end," according to which there is but a single highest end of nature, creation, and humankind. It is for the sake of our attainment of our supreme goal that this world exists (is created) and this nature is designed (cf. *Religion* 6:5, 6:60).

We can then fully endorse this creation, recognizing that the same supreme goal that gives a unified focus to all our moral conduct also animates the design of nature and would move a hypothetical creator to will our existence as beings inhabiting two worlds, with two causalities (of freedom and of nature). Even if any such creator could do no more than create rational-sensuous beings *under* moral laws (cf. *Opus postumum* 21:57, 21:66), placed within a nature that permits and stimulates the development of their capacities, we can still conceive him to be moved by the hope of bringing about human beings who follow moral laws. If he is rational, he, too, must be committed to "that which reason presents to all rational beings as the goal [*Ziel*] of all their moral wishes" (*KpV* 5:115). The meaningfulness of the universe, of nature, and of the human species thus lies in our hands as the only beings who are endowed with reason and can consciously have and freely adopt ends (*KU* 5:431). But any rational creator would be hoping for our success, for whose sake alone he would have created the world.

That the meaningfulness of the universe depends on sensuously inclined rational beings – "the warped wood of humanity" (*Idea* 8:23; cf. *Religion* 6:100) – is not a flaw in creation. The alternatives are, as far as we can conceive, worse. We can imagine a world inhabited by angels:

beings with holy wills, motivated solely by pure practical reason – but what could possibly be its point? We can add to this world Humean humans, to whose desires the angels might devote themselves – but that world, too, would strike us as meaningless. We can recognize as meaningful only a world that is not a preprogrammed display, that transcends creation by containing freedom: the possibility of good will, a genuinely open struggle for our supreme goal. Thus, the uncertainty of the outcome notwithstanding, we can be fully reconciled to our existence: Creation and nature are, and we have it in our power to be, entirely good.

VI. The Religious Conception of the Highest Good

I have suggested that our supreme goal is the highest end (in the loose sense) also of nature and creation. I will pursue this thought further in the final section by developing Kant's worldly conception of the highest good. First I must remark briefly, however, on Kant's competing religious conception.[33]

This conception defines the highest good as virtue (acting from duty) combined with proportional happiness.[34] Humankind can promote, and hence aim for (strictly speaking), only one of its components – our own inner moral perfection – and, since one can promote only one's own moral perfection and not that of others (*MdS* 6:386), each person can strictly aim for only a tiny aspect of this component. The matching of each person's virtue with an exactly (as Kant often stresses) proportional happiness must be left to God, who alone can fathom our motives[35] and who alone can rectify, perhaps by means of an afterlife (*KrV* A811/B839), temporary disproportions.

This religious conception of the highest good has been criticized by many, and I will therefore do no more than briefly state four of its main drawbacks.

(1) Although presented as being in principle fully attainable, this highest good is in fact forever out of reach, because our world contains unerasable lapses in moral character.[36] This fact – though we can still strive to come as close to the ideal as possible – must weaken the endorsement our reason can give to creation and must detract from the urgency, beauty, and authority of the highest good.

(2) This highest good does rather little by way of unifying human endeavors. It does not invite us to collaborate in a common project, but rather leaves each of us to work in a separate domain and without regard to the others.

(3) The concept of proportionality requires that happiness and virtue be representable on interval scales. It also requires two pairs of matching points across scales. Kant supplies one (dubious) such pair: The best possible moral character is to be matched with the greatest possible happiness. But he provides no second pair. Should someone who never acts from duty have zero happiness (and what does that mean?), or a life of the greatest possible pain, or what? And how can an answer to this question be nonarbitrarily justified?

(4) Kant offers no argument for his proposal. He claims that the goal of the highest good is prescribed by, or derived from, the moral law (*KU* 5:449, 5:470, 5:471n, 5:474, 5:485), but he never gives a substantive account of how this might be so. It would, in fact, be surprising if that goal were derivable from this law. For the former prominently involves an idea that has no place at all in the latter, namely the idea of proportionality of happiness and virtue.

These problems with the religious conception of the highest good are major (no accepted solutions have been produced in 200 years of scholarship) and too obvious for Kant himself to have been entirely unaware of them. That he clung to it so strongly nevertheless may be due to three reasons: This highest good can – or at least seems to – support practical faith in God and our immortality, which Kant wanted to support even while realizing that they cannot be supported (nor refuted) by theoretical reason. It allows Kant to retain his catchy and oft-repeated claim that our practical reason directs us to strive not for happiness but for the worthiness to be happy (*KrV* A808f/B836f.; *MdS* 6:481), which suggests that it would be a moral flaw in the world if some persons were virtuous (= worthy of happiness) but unhappy or unvirtuous (= unworthy of happiness) but happy (cf. *G* 4:393). And it opens up for the question "What may I hope?" an answer that satisfies the constraint that "all hoping is directed toward happiness" (*KrV* A805/B833).

In the end, Kant must have seen the untenability of the religious conception. As Förster shows in detail, he jettisons, in the *Opus postumum*, the belief in God as substance and guarantor of proportionality, and thereby presumably also the belief in immortality, leaving freedom as the only surviving member of the original triad, for faith in which his critical philosophy was supposed to have made room (*KrV* Bxxx). The concluding paragraph of Förster's essay is: "In Kant's final determination of transcendental philosophy, there is then nothing left to hope for. So be it. We know what we ought to do. That must suffice."[37] Without doubting that this was Kant's last thought on the matter, we

should nevertheless consider whether one could also reach a more optimistic Kantian position. It is clear where we should start: with the attempt to find in Kant, or to develop from his thoughts, a conception of
the highest good that is free of the untenable theological elements and
can fit the role of supreme goal sketched in the preceding section. We
must try, then, to specify for humankind a final end that is constructible
from the moral law, can fully unify the moral ends of all human beings,
and is one we can recognize as a suitable highest end (loose sense) of
creation. Such a worldly conception of the highest good would complete
the second Copernican revolution: the insight that we can be *fully* autonomous, that our reason contains not only the content of the moral
law, but also an always sufficient motive to follow it – without connecting
with it silly "promises and threats" (*KrV* A811/B839). For the worldly
highest good would inspire in us a hope that far transcends any petty
longing for proportionality or personal happiness,[38] a hope that is truly
divine in that we could also ascribe it to an imagined creator of the world
as His sole motive: the hope for the moral success of humankind.

VII. A Worldly Conception of the Highest Good

One obvious candidate for humankind's supreme goal is the realm of
ends of the *Groundwork*, defined as "a whole of all ends (both of rational
beings as ends in themselves and also of the personal ends that each may
set himself)" (*G* 4:433).[39] In this realm, all persons would adopt only
permissible maxims, and all their ends would therefore be mutually
consistent. Moreover, all persons would also adopt all obligatory maxims
and would therefore, by developing their talents and by receiving help
from one another, tend to attain their permissible ends.

Kant soon came to see that this ideal is not workable, for the moral law
underdetermines the realm of ends, and there may then be more than
one complete system of jointly universalizable maxims.[40] Thus, even
persons who act fully in accord with a self-constructed hypothetical
realm of ends in which conflict is impossible may then come into conflict
in the one real world they all must share. Moreover, persons may conscientiously differ about the content of morality and about its proper
application (*MdS* 6:401). And this, since each would then do "what
seems right and good to him" (*MdS* 6:312), poses another severe problem for the ideal of interpersonal harmony through morally motivated
self-restraint.[41]

Seeing these problems, Kant works out a more complex ideal based on
the realization that the political and legal institutions of a state are not
only possible, even among a nation of devils (*Peace* 8:366) – but also

necessary even among a nation of persons of good will. This ideal has two components, corresponding to the new division of the metaphysics of morals into a *Rechtslehre* and a *Tugendlehre*. The political component centers around a republican constitution that coordinates the self-restraint of individuals through a single, consistent, complete, and suitably enforced equal distribution of domains of external freedom. The other component adds the idea of an ethical commonwealth in which citizens of good will can unite under public noncoercive laws of virtue and, together, "gain the upper hand over the evil that is ceaselessly assailing them" (*Religion* 6:94, cf. 6:151). The overarching goal remains the realization of morality – and thus of reason – in this world: its realization both in just social institutions and in good moral dispositions.

Does Kant assert a special or further duty of promoting the highest good? Kant says of our final end that "harmony with [it], while not increasing the number of [morality's] duties, yet provides them with a special point of focus for the unification of all ends" (*Religion* 6:5). If promoting our final end were some further moral concern over and above the others, then it could not unify all of the latter. So it does not give rise to just another duty. And yet, thinking of it as our supreme goal to which all our conduct on obligatory and permissible maxims contributes and is ultimately directed makes a profound difference to how we view and specify all our moral duties and (moral and nonmoral) ends. It gives a point to fulfilling our duties of justice, in that morality can be realized only in a juridical state. And it guides our fulfillment of our duties of virtue. Being duties of "wide requirement" (*MdS* 6:390–5), these leave a great deal of freedom to choose what we shall do to improve ourselves and the lives of others. We can and should use this freedom, within the confines of positive law, with an eye to promoting the highest good.

The four mentioned drawbacks of the religious conception are all avoided by this worldly conception of the highest good. (1) Instead of giving us a moral task that is in principle fully attainable and yet factually forever out of reach (the moral perfection of every human being), it gives us an open-ended goal: to promote humanity's moral progress, which can transcend any given limit. (2) This task is a collective one, a "duty of humankind toward itself, [directing each human being toward] a shared end, namely the promotion of the highest as a shared good. [This] requires a union of persons . . . into a system of well-disposed human beings, in which and through whose unity alone it can come about" (*Religion* 6:97f., cf. 6:151). (3) The worldly conception eschews the problematic idea of a proportionality of happiness and virtue. And (4) its content derives directly from the moral law, because its highest good is a world in which human beings orient their conduct and willing toward this law.[42]

Taking off from the first two points, let me sketch in conclusion why the shift to this worldly conception (which Kant never fully made[43]) has such depth. The religious conception conceives the moral task in terms of good will. In this regard, moral perfection is accessible to the "commonest intelligence" (*KpV* 5:36; cf. *G* 4:403). A man who curbs his desires according to his primitive notions of morality may well exemplify inner moral perfection. That his morality is simplistic and laced with superstition cannot be held against him if he sincerely tries to lead a moral life as best he knows how.[44]

The worldly conception emphasizes the further task and duty to realize morality in human history (*Common Saying* 8:280n; *Religion* 6:151). This task is anything but simple. It requires that we overcome the divisions of race, gender, nation, and religion and together build just institutions on a global scale so as to overcome human inhumanity worldwide. Kant is quite adamant about the need for a global solution: Humanity's final end cannot be attained in one country. Even justice can only be achieved universally (*Idea* 8:24). So long as humankind does not enter a "universal cosmopolitan condition" (*Idea* 8:28), does not organize itself into a "moral whole" (*Idea* 8:21), we can expect human beings to be, at best, cultivated and civilized – "nothing but illusion and glittering misery" – but not moralized (*Idea* 8:26).[45]

One might try to square this task with the religious conception: Perhaps it is required because we can, after all, promote the inner moral perfection of others at least by removing temptations and obstacles.[46] Perhaps the historical triumph of morality will come about as a side effect of widespread inner moral perfection. Or perhaps this triumph is something we must hope for in order to maintain our moral disposition, because "reason cannot possibly be indifferent to what the answer may be to the question: *What will result from this right conduct of ours?*" (*Religion* 6:5, cf. 6:7n).

Such reductions rest on shaky (and wishful) empirical views that can hardly inspire conviction. But there is a deeper reason they will not work. They cannot include what is, for Kant, by far the most important aspect of historical moral progress: enlightenment. There can be good will, inner moral perfection, in a person lacking the capacity for independent critical thought. And a whole species of rational beings might then achieve universal inner moral perfection while making only minimal progress toward enlightenment. Could the hope for this achievement be my highest hope, when I place myself into the role of world creator? Kant's answer is an emphatic *No*. He insists that our moral life must be "cleansed of the idiocy of superstition and the madness of zealotry [*Schwärmerei*]" (*Religion* 6:101). Without betraying the respect Rousseau taught him to have[47] for the common man who conscientiously tries to live decently, Kant would say that this man, even when he leads the best life he can lead by his dim lights, is still not leading the best life possible for a human being: He is not thinking well and does not think for himself.

Each of us falls short in these respects to some extent. And although some of our immaturity may be our own fault (*Enlightenment* 8:35), we surely could not have helped all of it: Our intellectual achievements are constrained by our epoch, culture, and upbringing. But is it not a moral flaw in the world that every human being falls short in this way – that many have, for instance, lived committed to primitive moral notions? We can avoid this conclusion if we conceive the focus of creation to be humankind at large, a self-perfecting species of free rational beings which, together, can overcome any limits on its enlightenment: "In the human being (as the only rational creature on Earth) the natural endowments directed toward the use of his reason ought to develop completely – not, however, in the individual, but only in the species" (*Idea* 8:18). Elsewhere Kant likens humankind to a curve asymptotically approaching an ideal line:

No member of any generation of humankind, but only the species will fully reach its destiny [*Bestimmung*]. . . . The destiny of humankind as a whole is *unceasing progress*, and the completion [of its destiny] is a mere (but in all respects quite useful) idea of the goal [*Ziel*] toward which . . . we are to focus our efforts.[48]

On the worldly conception of the highest good, it is then part of our moral task to help our contemporaries and succeeding generations to think better and more independently, a task to which Kant meant to contribute and did contribute greatly. We should strive to bring about, maintain, and perfect a human environment – political, legal, economic, and educational institutions as well as a culture of mutual respect and toleration – in which persons can come to think well and freely. "For how much and how correctly would we *think*, if we did not think, as it were, in community with others with whom we exchange thoughts?"[49]

Morality is reason's noblest product. But reason is not a ready-made capacity fully available to any rational being willing to make full use of it. It develops over time, in each person and in the species. "Its pronouncement is never more than the agreement of free citizens of whom each must be able to express, without holding back, his objections, nay even his veto" (*KrV* A738f/B766f). This thought adds a last twist to the worldly idea of moral progress. On Kant's view, our supreme moral goal is not merely to advance toward the moral ideal projected by his moral theory. It also involves the task to rethink this theory, to deepen and specify – even revise or replace it, should that prove warranted. This is then our supreme moral goal: to advance human moral thinking and, through it, ourselves and the human world. We cannot know where this project may take humankind in centuries to come. "But what one must do to remain on the path of duty (according to rules of wisdom), for that and thus for the final end reason always shines enough light ahead" (*Peace* 8:370). We can and we do know what we must do here and now: The thoughts of our predecessors and contemporaries are readily available for reflection, discussion, and critique. Immaturity and prejudice are all around us. Starvation and brutality stare us in the face.

There is then an "inborn duty in every member of the sequence of generations – in which I am (as a human being), but not as good in terms of the moral quality required of me as I should and therefore could be – to influence posterity so that it should become better and better" (*Common Saying* 8:309). We cannot know whether there will be moral progress after us; and no human being will ever know our task to be completed. But we can live for the hope for such progress, thus joining hands with the most admirable persons our species has brought forth throughout the ages – and with the best yet to come, who will continue our work. A free species inspired by this hope and working together over many generations toward its realization; could it not be the highest purpose of all that exists?

NOTES

Kant's three *Critiques* are referred to as *KrV*, *KpV*, and *KU*, the *Groundwork* as *G*, the *Metaphysics of Morals* as *MdS*, and the first (draft) introduction to *KU* as *EE*. Key title words are used to refer to his other writings. Citations are by volume and page numbers of the Preußische Akademieausgabe, except for the *KrV*, where citations are to the first (A) and second (B) editions. All translations are my own. I want to thank Rüdiger Bittner, Hilary Bok, Taylor Carman, Sam Kerstein, Christine Korsgaard, Mary Mothersill, Brian Orend, and especially Andrews Reath for their extensive and very helpful comments on earlier versions of this essay.

1. The relevant writings from this period are *KU* (1790), *Failure* ("On the Failure of all Philosophical Endeavors in Theodicy," 1791), *Religion (Religion Within the Limits of Reason Alone)* (1793), *Common Saying (On the Common Saying: This May Be True in Theory, but It Does Not Apply in Practice)* (1793), *End* ("The End [*Ende*] of All Things," 1794), and *Peace (Perpetual Peace)* (1795).
2. The definition is repeated, almost verbatim, a few pages later (*MdS* 6:384). See also the definition in the *Religion*: "An *end* is always the object of an

inclination [*Zuneigung*], that is, of an immediate craving [*Begierde*] for possession of a thing through one's action" (*Religion* 6:6n).

3. Thomas Hill, noting the different senses of "end," interprets this expression as "reason for acting" (*Dignity and Practical Reason in Kant's Moral Theory* [Ithaca: Cornell University Press, 1992], p. 43). Perhaps "source of reasons for acting" would be more accurate. Cf. pp. 196ff. of Christine Korsgaard, "Kant's Formula of Humanity," *Kant-Studien* 77 (1986): 183–202.

4. Kant does this, for example, at *G* 4:427; *Religion* 6:6n; and *MdS* 6:389.

5. *MdS* 6:385. God and the angels would presumably lack this power of choice: Not sensuously inclined, they necessarily follow their reason-based motives; they have no others.

6. I assume here that events and states of affairs can be means to goals: I may be interested in bringing it about that the book is at home at t_1 only because and insofar as I am interested in reading it at t_2. Of course, things and persons can also be means to goals – though they cannot be goals (except in the special case of creation).

7. Here we must hold fixed, of course, whether we are talking about believed subjective, believed objective, true subjective, or true objective ends in themselves. One might still challenge the claim of exhaustiveness. Suppose Kant knew nothing about some island. One would then presumably say neither that he (ought to have) treated its inhabitants with respect, nor that he (ought to have) treated them without. I have tried to cover this point by adding the phrase "in its domain." It does not, in any case, affect the contrast I want to bring out.

8. It may be thought that this amounts to treating him as a *potential* means to goals. But I think this is not so. One may think of a person as having no worth, and be indifferent to his good and his goals, while also deeming it dishonorable or wrong to use him in order to attain one's own goals (as when one regards him as another's property or as a source of spiritual pollution).

9. To be sure, the categorical imperative is in the first instance a test for the permissibility of maxims (*G* 4:439). But Kant clearly holds that a person does not qualify for having acted from duty, nor her action for having moral worth, if she merely acted on a permissible maxim suggested by her inclinations – even if she has checked its permissibility (*G* 4:398–401, 4:406). Kant must then have thought that the categorical imperative can also (indirectly) *require* the adoption of some maxim – of helping others, say, when we find alternative maxims in this domain (never to help others) to be impermissible.

10. *Religion* 6:4f.; cf. *G* 4:413n. One may doubt whether the asserted structural difference between moral and nonmoral conduct is defensible: Isn't the moral agent, too, moved by a subjective goal that motivates and controls her adoption of maxims: the goal to make her conduct conform to the categorical imperative? Even if this were so, there would still be a structural difference: In nonmoral acts, the interest in the subsidiary goal (selling) derives from its presumed causal relation to an ulterior goal (making a profit). In moral action there is no such presumed causal relation: Getting Jim a good meal does not cause my compliance with the categorical imperative. I am indebted to Sam Kerstein for discussions of this point, which receives more extensive treatment in his dissertation, *Action, Hedonism, and Practical Law* (Columbia University, 1995).

11. The text strongly suggests that Kant thought of his claim that rational beings

are objective ends in themselves as fixing the scope of his universalization requirement: The preceding formulations of the first formula (*G* 4:402, 4:421) speak merely of universal law, while later formulations use the more exact phrases "universal validity for every rational being" and "universal law (of all rational beings)" (*G* 4:437f.). For more on this interpretation of the second formula, see my "The Categorical Imperative," in *Grundlegung zur Metaphysik der Sitten. Ein kooperativer Kommentar*, ed. Otfried Höffe (Frankfurt: Vittorio Klostermann, 1989), 172–93, at pp. 181–3.

12. *MdS* 6:443. As Nozick has argued, Kant's empirical assertion may well be false for persons who are genuinely convinced that animals have no moral standing at all. For them hitting a cow would be like hitting a baseball. See Robert Nozick: *Anarchy, State, and Utopia* (New York 1974), p. 36.

13. *MdS* 6:223; cf. *MdS* 6:434f.; *KU* 5:431, 5:434n, 5:435.

14. There is an alternative reading: We need treat with respect only persons who have, or are progressing toward, a good will; but since we can never be sure of anyone that they fail to meet this requirement (*G* 4:407f., *MdS* 6:392f., 6:447), we ought in practice treat every person with respect (act as if each were an objective end in itself).

15. Kant entertains the possibility of such beings, for example, at *MdS* 6:418, and also at *KU* 5:449.

16. That human beings fit this description seems to be, surprisingly, Kant's view in *KrV*, where he suggests that reason can make its moral laws effective only by postulating a God and an afterlife, because we could not follow the moral laws "if they did not . . . carry with them *promises* and *threats*" (*KrV* A811/B839).

17. A big "if": Given Kant's uncertainty about whether anyone has ever acted from duty (*G* 4:407f), how can he be so sure that everyone could have? Kant might respond that, feeling the authority of the moral law, one knows one can always follow it (*KpV* 5:30) and thus can know at least in one's own case that one is not a Humean agent. Can we know that those around us, too, are Kantian rather than Humean agents? I suspect that, when pressed, Kant would have defended this claim by appeal to reasonable faith (cf. *KpV* 5:126).

18. They would be more formidable competitors, of course. So we might find it advantageous to enter with them into a juridical state. We would then have legal duties toward them that, though backed by sanctions, would not be backed by corresponding "indirect-ethical duties" (*MdS* 6:221) and would thus lack all moral force. It is a precondition not only of duties of virtue, but of all morally binding duties that the being to whom they are owed be a *person*, i.e., capable of a good will.

19. Kant writes, in a letter to his student Jacob Sigismund Beck (dated 12–4–1792, 11:396 in the *second* edition of 1922), that he abandoned the draft introduction to *KU* only on account of its excessive length. I see other problems with it as well; but I will nevertheless cite it (*EE*) where it accords well with the published text.

20. *Zweckmäßig(keit)*, translated as "purposive(ness)," is closely related to *Zweck*. In what follows, I often use "purpose" for *Zweck* so as to flag this etymological connection. Unfortunately, "purpose" cannot be used to translate *Zweck* across the board, because the expression "end in itself" is now too deeply entrenched and also because it is often much less fitting than some

other word. So we will just have to remember that, unless otherwise noted, "end," "purpose," "goal," "aim," and also "point" are all translations of Kant's *Zweck*.

21. This must be taken with a grain of salt. Of course, what does and does not strike us as purposive in nature is not independent of our capacities. The objective–subjective distinction here hinges on whether something that strikes us (our cognitive faculties) as an intelligent creation also strikes us as having been created with us in mind.

22. See *KrV* A203/B248, where a ball at rest is said to cause a dimple in a cushion.

23. One might well ask whether a large number of substances or processes, each sustained by and also contributing to the sustaining of some of the others, could not suggest the idea of a system of purely extrinsic purposiveness. Seeing that we do ascribe (intrinsic) purposiveness to a tree with its complexly interrelated parts (roots, leaves, branches, etc.), why should we not ascribe extrinsic purposiveness to the relations among the various components of earthly weather (winds, currents, clouds, rain, etc.)? Kant's last line of defense against such a challenge appears rather weak today: He stresses repeatedly that we cannot "hope to understand in terms of merely mechanical causes the genesis of even a single blade of grass" (*KU* 5:409, cf. 5:378, 5:400).

24. For the distinction between the two teleologies, see *KU* 5:444 and 5:447f.

25. In a rare and somewhat tasteless joke, Kant offers the New Hollanders and the Fuegians as examples of beings with respect to whom it is difficult to see why they should have had to exist (*KU* 5:378).

26. This thought appears, well before Charles Darwin, in various eighteenth-century authors, such as Julien Offroy de La Mettrie, George Louis Leclerc Comte de Buffon, Erasmus Darwin (Charles Darwin's grandfather), and Jean Baptiste Pierre Antoine de Monet Chevalier de Lamarck. Kant was certainly familiar with the work of Buffon.

27. *KrV* A797/B825. See also A298–302/B355–9, A657ff/B685ff.; and *KpV* 5:107f., 5:120.

28. Recall how Kant appeals to teleological laws of nature in his *Groundwork* discussion of duties to oneself, asserting for example that the "function [*Bestimmung*] [of self-love] is to stimulate the furtherance of life" (*G* 4:422). Laws of nature to the effect that persons kill themselves when their expected future happiness falls below some threshold, or develop their talents only insofar as this increases their expected net happiness, would not fit into a totality of natural laws whose ultimate end is the full development of human capacities. Once we see how physical teleology is grounded in moral teleology (especially as regards the identity of nature's ultimate end), these arguments become much more plausible.

29. The regulative principle guiding our quest for more and more general mechanical laws of nature is, by contrast, a priori: Reason impels us to engage in this quest irrespective of what we find the particulars of the empirical world to be. The question of nature's objective purposiveness must be distinguished from the prior question of its susceptibility to systematization by us through repeatedly applicable empirical concepts and empirical generalizations.

30. *KU* 5:431, cf. 5:378, 5:444.

31. *KU* 5:455, cf. 5:458. The two final ends are also contrasted at *KU* 5:453 and 5:469.

32. *KU* 5:442, cf. 5:449f. Would a rational God have positive reason to create us? Our affirmative answer can grow out of a thought that we find "unavoidable and yet also unbearable: that a being, which we conceive as supreme among all possible beings, would as it were, say to itself: 'I am from eternity to eternity, and outside me there is nothing save what is through my will, *but whence then am I?*'" (*KrV* A613/B641). Infinite cognitive and practical powers mean nothing in the face of this existential predicament. By creating us, God would be creating (though Kant cannot quite *say* so) His equals . . . and even beings more interesting than Himself – not intrinsically perfect and moral, but free to perfect themselves, to become moral by their own lights. I return to this theme below.

33. In what follows I am indebted to Andrews Reath, "Two Conceptions of the Highest Good in Kant," *Journal of the History of Philosophy* 26 (1988): 593–619. For a qualified defense of the religious conception, see Stephen Engstrom: "The Concept of the Highest Good in Kant's Moral Theory," *Philosophy and Phenomenological Research* 52 (1992): 747–80.

34. Formulations of this sort are numerous throughout Kant's writings. See *KrV* A810f/B838f., A813f/B841f.; *KpV* 5:110–19, 144; *KU* 5:451, 5:453, 5:47ln; *Orientation* 8:139; *Common Saying* 8:280n; and *Religion* 6:8n.

35. *G* 4:407; *KpV* 5:99; *MdS* 6:392f., 6:447.

36. Kant holds that, to make the highest good fully attainable, we must assume an unending afterlife that would enable indefinite improvement of character (*KpV* 5:122). But even with this assumption, it would still remain true that Hitler, Caligula, and the rest of us could have (had) a better character than we (did) have in fact. I assume here that Kant must agree that approaching a good will in the indefinitely long run is not sufficient for having a flawless (noumenal) character.

37. Eckart Förster: "Was darf ich hoffen?" *Zeitschrift für philosophische Forschung*, 46 (1992): 168–85, p. 185.

38. There is nothing wrong with happiness. Part of what moral agents are striving for is that more human beings shall have a decent chance for it. But happiness cannot be the highest hope of an ideal moral agent, because it is not what such an agent lives for. What sustains one in this immoral age may well be the hope for an afterlife. But, if so, this is not an afterlife in which one gets to have some fun to compensate one for one's labors. It is an afterlife in which one's work lives on and, together with the work of many other moral persons, achieves the result on which one's energies were focused: succeeds in overcoming injustice and callousness, oppression, war, and hunger.

39. Kant explicitly points out the teleological significance of the idea of a realm of ends, calling it a practical idea to be employed for its own realization (*G* 4:436n).

40. See my "The Categorical Imperative," pp. 187, 190.

41. Another problem Kant comes to see is the moral variant of the assurance problem: Contrary to his earlier account (*G* 4:438f.), he now holds that one is not morally required always to restrain oneself pursuant to the moral law so long as one lacks assurances that others will not take advantage of such self-restraint (*Peace* 8:349n, *MdS* 6:307, 6:257). Kant's changing conception

of the metaphysics of morals is further discussed in sections I–III of my "Kant's Theory of Justice," *Kant-Studien* 79 (1988): 407–33.

42. I have been brief, because these points, or points much like them, have been raised, rather well, before. See, for instance, Hermann Cohen: *Kant's Begründung der Ethik* (Berlin: Bruno Cassirer, 1877), Yirmiahu Yovel: *Kant and the Philosophy of History* (Princeton: Princeton University Press, 1980), Harry van der Linden: *Kantian Ethics and Socialism* (Indianapolis: Hackett, 1988), and Andrews Reath: "The Concept of the Highest Good."

43. In particular, Kant never fully divorced himself from the proportionality conception, which he frequently mentions even when discussing the highest good in secular terms. This explains the indefinite article in the title of this section.

44. "When someone is conscious of having followed his conscience, then, as regards guilt or innocence, nothing more can be required" (*MdS* 6:401; cf. *Failure* 8:268).

45. Kant wavers in how he envisions this moral whole, mainly because, I believe, his endorsement of the dogma of absolute sovereignty leaves him only two alternatives: a world sovereign, which could lead to the most fearful despotism (*Common Saying* 8:311), and a free association of sovereign states, which, constantly endangered by possible breakdown, is only a negative surrogate for a world republic (*Peace* 8:357). At times, though, Kant comes within reach of what today must seem the most promising ideal: that of a global federalism involving a genuine vertical division of powers. Thus he envisions (*Idea* 8:26) a unification of states (*Staatenverbindung*) with a united power (*vereinigte Gewalt*) that enforces a law of equilibrium among states and thereby introduces a cosmopolitan condition of public security of states (*einen weltbürgerlichen Zustand der öffentlichen Staatssicherheit*). He writes that securing individual freedom "would require – if only human beings were smart enough to discover it and wise enough willingly to submit to its coercive power – a *cosmopolitan* whole [*weltbürgerliches Ganze*], i.e., a system of all states that are in danger of affecting one another detrimentally" (*KU* 5:432). And he asserts that "there exists no other remedy against this [oppressive burden of military expenditure] except an international law (in analogy to the civil or public law of individual men) founded upon public and enforced laws to which each state would have to subject itself" (*Common Saying* 8:312). See also *Religion* 6:34 ("Völkerbund als Weltrepublik"); *Peace* 8:379; *MdS* 6:311 ("Völkerstaatsrecht"); *Contest* 7:92 ("weltbürgerliche Gesellschaft"); and *Anthropology* 7:331, 7:333.

46. Kant holds that one may be able to promote one's own moral perfection in this way by promoting one's own happiness and that one then has an (indirect) duty to do so (*KpV* 5:93; *MdS* 6:388).

47. See Kant's notes toward his 1764 essay "Observations on the Feeling of the Beautiful and Sublime" (20:44).

48. This is near the end of the last installment of Kant's 1785 review of Herder (8:65).

49. *Orientation* 8:144. These concluding thoughts are partly inspired by Onora O'Neill: "Vindicating Reason" in *The Cambridge Companion to Kant*, ed. Paul Guyer (Cambridge University Press, 1993). See also her *Constructions of Reason* (Cambridge University Press, 1989), chapters 1–2, and Part III of Yovel, *Kant and the Philosophy of History*.

Community and Completion

DANIEL BRUDNEY

> Community is what takes place always through others and for others.
>
> Jean-Luc Nancy, *The Inoperative Community*

For over a decade – say, since Michael Sandel's *Liberalism and the Limits of Justice*[1] – communitarians have attacked John Rawls's theory of justice as fairness. Yet communitarian writers have said almost nothing about what kind or kinds of relationships among citizens or between citizens and the state a communitarian should advocate. In this essay I sketch a picture of communal relationships and use it to examine the nature of community in Rawls's work. In the first section I extract a picture of communal relationships from Karl Marx's 1844 *Comments on James Mill, Élémens d'économie politique*; in the second section I argue for this picture's distinctiveness; finally, in the last section I look at a shift in the nature of community between *A Theory of Justice* and Rawls's more recent book, *Political Liberalism*. In that last section I argue that a picture structurally similar to that in Marx is exhibited by the well-ordered society of *Theory*, although not by that of *Political Liberalism*. In the end the communitarian charge – that Rawls's view is at odds with an emphasis on community – turns out to be legitimate, but *not* with respect to *Theory*, the standard communitarian target. However, seeing this depends on seeing the possibility of different conceptions of community. And that points to the need for development of and debate about such conceptions. My larger goal is to take a step toward such development and debate.

I

1. "Suppose," Marx says in the *Comments*, "we had carried out production as human beings. Each of us would have *doubly affirmed* himself and the other person."[2] Marx actually goes on to list four forms of this affirmation, but they divide into two areas. The first concerns an agent's affirmation of her individuality.

In my *production* I would have objectified my *individuality*, its *specific character*, and therefore enjoyed not only an individual *life-expression* during the activity, but also when looking at the object I would have the individual pleasure of knowing my personality to be *objective, sensuously perceptible* and hence a power raised *beyond all doubt.*[3]

Marx's idea here is clear enough: in a communist society agents would find individual fulfillment in the process of production, both in the activity itself and in the fact that the activity's result is something external in which an individual can see a concrete manifestation of her individuality. The rest of the passage focuses on the agent's relation to other agents.

(2) In your enjoyment or use of my product I would have the *direct* enjoyment both of being conscious of having satisfied a *human* need by my work, that is, of having objectified *human* nature [*Wesen*], and of having thus created an object corresponding to the need of another *human* being [*Wesen*]. (3) I would have been for you the *mediator* between you and the species, and therefore would become recognized and felt by you yourself as a completion [*Ergänzung*] of your own nature and as a necessary part of yourself, and consequently would know myself to be confirmed both in your thought and your love. (4) In my individual life-expression I would have directly created your life-expression, and therefore in my individual activity I would have directly *confirmed* and *realized* my true nature [*Wesen*], my *human* nature, my *communal* nature.

Our products would be so many mirrors reflecting our nature.

This relationship would moreover be reciprocal; what occurs on my side has also to occur on yours.[4]

The sections labeled (2), (3), and (4) point to two connected concerns: a concern with agents' relations to each other one-to-one, and a concern with agents' relations to each other as members of the group, the human species. I will take these in turn.

At several places in the *Comments* Marx talks of how, in a communist society, agents would "complete" one another.[5] To begin with, the idea seems to be that in various ways agents would enable one another to attain their ends. In terms of the production of goods and services this is straightforward enough. Cooperation generates benefits for all: additional goods and services agents can use to pursue their ends.

Such reciprocal bestowal of benefits obtains in capitalism as well as in communism. However, Marx says, in market relationships people try to get the better of one another.

The social relation in which I stand to you, my labor for your need, is therefore also a mere *semblance* [*Schein*], and our reciprocal completion is likewise a mere *semblance*, the basis of which is reciprocal plundering.[6]

Agents in the market are not centrally concerned to provide objects others can use. They want simply to get the most for the least. A bit later in the *Comments* Marx muddies his point by stressing that under capitalism individuals deceive or coerce where they can. But many capitalist exchanges – say, trading pork bellies on a commodity exchange – occur with neither coercion nor deception, and for Marx these hardly instantiate proper human relationships.[7] What is needed, for Marx, is not that coercion and deception be absent but that the provision of something useful to others be central to what one is trying to accomplish.

To take an example, suppose Richard wants to write the score for a hit musical, while Oscar wants to write the lyrics. They agree to collaborate. Here there is no deception or coercion. Moreover, each knows he is completing the other. Yet their relationship could still be purely instrumental. It is as if they both want to open a vault needing two keys. By contrast, in a communist society part of the point of my activity would be to provide you with what you need to pursue your ends. I would not only provide you with the cauliflower for your soup; in growing that cauliflower my goal would be to provide you (anyway, to provide someone) with a cauliflower to use. Your use of it would thus contribute to attaining my end as well as to attaining one of your own ends. Our ends would not only not conflict, they would be complementary. And since you, on your part, would make something which I (anyway, which some other human being) would use, the complementarity would be reciprocal, at least within the community as a whole.

Such a relationship is, incidentally, an anticipatory gloss on the dictum from the *Critique of the Gotha Program* of 31 years later: "From each according to his abilities, to each according to his needs."[8] On the 1844 Marx's view, what I will call my *production activity* would be a good thing for me, a part of my self-realization (it would both express my individuality and help me to realize "my true nature, my *human* nature"). Here the idea of "from each according to his abilities" is not that I have an obligation to make my talents benefit the public or that I must make recompense for goods I've received. It is just a description of what communist life would be like. The exercise of my abilities would be simply a component of my own good.[9]

In the *Comments* Marx goes on to say that in the other's use of my product I would find satisfaction in "having thus created an object corresponding to the need of another *human* being." Suppose I have no personal financial worries, since I take what I need from the public till. I spend my time carving a chair. It is my form of self-realization. But I also want that chair to be used. My self-realization would be short-circuited if the chair were to rot in an attic. As with the cauliflower I grew, I want someone to use the chair I've made. Only then would I have helped to satisfy a human need, and only then would I "become recognized and felt by you yourself as a completion of your own nature."

In a communist society there would thus be a link between my production according to my abilities and your use according to your needs. My production would be *for* your needs, and your need satisfaction would be the final stage in my production. To help meet your (anyway, someone's) needs would be among my ends; actually meeting your (someone's) needs would also be a component of my good.

2. Marx lauds this relationship, but it has problems.

(i) First, there is the obvious coordination problem: how to ensure that while each produces as she pleases, together we generate the right mix of socially necessary outputs. The 1844 Marx does not share Fourier's view that a random sample of 1700 to 1800 people would have sufficiently complementary desires that each could do as she pleases and yet the socially necessary work be done, but he is clearly a bit too optimistic.[10]

(ii) A second coordination problem is somewhat whimsical. Complementarity within a communist community must – ideally – be absolutely perfect. It is actually crucial that *too much* not be produced. Otherwise some individuals would have made objects no one would use. With respect to that part of their production activities those individuals would not have the enjoyment of satisfying another's need, would not know themselves to be "confirmed" in anyone's "thought and . . . love." Marx does not require individuals to be altruistic in the sense of forgoing consumption on one another's behalf, but here an altruism of excess might be needed, where selflessness would be shown not by forgoing but by increasing one's consumption so as to confirm another person's production. The problem would be like that faced by the parent of a preschooler who must somehow find sufficient wall space to display the ceaseless stream of his child's drawings.

(iii) A final problem goes deeper. The requirement that we intend to facilitate one another's ends need not generate acceptable relationships. In Richard Connell's story "The Most Dangerous Game," the ruler of a small island deliberately wrecks passing ships, nurses the survivors to health, and then amuses himself by setting them free, arming them and then hunting them.[11] Assume it is important to this ruler that his prey is human, not a machine with a certain degree of strength and cunning. Assume further that he sees humans as essentially hunters of other humans. Imagine now that one day someone with the same conception of human nature is wrecked on the island. They exchange views and are delighted to find their deep agreement. Consumed with mutual admira-

tion, equally armed and in the best of moods, they set off to hunt one another.

Each hunter is determined to win, but each takes satisfaction in knowing that if he loses he will have made the other's triumph the right sort of triumph. Each not only seeks to attain his own end but to help the other attain his as well. These are not incompatible. Only if he is truly trying to win will each be a worthy foe, and so facilitate the right sort of triumph should he lose. In steadfastly seeking to kill the other each is doing all he can to help the other attain his end. There is thus the desired kind of complementarity of ends.

The point is simply that whether a relationship is acceptable goes to its content as well as its form. For the 1844 Marx, acceptable content is specified by his account of human beings as essentially producers, transformers of the natural world.[12] Communists would provide one another with products, not bullets.[13]

3. Now for Marx completing one another means more than just producing for one another's needs. In a communist society agents would also *mediate* for one another with the species. Marx says, more specifically, that the producer would mediate between the consumer and the species. I take the idea to be that under communism when another person uses my product she sees me as a representative of the species generally. In her use of the product she no doubt recognizes the specific use value I have produced, but she also recognizes that a human being has produced something with the intention that she use it. It is as if the species generally has produced something for her. I take the idea to be further – though this is not explicit in the text – that in seeing the species produce *for her*, she regards herself as having her species membership affirmed, as it were, going through what one might think of as a rite of affirmation.

Actually, I don't see why Marx wouldn't want to reverse the mediating relationship as well. Insofar as I am a producer under communism, couldn't the consumer similarly represent the species, and mediate between me and it? Her consumption with the recognition that I have produced something for human beings to use could be seen as the validation of my activity of producing (both to express my individuality and) for others, which for the 1844 Marx is the essential human activity. This too could presumably count as a way I can see my species membership affirmed. I suspect Marx has something like this in mind when he says that "therefore in my individual activity I would have directly confirmed and realized my true nature, my *human* nature, my *communal nature*."

An agent's species membership would be affirmed in these production/consumption interactions because these interactions involve the essential human activity (production), the activity through which Marx thinks human beings realize their nature as human beings. In such inter-actions agents would affirm one another not just as members of *some* group or other but specifically as members of the human species, as beings for whom the interactions in question are the way to realize their nature.

In a communist society, then, production and consumption would have a certain resonance. In their daily activities individuals would see their essential nature and their group (their species) membership writ large.

4. Marx says further that "Our products would be so many mirrors reflecting our nature."[14] Now suppose that the activity through which human beings realize their nature is the production of objects in order to express their individuality and to provide the means for others to attain their ends, and suppose that communists know this fact about them-selves. Then it would make sense for them to see the objects so produced as embodiments of their nature. And as such embodiments, the objects could be said to "reflect" their nature.

Note that products are Marx's mirrors, but that they can function as mirrors only if interpreted in a certain way. In themselves they are mere clay. To reflect human beings' essential nature they must be interpreted *as* embodying it: presumably, communists would so interpret them. And with products reciprocally mirroring our nature not only would I see both my product and your product as embodying human beings' essen-tial nature; I would also see that you see my product and your product as embodying human beings' essential nature; and I would see that you see that I see, etc.

So communists would see human nature reflected in their products (and would be aware of this fact about one another, and of one another's awareness, etc.), and would believe that this nature involves producing for one another. They would regard the objects of economic commerce as the expression of their common essential nature (and believe them to be regarded as such). The mirroring would express communists' belief that they share a common nature and that their current (and essential) relation to each other is that of intentional and reciprocal completing. Under such conditions, strong communal ties would presumably obtain.[15]

II

1. I have presented the 1844 Marx's picture of community. In this section I try to show the distinctiveness of the relationships involved.

Marx's community of the species is the generalization of a set of relationships. In these relationships individuals (i) engage in activities at

least part of whose point is to facilitate others' attainment of their ends;
(ii) recognize that fact about one another's activities; (iii) reciprocally
mediate for one another with the group; and (iv) recognize *that* fact
about one another's activities.

It would distort matters to think of such relationships as either simply
self-interested or simply altruistic. Take my desire to carve a chair others
will use. I would not attain my end were God to rain chairs from heaven
with the result that no one needed mine. My concern is not solely for
others' comfort. What I want is to satisfy a need; my desire is not merely
that somehow or other a need be satisfied. Yet this apparent egoism
cannot be understood apart from a focus on what others actually need. I
take care to make my chair durable and comfortable and pleasant to look
at. And I take satisfaction in others' use and appreciation of what I have
done. Although my end is not simply to benefit others, it *is* to make
something useful to others. For me to attain my end others must in fact
find what I have made useful.[16]

As for reciprocal mediation, on Marx's account one desires such mediation in order to realize one's nature as a communal being. However,
a person cannot receive such mediation unless she gives it back in the
right way. I must see myself and you in a certain light if I am in fact to see
us as engaged in a mediating activity. I must see myself as recognized as
engaged in an activity an important part of whose goal is the satisfaction
of your (anyway of some human being's) need. And since I want to
realize my nature, I must actually have the requisite goal in producing
(since, according to Marx, that is what my nature requires). Thus in order
to realize my nature I must produce objects useful to others, and I must
regard others as the kind of beings who can appreciate in the right way
that I have produced objects for them to use. And that means regarding
them also as beings who produce for me. It means appreciating *others'*
products in the right way. In effect, if you are to mediate between me and
the species I must satisfy the condition for me to mediate between you
and the species.[17]

2. In the relationships that Marx describes, individuals complete one
another, to use his term. On the one hand, your use of my object (with
the appropriate kind of appreciation) completes my project of producing
a particular object to be used, and is, more generally, part of the completion of my essential (human) nature (which centrally involves being a
producer of objects others can use); on the other hand, being mediated
with the human species completes me as a member of that group –
realizes my nature, Marx says, *qua* communal being.

The idea of completing one another may sound odd. It smacks of
Aristophanes' image in Plato's *Symposium* of a divided soul at last

finding its other half. But Aristophanes' spatial image makes it seem as if what we need from one another is merely some *thing*, merely some object with particular properties, and that is to miss the point. Crucial to both forms of their reciprocal completion is communists' *recognition* of their interactions as the reciprocal completion of one another. "Recognition" is not a fully adequate term. A communist would not merely note that something is the case, namely, that it is a human being who has produced this object I am using. Rather, recognition would involve both acknowledgment and affirmation. Marx thinks that under capitalism individuals acknowledge but regard as trivial the fact that they have produced objects for one another's use. They merely register this fact. He thinks that in a communist society individuals would regard this fact not as trivial but as vital. Only by seeing this fact *as* vital could communists see their production activity as a way to complete one another. That is, I take it that one would not regard an activity or state of affairs as completing oneself unless one saw it as picking out something vital to who one is. In the end the idea of completing one another is the idea that individuals can relate to one another in such a way that they do not merely acknowledge but also affirm their particular form of interdependence. The idea is that lived in the right way this interdependence would be a major part of an individual's good.[18]

3. Marx's view can be clarified further by contrasting the relationships in the *Comments* to those in two other pictures of good societies.

(i) Consider first a variation on Kant's notion of a realm of ends.[19] Imagine such a realm in which agents do not believe that other agents are acting as Kantians. Each believes others are motivated exclusively by their particular desires. Each believes no one else is even trying to act from a concern for the moral law (though each is in fact doing so). And each believes the others believe *she* is motivated exclusively by *her* particular desires.

These agents are interdependent. They need one another to pursue happiness under the conditions of human life. Still, consistent with Kant's requirements, their relationships of mutual aid could be altogether impersonal in the sense that, in principle, what such agents need from one another might be only those objects and services necessary to satisfy their various desires. Such agents don't necessarily need *help*, that is, the aid specifically of other human beings. An agent who by good luck was entirely self-sufficient would – *qua* Kantian – have lost nothing.

Further, Kantians do not need one another to express their essential nature, that is, their nature as rational beings. For this a Kantian needs neither aid nor recognition from others.[20] A Kantian can realize her nature on her own. In these ways the Kantian picture is individualist. There is no necessary reciprocal dependence.[21]

The contrast to the 1844 Marx should be clear. On his account agents realize their nature through a set of interactions which must be interactions of reciprocal dependence with other human beings who, moreover, must understand the content of the interactions. A communist cannot be self-sufficient. And she would not realize her nature if she did not have the proper beliefs about other communists and their ends and beliefs in producing and consuming, or if they did not have the proper beliefs about her and her ends and beliefs in producing and consuming. A communist cannot realize her nature on her own.

(ii) My second example is Gerald Cohen's sketch of life under communism. Cohen writes:

One way of picturing life under communism, as Marx conceived it, is to imagine a jazz band each player in which seeks his own fulfillment as a musician. Though motivated to secure his own fulfillment, as opposed to that of the band as a whole, or of his fellow musicians taken severally, he nevertheless fulfills himself maximally to the extent that each of the others also does so, and the same holds for each of them. . . . I do not say that no one cares about the musical fulfillment of the others . . . but no concern for others is demanded.[22]

Cohen is here focusing on a phrase from the *Communist Manifesto*. Communism, Marx says in the *Manifesto*, is "an association, in which the free development of each is the condition for the free development of all."[23] At issue is not Cohen's understanding of the *Manifesto* (I think he is accurate about that text) but the contrast of his view to that in the *Comments*. In Cohen's example "each player . . . seeks his own fulfillment as a musician." Each depends on the others to gain this fulfillment because he depends on the others' playing to create the context for his own performance. But nothing in Cohen's picture requires a player's fellow musicians to be humans rather than machines. If machines with sufficient musical proficiency could be constructed, Cohen's jazz musicians could attain fulfillment by playing with those machines rather than with each other.

The 1844 Marx says that communist individuals would mediate between one another and the species. This is something only human beings can do for one another.[24] "As a human being [*als Mensch*]," Marx complains, "[in a capitalist society] you stand in no relationship to my object."[25] This could be equally true in Cohen's jazz band.[26]

No doubt Cohen's musicians know they are playing with musicians not machines, but on his description this fact need not be important to them. In principle, they could attain their ends without recognizing (in the sense of both acknowledging and affirming) one another *qua* musicians.

Now Cohen's description of this jazz band seems to me too thin. Keith Graham faults him for not seeing that the members of a band have a shared final end – presumably to have a good performance – like the goal, Graham says, "of winning in a team sport."[27] But even this does not adequately specify the relationships among the individuals in the course of playing. (It also points to the wrong kind of focus; see the next subsection for two distinctions in types of shared ends.) Musicians in a band, especially a jazz band, are likely more or less consciously to play in continually shifting response to one another: they have a musical conversation. Implicit in that conversation is likely to be a reciprocal recognition (both acknowledgment and affirmation) of one another as members of a band with a shared end. And suppose part of these musicians' shared end *qua* musicians was to play music in which a conversation with another musician could occur. Musicians with such a shared end would help complete one another *qua* musicians.[28]

4. As a last way to get at the specificity of Marx's picture I want to look at two distinctions in how individuals might share ends. First, communists' shared end is an *internally oriented* end. Their shared end is simply to live in a society structured in a certain way. There is no further goal. Marx's communists seek to realize their nature as beings who simultaneously express their individuality and produce for others as part of the species' continual joint transformation of itself and the world. Their shared end is the creation of a society in which individuals can realize their nature so understood. There is no social goal distinct from this.[29]

By contrast, an *externally oriented* shared end involves attaining some goal held by the collectivity as a whole. This could take many forms: attaining God's kingdom on earth, attaining the nation's manifest destiny, etc. The point is that agents are concerned to promote something going beyond merely a certain form of living with one another.

The second distinction is between *overlapping* and *intertwined* shared ends. Ends overlap when agents have the same end but attaining it with and through others is not a necessary condition of attaining the end. Consider the donors to a fund drive to raise money for research to eradicate some disease. These people share an end, but they need one another only because a joint effort is required to raise money. It would hardly defeat their shared end if one donor gave enough to support all the research, or if fortunate natural circumstances made the disease disappear. By contrast, it is part of the description of a communist's activities that she is producing *for* other human beings (and that in consuming she appreciates what others have produced *for* her). Her ends would not be attained if her products were to rot or God were to rain manna. Persons with such ends in common – persons for whom it is crucial that they help satisfy one another's ends – have intertwined ends.

I take the standard communitarian view to be that having shared final external ends is the way to generate communal ties. Perhaps this is often true. But the appropriate comparison is not between external and internal overlapping shared ends. *That* comparison might be between a community united by a shared religious belief (external end) and a libertarian society in which agents share the end of living in a stable, minimal state (internal end). Some degree of communal ties could obtain among the latter group, but it would likely be weak. When final ends merely overlap, it may be that a shared external goal is needed to generate communal ties.

The proper comparison, though, is between external overlapping and internal intertwined shared final ends. Communists' shared final ends are intertwined. It is not a contingent fact that they need each other, and each knows and affirms this. Given their nature it is vital that they attain their ends through one another's assistance. Assuming this sort of relationship to obtain, it is reasonable to think strong communal ties would also obtain even in the absence of any shared external end.[30]

5. Communities formed via overlapping external shared ends are structurally different from those formed via internal intertwined shared ends. In a community characterized by external overlapping ends agents are bound to each other not one-to-one but through their shared final end. We do not necessarily see ourselves as doing things for others; nor do we necessarily see others as doing things for us. Rather, we see ourselves and others as doing things for the sake of the external end we share. That my actions contribute to attaining your end (the advent of God's kingdom) is a contingent consequence of the nature of my end (the advent of God's kingdom); it is not part of the content of my end. I want God's kingdom to come even if you don't. I might be pleased you do as well (but I also might not), and that you do might establish an important relationship between us (but it also might not). Here community would be a consequence of ends not themselves geared toward satisfying one another's needs.

An analogy to friendship is useful. People often become friends by pursuing a shared interest, and pursuing a shared interest is often part of a continuing friendship. But consider two shared interests. First, friends might share an interest in a particular brand of politics: they might share political commitments. Second, they might share an interest in tennis: they might enjoy smashing a fuzzy ball back and forth over a net.

I think for most people with a shared interest in politics the key concern would be to get the right candidate selected, elected, and so forth. In doing so it would be nicer to work with friends than with people you don't like, and the people you work with might become your friends, but your focus would be your particular political goal. Tennis is likely to be different. Of course a person could be passionately devoted to the game, and even devoted to winning every match, eager to play any time with anyone and always desperate to win. But that is not what tennis is like as an interest one shares with a friend. As such it is not just an activity one enjoys, but an opportunity to do something with one's friend. A significant part of one's enjoyment in playing tennis with X could be that one is playing tennis specifically with X. A significant part of the point of playing tennis with X could be to maintain one's relationship with X.

It has often been noted that many valuable things are essentially by-products of activities pursued for other reasons: one cannot attain these things by aiming directly at them.[31] But some things that are initially by-products can subsequently be aimed at, perhaps not directly but at least half-on. Friendship can be of this kind. Once one is in a relationship of friendship it is not odd to search for things to do *with* one's friend.

If pushed hard the analogy of friendship to community will break down. My claim is simply that it can be a feature of an activity that it is structurally the right sort of activity to promote a particular kind of relationship. The production and consumption activities of Marx's communists are structurally the right sort of activities to promote a particular kind of communal tie.[32]

III

1. In this final section I argue that the activities of citizens in *A Theory of Justice*'s "well-ordered society" can be seen this way as well.[33] That will set up a contrast between *Theory* and *Political Liberalism*.

For the 1844 Marx humans are essentially beings who pursue their particular production activities while simultaneously generating the means for others to pursue theirs. Production with the appropriate ends and beliefs under the appropriate social conditions is how Marx thinks a communist would realize her nature. The features of human beings that Rawls highlights are what in "Kantian Constructivism in Moral Theory" he calls our "two moral powers . . . the capacity to understand, to apply and to act from (and not merely in accordance with) the principles of justice . . . [and] the capacity to form, to revise and rationally to pursue a conception of the good."[34] In the well-ordered society, he says in *Theory*, "moral personality" – that is, the possession of what in "Kantian Constructivism" is referred to as the two moral powers – is regarded "as the fundamental aspect of the self."[35] I take *Theory*'s well-ordered society to represent the optimal conditions for the realization of this fundamental aspect of the self.

In *Theory* the desired relationship between citizens in the well-ordered society is that of reciprocal appreciation and confirmation of one another's talents. Individuals follow their own life plans, but, Rawls says, "our person and deeds [are] appreciated and confirmed by others."[36] Rawls refers to individuals' life plans as complementary, and says that each takes pleasure in what others do. "The successes and enjoyments of others are necessary for and complimentary [sic] to our own good."[37] And: "The members of a community participate in one another's nature: we appreciate what others do as things we might have done but which they do for us, and what we do is similarly done for them."[38]

This sounds vaguely like the relationships the 1844 Marx describes. Now Marx thinks that in their production/consumption activities communists complete one another both *qua* producers and *qua* communal beings. Do the citizens of the well-ordered society complete one another? I think they do, but not by the same kinds of activities or in quite the same ways as Marx's communists. To see the differences we need to consider four ways to regard an activity. An individual might regard an activity (i) as involving the pursuit of a particular local goal in which she finds short term satisfaction (e.g., building a chair); (ii) as contributing in some way to realizing her conception of her own good; (iii) as contributing in some way to realizing her essential nature as a human being; and (iv) as contributing to the maintenance of the proper form of society. For the 1844 Marx a communist's understanding of her production activity would involve all four elements. She would choose her specific activity (e.g., building a chair) to satisfy her immediate individual inclination, and in so doing she would presumably believe she was both attaining her own good (which would centrally involve production activity in some form) and helping to realize her essential nature as a human being (which centrally involves production activity), and that she was engaged in the activity basic to the maintenance of the proper form of society.

Under communism there would be variation among individuals at level (i) (not everyone would want to make chairs all the time) and at level (ii) (people would have different conceptions of how particular types of production activity fit into a conception of their own good). There would be no variation at levels (iii) or (iv). For everyone would see production activity as the way to realize their nature as human beings, and everyone would regard such activity as the basic contribution to the maintenance of the proper form of society.

It may seem redundant to talk of realizing both one's conception of one's good and one's essential nature as a human being. In fact these are connected but not identical. For example, one might think of human beings as essentially creators, but this would be compatible with choosing to be a novelist, a city planner, a politician, a builder of empires, and so on. Within the framework of "creative activity" one would still need to determine which kind of creative activity (or set of activities) would constitute one's own good. A conception of human beings' essential nature constrains but does not determine one's conception of one's good.[39]

In Rawls's well-ordered society there is variation with respect to both (i) and (ii). Indeed, there is probably wider variation among conceptions of one's good than in Marx's 1844 picture. Marx's account of human beings' essential nature does not determine a unique conception of an agent's good, but it does impose relatively narrow constraints: one's conception of one's good must involve production activity of some form. With moral personality seen as the fundamental aspect of the self the constraints are much looser. The only constraints are those imposed by considerations of justice.

More important, in the well-ordered society citizens do not complete one another in quite the same way as under communism. Communists complete one another, first, *qua* producers. For this to happen both producer and consumer must see (and be believed by the other to see) a specific activity, the activity of production, *as* the essential human activity. But in the well-ordered society the view that moral personality is the fundamental aspect of the self precludes any straightforward analogue to production activity. With moral personality rather than the capacity to produce seen as the fundamental aspect of the self, there is no specific type of activity most citizens believe is expressive of human beings' nature, no specific type of activity corresponding to the role of production for Marx. So citizens do not complete one another *qua* beings for whom a particular type of activity expresses their nature (since none is thought by most citizens to do so).

Still, communists also complete one another in a second sense, in the sense of confirming one another's communal nature. They help one another feel deeply identified with the collectivity, part of the larger whole. This does occur in the well-ordered society but in a more complicated way because element (iv) – contribution to the proper form of society – is more complicated. On the one hand, in the well-ordered society citizens appreciate one another's particular activities (e.g., producing, selling, administering) as contributing to the maintenance of the proper form of society. On the other hand, there is also what could be thought of as another form of activity in the well-ordered society that is equally or even more basic to the maintenance of the proper form of society: the giving and receiving of justice from one another. Day after day citizens abide by the principles of justice regulating the well-ordered society, and they do so because each believes those principles are just and believes others also abide by them from that belief.

Now as a social creation the well-ordered society has two key features: it is the aggregate of citizens' activities, and it is just. Whether citizens of the well-ordered society complete one another in this second sense (in the sense, as Marx puts it, of confirming one another's communal nature) depends on the role of these two features in their lives.

As for the first feature, Rawls says that citizens come to see other citizens' accomplishments as their own. In the well-ordered society, he says:

the good attained from the common culture far exceeds our work in the sense that we cease to be mere fragments: that part of ourselves that we directly realize is joined to a wider and just arrangement the aims of which we affirm. The division of labor is overcome not by each becoming complete in himself, but by willing and meaningful work within a just social union of social unions.[40]

We "cease to be mere fragments." We identify with the social whole.

As for the second feature, citizens' contribution to the maintenance of a just society should be thought of in two ways: as actual political partici- pation, and as a stance toward one another in daily life. To begin with, citizens share the end of maintaining just institutions, and it is reasonable to think most engage in some degree of political participation, if only in the sense of sincere debate with fellow citizens about the issues of the day.[41] Citizens provide one another not with products but with argu- ments and ideas, with the intention to promote just institutions read into such interactions. By this means individuals' sense of themselves as part of the well-ordered society is strengthened.

In addition, in a less explicit but more pervasive way the same thing happens throughout daily life. Indeed, the giving and receiving of justice in the well-ordered society should be thought of as a kind of secondary quality of daily actions. Commitment to the social form in which they live should be thought of as read into citizens' law-abiding actions generally, just as the intention to produce something others can use is read into the production activities of communists.

For the 1844 Marx production activity is the way agents mediate for one another with the collectivity, the way they come to see themselves and others *as* members of a collectivity. In *Theory* the activity of con- forming one's conduct to society's laws, where it is publicly understood that one does so because one believes those laws to be the publicly acknowledged output of just institutions, plays this role. "What binds a society's efforts into one social union," Rawls says, "is the mutual recognition and acceptance of the principles of justice; it is this general affirmation which extends the ties of identification over the whole community."[42] Such mutual recognition and acceptance (what I earlier talked of as acknowledgment and affirmation), and the reciprocal recognition *of* the mutual recognition and acceptance, generates identification with the community so that through their interactions with one another citizens cease to be mere fragments and feel themselves part of a larger whole.

At this point we can also see a way in which ordinary daily activities in the well-ordered society do involve a parallel to that completion of one another's essential nature characteristic of production/consumption activities in the 1844 Marx's picture of communism. For suppose that read into one's actions in the well-ordered society were one's intention to pursue one's own conception of the good *while remaining within the bounds of just social rules.* On the assumption that moral personality (including, importantly, a willingness to apply and to act from principles of justice) is in fact and is publicly believed to be the fundamental aspect of the self, citizens' confirmation of one another's actions *as* having this structure would be reciprocal confirmation of the fundamental aspect of the self – and I take this to be more or less equivalent to reciprocal completion of one another's essential nature. Were citizens to read the relevant intentions and beliefs into one another's actions (and to read their readings), they would be completing one another's nature in a manner structurally similar to that depicted by the 1844 Marx.[43]

So citizens in *Theory's* well-ordered society do complete one another *qua* communal beings, and also *qua* beings for whom moral personality is the fundamental aspect of the self.[44]

2. Such citizens also share an important final end, namely, the maintenance of a just society. Rawls calls the maintenance of a just society a great good. Indeed, he calls it "the preeminent form of human flourishing" and says that "persons best express their nature" by maintaining just institutions.[45] For all citizens this is a central accomplishment, a shared final end.[46] And it is an internally, not an externally oriented shared end, for the shared end is simply to live in a society organized in a certain way.[47] Moreover, citizens' shared end is an intertwined, not an overlapping shared end. Citizens need one another to realize the good of living in a just society not merely because they need one another's strength and cooperation and forbearance from injustice; they need one another to realize this good because this good involves the reciprocal recognition (the acknowledgment and affirmation) of one another as

contributors to the maintenance of just institutions and as beings for whom moral personality (including a willingness to apply and to act from principles of justice) is the fundamental aspect of the self. Indeed, that citizens do complete one another as beings for whom moral personality is the fundamental aspect of the self is a consequence of the fact that in the well-ordered society they have successfully attained their shared final end of maintaining just institutions (just as the fact that Marx's communists complete one another *qua* producers is a consequence of their having attained their shared final end of living in a communist society).

3. In his more recent book, *Political Liberalism*, Rawls claims that in the well-ordered society of *Theory* "all citizens endorse [justice as fairness] on the basis" of what he terms "a comprehensive philosophical doctrine," that is, a general view of what is of value in human life.[48] Rawls says little about the content of *Theory*'s comprehensive doctrine but it very likely involves such claims as that moral personality is the fundamental aspect of the self and that the collective activity of justice is the preeminent form of human flourishing.[49] I take such claims to be what the new book refuses to endorse.[50]

Nevertheless, Rawls continues to hold to a great deal from *Theory*. He says that in a well-ordered society (as he now understands it) agents are "fully cooperating members of society" and want to be recognized *as* fully cooperating members.[51] He fills this out as the claim that agents "want to realize . . . and have it recognized that they realize, [a certain] ideal of citizens."[52] And he says that in the well-ordered society "the exercise of the two moral powers is experienced as a good."[53] He continues to think of society as a social union of social unions and says that, so conceived, "the ties of reciprocity are extended over the whole of society and individual and group accomplishments are no longer seen as so many separate personal or associational goods."[54] Moreover, in *Theory*, Rawls defines autonomy as "acting from principles that we would consent to as free and equal rational beings," namely, the principles of justice that would be adopted in the original position.[55] Citizens of *Theory*'s well-ordered society satisfy this definition. In *Political Liberalism* Rawls says of what he there calls "full autonomy" that "it is in their public recognition and informed application of the principles of justice . . . that citizens achieve full autonomy."[56] And he goes on to say that full autonomy is "realized in public life by affirming the political principles of justice and enjoying the protections of the basic rights and liberties; it is also realized by participating in society's public affairs and sharing in its collective self-determination over time."[57]

Where, then, is the difference between the earlier and the later view? It comes in *Political Liberalism*'s insistence that full autonomy is "a political and not an ethical value," and in *Political Liberalism's* separation of the political from any value "which may apply to the whole of life, both social and individual."[58] The underlying idea is that for many people the central goods of life are not to be found in the sphere of political institutions, and whatever value political philosophy puts on that sphere must not impugn the value many people put on other areas of life. On the new account, in abiding by and self-consciously living within the laws of a just society, and in participating in its collective self-determination over time we are indeed engaging in a set of reciprocal activities by which we realize part of our nature; nevertheless, what we realize in these ways is merely part, and not necessarily the most important part, of our nature. For the purposes of political philosophy, the collective activity of justice is no longer taken to be the *preeminent* form of human flourishing.

The new version of justice as fairness is clearly going to be less communitarian than the old. For imagine three spots on a continuum. At one end is the *non-communitarian well-ordered society*. There agents abide by the two principles of justice and think themselves obligated to do so. They engage in political activity, voting conscientiously and even standing for office when they think it their duty. Such agents exercise their capacity for a sense of justice. However, they do not regard this as a significant good. They believe nothing would be lost if the circumstances requiring the excercise of that capacity, the circumstances of justice, were to disappear. Like early Christians complying with Roman authorities they do what they ought but their real life is elsewhere. They acknowledge the obligations that come with living with others, but for them these are *only* obligations. They do not also represent an important opportunity. In daily life these people might read their own and others' actions as the actions of beings exercising their capacity for a sense of justice, but such an interpretation would not generate communal ties because that requires believing it important to belong to a group of beings exercising their capacity for a sense of justice, and it requires believing that most other group members believe this as well. Missing here is the belief that what is shared with all other citizens – moral personality – both is paradigmatically expressed via interactions specifically in one's capacity as a citizen, and is, and is widely believed to be, a very important part of one's nature.

At the other extreme we find the well-ordered society of *Theory*. There the circumstances that make the collective activity of justice necessary represent a fortunate fall. They provide the opportunity to regulate our conflicts of interest via the principles of justice and so to realize what is believed to be the fundamental aspect of the self. In this society communal ties flow through the activity of supporting just institutions.

The third society on the continuum – that of *Political Liberalism* – is somewhere in between. The question is where. There are two variables: how many people see the exercise of a sense of justice as a good in itself; and, for those who do, how heavily they weight that good.[59] For participation in public life to generate communal ties (a) an agent must regard her identity as a citizen as very important, that is, she must put a high value on her activities in the sphere of political institutions (whether this involves direct political participation, debate with others, or merely daily compliance with just institutions); and (b) there must be, and be publicly believed to be, a critical mass of agents who also put a high value on such activities. Depending on the beliefs agents attribute to one another, they will or will not regard interactions with other citizens as realizing a very important part of their nature; and if these interactions are *not* so regarded they cannot be a way individuals "mediate" for one another with the group (Marx's phrasing), they cannot extend "the ties of identification over the whole community" (Rawls's phrasing). The less that complying with just institutions and engaging in political life are and are publicly believed to realize a very important part of a citizen's nature, the less such activities can function in this way.

Rawls does still say that the end of "supporting just institutions and of giving one another justice accordingly" is a shared final end.[60] However, for at least some and perhaps for many citizens in the well-ordered society of *Political Liberalism* this shared end will be relatively unimportant. It is no longer said to be the case that by maintaining just institutions citizens tend to see themselves as thereby realizing the fundamental aspect of the self. And it would not be rational for those who would like to see the maintenance of just institutions that way to believe that a sufficient number of their fellow citizens have the same view. Of course a sufficient number might have the same view. But this seems unlikely given the pluralism with respect to comprehensive doctrines to which the new theory is adapted. Given such pluralism, it seems unlikely that a sufficient number of citizens will see the maintenance of just institutions as the way to realize the fundamental aspect of the self. And then it would not be rational, even for those who would like to do so, to regard the activity of supporting just institutions as a collective activity in the full sense, as a common activity citizens do not merely acknowledge but also affirm. Given the fact of pluralism, it seems unlikely that communal bonds could now flow through the activity of supporting just institutions.

4. This is hardly surprising. Rawls explicitly denies that the well-ordered society of *Political Liberalism* is a community, for its citizens do not share a comprehensive doctrine.[61] But Rawls believes that considerable social unity remains. Here I think he is mistaken. The problem can be seen by looking at the good of social union in the context of the new view.

Rawls concedes that a condition for everyone to regard "the richness and diversity of society's public culture as the result of everyone's cooperative efforts for mutual good" is that "citizens . . . be able to recognize their shared public purpose and common allegiance."[62] But for a citizen to relate to the public culture – something created largely by others – as in a sense her creation, she must not only see that others have the relevant shared purpose (namely, to support "just institutions and [give] one another justice"), and the relevant shared purpose must not only play a very important role in her conception of her own overall good; she must also believe it plays such a role for many others.

My claim here is psychological. It is easy to acknowledge that society's public culture is the result of everyone's efforts (how else could it have been generated?), but Rawls intends that fact to have impact. He intends it to enable one to relate to the public culture in a certain way, to take pleasure and pride in it. But one's ability to see the works of others as also one's own depends on believing that others will see one's own work as also theirs. If I believe others will merely acknowledge the fact that the public culture is a shared creation but not also affirm that shared creation as important to them, so not also affirm *my* work as important to them, then it will be difficult for me to affirm *their* work as important to me. It will be difficult for me to take pleasure and pride in their work. But in Rawls's new well-ordered society I will know that, given the fact of pluralism, it is unlikely that most people will affirm my work in the required way, for I will know that it is unlikely that most people will see our shared creation of society's public culture as a very important element in their overall good. I think it would then be hard to avail myself of the good of social union. Rawls admits that perhaps only a few people will avail themselves of it.[63] But social union is not the sort of thing only a few people can avail themselves of. Some threshold (and, I suspect, relatively large) number of citizens must do so and be believed to do so. As a good, social union not only has a social content; the psychological conditions for its enjoyment are social as well.[64]

5. Citizens in Rawls's new well-ordered society do not complete one another. That is not because they no longer share an internally oriented intertwined end. It is because they no longer share what most see (and are believed to see) as a very important final end. They no longer need one another to attain the shared very important final end of maintaining just institutions, because for most that is not – certainly not believed to be – a shared very important final end. And it will be difficult for them to see their shared culture as a social union of social unions: it will be

difficult for them to affirm rather than merely to register it as the result of what they do for one another.[65] They complete one another neither *qua* communal beings nor *qua* beings for whom moral personality is the fundamental aspect of the self.

A community is a set of relationships. If a community has no external end, then its citizens must, in general, be committed to their reciprocal dependence. They must believe such dependence to be an opportunity as well as a burden; and they must believe that others believe this. In the well-ordered society of *Political Liberalism* such commitment and such beliefs don't seem sufficiently to obtain.

My aims have been primarily exegetical. I have tried to link two writers not usually put together, the 1844 Marx and the Rawls of *A Theory of Justice*: the young Marx and the young Rawls. In doing so, I have presented a picture of communal relationships different from the standard one. But all communal relationships rest on substantive shared beliefs, what Rawls calls a comprehensive doctrine (including, presumably, beliefs about the fundamental aspect of the self). Now in general one might worry that, because particular communities rest on particular comprehensive doctrines, stressing the value of community will lead to scanting the liberties of those who don't share the local comprehensive doctrine. The worry is that a commitment to community is liable to be at odds with a commitment to liberty.

This is a legitimate concern but I think, for two reasons, that it is often raised too quickly. First, the theories of academic philosophers will not soon be embodied in constitutions or legislation, and at this point we should not allow the worry about what might happen if they were so embodied to keep us from debating the varied *desiderata* of a good society. Second, internally oriented communities might be quite compatible with the classic individual liberties, the well-ordered society of *Theory* being a case in point. At least in principle such communities could provide room for individuals to go their own way. No general social goal is promoted, and so it is not obviously likely that there would be a threat to individual liberties. Of course there remains Rawls's recent worry that even an internally oriented community involves a comprehensive doctrine and so is inappropriate for a pluralist society. But it is worth pointing out that this worry is not the same as the usual worry about the suppression of individual liberties by a society with a dominant end.

Perhaps it will turn out to be impossible to reconcile community with a pluralism of comprehensive doctrines. And perhaps it will turn out that, between these two, it is the aspiration to community that should be abandoned. Still, it will be worth knowing what is being abandoned, what the value of community amounts to. I don't think we know this yet, because I don't think we know the range of relationships a community might involve. Recent decades have seen the development of a rich array of liberal conceptions on the one hand, and on the other hand mostly abstract and polemical remarks by communitarians. There has been little attempt to investigate the various relationships community might involve and even less to assess which is best. Productive engagement between the communitarian and the liberal requires a better account of what the structure of a community should be.

NOTES

My debt to John Rawls is several-fold. It is of course a student's debt to the teacher who taught him his trade (and whose works renew the teaching with each re-reading); and it is the debt of everyone who does or is affected by political philosophy to the writer who transformed the subject; but it is perhaps most of all a debt to the person who has been, for me (and I suspect for all of his students) the absolute model for the depth, the intellectual integrity, and always for the fundamental decency of a true philosopher.

I am grateful to Michael Hardimon, Edward Minar, Andrews Reath, and Candace Vogler for helpful comments on earlier drafts of this article.

1. See Michael Sandel, *Liberalism and the Limits of Justice* (Cambridge University Press, 1982).
2. Karl Marx, *Comments on James Mill, Elémens d'économie politique*, in Karl Marx and Friedrich Engels, *Collected Works* (New York: International Publishers, 1968), Vol. 3, pp. 227–8; "Auszüge aus James Mills Buch *Elémens d'économie politique*," in Karl Marx, Friedrich Engels, *Werke* (Berlin: Dietz Verlag, Ergänzungsband), p. 462. I cite the *Collected Works* edition because of its availability. At a number of places I have amended the translation. See note 5. Emphasis is in the original unless otherwise noted.
3. Marx, *Comments*, p. 227; "Auszüge," p. 462.
4. Marx, *Comments*, pp. 227–8, "Auszüge," pp. 462–3.
5. Marx, *Comments*, pp. 217, 226, 228; "Auszüge," pp. 451, 460, 462. The German I have translated as "completion" is *Ergänzung*. Translators of the *Comments* have rendered *Ergänzung* in the three cited places variously as "completion," "complement," "supplement," and "redintegration." (*Ergänzen* and *Ergänzung* are each used one other time in the *Comments* – pp. 212 and 220 – but with a different reference, i.e., not with reference to human agents and what they do for one another.) I prefer "completion" for its suggestion that what agents provide one another is something crucial, something that fills a fundamental gap. "Supplement" suggests something relatively unimportant. "Complement" is better but still not quite right. It suggests something that is fitting but perhaps not necessary: something whose absence is not obviously very bad. "Redintegration" (defined by the OED as "restoration, reestablishment, reconstruction, renewal") is better still but it both is awkward and suggests that Marx is after the *re*establishment of something that existed prior to capitalism and that capital-

ism has destroyed, and I think that is not in fact his view. I should note that the translator for the *Collected Works* translates *Ergänzung* on p. 228 as "completion," but on pp. 217 and 226 as "complement." In quoting the passage from p. 226 I have amended the translation. I am indebted to Candace Vogler for urging that, in the relevant places, "completion" is the best translation.

6. Marx, *Comments*, p. 226; "Auszüge," p. 460.
7. Marx himself makes this point in the *Grundrisse*. See Karl Marx, *Grundrisse*, trans. Martin Nicolaus (New York: Vintage Books, 1973), p. 241. No doubt Marx would argue that capitalism impels agents to deceive or coerce, but to rest the 1844 critique of capitalism on its tendency toward such things would raise the possibility that an increasingly regulated capitalism would be increasingly acceptable to Marx. And that is false.
8. Marx, *Critique of the Gotha Programme*, in Karl Marx and Friedrich Engels, *Selected Works* (New York: International Publishers, 1984), p. 325.
9. Gerald Cohen makes this point. See Gerald Cohen, "Marxism and Contemporary Political Philosophy, or: Why Nozick Exercises Some Marxists More than He Does Any Egalitarian Liberals," *Canadian Journal of Philosophy*, Supplementary Volume 16 (1990): 381–2. See also Gerald Cohen and Keith Graham, "Self-Ownership, Communism and Equality," *Proceedings of the Aristotelian Society*, Supplementary Volume 64 (1990): 31–2. See also Allen Buchanan, *Marx and Justice* (Totowa, NJ: Rowman and Littlefield, 1982), p. 24.
10. See Frank E. Manuel and Fritzie P. Manuel, *Utopian Thought in the Western World* (Cambridge: Harvard University Press, 1982), p. 659.
11. See Richard Connell, "The Most Dangerous Game," in *O'Henry Prize Stories, 1924* (New York: Doubleday, Page, & Company, 1925), pp. 71–92.
12. Marx's account of human nature is scattered throughout the works of 1844, especially the *Economic and Philosophic Manuscripts*. See in particular the manuscripts "Estranged Labor" and "Private Property and Communism."
13. There is actually a further question for Marx's picture. Would it matter to me *how* you used my product? I carve the chair and you use it in a piece of conceptual art or a theater production such that (i) you have to paint it magenta, and (ii) no one ever sits in it. It is vital to the pursuit of your ends. Has this use of it helped me attain mine?
14. Marx, *Comments*, p. 228; "Auszüge," p. 463 (translation amended).
15. Marx is claiming that one's products would reflect both one's individual and one's species nature, but for the most part other people could register only the latter. Marx speaks of having "the individual pleasure of knowing my personality to be *objective, sensuously perceptible* and hence a power raised *beyond all doubt*." The implicit model seems to be an artist's individual expression in a book, painting, etc. Perhaps a farmer could see her cauliflowers that way. They embody her sweat and forethought, her anxiety about the weather, and so on. Still, a cauliflower is a cauliflower is a cauliflower. Those produced by different farmers are indistinguishable. A batch of cauliflowers could express a person's individuality in the sense that producing them is part of her life plan and that is unique. But cauliflowers are not themselves unique. A consumer could not see one as the product of a particular individual. Mass consumption objects cannot mirror unique individuals.

16. This example is structurally identical to one Christine Korsgaard uses in "The Reasons We Can Share: An Attack on the Distinction between Agent-Relative and Agent-Neutral Values," *Social Philosophy & Policy*, 10 (1993) pp. 37–8.

17. There is an apparent similarity to Hegel's master–slave relationship here, so it is worth a note to locate the difference. Hegel's agents seek to negate the external world in three ways: (a) by risking their lives and so affirming that they are not merely material objects; (b) by transforming the world through work; and (c) by consuming the world. In the situation Marx describes it is clear that (b) and (c) are satisfied; however, bees, beavers, and other creatures that work on nature and are interdependent also satisfy (b) and (c). For Hegel, the key in (a) is the element of recognition the master wishes to extract from the slave. But this recognition is supposed to be recognition precisely that the master is a being who is *not* essentially material, who is also crucially and in fact essentially consciousness. For the 1844 Marx this is a false dichotomy and a misunderstanding of the kind of beings we are. It is the mistake characteristic of alienated thought under capitalism. For Marx the desired recognition is rather recognition as a material being who is a conscious transformer and consumer of the material world. In the section on the master and the slave Hegel says:

> The presentation of itself, however, as the pure abstraction of self-consciousness consists in showing itself as the pure negation of its objective mode, or in showing that it is not attached to any specific *existence* [*Dasein*], not the individuality common to existence as such, that it is not attached to life. (G. W. F. Hegel, *Phenomenology of Spirit*, trans. A. V. Miller [Oxford: Oxford University Press, 1977], p. 113)

For Hegel this independence from any specific existence is key. By contrast, for Marx agents are in fact tied to a specific existence or at least to a specific *kind* of existence – that is, they are conscious transformers and consumers of the material world – and they recognize one another under that description. For Marx there is no need for a separate recognition as a being not attached to life, as mere consciousness, and so no need to risk one's life.

There is a further difference. For Hegel the fight for recognition obtains in its extreme form of a fight to the death only

> in the natural state, where men exist only as single, separate individuals; but it is absent in civil society and the State because here the recognition for which the combatants fought already exists. . . . What dominates in the State is the spirit of the people, custom, and law. (G. W. F. Hegel, *Philosophy of Mind*, trans. William Wallace and A. V. Miller [Oxford: Oxford University Press, 1990], §432, p. 172)

For Marx the recognition for which people strive would obtain in their direct economic interactions. Its primary occurrence would not be through such things as customs and laws. See also note 32.

18. As I attribute its use to Marx, the notion of completion is "essentialist" in the sense that it assumes that human beings have a specific nature to be completed. However, the degree of metaphysical commitment will vary with what is to be completed. For instance, completing oneself *qua* citizen presupposes some relatively determinate conception of what it is to realize one's nature as a citizen, but this could be spelled out in a rough and ready way, e.g., citizens participate in public affairs and put the concerns of the state

high on the list of their own concerns. There need be no commitment to the view that human beings are essentially citizens, but only a view of what it is to complete oneself under the description "citizen." Completing oneself is always doing so under a particular description, and that description must have a relatively determinate content. The degree of metaphysical commitment embedded in the description is a separate question.

19. See Immanuel Kant, *Grounding for the Metaphysics of Morals*, trans. James W. Ellington (Indianapolis: Hackett Publishing Company, 1981), pp. 39ff.

20. I have said "in principle" since perhaps in practice benign external circumstances make it easier to express one's nature as a rational being. Kant remarks that adversity might tempt one "to violate one's duty" (see Immanuel Kant, *The Metaphysics of Morals*, trans. Mary J. Gregor [Cambridge University Press, 1991], pp. 192–3). But benign circumstances are not a necessary condition for expressing one's nature as a rational being.

21. Robert Pippin raises this question about Kant. See his "Hegel on the Rationality and Priority of Ethical Life," *Neue Hefte für Philosophie* 35 (1995): 109n33. For an argument that Kant's realm of ends necessarily involves reciprocal recognition, see Andrews Reath, "Legislating for a Realm of Ends: The Social Dimension of Autonomy," this volume.

22. Cohen, "Marxism and Contemporary Political Philosophy," p. 381. See also Cohen and Graham, "Self-Ownership, Communism and Equality," p. 32. Jon Elster uses a similar analogy; see Elster, "Self-Realization in Work and Politics: The Marxist Conception of the Good Life," in Ellen Frankel Paul, Fred D. Miller, Jr., Jeffrey Paul, and John Ahrens, eds., *Marxism and Liberalism* (Oxford: Blackwell, 1986), p. 121.

23. Karl Marx and Friedrich Engels, *Manifesto of the Communist Party*, in Marx and Engels, *Selected Works*, p. 53.

24. In the *Grundrisse* Marx insists that – in principle – the way human beings satisfy each other's needs involves awareness of one's species being:

The fact that this need on the part of one can be satisfied by the product of the other, and vice versa, and that the one is capable of producing the object of the need of the other, and that each confronts the other as owner of the object of the other's need, this proves that each of them reaches beyond his own particular need, etc., as a *human being* [*als Mensch*], and that they relate to one another as human beings [*als Menschen*]; that their common species-being is acknowledged by all [*daß ihr gemeinschaftliches Gattungswesen von allen gewußt ist*]. (p. 243)

25. Marx, *Comments*, p. 226, "Auszüge," p. 461.

26. For a good reading of Marx emphasizing sociality rather than harmony (Cohen's picture is merely of harmony), and in general stressing some of the themes I have stressed, see David Archard, "The Marxist Ethic of Self-realization: Individuality and Community," in *Moral Philosophy and Contemporary Problems*, ed. J. D. G. Evans (Cambridge University Press, 1987).

27. Keith Graham, in Cohen and Graham, "Self-Ownership, Communism and Equality," p. 53.

28. Charles Taylor seems to be seeing this point in his essay, "Cross-Purposes: The Liberal–Communitarian Debate," in *Liberalism and the Moral Life*, ed. Nancy Rosenblum (Cambridge: Harvard University Press, 1989). There he too uses the image of a musical group, this time a symphony, and stresses the dialogue between orchestra and audience. This is supposed to be an example

of what Taylor calls an "'immediately' common good" (see "Cross-Purposes: The Liberal–Communitarian Debate," p. 169). It is worth remarking that the metaphor, in revealing variations, of a band for society recurs again and again in contemporary debates. Warner Wick uses a string quartet as a metaphor for Kant's realm of ends, and John Rawls uses an orchestra to illustrate the idea of social union. See Warner Wick, Introduction to Immanuel Kant, *Ethical Philosophy* (Indianapolis: Hackett Publishing Company, 1983), p. xvi, and John Rawls, *A Theory of Justice* (Cambridge: Harvard University Press, 1971), p. 524n, and *Political Liberalism* (New York: Columbia University Press, 1993; paperback edition with new material, 1996), p. 321.

29. Another instance of a society with internally oriented shared ends is the well-ordered society sketched in *A Theory of Justice* (see below, Section III). Although of course Rawls does not use this terminology, he makes the point explicit at p. 528. I suspect that T. H. Green's picture of a proper society is also of this kind. See his *Principles of Political Obligation* (Cambridge University Press, 1986), §§24, 25, and especially 62.

30. In principle, externally oriented ends are similarly divisible into overlapping and intertwined ends. However, here there could be conflict. For the conditions for having the ends be intertwined might, conceivably, inhibit the attainment of the collectivity's goal. This could not happen with internally oriented shared ends, since there is no such goal.

31. See Jon Elster, *Sour Grapes* (Cambridge University Press, 1983), p. 100.

32. Another word on Hegel. The state he depicts (in the *Philosophy of Right* and the *Philosophy of Mind*) is basically an externally oriented community. It is toward the state not toward one another that agents' eyes are primarily turned. But agents' eyes are *also* at times turned toward one another. Hegel's state is complex. Agents play various social roles at various times and relate to one another differently depending on the role. In some respects their relations are in fact direct, one-to-one (e.g., in their reciprocal recognition of one another's "honor" from the trade each plies; see *Philosophy of Mind*, §432, *Zusatz* and *Philosophy of Right*, §207). Still, I think the overall orientation of a Hegelian community is external.

33. See Rawls, *A Theory of Justice*, §69.

34. John Rawls, "Kantian Constructivism in Moral Theory," *The Journal of Philosophy*, volume LXXVII, No. 9, September 1980, p. 525.

35. Rawls, *A Theory of Justice*, p. 563.

36. Ibid., p. 440.

37. Ibid., pp. 522–3.

38. Ibid., p. 565.

39. I suppose someone could have a conception of humanity's essential nature that is so narrowly drawn as to determine a unique conception of the good, but this seems unlikely.

40. Rawls, *A Theory of Justice*, p. 529. See also p. 525n.

41. On this point, see H. L. A. Hart, "Rawls on Liberty and Its Priority," in *Reading Rawls*, ed. Norman Daniels (Stanford, CA: Stanford University Press, 1989), p. 252.

42. Rawls, *A Theory of Justice*, p. 571.

43. Rawls distinguishes the concept of social union from the idea of the flourishing of the many-sided individual, and he attributes the latter to the

1844 Marx (see *A Theory of Justice*, pp. 523–5n). I have not discussed an analogue in Marx's work to social union's stress on the satisfaction citizens take in one another's activities. However, in fact for the 1844 Marx, communists do take pleasure in one another's accomplishments (he says that "the senses and enjoyment of other men have become my own appropriation"; *Economic and Philosophic Manuscripts*, in Marx and Engels, *Collected Works*, Vol. 3, p. 300) and do appreciate one another's accomplishments as the species' accomplishments.

It is worth noting, incidentally, that, in the long footnote Rawls devotes to the history of the idea of social union (pp. 523–5n), he invokes the ubiquitous metaphor of a musical group as a model for community, but on his account (by contrast, say, to Gerald Cohen's) the musicians have "a kind of tacit agreement . . . to realize the powers of all in their joint performances." Rawls's musicians have a shared end and one that is intertwined.

44. There is a further feature relevant to the well-ordered society as a social creation. Rawls says that citizens appreciate "one another's excellences and individuality elicited by free institutions" (p. 523). This appreciation of one another's accomplishments as things that could not be achieved but for the social arrangements citizens have jointly created is likely to be a further way through which citizens are bound together. It may also be an element in citizens' completion of one another in the sense I am using. For that to be the case, it would have to be essential to citizens' natures to participate in some way in achievements greater than they could possibly accomplish as individuals. Now I have attributed to Rawls the view that citizens of the well-ordered society are communal beings (that is why they can be completed *qua* communal beings). Perhaps the (slightly perfectionist) capacity to appreciate and to take satisfaction in joint achievements is part of what that amounts to.

45. Rawls, *A Theory of Justice*, p. 529.
46. See ibid., pp. 522 and 527.
47. See ibid., p. 528.
48. See Rawls, *Political Liberalism*, p. 13.
49. Rawls, *A Theory of Justice*, pp. 563 and 529.
50. More generally, I take the notion of a comprehensive doctrine to be at the same level as the notion of the fundamental aspect of the self, and indeed at the same level as a conception of *the* good as distinct from a conception of *one's own* good. These all constrain without determining one's conception of one's own good. They are broader or, to use Rawls's term, more comprehensive notions.
51. Rawls, *Political Liberalism*, pp. 81–2.
52. Ibid., p. 84.
53. Ibid., p. 203.
54. Ibid., p. 323.
55. Rawls, *A Theory of Justice*, p. 516.
56. Rawls, *Political Liberalism*, p. 77.
57. Ibid., pp. 77–8.
58. Ibid.
59. This point is similar to one Kurt Baier makes about the dimensions involved in the existence of an adequate overlapping consensus. See Kurt Baier, "Justice and the Aims of Political Philosophy," *Ethics*, 99 (4) (July 1989), pp. 776–7.

60. Rawls, *Political Liberalism*, p. 202.
61. Ibid., p. 42.
62. Ibid., p. 322.
63. Ibid., p. 320.
64. The problem of interpreting one's social interactions can be seen by looking at Rawls's statement that "the values of the political . . . govern the basic framework of social life – the very groundwork of our existence" (*Political Liberalism*, p. 139). The idea that the basic framework of social life counts as "the very groundwork of our existence" (a phrase Rawls takes from J. S. Mill) can be given two readings. As a fact about creatures who must live with other human beings in the world, the idea is straightforward: the basic structure provides the concrete elements necessary for humans to survive, at least in a form in which they can care about anything beyond survival. But "our existence" need not be glossed so crassly. It could refer to our existence as, say, beings with souls, or as inhabitants of a particular stage in the evolution of *Geist*, and then the basic structure would not provide the groundwork of our existence. That would come from elsewhere. The basic structure *would* provide the groundwork of our existence in this stronger sense if it were animated by a comprehensive doctrine, but this is just what Rawls now rejects. Citizens of the new well-ordered society are likely to see the groundwork of their existence in the basic structure only in the first, the weak sense.
65. It is ironic that the changes from *Theory* are in part a response to communitarian critics who felt *Theory* insufficiently sensitive to the specifics of American life. It is just Rawls's attempt to work from within current conditions (that is, his acceptance of and emphasis on "the fact of reasonable pluralism"; see *Political Liberalism*, p. 36) that prompts his rejection of the comprehensive doctrine he finds in *Theory*. And this rejection undermines the ability of citizens to complete one another and so to form a certain kind of communal bond in the way they do in the well-ordered society of *Theory*. I owe this point to Michael Hardimon.